EDUCATING ONESELF IN PUBLIC

EDUCATING ONESELF IN PUBLIC

Critical Essays in Jurisprudence

MICHAEL S. MOORE

OXFORD
UNIVERSITY PRESS

OXFORD
UNIVERSITY PRESS
Great Clarendon Street, Oxford OX2 6DP

Oxford University Press is a department of the University of Oxford.
It furthers the University's objective of excellence in research, scholarship,
and education by publishing worldwide in

Oxford New York
Athens Auckland Bangkok Bogotá Buenos Aires Calcutta
Cape Town Chennai Dar es Salaam Delhi Florence Hong Kong Istanbul
Karachi Kuala Lumpur Madrid Melbourne Mexico City Mumbai
Nairobi Paris São Paulo Singapore Taipei Tokyo Toronto Warsaw
and associated companies in Berlin Ibadan

Oxford is a registered trade mark of Oxford University Press
in the UK and in certain other countries

Published in the United States
by Oxford University Press Inc., New York

First published 2000

British Library Cataloguing in Publication Data
Data available

Library of Congress Cataloging in Publication Data
Moore, Michael S., 1943–
Educating oneself in public: critical essays in
jurisprudence / Michael S. Moore.
p. cm.
Includes bibliographical references and index.
1. Jurisprudence. 2. Law—Philosophy.
3. Critical legal studies. I. Title.
K235.M664 2000 340'.1—dc21 00–032361

ISBN 0–19–826879–3

1 3 5 7 9 10 8 6 4 2

Typeset by Hope Services (Abingdon) Ltd.
Printed in Great Britain
on acid-free paper by
Biddles Ltd.,
Guildford & King's Lynn

For Sharon and Jean

intellectual mentors from an early age.

Preface

The essays that follow were not written with an eye towards publication as a book. Each was intended to be a bit of critical analysis capable of standing on its own. Still, the essays together form a coherent whole. As is explored in some depth at the beginning of Chapter 10, jurisprudence is best organized along metaphysical lines, and in metaphysics there are only three interesting positions about any things: conventionalism, scepticism, and (philosophical) realism. In jurisprudence, this plays out to three leading schools: legal positivism, Legal Realism (and its post-modernist descendants), and natural law, respectively.[1] The essays in this volume organize themselves naturally into these three groupings. (The last two essays, Chapters 10 and 11, deal with the attempt of Ronald Dworkin and others to have a non-metaphysical, 'interpretivist' jurisprudence, the logical space for which I argue in Chapters 8 and 10 does not exist.)

Beyond this thematic unity, I would hope that the essays share a common approach to critical analysis of the works of others. The late Herbert Hart once wrote that jurisprudence has too often been about what other books have said.[2] Preferable, Hart thought, was a jurisprudence that seeks positively to describe its subject matter, allowing the nature of that subject matter to dictate one's organization rather than have such organization dictated by the thoughts (or 'schools' of thoughts) of others. One can and should concede this primacy of original work, and yet still find a place for critical analysis of the jurisprudential thoughts of others. At the least, such critical analysis clarifies one's own position by clarifying what it is not. Even better, such critical analysis is the usual heuristic for most philosophers in working out what it is that they do ultimately believe about a subject matter like law or legal reasoning. Such a working out is admittedly a preliminary task to the more synthetic and creative task of carving out one's own position in philosophy. After Hegel had finally disgorged his *Phenomenology*, he allowed himself to comment in his lectures about his former friend, Schelling, who had published much preliminary, critical work while Hegel was yet unpublished. Hegel quipped that he (Schelling) had merely educated himself in public.[3] As an alternative to waiting upon the completion of Hegel-like systems of thought, my own choice is like that of Schelling, which is to favour such public education.

[1] A division of jurisprudence owing to Herbert Hart, who divided *The Concept of Law* into this threefold division: first (Austinian and then his own version of) legal positivism (chapters 2–6); second, sceptical legal realism (chapter 7); and finally, natural law (chapters 8–9). H. L. A. Hart, *The Concept of Law* (Oxford: Clarendon Press, 1961).

[2] Ibid., p. vi.

[3] Quoted in Walter Kaufmann, *Hegel: A Reinterpretation* (Garden City, NY: Anchor Books, 1966), 38, 166.

There is another benefit of critical analysis, more important than these two, achievable if the critical analysis is not only critical. That benefit is the furtherance of the insight most respectable thought contains. If criticism is sympathetic, in the sense that the critic steps inside the enterprise being criticized enough to grasp its temptations, then such criticism can further the insights of the subject even if ultimately rejecting the conclusions.

Such contributing criticism thus has the potential of making the thought criticized better than it was. It also, to my mind, makes for more interesting reading. Few things are more boring than fine-grained criticisms of particular authors for particular inconsistencies in their statements, or for errors in the way they have defended their positions, or, even worse, for *ad hominems* directed against the authors themselves. It is very difficult to sustain interest, for example, in the law review literature of the 1930s defending or attacking American Legal Realism for these reasons. Much of the criticism of 'liberalism' by critical legal studies scholars in the 1980s I find boring for the same reasons. Depth of understanding is achieved, and interest maintained, only if those who would be critical respect their targets enough to interpret them charitably, even if this is on the way to rejecting them entirely.

Such contributing criticism is psychologically possible and epistemologically worthwhile, of course, only if one selects the targets of the criticism with some care. It is an empty exercise to critique a view one knows to be bankrupt from the start; perception of such bankruptcy by a critic limits his criticism to the merely clever and cutting, at best. One thus has to criticize views that are worth taking seriously.[4] Although the subjects of such criticism rarely think so, being such a subject is thus a kind of compliment. The act of criticism says that the view being criticized is tempting enough to be learned from, even while being rejected.

In truth, there is some variation in the sympathy I can muster for the views discussed in these essays. Joseph Raz's central notion of exclusionary reasons, the early Ronald Dworkin's rights and right answer theses, Herbert Hart's idea of a purely external, general jurisprudence, Lon Fuller's general idea for a functionalist jurisprudence, and John Finnis's idea of the common good, are all ideas with which I have considerable sympathy; the criticism of those ideas thus hopefully furthers them while critiquing them. The American Legal Realists, by contrast, were so stubbornly unphilosophical that I have very little sympathy with their writings. I fear that that lack of sympathy shows in the impatience expressed in my essay on them in Chapter 6. Some of the impatience with them undoubtedly rubs off onto the nominal target of Chapter 6, Robert

[4] Cf. Nietzsche, *Untimely Meditations*, trans. R. J. Hollingdale (Cambridge: Cambridge University Press, 1997).

Summers, whose book on the Realists sought to portray them as serious theorists of law.

I did not find the exchange with Summers that my essay prompted to be a very productive one, so in critiquing other views with which I have equally little sympathy I sought to be more patient. I refer to the views I lump together as 'the interpretive turn'. My impatience with these currently very fashionable views is pretty clearly revealed in the rather grumpy beginning of Chapter 11. Nonetheless, in the essay on the interpretive turn in Chapter 10 I sought to suppress such impatience in order to give the interpretivists their due. The reader can judge with what success I was able to clarify and to capture the temptations of the interpretive turn while refusing to take the turn myself. (Brian Langille's comment to me while I was defending this essay in Toronto—that my essay in Chapter 10 has a misleading subtitle because of a question-mark rather than an exclamation point as its punctuation—suggests that I have had only limited success here.)

Each of the essays has prompted a response, either by the subject of the essays or by others on their behalf. In lieu of including such responses in a volume already long enough, I have written an introductory chapter that summarizes their principal arguments and refers readers to where they may find the complete text of such responses. To render such responses intelligible, I also do there what I would do anyway in order to preview the contents of the volume, namely, summarize my own critiques very briefly.

As is indicated in the Acknowledgements that follow, preliminary versions for these chapters have been given at numerous workshops and colloquia. The comments and suggestions that I received at each of these presentations were quite helpful and I thank all those who participated in such discussions for making the papers better. Special thanks go to Larry Alexander, Soterios Barber, Gilead Bar-Elli, Chris Boorse, Peter Clark, Jules Coleman, Dick Craswell, Ronald Dworkin, John Finnis, Stanley Fish, Ruth Gavison, Robert George, the late Herbert Hart, Don Herzog, Tony Honoré, Leo Katz, Ken Kress, Brian Languille, Andrei Marmor, Stephen Morse, Hans Oberdiek, Michael Perry, Stephen Perry, Robert Post, Joseph Raz, Ed Rock, Richard Rorty, Fred Schauer, Michael Smith, and Jeremy Waldron, each of whom provided me with separate comments on one or more of the chapters. My research assistant for Chapter 10 was (now Professor) Linda Helyar, who did an admirable job of wading through the literature of Critical Legal Studies to provide me with examples of interpretivists in law. As always, the person to whom most thanks are due is my wife and philosophical collaborator, Heidi Hurd. She has been the kind of insightful, constructive, and dedicated critic of these essays that one only hopes for but never expects. (I should say that the one piece of her advice that I did not follow was with regard to the title for this book, which she did her best to dissuade me from using.)

I have been generously supported in the production of this book (and most of the essays comprising it) by the University of Pennsylvania Law School Summer Research Fund. The University of Pennsylvania Law Library staff, notably my liaison librarians Catharine Krieps and Edwin Greenlee, have done yeoman's work in assembling the reference and bibliographic material for this volume. They have made the telephone an extremely efficient research tool for me.

Lastly, thanks go to my secretaries at the University of Pennsylvania, Betty Burks and Patricia-Anne Meier, who between them translated my primitive scrawlings on yellow pads into a printable manuscript.

M. M.

Idyllwild, California
July, 1999

Acknowledgements

Chapter 1: Given at the Methods of Jurisprudence Conference, Center for Law and Philosophy, Columbia University, 2000; never before published.

Chapter 2: Written for the Legal Classics edition of H. L. A. Hart's *The Concept of Law* (Birmingham, Ala: Gryphon Press, 1990).

Chapter 3: Written for the Symposium on Hart's 'Postscript' to *The Concept of Law*, *Legal Theory*, iv (1998), 301–27.

Chapter 4: Given at the Conference on Rules and the Rule of Law, University of San Diego Law School, 1990, first published in *Harvard Journal of Law and Public Policy*, 14 (1991), 771–95.

Chapter 5: A very preliminary version given as a commentary on Raz's theory of authority, annual meeting, Pacific Division, American Philosophical Association, Long Beach, Calif., 1984; a more complete version given at the 2nd annual USC/Oxford Institute for Legal Theory, All Souls College, Oxford, 1988; first published in *Southern California Law Review*, 62 (1989), 827–96.

Chapter 6: First published in *Cornell Law Review*, 69 (1984), 988–1013.

Chapter 7: A preliminary version given at the Center for Law and Humanities, Harvard University, 1977; first published in a symposium issue on legal principles, *Iowa Law Review*, 82 (1997), 867–91.

Chapter 8: Given at the Legal Theory Workshop, University of Michigan Law School, Ann Arbor, 1987; first published in *Southern California Law Review*, 60 (1987), 453–506; and then defended at the first annual USC/Oxford Institute for Legal Theory, All Souls College, Oxford, 1987.

Chapter 9: Initially written during my teaching of seminars on natural law jurisprudence at UC-Berkeley's Program for Jurisprudence and Social Policy, 1988, and the University of Pennsylvania Law School, 1989, and then given as an Ad Hoc Faculty Workshop, University of Pennsylvania Law School, 1989, and at a meeting of the Philosophy of Law Reading Group, Greater Philadelphia Philosophy Consortium, and then as part of my presentation to the Panel on Natural Law at the 1990 annual meeting of the Midwest Political Science Association; first published in R. George (ed.), *Natural Law Theories* (Oxford: Oxford University Press, 1992).

Chapter 10: Given at the 1st annual USC/Oxford Institute for Legal Theory, All Souls College, Oxford, 1987, at the Faculty Colloquium, School of Law (Boalt Hall), University of California, Berkeley, 1988, at the Legal Theory Workshop, University of Toronto Law School, Toronto, 1988, and at the Humanities Research Institute, University of California at Irvine, 1989; first published in *Stanford Law Review*, 41 (1989), 871–957.

Chapter 11: Derived from Lectures on Interpretation, given by me at the Eighth Annual Session of the International Institute for Semiotic and Structural Studies, held in 1986 at the English Department, Northwestern University, Evanston; first given as a paper at the Tel Aviv University Conference on Interpretation and Legal Theory, Tel Aviv, May, 1993; first published (in Hebrew) in the *Tel Aviv University Law Review*, 18 (1994), 359–86, and then in A. Marmor (ed.), *Interpretation and Legal Theory* (Oxford: Oxford University Press, 1995).

Contents

Table of Cases and Legislation

Cases

Legislation

Introduction

1

Overview

I. CHAPTER 2: H. L. A. HART'S LEGAL POSITIVISM

In this overview I shall do three things by way of introducing the essays that follow: I shall summarize each of the essays, then give the response of those criticized, and then give my rejoinders to such responses. The first part of the volume is on legal positivism, and the first two chapters of that part are on the central figure of that movement in this century, H. L. A. Hart. The first essay, Chapter 2, is largely biographical and expository, summarizing Hart's professional life and his major works. This was written as an introduction to a reprinted, American edition of *The Concept of Law* and thus was not intended to be a critique of Hart's work. Nonetheless, two critical remarks are ventured, the first having to do with Hart's ordinary language-based rejection of more metaphysical approaches to jurisprudence, and the second having to do with Hart's steadfast refusal to acknowledge that officials within a regime must at least believe that the master rule for that regime (what Hart called a 'rule of recognition') was just for there to be a legal regime in place. Upon publication of the essay, Hart wrote to thank me for what he regarded as the 'careful and insightful presentation of my views' as well as to express, with characteristic modesty, 'doubts as to whether I deserve all that praise'.[1] Hart did not respond to the first of the two criticisms, other than to note generally that he was 'acutely aware of the defects in my various works . . .'[2] With regard to the second criticism, Hart responded with the position he had defended throughout his life:

> I see you wonder why I don't settle for a less extreme form of positivism which would be content with the assertion that officials must *believe* in the justness of their system but not that the system must *be* just if it is to be law. I myself wonder at times why I do not take the easier line; what prevents me is the simple empirical doubt as to whether all officials do believe this (Oliver Wendell Holmes did not!) and if they do not whether a system with all the other features of law cannot exist as a legal system.[3]

In assessing Hart's position, one must remember the question Hart put to himself: from a perspective external to any particular legal system, wouldn't our concept of a legal system be satisfied when officials accepted the rule of recognition for their system for any reason (not just moral ones)

[1] Personal communication, Herbert Hart, 13 Feb. 1990.
[2] Ibid. [3] Ibid.

or for no reason at all but mere habit?[4] This is the external, conceptual question of a non-participant in the legal system in question, and to that question Hart consistently maintained that the answer was, 'yes'. But does such an answer square with Hart's attempt to account for the 'normativity' of law, for the difference between being obliged to yield to the threats of the gunman and being obligated to yield to the demands of law?[5] My own sense when I wrote the essay to which Hart responded, and my sense still, was and is that Hart's thin acceptance by officials hardly distinguishes his legal positivism from that of Austin and Bentham; ultimately, for all three, law and legal obligation are matters of habits of obedience, induced either by fear of legal sanctions (Bentham and Austin) or by the *believed* legitimacy of the government by officials (Hart).

Yet perhaps legal positivists should not seek to distance themselves from Bentham and Austin. What if Hart had chosen the other option, proclaiming that there is no law unless judges within a system not only accept the rule of recognition as legitimate but do so because they believe such a rule is just? That would not have affected the value-free nature of Hart's external (or 'general') jurisprudence, because the external theorist would be making no evaluations of the justness of political orders in order to see if they had a legal system. Yet for internal participants of some particular system applying such a concept of law when they ask whether they are participating in something properly called a legal system, the situation is not so clear. Such participants, if they are officials, presumably must believe that the rule of recognition is a just one before they can accept the rule as legitimate, and such acceptance is itself a precondition of their recognizing their system as a legal one. That is, from their point of view the system must be just to be legal. And that sounds, *prima facie* at least, like an embarrassing thing to say for a legal positivist. Such an admission might become the beginning of an argument by a natural lawyer that (from the internal point of view of a judge in a particular legal system) the justness of particular standards must be judged if those standards can obligate her *qua* judge, i.e. if those standards are law.[6] So perhaps Hart was wise to limit his legal positivism in the way that he did. Doing so makes no concessions towards the natural law view. True enough, so limiting his legal positivism does not allow Hart to distinguish law from the orders of a gunman in terms of obligation. But perhaps a legal positivist should not seek to answer St Augustine's query any better than did Bentham and

[4] H. L. A. Hart, *The Concept of Law* (Oxford: Clarendon Press, 1961), 198.

[5] Ibid. at 82.

[6] One of the two main openings sought to be exploited in Ronald Dworkin's critique of Hart. See Dworkin, *Taking Rights Seriously* (Cambridge, Mass.: Harvard University Press, 1978), 36–8, 105–15. For an exploration of these issues, see Richard Hulton, 'Positivism and the Internal Point of View', *Law and Philosophy*, 17 (1998), 597–625.

Austin: law necessarily 'obligates' only in the Pickwickian sense that law gives rise to liability to sanctions and that liability induces habits of obedience in citizens and perhaps even beliefs of legitimacy. Such a positivist can concede that the more interesting sense of 'obligation' is that of moral obligation, but in that sense, he would say, law does not *necessarily* obligate anyone and it is law nonetheless.

II. CHAPTER 3: HART'S METHOD IN JURISPRUDENCE

This is one of the points picked up in the next chapter, Chapter 3. More generally, the chapter aims to contrast two ways of doing jurisprudence. Hart's jurisprudence is used to exemplify a general jurisprudence. Such a jurisprudence is general in the sense that it asks the central question of jurisprudence, 'What is law?', from a perspective external to any particular legal system. Moreover, the focus of such a jurisprudence is on 'law' in the sense of legal system, so that the enquiry is into the attributes a society must have before it can be said to have 'law', i.e. a legal system.

Such a jurisprudence is also descriptive in the sense that it seeks to describe the phenomenon, law; it does not seek to prescribe that we use the word, 'law', to name one thing or another. Nor does such a jurisprudence vicariously occupy the role of some particular actor within legal systems, such as that of the judge, and ask the normative question of what standards obligate such occupants of such roles.

Finally, Hart's jurisprudence is construed to be descriptive of the phenomenon, law. This does require Hart to abstract from various social practices we recognize as *legal* practices, so as to capture their essential features. It does not require Hart to engage in a linguistic analysis into the concept of law presupposed by ordinary English usage of the word 'law'. Hart's general jurisprudence is sociological, not semantic (in this sense).

The jurisprudence contrasting most sharply with Hart's is a kind of particular jurisprudence partly exemplified by the work of Ronald Dworkin. Such a jurisprudence is particular in the sense that it asks the, 'What is law?', question from the perspective of a participant within some particular legal culture. Such a jurisprudence thus bypasses Hart's enquiry into the universally necessary conditions for law (legal system) to exist, by presupposing that one is within a legal system; within such a system, a participant asks, 'What is law?', meaning, 'What are the standards binding on legal actors *qua* legal actors within this system?' Such an internal jurisprudence thus focuses on laws and the laws of cases, often called, respectively, general and singular propositions of law. This is in marked contrast to Hart's external jurisprudence, which focuses on propositions *about* law.

Such an internal jurisprudence cannot be non-normative. Since the viewpoint adopted is that of the occupant of some legal office within some legal system, law will be conceived as that which binds the occupant of such office (such as, typically, that of a judge). Laws can bind judges only if it obligates them, i.e. tells them what they ought to do. Propositions of law will thus necessarily be normative, and so will be a theory that is itself a proposition of law within that system.

Such an internal jurisprudence will no more engage in a linguistic analysis of the concept of law extracted from ordinary usage than does Hart's external jurisprudence. Rather, substantive moral theory will determine what standards are good enough for government work, i.e. are good enough (in terms of their content and their pedigree) to obligate obedience to them by legal actors.

The chapter concludes on an ecumenical note by urging that both sorts of jurisprudence are worthy of academic energies. Particular jurisprudence is more directly practical but some general jurisprudence is a presupposition of any successful particular jurisprudence. In particular, I urge that Dworkin's imperialist claims on behalf of particular jurisprudence—that general jurisprudence is either an impossible or a useless enterprise—are false.

Chapter 3 was written and published after Hart's death. Although he had no chance to read it (as he did Chapter 2), I suspect that he would have agreed with my interpretation of his views. Chapter 3 was solicited by the editors of *Legal Theory* for a symposium issue on the partly finished 'Postscript' to *The Concept of Law* that Hart had been intermittently drafting for years.[7]

Among the symposiasts Gerald Postema and Stephen Perry most directly picked up the cudgels against Hart and, implicitly, against my interpretation of Hart.[8] Perry's and Postema's arguments can most clearly be seen against the backdrop of Dworkin's similar argument against Hart in 1972. The Dworkin of the 'Social Rules' article of 1972 interpreted Hart to be seeking to give an analysis of when judges are actually obligated, by laws or by anything else.[9] This is what Dworkin construed Hart to mean when Hart criticized Bentham and Austin for insufficiently accounting for the 'normativity' of law; what is missing in the sanction view of legal

[7] H. L. A. Hart, 'Postscript', *The Concept of Law*, 2nd edn. (Oxford: Oxford University Press, 1994).

[8] Gerald Postema, 'Jurisprudence as Practical Philosophy', *Legal Theory*, 4 (1998), 329–58; Stephen Perry, 'Hart's Methodological Positivism', *Legal Theory*, 4 (1998), 427–67.

[9] Ronald Dworkin, 'Social Rules and Legal Theory', *Yale Law Journal*, 81 (1972), 855–90, reprinted in *Taking Rights Seriously* (above n. 6), 47–58. Thus, Dworkin attacks 'a thesis that Hart defended in *The Concept of Law*, a thesis . . . that no rights or duties of any sort can exist except by virtue of a uniform social practice of recognizing these rights and duties.' Ibid. at 47–8.

obligation, on Dworkin's version of Hart, is an account of what actually justifies officials in following the rules that *obligate* them.

Having construed Hart to have asked this question, Dworkin then stuck him with a particularly stupid answer to it: an official is actually (and not merely said to be, or believed to be) obligated by a rule when: (1) he adopts the internal attitude towards the rule, marking the rule as a social rule and not a mere habit;[10] (2) 'the general demand for conformity is insistent and the social pressure [not to deviate] is great';[11] (3) the content of the rule is thought important because what it protects is 'believed to be necessary to the maintenance of social life or some highly prized feature of it';[12] (4) what the rules demand may 'conflict with what the person who owes the duty may wish to do'.[13] This familiar answer by Hart is taken by Dworkin to be an answer to the ethical question, 'When do rules actually obligate obedience?' Dworkin then criticizes Hart for a glaringly naive instance of the naturalistic fallacy, inferring a moral conclusion (about the actual obligatoriness, or 'normativity' of law) from a set of social and psychological facts.

The only way such naivety could be avoided by Hart, Dworkin urges, is for Hart to assert that *judicial* obligation (not obligation in general) depends on the existence of a general judicial practice. That is, even-handed, like-minded judging is a virtue, so that if a judge co-ordinates with his fellow judges through some social rule that they all accept, some real good is achieved. Then Hart would not be guilty of some sophomoric instance of the naturalistic fallacy when he makes judicial obligation depend on the existence of certain social rules. That other judges accept the rule of recognition and follow it then can constitute a reason—an obligating reason—for any individual judge to do so too.

Having reconstrued Hart in this direction, Dworkin then has no problem shooting down any such attempt to derive actual obligation from social convention. As Dworkin points out, judicial obligations are not plausibly confined to situations where judges accept some rule so as to co-ordinate their behaviour.

Hart's conventionalist answer would surely be a bad answer to Dworkin's ethical question, if that were the question Hart had asked. Yet Hart did not ask such a question of ethics. Hart did not see himself as accounting for the actual normativity of law for the simple reason that he did not think rules had to be actually obligating of anyone in order to be law. The 'normativity' law had to possess to be law was only a believed normativity by those administering the law: such actors practising law internal to some legal system had to accept the rule of recognition, and that acceptance had to have the conventional characteristics (of social pressure,

[10] Hart, *Concept*, above n. 4, at 85. [11] Ibid. at 86. [12] Ibid. at 87.
[13] Ibid.

etc.) Hart identifies. Only then would such actors regard themselves as obligated by such rules; only then would we external observers say of such actors, they have law because of such 'internal attitudes' toward their master rule.

In short, Hart was only doing a sociology of ethics when he analysed obligation in general and legal obligation in particular.[14] He was not doing ethics itself, because on his view of law's normativity, none needed doing in order to ascertain whether a system of rules possessed sufficient 'normativity' to be a legal system. Jurisprudence in the last half of this century is rife with the attempt to force Hart into answering questions he did not ask, and Dworkin's argument in 1972 was a prime instance of this unfortunate tendency.

Postema's recent continuation of Dworkin's argument recognizes that Hart thought he was giving a sociological account of law's normativity with his concept of the 'internal attitude' officials must have (on Hart's account) towards the rule of recognition of their legal system.[15] Postema recognizes that Hart thought he could do such sociology (of law's essential normativity) by describing the psychological states cum behaviour that officials must have; no evaluative judgement need be made by such a sociologist, because no attempt to show that law actually obligates officials is needed by such sociology. Nonetheless, Postema concludes that Hart cannot account for law's essential normativity without abandoning such descriptive sociology for a prescriptive ethics—which is essentially Dworkin's earlier conclusion.

Part of Postema's argument to this conclusion seems to be based on the same elision of ambiguity that pervades Dworkin's older critique. Notice that when one talks of 'law's essential normativity', of law's 'authority', of law's capacity to give the actors subject to it 'reasons for acting' in conformity to it, of law 'obligating' judges, there is a fundamental ambiguity. Take 'authority'. When we say that a rule has authority for a person, we can mean that the rule is regarded by him as giving him a reason to act in conformity to it. On such occasions the authority of which we speak is a social fact. Alternatively, with equal idiomatic propriety we may mean to be saying that the rule gives him a reason to act in conformity with it, whether he thinks so or not. Now the authority of which we speak is a moral fact.

This ambiguity is pervasive. 'Reasons for actions' is notoriously ambiguous between: subjective reasons which motivate behaviour, versus objective reasons which justify (and thus, *ought* to motivate) behaviour,[16]

[14] As Hart himself consistently said. See ibid. at 169. See also H. L. A. Hart, 'Legal Duty and Obligation', in his *Essays on Bentham* (Oxford: Clarendon Press, 1982).

[15] Postema, 'Jurisprudence', above n. 8, at 330–2.

[16] See e.g. the discussion in Ch. 5 herein.

'obligation', between regarded-as-obligating versus actually obligating, 'normativity', between treated-as-normative versus actually normative. Sometimes Postema's argument seems to be no more than a trading on this ambiguity, sticking Hart with the objective version of each of these concepts when he plainly meant to be framing his questions with the subjective version only. Consider by way of example Postema's revival of his old critique[17] of Hart's account of the authority the rule of recognition must possess with the judges of some system if that system was to be a *legal* system. Postema recognizes that for Hart 'the authority of the rule of recognition lies simply in the facts of the practice of law-applying officials. . . . This argument is unpersuasive. For one thing, the appeal to the facts of regular patterns of behaviour, even if supplemented by facts about the volitions of the agents, will not answer the practical question posed by the inquiry into the practical authority of the rule of recognition'.[18] According to Postema, Hart had to make a 'practical' argument—that co-ordination by judges is good because promotive of equality and predictability, for example—in order to account for the authority of a rule of recognition for the judges of the system whose rule it is. This is just to force Hart to answer a question (about actual authority) that he did not ask.

Fortunately, the main thrust of Postema's account lies elsewhere. Unfortunately, that thrust by Postema essentially consists in his attempt to find a middle ground in the dichotomies just charted. Thinking as I do that there is no middle ground to be found here, I conclude that Postema's critique of Hart collapses back into Dworkin's, and fails for the same reasons. Let me briefly describe Postema's hoped-for middle ground.

Postema recognizes the difference between theoretical inquiries and practical inquiries. With some qualifications not here important,[19] this is Hart's distinction between descriptive social science and evaluative ethics. Roughly, theoretical inquiries are purely cognitive: they seek reasons for belief, whereas practical inquiries are motivational, seeking reasons for action.

Despite his recognition of two inquiries corresponding to the subjective/objective ambiguities earlier mentioned, Postema seeks to find a kind of practical inquiry that Hart had to be doing (despite his own exclusively theoretical ambitions). This is a practical inquiry that *looks* partly sociological because the reasons such an inquiry seeks are what we might call 'practice-dependent reasons', that is, reasons whose existence and force depends on the existence in a society of certain practices.[20] Postema seeks

[17] G. Postema, 'Coordination and Convention at the Foundations of Law', *Journal of Legal Studies*, 11 (1982), 165–203, at 170–1. See also Postema, 'The Normativity of Law', in Ruth Gavison (ed.), *Issues in Contemporary Legal Philosophy* (Oxford: Oxford University Press, 1987).

[18] Postema, 'Jurisprudence', above n. 8, 337.

[19] See ibid. at 332–5.

[20] Ibid. at 337–41.

to make his idea of practice-dependent reasons more precise through three ideas: (1) that there are 'logical points of view', as opposed to personal points of view. Such a logical point of view 'defines a region of practical, logical space, not anyone's psychological set';[21] (2) that there are non-ideal inquiries as well as ideal practical inquiries. Such non-ideal inquiries seek to justify behaviour within existing practices, giving those practices the normative weight that they deserve even though they are admittedly non-ideal;[22] (3) that there are a class of reasons for action Postema calls 'compliance reasons'. Compliance reasons are given by a rule that requires conformity, as opposed to a rule that only prompts or favours actions conforming to the rule. Because compliance reasons are 'intrinsically action-guiding,' we must ask for the point or rationale of any rule that purports to provide a compliance reason; if the rule is 'one for which no intelligible rationale can be discerned, [then it] cannot provide an agent with a compliance reason'.[23]

None of this goes any distance towards establishing the middle ground that Postema seeks. One should grant that there are 'logical points of view' in the sense that a social practice can have a structure and a function such that we can inquire what actors have reason to do when they act within such a practice. We should remember, however, that such a practice is a social phenomenon and its existence is a social fact that can be studied like any other, in a theoretical inquiry. Such a practice consists of no more than the roles, habits, social rules, convergent behaviour, shared goals and beliefs, of the actors who practise the practice, and studying these can be a purely theoretical (or as Hart would say, descriptive) inquiry. Moreover, the gulf between the objective and the subjective inquiries will still persist no matter how Postema's 'logical point of view' is construed. We can ask (subjectively) whether, from the point of view of some practice, an action is justifiable; and we can ask (objectively), whether the action is really justifiable. These are not the same inquiries. An opponent of the death penalty can easily recognize the justifiability of a particular sentence of death from the point of view of retributive punishment practices while not for a moment conceding such a sentence really to be justified.

Likewise, one can distinguish practices (like those involving requests between friends) that create 'prompting' reasons for action, from practices (like those involving promises) that create 'compliance reasons'. This differential force does not eliminate the possibility of studying either kind of such practice from the outside, as Hart (and later, Raz) wished to do. Such a sociology describes two forms that the normative practices of others might take.

[21] Postema, 'Jurisprudence', above n. 8, at 345.
[22] Ibid. at 344–5.
[23] Ibid. at 348.

Finally, all of us lead most of our lives speculating about and putting into practice non-ideal theories. We live in a social world already made, so of course we have to take that into account as we decide what changes to recommend in our society. Two points, however. First, such daily need for non-ideal theory hardly rules out speculation about ideal theory; all we need do is imagine, contrary to fact, that we are writing on a clean slate, which is to say, from a point of view external to our current practices. Second, and more to the point for Hart, non-ideal theory can be done in either the first or the third person. That is, we can ask what parts of our practices actually obligate us, or we can ask what parts of our practices are regarded by most of our fellow practitioners as being obligatory. The subjective/objective dichotomy does not get finessed by this distinction any more than by the other two.

If I understand Postema, he nonetheless thinks that the desired middle ground is to be found in the idea that practices must be *intelligible* for us if we are to understand them even in a theoretical (external, descriptive) enquiry. Our ability to understand a logical point of view, the point of any rule giving a compliance reason, or how *non*-ideal practices can still motivate behaviour, depends on such practices being *intelligible* to us. 'This', Postema tells us, 'necessarily engages our own moral beliefs, for what is morally intelligible to us depends on what we take to be morally true.'[24]

This last claim by Postema is an old one.[25] It is also, although true enough psychologically, barren of any interesting methodological or theoretical implications, Postema's included. As a bit of psychology, Postema's thesis accurately enough describes how we usually understand the differing evaluations of others: we must see their aims as intelligible, and this we can do usually by relating those aims to some goal we think to be valuable. But even as a matter of psychology it is not inevitable that we rely on the heuristic provided by our own moral beliefs in order to see others as intelligible; an anthropologist studying Martians or very crazy people, may show us such intelligibility by the brute facts of repeated behaviours by the Martians explicable only by their (previously unintelligible) ends. Such radical anthropology can make us less parochial than Postema's 'true moral beliefs' heuristic would make us. Furthermore, even if I am wrong about this, so that we inevitably and necessarily must rely on this moral heuristic to understanding the goals of others, that still does not mean that we are evaluating people's goals—even weakly—while we

24 Ibid. at 333.

25 On intelligibility generally, see G. E. M. Anscombe, *Intention*, 2nd edn. (Ithaca, NY: Cornell University Press, 1963); A. J. Watt, 'The Intelligibility of Wants', *Mind*, 81 (1972), 553–61. A. R. Louch used the necessity of intelligibility judgements to reason-giving explanations, to argue that social science could neither be causal nor value-free. *Explanation and Human Action* (Berkeley: University of California Press, 1966).

are describing them. Use of such a moral heuristic may be our way of coming to understand something, but what we understand is a psycholological, not a moral fact. We understand what goals, desires, moral beliefs, they actually have and that move them to action. Such understanding is part of descriptive psychology, not substantive ethics.

Without any 'middle ground' in which to locate Hart's enterprise, the result is that Postema joins Dworkin in reconstruing Hart's external questions of sociology into internal questions of ethics. Doing so makes Hart's social rules kind of answer look glaringly stupid. The apparent stupidity, however, is all in the mismatching of Hart's answer to a question he never asked, and never needed to ask in his theoretical inquiry about law.

Stephen Perry joins Postema in conceding that Hart did not intend to be answering the question of whether any rule of recognition actually obligates judges; Hart, as Perry sees, only sought to show when judges regard themselves as obligated. Nevertheless, Perry too seeks to sustain Dworkin's older conclusion that Hart had to engage in the practical inquiry involving a judge's actual obligation. Not surprisingly, having forced Hart into asking this sort of question, Perry too concludes that Hart's social rules kind of answer is obviously inadequate.

As I understand him, Perry advances two arguments for his forcing of Hart into an inquiry into the actual obligatoriness of law. The first and less interesting of these two is to take seriously Hart's desire to distance himself from Austin's sanctions-oriented analysis of legal obligation. This is to credit Hart with the insight that (in Hart's words), 'The most prominent general feature of law at all times and places is that its existence means that certain kinds of human conduct are no longer optional, but in *some* sense obligatory.'[26] If the sense in which law must be obligatory in order to exist is not Austin's fear of sanctions inducing habits of obedience, then in a way Perry (and behind him, Dworkin) are right: the only alternative is the position of Aquinas and the natural lawyers, according to whom law exists only if it (morally, actually) obligates someone, judges at least.

This is to deny the existence of any middle ground between Austin's view—that law exists only when there are sufficient habits of obedience and fear of sanctions to create 'legal obligations', in his reductionist sense—and the natural law view—that law exists only when the basic social system is sufficiently just that it can create 'legal obligations' in the sense that it can morally obligate obedience to law. What is right about this denial of middle ground to Hart is that the big divide is between Austin and Hart, on the one hand, and the natural law view on the other. Hart distances himself not at all from Austin in giving 'legal obligation'—the kind

[26] Hart, *Concept*, above n. 4, at 6. Quoted by Perry, 'Hart's . . . Positivism', above n. 8, at 445.

of obligation *law* creates—a factual and not a moral reading. In that sense, he has not at all accounted for the essential normativity of law.

The only way Hart could have had any middle ground on which to stand (in *this* divide) is if he could sustain the view that there exists a kind of obligation that is neither moral nor legal (in Austin's reductionist sense). Then law could be seen to create this kind of social obligation and still not reduce to mere threats and force. Yet Perry is right (about a view that I join him in thinking did tempt Herbert Hart): the view is not sustainable, and Hart did see that clearly enough to disdain such a view.[27]

Once we put away any hopes for a middle ground, the question for Hart then becomes which way he should take his enterprise. What is wrong about the Perry/Dworkin critique is the assumption that Hart had to jump to the natural lawyer's conclusion that law *morally* obligates to be law (and thus likely has a moral pedigree in order to sustain this obligation-creating power). It is much more consistent to interpret Hart as basically redoing Austin but staying on Austin's side of the divide. For both Hart and Austin, law necessarily obligates (creates 'legal obligations') only in the sense that those subject to such law by-and-large obey it. For Austin, such obedience can be because of habits or fear, while for Hart, a subset of people (judges) at least must obey some of the rules (the rule of recognition) because they believe them to be morally obligatory. But for Hart no less than Austin, law's existence depends on its 'obligatoriness' only in this behavioural sense, a sense that has nothing to do with actual moral obligation.

Of course, Perry can join Aquinas in positively asserting (rather than interpreting Hart to have been asserting) that law must morally obligate in order for law to exist, i.e. in order for law to create legal obligations. Yet it would be an odd criticism of Hart's *method* of doing jurisprudence to say that it did not begin with the natural lawyer's identification of legal and moral obligation. I and other natural lawyers of course criticize Hart's legal positivism for not *ending* here, but it never occurred to me to find Hart's methods of doing legal philosophy deficient because he did not start here. I take the identification of the obligations law necessarily creates ('legal obligations') with moral obligation to be one of the central bones of contention between natural lawyers and legal positivists. It takes considerable substantive argumentation to sustain either position about this identification, and one cannot shortcut this process with methodological considerations.

Despite this, I take Perry's second argument against Hart to attempt just such a shortcut. Following what I call in Chapter 3 Dworkin's imperialist claim, Perry argues: (1) That the kind of legal theory that I call in Chapter 3

[27] Perry, 'Hart's . . . Positivism', above n. 8, at 447 n. 18.

'internal jurisprudence' is a jurisprudence in which law is necessarily (actually, morally) obligating, and (2) That the only possible jurisprudence is internal jurisprudence. Therefore, according to jurisprudence, law is necessarily (actually, morally) obligating.

One will find in Chapter 3 why I agree with premise (1) above. My disagreement with Dworkin in Chapter 3 is with premise (2). Perry's elaboration of Dworkin's imperialist defence of that premise does not lead me to alter my conclusion in Chapter 3: following Hart, I find the claim so counterintuitive as to be 'extravagant'.

Perry here pursues what might be called a 'divide and conquer' strategy. He imposes four distinctions on jurisprudence, hoping to show that Hart's kind of external jurisprudence is lost in the resulting matrix. The four distinctions are, *first*, the distinction between jurisprudence that is general, in that it studies law in general and not law as it exists in any particular legal system, and jurisprudence that is local or particular, in that it studies law as it exists within some particular legal system or legal culture (such as the Anglo-American legal culture). *Second*, focusing on Hart's ambition to do general jurisprudence, Perry distinguishes two putative kinds of general jurisprudence: there is the scientific approach, where one treats law as a theoretical construct whose parameters are discovered as one discovers more and more about the descriptive/explanatory/predictive power of alternative conceptualizations of law; and there is the philosophical approach, which seeks to articulate a concept of law as that concept is actually used by some group of people. *Third*, such conceptual (or philosophical) analysis of law is parsed into an analysis of all cultures' shared criteria for law—a cultural universal—and an analysis of some particular culture's understanding of what law is, such as the English concept of law. *Fourth*, Perry distinguishes conceptual analysis that is descriptive (detached), in the sense that the theorist doing the analysis need make no moral evaluation, from conceptual analysis that is evaluative (committed), in the sense that the theorist doing the analysis is recommending one concept of law over others on morally evaluative grounds.

Using these distinctions, Perry characterizes Hart's external jurisprudence to have as its ambition that it be a jurisprudence that is: (1) general; (2) philosophical; (3) universal; and (4) descriptive. Perry's argument is that because Hart's jurisprudence is philosophical (i.e. conceptual), it is not general, universal, or descriptive. Such an argument invites two queries. First, was Hart's jurisprudence not a scientific sociology of law, as he himself described it at times, but rather, a philosophical jurisprudence of a kind that Perry (and Oxford ordinary language philosophy circa 1961) would call 'conceptual analysis'? Second, if Hart's jurisprudence was an effort at analysing some concept of law, does that methodological aim preclude his jurisprudence from being general, universal, and descriptive?

Take the first query first. Perry gives two reasons for interpreting Hart not to be doing what he says he is doing in *The Concept of Law*, which is to give a social scientific description of law. One is that Hart also says things of a conceptual analysis sort (as well as of a social sciency sort).[28] The second is that a social scientific approach to law may generate a concept of law that has little relation to any ordinary concept of law that we or others share.[29] Nothing succeeds like success in theory construction in science, and why should we think that our historically held concept of law is the (descriptively, explanatorily, predictively) most fruitful conceptualization of the phenomenon?

My reasons for rejecting both of these arguments by Perry are the same: Hart did not in fact distinguish descriptive/explanatory social science from conceptual analysis and he was right not to do so. Perry's second dichotomy ('conceptual vs. scientific') is a false one and Hart did not order his methodological thoughts around it. It is thus unavailing to seek to divine Hart's real views on his method—relative to this divide, he had none—or to seek to force Hart one way or the other, despite the lack of any views by him on the matter.

Consider an analogy in an indisputably social scientific enterprise, psychology. There have been approaches to understanding human behaviour and the motivations behind it that correspond to Perry's picture of descriptive/explanatory social science. A generation ago, these were called 'methodological behaviourism'[30] and today, 'eliminative materialism'.[31] Such approaches eschew our ordinary concepts of voluntariness, agency, freedom, intention, and the like, because, such psychologies say, the best explanation of human behaviour will not use these concepts or anything like them; rather, those better explanations will use concepts of environmental stimuli (methodological behaviourism) or of neurophysiology (eliminative materialism).

If these approaches exhausted the social science we call psychology, Perry's contrast between descriptive/explanatory social science and conceptually analytic philosophy would hold. The latter would analyse the concept of intention as we use that concept in everyday descriptions and explanations, while the former would replace those everyday descriptions and explanations with others having no place for our ordinary concept of intention.

Yet current cognitive science has developed otherwise. Current cognitive psychology uses conceptual analysis of concepts like intention

[28] Perry, 'Hart's . . . Positivism', above n. 8, at 436–7. [29] Ibid. at 437.

[30] I discuss methodological behaviourism and its challenge to ordinary concepts, in M. Moore, *Law and Psychiatry: Rethinking the Relationship* (Cambridge: Cambridge University Press, 1984), ch. 1.

[31] See John Greenwood (ed.), *The Future of Folk Psychology* (Cambridge: Cambridge University Press, 1991).

because it bets that the best explanation of human behaviour will not replace such concepts even if does deepen them.[32] Conceptual analysis is the handmaiden of cognitive science so conceived. It is part of the 'top down' approach of researchers as they seek to find, for example, more about the neurophysiology of intentional motor behaviour.[33]

Hart was right to place his social science bets in the same direction. He did not distinguish conceptual analysis from descriptive/explanatory social science because he thought it unlikely that the best explanation of social behaviour would use a concept of law alien to the understanding of law of those whose behaviour it was. It would be remarkable if our understanding of ourselves or our societies (in terms of concepts such as those of intention or of law) had no place in such explanations. Perry is right this far: radical surgery to our self-understanding is possible; explanatory success of a radical behaviourism, a radical neurophysiology, or even the kind of radically revisionist sociology of law that some Legal Realists had in mind, cannot be ruled out *a priori*. Possibility is not likelihood, however, and Hart was right to bet that the more successful social science of law would use, not replace, the concept of law with which we understand our society and ourselves.

Even if I am wrong about this, I also doubt that the second step of Perry's argument can be sustained. Suppose we distinguish descriptive/explanatory approaches to law from conceptual ones. Suppose further Hart is, or must be construed to be, doing conceptual analysis, not sociology. Even with these suppositions, there is little reason to infer that Hart must be engaged in a non-general, non-universal, non-descriptive (and thus, 'internal') kind of jurisprudence.

Perry's central argument here stems from what he regards as the necessary failure of any kind of conceptual analysis if that analysis is not: about legal institutions in a particular culture; grounded in the self-understanding (concept of law) of the practitioners within such institutions; and evaluatively loaded in the sense that one seeks to display the culture's concept of law in the morally best light possible.

I emphasize the idea of *necessary* failure here, because it is one thing to show that Hart's actual analyses of obligation, authority, and law are not successful. It is quite another to show that such failure was inevitable because of the kind of conceptual enterprise in which Hart was engaged. One might well conclude, as does Perry, that Hart's analysis of when

[32] Thus, Michael Bratman characterizes his book as an exercise in functionalist cognitive science, even though he analyses the concept of intention. Bratman, *Intentions, Plans, and Practical Reasoning* (Cambridge, Mass.: Harvard University Press, 1983). For a similar view about conceptual analyses of intention, see Myles Brand, *Intending and Acting* (Cambridge, Mass.: MIT Press, 1984).

[33] See M. Moore, *Act and Crime: The Implications of the Philosophy of Action for the Criminal Law* (Oxford: Oxford University Press, 1993), ch. 6.

people regard themselves as obligated is unsuccessful because circular: people regard themselves as obligated whenever they *accept* (for whatever reason) that they are. This is, in truth, not much of an analysis. But this failure of Hart's is contingent. Contrast Hart's shallow analysis with Joseph Raz's deeper (but equally external) analysis of obligation in terms of the *form* taken by obligating reasons within the family of reasons. I examine Raz's analysis in Chapter 5. But briefly, Raz tells us that an obligation is best analysed in terms of exclusionary reasons (negative second-order reasons, i.e. reasons not to act for certain reasons) and that a legal obligation is a new first-order reason created by law when that reason is protected by a second-order, exclusionary reason.

Perry urges that such analyses of concepts have to be barren if they are truly external. He urges this because such detached, uncommitted analyses of others' concepts cannot be revisionary. Such analyses can only report the vagaries, inconsistencies, and disagreements inevitably present with any group's concept of anything. Lacking any evaluative ideal, such analysis cannot revise, unify, and thereby improve the concept in question.[34]

This response by Perry supposes that everyone's concepts need such improvement. It is possible that they don't because our shared concepts have a coherent structure to them. Perry seems to think that in this event, we cannot learn anything from such conceptual analysis that we didn't know already. Yet we may well be surprised by analyses that we instantly recognize, once they are pointed out to us, as right. In one sense we always did know it, but in another, we didn't because we couldn't articulate it prior to doing the conceptual analysis.

As with obligation, Perry similarly faults Hart's conceptual analysis of law itself: Hart attempts to analyse the concept of law descriptively and from the outside rather than by 'going native' and joining the practitioners of law in *their* concept of law. One criticism of Hart's method that Perry advances here is that Hart supposedly relies on his own evaluative judgements about why a system with secondary rules is a *better* legal system than one with only primary rules.[35] This is probably inaccurate to Hart, who *explains* the rise of municipal legal systems by the greater efficiency such systems possess and who judges the later systems to be the more developed variety, and thus our current central case of the concept. But this is by-the-by to the point here: if Hart happened to slip into an evaluative argument, that is not to say he had to.

Perry again is thrust upon his argument that an external, detached conceptual analysis cannot clarify, unify, or elucidate our concept of law. Yet again, this is a contingent claim about the sad shape Perry thinks our

34 Perry, 'Hart's . . . Positivism', above n. 8, at 449.

35 Ibid. at 437–9.

concept of law to be in. Once Perry concedes that 'our conceptual scheme, as it exists at any given time, can be neutrally described from the outside',[36] he has conceded the possibility of Hart's enterprise. All that is needed is a more optimistic view of the coherence of our concept of law than Perry possesses in order to concede Hart a worthwhile and possible task.

For my own part, as I say in Chapter 3, I have never found Hart's external, general jurisprudence to be sufficiently interesting to pursue it very far myself. Internal jurisprudence has much more immediate practical appeal, and that is the kind of jurisprudence I have preferred to practise. What baffles me is why Dworkin, and now Postema and Perry, want stronger grounds on which to justify their own internal jurisprudence than this. It seems a bit ungracious, in addition to being false.

III. CHAPTER 4: FRED SCHAUER'S 'PRESUMPTIVE POSITIVISM'

Chapter 4 deals with the continuation of Hart's jurisprudence of rules done recently by Fred Schauer. Schauer both expanded Hart's enquiry by expanding the topic to include rules in all contexts of decision, not just in law, and amended Hart's recommended decision procedure for judges in the 'core' of authoritative rules, from Hart's Rawls-like practice rule conception to what Schauer calls 'presumptive positivism'. Nonetheless, Schauer's approach to rules is highly reminiscent of Hart's: both focus on what are standardly called social rules. Social rules, as I describe them in Chapter 4, are aids to the decisions of subordinate officials that an institutional designer may or may not choose to employ in order to optimize those decisions. Such rules are means chosen by an institutional designer to preclude non-rule-governed decisions by judges or other officials. Such rules thus require historical formulation to make their content accessible to their subjects, and they often require sanctions to motivate compliance.

My main point in Chapter 4 is to point out two other concepts of rules needed to make sense of much of what has been debated about when rules are at issue in jurisprudence, ethics, and political theory. Those debates have been six in number and have been about: (1) the place of rules in morality; (2) the place of rules within the utilitarian's version of morality; (3) the kinds of reasons that are created by such rules as are issued by legitimate practical authority; (4) whether citizens are obligated, at least *prima facie*, to obey the law; (5) whether law (in the sense of legal system) consists of a set of rules; (6) whether judges do or ought to simply follow the plain

[36] Perry, 'Hart's . . . Positivism', above n. 8, at 458.

meaning of statutory, constitutional, or common law rules. I argue that none of these debates can be understood exclusively in terms of the social rules concept of rules. Needed are two other concepts of rules: what I call the 'real rules' concept, where the rules are true moral laws, not pronouncements by anyone; and what I call the 'authoritative rules' concept, where the rules are the content of a promise, request, command, or other exercise of a valid normative power by one possessed of that power. I argue that the first debate (about morality) can only be understood in terms of the real rules concept; that the second debate (about utilitarianism) is two debates, one in terms of the social rules concept and the other in terms of the real rules concept; that the third and fourth debates (about authority in general, and legal authority in particular) can only be understood in terms of the authoritative rules concept; that the fifth debate (about the general nature of law) is precisely a debate between those equating law with social rules and those equating law with real rules and/or authoritative rules; and that the sixth debate (about how judges should adjudicate under rules) is in reality two debates, one about the proper psychological decision-procedures for judges framed in terms of the social rules concept, and the other, about the truth conditions of those singular propositions of law that decide concrete cases, framed in terms either of the real rules, or of the authoritative rules concepts.

At the written symposium in which Chapter 4 first appeared Fred Schauer responded to my suggested reorientation of his enterprise. In his response Schauer admits the need for the real rules concept of rules in order to make sense of the first debate about the rule-ness of morality.[37] Schauer unfortunately does not address whether the authoritative rules concept of rules is needed in any of the debates which I reference, nor whether he agrees with me in thinking that this concept of rules differs significantly from his social rules concept. Schauer also is silent on what concept of rules is at issue in the second, third, fourth, and fifth debates that I discuss.

Schauer does respond on the sixth debate, which is about proper judicial decision procedures. Schauer finds 'problematic, albeit interesting, [the] distinction between the idea of a correct judicial decision and the procedure that some judge might employ to reach it'.[38] Schauer thus seeks to cloud my distinction between two versions of the sixth debate, one version being about the best decision-procedures for judges and the other version being about what are the correct decisions for judges to reach (however they reach them). Yet the cost of eliding this distinction is simply

[37] F. Schauer, 'The Rules of Jurisprudence: A Reply', *Harvard Journal of Law and Public Policy*, 14 (1991), 839–52, at 842.
[38] Ibid. at 843.

confusion. In science,[39] in ethics,[40] as well as in law,[41] it has long been recognized that we must distinguish what makes a decision right (or a proposition true) from how best to get decision-makers to reach those right results. Without answering the question of correctness, how could we judge various decision-procedures to be better or worse? We judge some decision-procedures to be better than others precisely because those procedures yield a higher percentage of correct results—assuming we know first what makes a result correct.

Schauer has (what he regards as) a separate point to make in response to me on judicial decision-making. This point concedes that we should be talking about what makes a decision correct, and not about how one should go about discovering the correct decision to make. Nonetheless, Schauer is a perspectivalist about the correctness of decisions under rules. Schauer believes that there is an 'unbridgeable gap' between how authority looks from the perspective of the subject and how it looks from the perspective of the authority.[42] What this means for individual judges vis-à-vis those who would design judicial institutions is that the right answer about what judges should do for institution designers may differ from the right answer for individual judges about what they should do in their judging.[43] An institution designer may be correct in barring resort to certain considerations by judges while judges might be correct to pay attention to just those considerations in their judging. Thus, Schauer wishes to say, even if I am right about the answers judges should seek to find (in terms of real or authoritative rules), Schauer claims that he is right from the perspective of a designer of legal institutions in his recommendation that judicial discretion be limited by social rules.

This response by Schauer reminds me of the familiar tale of the indecisive rabbi:

> [A] rabbi was once asked to adjudicate a dispute between two women. The rabbi heard the first and said immediately, 'You're right!' An associate of the rabbi's reminded him that he had also to hear the other side of the story. The second woman spoke, and the rabbi said again, 'You're right!' Calling him aside, his associate whispered, 'They can't both be right.' The rabbi replied, 'You're right!'[44]

[39] See e.g. Israel Scheffler, *Science and Subjectivity* (Cambridge, Mass.: Harvard University Press, 1967), 68–73; Hans Reichenbach, *Experience and Prediction* (Chicago: University of Chicago Press, 1938), 4–5.

[40] See e.g. Samuel Scheffler, *The Rejection of Consequentialism* (Oxford: Oxford University Press, 1982), 44–52.

[41] See e.g. Neil McCormick, *Legal Theory and Legal Reasoning* (Oxford: Oxford University Press, 1978), 14–16.

[42] Schauer, 'Reply', above n. 37, at 849.

[43] Ibid. at 844.

[44] Recounted in Sandra Peterson, 'Remarks on Three Formulations of Ethical Relativism', *Ethics*, 95 (1985), 887–908, at 887.

I find myself in the position of the associate to the rabbi, in this case Rabbi Schauer. The institution designer and the judge cannot both be right in their differing conclusions about correct judicial behaviour.

Showing why this is so is a complicated business. Fortunately Heidi Hurd has written two detailed and powerfully argued pieces, one showing why the meta-ethical version of perspectivalism (in meta-ethical relativism and subjectivism) is false[45] and the other showing why the ethical version of perspectivalism is also false.[46] Since Schauer appears to be of the second kind of perspectivalist, let me summarize very briefly Hurd's argument against this version.

Briefly, such a role-relative morality makes a mockery of the universalizability of moral judgements. If it is right for a judge to construe a criminal statute against the plain meaning of the words contained within it so as better to promote justice, then it is right for any one else that the judge engage in such purposive interpretation. The correct result to reach in such a case, in other words, does not change depending on whose perspective one adopts. The goods achieved by purposive versus literal construction of criminal statutes are goods for everyone, no matter what their position within the legal system. The goods of giving fair warning to citizens, of yielding to democratic decision-making, of substantive justice being achieved in punishment, do not vary by perspective, so how can any combination of those goods in a particular decision vary by perspective or role?

The only way that Schauer garners plausibility for his perspectivalism is by eliding the distinction he finds 'problematic'. For it is plausible for an institution designer to calculate as follows: the average run of judges either lack moral wisdom, are too subject to the emotional appeal of real people before them in hard cases, or insufficiently appreciate the rule of law values and the values of democracy, that they will get it wrong more often than they will get it right if they depart from the plain meaning of statutory language in their decisions. Therefore, it is best to *tell* judges that their duty is to follow that plain meaning without exception. Granted, for some judges this is not the optimal decision strategy, but since at the level of institutional design one cannot separate such judges the best general rule to tell all of them is, 'stick to the plain meaning of statutory language'.

I have argued elsewhere in detail that this is bad advice for an institution designer to give to judges about how they should decide,[47] but the

[45] H. Hurd, 'Relativistic Jurisprudence: Skepticism Founded on Confusion', *Southern California Law Review*, 61 (1988), 1417–509.

[46] H. Hurd, 'Justifiably Punishing the Justified', *Michigan Law Review*, 90 (1992), 2203–324, expanded into a book-length treatment in her *Moral Combat* (Cambridge: Cambridge University Press, 1999).

[47] Michael Moore, 'The Semantics of Judging', *Southern California Law Review*, 54 (1981), 151–294, and 'A Natural Law Theory of Interpretation', *Southern California Law Review*, 58 (1985), 277–398.

relevant point here is what sort of advice it is. Such an institution designer does not disagree at all with judges about what *are* the right results to reach in particular cases. The correct decisions for judges are the correct decisions for the institution designer and vice-versa. What the institution designer is calculating is what decision-procedure he should require judges to use in order to reach the maximal number of those (universally) correct results. Somewhat paradoxically, such a designer would preclude judges from resorting to one of the considerations that is actually a right-making characteristic of judicial decisions. Whether that is right or wrong, one must be clear about what is: it is a recommended decision procedure, having nothing to do with the correctness of the decisions to be reached.

Schauer thus must fudge the distinction between what are good psychological decision procedures and what are legally good decisions in order to have a plausible point to make here. Yet this distinction will not and cannot be collapsed. Where one should get to is one question, and how one should get there is another, whether one is talking about vacation destinations or judicial decisions. And as a matter exclusively of where one should get to in judicial decisions, it is wildly implausible to think that what is right for judges is wrong for institution designers or vice-versa.

IV. CHAPTER 5: JOSEPH RAZ'S REASON-BASED LEGAL POSITIVISM

The last chapter in Part I on legal positivism, Chapter 5, considers the most sophisticated version of legal positivism with which I am familiar, that articulated by Joseph Raz. As I note early in the chapter, Raz's legal theory, unlike that of Hart, asks the perennial jurisprudential question, 'What is law?', as part of a more general enquiry about practical rationality. For Raz, law is a subset of a special kind of reasons, and asking what law is, is to ask what makes those reasons special and how those special reasons interact with the other, more ordinary reasons we have for acting. Despite this difference with Hart, Raz's jurisprudence is fundamentally like Hart's in being an external jurisprudence. While on Raz's account law to be law must be practical in a way that presupposes (or 'claims') to give actors subject to the law certain kinds of reasons for action, Raz's external or 'detached' position allows him to note this fact without endorsing it. Raz's location of law within a general theory of practical rationality does not betoken any (internal) commitment by Raz to the view that laws must actually give actors subject to them reasons for action in order to be laws.

Following Raz's own lead here, the chapter focuses on the sort of reasons that laws and other directives of legitimate practical authorities might plausibly be thought to give. It thus enters into the third debate distinguished above with respect to Fred Schauer. In that debate Raz has staked out a finely honed, elegantly structured position, the keystone of which is Raz's notion of exclusionary reasons. Exclusionary reasons are negative second-order reasons, by which Raz means, they are reasons not to act for certain reasons.

The chapter raises essentially three sorts of questions about Raz's notion of exclusionary reasons: (1) Might it not be the case that the idea of second-order reasons is built on a problematic model of practical rationality, which is that to act rationally is to act on *a balance* of conflicting reasons? (2) Are there not three quite different readings of what an exclusionary reason might be, changing considerably the claims one would be making about law and authority in terms of that concept, depending on which conception of it one had in mind? And (3), are there not serious moral, psychological, and legal objections to the use of each of these three conceptions to unpack our notions of law, legal obligation, and authority?

The paper that became Chapter 5 was presented at All Souls College, Oxford, in the summer of 1988. Joe Raz was the respondent. Predictably, he disagreed with each of my three levels of criticism.[48] In summarizing his responses I shall detail as much of my original criticism as is necessary to understand Raz's thought. The detailed exposition of the criticism is of course to be found in Chapter 5.

Suppose one views practical rationality as a set of objective reasons we each have to act in certain ways and not others. Then in the simplest case where only one such reason bears on the contemplated action it is easy to state what it is rational to do: act in conformity with that reason. Rarely if ever are things that simple, however. More typically, more than one reason bears on any contemplated action, and the question then arises, what is it rational to do? Raz's answer is a familiar and an intuitively plausible one: act on the balance of conflicting reasons.

In Chapter 5 I rather glancingly suggest that reasons are not the sort of things that can conflict, that they have no dimension of weight but rather are all-or-nothing applicable, and that rational action accordingly cannot be acting on the balance of reasons. In this, I align myself with Kant, who with respect to moral reasons held that 'a conflict of duties and obligations is inconceivable'.[49] The alternative model of practical rationality is sketched in Chapter 5: when the content of reasons is fully spelled out, so as to include the exceptions to what we normally have reason to do, there are no conflicting reasons to be balanced off against one another, so that acting rationally is to act in conformity with (non-conflicting) reasons.

[48] Raz's commentary became part of his printed reply in the symposium in which my paper eventually appeared. See J. Raz, 'Facing Up: A Reply', *Southern California Law Review*, 62 (1989), 1153–235, esp. at 1154–62, 1164–78.

[49] Kant, *The Metaphysical Elements of Justice*, trans. John Ladd (Indianapolis: Bobs-Merrill, 1965), 25.

Raz's reply goes to some fundamental issues of moral ontology. Raz urges that 'reasons for an action are considerations that count in favor of that action. . . . That considerations which establish the disadvantages of the action obtain as well, does not in the least show that the reasons do not exist, nor does it show that the reasons are subject to an "exception". The original reason is still there.'[50] Moreover, Raz accuses me of a kind of category mistake in thinking that reasons could have exceptions: 'Exceptions are at home when we consider rules, especially authoritative, institutionalized rules. There are no exceptions to a reason.'[51]

With regard to the basic question of what reasons are, clarity is achieved only by distinguishing reasons for action from reasons for believing what our reasons for action are. The latter are epistemic considerations that we indeed balance when we decide what is true; they are what we more idiomatically describe as evidence. Reasons for action are different. Their content are the norms of morality (or of prudence), telling us what we ought (at least *prima facie*) to do. The norm, people ought to keep their promises, is the content of an objective reason binding on all of us; it is a reason for actor X to do act A on the occasions when he has promised to do A. Various facts evidencing the fact that X did promise to do A, or various considerations evidencing the truth of the moral norm that we ought to keep our promises, are reasons for X to believe that he has a reason to do A.

Now it is obvious what I am going to say: talk of balancing considerations is most at home when what we balance are epistemic considerations about what we ought to believe are our reasons for action. There is no need in addition to think that the things evidenced by these epistemic considerations—reasons for action—themselves conflict and need to be balanced. It is true that we experience conflicts of reasons for actions too, but as I argue in Chapter 5, such experience simply betokens our imperfect grasp of the full content of those reasons for action, which is the relevant moral norm with all of its exceptions.

This brings me to the second of Raz's points in reply to my first critique, the distinction between rules and reasons.[52] If Raz were to mean by 'rules' either the real rules or the authoritative rules that I discuss in Chapter 4, then I fail to see the difference he supposes to exist between rules and reasons; for such rules simply are the content of the reasons we have to act in conformity with them. As such, any exceptions to the rules will be exceptions in the content of reasons, and vice-versa. Such reasons will conflict no more than the rules that are their content.

Perhaps Raz has in mind what I call in Chapters 3 and 4 social rules. These do differ from reasons in the way Raz suggests, for such social rules

[50] Raz, 'Reply', above n. 48, at 1155. [51] Ibid. at 1154. [52] Ibid. at 1155–6.

are instrumental means that a society might adopt so as to optimize the conformity of its individual actors to the reasons for action that bind them. As such, such social rules will not be reasons for action themselves, even though we have reason to adopt them, as Raz suggests. But this suggestion goes no distance towards establishing that reasons for action do not have as their content rules in the other senses I discuss and that such reasons/rules have exceptions to rule out conflict between them in particular cases.

Suppose that my view of practical rationality were adopted; how would that change Raz's account of law and authority in terms of exclusionary reasons? When I wrote the essay that is now Chapter 5, I assumed that how one came out on this issue (about the ontology of reasons) did not affect Raz's hierarchical account of first- and second-order reasons, and thus, his account of law and authority. Raz's reply to my essay has convinced me otherwise.

To see this, we need to turn to the second of the three questions about exclusionary reasons that I earlier distinguished. This was the question about potential ambiguities in what Raz meant by 'exclusionary reasons'. In Chapter 5 I urge that Raz has three distinct concepts elided together. The first I call the justificatory sense. In this sense an exclusionary reason affects the rightness of the decision in question by excluding from counting certain first-order reasons (that would have counted in assessing the rightness of an action, in the absence of the exclusionary reason). The second I call the motivational sense. In this sense, an exclusionary reason does not affect the rightness of an action, only the rightness of doing that action with a certain motive. The third I call the decision strategy sense. In this sense, an exclusionary reason affects the processes by which one decides on the doing of some action; it does this by excluding certain reasons from being considered anymore as reasons justifying the action.

In his Reply Raz states that the only sense of 'exclusionary reason' he ever employed, or intended to employ, was the second or motivational sense.[53] He thus refuses to concede that any of his examples of exclusionary reasons instantiate my justificatory or decision-strategy senses. Let us examine these separately, beginning with the decision-strategy sense.

Take poor old Jill, who is still worrying, after all these years, where to go on her vacation.[54] Raz still thinks that when Jill decides in general always to take her vacation in France, because it is too much trouble to debate about the question every year, that the rule (or general decision) that she has adopted operates as an exclusionary reason. I think that the only sense

[53] Ibid. at 1156.

[54] Jill began her deliberations in Raz, 'Reasons for Action, Decisions, and Norms', in J. Raz (ed.), *Practical Reasoning* (Oxford: Oxford University Press, 1975), at 140–1. See also Raz, 'Reply', above n. 48, at 1156–7.

that can be made of this is by using 'exclusionary reason' in my decision-strategy sense. Raz thinks I am wrong about this.

Our disagreement here harks back to our disagreement about the ontology of reasons. Raz's 'balance of reasons' account of rationality, and his accompanying view that 'reasons for action are considerations that count in favor of that action', leave him bereft of the resources with which to make the needed distinctions here. When reasons for action are merely 'considerations that count', then far too many items are reasons for action. Jill's general decision to take vacations in France, for example. Whereas on my view, such decisions (intentions, rules) are merely intellectual breathing points, way stations along the way to deciding what to do on particular occasions. They are only heuristics, decision procedures, about how best to decide something. At best, they can give actors who adopt them only *subjective* reasons for action. They do not give actors objective reasons of any kind, first order or second order—so long as one's idea of objective reasons is not Raz's ultimately epistemic one of 'considerations that count'.

Contrast Jill's decision, where she subjectively embeds a social rule, to Raz's example of promises and commands. There, the generalizations that describe what was promised or commanded constitute authoritative rules, giving objective reasons for action that are not mere decisional aids. This is why I would still allocate examples like Jill to a decision-procedure sense of exclusionary reasons. On my view of what are reasons for action, her rule gives no reason for action. It is simply a subjectively embedded social rule she makes use of as a decisional aid.

Raz would reply to this that he has no concern with where Jill should go on vacation, nor with how she decides where she should go. He would thus refuse my distinction between decisions (like Jill's) and promises. Both, he would say, create exclusionary reasons in his only sense, namely, the motivational sense. Jill's decision gives her a second-order reason not to go to France on vacation for any motive save that she had earlier decided that France was where she would always go on vacation.[55] I remain steadfast in my belief that this motivational reading of the reasons created by Jill's rule will not go through. The benefits of Jill's having such a rule are the elimination of the uncertainty, anxiety, time lost, etc., of making up her mind on each occasion where she should go on vacation. These benefits are obtainable only if she excludes other possible vacation destinations, and the reasons that favour such destinations, from her deliberations. These benefits are not obtained by Jill acting for Raz's austere reason: reverence for her own rule. For she may well follow her rule (by going to France), and do so only because that was her rule, yet waste her

[55] Raz, 'Reply', above n. 48, at 1157.

time, be anxious and uncertain, because she allowed herself to consider where else to go.[56] Relatedly, she may also follow her rule (by going to France), obtain the benefit of her rule (by not deliberating at all), and yet *not* be motivated in Raz's preferred way. She may go to France because she loves the food there, because her lover is there, etc., etc., even though none of these possible motives entered into her deliberations.

Raz also refuses my justificatory reading of his idea of exclusionary reasons. This I regard as particularly unfortunate, because as I say in Chapter 5 I think the justificatory reading is the best reading of Raz's 'exclusionary reasons'. It is true that in Chapter 5 I ultimately urge that neither promises nor authoritative rules give exclusionary reasons in the justificatory sense. I urge this because to exclude relevant considerations inevitably warps decisions from what would be ideal. Yet this is a *moral* argument by me. The best *conceptualization* of exclusionary reasons remains the justificatory one, even though on moral grounds, I reject its applicability to certain items.

I say that this is the best conceptualization because it presents an intuitively attractive picture of the effect of promises and authoritative rules on practical reasoning, a picture well in line with common sense understandings of these matters. The picture is this: a promise both gives us a new reason to do the action promised, 'A', and it excludes other reasons from counting against doing A (even though these reasons would be quite good reasons for not doing A absent the promise). The new first-order reason created by the promise is thus 'protected' (Raz's term) from competition by the exclusionary nature of the second-order reason created by the promise. The new first-order reason does not have to *outweigh* those other first-order reasons; it *excludes* them from competition. The upshot is that while it may have been right to not-A in the absence of the promise, with the promise it is right to do A.

So construed, Raz would be giving a better analysis of the phenomenon Rawls attempted to capture with his idea of a 'practice rule'.[57] Yet Raz eschews this interpretation. He sees very clearly the kind of case that tests whether his concept of exclusionary reasons is justificatory or motivational: 'while completely disregarding the excluded reasons and letting them play no part in his motivations, John nonetheless performed the action which is in fact indicated by the balance of all the first-order reasons.'[58] About such cases, Raz concludes, the actors are lucky: they do the right thing (i.e. the thing indicated by the balance of *all* first-order reasons, including the excluded ones) *and* they exclude the excluded reasons from their motivations. In Raz's motivational sense of 'exclusionary reasons',

[56] Raz recognizes as much, at least in some such cases. Ibid. at 1157 n. 8.

[57] John Rawls, 'Two Concepts of Rules', *The Philosophical Review*, 64 (1955), 3–30.

[58] Raz, 'Reply', above n. 48, at 1159.

they have acted in accordance with their exclusionary reasons. Since such excluded first-order reasons are only excluded motivationally, but still count for the rightness of the action chosen, such lucky actors still do the right thing.

There is thus no confusion by Raz on the differences between the motivational and the justificatory senses of 'exclusionary reason'. Our disagreement centres on which sense captures the most morally interesting phenomenon. Raz joins Kant in thinking that morality mostly cares about the reasons that motivate our actions; I and many others think that morality mostly cares about the actions themselves. On this latter view, it is thus the ability of an exclusionary reason to affect the rightness of actions that should capture our interest. This is, after all, what authoritative rules, promises, commands, and requests purport to do.

Furthermore, Raz has to recognize that *sometimes* exclusionary reasons must exclude certain first-order reasons from counting as considerations affecting the rightness of action. These exclusionary reasons, in other words, are not merely motivationally excluding. I refer to what Raz calls 'pre-emptive reasons'.[59] A pre-emptive reason, as the name suggests, is the combination of: (1) a new first-order reason that 'depends' for its force on other first-order reasons; and (2) a second-order, exclusionary reason that excludes just those first-order reasons on which the new first-order reason depends. As Raz implicitly recognizes, the very concept of a pre-emptive reason requires the concept of an exclusionary reason in my justificatory sense, not in his motivational sense.

With this concession about those exclusionary reasons involved in pre-emptive reasons, I simply do not understand Raz's refusal to extend the concession. For pre-emptive reasons are very special sorts of protected reasons having no application to some of Raz's best examples of protected reasons, such as promises. A pre-emptive reason excludes only those first-order reasons as were given, pro and con, in the justification of the pre-emptive reason. In Raz's language, the scope of the exclusionary reason is limited to those first-order reasons justifying the new, dependent reason. This is fine as an analysis of arbitrator's decisions and the like; it is not satisfactory for Raz's main targets, promises and laws.

If promises create exclusionary reasons, surely the first-order reasons excluded include more than the considerations on which the force of the promise depends. These first-order reasons are excluded, as Raz recognizes[60] but surely *all* first-order reasons are similarly excluded. To understand the practice of promising, Rawls urged, is to understand that the promisor does not get to count all the many things, pro and con, bearing

[59] Joseph Raz, *The Morality of Freedom* (Oxford: Oxford University Press, 1987), chs. 2–4.
[60] Raz, 'Reply', above n. 48, at 1161.

on the desirability of the action promised; the promisor, as long as there is no exception he falls under, simply counts the promise as his sole and sufficient reason to do the action promised. If this is right, then Raz's concession regarding pre-emptive reasons needs to be broadened. Raz needs a concept of exclusionary reasons in my justificatory sense more generally, if he is to align himself within the categorical tradition on the moral force of promises, rules of morality, and the law.

My third question about Raz earlier distinguished goes to the merits of his analysis of the moral force of promises, laws, etc. Chapter 5 is divided into three parts, corresponding to Raz's claims being taken in each of my three senses of 'exclusionary reason'. My arguments in Chapter 5, and Raz's rejoinders, are too nuanced to be summarized here. The interested reader is referred to both essays for their pursuit of such topics as: can we will the reasons on which we act? Can any exclusionary reason account be given of common law rules, given the powers reserved by all common law courts to overrule retroactively such rules? Can any exclusionary reason account be given of the plain meaning of statutory rules, given the power reserved by most courts to overrule retroactively any such plain meanings? How can we justify our belief, pro or con, that morality's reasons have the hierarchical structure Raz depicts? Do laws concern themselves with an actor's motive, or are their prescriptions usually aimed at actions only (and not against actions for certain reasons)? Should judges reason in a way that blindfolds them from considering certain sorts of considerations, considerations that they would have relied upon if they were not a judge?

V. CHAPTER 6: ROBERT SUMMERS AND THE LEGAL REALISTS

In Part II I turn from conventionalist theories of law—various forms of legal positivism—to sceptical approaches to law. Part II consists of but one chapter, Chapter 6. This, because of my disdain for most forms of scepticism in law. In the abstract, scepticism in many realms of thought is an interesting position with a long and distinguished tradition. Indeed, in some realms of thought such as religion, scepticism is not only interesting but true.

About law and propositions of law, scepticism could also be an interesting position. But to be interesting, such scepticism has to be earned. When it is simply the expression of a juvenile exuberance in trashing others' work, it is not interesting. Scepticism can be interesting when it is the last position one adopts, not the first. That is, an interesting sceptic is one who has tried to account for legal phenomenon in a (philosophical) realist or a conventionalist way; only, having given these positive theories their best run does the interesting sceptic become a sceptic. Then such scepticism is partly earned and deserves some respect.

Sceptical positions are fully earned when those who would be sceptical have also taken the trouble to acquaint themselves with the most sophisticated expressions of the sceptical tradition in their area. There are, for example, sophisticated sceptics about such basic matters as induction, the past, other minds, and even the external world. Those who are sceptical about objective knowledge in general—which broad scepticism is so fashionable in some quarters today—only become interesting if they can advance the argument over their sophisticated forebears in the sceptical tradition. Such advancing of the ball is of course only possible if the would-be sceptic bothers to read and to understand his sophisticated antecedents.

In American legal thought we have seen two waves of scepticism about law, the badly labelled 'Legal Realists' of the 1920s and 1930s, and the Critical Legal Studies Movement of the 1970s and 1980s. Both movements generated far more heat than light. Neither had the patience or the sophistication to become an interesting scepticism about law. Their practitioners were too ill-read, too motivated by the political bottom line, too anti-philosophical in their interests, or just too stupid or sloppy, to be interesting.

That is why in Chapter 10 I could not bring myself to work through the hyperbole of the crits, even though they were the best legal examples in law of the kind of interpretivism I generally critique. Instead, I found more interesting, and thus more worthy adversaries, the likes of Richard Rorty, Stanley Fish, and the dualist hermeneuts. In Chapter 6 I deal more directly with the earlier sceptics about law in America, the Legal Realists. The chapter appeared originally as a book review of Professor Robert Summers's book on the Realists. The main bone of contention between myself and Summers was whether the Legal Realists had a sufficiently sophisticated view about law that they were worthy of much attention.

The view I advance in Chapter 6 is that the Legal Realists were not very interesting thinkers about law. Summers disagreed, both in his book and in the extended reply he wrote to my book review.[61] According to Summers, the Realists collectively created a fourth great tradition in legal theory, to be compared to analytical positivism, historical jurisprudence, and natural law.[62]

Part of the disagreement between us is factual: I say that the Legal Realists held some pretty defective views on precedent, for example, and

[61] Robert S. Summers, 'On Identifying and Reconstructing a General Legal Theory—Some Thought Prompted by Professor Moore's Critique', *Cornell Law Review*, 69 (1984), 1014–46.
[62] Ibid. at 1021.

Summers says that the very thinkers I cite did not hold these views.[63] Part of the disagreement is as to whose views count as 'Realist': I think of Llewellyn and Frank as central Realists, while Summers relegates them to 'the extremist wing'.[64] But the most interesting disagreement is on the questions of how we should construct an idea of what legal theory should be about, and what a complete legal theory would look like (in terms of the questions it asks and the range of answers it finds acceptable).

Chapter 6 advances the view that one has to have one's own concept of what legal theory should be about in order to assess the contributions of a group of people such as the Legal Realists. I call this 'imperial' (as opposed to 'modest') intellectual history. I then outline my own version of that subpart of legal theory of most interest to the Legal Realists, which was the theory of adjudication. I then assess the Legal Realists' answers to the major questions my own best theory of adjudication would ask, finding in almost all cases the Legal Realists' answers to be wanting or absent.

Summers's response was to disagree at all levels of this analysis. He opposed my imperialist methods in historiography, disagreed with my general outline of legal theory, disagreed that my version of the theory of adjudication was the proper one to use in assessing the Legal Realists' contributions, and disagreed that the Legal Realist answers were either absent or obviously wrong even if one were to ask my preferred questions of them.

In truth, there is no consensus to which either Summers or I could appeal about what activities are referred to by 'jurisprudence', 'legal philosophy,' 'legal theory', or 'philosophy of law'. We should not find this disturbing. Philosophy in all of its branches picks itself up by its own bootstraps, in the sense that what one should be doing is as much up for grabs as the positions one stakes out in doing it. By my lights, the most interesting activity going under these rubrics is a normative one. Within the theory of adjudication, for example, I find the normative question of how judges ought to reason in their decisions of disputed law cases, to be an interesting one. It combines theoretically loaded questions with those of a quite practical import.

Such a jurisprudence is not necessarily internal to some particular legal system. That is, it does not have to proceed from the point of view of a participant in some one legal system, and thus such analyses can be a 'general jurisprudence', in one sense of that phrase.[65] Still, such a normative general jurisprudence differs considerably from the sort of general jurisprudence practised by Herbert Hart, for example. As Summers noted in his

[63] Ibid. at 1031.

[64] Ibid. at 1024.

[65] Ruth Gavison notes this about my sort of theory of adjudication. See Gavison, 'Comment', in her *Issues in Contemporary Legal Philosophy: The Influence of H. L. A. Hart* (Oxford: Oxford University Press, 1987), 26 n. 5.

reply to me,[66] Hart's jurisprudence was not only external to any particular legal system, it was also sociological, not normative. Hart was concerned to describe the concept of law implicit in legal practices, and such description was not done from the point of view of some judge working out a theory of adjudication. Hart as a sociologist simply wanted to enquire into the notion of one social practice, that commonly called law (or legal system).

Summers would use this fact to pave the way for one of his theses about the Legal Realists: their social scientific concerns should also be seen as part of jurisprudence and legal theory. Yet I still believe what I say in Chapter 6: 'much of Summers's sociological work leaves the impression of being an answer to a question that is not asked by any properly focused legal theory.' As I explore in Chapter 9, one might view 'law' and 'legal system' as words whose meaning is given by a concept in Locke's sense, not by the nature of some kind; if so, then one will have to do some of the sociological work of the sort that Hart and others have done. Yet such work will still not become the kind of social science that interested some of the Legal Realists and still interests Summers. Indeed, historically such social science (such as the behaviouralist study of judicial behaviour, in terms of scalograms, game theory, and the like) became the Legal Realists' agenda after they had rejected traditional legal theory. Theirs was the naive faith that social science could fill the gap created by their own scepticism about law. This faith, as Hart himself pointed out,[67] was simply a category mistake by them. Such social science may give us reasons to believe that a judge will decide in a certain way; it cannot give that judge a reason (for action) to decide in that way.

It is at precisely this point that Brian Leiter has picked up a lance in favour of the Legal Realists. Leiter recognizes that Robert Summers's project and his own are the same, namely, to depict the Realists as sophisticated legal theorists.[68] Leiter agrees with me in Chapter 6 herein, to the effect that Summers failed in his attempted resuscitation of the Realists precisely because of Summers's own lack of any theory of what jurisprudence should be about or how it should be done.[69]

Taking the lesson to heart, Leiter brings a theory to Legal Realism with a vengeance. Utilizing his considerable philosophical sophistication, Leiter would reconstruct the Realist programme in light of the contemporary philosophical movements known as naturalism and pragmatism. Naturalists in epistemology seek to show how the normative task of justifying belief depends on the descriptive task of causally explaining belief.

[66] Summers, 'On . . . a General Legal Theory', above n. 61, at 1034.

[67] Hart, *Concept*, above n. 4, at 86–8, 143–4.

[68] Brian Leiter, 'Rethinking Legal Realism: Toward a Naturalized Jurisprudence', *Texas Law Review*, 76 (1997), 267–315, at 275 n. 37.

[69] Ibid.

Pragmatists in epistemology seek to show how ultimately justified belief depends on the practical importance of belief to human ends. On Leiter's reconstruction, the Legal Realists had good naturalist and pragmatist grounds for turning jurisprudence into a social science of judicial behaviour. So seen, Leiter concludes that the Realists were not guilty of any simple category mistake, confusing the cause that explains judicial decisions with the reasons that justify judicial decisions. Thus, 'the Realists were not bad legal philosophers, but rather prescient ones, philosophical naturalists before their time'.[70]

Leiter's reconstruction of the Legal Realists is an intriguing one. If Leiter could make the case historically that the Legal Realists put forward the pragmatic, naturalistic theory of jurisprudence that Leiter describes, I would withdraw my conclusion about the Legal Realists. Irrespective of whether such a sceptical theory was right or wrong, it would be an *earned* scepticism and thus worthy of respect, in marked contrast to the unearned scepticisms of the crits and their post-modernist fellow-travellers.[71]

My doubt about Leiter's project is historical: I do not think the Legal Realists had anything like Leiter's philosophically sophisticated reasons for replacing a conceptual and normative jurisprudence with an explanation-giving social science. I think they were simply confused. True enough, some of their views can be fitted to the philosophically sophisticated views Leiter describes; yet as the sayings go, even a broken clock tells the correct time twice every twenty-four hours, and even paranoids do on occasion have real enemies. We rightfully do not honour such accidentally correct judgements.

Consider three central examples of the historical contortions Leiter must go through to turn Karl Llewellyn into Willard Quine. These contortions are about (1) the Legal Realist's concept of law; (2) the Legal Realist thesis on the indeterminacy of law to decide disputed cases; and (3) the Legal Realist replacement of *arguments* giving judges justifying *reasons* (legal or otherwise), with *explanations/predictions* of judicial decision-making in terms of underlying *causes*. The standard interpretation of the Realists on these three items—an interpretation taken by Hart and by myself, as Leiter notes—is this: (1) following Holmes's famous dictum, law is nothing more than a prediction of what judges will do in future cases, real or imagined; (2) the rules that make up a body of law are merely 'pretty playthings' (in Llewellyn's famous phrase), in that such rules can always be reformulated or reinterpreted so as to give either result in any case; (3) predictions of what judges will do are given not only from an external point of view (say,

[70] Ibid. at 315. See also B. Leiter, 'Legal Realism', in D. Patterson (ed.), *A Companion to Philosophy of Law and Legal Theory* (Oxford: Blackwell, 1996), at 264.

[71] Leiter in both of the cited pieces, above nn. 68 and 70, is refreshingly honest about how unsophisticated and silly are the latter kind of sceptics.

to a 'bad man' client who wants only this knowledge about the law) but also from the internal point of view of a lawyer trying to give a judge a reason to do what the judge is predicted to do.

Leiter concedes that if the Legal Realists held such views, then they held a bad philosophy—one so bad that it arguably was not philosophy at all. Leiter's reconstruction of the Realists, however, has them holding none of these views. I take them one at a time.

1. Leiter's Realists are portrayed as legal positivists in the concept of law that they really held. We can know this, Leiter tells us, because of the concept of law implicit in their arguments about the indeterminacy of *law*; presupposed in such arguments is a fairly conventional, positivistic identification of law with statutes and case-rulings.[72] The only reason Realists repeated Holmes's epigram in mantra-like fashion was to make the limited point Holmes himself is construed to have cared about: that any *citizen's* interest in law is predictive because that is where law affects him.

2. The Realists were not globally sceptical about law's indeterminacy. Really they were more like Cardozo than like Frank, the Cardozo who opined that in the vast majority of the cases he had seen there was no indeterminacy in the legal materials.[73] It thus is only in 'a percentage, not large indeed' of the argued cases in an appellate court that the law runs out, and that rules are then merely 'pretty playthings', decorative ornaments in an opinion that is in no way based on them. The only reason Realists often said more extreme things about legal indeterminacy was because they were making a point of behaviourist psychology: to a trained judge, whose knowledge of the law has receded into the intuitive locale of the skills of a trained pianist, attention to the 'brutal facts' of the case before them is all that is required to reach a decision.

3. The Realists never confused normative justification (by giving reasons) with causal explanation/prediction (by giving causes). Rather, they were making one of two moves. Sometimes they were making a point about *non-legal* reasons: when the law is indeterminate, judges are and should be making judgements of policy and justice. Such judgements are justified by justifying (not explanatory) reasons, even if those reasons stem from morality and pragmatic common sense, not from legal materials. Alternatively, sometimes the Realists were making the pragmatist's point that normative (or justifying) reasons cannot be grounded, at least not ultimately; in that sense they lack a foundation. At such an ultimate level, the best we can do, in law or elsewhere, is look to our justifying practices in order to see what counts as a good reason to decide one way or another. In this way good justifying reasons do depend on descriptive/explanatory/

[72] B. Leiter, 'Naturalism and Naturalized Jurisprudence', in Brian Bix (ed.), *Analyzing Law: New Essays in Legal Theory* (Cambridge: Cambridge University Press, 1998).

[73] Benjamin Cardozo, *The Legal Process* (New Haven: Yale University Press, 1923), 164–5.

predictive truths of social science, and it is no category mistake to use such truths in framing reasons justifying a judge in deciding one way rather than another.

Leiter's reconstruction reminds me of a tenure case with which I was once concerned. One of my tenured colleagues proudly declared that the candidate's views were good, and, indeed, much better than they had been before the considerable talents of my colleague had been enlisted by the candidate to improve upon them. My response was that I had no doubt of the quality of the views, only doubt as to whether they could now be said to be the candidate's views.

1. On the Realist's concept of law, Leiter knows as well as any of us that the only *explicit* concept of law the Realists held was the predictive definition of Holmes. It is a curious historiographic method to attribute beliefs to individuals in a way that: (*a*) discounts what they explicitly said, in favour (*b*) of a concept allegedly implicit in their discussion of something else. Leiter attempts to diminish the curiosity of (*a*) by confining their 'law is prediction' pronouncements to contexts of practical advice by lawyers to clients. Yet the very texts Leiter cites support no such confinement; they propounded the Holmesian identification (of law with predicted judicial force) as an eye-opening, refreshingly frank, general theory of law applicable to judges and laypersons alike.[74]

[74] To quote Leiter: 'Holmes makes clear on the very first page of 'The Path of the Law' that he is talking about the meaning of law *to lawyers*, who will "appear before judges, or to advise people in such a way as to keep them out of court" ' (Leiter, 'Legal Realism', above n. 70, at 263). Leiter has written that he is puzzled by my reference to this quotation of Holmes: 'especially puzzling was note [74] where you simply deny what I assert, without citation; it would help . . . if you could offer up some contrary quote from Holmes . . .' Leiter, personal communication, 20 July 1998. Yet no other quote is needed. Notice that Holmes sees clearly that lawyers perform two different services for clients: they advise clients how to stay out of court and they represent clients in court. The first task is predictive, but the second surely is not. To do the second task, a lawyer must vicariously be a judge; he must offer up good justifying reasons for deciding in his client's favour. If the law is one of those reasons—as it surely is—the law cannot be simply a prediction of how the judge will decide. Yet Holmes explicitly identifies law with 'what the courts will do in fact' *and* takes this to be the answer needed by the legal profession 'in order to appear before judges' no less than to advise clients. This strikes me as seeking a general answer to the question of what law is—general enough at least for lawyers to use in their professional tasks—and to be a very bad answer to that question.

The second half of Holmes's famous essay, 'The Path of the Law', deals with judicial duty when the settled doctrines either must be extended in new directions or even changed (when such doctrines point to results that make no sense in changed circumstances). Holmes concludes that 'the judges themselves have failed adequately to recognize their duty of weighing considerations of social advantage. The duty is irresistible . . .' Yet Holmes had earlier reduced any legal duty into a 'prophecy that if he does certain things he will be subject to disagreeable consequences', and tells us that this predictive interest is what motivates our talk of a judge's legal duties no less than a citizen's legal duties. This is again to ask a general question about legal duty—general enough for judges as well as citizens—and then to give a very bad answer, in terms of predictions.

Leiter also cites Jerome Frank as another Realist who limited his theory of law (as prediction) to the predictive needs of clients of lawyers. That Frank had no such limits in mind is

As to the evidence for (*b*), Leiter relies on what were at best *arguendo* concessions by the Realists. They conceded for purposes of argument that law was just as their positivist and formalist adversaries conceived it to be, a matter of duly enacted statutes and historically formulated common law rules. Even so, they argued, that stuff (that their opponents prized as law) was indeterminate in the decisions of judges. Such use of an opponent's concept in order to show him the uselessness of that concept, hardly betokens one's own subscription to the concept.

2. About the indeterminacy of legal materials to dictate outcomes in particular cases, Leiter would make the Realists such reasonable fellows you have to wonder what all the fuss was about. The conventional wisdom has always been that if there are hard cases, where the legal materials do not yield unique answers, so there are easy cases where they do. All save certain (but not all) formalists and certain (but not all) natural lawyers subscribe to this wisdom, making it extremely conventional, and Leiter would paint the Realists as just another instance of this dominant view.

Unless the contemporaries of the Realists of the 1920s and 1930s were paranoid, Leiter's low-key interpretation of the Realists cannot be right. Mainstream views can hardly generate the apoplexy the Realists generated within the more traditional legal academy. We should understand the Realists as their contemporaries understood them, as radicals about the indeterminacy of law.

Leiter's explanation of why the Realists seemed to say so many radical things about global indeterminacy in law is symptomatic of the extreme charity that Leiter exhibits generally towards the Realists. The Realists *were* focused on what Leiter calls their 'core claim', that the salient *causal* determinants of judicial discussions were the facts of cases.[75] The Realist phenomenology of judging is indeed replete with descriptions of listening carefully to the facts of disputed law cases and then using intuition, emotion, and hunches—not logic, legal rules, and deduction—to decide the case. Yet unlike Leiter, the Realists never saw the difference between what

betrayed by the following: 'Of course, anyone can define "law" as he pleases. The word "law" is ambiguous and it might be well if we could abolish it. But until a substitute is invented, it seems not improper to apply it to that which is central in the work of the practicing lawyer. *This book is primarily concerned with "law" as it affects the work of the practicing lawyer and the needs of the clients who retain them*' (Jerome Frank, *Law and the Modern Mind* (Gloucester, Mass.: Peter Smith, 1970), 51–2, n. 4 (emphasis in original)). Like Holmes, Frank recognized that clients expect, and lawyers perform, two distinct tasks: 'The major portions of a lawyer's time is today devoted to predicting or bringing about decisions of judges . . .' (ibid. at 51 n. 4). Despite the second, non-predictive task of lawyers, Frank adopts the particularistic view of law distinctive of Legal Realism; for Frank, 'actual law' is a specific past decision and 'probable law' is a guess as to a specific future decision. Ibid. at 50–1. This is a very bad answer for at least half of what lawyers (and their clients) need from a concept of law.

[75] Leiter, 'Rethinking Legal Realism', above n. 68, at 269.

Leiter calls the rational indeterminacy of legal materials—a logical question—and what Leiter calls the causal indeterminacy of legal materials. The Realists thought that if the psychology of judging were as they described it, then they would have shown the rational indeterminacy of legal materials. They unlike Leiter did not see the difference between the psychology of discovery—an empirical causal question—and the logic of justification—a logical question about possibilities.[76] Their 'core claim' thus does not explain why they looked like they were radical in their claims of indeterminacy but were not in fact, which is Leiter's use of it. Rather, their confusion was such that they took their core claim in psychology to be as well a core claim about the determinacy of legal materials. They were thus not only radicals about legal indeterminacy, but deep muddle lay at the root of their radical views.

3. Leiter's charity towards the Realists is most evident in his interpreting them as prescient precursors to post-Quinean naturalized epistemology. Even if it turned out to be the case that normative, justifying reasons in law must ultimately be grounded in the beliefs and conventions studied by social science, the complex argumentation needed to sustain that conclusion was far beyond the interests and abilities of the Realists. They may have arrived at the point also arrived at by a sophisticated, naturalized jurisprudence; but surely how they got there makes all the difference in assessing their place in history. There is a world of difference between someone who sees a deep divide and cleverly finds a new and ingenious way across, and someone who never sees the divide to begin with but who stumbles across it in his blindness. The Legal Realist supplanting of reasons which justify, with causes that explain, is much more the latter than the former.

It is a bit iurenic of Leiter to articulate a philosophically sophisticated view and then to pass off his discovery as a rediscovery of the real views of a group of people who would not know what he is talking about. I thus remain unconvinced that the Legal Realists were any different than the more recent crits: sceptics whose scepticism is unearned and thus uninteresting and unworthy of much attention. Contemporary philosophers of law who wish to describe or defend an earned scepticism should adopt Priscilla's advice to John Alden when he proposed marriage on behalf of Myles Standish: 'speak for yourself, John.'

VI. CHAPTER 7: RONALD DWORKIN AND THE RIGHTS THESIS

In Part III I turn to a decidedly non-sceptical view about law. This is the view according to which morality is a matter of objective fact, and law is

[76] See text at nn. 39–42, above.

in some way intimately related to morality. As I explore in Chapter 9, the combination of these two theses is often referred to as a 'natural law' view.

In each of the three essays collected in this part Ronald Dworkin figures prominently. This may be surprising in light of the contentions advanced here and elsewhere, that Dworkin is not a natural lawyer. Yet it is Dworkin's meta-ethics that disqualifies him from being a natural lawyer, as I shall explore shortly. About the relational thesis (between law and morality), Dworkin's has been a powerful and interesting voice.

In the 1960s and 1970s Dworkin was intrigued by the seeming complexities of law in well-established legal systems such as those of England and America. He took seriously the old maxim that decorates a number of law school façades in America, that law is a 'seamless web'. Dworkin extracted two theses out of this hoary old maxim. One he called the rights thesis, according to which litigants in disputed law cases were not supplicants of a favourable exercise of judicial discretion but rather, they were holders of legal rights. The second thesis Dworkin dubbed the right-answer thesis. According to this thesis litigants even in the hardest of cases (where there was no obvious law bearing on the question, or where there was too much law in the sense that the relevant standards conflicted with each other in their recommended decision) had either the legal right to prevail or the legal duty to lose. There was, in other words, a right answer in all cases.

In Chapter 7 I explore the first of these theses, the rights thesis. In order to make the thesis plausible, Dworkin argued that 'the law'—the stuff that binds judges, and that is not merely discretionary with them—includes more than its obvious components like statutory and common law rules. It includes more general standards Dworkin called legal principles. In the first half of Chapter 7 I describe my own reconstruction of what I took to be Dworkin's argument for the existence of legal principles and for why law is best seen as a constellation of such principles rather than as a set of source-based rules. Not surprisingly, with such a sympathetic reconstruction of his argument Dworkin found little to dispute. Although not published until recently, this reconstruction was presented by me at a symposium I put on at Harvard in the spring of 1977 as part of the Law and Humanities Programme. Dworkin was kind enough to attend and to respond.

The one critical point on which Dworkin and I disagreed was with respect to what I distinguish in Chapter 7 as Dworkin's fourth question: can there be a source-based test—a factual pedigree of the kind Hart called a rule of recognition—for legal principles? To escape the charge that his coherentist and holistic view of law was simply a different form of legal positivism, Dworkin needed the answer to that question to be 'no'.

As I explore in Chapter 7 and elsewhere, 'no' is probably the right answer here, but not for the reasons Dworkin had advanced in his three main jurisprudential essays of the 1960s and 1970s. The example considered in our discussion was that mentioned in Chapter 7, C. C. Langdell's principle of contract law, to the effect that there could be no contract unless there was a 'meeting of the minds' of the parties to it. I proposed such a principle as a seeming example of value-free derivation: Langdell claimed to derive it inductively from his reading of Anglo-American contract cases. Dworkin's response was to deny Langdell's claim. It was because Langdell thought that only communicated promises gave rise to expectations, or some such moral notion, that led Langdell to posit this as his most basic principle of contract law. Dworkin then pressed on to make a stronger claim of necessity: what else could justify a judge in using such a principle to decide future cases but a principle having moral content? As Dworkin sloganized this claim: 'What else can justify but a justification?'

Dworkin's contingent claim about Langdell is probably true. Langdell probably was influenced by his sense of when promises ought to bind so as to read contract law in the way that allowed him to extract his famous 'meeting of the minds' principle. But for his argument Dworkin needed the stronger claim, that of necessity, and this the argument failed to establish. As I mention in Chapter 7, a judge might be justified in using a legal principle like Langdell's, not by the goodness of the principle's content, but rather by the enhancement of the rule of law values such use of the principle makes possible. Whether such an enhancement occurs is a matter that has to be shown, but there is nothing in Dworkin's argument thus far that shows such enhancement to be impossible.

The second half of Chapter 7 defends my reconstruction of Dworkin's early treatment of legal principles against the recent critique of Larry Alexander and Ken Kress.[77] In Chapter 7 I construe Alexander and Kress to be making two points against Dworkin's legal principles: (1) the generalizing of past law implicit in Dworkin's idea of legal principles will not in fact enhance the rule of law values, such as the values of equality, liberty, and fairness; and (2) even if there can be some enhancement of such values by judges generalizing legal rules in the way Dworkin recommends, such generalizing efforts do not need distinctively legal principles since correct moral principles will both achieve such virtues *and* be morally preferable.

My argument in the second half of Chapter 7 seeks to dispute both of these points. Against the first, I urge that generalizing more particular legal rules *may* enhance predictability, and *does* enhance equality, two rule of law virtues. Against the second, I urge that generalizations about how such generalizing should go in its attempt to enhance such rule of law

[77] Larry Alexander and Ken Kress, 'Against Legal Principles', in A. Marmor (ed.), *Law and Interpretation* (Oxford: Oxford University Press, 1995), reprinted in *Iowa Law Review*, 82 (1997), 739–86.

values will constitute the content of principles that will not be the same as the content of correct moral principles; such generalizations are appropriately called, therefore, *legal* principles.

In their response to my essay, Kress and Alexander deny that equality does the generalizing work I claim.[78] They reassert their original claim that equality is never a powerful enough value to justify projecting morally mistaken legal decisions into the future; the values that make such decisions mistaken will always outweigh equality. On this, issue is joined, so I leave to the reader whether Chapter 7 makes its case.

VII. CHAPTER 8: RONALD DWORKIN AND THE RIGHT-ANSWER THESIS

Chapter 8 takes a hard look at Dworkin's right-answer thesis. The analysis specific to the right-answer thesis will be found in the second of the three major sections of this chapter. In that section I first clarify what the right-answer thesis asserts, what its presuppositions are, and the extent to which Dworkin's rights thesis commits him to a right-answer thesis. The major portion of that section is then devoted to an examination of the arguments, pro and con, about whether there are right answers to all disputed law cases in a legal system such as ours.

My agreement with the right-answer thesis will become apparent to any reader of Chapter 8. My disagreement with other views of Dworkin will be equally apparent on a reading of the first and third sections of Chapter 8. In the first section of that chapter I describe in detail Dworkin's conventionalist metaphysics about law, literature, and morality. A central thesis of Chapter 8 is that one cannot simultaneously assert conventionalist metaphysics and the right-answer thesis about any field of discourse, legal discourse included.

Dworkin strongly disagrees with my attribution of conventionalist metaphysics to him, particularly about morality. Chapter 8 had originally been solicited by Peter Clark on behalf of the *Philosophical Quarterly* in Scotland, as a book review of Dworkin's *A Matter of Principle*. The essay became too expanded for that format and so was transferred over to an American law review, for whom length was less of a problem. Prior to the original publication of Chapter 8 as a book review, Dworkin took it upon himself to obtain a manuscript copy and to urge me that he was 'not even in your sense, a conventionalist about morals'.[79] Dworkin conceded that he 'would write the passage about natural and constructed theories in my article on Rawls in *Taking Rights Seriously* differently now'.[80] Dworkin

[78] L. Alexander and K. Kress, 'Replies to Our Critics', *Iowa Law Review*, 82 (1997), 923–41, at 930–2.

[79] Personal communication, 9 March 1986.

[80] Ibid.

thought he '*was* a moral realist, and in any case cheerfully agree to become one' because he certainly agreed 'that many of the various claims I make very much depend on the kinds of claims about morality that you take to comprise moral realism'.[81]

One thing that these remarks make clear is that Dworkin thinks that he is a moral realist, in some sense of that phrase. Yet Dworkin would be the last to claim any incorrigible authority for any author, himself included, about what his true views are on any subject. Anyone who reconstructs what people say they believe on a given subject in light of their other beliefs, has to allow that he might be mistaken in the views he attributes to himself. I wrote the first section of Chapter 8 quite aware that Dworkin never has thought of himself as a conventionalist about morality. Yet such a conventionalist metaphysics is the best rational reconstruction I can make of the many things Dworkin has said and believed. Dworkin's stated beliefs in this regard are copiously quoted and referred to in Section I of Chapter 8, and I invite readers to judge this issue for themselves.

What Dworkin thinks he is in metaphysics, I describe in Section III of Chapter 8. Despite the quotations earlier, Dworkin's avowed metaphysics is not realist about morality or laws, for Dworkin qualifies his 'realism' thusly:

> Our only disagreement, I think, is about what realism is or can be in morals. I believe it is a moral position. You apparently believe that it is a *causal* position, the thesis that moral beliefs are caused by moral facts.[82]

As I detailed in another article,[83] there are lots of philosophers who call themselves moral realists today. Only some of these actually advance the ontological and semantic claims about truth distinctive of metaphysical realism about morality. The rest, Dworkin included, appropriate the label, 'moral realist', as a rhetorical ploy by which they hope to reap the many advantages of realist metaphysics without having to pay the price in terms of (what they regard as) queer ontological commitments.

The logical space Dworkin hopes he can occupy about morality is a kind of deflationism.[84] Using Dworkin's distinctions (discussed in Section III of Chapter 8), Dworkin thinks that the only criticism or support that can be

[81] Ibid. Dworkin eventually came to elaborate on his kind of 'moral realism' in R. Dworkin, 'Objectivity and Truth: You'd Better Believe It', *Philosophy and Public Affairs*, 25 (1996), 87–139.

[82] Personal communication, 9 March 1986.

[83] Michael Moore, 'Moral Reality Revisited', *Michigan Law Review*, 90 (1992), 2424–53, at 2445–6.

[84] 'Deflationism' is usually restricted to label a position about truth. I intend a broader meaning, in that Dworkin seeks to deflate all kinds of metaphysics, ontological as well as truth-related, about morality and law. One of Dworkin's admiring interpreters, Nicos Stavropoulos, prefers the label 'quietist' for Dworkin's (and his own) attitude towards metaphysics. Stavropoulos, *Objectivity in Law* (Oxford: Oxford University Press, 1996), 161.

made for substantive moral conclusions will be *internal* to our practice of morality; and further, such criticisms or support are usually only usefully made at *retail*, challenging or justifying a limited subset of our moral beliefs, not at *wholesale* where the justifiability of all of our moral beliefs would be up for grabs. This is what Dworkin means when he says that he is a moral realist on moral, not on causal, grounds. He means that only substantive moral arguments can be given for the moral realist tenets, not a causal, external, global argument of a true realist metaphysics.

My reason for refusing to take Dworkin's deflationism seriously is because there is no logical space for such a position. It is instructive to contrast Dworkin's stated deflationism with the most sophisticated form of contemporary non-cognitivism, that of Simon Blackburn[85] and Jeremy Waldron.[86] Blackburn and Waldron call themselves 'quasi-realists'. This, because they like Dworkin help themselves to the many implications of metaphysical realism about morality (such as truth conditional semantics, bivalence, claims of knowledge, divorce of critical judgement from any conventional mores), and yet, again like Dworkin, eschew any ontological commitment to moral entities like rights or to moral qualities like goodness.

One might picture quasi-realism this way: on Monday through Friday, when the quasi-realist is doing substantive ethics, he takes his practices with full realistic seriousness. He says his moral judgements are true or false, he proclaims their correspondence with moral facts, he proclaims his independence from moral conventions, he recognizes his own moral fallibility. It is only on the weekends, when he is reflecting on his work-week activities, that he reverses field: all that seemingly realist talk is not to be taken at face value, for all he was doing was staining the world with his own projected 'qualities'. He was reporting no independent moral facts, because he was reporting no facts at all. He was merely expressing his attitudes.

Dworkin is no quasi-realist. For there is an untenable external/internal distinction crucial to maintaining quasi-realism. In the terms of the work-week metaphor above, the problem is this: what prevents the sceptical meta-ethics the non-cognitivist discovers on his weekends, from penetrating the practice of substantive ethics during the week so as to rob the latter of its full realistic seriousness? If one can get external to the practices of morality—to say, 'it's all a game we play to express our attitudes in a cer-

[85] Simon Blackburn, *Spreading the Word* (Oxford: Oxford University Press, 1982). Blackburn himself has seen the similarity between his quasi-realism and Dworkin's deflationism. See Blackburn, 'Symposium on Ronald Dworkin's "Objectivity and Truth"', Brown University Philosophy Department Website, 11 Nov. 1996.

[86] Jeremy Waldron, 'The Irrelevance of Moral Objectivity', in R. George (ed.), *Natural Law Theories* (Oxford: Oxford University Press, 1992).

tain way'—why doesn't that externally generated scepticism come back inside the practice of morality? One can boldly proclaim, as Simon Blackburn does, that it is a kind of category mistake to conjoin the concepts of meta-ethics with those of ethics, as in the statement, 'if my emotions about slavery were different, then the truth of the judgement that slavery is unjust would also be different'.[87] Yet as Quine asked of Ryle's similar strategy in the philosophy of mind, what *in language use* could possibly show there to be a category mistake here?[88]

Dworkin may be a queasy realist, but he is no quasi-realist. For he would not utter the sceptical statements about morality that the quasi-realist utters from a perspective external to that morality. Indeed, Dworkin denies sense to such external, wholesale scepticism, as I examine in Section III of Chapter 8. But this should lead one to ask of Dworkin, where he is on the weekends. Dworkin's answer apparently is that of the workaholic: there are no weekends. Ethics is a seven-day-a-week business, with no chance to step back and reflect on its deepest presuppositions from some external, amoral (read, metaphysical) viewpoint.

Yet if Dworkin were right about this, then he should be an unqualified metaphysical realist about morality. For Dworkin, like the quasi-realist, aspires to practise his substantive ethics with full realist seriousness. And if there are no fireside moments—where in reflective moods, external to one's practice, one doubts the presuppositions of that practice—then there is only the full realist seriousness as the appropriate metaphysics for morality.

As much as I suspect that Dworkin thinks that he holds exactly this position, there are three reasons to doubt it. The first doubt stems from the reasons (given in Section III of Chapter 8) to reject Dworkin's supposed impossibility of judging our moral practices from an amoral, metaphysical viewpoint. Because we can and do judge our moral practices in terms of the metaphysics that they presuppose, any supposed deflationism is surely an incomplete theory. That is, suppose one adopts a deflationary account of the truth predicate, according to which the statement, 'p is true' adds nothing to the assertion of 'p' by itself. The predicate, 'is true', on this familiar analysis is redundant to the proposition of which the predication is made. One may well be able to adopt this familiar deflationist analysis, and yet the question will remain: what is the reference and the extension of the singular terms and predicates that occur in some moral statement, p? Deflationism only defers slightly, but does not eliminate, the need for some kind of metaphysics, be it realist, conventionalist, or sceptical.

[87] See my discussion of Blackburn and Waldron on this point, in Moore, 'Moral Reality Revisited', above n. 83, at 2456–9.

[88] W. V. Quine, *Word and Object* (Cambridge, Mass.: MIT Press, 1960), 131.

Given this possibility of an external perspective on morality, and given the necessity for a theorist to have some ontological commitments from that perspective, it is no surprise how many things Dworkin allows himself to say from a perspective external to our substantive moral practice. These are detailed in Section I of Chapter 8, and form the basis of my second doubt here. Dworkin does spend his weekends outside his own moral practices, and what he sees in such moments is the relativity of the sense of this enterprise to the deepest conventions that we share. That is why at bottom I characterize Dworkin's metaphysics as conventionalist.

My third doubt stems from Dworkin's ontological queasiness even inside his own moral practices. For in fact, Dworkin does not match the quasi-realist stride for stride in practising substantive ethics with full realist seriousness. Dworkin's queasiness prevents him from talking about the 'mind-independent moral facts' that are distinctive of any form of moral realism. Thus, even if Dworkin were right that there is no perspective external to our moral practices from which we can judge those practices' deepest presuppositions, he himself maintains an internal perspective that is not realist. What Dworkin's ontological commitments might be, he will not say. At a lengthy public debate on this topic at All Souls College, Oxford, in 1987, I asked Dworkin whether his metaphysics allowed him to assign a truth value to statements using moral concepts like justice in ways totally alien to our practices of justice. Suppose, that is, there was no plateau of agreement (concept) about justice that made possible disagreements (conceptions) about what was just. For example, one discussant's position is that killing babies for fun is the central demand of justice. Since for Dworkin, 'justice is an institution',[89] not a mind—and convention—independent moral quality, one might expect there to be no sense to be assigned to such statements outside *our* concept of justice. Dworkin, however, holds such statements to have a truth value even internal to our practices (namely, the truth value, 'false'). Yet when asked, 'By virtue of *what* are such statements false?', Dworkin's (even internal) deflationism forces him into silence.

Not so silent has been Nicos Stavropoulos, who has come to Dworkin's defence at just this juncture. Stavropoulos joins Dworkin in his metaphysical abstinence,[90] but unlike Dworkin gives a detailed answer to questions such as mine. Stavropoulos's answer is I think Dworkin's intended answer, so I shall lay it out before I question it.

In one sense, it is by virtue of nothing but our own conventional practices that we can assign a truth value to statements using concepts alien to

[89] Ronald Dworkin, *Law's Empire* (Cambridge, Mass.: Harvard University Press, 1986), 73.

[90] In response to my suggestion (as referee for the book) that he clarify this issue, Stavropoulos now explicitly joins 'Dworkin's quietist conclusions' about metaphysics. Nicos Stavropoulos, *Objectivity*, above n. 84, at 162.

our practices. As Stavropoulos puts it in his explicit attempt to join Dworkin on this issue, the only constraints that exist are the 'paradigmatic applications and abstract characterizations of the relevant practice of application' that we are practising.[91] Paradigmatic exemplars and deep concepts ('abstract characterizations') are the traditional tools of the deep conventionalist, as I have sought to show in detail elsewhere.[92] That is why in Section I of Chapter 8 I keep calling Dworkin (and now, Stavropoulos) a conventionalist.

A clear-headed deep conventionalist, however, would not find my revolutionary question sensible.[93] After all, if there is no moral reality against which such questions can be checked, and if such questions use a concept of justice wholly alien to our concept of justice, then my sort of question is not false but senseless. This is, indeed, precisely what Dworkin seems to say of such questions. Dworkin imagines the revolutionary judgement that abstract art is unjust. Dworkin then urges the conclusion of my clear-headed deep conventionalist:

> The thesis that abstract art is unjust is not even unattractive; it is unintelligible as a theory about justice because no competent preinterpretive account of the practice of justice embraces the criticism and the evolution of art.[94]

Likewise, consider the example fed to Stavropoulos by Dworkin:

> Suppose an art critic looking at a painting says 'there is a unicorn there'. It is intuitively inappropriate for a biologist to object that unicorns do not exist. It seems that we know *a priori* that this is inappropriate, it seems that we do not simply count this as a wrong remark about the painting but as a remark about something else altogether.[95]

Such analyses of such examples is why Joseph Raz, attending the All Souls exchange between myself and Dworkin, accused Dworkin of 'cheating' (by Dworkin's giving the truth value, 'false', to such revolutionary questions). By 'cheating', Raz meant, illicitly seeking to avoid the embarrassing implications of Dworkin's own deepest metaphysical commitments.

Stavropoulos would urge that there is no cheating going on here, because my revolutionary questions are never really rejected *a priori*, on the conventionalist's ground that they abuse the concept of justice. Rather, Dworkin/Stavropoulos reject my revolutionary questions on grounds of a substantive theory about justice.[96] It is because they (and all sensible people, myself included) have substantive theories of art, biology, and

[91] Ibid. at 160.
[92] Moore, 'A Natural Law Theory', above n. 47, at 291–301.
[93] On 'revolutionary judgements' and 'revolutionary questions', see Moore, 'Moral Reality Revisited', above n. 83, at 2467–8.
[94] Dworkin, *Law's Empire*, above n. 89, at 75.
[95] Stavropoulos, *Objectivity*, above n. 84, at 181.
[96] Ibid. at 180–6.

justice, and because those theories (not conventions or shared concepts) make justice and biological existence not the kind of qualities appropriately ascribed to art that gives my revolutionary questions their external flavour. What is actually going on is that it is our substantive theories of these matters that determine when a question is sensible, and hence capable of being either true or false, and when that question is senseless because external to our practices of art, biology, and justice.

Stavropoulos unblinkingly endorses the obvious implication of his position: all *sensible* questions—questions capable of having a truth value—are internal to our practices. The only items external are senseless questions. The trick is to see that what bounds and individuates our practices is *not* any items of conventional agreement, be they shared paradigmatic exemplars, abstract concepts, or Dworkin's 'pre-interpretive data'. That is what allows our substantive theories of justice, art and biology to move the boundaries of our practices to include (namely, make internal) all revolutionary questions that are sensible enough to have a truth value.

I shall close with one observation about this position. This is to notice that Stavropoulos has come full circle to the point at which we began. His argument gives no more an answer to my question than did Dworkin's silence: by virtue of what can revolutionary judgements have a truth value, according to a theory that rejects both a mind-independent quality of justice and any deep concept of justice shared enough to provide the plateau of agreement that makes disagreement possible? What are our substantive theories (that patrol the borders of the external/internal and that adjudicate what is sensible) *of*, if they are not either theories of the things, justice, beauty, and biological existence, or of the concepts of justice, beauty, and biology? What motivates us to move the boundaries of our practices so as to accommodate some revolutionary judgements as internal and thus sensible, and others as external and thus senseless, if it is *not* some new insight about either the thing, justice, or a deep concept of justice that our (surface) practices hitherto have failed to capture? That question of reference and sense is not answered by Stavropoulos's argument any more than it was by Dworkin.[97]

[97] Separately from the argument just discussed in the text, Stavropoulos does give an answer to my ontological question. Legal properties supervene upon both institutional facts and moral properties, and moral properties supervene upon natural ones. Ibid. at chs. 3, 4. Although Dworkin in private correspondence has advocated the latter of these supervenient relations (we must take 'moral properties to be supervenient properties, as I believe they plainly are'), Stavropoulos is correct to say that 'Dworkin does not talk, or talks very little, about properties, entities, reducibility, supervenience and so on' (ibid. at 161). Stavropoulos is not nearly as quiet as Dworkin on these issues. Indeed Stavropoulos reveals himself in detail to be a naturalist realist about morals of a very similar stripe to my own naturalist-realism, in that we both defend a supervenience of moral properties upon natural ones with irreducibility. Compare ibid. at 103–11, with Moore, 'Moral Reality Revisited', above n. 83, at 2491–533. We both defend the existence of moral properties in part by their role in the best

I understand that both Dworkin and Stavropoulos would like to help themselves to the many advantages of a realist semantics for both law and ethics, and to do so without what they regard as the embarrassing ontological commitments of a realist metaphysics. I fear that this is very much like wanting to fly but refusing to accept airplanes for the purpose. That is why I ultimately deny that there is any logical space for their 'position', and why I ultimately construe them both to be deep conventionalists. So construed, they do indeed 'cheat' when they pretend to find sense (or at least the possibility of sense) in revolutionary uses of shared concepts.

VIII. CHAPTER 9: THE FUNCTIONALIST APPROACH TO NATURAL LAW

The last chapter of Part III, Chapter 9, was written for what was to be an Oxford Series student reader on natural law. The essay thus develops no natural law theory of its own. Rather, it seeks to lay out the general structure natural law positions tend to take. I use three contemporary theorists for this purpose, Lon Fuller, Ronald Dworkin, and John Finnis, with most emphasis on the work of the latter. Chapter 9 attempts to set forth the structure common to all such theories, a structure cast in terms of a functionalist jurisprudence. As Chapter 9 explores in greater detail, a functionalist approach to jurisprudence seeks to find the (real or nominal) essence of law in the functions served in the promotion of some value or discrete set of values. This approach is to be distinguished from a structuralist approach, where one seeks to find institutional structures (such as sanctions, or habits of obedience) that are necessary for there to be law.

Whether a functionalist approach to jurisprudence can generate a natural law view of human law is the central critical question posed (but not answered) by the chapter. The central problem is this: to be a functional kind, law must be a thing in the service of some discrete set of values that is smaller than the set of all values there are. Yet if some structure is law just because it serves such a subset of values, then how can it be necessarily true that law is sufficiently just that it obligates citizen obedience, a crucial premise in the natural law argument? After all, a kind can serve one value well (such as food preparation), and yet disserve other values greatly. Unless a functional kind serves some end so valuable that its

explanation of our moral beliefs. In this, both Stavropoulos and I differ from Dworkin, who believes that 'the thesis that moral beliefs are caused by moral facts . . . seems to me at variance with taking moral properties to be supervenient properties, as I believe they plainly are' (Dworkin, above n. 79). Stavropoulos disagrees with this, as he should. What I do not understand is how such full-blown realism about morality is in any sense a relative of Dworkin's metaphysical quietism. See Stavropoulos, *Objectivity*, above n. 84, at 162. Such realism should allow Stavropoulos to say (as well as I), that it is the nature of justice that guides and motivates the boundaries of our practices and our concepts of justice.

attainment always outweighs other ends—not a very likely possibility—then something can serve the requisite function sufficiently to be of the kind and yet fail to be all-things-considered valuable.

Or so it seems. I urge that Dworkin's equality/integrity, Finnis's common good, and Fuller's inner morality of law all should be seen as attempts to get around this problem. The general strategy I attribute to each is to locate law's function in the service of a value that is *both* a discrete value in its own right, and yet is connected to all other values there are. (Equality, for example, is a discrete value and yet depends on all other values to spell out the *relevant* respects in which people or situations are similar enough to deserve like treatment.) Then if something serves such a value, it also serves all other values too.

The response of each of these three thinkers to this characterization must mostly be reconstructed. Fuller had died years before this essay appeared, and Dworkin has never responded to this functionalist interpretation of his jurisprudence. The problems for Fuller's functionalism are daunting. In the first place, Fuller's 'governance of human behaviour by rules' is an implausible candidate for an intrinsic good (in whose service law could be the means). As I explore in Chapter 9, we thus have to supply a more plausible value, such as liberty or substantive fairness here. Second, there is the well-known problem of deriving the justness (and thus, the obligating force of law) from its service of Fuller's proceduralist end(s) for law. As Herbert Hart said many times, the most evil regimes can nonetheless be scrupulous and meticulous in their observance of Fuller's rule of law desiderata.[98]

Fuller's response to this second charge was always to assert his 'faith' (his language) that observance of the requirements of the rule of law has more affinity with substantive goodness than with evil. This, however, is a faith very few people share. One might attempt to replace this faith with the empirical observation that thoroughly unjust regimes, as a matter of contingent fact, do not find it worth their time to observe the niceties demanded by the rule of law. Yet this is not the strong claim needed by the natural lawyer. As I explore in some detail in Chapter 9, in some sense of 'necessity' the natural lawyer asserts that necessarily, law bears some intimate relation to morality. In addition, even as a contingent matter, meticulous Nazis are not unknown to us.

Ronald Dworkin would no doubt resist recasting his explicitly interpretivist jurisprudence into Fuller's functionalist form. Dworkin, like Hart before him, had little respect for Fuller as a legal philosopher. Yet, as I mentioned earlier, even a broken clock tells the correct time once in a

[98] H. L. A. Hart, 'Book Review—*The Morality of Law*', *Harvard Law Review*, 78 (1965), 1281–96.

while. The reader should compare the functionalist Dworkin of Chapter 9 with the modestly interpretive Dworkin of Chapter 10. Both are reconstructions that require some reworking of what Dworkin has explicitly said, and it is not clear which makes his jurisprudence the best it can be.

The problems for Dworkin's jurisprudence (when construed as a natural law jurisprudence pursuing a functionalist method) are the same two kinds of problems as exist for Fuller: First, is equality (or integrity) an intrinsic good? And second, is it sufficiently connected to all other intrinsic goods that a means (law) that serves the one also serves the other? The first of these questions we pursued in Chapter 7, and the second I simply leave open in Chapter 9.

John Finnis's *Natural Law and Natural Rights* is my primary example in Chapter 9 of a fully spelled out functionalist jurisprudence with a natural law conclusion.[99] The common good, as Finnis reconstrues it from Aquinas, is both the intrinsic good that law serves, and is connected to all other intrinsic goods because it is the way those goods can be realized through social co-operation. In Chapter 9 I explore whether this function for law is sufficient to guarantee that particular laws must pass some threshold of justice in order to be laws at all, the natural lawyer's conclusion. As I mention there, Finnis responded to a preprint of this chapter by claiming that 'law' has a primary or focal meaning that itself guarantee law's necessary obligatoriness (and thus, its necessary degree of justness).[100] I urge in Chapter 9 that any attempt to guarantee a natural law conclusion in this analytic way is an illegitimate shortcut for one pursuing a functionalist method in jurisprudence. Unless 'law' names a purely nominal kind, it is also doubtful that such analytic truths exist.

Chapter 9 ends with some agnosticism on the question of whether a functionalist method in jurisprudence can result in a substantive jurisprudence of natural law. Still, it should be obvious where my sympathies lie. My own temptation is to say that jurisprudence should be functionalist 'all the way down'. That is, not only is law (legal system) in general a functional kind; but so also are: areas of law, such as criminal law, whose identity and boundaries are guided by the function such kind of law serves;[101] individual laws, such as the common law rules of negligence, where the formulation of the rule depends as much or more on the function such a rule serves as on any prior formulation of it by courts or restatements; [102]

[99] John Finnis, *Natural Law and Natural Rights* (Oxford: Clarendon Press, 1980).

[100] Personal communication, Jan. 1990.

[101] So argued in M. Moore, 'A Theory of Criminal Law Theories', in D. Friedman (ed.), *Tel Aviv University Studies in Law* (Tel Aviv: Tel Aviv University Press, 1990), revised and reprinted as ch. 1 of Moore, *Placing Blame: A General Theory of the Criminal Law* (Oxford: Oxford University Press, 1997).

[102] See M. Moore, 'Precedent, Induction, and Ethical Generalization', in L. Goldstein (ed.), *Precedent in Law* (Oxford: Oxford University Press, 1987).

singular propositions of law that interpret law so as to decide concrete cases, such as those singular propositions of statutory law that depend as much on the function (purpose, spirit) of a statute as on the plain meaning of its terms.[103]

The dilemma that we have seen for a functionalist approach to general jurisprudence (about law in general) will recapitulate itself at these other levels. That is, if criminal law as an area of law is defined by service of the goal of retributive punishment (as I argue elsewhere it is),[104] then sometimes service of that function will disserve other values, such as formal equality or minimizing crime; and mightn't such other values sometimes win out because they are weightier than the attainment of retributive justice, and yet the law that results be of the kind, criminal law? Similarly, even if the function of some statute is rapid interstate passage of the mail, sometimes that good will lose out to other goods that are more important, such as the good of getting a murderous mail carrier out of circulation;[105] yet when the purpose or spirit of a statute loses out to other values in this way, do we not still count this as the same statute, even though not individuated by its function?

My sense is that here as well as in general jurisprudence about law as such the natural lawyer must supplement his functionalist method with some other route for infusing value into law. Even so, functionalism may well remain his starting point.

My reliance on such a functionalist method, thus qualified, is still a heavy one. A number of criticisms of that method that have arisen are thus of importance to me. One was an ambiguity in the functionalist claim pointed out by Jeremy Waldron in his referee's report on Chapter 9 for the volume in which it originally appeared. The ambiguity is in the idea of there being a value that law *uniquely* serves. A strong form of this idea would be that there is some value that only law can serve. A weaker form would be that there is some value that anything must serve to be law, although things besides law can serve such a value too. The weakest form would be that there is some value that law usually serves, and yet: (1) not only law serves this value; and (2) even law need not always serve this value to preserve its character as law.

A *purely* functionalist definition of law would require the strong form of this claim, for then we could say, anything that serves such-and-such a value is law, no matter what its structural features. Yet as Waldron pointed out, no candidates for such a value seem very plausible. Many things besides law serve equality, integrity, the common good, or liberty

[103] See Moore, 'Semantics of Judging', above n. 47, at 277–81; and Moore, 'A Natural Law Theory', above n. 47, at 383–8.

[104] Moore, 'Criminal Law Theories', above n. 101.

[105] The facts of *Kirby v. United States*, 74 U.S. (7 Wall.) 482 (1869).

and fairness. Thus one cannot say that anything that furthers one of these values is law, as a pure functionalist jurisprudence would like to say. This is enough to require the functionalist to import some intuitions about law's structure, intuitions about the means of serving law's point that are peculiarly *legal* means. Further, the functionalist who wishes to reach the natural lawyer's conclusion that law is necessarily obligating and therefore just, must allow for law sometimes existing even when the value behind law is not being served. This, because to align law with justice sometimes requires values (other than that claimed to be law's point) to determine law's content. This further qualification forces the functionalist (who would also be a natural lawyer) to the weakest of the three claims.

Another query for the functionalist approach to jurisprudence was also put forward by Waldron and seconded by Chris Boorse in his commentary on Chapter 9 at one of its public presentations. The query was how such functionalism in jurisprudence fits in with more recent accounts of functional explanation in the philosophy of science. On these latter accounts, significant function assignments only take place when the existence of the thing doing the functioning is best explained by that thing having a certain function.

My suspicion is that this biologically inspired account of function assignment is too narrow even for the philosophy of science. But in any case, the function assignments I have in mind for medicine (my example in Chapter 9) and law do not involve functional *explanation*. Rather, the functions of a thing are simply those of its uses that are valuable. Function assignment, accordingly, is a task in applied ethics, isolating what various things are good for because productive of valuable consequences. 'Instrumentalism' would be as apt a name for this kind of functionalist jurisprudence, but I think my use of 'function' is perfectly idiomatic English and so I retain it.

This last clarification also dispatches another criticism by Boorse, which had to do with my evaluative basis for function assignments. It has been Boorse's long-held view that assignment of function is not relative to some value, but rather, is relative to some naturally occurring homeostatic state such as the human body's temperature.[106] I doubt that this claim squares with our usage of 'function' in ordinary speech or even in science, but again, this doesn't really matter. I intend my usage of 'function' to be stipulative: it simply means, 'instrumentally in the service of some value(s)'. Nothing turns on whether there is some other usage of 'function' that informs good explanations in science.

[106] See the numerous articles by Boorse cited in the References for my *Law and Psychiatry: Rethinking the Relationship* (Cambridge: Cambridge University Press, 1984), at 497. Boorse also reiterated this criticism of my use of function assignments in his extensive commentary on the manuscript for the latter book in 1983.

Daniel Robinson apparently shares this criticism of my value-laden functionalism with Boorse. Robinson proposes the following *reductio* on my analysis of how functions are assigned to the human body:

We ascertain of all the human goods which one or ones could be served by the human body. An early death in the pink of life being better than the ravages of wasting age, we hypothesize that the soon-to-burst cerebral aneurism is the goal of the body: i.e., what the body is good for.[107]

There is an old saying about *reductio* arguments, namely that one man's *reductio* is another man's valid inference. I fear that I find nothing absurd about Robinson's redoing of a value-based functional organization of the human body. As Joel Feinberg argued years ago, if one didn't value a longer life, free of pain, with the normal abilities, then one's function assignments to body parts would be very different.[108] What makes Robinson's function assignments seem absurd is that we do not in the least share the value judgements relative to which his function assignments are made.

Finally, Robinson also appears to advance another criticism of functionalist approaches to jurisprudence that is discussed in Chapter 9. This is the worry that functionalism already assumes a natural law theory from the start, so the method cannot be used to argue for a natural law position. The charge is that to conceive of law in functionalist terms—as necessarily being good for something—is already to conceive of law as necessarily connected to morality in the way the natural lawyer asserts.[109]

There are two answers to this worry, both given in Chapter 9. One is that the necessary connection between law and morality required by functionalism is not the relationship needed by the natural lawyer. The latter relationship is stronger, in that law is connected to all values (and not simply to the value(s) in the service of which law is functionally defined). Recall from our earlier discussion that the natural lawyer needs this stronger connection if he is to assert the natural lawyer's slogan, 'an unjust law is no law at all'. Second, the necessity hypothesized by functionalism is only hypothesized, not posited or assumed. It is not an analytical or a priori necessity that we can know with certainty and without observation. It is only a metaphysical necessity whose existence we must verify as we observe whether law is capable of working towards whatever end we hypothesize to be law's end.

[107] Daniel L. Robinson, 'Antigone's Defense: A Critical Study of *Natural Law Theory: Contemporary Essays*', *Review of Metaphysics*, 45 (1991), 363–92, at 382.

[108] Joel Feinberg, 'Crime, Clutchability, and Individuated Treatment', in his *Doing and Deserving* (Princeton: Princeton University Press, 1970), 253–4.

[109] Robinson, 'Antigone's Defense', above n. 107, at 382–3.

IX. CHAPTER 10: THE INTERPRETIVE TURN IN MODERN THEORIZING

The two essays in Part IV, Chapters 10 and 11, examine the currently fashionable view that there is some fourth way of doing jurisprudence (in addition to conventionalist, sceptical, and realist approaches examined in the first three parts). This 'fourth way' is variously styled as a 'pragmatic', 'hermeneutic', or 'interpretive' approach. This approach is touted by its devotees to offer fresh questions, and thus new answers to the old conundrums that beset the other three types of jurisprudence.

Both essays seek to explode this fashionable myth. Chapter 10 begins with a description of how the traditional schools in jurisprudence (legal positivism, natural law, Legal Realism) are best seen in the metaphysical categories of conventionalism, realism, and scepticism. This is a metaphysics-soaked view of jurisprudence. I then preview how various forms of 'interpretivism' seek to avoid the terms in which the traditional debates between these three schools have been carried on. Interpretivism thus aspires not to answer the traditional questions of jurisprudence, but to replace them with its own questions.

Chapter 10 divides interpretivists into three camps. All three seek to avoid any of the three traditional metaphysical positions, but how each does so differs. The very ambitious interpretivist is so named because he seeks to show that everything we claim to know in all fields of knowledge is in reality an interpretation by us. The merely ambitious interpretivist, by contrast, is some kind of dualist: knowledge in the physical sciences is a matter of propositions corresponding to a reality, but in the humanities and social sciences there is something categorically different, the understanding of the meaning of various social texts that can only be gained through interpretation. The modest interpretivist, by contrast, only distinguishes interpretation from explanation on practical grounds and on a case by case basis; still, such an interpretivist may claim that jurisprudence is one of those areas that is interpretive and, because of this, outside the normal descriptive/explanatory realm in which the traditional metaphysical positions make sense.

Chapter 10 proceeds by examining these three forms of interpretivism *seriatim*. About very ambitious interpretivism, I conclude that its practitioners do not offer some new, fourth way of viewing the world that eliminates the need to choose between realist, idealist, or sceptical metaphysics. Indeed, I seek to show in some detail how such very ambitious interpretivism waffles between a kind of closet idealism and a kind of outright scepticism. About ambitious interpretivism, I reject the dualist metaphysics presupposed by those claiming that the human sciences study a special realm of meaningful phenomena. I also reject the rejection of traditional metaphysics by 'philosophical hermeneutics', in part because such a variant of interpretivism finds significance (which I do not) in the study of 'being qua being', and partly because such interpretivism is empty of practical interest. I also reject the linguistic dualism that lies at the base of the third strand of ambitious interpretivism, that worked out in ordinary language philosophy in the 1950s and 1960s. I do not reject modest interpretivism as an apt description of some activities in some disciplines such as law, psychoanalysis, literary criticism, and theology, but I argue that legal theory (unlike some of legal practice) is not even modestly interpretive. I then conclude that the debate in legal theory between natural lawyers, legal positivists, and various legal sceptics, are guided by the deeper divides in metaphysics.

When I wrote Chapter 10 I was under no illusions as to its impact. The contemporary legal academy is sufficiently divided that the only ones to read the essay carefully are those philosophically trained jurisprudes who already agreed with it; those who most needed to take the essay seriously—the critical this and thats—predictably would and did dismiss the essay with the most cursory of swipes.[110] If one believes that it has been conclusively demonstrated that nothing can be conclusively demonstrated—as muddled as such a belief is—then it is no surprise that any challenge to this new orthodoxy would be put aside.

Richard Rorty, one of my two examples of very ambitious interpretivism in Chapter 10, does not make the kind of unsophisticated errors just instanced. Rorty used the article that has become Chapter 10 in his Theory Seminar at the University of Virginia and he was kind enough to host a day-long symposium on Moorean interpretive theory when I visited the University of Virginia academic year 1997–8. Rorty's main response to me was at the level of motivation. He finds metaphysical types like me doubly peculiar, first in needing some kind of back-up to justify the activities I find worth doing, and second, in the credulity to accept metaphysics as adequate to the task. Like Dworkin, Rorty believes that each activity we find worth doing 'rests on its own bottom' (as English judges are inclined to put it) and neither needs nor can receive any support external to it. Rorty at one point has likened me to Allan Bloom in that the two of us are about the only two people in America silly enough to care whether realism about morality and law is true.[111]

At the level of motivation Rorty and I do disagree. As I said at the Virginia Symposium, if I believed what Rorty believes I would not be a legal philosopher, nor even an academic of any kind. It seems an indul-

110 e.g. Alan Hutchinson, 'Book Review of *Contingency, Irony, and Solidarity*', *Harvard Law Review*, 103 (1989), 555–85, at 556, 560.

111 Richard Rorty, 'The Banality of Pragmatism and the Poetry of Justice', *Southern California Law Review*, 63 (1990), 1811–19, at 1813.

gent, wasteful thing to accept a position in the beautiful garden that is the academy only to 'carry on conversation' with other academics. On straight pragmatist grounds, both we academics and society would be better off if we did something useful, like tending sheep. So my metaphysics do matter to my motives for being an academic. What I don't understand is why Rorty's alleged lack of metaphysics do not demotivate his own academic pursuits.

Stanley Fish, my other main stalking horse in the part of Chapter 10 dealing with very ambitious interpretivism, is of course no more convinced by my critique of him than is Rorty. Fish and I have debated his 'no-theory theory' on numerous occasions over the past fifteen years, and we discussed Chapter 10 in detail during my day-long presentation of Chapter 10 to The Humanities Research Institute of the University of California at Irvine, where Fish and I were Resident Fellows for a term.[112]

Fish was gracious enough to acknowledge that Chapter 10 at least states his views accurately. But Fish stubbornly clings to his central view that knowledge is everywhere and always tacit and particular. Theories such as mine, accordingly, may grace a practice like ornamental sculpture on a building, but such theories in no way influence the practice.

A recent exchange with Fish was over his application of his very general thesis to semantics. Fish, no surprise, is a contextualist about both word-meaning (lexical semantics) and sentence-meaning (compositional semantics). Words can mean just about anything in different contexts, according to Fish, which is why the general theories propounded by semantics cannot be true. Among other things, this would doom any legal rule (such as the parol evidence rule of contract law) that purported to interpret a legal document by the meanings of the terms alone, *sans* context. Fish presented these conclusions about semantics at a workshop at the University of Pennsylvania in 1989. My main comment on Fish's paper consisted of the single phrase, 'gleeg, gleeg, gleeg!'[113] Fish responded, 'glug, glug, glug', but then saw what I had meant by 'gleeg, gleeg, gleeg': if all words were as devoid of semantic (i.e. context-independent) meaning as he claimed, why couldn't one communicate with any symbols whatsoever, no matter how arbitrary? Indeed, why couldn't Fish simply have said 'glug, glug, glug' to start with, communicating everything communicated by his much longer and more conventionally composed paper?

[112] This was a term-length study group on interpretation which included J. Hillis Miller, Murray Krieger, Geoffrey Hartmann, Martha Minnow, Jacques Derrida, Joseph Raz, Sanford Kadish, Tom Heller, Jeremy Waldron, Robin West, Patricia Williams, and others. Needless to say such a group generated no consensus as to the nature of interpretation (or much else).

[113] 'Gleeg, gleeg, gleeg', was Paul Ziff's response to the speech-act approach to semantics proposed by the late Paul Grice. See Ziff, 'On H.P. Grice's Account of Meaning', *Analysis*, 28 (1967), 1–8.

Like most of us, Fish thought of his best response only after the workshop, on his plane ride back to Durham. Unlike most of us, Fish wrote out his response and sent it as an open letter to the Penn faculty:

You will recall that Michael Moore asked me a two-part question. The first part was of the 'If you say x, how do you account for y?' variety; the second part, which he introduced by declaring it was 'shorter,' was simply 'Gleeg, gleeg, gleeg.' After answering the first part, I then answered the second part, and I began by explaining what the question meant, i.e., that Michael was saying that if words, as I claim, could in persuasive context sufficiently elaborated mean anything, why then didn't a judge in delivering an opinion, say, 'Gleeg, gleeg, gleeg,' or why couldn't any of the sentences of the paper I read be replaced by 'Gleeg, gleeg, gleeg,' or why couldn't the various parts of the Constitution or a statute be replaced by 'Gleeg, gleeg, gleeg?' What I should have realized—and realized only on the airplane going back—is by understanding the question, I had already answered it. Michael said only, 'Gleeg, gleeg, gleeg,' and yet I was able to repeat to him in more elaborate terms the import of his question, and, as he agreed, I got it right. How did I do that? Well, I did that in the way in which one always does things with words—hears them with ears informed of the present context—focus, emphasis, concerns, strategies, desires, etc. In this case I knew without reflecting on it that I was in the middle of a discussion of linguistic-epistemology; I knew (in my bones) what kinds of questions were likely to come from Michael's side of the street to someone who had been advancing theses on my side of the street; I know his previous writings and knew that he knew mine. I knew and knew he knew the history of such arguments and debates, and within that knowledge and a great deal else what he meant by 'Gleeg, gleeg, gleeg' couldn't have been clearer, as my performance indicated. The second part of course is that utterances less obviously curious (like 'France is hexagonal' or 'Pass the salt please') are understood in exactly the same way, i.e., the meaning they are perceived to bear is the property not of some formal features or of some semantic constant but of the interpretive conditions within which they are heard. I ask you to share this post-seminar analysis of a moment in the seminar with those students and faculty who were present, and I ask you to thank Michael for an example I will be trading on for years.[114]

Had Fish not figured out what I meant by 'gleeg, gleeg, gleeg', I had intended to use his bafflement as evidence of the falsity of his thesis. The point would have been that Fish like all of us needs words *not* to be chameleons in order to use them to communicate our intentions. That Fish was clever enough to figure out what I meant cut off the point I had hoped to make. However, Fish's success in understanding what I meant cuts less favourably in his direction than his bafflement would have cut in mine. Given our prior exchanges, Fish knew what I was going to say before I said it. His success only shows that our exchanges have become rituals unto themselves, a kind of semantics that can shortcut normal English semantics. Such communicative shortcuts go no distance to establishing the

[114] Letter from Stanley Fish to Stephen Morse, 17 Nov. 1989.

impossibility of semantics nor even to any absence of its general necessity. Most speakers most of the time can only communicate their thoughts by using semantic conventions that they do not create and that are not unique to the particular context of speech. Fish thus makes out his general view—that there can be no useful employment of general views—no more in semantics than in the other disciplines I explore in Chapter 10.

Turning to the ambitious interpretivism I also discuss in Chapter 10, surprisingly the most influential kind of ambitious interpretivism has been the 'philosophical hermeneutics' of Heidegger and Gadamer. William Eskridge, for example, has written extensively about statutory interpretation and thinks that he has been influenced in his thought by Gadamerian hermeneutics.[115] Similarly, Stephen Feldman has sought to show how Heidegger and Gadamer have significant implications for how we practise constitutional interpretation.[116]

One of the criticisms I advance in Chapter 10 against philosophical hermeneutics is that it is empty of interest because devoid of any practical interpretations. So Eskridge and Feldman purport to respond directly to such a charge by showing how legal interpretive practices are affected by adoption of philosophical hermeneutics. Yet I am afraid I still fail to see this. Feldman correctly concedes that neither Heidegger nor Gadamer concern themselves with the question of validity of interpretations. Theirs are simply abstract generalizations about what we do when we interpret. As Feldman summarizes their insights:

> Philosophical hermeneutics describes interpretation as an ontological event in which meaning comes into being. We live in tradition, in the form of language, and thus we each have a horizon, formed by our prejudices, that limits our vision and understanding. Interpretation requires one to fuse the horizon of the present with the horizon of the text. This process is dialectical and dialogical: there is a play between the interpreter and the text that resembles a conversation between two speakers. And as meaning comes into being, tradition changes and one's horizon shifts, thus leading to new meanings for the same text in the future.[117]

Recognizing that 'it is not immediately clear that hermeneutics generally . . . provides my insight into statutory interpretation',[118] here is Eskridge's description of that insight:

[115] William N. Eskridge, Jr., *Dynamic Statutory Interpretation* (Cambridge, Mass.: Harvard University Press, 1994), 58–65. At a symposium on Law and Linguistics in Chicago in 1995, I attempted to convince Eskridge that Gadamerian hermeneutics were empty of implications for Eskridge's theory of legal interpretation and so could have influenced him causally only in some non-rational way. See Symposium Transcript, *Washington Law Quarterly*, 73 (1995), 800–970, at 881–4.

[116] Stephen Feldman, 'The New Metaphysics: The Interpretive Turn in Jurisprudence', *Iowa Law Review*, 76 (1991), 661–99.

[117] Ibid. at 699.

[118] Eskridge, *Dynamic Statutory Interpretation*, above n. 115, at 61.

[T]he central insight of hermeneutics would be relevant for legal interpretation: the horizon of the interpreter affects the way she approaches the text—what questions she asks of it, how she responds to words and phrases, and what text and surrounding context she finds important. Hermeneutics suggests that statutory interpretation . . . involves an interaction between interpreter and text that creates new and perhaps unexpected meaning over time.[119]

If this isn't just idealist metaphysics in rather woolly clothing, then it is empty. If, that is, 'horizons', 'traditions', 'prejudices' are not idealist criteria for correct interpretation (as they should not be for the truly philosophical hermeneut), then they give no guidelines to an interpreter as to how to proceed. 'Keep talking' is about as much help as one gets from this brand of ambitious interpretivism. Philosophical hermeneutics is empty of practical interest in the same way as was the behaviouralism of the older Legal Realists. Both make a number of social science pronouncements about how legal actors are behaving, but such external explanations and predictions are no help whatsoever to those actors as they decide how to interpret or otherwise behave.

Turning to modest interpretivist enterprises, the third of my targets in Chapter 10, I have no quarrel with such enterprises so long as they remain appropriately modest. The objection I make to Dworkin's version of a modestly interpretive jurisprudence in Chapter 10 is twofold: (*a*) some of legal practice, and all of legal theory, is not even modestly interpretive in character, and (*b*) even where such practice is modestly interpretive, there are no anti-metaphysical conclusions to be drawn from this fact. Dworkin too cannot prescind from the metaphysical debate between realists, idealists, and sceptics about law, as his interpretivist jurisprudence aspires to do. (This is the same conclusion as I defended earlier in this Introduction in connection with Chapter 8, so I shall not revisit the issue here.)

X. CHAPTER 11: FINDING SOMETHING TO LIKE ABOUT INTERPRETATION

Chapter 11 steps back from the purely critical work of Chapter 10 in order to take stock of the implications of that work for a usable concept of interpretation. Chapter 11 attempts to work out in a more positive way what the notion of modest interpretivism comes to. Three basic questions about any properly modest interpretivism are distinguished: first, what is a text (and thus, when is interpretation an appropriate activity); second, when is an interpretation valid? And third, what justifies anyone in engaging in the activity we call interpretation? I pursue these questions through various competing models of interpretation and through various disciplines.

[119] Eskridge, *Dynamic Statutory Interpretation*, above n. 115, at 62.

The most troubling criticism that I received at the Tel Aviv University Conference at which the essay was originally presented was that of my commentator Gilead Bar Elli, and seconded by Joseph Raz. The criticism was that I had not answered my first question adequately because (on their view of my answer) anything could be a text and then, anything could be an interpretation of some text. I do not so much disagree with this *reductio* of my views as I disagree that it is absurd or undesirable. On the general view of interpretation advanced in Chapter 11, anything in principle can be a text. Yet to be a text, there must be good reasons for people to treat that thing as a text, and I deny that those reasons are very widespread. The alternative view, that ties text-hood to authorial intention, still strikes me as much too parochial a view of when (modestly) interpretive enterprises are appropriate. Such alternative view would exclude, for example, the interpretation of dreams as a possible enterprise, because there is no author of dreams to have the requisite, text-creating intentions.

Chapter 11 closes by concluding that there is no fourth school of jurisprudence based on an interpretive methodology. If that is so, and if there is no other alternative, then in jurisprudence we are thrust back to the familiar triad of jurisprudential theories between which we must choose as we carry on this activity. These are the three sorts of theories examined in the preceding parts of this book.

Part I
Legal Positivism

2

Introduction to The Concept of Law

I. HART AND LEGAL PHILOSOPHY

In March of 1984 a number of well-known legal philosophers met in Jerusalem. The purpose of the meeting was to honour Herbert Hart in the way most fitting to his own status as the world's pre-eminent legal philosopher: to present papers pursuing the questions he had made central to legal philosophy.[1] At the end of the conference, in the encomium to Hart personally, we unanimously agreed that Hart had made the field of legal philosophy what it is today, a challenging, interesting, politically relevant field in which to work.[2] In that sense Hart had made a personal gift to each legal philosopher working today.

It would be difficult to overstate Hart's influence on contemporary legal philosophy. Ruth Gavison, the organizer of the conference, accurately noted that '[t]here is hardly a subject or issue in legal philosophy on which it is not natural, almost inevitable, to start with his views'.[3] As Joseph Raz and Peter Hacker observed seven years earlier in the preface to their own volume of essays honouring Herbert Hart:

> At mid-century political philosophy was said to be dead and legal philosophy appeared to be dying. . . . A quarter of a century later a transformed landscape is revealed—legal philosophy flourishes as never before. The responsibility for this renaissance is H. L. A. Hart's. His work provides the foundations of contemporary legal philosophy in the English-speaking world and beyond.[4]

The reason that contemporary legal philosophy takes the work of Herbert Hart as its point of departure lies in the kind of break with the past that Hart's work represented. With occasional exceptions, such as Morris Cohen, legal philosophy in the English-speaking world for a century and a half after Bentham had been amateurish and dilettantish in its philosophy, methodologically un-self-conscious, and often 'academic' (in the pejorative sense of that word) and unconnected to practical concerns. In each of these three respects Hart left legal philosophy better than he found it.

[1] The papers of the Conference were published on the occasion of Hart's eightieth birthday in Ruth Gavison (ed.), *Issues in Contemporary Legal Philosophy: The Influence of H. L. A. Hart* (Oxford: Oxford University Press, 1987).

[2] See Gavison's 'Introduction', ibid. at 5.

[3] Ibid. at 2. Ruth Gavison, the H. Cohen Professor of Human Rights in the Faculty of Law, Hebrew University, Jerusalem, was a student of Hart's at Oxford.

[4] P. M. S. Hacker and J. Raz (eds.), *Law, Morality and Society: Essays in Honour of H. L. A. Hart* (Oxford: Clarendon Press, 1977), p. v.

Clemenceau once remarked that military justice stands to justice as military music stands to music. Before Herbert Hart, much the same could be said about the nineteenth- and twentieth-century legal philosophy and its relation to philosophy. Much of what passed for legal philosophy consisted of the vague gesturings towards grandeur of lawyers or judges who, having grown older and tired of detailed work in contracts, commercial law, etc., put their feet up on their desks and pontificated about law, or common law, or judging, in general. Such lawyers often knew a great deal about the history of law and of legal thought, spicing their own verities with references to Roman law, the laws of the German tribes, quotations from Pfuffendorf, Grotius, Coke, Von Ihring, Stammler, etc. Yet when they were not explicitly anti-philosophical (as were many of the American Legal Realist theoreticians), they were at best dabblers in the philosophy of their time.

Herbert Hart has never been a dilettante in philosophy. Nor has he been a mere applier of general philosophical insights worked out by others. Hart was himself a philosopher of the first rank when he began his remaking of legal philosophy following the end of World War II. Ever since, he has been a participant in the central philosophical debates of his times—debates in the philosophy of language, in the philosophy of mind, in the philosophy of action, in ethics, and in political philosophy. The insights that he applied to legal philosophy from philosophy generally were his own worked out views about the meaning of language, the nature of causation, the meaning of mental state concepts, etc. After Hart it will be impossible for a legal philosopher to be taken seriously if he or she is not also a participant in philosophy's more general concerns.

The second respect in which Hart gave legal philosophy a fresh start is the methodological self-consciousness that Hart's work exemplifies. Hart tells us in the preface of *The Concept of Law* that he wants to 'discourage the belief that a book on legal theory is primarily a book from which one learns what other books contain'.[5] Hart thus never contents himself with the trotting out of some tired old scheme for classifying others' thoughts and explicating those thoughts with such scheme, be it 'analytical versus sociological vs. historical jurisprudence', 'legal formalism vs. legal realism', 'natural law vs. legal positivism'. Legal philosophy in Hart's hands became critical, seeking the solution to problems, not expositions of others' thoughts (except insofar as they could contribute to solutions). To have any depth, Hart realized that such critical legal philosophy had constantly to turn its critical gaze upon itself, to ask whether the methods it employed were up to answering the questions it posed. Thus, in his inaugural lecture in 1953 as Professor of Jurisprudence at Oxford, Hart

[5] H. L. A. Hart, *The Concept of Law* (Oxford: Oxford University Press, 1961), p. viii.

attacked the methods used by his predecessors in legal philosophy, who had made central the question, 'What is law?'[6] Such methods consisted of the seeking of definitions of 'law' either in the form of necessary and sufficient conditions that give the essence of our *concept* of law or (even worse in Hart's eyes) in the form of some real essence law itself (the phenomenon, not the concept) possessed. As Hart said, in later defending his methodological enquiry from criticism:

In 1952 . . . I formed the view that analytical enquiries into the nature of law and legal concepts had come to a premature standstill. . . . Very often progress in a science is held up not because wrong answers have been given but because the wrong sort of question has been asked; and this, I think, had for long been the case with analytical enquiries into the nature of legal concepts. Those enquiries had taken the form of requests for definition issuing in the standard type question 'What is *X*?,' e.g. 'What is *duty*?' . . . The 'What is *X*?' form of question takes a single word and asks what it means (or worse, 'stands for') and this has led to confusion because it insidiously suggests the type of answer to be given *must* be answered in the specification of some thing or quality with which the word is supposed to be directly aligned.[7]

Hart continues this methodological concern into how general jurisprudence is to be done in his own major work in general jurisprudence, *The Concept of Law*. In the final section of chapter 1, for example, Hart gives three reasons why he does not proceed by seeking a definition of 'law' in terms of necessary and sufficient conditions.

After Hart's example, few legal philosophers begin major works without similar methodological self-consciousness. Even those proposing theories and using methods quite different than Hart's, such as more recent books by John Finnis[8] or Ronald Dworkin,[9] devote considerable attention to the question, 'Is the method of this enquiry suited to its subject matter?' Such methodological self-consciousness is a hallmark of contemporary legal philosophy's truly *philosophical* nature, for all philosophy begins somewhat at sea as to what can be held constant while something else is being examined.

The third way in which Hart has left legal philosophy better than he found it stems from his exemplary unwillingness to tolerate abstract philosophizing that had no real point. An example is provided by *The Concept of Law* itself. In 1945 the eminent English criminal law theoretician, Glanville Williams, excoriated legal philosophers for wasting their time

[6] Hart, *Definition and Theory in Jurisprudence* (Oxford: Clarendon Press, 1953). (This is reprinted in H. L. A. Hart, *Essays in Jurisprudence and Philosophy* (Oxford: Clarendon Press, 1983).)

[7] H. L. A. Hart, 'Analytic Jurisprudence in Mid-twentieth Century: A Reply to Professor Bodenheimer', *University of Pennsylvania Law Review*, 105 (1957), 953–75, at 957, 960.

[8] John Finnis, *Natural Law and Natural Rights* (Oxford: Clarendon Press, 1980).

[9] Ronald Dworkin, *Law's Empire* (Cambridge, Mass.: Harvard University Press, 1986).

arguing about competing answers to the question, 'What is law?' Such a question, Williams asserted, was 'only a verbal one' of no practical or theoretical importance.[10] Reading through the definitions of law of a John Austin or a Hans Kelsen may well give one some sympathy for Williams's criticism, for such legal philosophy rarely asks, 'Why are we asking the question, "What is law?", and what difference could different answers to that question make?'

Sensitive to this criticizing of his predecessors in legal philosophy, Hart begins *The Concept of Law* by urging that we 'defer giving any answer to the query "What is law?" until we have found out what it is about law that has in fact puzzled those who have asked or attempted to answer it . . .'[11] Hart then proceeds to list three concerns that should motivate the question: What is the difference between being *obliged* by force, and *obligated* by law? What is the difference between *legal* obligation and *moral* obligation? What is it to follow a *rule*?[12] The first two of these concerns form the conceptual preliminary to the age-old, practical question of how law affects citizens' obligations. The last of these concerns forms the bedrock of any scientific study of law as a social phenomenon. The three together give the practical and theoretical payoffs for asking the question, 'What is law?', and allow Hart to avoid the unmotivated and thus unguided asking of that question so typical of his predecessors.

II. HART AND THE ORDINARY LANGUAGE PHILOSOPHY MOVEMENT AT OXFORD

The man who transformed twentieth-century legal philosophy was born in July of 1907.[13] He studied at New College, Oxford University, focusing on classics, ancient history, and philosophy and taking a first in 'Greats' in 1929. He then decided upon a legal career, reading for the Bar Examinations and passing them in 1932. Throughout the 1930s he practised law as a Barrister in Chancery, dealing with such technical matters as trusts and estates, as well as related taxation matters.

With the coming of World War II Hart began work in Great Britain's military intelligence. He worked there throughout the war, having the good philosophical fortune to have the companionship of Gilbert Ryle and Stuart Hampshire, who were also working for British intelligence. Hart was later to co-author an important article with the latter, and to Ryle Hart owed much in the way of inspiration in the philosophy of language.

[10] Glanville Williams, 'International Law and the Controversy Concerning the Word "Law"', *British Year Book of International Law*, 22 (1945), 146–63.

[11] Hart, *Concept*, above n. 5, at 5.

[12] Ibid. at 6–13.

[13] Those facts of Hart's biography that are not of my own knowledge come from the biographical sketch of Hart in Neil MacCormick's *H. L. A. Hart* (Stanford: Stanford University Press, 1981).

At the close of World War II Hart did not return to law practice. He had had such success in studying philosophy at Oxford in the 1920s that during the 1930s he had been asked to become a philosophy tutor at his former College, New College. Although he had declined the earlier offer, in 1945 he accepted a renewed offer, and for seven years taught philosophy as a Fellow and Tutor in Philosophy. During this period Hart was not focused on legal philosophy. His interests were in the central questions of philosophy proper, and it appeared he had made a clean break with things legal.

Nonetheless, this period is crucial to understanding Hart's later developed legal philosophy. The Oxford to which Hart returned was the Oxford of Gilbert Ryle and J. L. Austin, the two best-known representatives of the style of philosophy that came to be known as 'ordinary language philosophy'. Like the logical positivists on the Continent in the 1920s and 1930s, and like the views of the later Wittgenstein, which were also flowering during this same period at Cambridge University, the Oxford ordinary language philosophers saw much they did not like in the 2,000-year-old history of Western philosophy.[14] Such a history seemed replete with failures, failures inevitable because of the nature of the problems posed. Specifically, the Oxford philosophers, like their Cambridge and logical positivist counterparts, sought to *dissolve* such problems through more careful attention to language, not to *solve* them through some new metaphysics.

In the 1940s a number of Gilbert Ryle's colleagues asked him to illustrate the power of Oxford's new ordinary language approach to dissolving traditional problems in philosophy. Ryle chose the ancient problem of how mind relates to matter for the purpose, and the result was the 1949 publication of *The Concept of Mind*.[15] In that book Ryle steadfastly refused to take any of the traditional positions about how mental states like intentions, hopes, desires, emotions, were related to physical states such as those of the brain and central nervous system. Ryle came to praise neither idealism (reducing matter to mind), nor physicalism (reducing mind to matter), nor dualism (allowing there to be two different kinds of 'stuffs' in the universe); he came to bury all three of them, along with the question to which they purported to be the answer.

One kind of question that we do not have to answer is a question that makes no sense. 'Does the moon love the sun?' seems to be such a question, because 'love' as a word does not seem to be appropriately joined in

[14] An accessible overview of the ordinary language movements of both Ryle and Wittgenstein, and a comparison to the ideal language aspirations of the logical positivists, will be found in Richard Rorty's 'Introduction', *The Linguistic Turn* (Chicago: University of Chicago Press, 1967).

[15] Gilbert Ryle, *The Concept of Mind* (London: Hutcheson, 1949).

the same sentence with words like 'sun' and 'moon'. (The example is the late Peter Hempel's , who actually unearthed a theological text proclaiming love as a substitute for gravity.) We know this inappropriateness, it seems, not by doing astronomical research, but simply by observing how the words 'moon', 'sun', and 'love' are used in ordinary speech; the rules of correct usage do not allow for such joinder.

Ryle argued that the question, 'Do minds and bodies exist?', was as senseless as my question about the love of celestial bodies, and on the same ordinary language grounds. This meant that philosophers could not sensibly ask how mind was related to body, rendering all metaphysical answers as senseless as the question to which they were answers. The task this left the ordinary language philosopher was the task of 'cleaning up' our conceptual tools (words) by showing in detail how such words were appropriately used.

This was a task in which J. L. Austin, Hart, and scores of other Oxford philosophers eagerly busied themselves. In the late 1940s Hart attended the Saturday discussions in Austin's room at Oxford, and in the late 1940s and into the 1950s Hart and Austin taught a joint seminar at Oxford. Both Austin and Hart had the common insight that words could be used in many interesting ways besides in sentences expressing statements that could be true or false. 'I do', said in a marriage ceremony, does not *describe* some state of affairs; the saying of it *creates* a new state of affairs. There is thus no *doing* to be looked for as the referent of the word 'do', because the word does not refer and the statement in which it appears is neither true nor false. This insight of Austin's and Hart's was similar to Ryle's, and it led in the same direction: philosophers should not look for the essence of 'things' like voluntariness, intentions, will, or contract. Rather, to understand these 'things' is to know how the words, 'voluntary', etc., are used (to rebut claims of excuse, for example).[16]

Aside from greatly influencing Hart's method—including his method in writing *The Concept of Law*—the Ryle/Austin ordinary language philosophy led Hart back to the law. For much of Oxford philosophy followed Ryle's lead into the philosophy of mind, applying ordinary language analysis to 'desire', 'motive', 'intention', 'action', 'voluntary action', and like words.[17] The law was seen as a companion source (to ordinary English usage) of intuitions uncontaminated by philosophical theory in these matters, and the person who knew that source best at Oxford was Herbert

[16] Two papers expressing these views were H. L. A. Hart, 'The Ascription of Responsibility and Rights', *Proceedings of the Aristotelian Society*, 49 (1949), 171–94; J. L. Austin, 'A Plea for Excuses', *Proceedings of the Aristotelian Society*, 57 (1956), 1–30. Both papers were worked out via the joint Hart/Austin seminar mentioned in the text.

[17] See e.g Richard Peters, *The Concept of Motivation* (London: Routledge and Kegan Paul, 1958).

Hart. Moreover, in developing this view of 'performative utterances' (Austin's initial term for expressions like 'I do') Austin and his followers often used legal examples, for legal practice is rich in examples where a saying such and such makes it the case that 'such and such' is true. (Baseball is another, captured by the umpire's slogan that 'they ain't nothin' 'til I call 'em'.) Hart was again the source of learning about such legal examples.

The result was that in 1952, when A. L. Goodhart resigned the Chair in Jurisprudence at Oxford, Hart was the natural representative of the new style of philosophy to hold it. Hart's appointment to the chair in 1952 (and his appointment as a Fellow of University College, Oxford) marked Hart's return to law, this time not as a practitioner but as a philosopher intent on reshaping legal philosophy in philosophy's new image.

Hart's inaugural lecture in 1953, 'Definition and Theory in Jurisprudence',[18] was his explicit announcement that the new method was to be applied to legal philosophy. As is evident from the earlier quoted summary of that lecture by Hart,[19] Hart like Ryle and Austin thought it bankrupt to seek essences—real or conceptual—as the meaning of words like 'mind', 'intention', 'law', or 'legal right'. This was to try to make definitions do the work only a substantive theory could do. What would be helpful to theoreticians about law would be an explication of the concept of law, which explication would not provide necessary and sufficient conditions for law but only rules for appropriate usage of 'law'. In his lecture Hart did not go after law itself, but illustrated his point with an explication of the phrase, 'X has a legal right'.

The next main target for Hart's new method in legal philosophy was the concept of causation. In the mid-1950s Hart and his colleague at Oxford, Tony Honoré, holder of the Regius Chair in Civil Law, embarked on an ambitious analysis of causation both within the law and outside it. This resulted in a series of articles in the *Law Quarterly Review* in 1956,[20] and, ultimately, in the massive *Causation in the Law*, published by Oxford in 1959.[21] The latter book is a truly impressive achievement, illustrating as well as any work of Hart's how first-rate legal philosophy (here, about the law's concept of causation) can only be done by one capable of contributing to philosophy generally (here, about causation in general). Although overshadowed in reputation by *The Concept of Law*, Hart and Honoré's

[18] See n. 6 above.

[19] See text at n. 7 above.

[20] H. L. A. Hart and A. M. Honoré, 'Causation in the Law I—A Survey of Common Sense Principles', *Law Quarterly Review*, 72 (1956), 58–90; 'Causation in the Law II—Factors Negating Causal Connection', *Law Quarterly Review*, 72 (1956), 260–81; 'Causation in the Law III—Factors Negating Causal Connection (Continued)', *Law Quarterly Review*, 72 (1956), 398–417.

[21] H. L. A. Hart and A. M. Honoré, *Causation in the Law* (Oxford: Clarendon Press, 1959). A 2nd edn., revised exclusively by Tony Honoré, was issued in 1985.

1959 book on causation was and is regarded as a major contribution both to a purely philosophical analysis of causation and to the legal analysis of causation in the law. This is true despite the fact that Hart came to see serious problems for the analysis of causation done in that book, problems both of method and of substance.[22]

III. OVERVIEW OF *THE CONCEPT OF LAW*

With the publication of *The Concept of Law* in 1961 Hart secured his preeminent place in legal philosophy. The book's method was presaged in Hart's inaugural lecture, and its content was partly presaged in Hart's famous 1958 debate with Lon Fuller in the pages of the *Harvard Law Review*.[23] But the book drew together the strands of Hart's thoughts about jurisprudence in one place and gave them the kind of organized, clear expression for which the book is justly famous.

The Concept of Law is usefully read as having five parts to it. The first part is constituted by chapter 1, which addresses some of the methodological preliminaries that we have already previewed. Hart there asks, 'What is the central question of jurisprudence?', surveys some traditional answers, asks why we should care about the question, and closes with a discussion of his non-definition-seeking method.

One question that Hart does not much discuss, but which we can fruitfully raise here, is what kind of jurisprudence he is doing in the book. Is his a *descriptive* jurisprudence, describing the concept of law we presently employ, or is it a *prescriptive* jurisprudence, recommending to us what concept of law we ought to employ? Consider each possibility separately. Hart prefaces the book by allowing us two alternative interpretations of what he is up to: (1) in the book, he tells us, he has 'raised questions which may well be said to be about the meanings of words',[24] and (2) 'Notwithstanding its concern with analysis the book may also be regarded

[22] I raise these problems in Michael Moore, 'Causation and Responsibility', *Social Philosophy and Policy*, 16 (1998), 1–51; and in Moore, 'The Metaphysics of Causal Intervention', forthcoming, *California Law Review*, (2000).

[23] H. L. A. Hart, 'Positivism and the Separation of Law and Morals', *Harvard Law Review*, 71 (1958), 593–629; L. Fuller, 'Positivism and Fidelity to Law—A Reply to Professor Hart', *Harvard Law Review*, 71 (1958), 630–72. The exchange between Hart and Fuller actually begins with Fuller's 'Human Purpose and Natural Law', *Journal of Philosophy*, 53 (1956), 697–709. The exchange continued beyond 1958 in Hart's *The Concept of Law* of 1961 (esp. 202); Fuller's *The Morality of Law* (New Haven: Yale University Press, 1965), ch. 3; Hart's review of Fuller, 'Book Review—*The Morality of Law*', *Harvard Law Review*, 78 (1965), 1281–96; and Fuller's reply in the 'Reply to Critics' in the 2nd edn. of *The Morality of Law* in 1969. Despite this attention, I doubt that Hart ever took Lon Fuller very seriously as a legal philosopher, for Fuller was something of a dilettante in philosophy proper.

[24] *Concept*, above n. 5, p. vii.

as an essay in descriptive sociology . . .'[25] These are both descriptive tasks, for a philosopher doing either of them seeks to describe something as it is—either the meaning of the word 'law' or the concept of law presupposed by social practices (including but not limited to linguistic social practices).

Contrast both of those descriptive tasks with two possible prescriptive tasks Hart could be seeking to perform in the book: (1) Hart could be recommending a concept of law to us for moral reasons, i.e. reasons having to do with the better moral consequences that would follow if people were to adopt one concept of law over another; or (2) Hart could be recommending a concept of law to us for reasons of theoretical advantage, i.e. reasons having to do with more successful theory-building in social science. By the end of the book Hart seems to be defending his concept of law on these two normative grounds, for he tells us that if 'we are to make a reasoned choice between these concepts [of law], it must be because one is superior to the other in the way in which it will assist our theoretical enquiries, or advance and clarify our moral deliberations, or both'.[26]

The second part of the book is constituted by chapters 2, 3, and 4. Here, Hart criticizes the nineteenth-century views of John Austin, according to whom (following Hobbes and Bentham) law is always the command of some identifiable sovereign in a society.[27] In these chapters Hart raises a number of objections to Austin's definition of law, many of which Hart later recognized would not have been telling objections to the similar but more sophisticated views of Jeremy Bentham.[28] One objection, however, is central, and it is equally telling against Bentham as well as Austin. At bottom, the Austin/Bentham view identifies law with coercive force and with citizens' habits of obedience. These ideas, Hart contends, are insufficient elements out of which to account for what we might call the 'normativity' of law. Whatever else law is, Hart observes, 'where there is law, there human conduct is made in some sense non-optional or obligatory'.[29] The problem with analysing law as orders habitually obeyed and backed by coercive sanctions is that it doesn't distinguish legal obligation from the 'obligation' to obey the gunman who orders you to hand over your money or suffer the consequences. Hart agrees with natural law theoreticians like St Augustine, who held that law has to be normative (obligating) in some sense stronger than this.

This sets up Hart's project for him in the third part of the book (chapters 5 and 6): can one give an analysis of law that does not collapse it into

[25] Ibid. [26] Ibid. at 204–5.

[27] John Austin, *The Province of Jurisprudence Determined*, ed. H. L. A. Hart (New York: Noonday Press, 1954). (John Austin, the 19th-cent. legal philosopher, is to be distinguished from J. L. Austin, the 20th-cent. ordinary language philosopher.)

[28] See Hart, *Essays on Bentham* (Oxford: Clarendon Press, 1982), 108–9.

[29] *Concept*, above n. 5, at 80.

habitual obedience and coercive sanctions, on the one hand, or into the moral obligation favoured by the natural lawyers, on the other? Hart's answer in these two chapters is 'yes'.

The key to understanding how Hart makes out his answer is his distinction between the 'internal' and 'external' aspects of rules. Although Hart twice introduces this distinction in criticizing the Austin/Bentham account of legal obligation in terms of predicted sanctions,[30] the distinction is in fact crucial to Hart's own positive account of law. Only when officials within some society adopt the 'internal attitude' towards that master rule Hart calls the 'rule of recognition' does that society have a legal system (or law). Such an internal attitude towards a rule consists in an endorsement of the rule as one that ought to be followed.[31] Thus, law differs from the threats of a gunman writ large in that for one but not the other someone must believe that the rule authorizing the threat is in some sense legitimate.

More than this cannot here be said, for any summary of chapters 5 and 6 could not do justice to Hart's theory of law (as the union of primary and secondary rules) and remain within the limitations of length here appropriate. Suffice it to say that these chapters form the core of the book. They in any event are clear enough, and succinct enough, that they can speak for themselves.

In the fourth part of the book, chapter 7, Hart gives a critical examination of the sceptical attitude towards law of American Legal Realism. Defusing the 'rule-scepticism' of the Legal Realists was an important task for Hart. As he early recognized, if the Legal Realists were right, then he would have to give up 'the very possibility of describing a legal system even partly in terms of *rules* . . .'[32] The answer to the Realists Hart gives in chapter 7 echoes the answer he gave three years earlier in his debate with Lon Fuller: if legal rules have a penumbra of uncertainty attached to some of their applications, they also must have a core of certain applications. Otherwise, communication, let alone law, becomes impossible.

In the fifth and last major part of the book, chapters 8 and 9, Hart seeks to lay to rest the natural law theory of law, according to which there is some intrinsic link between morality and law that accounts for law's normativity. Having accepted St Augustine's point that law's normativity cannot be analogized to the obliging done by the gunman's force, Hart needed to underscore the fact that his own theory did not slide unwittingly into St Augustine's moralistic account of legal obligation. This Hart does when he tells us that the internal attitude essential for law to exist need not involve any *moral* beliefs of the officials who accept the rule of recognition:

[30] *Concept*, above n. 5, 55–6, 86–8. [31] Ibid. 55.
[32] Hart, 'Analytic Jurisprudence', above n. 7, at 957.

> [I]t is not even true that those who do accept the system voluntarily, must conceive of themselves as morally bound to do so . . . In fact, their allegiance to the system may be based on many different considerations: calculations of long-term interest; disinterested interest in others; an unreflecting, inherited or traditional attitude; or the mere wish to do as others do.[33]

This was perhaps an excess of zeal on Hart's part, for he could have distinguished himself from the natural lawyers by simply pointing out the difference between statements *about* moral belief from statements *of* moral belief. Hart could assert that there is no law unless the officials of the system believe in the justness of their system, without himself asserting that there is no law unless the system is just. Only the latter assertion makes one a natural law theorist, although Hart was at pains even to deny the first.

IV. CRITICISMS OF *THE CONCEPT OF LAW*

The reaction to *The Concept of Law* when it was first published was immediate and enthusiastic. Early on it was recognized for the classic in legal philosophy that it is, and over the years its stature has only grown. Hart has never revised it, although he intended to do so at one time in order to answer the considerable critical literature that grew up around it.[34] My own hypothesis is that Hart has never thought he was in error in any of the central tenets of the book, how ever much he might have expressed them differently in later years.

The best-known criticism of the book came from one of Hart's former students at Oxford, Ronald Dworkin, who was appointed to succeed Hart in the Chair in Jurisprudence at Oxford after Hart resigned the Chair in 1968. Beginning in 1967, Dworkin attacked Hart's central idea that law should be conceived as a system of *rules*.[35] Rather, Dworkin has argued, the law of any legal system (such as that of England or America) that is rich in institutional history, should be seen as an organic whole, not as a set of discrete rules. The result, argued Dworkin, is a fusion of moral and legal principles, since there can be no master rule at all like Hart's rule of recognition that picks which principles are moral and which are legal.

[33] *Concept*, above n. 5, at 198.

[34] Since this chapter was originally published in 1990 Hart's partially completed 'Postscript' to *The Concept of Law* has been published posthumously. It appears in the otherwise unaltered 2nd edn. of *The Concept of Law* (Oxford: Oxford University Press, 1994).

[35] Ronald Dworkin, 'The Model of Rules', *University of Chicago Law Review*, 35 (1967), 14–54. Dworkin continues his criticism of Hart in *Taking Rights Seriously* (Cambridge, Mass.: Harvard University Press, 1978), chs. 3–4, and in *Law's Empire*, above n. 9.

Hart has responded in detail to Dworkin's criticism.[36] Hart's most general response—and one gaining much support from other legal philosophers—is that Dworkin wilfully ignores the question Hart set himself, and wishes Hart had asked a different one. Hart in *The Concept of Law* did not ask Dworkin's *internal* question: 'From the perspective of a judge in some particular legal system, does the law that binds me as a judge include more than explicit rules?' Rather, Hart asked, 'From the vantage point of a social scientist *external* to my or any legal system, what is law?' Criticisms that he failed to accommodate American judicial practice are not, Hart thought, criticisms of the book he wrote, only the wish that he had written a different book.

Aside from Dworkin, other well-known criticisms of the book were made by Hart's old foe at Harvard, Lon Fuller, and by a fellow legal positivist, friend, and former student of Hart's, Joseph Raz, now Professor of the Philosophy of Law at Oxford University. Fuller's criticism, which appeared in the first edition of *The Morality of Law* in 1965, elaborated on and refined one of the criticisms he had advanced against Hart in the famous 1958 debate. This was the criticism that there could be no law in a system that did not respect what Fuller called the 'inner morality' of law—norms such as those demanding public, prospective, consistent rules that citizens *can* obey if they are of a mind to do so. Hart's 1965 response[37] was the same as it was in the 1958 debate and in *The Concept of Law* itself: strict compliance with such norms of procedural fairness is 'compatible with very great iniquity'.[38] Or, as Grant Gilmore put the same point at the close of his Storrs Lectures at Yale some years later: 'In Hell there will be nothing but law, and due process will be meticulously observed.'[39]

Joseph Raz, although developing and extending Hart's insights in his own work,[40] criticized Hart's unwillingness to acknowledge that officials must at least believe or claim that the ultimate rule of a system is just before that system is a legal system. Raz observed that such an acknowledgement was compatible with Hart's legal positivism, for the legal theorist did not himself have to believe in the justness of some system for that to be a legal system. Yet how, Raz asked, could Hart accommodate the obligation of a judge to follow the law if such judges did not have such

[36] H. L. A. Hart, 'Law in the Perspective of Philosophy: 1776–1976', *New York University Law Review*, 51 (1976), 538–51; Hart, 'American Jurisprudence Through English Eyes: The Nightmare and the Noble Dream', *Georgia Law Review*, 11 (1977), 969–89 (both of these articles are reprinted in Hart, *Essays in Jurisprudence and Philosophy*, above n. 6); Hart, *Essays on Bentham*, above n. 27, at 147–53; and Hart, 'Comment', in Ruth Gavison, above n. 1, at 35–42. See also the posthumously published 'Postscript', above n. 34.

[37] Hart, 'Book Review', above n. 23.

[38] *Concept*, above n. 5, at 202.

[39] Grant Gilmore, *The Ages of American Law* (New Haven: Yale University Press, 1977), at 111.

[40] See esp. J. Raz, *The Concept of a Legal System* (Oxford: Oxford University Press, 1970) (2nd edn. 1980).

beliefs?[41] Hart's response has been to reiterate his account of the judge's 'internal' attitude towards the rule of recognition of his system. Although finding much of Raz's criticism to be 'a valuable supplementation to my own distinction drawn in *The Concept of Law* between external statements about law and internal statements made by those who accept the law',[42] Hart ultimately thinks that the needed internal attitude of officials does not demand any more than an acceptance of the rules for *any* reason, not just because of some belief in the justness of the rules. A judge's 'view of the merits may be favourable or unfavourable, or simply absent, or, without any dereliction of his duty as a judge, he may have formed no view on the moral merits'.[43]

My own criticism of *The Concept of Law* has focused on its ordinary language philosophy method.[44] The revolution in philosophy begun by Gilbert Ryle, J. L. Austin, and Herbert Hart at Oxford in the 1940s did not have the outcome they envisioned. In particular, the methods of ordinary language analysis did not supplant the perennial quest in philosophy for metaphysical answers to questions such as, 'How does mind relate to the material world?' The philosophy of mind current today pursues that question with a vengeance, joining hands with linguistics, cognitive psychology, and artificial intelligence in search of increasingly sophisticated answers. Even so, the work of Ryle, Austin, and Hart has not been put aside. Stuart Hampshire was prescient about this when he wrote in his 1950 review of *The Concept of Mind* that one measure of the greatness of such a work is the rewards it would offer to patient nibbling by critics over the years.[45] If one surveys those currently in the forefront of work in the philosophy of mind, one sees that such nibbling is still going on.[46]

The same has been and will continue to be true of *The Concept of Law*. It has been nibbled at by critics for over 30 years, and even for those of its critics who do not share its method—in which I include myself—it still represents the starting point for serious thought about law.

[41] Raz, *The Concept of a Legal System*, above n. 40 (2nd edn., 1980), 234–8; Raz, *Practical Reason and Norms* (London: Hutchinson, 1975), 123–9, 146–8, 162–77; Raz, *The Authority of Law* (Oxford: Oxford University Press, 1979), 28–33, 153–7; Raz, 'Hart on Moral Rights and Legal Duties', *Oxford Journal of Legal Studies*, 4 (1984), 123–31.

[42] Hart, *Essays on Bentham*, above n. 27, at 154–5.

[43] Ibid. at 159.

[44] See e.g M. Moore, 'The Interpretive Turn in Modern Theory: A Turn for the Worse?', *Stanford Law Review*, 41 (1989), 871–957, at 927–34 (now Ch. 10 herein).

[45] Stuart Hampshire, 'Review of *The Concept of Mind*', *Mind*, 59 (1950), 237–55.

[46] See e.g. a recent book by one of the foremost philosophers of mind of our time, Daniel Dennett, who while pursuing the relation of mind to brain, acknowledges his deep debt to Ryle. Dennett, *Elbow Room* (Cambridge, Mass.: MIT Press, 1984), p. ix.

V. HART'S CAREER AFTER *THE CONCEPT OF LAW*

Aside from his rearguard actions against Fuller, Dworkin, and Raz, Hart has let his theory of law rest as it is stated in *The Concept of Law*. This has hardly been because Hart stopped writing upon the publication of this book. He turned his attention to other topics within political and legal philosophy.

One of those topics was a topic made central to political theory by John Stuart Mill in the nineteenth century: What principled limits might there be to the power of a legislature in a democracy to control the behaviour of individuals through coercive legal sanctions? The book that followed *The Concept of Law* was *Law, Liberty, and Morality* in 1963, a write-up of Hart's 1962 lectures at Stanford on this topic. In the latter book Hart demolished the popular view that society was entitled to protect itself (with legislation) against immoral behaviour as it was entitled to protect itself against treason. Hart three years before had addressed this topic,[47] and did so again four years later.[48]

Hart's work on the theory of legislation represents the core of the political liberalism that he so eloquently defended. As Neil MacCormick, Dean of the Faculty of Law at the University of Edinburgh, has said of this branch of Hart's writings: 'As thinker and as writer Hart has been one of the most important and influential contributors of the post-war period to the liberal/social democratic way of thought and action.'[49] In addition to his work on the liberal theory of legislation, Hart's work in this vein includes essays on the natural right to freedom, on constructive criticism of the philosophers who have done the most to revive political philosophy in the 1970s and 1980s, John Rawls and Robert Nozick, on the ideas of rights in terms of the choices of individuals as to whether or not to exercise such rights (a view that came to be known as the 'choice theory of rights'), on the meta-ethical depths of political philosophy and ethics, and on utilitarianism.[50]

Hart's other main area of writing since *The Concept of Law* has been a return to the issues of responsibility and punishment with which he began his academic career. In the philosophy of the criminal law Hart has writ-

[47] H. L. A. Hart, 'Immorality and Treason', *Listener* (30 July 1959), 162.

[48] H. L. A. Hart, 'Social Solidarity and the Enforcement of Morality', *University of Chicago Law Review*, 35 (1967), 1–13.

[49] MacCormick, *H. L. A. Hart*, above n. 13, at 10.

[50] H. L. A. Hart, 'Are there Any Natural Rights?', *Philosophical Review*, 64 (1955), 175–91; 'Rawls on Liberty and Its Priority', *University of Chicago Law Review*, 40 (1973), 543–55; 'Between Utility and Rights', *Columbia Law Review*, 79 (1979), 828–46; 'Book Review of Gilbert Harman, *The Nature of Morality* and J. L. Mackie, *Ethics*', *New York Review of Books*, 25 (1978); 'Utilitarianism and Natural Rights', *Tulane Law Review*, 53 (1979), 663–80.

ten extensively and systematically. His collection of essays, published by Oxford in 1968 is still the most influential book in criminal law theory.[51] For in that book Hart lays out his widely adopted 'mixed' theory of punishment, analyses moral responsibility's role in punishment, and proceeds to analyse various key elements in the ascription of responsibility, notably action and intention. Much of Hart's other work was related to responsibility/punishment theory, even when not specifically directed towards it. His first essay in 1949 was in action theory,[52] his co-authored paper with Stuart Hampshire in 1958, on a central concept to responsibility, the concept of intention,[53] and his already mentioned work on causation bore directly on responsibility issues.[54]

When Hart resigned his Chair in Jurisprudence at Oxford in 1968, he did so in part to devote more time to his editorial duties with respect to the Bentham papers he was instrumental in having published during the 1970s. Hart also wrote a series of essays on Bentham, collected eventually into another fine book, *Essays on Bentham: Jurisprudence and Political Theory*, published by Oxford in 1982. These essays together with his Bentham editorship represent something of a labour of love for Herbert Hart. He clearly respects his only true predecessor in legal philosophy, as well he might, since he in so many ways resembles him. As Joseph Raz and Peter Hacker wrote of Hart on the occasion of his seventieth birthday:

> Herbert Hart has done for twentieth-century legal philosophy what Bentham did for eighteenth-century jurisprudence. He has integrated it into the mainstream of general philosophical thought. He has brought his knowledge of contemporary philosophical method to bear upon the questions of the philosophy of law, and, as he has said of Bentham, 'We are too often forced to the conclusion that . . . [he] . . . has provided us with a new question, rather than merely a new answer, for his innovation to be considered a matter of method alone.' He has clarified and strengthened the links between legal philosophy and moral and political philosophy, philosophy of mind and of language, and philosophical logic. To each of these subjects he has made a serious contribution. Finally, again following Bentham's footsteps, he has been a forceful spokesman for the liberal tradition in morals and politics. The endeavor to strike a judicious balance between the liberty of the individual and the social good lies at the core of his political morality.[55]

Upon resignation of his Chair in Jurisprudence in 1968 Hart held a Senior Research Fellowship at University College of Oxford University. In 1972 he became Principal of Brasenose College, Oxford, a position he occupied until his retirement in 1978 at the age of 71.

[51] H. L. A. Hart, *Punishment and Responsibility* (Oxford: Oxford University Press, 1968).

[52] Hart, 'Ascription', above n. 16.

[53] H. L. A. Hart and S. Hampshire, 'Decision, Intention, and Certainty', *Mind*, 67 (1958), 1–12.

[54] Hart and Honoré, *Causation in the Law*, above n. 21.

[55] Hacker and Raz, above n. 4, p. v.

Hart at the time this was originally written (1989) was approaching his eighty-third birthday. He continued to reside in Oxford with his wife Jennifer, although they split their time between Oxford and their house in Cornwall. Although formally retired, he remained actively interested in the world of philosophy to which he had been such a contributor. At gatherings of legal philosophers to discuss work-in-progress, held in the 1980s in Tony Honoré's rooms as Warden of All Souls College, Oxford, Hart was the same keen-sighted and sophisticated participant that he had been as a student at Oxford in the 1920s. His has been an exemplary illustration of how the life of the mind can be worthwhile, when it is carried on with such intelligence, integrity, and grace.

3

Hart's Concluding Scientific Postscript

I. INTRODUCTION

It has often and correctly been remarked that the Hart–Fuller debate of 1956–69[1] set the agenda for Anglo-American jurisprudence in the last half of this century. The nature of law, of legal obligation, of legal authority, and of law's relation to morality, were the questions that debate made central to jurisprudence as we have since practised it.

It is thus fitting that in his final contribution to jurisprudence—his 'Postscript' to *The Concept of Law*[2]—Hart re-examined the agenda that he had set in his debate with Fuller. That re-examination took place as a response to the criticisms of Hart offered up by Ronald Dworkin over the years. As Hart recognized, Dworkin 'called in question the whole conception of legal theory and of what it should do' that was implicit in Hart's work.[3] Dworkin thus provided Hart with a convenient foil against which to reaffirm Hart's own long-held views about how jurisprudence is most fruitfully conceived and practised.

Current practitioners of jurisprudence should welcome this 'Hart–Dworkin debate', if we may call it that. For such a debate allows us to reassess our own focus on the agenda set forty years ago by Hart and Fuller. It allows us, in other words, to step back and to reassess what kind of activity we should carry on as 'jurisprudence'. This may be more important to do now than it was forty years ago, since so many different activities (e.g. legal storytelling) have appropriated the title, 'jurisprudence', for themselves.[4]

[1] The first salvo in this debate should probably be given to Fuller in his exchange with Ernst Nagel. L. Fuller, 'Human Purpose and Natural Law', *Journal of Philosophy*, 53 (1956), 697–709, reprinted under the same title, *Natural Law Forum*, 3 (1958), 68–76. Hart responds to Fuller's arguments in his justly celebrated article, 'Positivism and the Separation of Law and Morality', *Harvard Law Review*, 71 (1958), 593–629. Fuller's response was 'Positivism and Fidelity to Law—A Reply to Professor Hart', *Harvard Law Review*, 71 (1958), 630–72. Hart restated his views in *The Concept of Law* (Oxford: Clarendon Press, 1961), and Fuller, his in *The Morality of Law* (Stanford: Stanford University Press, 1964). Hart's response to the latter was 'Book Review—*The Morality of Law*', *Harvard Law Review*, 78 (1965), 1281–96. Fuller's rejoinder is in his *The Morality of Law*, 2nd edn. (Stanford: Stanford University Press, 1969).

[2] H. L. A. Hart, 'Postscript', in *The Concept of Law*, 2nd edn. (Oxford: Clarendon Press, 1994).

[3] Ibid. at 239.

[4] At a recent AALS Planning Committee Meeting organizing a mini-workshop on 'Jurisprudence', one sceptical type suggested we just go by the titles of various professors in picking our participants; if their title included the word, 'jurisprudence', they were in.

There is a second reason to welcome the Hart–Dworkin debate. Some of Dworkin's positions restate those defended by Fuller in the earlier debate.[5] Since this part of the present debate rehashes issues identical to those in the debate between Hart and Fuller, we should also welcome an updated version of what often should be seen as but one debate. Hart's views over the fifty years have remained constant, and Dworkin's positions in the debate have often shown a surprising similarity to those of Fuller. Since Dworkin is plainly better armed philosophically than was his predecessor, the updated debate also allows us to see what the Hart–Fuller debate might have looked like had Fuller's side been better represented.

II. HART'S IDEA OF AN EXTERNAL JURISPRUDENCE

I begin with Hart's theory about how jurisprudence ought to be carried on. Hart's ideas are most usefully clustered into three groups: those connected to the generality of law and of legal theory; those connected to the normativity of law and of legal theory; and those connected to the semantics of law and of legal theory. I shall discuss each in turn.

A. The Generality of Law and Legal Theory

Hart from first to last saw himself as doing what John Austin would have called 'general jurisprudence'.[6] Such jurisprudence 'is *general* in the sense that it is not tied to any particular legal system or legal culture . . .' The thesis underlying such a general jurisprudence is that 'this institution [law], in spite of many variations in different cultures and in different times, has taken the same general form and structure . . .'[7]

Particular jurisprudence, by contrast, studies law as it is conceived and practised within a particular legal system or legal culture. Here one seeks, not the 'general form and structure' of law as such, but rather, whether for example law *in the United States* consists of more than statutes, including perhaps the Constitution and the common law of judges.

An easy way to miss this distinction is to think that Hart must really have been charting the *English* concept of law, whatever his pretensions to generality might have been. This argument, popular among students introduced to Hart's book for the first time,[8] goes like this: Hart is using a

[5] I chart some of these affinities in Chs. 7 and 9, below.

[6] John Austin, *The Province of Jurisprudence Determined*, ed. Hart (New York: Noonday Press, 1954).

[7] Hart, 'Postscript', above n. 2, at 239–40.

[8] The first year graduate students who took my and Waldron's introductory jurisprudence seminar in the Jurisprudence and Social Policy Programme at UC-Berkeley introduced me to this reaction to Hart.

concept of law derived from the English language and from English legal practices; no matter how universal may be the intended *application* of this concept, the *source* of the concept cannot be hidden; Hart is really asking when other cultures have 'law' *in the sense the English think they have law*; his jurisprudence is thus parochial despite its cosmopolitan ambitions.

The problem with this attempted demotion for Hart's general jurisprudence is the problem with all such modestly conceived social science.[9] Modest social science desperately wants to be fair to the differing social practices of other cultures. It thus thinks that somehow we are imposing something on other cultures if we impose our categories on their practices. For example, if we are studying religions around the world, we shouldn't impose our concept of religion onto other cultures; we should use *their* concept of religion. Perhaps their mating behaviour is really a religious rite for them, by their concept of religion even if not by our own.

This is pretty obviously dotty, even if well intentioned. Social science cannot proceed with such conceptual anarchy. If we want to compare institutions such as law or religion in different cultures, we will have to have some idea of what law or religions are. We will have to have some idea about what functional or structural features make an institution of the kind, legal or religious, to have any chance of studying the same kinds of things in our cross-cultural studies. We have at least to start with a provisional theory about the nature of such kinds in order even to know what to look for. That such theory is influenced by our own cultural conditioning is true but harmless. Our best theories of anything all have such influences behind their acceptance, but to let the fact of such influences undermine our confidence that this is the best theory is a fallacy—indeed, one with its own name, the 'genetic fallacy'.

Hart's kind of jurisprudence is thus general in the sense he describes, secure against what I shall call the 'standard sophomore objection'. Hart's jurisprudence was also general in a second sense quite distinct from that he articulates in the Postscript. This second sense of generality is best seen by repairing to a threefold distinction about the subject matter of legal theory (namely, law) that Hart introduced in his 1958 debate with Fuller. There Hart distinguished: (1) law, in the sense of legal system, from (2) laws, which are logically general standards binding on legal actors, from (3) the laws of cases, which are those singular propositions of law that make reference to particular actors and particular legal situations and which resolve particular cases in legal dispute.[10] Hart drew this distinction so as to isolate the three possible points of contact that a natural lawyer might urge to exist, between 'law' and morality. However, we can use the distinction to clarify Hart's own focus for jurisprudence.

[9] I describe such 'modest' social science in Ch. 6 herein.
[10] Hart, 'Positivism', above n. 1, at 600–1.

Even a casual reading of *The Concept of Law* will show that Hart's central concern is with law in its most general sense, namely, legal system.[11] The traditional question with which the book begins, 'What is law?', is translated by Hart into the question that interests him: 'When does a society have a legal system?' It is true that Hart's answer to this question requires him to take some position about the nature of laws and of the laws of cases. That is, if a mature legal system exists only when there is a 'union of primary and secondary rules', then in order to understand more fully what a legal system is we need to know something about such rules. Moreover, if the crucial secondary rule needed for there to be a legal system is what Hart calls a 'rule of recognition'—a rule that quite literally recognizes other rules as valid laws—then this attribute of a legal system will also have implications for what laws within such a system can be. Valid laws are those standards recognized by the rule of recognition itself accepted by the relevant officials within that legal system.

Further, Hart's answer that legal systems exist when primary rules of obligation are obeyed by citizens and the secondary rules are accepted by judges, dictates at least this much of an answer about the nature of the laws of cases: prior to judicial decisions, all singular propositions of law cannot lack a truth value, although some of them can. Hart at least needed enough of a theory of adjudication to defuse what he calls 'rule scepticism'.[12] For if extreme Legal Realism were correct, so that general legal standards were completely indeterminate in their implications for particular cases, then an analysis of legal system in terms of such standards would be empty. In such an event, legal systems could well be just as Hart's analysis says they are; but such an analysis would hold no one's interest because legal systems would be of no interest.

Despite these implications for the ideas of law that figure so prominently in the theory of adjudication—laws and laws of cases—Hart's central focus is on something much more general. His question is when a society has law, by which he means, legal system.

There is yet a third dimension of generality we need to distinguish. This has to do with the role-specific nature a jurisprudence may or may not have. That is, one can ask about law from a kind of 'view from nowhere', in the sense that one is not asking after law as it limits or defines a particular role or office. Alternatively, one can ask about law from the point of view of some role within legal systems. Most famously, one might reasonably think that judging is a role that is virtually defined by law in this role-specific sense; law, so conceived, is whatever standards are obligatory

[11] Argued convincingly by Joseph Raz, *The Concept of a Legal System*, 2nd edn. (Oxford: Clarendon Press, 1980).

[12] Hart, *Concept*, above n. 1, at ch. 7.

on a judge (*qua* judge) as she reaches and justifies her decisions in particular cases.[13]

Hart's jurisprudence is general in this further sense that it is not role-specific. Hart's jurisprudence is an academic enterprise in that it seeks to answer the academic question, 'What is law?', without vicariously assuming some role within some legal system. It is not a practical jurisprudence of the kind each sitting judge must possess, a jurisprudence that defines law to be whatever obligates judges as standards of decision.

It is true that Hart's answer to his academic question is an answer focusing mightily on judges. A mature legal system exists, Hart tell us, only when judges (Hart's 'legal officials') *accept* the rule of recognition for their systems;[14] such acceptance, Hart further tells us, occurs only when judges adopt an 'internal attitude' towards the rule of recognition,[15] and when such judges regard this master rule as obligatory for one reason or another.[16] Thus, judges must have a role-specific theory of law in order for there to be a legal system. That, however, does not transform Hart's jurisprudence into a role-specific jurisprudence. Hart's is a general jurisprudence outside of any practical role, even if the answers given to questions asked from such a general point of view turn out to require legal actors to practise a jurisprudence more specific to their role.

Hart's jurisprudence in *The Concept of Law* was general in each of these three dimensions. These dimensions are not so interconnected that if one is doing general jurisprudence in one sense, he must be doing it in all three senses. Some of my own jurisprudential writings on interpretation, for example, are general in the first sense but particular in the second and third senses. I urge certain truth conditions for singular propositions of law, and certain theories of law for judges, without limiting the recommendations to judges in any particular legal culture.[17]

Given this lack of interconnectedness between the generality of jurisprudence in these three senses, Dworkin's jurisprudence is a particularly apt contrast to Hart's. For Dworkin, as we shall see, promotes a particular jurisprudence in all three senses of the word.

[13] On whether there can be role-specific ethics, see Heidi Hurd, 'Justifiably Punishing the Justified', *Michigan Law Review*, 90 (1992), 2203–324; and *Moral Combat* (Cambridge: Cambridge University Press, 1999).

[14] Hart, *Concept*, above n. 1, at 115–17.

[15] Ibid. at 56–7, 84–5, 115–17.

[16] Ibid. at 115.

[17] Michael Moore, 'A Natural Law Theory of Interpretation', *Southern California Law Review*, 58 (1985), 277–398. Ruth Gavison notices this separation in this work, in her 'Comment', in R. Gavison (ed.), *Issues in Contemporary Legal Philosophy: The Influence of H. L. A. Hart* (Oxford: Oxford University Press, 1987), at 26 n. 5.

B. The Normativity of Law and Legal Theory

Every theory of law has had to take some position on the ability of law to create obligation. The hard legal positivist line on this was that of Austin and Bentham: law obligates only in the Pickwickian sense that law gives prudential reasons for action by virtue of the sanctions attached to non-compliance. The natural law position is that there is only one kind of obligation and that is moral obligation; further, that a standard must (prima facie at least) morally obligate obedience if it is to be law.

Hart famously tried to find some middle ground between the hard positivist and the natural lawyer on this issue. Hart took seriously St Augustine's question to the hard positivist: on their view, how does law differ from the threat of a gunman? Austin's answer was that law is general in a way that the order of a gunman is not. Hart, by contrast, sought to soften legal positivism by granting that in some sense law obligates.[18] The task for Hart was to accomplish this softening of legal positivism without collapsing into the natural law view that because law morally obligates only morally correct standards could be law.

Hart's attempt to answer St Augustine begins with the idea of a social rule. A social rule is more than a generalization about convergent behaviour of individuals. Habits when shared constitute such convergent behaviour but habits are not described by a social rule. Needed, Hart argued, was a distinctive attitude of the actors towards the rule. This is the attitude of one who has the 'internal point of view' towards the rule. Such an individual regards the rule as a standard by which to guide his own behaviour and by which to evaluate such behaviour, whether by himself or others.[19] A social rule, in other words, is a prescriptive rule for those actors who adopt the internal viewpoint towards it.

Moral obligations, as Hart analyses them, are imposed by social rules with three characteristics (in addition to the convergent behaviour plus internal attitude making it a social rule). First, 'when the general demand for conformity is insistent and the social pressure . . . is great', there may be an obligation.[20] Whether this is so depends on, second, whether the social rules 'are thought important because they are believed to be necessary to the maintenance of social life . . .'[21] Third, 'obligations and duties are thought of as characteristically involving sacrifice or renunciation' since what such rules demand often conflicts with the self-interests of the persons to whom they apply.[22]

Before coming to Hart's use of this idea of moral obligation to account for the obligatoriness of law, it is worth pausing to be clear what kind of

[18] Hart, *Concept*, above n. 1, at 82, 85.
[19] Ibid. at 55–8.
[20] Ibid. at 86.
[21] Ibid. at 87.
[22] Ibid.

analysis this is on Hart's part. Hart is not doing ethics. He is not giving an analysis of when people are actually obligated. His is a viewpoint (in his own language) external to ethics, from which viewpoint he is assessing when people *regard themselves* as obligated. As an analysis of when people *are obligated*, this would be a hopelessly relativist and conventionalist kind of ethics. Despite Ronald Dworkin's one-time attempt to paint Hart into this kind of corner,[23] it is clear that that was not his meta-ethical view.[24]

Hart is thus giving us a sociology of ethics. He is analysing when people regard themselves as bound by prescriptive rules, and, more particularly, when people regard themselves as bound by the social rules of *obligation*. Hart remains the trenchantly and consistently external sociologist when he turns to analyse the obligatoriness of law. Hart nowhere concedes that law necessarily obligates, not really; this is as true of judges as it is of citizens. At most, Hart locates law's normativity in judges' regarding themselves as obligated by the rule of recognition of the legal system in which they are judges. Judges must adopt the internal attitude towards the rule of recognition, and, unlike the citizen a judge must 'think of his conforming behaviour as "right", "correct", or "obligatory"' for there to be law.[25]

It is worth stressing that Hart's external sociological jurisprudence and ethics takes no position on whether the law of America (or any other legal system) actually obligates judges, citizens, or any other legal actors.[26] Hart's question was what is necessary for law (in the sense of legal system) to exist. His answer with respect to obligation was both clear and plausible: law exists only if judges believe the rule of recognition obligates their obedience to it. There is little comfort to be found here by the natural lawyer, because a judicial belief in the obligatoriness of secondary rules is but another social fact, not any kind of moral fact.

Left open by Hart's purely external jurisprudence is the following possibility. Perhaps for those pursuing particular jurisprudence law does have some necessary connection to morality. In particular, if the 'law' one cares about is the law of some particular legal system; if it is 'law' in the sense of individuated *laws*; if it is 'law' in the sense of defining the role of a judge—then it may well be consistent with everything Hart has said, that laws must be sufficiently connected with morality that they actually can obligate judicial obedience. Indeed, perhaps Hart's own internal jurisprudence—a purely hypothetical jurisprudence, since Hart did not engage in

[23] Ronald Dworkin, 'Social Rules and Legal Theory', *Yale Law Journal*, 81 (1972), 855–90, reprinted as ch. 3 of *Taking Rights Seriously* (Cambridge: Harvard University Press, 1978).

[24] See e.g. Hart, 'Book Review of Gilbert Harman, *The Nature of Morality* and J. L. Mackie, *Ethics*', *New York Review of Books*, 25 (9 Mar. 1979), 35–8.

[25] Hart, *Concept*, above n. 1, at 115.

[26] Joseph Raz, carrying on Hart's style of external, general jurisprudence, also avoids this ethical question of internal jurisprudence. See Raz, 'Facing Up: A Reply', *Southern California Law Review*, 62 (1989), 1153–235, at 1170 n. 28.

such an enterprise—would at least require the rule of recognition for this legal system to be sufficiently just that the laws it validates could be actually obligatory on judges. After all, such a judge doing internal jurisprudence might well take Hart's external analysis of law to heart. Such a judge would say the statutes, etc., of my legal system can only be *law* binding on me if they have the character of law in general; given Hart's analysis of when there is law in general, this means there can only be *law* binding on me if I (and other judges) believe that we are obligated by the Constitution (our rule of recognition); we can believe we are obligated by the Constitution only if we believe in the (all things considered, overall) justness of the Constitution; and I can only say that I believe the Constitution is both just and binding on me, if I also say that, as a matter of moral fact, the Constitution *is* both just and binding on me. Therefore, something is law (in the sense of obligating me in my role as a judge) only if at least the basic features of the legal system of which this law is a part, are just.

It is unclear to me how much Herbert Hart anticipated this kind of move, a move that takes his limited concession to the normativity of law in general jurisprudence and transforms the concession into a full-blown natural law view in particular jurisprudence. In any event, Hart cut off such a move by his lifelong insistence on the thinness of acceptance needed for there to be a legal system. According to Hart, for a legal system to exist does require that judges believe themselves to be obligated by the rule of recognition for that system. However, for such a belief by judges, it is not required that judges believe in the justness (or moral desirability in any sense) of the rule of recognition. As Hart put it:

> [I]t is not even true that those who do accept the system voluntarily, must conceive of themselves as morally bound to do so . . . In fact, their allegiance to the system may be based on many different considerations; calculations of long-term interest; disinterested interest in others; an unreflecting, inherited or traditional attitude; or the mere wish to do as others do.[27]

[27] Hart, *Concept*, above n. 1, at 203. In the passage quoted in the text it is unclear whether Hart is referring to officials' acceptance of the rule of recognition or to citizens' acceptance of the primary rules of obligation. I take the former interpretation because of Hart's later statement that, 'though the judge is . . . committed to following the rules his view of the moral merits of doing so . . . is irrelevant. His view of the merits may be favourable or unfavourable, or simply absent, or, without dereliction of his duty as a judge, he may have formed no view on the moral merits' (H. L. A. Hart, *Essays on Bentham* (Oxford: Clarendon Press, 1982), 159). In the Introduction I wrote for the Legal Classics edition of *The Concept of Law* (Birmingham, Ala.: Gryphon Press, 1990), I opined that this disclaimer by Hart was 'an excess of zeal' on his part because he could do his kind of external jurisprudence without it and yet remain an external legal positivist. Upon publication of the Introduction Hart received a copy, and wrote to reaffirm his 'excessive' zealousness: 'I see that you wonder why I don't settle for a less extreme form of positivism which would be content with the assertion that officials must *believe* in the justness of their system but not that the system must *be* just if it is to be law. I myself wonder at times why I do not take the easier line; what prevents me is the simple empirical doubt as to whether all officials do believe this (Oliver Wendell Holmes did

By this disclaimer Hart cut off the possibility of inferring a natural law particular jurisprudence from his legal positivist general jurisprudence. My above-imagined judge reasoning from the latter to the former now cannot say that for there to be law at all in his legal system requires that he (and other judges) believe in the justness of the rule of recognition for this system. It is enough that he and his fellow judges accept their rule of recognition as being obligatory for whatever reason, and this breaks any necessary connection between law and morality even within particular jurisprudence.

Hart recognized that not only might law be thought to be normative, but that theorizing about law in jurisprudence might also be thought to be a normative enterprise.[28] Jurisprudence is normative when it eschews the task of describing law or some concept of law, for the task of giving normative recommendations about the concept of law that we *ought* to employ. Hart seemed to recognize the possibility of doing two kinds of normative general jurisprudence. The first uses moral arguments to back up its normative recommendations. Such a jurisprudence might argue, for example, that widespread acceptance of legal positivist conceptions of law make evil regimes like those of the Nazis more likely. Or one might argue that natural law concepts of law make people too quiescent in their conformity to legal authority, since they will believe that any legal institution is also morally desirable.[29] This kind of jurisprudence recommends a concept of law based on the net desirable moral consequences that are brought about by acceptance of such a concept.

Jerry Postema presents Jeremy Bentham as an example of such a morally normative jurisprudence.[30] Bentham's ideal for law was that of giving notice to citizens of what the law expected of them. As Bentham put it in one of his more exuberant moments, law should be such that each citizen could open the great book of laws and know thereby the legal consequences attached to any conceivable action he might wish to perform. A hard legal positivist concept of law promoted this ideal, according to Bentham, because it validated as law statutes and not common law.[31] The result of acceptance of such a concept of law would thus be greater predictability of law.

not!) and if they do not whether a system with all the other features of law cannot exist as a legal system' (Herbert Hart, personal communication, 13 Feb. 1990).

[28] See generally Phil Soper, 'Choosing a Legal Theory on Moral Grounds', in J. Coleman and E. F. Paul (eds.), *Philosophy and Law* (London: Basil Blackwell, 1987).

[29] The kind of arguments Fuller and Hart glancingly consider in their 1958 debate. See Hart, 'Positivism', above n. 1; Fuller, 'Positivism and Fidelity', n. 1.

[30] Gerald Postema, *Bentham and the Common Law Tradition* (Oxford: Clarendon Press, 1986).

[31] Argued for in A. W. B. Simpson, 'Common Law and Legal Theory', in *Oxford Essays in Jurisprudence*, 2nd ser. (Oxford: Oxford University Press, 1973).

Hart alternatively glimpsed the possibility of a non-moral but nonetheless normative jurisprudence. This kind of jurisprudence would recommend a concept of law for reasons of successful theory construction in social science. Suppose, for example, that the hard positivist concept of law fitted in with one's empiricist ideals for social science. This would recommend such a concept of law to any social scientist with such ideals because to such a person explanations framed with this concept of law would not make exorbitant demands on what one's explanations require to exist in order to be true.[32]

In his 'Postscript' Hart reaffirms what had always been obvious anyway: his kind of jurisprudence was not only general but also descriptive.[33] Hart seeks to describe the concept of law that we presently employ. He has no reformer's aims here, not for reasons of morality, and not for reasons of good theory construction in social science.

Ronald Dworkin has created a fictionalized Hart who despite the real Hart's protestations finds himself doing a kind of morally normative jurisprudence.[34] This is Dworkin's attempt to turn Hart into Bentham. I shall examine later Dworkin's supposed reason for this fictionalization (in terms of the supposed impossibility of a purely descriptive, general jurisprudence). For now it is sufficient to note what Hart himself reaffirms in his 'Postscript':

> Like other forms of positivism my theory makes no claim to identify the point or purpose of law and legal practices as such . . . In fact, I think it quite vain to seek any more specific purpose which law as such serves beyond providing guides to human conduct and standards of criticism of such conduct.[35]

Hart's was always in its intent a purely descriptive jurisprudence, which everyone (including Dworkin) has always known.

C. The Semantics of Law and of Legal Theory

It is legitimate to enquire of any purely descriptive jurisprudence just what it is it takes itself to be describing. One possibility is that one is describing a set of semantic (and pragmatic) conventions which give the meaning (and the conditions of appropriate use) of the word 'law' in the English language. This is, for example, probably a fair reading of John Austin's descriptive jurisprudence, for Austin proceeds by analysing the various primary and derived senses of the word, 'law'.[36]

32 Hart notices such empiricist-grounded normative arguments in *Concept*, above n. 1.
33 Hart, 'Postscript', above n. 2, at 240.
34 Ronald Dworkin, *Law's Empire* (Cambridge, Mass: Harvard University Press, 1986), ch. 4.
35 Hart, 'Postscript', above n. 2, at 248–9.
36 John Austin, *Province of Jurisprudence*, above n. 6.

We can pinpoint what it is that Hart's descriptive jurisprudence purports to describe by working through Dworkin's intentional misreading of Hart in this regard. In chapter 1 of *Law's Empire* Dworkin treats Hart as if he were John Austin pursuing an analysis of the semantic and pragmatic conventions governing the usage of the word 'law' in the English language.[37] This supposedly makes Hart subject to the 'semantic sting', which is Dworkin's phrase for the error of limiting the meaning and extension of a word to those situations covered by the conventions that have hitherto governed its usage.

Hart is rightfully indignant in his 'Postscript' at such a deliberate misreading of his kind of jurisprudence: 'in fact nothing in my book or in anything else I have written supports such an account of my theory.'[38] Indeed, in the 'Preface' to the original edition of *The Concept of Law* Hart was quite clear in this respect. Hart there recognized that he had 'raised questions which may well be said to be about the meanings of words'.[39] Yet, Hart continued, 'the book may also be regarded as an essay in descriptive sociology'.[40] What such a sociology describes is the phenomenon, law, a kind of social institution universally found in civilized societies. Hart shared the ordinary language philosopher's faith that a way to better understand a phenomenon like law is to first understand how words like 'law' are used. But the ultimate thing Hart sought to describe was not the conventions governing the usage of 'law'; rather, Hart sought to describe law itself.[41]

Thus, in the body of *The Concept of Law* Hart recognizes precisely the view Dworkin attributes to him. Linguistic usage of the words, 'law' and 'legal system', gives all competent speakers a 'standard case of a legal system';[42] when questions are raised, one could then 'simply say, such is the standard case of what is meant by "law" and "legal system" ';[43] for non-standard or borderline cases, we can reason by analogy to the standard case, remembering that where there 'are disputed cases . . . there can be no conclusive argument for or against this classification as law'.[44] Contrary to Dworkin's interpretation of him, Hart utterly rejects this semantic approach to jurisprudence's question, 'What is law?':

[37] Dworkin, *Law's Empire*, above n. 34, at 31–5.

[38] Hart, 'Postscript', above n. 2, at 246.

[39] Hart, *Concept*, above n. 1, at p. v.

[40] Ibid.

[41] Ruth Gavison sees this clearly: 'Dworkin is constructing a straw man here. Classical legal theories have always been attempts at understanding the phenomenon of law, and not at defining the word "law". . . . The linguistic formulations of the question concealed a belief that linguistic usages reflect social reality in some way, and that there was something to be gained from attending to them. But the search has always been the same: an attempt to understand the nature of law' (Gavison, *Issues*, above n. 17, at 23).

[42] Hart, *Concept*, above n. 1, at 4.

[43] Ibid. at 5.

[44] Ibid.

> Such a way with the question would be agreeably short. But it would have nothing else to recommend it. . . . The deep perplexity which has kept alive the question, is not ignorance or forgetfulness or inability to recognize the phenomenon to which the word 'law' commonly refers. . . . This short way with the question, which does little more than remind the questioner of the existing conventions governing the use of the words 'law' and 'legal system', is therefore useless.[45]

Hart's jurisprudence is a descriptive theory about the structure of law,[46] not an attempt at lexical semantics for the word 'law'.

It is true that the kind of nature Hart found law to possess was itself a kind of social convention. Law according to Hart is the union of primary and secondary rules, the first at least being obeyed and the second being obeyed because it is accepted at least by judges. These are social conventions forming the essence of law for Hart.[47] Yet nothing in this answer requires that one discover or justify that answer through the semantic/pragmatic conventions of language. Hart did not join Austin in describing such linguistic conventions, however much Dworkin wishes to read him that way.

Dworkin may have perhaps been misled by Hart's kind of analysis of propositions of law (as opposed to propositions about law, that is, of legal theory, our present topic). In Hart's 1953 inaugural lecture Hart did articulate his ordinary language philosopher's faith that to seek the meaning of a proposition of law (such as, 'x has a legal right') is to describe the semantic and pragmatic conventions governing the speech acts one typically does with such expressions. This is a semantic analysis of a kind.[48] Yet unlike Dworkin, Hart clearly distinguishes propositions *about* law from propositions *of* law.[49] The latter are propositions internal to some particu-

[45] Hart, *Concept*, above n. 1, at 4.

[46] Hart's later characterization in the article he wrote for Paul Edward's *Encyclopedia of Philosophy* in 1967. Hart, 'Problems of the Philosophy of Law', *Encyclopedia of Philosophy*, ed. Paul Edwards, vi (New York: MacMillan, 1967), 264–76, reprinted in H. L. A. Hart, *Essays in Jurisprudence and Philosophy* (Oxford: Clarendon Press, 1983), at 91.

[47] It is thus true that Hart's *answer* is given in terms of the conventions (that make up law) even if his *method* in arriving at that answer is not one relying on semantic conventions (surrounding usage of the word, 'law'). This conventionality of Hart's answer is enough for Dworkin to press his 'semantic sting' objection, directed against Hart's legal positivist theory of law but not against Hart's method of jurisprudence. In fact as we shall see, Dworkin is actually more subject to the 'semantic sting' than is Hart, for *both* Dworkin's answer and his methods are too conventionalist to justify belief in determinate answers in cases of radical disagreement in either law or in legal theory.

[48] H. L. A. Hart, 'Definition and Theory in Jurisprudence', *Law Quarterly Review*, 70 (1954), 37–60, reprinted in Hart, *Essays*, above n. 46. Hart himself came to see that like other Oxford ordinary language philosophers of the time he had merged force into meaning. Hart, 'Introduction', *Essays*, above n. 46, at 2–6. Hart also came to see that a purely semantic analysis even of more particular legal concepts used within a legal system did not resolve the controversies that have arisen in the application of such concepts. Ibid. at 5.

[49] Hart, 'Postscript', above n. 2, at 247: Dworkin 'seems to me to confuse the meaning of "law" with the meaning of propositions of law'. See also Gavison, *Issues*, above n. 17, at 26

lar legal system, while the former are the propositions expressed by a legal theory external to any legal system. Since Hart's jurisprudence is only of the latter kind, his ordinary usage approach to propositions *of* law cannot be taken as indicative of a similar approach to propositions *about* law.

Despite my rejection of Dworkin's attempt to force-fit Hart's external jurisprudence either into an internal jurisprudence analogue or into John Austin's semantic version of an external jurisprudence, there is a sense in which semantics for the propositions about law of Hart's external jurisprudence, is conventional. We can get at the conventional nature of Hart's semantics for legal theory by asking how Hart's descriptive jurisprudence is to make the separation between social conventions that are legal and all others? A normative jurisprude such as Bentham can answer in terms of the value he sees law as serving; Bentham's is a view according to which a legal system will have a kind of functional integrity and any convention that serves the value (function) of such a system *ought* to be called 'law'. But Hart as we have seen eschews any theory of law's point or value and thus is bereft of these resources.

It seems to me that Hart's descriptive jurisprudence is left with the intuition that certain kinds of social institutions stand to sociology and the social sciences the way that certain kinds of natural phenomenon stand to physics and the natural sciences. That is, just as there are 'natural kinds' in the natural world,[50] so there are 'social kinds' in the social world, and law is one of them. Such kinds exist and have a nature that can be discovered. Since the nature of such social kinds is not functional for Hart, it must be structural. Such structures are I gather what Hart claims to have discovered with his twofold essentialist analysis of law.[51]

Having made the discovery of a social kind, law, existing in all civilized societies, Hart's sociological, external jurisprudence refers to this kind of kind through a concept. Thus, the title of his book, *The Concept of Law*. As we have seen in our discussion of Dworkin's 'semantic sting', the concept of law is not to be equated with a lexical definition of the word, 'law', teased out of that word's ordinary usage in English. Rather, Hart's

('Dworkin is weakening considerably the distinction between law and theory of law . . . the law is what is binding on us, and a theory of law is our way of understanding what is binding on us').

50 Natural kinds have been a frequently discussed topic in contemporary philosophy. For an introduction, see Michael Moore, 'The Semantics of Judging', *Southern California Law Review*, 54 (1981), 151–295.

51 I do not think that this answer actually works for Hart, but why it does not gets us too far ahead of the story. The bottom line I shall defend later is this: Hart needed to have a functionalist essence to law, not a structural one, but this did not require him to abandon his descriptive kind of jurisprudence. Such a descriptive jurisprudence, however, will look quite different from Hart's because *what* it is describing will include some moral facts (about the ends of law) as well as some non-moral facts (about the efficacy of certain kinds of social institutions in effecting the ends of law).

sociology mines the social practices of civilized societies for the concept of law implicit in those practices to give the word, 'law', a meaning. Hart's semantics is thus conventional in that his kind of jurisprudence aims to refer to the phenomenon, law, through a concept of law.

A less conventionalist semantics would seek to refer to the phenomenon, law, more directly.[52] One would then write a book called something like, '*The Nature of Law*'. Still, the difference here is not great. Hart is seeking to describe the phenomenon, law, with his sociology. He is not seeking to rely on ordinary language in the way his contemporaries did who wrote similarly titled books.[53]

There is an aspect of Hart's semantics for legal theory that is puzzling. Hart consistently urged that words used in propositions of law did not have criteria that defined their meaning. From his 1949 essay to his 1958 debate with Fuller Hart disclaimed the logical positivist semantics according to which the meaning of a word is to be found in the necessary and sufficient conditions of that word's correct usage.[54] The puzzle is that this logical positivist ideal for meaning is the most obvious sense to be given the idea of a *concept*.[55] Moreover, Hart in the *Concept of Law* seemingly gives us just such a criterial definition of law:

> There are therefore two minimum conditions necessary and sufficient for the existence of a legal system. On the one hand, those rules of behaviour which are valid according to the system's ultimate criteria of validity must be generally obeyed, and, on the other hand, its rule of recognition specifying the criteria of legal validity and its rules of change and adjudication must be effectively accepted as common public standards of official behaviour by its officials.[56]

Because Hart distinguishes the propositions of law characteristic of an internal jurisprudence, from propositions *about* law characteristic of an external jurisprudence, it was open to him to adopt a different semantics for each. To see if this is a plausible interpretation of Hart, we need to repair to his reasons for his anti-criterial stance about the semantics of propositions of law.

52 I discuss theories of 'direct reference' (also called 'Kirpke–Putnam semantics', after two leading philosophical explications of it) in Moore, 'A Natural Law Theory', above n. 17; and 'Semantics of Judging', above n. 50.

53 e.g. Gilbert Ryle, *The Concept of Mind* (London: Hutcheson (1949); Richard Peters, *The Concept of Motivation* (London: Routledge and Kegan Paul, 1958).

54 H. L. A. Hart, 'The Ascription of Responsibility and Rights', *Proceedings of the Aristotelean Society*, 49 (1949), 171–94; Hart, 'Definition and Theory', above n. 47; Hart, 'Positivism', above n. 1.

55 See Moore, 'A Natural Law Theory', above n. 17, at 291 n. 25.

56 Hart, *Concept*, above n. 1, at 116. As Peter Hacker noted in his essay, 'Hart's Philosophy of Law', in P. M. S. Hacker and J. Raz (eds)., *Law, Morality and Society: Essays in Honour of H. L. A. Hart* (Oxford: Clarendon Press, 1977), 1–25, this certainly looks like the kind of explicit definition of 'law' that Hart throughout his career eschewed for more particular legal terms.

I take Hart's anti-criterial stance here to be due mainly to his general outlook in semantics.[57] Hart was plainly influenced in his general outlook in semantics by 1950s style Oxford paradigm case argument (PCA) semantics.[58] According to PCA semantics, one finds the meaning of a word by finding the paradigmatic exemplars shared by the linguistic community that uses the word. There will be things to which the word so clearly applies that anyone who doubts the word's application to such things will be said 'not to know the meaning of the word'. To determine the word's application to things that are not paradigms for that word, one reasons by analogy to the paradigms. Such analogical reasoning relies on there being primitive similarity relations between such paradigms and other things; for one cannot abstract properties shared by the paradigms, and construct a concept (in the sense of criterial definition) out of those.

For propositions of law used internal to some legal systems Hart correctly saw that the ordinary meaning of English words was relevant. If a statute uses the word 'vehicle' in its prohibition, 'no vehicle shall be allowed in the park', the ordinary meaning of 'vehicle' is prima facie relevant to the legal meaning of the word in this statute.[59] For Hart, that meant that an interpreting judge should repair to the 'standard instances' of the word in framing the singular proposition of law that will decide his case.[60]

However, when we turn to the propositions about law used in an external jurisprudence, we find no analogous reason to repair to our general outlook in semantics. As Hart saw clearly, when we do external jurisprudence we are not (and should not be) seeking to discover the ordinary meaning of the English word, 'law'.[61] Requests for a definition of law are not requests for such a semantic analysis. Rather, such requests are requests to understand the structure of the thing, law. Such a structure has puzzling elements that are interrelated in various complex ways, and a good external jurisprudence describes that structure.

In this sociological task of external jurisprudence, there is thus no reason to treat the ordinary English meaning of 'law' with the respect we should give the ordinary English meaning of e.g. 'vehicle', in internal jurisprudence. There is no text using 'law', as there is a (statutory) text

[57] Hart on occasion did marshal other arguments against criterial definitions. In 'Ascriptivism', above n. 54, Hart based his anti-criterial conclusion on: (1) the case law origins of legal concepts; (2) the lack of any unitary thing named by legal concepts; and (3) the supposedly non-descriptive use of legal concepts because of their ascriptive force. These themes are repeated in 'Definition and Theory', above n. 47, and in Hart, 'Analytic Jurisprudence in Mid-Twentieth Century. A Reply to Professor Bodenheimer', *University of Pennsylvania Law Review*, 105 (1957), 953–75.

[58] On PCA semantics, see Moore, 'Semantics of Judging', above n. 50.

[59] Hart, 'Positivism', above n. 1. Hart later softened but did not eliminate the reliance on ordinary English semantics in the interpretation of statutes, in his 'Introduction', above n. 48, and in his 'Problems', above n. 46.

[60] Hart, 'Positivism', above n. 1.

[61] See text at nn. 30–46, above.

using 'vehicle', that commands our attention as the source of our reasoning in external jurisprudence. Hart was thus free of his own views (PCA, apparently) about semantics in doing external jurisprudence. He could thus give the output of his descriptive efforts the form of a criterial definition of 'law' without contradicting himself.

III. THE IDEA OF AN INTERNAL JURISPRUDENCE

Since we have already outlined the main dimensions of comparison, we can more briefly describe the contrasting kind of internal jurisprudence.

A. The Generality of Law and of Legal Theory

Ronald Dworkin eschews Hart's general, external jurisprudence. Dworkin recognizes that the historian and the sociologist will do their theorizing about law from a point of view that is external to the practice of law in any legal system.[62] Dworkin recognizes that some have tried to do jurisprudence from that external perspective, giving Holmes as an example.[63] Yet finding jurisprudence of this sort to be 'perverse', 'impoverished', and 'defective',[64] Dworkin firmly takes up the task of an explicitly internal jurisprudence.

This is jurisprudence done from within our legal system. Here we theoreticians vicariously share with practitioners the concern with *our* law, not law in general. It is because of this that Dworkin sees jurisprudence as being continuous with law practice. Legal theoreticians trying to account for our law are making the same sorts of claims and arguments as practitioners, the only difference being in the generality of the issues dealt with by theoreticians: 'Jurisprudence is the general part of adjudication, silent prologue to any decision at law.'[65]

Given internal jurisprudence's focus on *our* law, not surprisingly such a jurisprudence also eschews analysis of law in the sense of legal system, for the other two, less general notions of law Hart distinguished in 1958, namely, laws and laws of cases.[66] Dworkin calls both of these, 'propositions of law', which are 'all the various statements and claims people make about what the law allows or prohibits or entitles them to have'.[67] Laws Dworkin calls general propositions of law, and laws of cases Dworkin calls concrete propositions of law.[68] Both are the sort of *law* one cares about if one is an American wondering what his legal rights and duties may be under US law.

[62] Dworkin, *Law's Empire*, above n. 34, at 13–14.
[63] Ibid. at 14.
[64] Ibid.
[65] Ibid. at 90.
[66] See text at n.10 above.
[67] Dworkin, *Law's Empire*, above n. 34, at 4.
[68] Ibid.

Dworkin is also explicit that his is a viewpoint within one particular role within our legal system, and the role is that of the judge.[69] As Dworkin puts it, we should do our jurisprudence:

from the judge's viewpoint, not because only judges are important or because we understand everything about them by noticing what they say, but because judicial argument about claims of law is a useful paradigm for exploring the central, propositional aspect of legal practice. Citizens and politicians and law teachers also worry and argue about what the law is and I might have taken their arguments as our paradigms rather than the judge's. But the structure of judicial argument is typically more explicit, and judicial reasoning has an influence over other forms of legal discourse that is not fully reciprocal.[70]

Dworkin's internal jurisprudence thus continues what H. L. A. Hart once called 'a concentration almost to the point of obsession, on the judicial process' characteristic of American jurisprudence.[71] Whether this distinctively 'American obsession' in jurisprudence is a good idea I shall address in the last section.

B. The Normativity of Law and of Legal Theory

From the point of view of internal jurisprudence law is necessarily normative. That is, if one's interest in law is the interest of a sitting judge in a specific legal system, the law is defined by its normative aspect: law is what a judge is obligated to use as a standard for decision. Indeed, the role of a judge and the reason-giving capacity of law reciprocally define each other in this kind of jurisprudence. Not only is law conceived as whatever obligates judges, but the role of judging is conceived in terms of decision-making constrained by those standards we think of as law.[72]

Because law from this viewpoint is necessarily obligating for a judge does not mean that it is also obligating for citizens.[73] If one thinks that there can be such a thing as role-relative morality, then it might be correct that a citizen is not obligated by a law that a judge nonetheless is obligated to use in judging her behaviour. The focus on judicial obligation is thus not to be justified as a place-holder for everyone's obligation towards the law of a particular legal system.

[69] Ibid. at 18.

[70] Ibid. at 18–19.

[71] H. L. A. Hart, 'American Jurisprudence Through English Eyes: The Nightmare and the Noble Dream', *Georgia Law Review*, 11 (1977), 969–89, reprinted in Hart, *Essays*, above n. 46, at 123.

[72] This tight connection between judicial obligation and law held for the early Dworkin. See Dworkin's 1967 article, 'The Model of Rules', *University of Chicago Law Review*, 35 (1967), 14–54, reprinted as ch. 2 of *Taking Rights Seriously* (Cambridge, Mass.: Harvard University Press, 1978), where Dworkin treats the question of whether principles are part of the law as equivalent to the question of whether principles are obligatory or discretionary with judges.

[73] See the illuminating discussion of this possibility in Hurd, 'Justifiably Punishing the Justified', above n. 13.

It is true that a legal theorist can describe the normativity of the laws and of the laws of cases of some legal system without himself being committed to thinking that such laws actually obligate the judge in that system. Joseph Raz has long so practised jurisprudence, making what he would describe as 'detached normative statements' about the obligations of judges.[74] Yet this is an external jurisprudence about such laws. Internal jurisprudence is not uncommitted in this way. A standard must actually obligate judges, and not merely be thought or claimed to obligate, if it is to be law for a sitting judge or a legal theorist arguing from the point of view of such a judge.

It is also possible to imagine an internal jurisprudence that did not tie law to judicial obligation in the tight way that I have described. Andrei Marmor, for example, urges that even for a judge sitting within a legal system it should make sense to say that some standard is law but that my obligation is not to follow it.[75] Justified civil disobedience by judges ought to be conceptually possible, and divorcing law from obligation is the seemingly obvious way to do this.

Even the later Dworkin seems to have caught some of this incubus. Dworkin now seems to believe that the necessary obligatoriness of American law for an American judge is only a posit we adopt whilst we are examining the grounds or structure of laws. We have two-legged trousers to put on, and this is just the keeping of one foot on the ground while we move the other. Really, however, we *can* shift to the other foot, hold the structure of law constant, and enquire into whether that stuff—'law'—really obligates judges in our system.[76]

A properly conceived internal jurisprudence should not make this concession. Such a jurisprudence should tie law strictly to judicial obligation, so that if a standard does not give a judge an obligation it is not part of the law. One can accommodate the conceptual possibility of justified judicial civil disobedience by distinguishing the prima facie obligations of role from all-things-considered obligations. Law obligates judges *in their role as judges;* that does not mean that sometimes judges will not be justified in stepping out of the judicial role because other values are more important than those (rule-of-law) values that normally justify conformity to the judicial role.[77]

74 See the discussion and citations in J. Raz, 'Hart on Moral Rights and Legal Duties', *Oxford Journal of Legal Studies*, 4 (1984), 123–31.

75 Andrei Marmor, *Interpretation and Legal Theory* (Oxford: Clarendon Press, 1992).

76 Dworkin, *Law's Empire*, above n. 34, at 108–13.

77 See ibid. at 112, where Dworkin concludes that after we have shifted from one foot to the other and have our trousers fully on, law 'must be understood as saying what judges should do in principle, unless circumstances are special in the way just noticed'. If 'what judges should do in principle' is equated with their role-defined obligations, this is the position I describe in the text.

The main virtue of internal jurisprudence is its practicality. It speaks to officials in power directly. One can maintain this practicality only by tying law to the obligations that define the offices such officials occupy. This is the main reason not to break the tie between law and judicial obligation sketched above.

Another virtue of this moralistic conception of law in internal jurisprudence can be seen if we think of judicial activities like distinguishing or overruling a common law precedent, or overruling the plain meaning of some statute in favour of that statute's perceived purpose. These are not usually thought of as instances of civilly disobedient judicial activities. Common law distinguishing or overruling, together with purposive interpretation of statutes, are well accepted aspects of the judge's role as we know it. If we freed law from its close tie to judicial obligation, we might think of these judicial activities as proper but as going *against the law*. Yet we find it simpler and closer to our ideals not to conceptualize these activities in this way. Instead, we conceptualize the law as always having been that which the overruling/distinguishing/purposefully interpreting court has discovered for the first time. Our conceptualizations here reveal the desirability of keeping our ethics of role simple, even at the expense of complicating our account of law's structure.

Because law is necessarily normative for the kind of internal jurisprudence here considered, does that mean that that jurisprudence itself must also be normative? A normative internal jurisprudence would not rest content with the task of describing the standards that judges in the legal system regard as law, nor in describing the interpretive or analogical reasoning practices that judges in fact employ in order to reach and to justify the laws of disputed cases. Rather, a normative internal jurisprudence recommends to judges both what standards they *ought* to regard as law in this legal system, and what methods they *ought* to use in applying those standards so as to discover and to justify the particular laws that decide individual cases.

Necessarily, by adopting the viewpoint of a sitting judge within a particular legal system, this kind of jurisprudence is as normative as the law about which it is a theory. After all, the conclusions of such a jurisprudence are conclusions about what is the law (laws, laws of cases) of this legal system, and as we have seen such conclusions about law are conclusions of what obligates judges in their role as judges. What else can tell judges what their obligations are—i.e. what they ought to do—but normative statements about what they ought to do? If law obligates judicial obedience, a jurisprudence about such law must be normative.

Such a normative jurisprudence might well on occasion take certain institutional facts into account in making its normative recommendations to judges. Suppose, for example, all judges in our system interpreted statutes in a plain meaning fashion, and they found the holding of precedent cases to be the stated holding in the precedent courts' opinions. Suppose further that citizen reliance had built up around these judicial practices. Such reliance would give a theorist of our system some reason to recommend these practices and the singular propositions of law that they would justify. Yet the bare fact that judges practise these practices recommends nothing.[78] It is only the normatively weighted social fact that counts. As it turns out, the other sorts of reasons disfavouring these two practices on the merits rather easily outweigh the normative power of the reliance fact imagined, so that a properly normative, internal jurisprudence would recommend against continuation of these practices no matter how universally they have been practised by judges in our legal system.[79]

These last considerations reveal the possibility of a slight wedge being driven between the viewpoint of a sitting judge within our legal system and a legal theorist arguing to such a judge. This possibility arises because an internal jurisprudential theorist might see himself as prescribing legislatively for the class of *all* sitting judges, whereas an individual sitting judge knows that the impact of his adoption of some theory of law is confined largely to his own decisions. (This empirical fact is of course untouched by the logical fact that the judge like the theorist is committed to universalizing his prescriptions.) If all or almost all other judges were practising their craft uniformly even if erroneously, that could give an individual sitting judge a reason to do likewise. Equality and predictability, for example, would be enhanced by his adopting such a practice.[80] Such reasons to conform will not exist for my imagined system-designing theorist, whose recommendations are free of the pull of uniform practice because he is urging the change of that practice by all judges. His only deference to the imagined uniform but less than ideal judicial practice will exist only to the extent that there are costs imposed by a one-time change to his new, equally uniform practice.

[78] As Lon Fuller exclaimed, 'It is incredible to think that obligation can arise from some such morally inert fact.' What Fuller was railing against is a view of jurisprudence that regards its task as purely descriptive and then (unlike Hart and Raz) turns to the question of the obligatoriness of law and without more ado blithely assumes that law of course obligates obedience, at least prima facie.

[79] For the argument against the classical theory of holding, see Michael Moore, 'Precedent, Induction, and Ethical Generalization', in L. Goldstein (ed.), *Precedent in Law* (Oxford: Oxford (University Press, 1987). For the argument against plain meaning interpretation of statutes, see Moore, 'A Natural Law Theory', above n. 17; and 'Semantics of Judging', above n. 50.

[80] Gerald Postema argues that such values can make judging a kind of co-ordination game, in that each judge has these reasons to seek to coordinate his kind of judging with that of other judges. Postema, 'Co-ordination and Convention at the Foundation of Law', *Journal of Legal Studies*, 11 (1982), 165–203.

I have described the normativity of legal theory without reference to Dworkin. This is because it is unclear whether we should attribute this purely normative internal jurisprudence to Dworkin. I have elsewhere separated Dworkin's early jurisprudence between its descriptive and its normative tasks.[81] Consider his well-known argument for treating the soundest theory of law ('principles') as part of the law of which it is a theory.[82] Dworkin argued descriptively that our practices of arguing and deciding hard cases as a matter of pre-existing legal right presuppose sufficient law to generate such rights; since in hard cases we have run out of obvious law, some unobvious stuff—'principles'—must be part of the law. Dworkin also argued normatively that our ideals of the separation of powers and of prospectivity of new law would be flouted if one did not regard the law as sufficiently rich that hard cases could be decided as a matter of pre-existing legal rights. Since for Dworkin, the practices we have are those that we ought to have, he did not need to decide whether he was describing how we practise law or prescribing to us how we ought to practise it.

The later Dworkin tries to finesse this question. The internal jurisprudence of *Law's Empire* is 'interpretive jurisprudence', which is both (Dworkin tells us) descriptive and normative.[83] Such jurisprudence is descriptive in that it takes our present judicial practices to be the 'pre-interpretive data' that it is a theorist's job to interpret; it is normative in that it interprets present judicial practices to 'make them the best they can be' while still being the same practices and not new ones.

Such an interpretive, internal jurisprudence is a possible kind of jurisprudence, but it is not an attractive one precisely because it is insufficiently normative.[84] It is unduly conservative towards existing theories of law and of legal reasoning as those theories are embedded in present judicial practice. It treats such practices as a kind of text that legal theorists (and the judges who are their audience) must interpret to find out what they ought to do. Yet there is no normatively persuasive argument to treat such practices as a kind of text. We should thus do our internal jurisprudence in a more purely normative way, if we are to reach plausible conclusions about what standards and modes of reasoning are obligatory on judges. As a theorist or as a judge, we are right to disdain the plain meaning rule of statutory interpretation and the classical theory of a case's

[81] Below, Ch. 7.

[82] Dworkin, 'The Model of Rules', above n. 72, and 'Hard Cases', *Harvard Law Review*, 88 (1975), 1057–109, also reprinted in *Taking Rights Seriously*, above n. 72.

[83] Dworkin, *Law's Empire*, above n. 34.

[84] For this argument in greater detail, see Chs. 10 and 11 below. Herbert Hart was present when I presented a draft of the former paper (now Ch. 10) at All Souls College, Oxford, with Dworkin commenting; I gather I won Hart's assent (if not Dworkin's) on this point. See 'Postscript', above n. 2, at 241 n. 15.

holding, no matter how many other theorists have recommended it and no matter how many other judges have acted on such defective recommendations.

So the internal jurisprudence that clearly contrasts to Hart's external jurisprudence is not quite Dworkin's. Dworkin might call this an interpretation of him making him the best he could be. I prefer to think of this as what he ought to believe even though he doesn't. In psychology no less than in jurisprudence it serves both honesty and clarity if we keep our recommendations separate from our descriptions.

C. The Semantics of Law and of Legal Theory

The best semantics for propositions of law, whether uttered by a judge or by an internal legal theorist vicariously speaking in the judicial role, is what I have elsewhere called a 'realist semantics'.[85] According to such a semantics, the meaning of words like 'contract', 'malice', 'law' itself, are not given by either criterial definitions or paradigmatic exemplars; rather, both such criteria and paradigms as may guide usage are 'defeasible'[86] in the sense that they are subject to correction in light of an improved theory of the nature of the kind of thing to which such words refer. It is the nature of law that gives the meaning of the word, 'law', the nature of contract that gives the meaning of 'contract', etc. Meaning is thus sought in a theory about such natures, not from any paradigms or definitions drawn from conventional usage of such words.[87]

The advantages of such a semantics for law and internal jurisprudence I earlier taxonomized as fourfold: (1) a judge or a theorist does not run out of meaning as fast as she runs out of conventions, be they paradigmatic exemplars or criterial definitions; (2) when such a judge or theorist adopts an improved theory of contract, etc., he is not changing the meaning of the law, or changing the law, because the meaning is the actual nature of the thing referred to, and that actual nature has not changed just because one's theory about it has changed; (3) such a semantics will usually better reflect

[85] Moore, 'A Natural Law Theory', above n. 17, and 'Semantics of Judging', above n. 50; Moore, 'Do We Have an Unwritten Constitution?', *Southern California Law Review*, 63 (1989), 107–39. I apply such a realist semantics to moral discourse in Moore, 'Moral Reality', *Wisconsin Law Review*, [1982], 1061–156, Moore, 'Moral Reality Revisited', *Michigan Law Review*, 90 (1992), 2424–533.

[86] Hart's old term for the provisional nature of semantic criteria. Hart, 'Ascriptivism', above n. 54.

[87] We do need intimations that there is a kind, and we may use paradigms in a weak sense to make this discovery. The paradigm from which we learned of flatness, for example, may have been the earth's surface. As this example shows, such paradigms may turn out not to be instances of the kind once we develop a proper theory of the kind's nature. Such learning paradigms thus do not fix the meaning in the style of PCA semantics. See Moore, 'Semantics of Judging', above n. 50.

the semantic intentions of the author of such language (if there is a determinate author and if one cares about his intentions); and (4) use of such a semantics in the interpretation of legal texts will often promote both better results and the purpose of the rules in which the words appear.[88]

Throughout his jurisprudential career Dworkin has relied heavily on the first two advantages. In the decision of hard cases both judges and the lawyers arguing to them do not run out of law (because they run out of the meaning of the words contained in such law).[89] In internal legal theory theorists can radically disagree with one another about what the law requires but also about what the nature of law might be; such radical disagreements are possible (in the sense of meaningful) only because such disagreeing theorists are not talking past each other, and they are not talking past each other only because they are talking about the same thing.[90] Hilary Putnam has long used realist semantics to make the same point about radical disagreements in science, both at a time and between different ages.[91]

These advantages of a realist semantics do not by themselves justify the adoption of such a semantics for the practice of law and internal jurisprudence. Such advantages only make it worthwhile to enquire whether the law and its theory can adopt such a semantics. Such advantages, in other words, motivate the enquiry but they do not answer it. Dworkin thinks that use of such semantics to be justified by a kind of social fact. We are to look to our legal practices to see whether or not they are 'interpretive', by which Dworkin means, whether they are carried on by us with what he calls the 'interpretive attitude'.[92] Part of such an attitude—the part relevant here—lies in how we regard our concepts. If we regard them as having a kind of 'semantic depth', so that they admit of theoretical exposition in terms of competing conceptions (or interpretations) of them, then we have such an attitude, and if that attitude is shared, then we have an interpretive practice.

In this foray into legal sociology Dworkin is right only this far: before we can use realist semantics we must find our own usage intentions to be 'indexical' (or 'referential').[93] Take the phrase, 'John's widow'. We can use

[88] Moore, 'A Natural Law Theory', above n. 17.

[89] See esp. Dworkin, 'Is There Really No Right Answer?', in R. Dworkin, *A Matter of Principle* (Cambridge, Mass.: Harvard University Press, 1985).

[90] Dworkin, *Law's Empire*, above n. 34.

[91] Hilary Putnam, 'The Meaning of "Meaning"', in his *Mind Language and Reality* (Cambridge: Cambridge University Press, 1975).

[92] Dworkin, *Law's Empire*, above n. 34, at 47.

[93] An indexical intention is Putnam's term for the intention to refer to some kind of thing, no matter what the nature of the kind may turn out to be. Putnam, 'Meaning of "Meaning"', above n. 91. A referential intention is Keith Donellan's name for such rigid designation of a particular or a kind. Donellan, 'Reference and Definite Descriptions', *Philosophical Review*, 75 (1966), 281–94.

such phrase to pick out Mary, John's present wife, when we convey now a property interest to take effect in the future; alternatively, we can use the phrase 'attributively', so that whoever possesses the property, married to John when he died, will be the designated taker.[94] The latter usage may pick Mary out, but only if it turns out to be she who possesses the property that defines the holder of the interest.

For concepts to have semantic depth they must be used referentially and not attributively. This much of a usage fact is necessary. But also necessary is a non-usage fact, a fact about the world, namely is there something whose nature can be referred to indexically? We may use the word 'jade' referentially and yet it may turn out that there is no natural kind whose unitary nature can give the meaning of the word.[95] Our referential intentions, in other words, have to answer to the facts.[96]

It is here that Dworkin's internal jurisprudence abandons the only semantics that can make sense of it.[97] For Dworkin cannot stomach the ontological commitments required by a realist semantics. He does not believe that it is either true or even sensible to talk of either mind-independent moral qualities or legal qualities that supervene on some combination of such moral qualities and certain institutional facts.[98] Thus, justice for Dworkin is not a quality that exists along with wetness and stupidity; rather, for Dworkin:

[94] In the famous 'unborn widow' case, *Jee v. Audley*, 1 Cox 324, 29 Eng. Rep. 1186 (Ct. Chancery 1787), the court took the phrase to be used attributively by the testator, which meant that the widow was not necessarily John's present wife Mary or any other life in being at the time the will took effect.

[95] Putnam's example, 'Meaning of "Meaning"', above n. 91.

[96] Here some of those who have followed me in applying realistic semantics to propositions of law have disagreed. See David Brink, 'Legal Theory, Legal Interpretation, and Judicial Review', *Philosophy and Public Affairs*, 17 (1988), 105–48; Brink, 'Semantics and Legal Interpretation (Further Thoughts)', *Canadian Journal of Law and Jurisprudence*, 2 (1989), 181–91; Nicos Stavropoulos, *Objectivity in Law* (Oxford: Clarendon Press, 1996). Brink and Stavropoulos appear to believe that we are justified in using realist semantics for any discourse whose practitioners speak and argue as if their concepts were theoretical terms. I think on the contrary that such a discourse necessarily degenerates into Dworkin's deep conventionalism, below discussed. For without the ontological commitments to kinds with natures, what is there to have a theory *about* except those deeply shared conventions Dworkin calls concepts? This is where Stavropoulos ends up, finding that the substantive theory that seeks to give the meaning of some legal concept is only 'constrained by paradigmatic applications and abstract characterizations of the relevant practice of application'. Ibid. at 160.

[97] Stavropoulos, *Objectivity*, above n. 96, at 160, makes a loyal effort to show that Dworkin's theory 'is perfectly compatible with K–P semantics'. Yet this stretches what Dworkin has said (particularly about interpretation) too far to be credible. Compare Ken Kress, 'The Interpretive Turn', *Ethics*, 97 (1987), 834–60, who sees more clearly the incompatibility between Dworkin's interpretive methodology and any version of realist semantics.

[98] I document Dworkin's conventionalism in this regard in Ch. 8 below.

Justice is an institution we interpret . . . it has a history; we each join that history when we learn to take the interpretive attitude toward the demands, justifications, and excuses we find other people making in the name of justice.[99]

Justice is thus a set of social conventions for Dworkin. Out of these conventions we try to locate the most abstract but most widely shared, which we may call a *concept* of justice:

Political philosophers . . . try to capture the plateau from which arguments about justice largely proceed, and try to describe this in some abstract proposition taken to define the 'concept' of justice for their community . . .[100]

Then, 'arguments over justice can be understood as arguments about the best conception of that concept'.[101]

This should be seen clearly for the 'deep conventionalism'[102] that it is. It is not the thing, justice, that makes sense of radical disagreements about *it* and that prevents radical change in our theories of justice from simply talking about different things. For Dworkin, it is that plateau of agreement that he calls a concept that provides the common coin needed here.

The problem for this deep conventionalism is that it is not (and cannot be) deep enough. It betrays the very advantages (of a truly realist semantics) that Dworkin hoped to achieve with it. Suppose that we should discover that the best theory of justice is one according to which certain forms of art are just, and others, unjust. Such a theory prompts us to say such things as, 'abstract art is unjust'. Such statements betray a theory of justice that is beyond any plateau of agreement we may have as a shared concept of justice; it is even outside any of the 'pre-interpretive data' of justice, which is Dworkin's label for the 'rough boundaries of the practice on which our imagination must be trained'.[103] Dworkin would thus be committed to saying what he in fact says about this example:

The thesis that abstract art is unjust is not even unattractive; it is incomprehensible as a theory about justice because no competent preinterpretive account of the practice of justice embraces the criticism and evaluation of art.[104]

Deep disagreements about justice will thus not make sense for Dworkin, because the participants will not be talking about the same things, each having different concepts of justice.

Since Dworkin applies this conventionalist approach to legal propositions equally with moral propositions,[105] his semantics for internal jurisprudence is subject to his 'semantic sting' no less than is John Austin's. A properly conceived internal jurisprudence would not make this mistake. We should thus discard Dworkin's conventionalist and

[99] Dworkin, *Law's Empire*, above n. 34, at 73.
[100] Ibid. at 74.
[101] Ibid.
[102] Moore, 'A Natural Law Theory', above n. 17, at 298–300; Ch. 8 below.
[103] Dworkin, *Law's Empire*, above n. 34, at 75.
[104] Ibid.
[105] Ibid. ch. 3.

interpretivist semantics and substitute the realist semantics sketched earlier. The resulting internal jurisprudence is both internally more coherent and it presents a more plausible contrast to Hart's kind of external jurisprudence.

IV. THE TASK OF JURISPRUDENCE: EXTERNAL, INTERNAL, OR BOTH?

External jurisprudence is a very different enterprise than is internal jurisprudence, whether the latter is of Dworkin's kind or my own reconstruction of it along roughly Dworkinian lines. It is thus something of an understatement for Hart to query that 'it is not obvious why there should be or indeed could be any significant conflict between enterprises so different as my own and Dworkin's conceptions of legal theory'.[106] I take that to be the polite and reserved, typically English way of saying that it is obvious that such different types of theory cannot conflict with each other.[107]

Rather remarkably, Dworkin has disagreed. As I have sought to show in detail elsewhere,[108] Dworkin makes both the imperialist claim that a jurisprudence done external to a culture's legal practices is impossible and the more modest claim that such an external jurisprudence, if not senseless, is at least irrelevant to any practical concern about law.

In his 'Postscript' Hart observes that Dworkin has withdrawn his imperialist claim.[109] But the only general withdrawal Dworkin has made was done orally at the discussion of a paper of mine at which both Hart and Dworkin were in attendance.[110] Dworkin's printed beliefs are that external jurisprudence is impossible. This is, as Hart describes it, an 'extravagant' claim.[111]

It is also a plainly false one. Dworkin's only basis for advancing it is his adoption of Peter Winch's old thesis (characteristic of some views of Wittgenstein and of dualist hermeneutics) that to *understand* a practice one must get inside the practice.[112] Getting inside the practice means adopting

[106] Hart, 'Postscript', above n. 2, at 241.

[107] Not being English I put it this way in my 'Introduction' to *The Concept of Law* (now Ch. 2) that Hart approved: 'Hart's most general response . . . is that Dworkin wilfully ignores the question Hart set himself, and wishes Hart had asked a different one. . . . Criticisms that he failed to accommodate American judicial practice are not, Hart thinks, criticisms of the book he wrote, only the wish that he had written a different book.'

[108] Chs. 10 and 8, below.

[109] Hart, 'Postscript', above n. 2, at 243.

[110] This was at All Souls College, Oxford, in July 1987. The paper was 'The Interpretive Turn', now Ch. 10 herein.

[111] Hart, 'Postscript', above n. 2, at 243.

[112] Peter Winch, *The Idea of a Social Science* (London: Routledge and Kegan-Paul, 1958). I discuss other varieties of dualistic hermeneutics in Ch. 10 below.

the viewpoint of the practitioners, including their attitudes toward the practice, their own standards of validity, objectivity, etc.[113]

As Hart notes, this old view is so obviously false, and has been shown to be such so many times, that one is loathe to attribute the view to Dworkin.[114] Nicos Stavropoulos has picked up the lance in Dworkin's defence here, but his 'defence' turns out in reality to be a confession of defeat.[115] According to Stavropoulos, exactly what practices we count as the legal practices of some particular culture is itself the subject of substantive theory.[116] Thus, the boundaries of 'external' critique or support, versus 'internal', are themselves movable by a superior theory. It thus is possible for an external jurisprudence to be practical, for its theoretical power may be such that it cannot be considered external anymore. Yet if no argument, consideration, or theory can be ruled out in principle as 'external', then I fail to understand the sense of Dworkin's categorical denial of sense to Hart's external jurisprudence.

Dworkin does better with his more modest claim, which is that external jurisprudence is not a sensible enterprise but it is a bootless one. It is bootless, we are told, because it is irrelevant to practitioners of law (including internal theorists) within any legal system.

It is certainly true that in comparison with the direct practical interest (for sitting judges and for those lawyers and theorists who would influence such judges) of a properly conceived internal jurisprudence, Hart's kind of external jurisprudence looks academic. Yet often academic pursuits carry their own justifications pretty much on their sleeves. As George Mallory said of Everest, so a social scientist might well say of legal systems: they are worth examining simply because they are there. Law is a major kind of social practice, and describing it needs no more justification than does the describing of religions, co-ordination games, two-party politics, etc.

As I intimated earlier,[117] there is also a non-academic interest to Hart's kind of external jurisprudence. This is because of the indirect influence of

[113] See the citations to Dworkin in Chs. 8 and 10, below.

[114] Hart, 'Postscript', above n. 2, at 242–3.

[115] Stavropoulos, *Objectivity*, above n. 96, at 179–86. I note in passing that Stavropoulos in these pages attributes to me a view (about discourse autonomy) that he knows I do not hold, and then uses the view I do hold to answer it!

[116] This movable feast view of a practice's boundaries can indeed be accommodated within the Dworkin/Stavropoulos kind of interpretivism. As Dworkin himself puts this, 'since even the preinterpretive stage requires interpretation, these boundaries around the practice are not precise or secure' (*Law's Empire*, above n. 34, at 425 n. 22). What cannot be accommodated is the possibility of radical mistake, not at the boundaries, but root and branch. Thus it is unclear how an interpretive practice (such as the internal jurisprudence of some legal culture is supposed to be) could move its boundaries sufficiently so as to recharacterize all of external jurisprudence as if it were interpretive of some culture's practice of law. Dworkin's attempt to do this to Hart's jurisprudence is hardly a reassuring example of such a possibility.

[117] See text at nn. 26–7 above.

a notion of law in general, for law in some particular legal culture. Part of what an American judge needs, to develop her theory of what standards obligate her in her role as an American judge, is a theory of what law, in general, is. Such standards cannot be *American* law without sharing the character of law in general. As much I take to be tacitly conceded by Dworkin in his own attempt to state a general concept of law, in terms of justified legal coercion.[118]

I have always thought that the kind of internal jurisprudence sketched here is a worthwhile enterprise for a legal philosopher. It is accordingly the main kind of jurisprudence that I have practised. Yet one shouldn't need to disparage those working the other side of the street. Our own activity can stand on its own two feet without having to denigrate the activities of others.

V. CONCLUSION

My prediction is that the long-term challenge to Hart's kind of external jurisprudence will not come from Dworkin's kind of internal jurisprudence. Not only is Dworkin's jurisprudence clothed in the passing fashion of 'interpretivism', but it also passes Hart's like the proverbial ship in the night, as we have seen. It may well be Lon Fuller's own kind of external jurisprudence that continues to give Hart's a run for its money. For what if Fuller were right, that law is a functional kind whose general nature can therefore only be described in terms including the value(s) law distinctively serves in order to be law?[119] Hart's descriptive general jurisprudence would then be partly evaluative, for law's function is not a purely descriptive question of cause and effect but is as much an evaluative question of the goodness of the states of affairs that law can promote. This would not collapse the distinction between an external and an internal jurisprudence, nor would it even collapse the distinction between a descriptive and a normative jurisprudence. It would, however, make a *purely* descriptive jurisprudence impossible, whether carried on externally or internally.

Hart's jurisprudential epitaph for Fuller was I fear quite accurate:

> The author [Fuller] has all his life been in love with the notion of purpose and this passion, like any other, can both inspire and blind a man . . . I wish that the high romance would settle down to some cooler form of regard. When this happens, the author's many readers will feel the drop in temperature; but they will be amply compensated by an increase in light.[120]

[118] Dworkin, *Law's Empire*, above n. 34, at 93.

[119] I give what I understand to be the general form of this kind of jurisprudence without deciding on the merits whether it can be successful, in Ch. 9 below.

[120] Hart, 'Book Review', above n. 1, at 1296.

I am sure that Hart's own opinion of Fuller was such that he knew that such an 'increase in light' was not to be forthcoming by Fuller in the last years of Fuller's career. But the position, at least as old as Aquinas, remains for others to develop. I am sorry that we shall not hear Herbert Hart's response to it, developed with the insight, honesty, and modesty that were so characteristic of him.

4
Three Concepts of Rules

The article by Professor Frederick Schauer[1] to which this chapter was a reply was an explication of parts of a much richer manuscript then about to be published by the Oxford University Press.[2] In the latter work Schauer probes the nature of rules, ruleness, and rule-based decision-making generically, that is, without particular regard to the law. Professor Schauer presents his jurisprudential theory, which he calls 'presumptive positivism', as one spin-off of his more general theses about the role of rules in all decisional environments.

In both works, Schauer has given us a well-organized, comprehensive, well-versed overview of how rules do and should enter into our decisions. He has drawn together the large bodies of literature that have developed regarding rules since 1950. These literatures have separately focused: on the later Wittgenstein's preoccupation with rule-following,[3] on H. L. A. Hart's model of law as the union of two kinds of rules,[4] on Joseph Raz's lifetime study of rules as they impact upon our practical rationality both within and without the law,[5] and on the varieties of indirect utilitarianism that have flourished in ethics since John Rawls's seminal article in 1955.[6]

My own contribution in this chapter is intended to clarify which, of the possible enterprises in which one could be engaged in the study of rules, is the one in which Schauer is actually engaged. I choose this largely clarificatory task because my reading of Schauer's work leaves me uncertain of the extent to which Schauer himself has accurately located his enterprise. In any case, I intend such clarifications to help others who think about rules to grasp what possible subject matters there are that are worth talking about.

[1] F. Schauer, 'Rules and the Rule of Law', *Harvard Journal of Law and Public Policy*, 14 (1991), 645–94.

[2] F. Schauer, *Playing By the Rules*, (Oxford: Oxford University Press, 1991).

[3] Ludwig Wittgenstein, *Philosophical Investigations*, 3rd edn. (London: Blackwell, 1958). The literature of the 1950s on rules inspired by Wittgenstein prominently included: Peter Winch, *The Idea Of A Social Science* (London: Routledge, 1958); Richard Peters, *The Concept of Motivation* (London: Routledge, 1958); A. I. Melden, 'Action', *The Philosophical Review*, 65 (1956), 523–41. There has recently been a revival of interest in Wittgenstein's treatment of rules. See e.g. Saul Kripke, *Wittgenstein On Rules And Private Language* (Cambridge, Mass.: Harvard University Press, 1982); S. Holtzman and C. Leich (eds.), *Wittgenstein: To Follow A Rule* (Boston: Routledge and Kegan Paul, 1981).

[4] H. L. A. Hart, *The Concept of Law* (Oxford: Oxford University Press, 1961).

[5] See particularly Joseph Raz, *Practical Reason and Norms* (Oxford: Oxford University Press, 1975).

[6] John Rawls, 'Two Concepts of Rules', *The Philosophical Review*, 64 (1955), 3–32.

Let me begin with the familiar distinction between *describing* how we and others use rules in our reasoning and acting, and *prescribing* to ourselves and others how we ought to use rules. This is *not* the distinction with which Schauer begins his book, the distinction between descriptive and prescriptive rules.[7] With his distinction, Schauer intends to differentiate between the two tasks others engage in when they use rules: sometimes they describe regularities with universally generalized statements ('descriptive rules'), and other times they prescribe to themselves or others what they ought to do in similarly general terms ('prescriptive rules'). In either case, when drawing his distinction Schauer is not prescribing how we ought to use rules; he is describing two ways in which rules are in fact used.

Schauer's book, *Playing By the Rules,* is descriptive of how people use prescriptive rules. It is an essay in what Herbert Hart would call 'descriptive sociology'.[8] The latter phrase was Hart's characterization of what he himself had done in his classic *The Concept of Law,* a book with which Schauer's *Playing By the Rules* may be fruitfully compared. In *The Concept of Law* Hart distinguished an 'external attitude' toward rules from what he called an 'internal attitude'.[9] The external attitude towards a rule was the attitude of one who did not accept the rule as having any guiding force for his own or others' behaviour, although he might recognize that the rule was believed to have such force by others. For example, the anthropologist studying primitive religious practices often exhibits such a detached attitude insofar as he does not accept such practices as desirable standards for his own or others' religious observances; he merely studies such standards as they are in fact employed by the natives being studied. By contrast, the anthropologist who 'goes native' by coming to accept the practices as regulative ideals for his own and others' behaviour exhibits an internal attitude towards such practices. He sees them, that is, as standards of justification (for conforming behaviour) and of criticism (for deviating behaviour).

When Hart described his own book as 'an essay in descriptive sociology', he realized that, as we explored in the last chapter, he had written the book from the external point of view. Occasionally Hart's descriptions ignore the participant's own internal attitudes toward a rule and describe mere behavioural regularities. (Hart called this the extreme external point of view;[10] in Schauer's terminology, this would be called a descriptive rule.) More often Hart's descriptions refer to the actors' internal attitudes towards a rule as essential to understanding what they are doing. Hart called this a moderate external point of view; in Schauer's terminology,

[7] See Schauer, *Playing,* above n. 2, at 1. See also Schauer, 'Rules', above n. 1, at 647–8.
[8] Hart, *Concept,* above n. 4, at p. v. [9] Ibid. at 54–6, 86–8. [10] Ibid. at 87.

this would be called a prescriptive rule. In either case, Hart does not reveal his own attitude toward the rules in question. He does not purport to tell us whether such rules are a good thing, that is, whether they give us reasons to act in conformity with them. He is the detached observer of other people's use of rules. 'Descriptive sociology' is an accurate label for such a purely descriptive task.

In his book Schauer like Hart engages in a purely descriptive sociology of how people in general use prescriptive rules in their reasonings. This is most evident in Schauer's conception of what a rule is, and in what sense it can be said that a rule exists. Because *qua* sociologist Schauer is describing a social phenomenon, rules exist for Schauer only relative to a person or group of persons; as he puts it, 'the existence of a rule is in an important way agent-specific'.[11] What Schauer means by this is that a generalization is a rule only when some agent treats it as a rule, namely, when some agent treats the generalization as itself providing a reason for him to act in conformity with it.[12] The existence of a rule for Schauer is thus a social fact as it was for Hart. For both Hart and Schauer the crucial social fact is not the mere coincidence of behaviour in conformity with some generalization, but rather the attitude of individuals towards that generalization.

Such social existence conditions for rules demands a similarly social ontology for rules. 'Rules . . . are neither entities nor properties',[13] according to Schauer. In particular, they are not abstract universals as are scientific and moral laws. Rather, 'a rule is most usefully understood as a *relationship*, or better yet, a *status*'.[14] The relationship or status Schauer has in mind is that attained when a generalization is 'entrenched' vis-à-vis its 'background justification'. The social nature of this ontology can be seen clearly when one sees what Schauer means when speaking of the 'entrenchment' of a rule and a rule's 'background justification'. For Schauer, as for Nelson Goodman, who also spoke of 'entrenched predicates',[15] the 'entrenchment of generalizations . . . is in large part a psychological phenomenon'.[16] A rule is entrenched whenever it is regarded by its addressee as itself providing him a reason for acting in conformity with it. This is a psychological and social criterion of entrenchment because it takes the addressee's attitude towards the rule as it happens to be; it is not a notion saying anything about the normative force a rule may truly have for that agent. Similarly, the 'background justifications' that Schauer sees rules entrenched against are not moral values, for that would require Schauer to abandon his external, sociological stance in order to tell us what

[11] Schauer, *Playing*, above n. 2, at 103. [12] Ibid. at 112, 126. [13] Ibid. at 112.
[14] Ibid.
[15] Nelson Goodman, *Fact, Fiction, and Forecast*, 4th edn. (Indianapolis: Bobbs–Merrill, 1983).
[16] Schauer, *Playing*, above n. 2, at 42.

those values are. Rather, a background justification for Schauer is 'the evil sought to be eradicated or the goal sought to be served' by the rule-maker—again, a psychological and social criterion of justification, not a moral one.[17]

The 'regulative' or 'mandatory' rules that interest Schauer have 'normative force' to them, as he describes it. Yet 'normative force' betrays no normative attitude by Schauer any more than it does for Herbert Hart. 'Normative force' (or the 'normativity of rules') only meant for Hart the acceptance of (internal attitude towards) a rule by some group of people; for Schauer, it simply means that such a rule constitutes a *subjective* reason for action. A subjective reason for action is the reason some determinate person has by virtue of his psychological makeup. If such a person desires to eat cheese, then that person has a reason to act so as to acquire some cheese. Absent the desire, such a person has no subjective reason so to act. Schauer is quite clear that when he talks of the 'normative force' of a rule in terms of that rule providing a 'reason for action' to an agent, he refers only to subjective reasons. As Schauer puts it, rules are applicable only insofar as they supply reasons for action for some addressee of a rule, but their ability to supply such reasons for that addressee is not a function of that rule itself. Rather, the applicability of a rule is necessarily dependent on the addressee of the rule *treating* the rule as supplying a reason for action.[18] Schauer, in other words, is *not* in the business of charting what sort of rules actually affect the reasons for action we all have as rational and moral agents. He is not, in other words, dealing with objective reasons, reasons we have for doing or not doing certain actions irrespective of what we happen to desire.[19] *Qua* sociologist, Schauer no more than Hart wishes to fish these moral waters.

The use of subjective reasons for action to mark prescriptive rules' 'normative force' leads Schauer to another aspect of rules that reflects in another way rules' essentially social nature for Schauer. Since rules give only subjective reasons for action for Schauer, the degree to which they constrain an agent's decisional space (a dimension of rules Schauer aptly calls 'ruleness') will also be a *psychological*, not a logical, matter. Thus, Schauer eschews specificity/vagueness as criteria of ruleness for an agent-specific criterion: how much does the agent already (i.e. absent the rule) want to do the act the rule dictates? 'Ruleness', thus for Schauer, 'will be greatest where rules command the highest proportion of extensionally divergent results for a given agent or class of agents. Conversely, the property of ruleness will diminish insofar as a rule does not indicate, for an

[17] Ibid. at 26.

[18] Ibid. at 121.

[19] For the distinction between subjective (or descriptive/explanatory) reasons and objective (or normative/justifying) reasons, see the chapter following. See also Tom Nagel, *The View From Nowhere* (New York: Oxford University Press, 1985).

agent or a class of agents, actions different from those the agent or agents would have performed in the absence of the rule.'[20]

Not surprisingly, this social conception of ruleness yields another aspect to Schauer's descriptive sociology of rules: not only do rules exist only relative to an agent or class of agents (see above); but even relative to any given agent their existence is itself a more-or-less affair, not a matter of yes/no. This scalar nature to rules follows for Schauer because rules, to exist, must have ruleness; and since ruleness for Schauer 'is a variable dimension rather than a single condition that either obtains or does not',[21] the existence of a rule for an agent must also be a scalar phenomenon, not a bright line affair. The scalar nature of ruleness, in turn, follows from the social nature of ruleness: for the social facts that make for ruleness—patterns of some agent's subjective desires without a rule, the patterns with the rule, and the difference between the two patterns—is surely a matter of degree that can vary on a smooth continuum.

Another aspect of Schauer's treatment of rules where his sociological focus surfaces is the individuation of rules. Rules have to have a social existence to exist at all for Schauer. This means that rules, to exist, will have an historical formulation. Such formulation may be a canonical laying down of a discrete set of symbols, as is done by a legislature passing a statute; it may be a non-canonical set of statements, each of which is equally authoritative even though syntactically divergent because each means the same thing, as (sometimes) is the case with common law rules; such formulation may even consist of unspoken thoughts, the content of which is nonetheless an entrenched rule for the person whose thoughts they are.[22] Whichever kind of historical formulation there is, for Schauer, without some authoritative formulation there is no rule at all;[23] 'rules lie much more in rather than behind their formulations.'[24] This identification of rules with their formulations creates a social theory of rules' individuation: if one formulation is more specific, more general, or in any way means something different than another formulation, then we have formulations of two different rules, not two different formulations of the same rule. As Schauer puts it, '"No boisterous and annoying dogs allowed" is simply a different rule from "No dogs allowed" . . .'[25]

This formulation-specific individuation for rules leads Schauer to treat exceptions to rules as destroying their ruleness, and thus, their very existence as rules. More exactly, Schauer urges that a rule with an exception is a different rule than 'the same rule' without it. 'Don't kill except in self-defence' is a different rule from 'Don't kill'. Moreover, if the rule 'Don't kill' is subject to a host of unformulated exceptions—like self-defence, defence of others, killing in a just war, etc.—then it loses its ruleness

[20] Schauer, *Playing*, above n. 2, at 104.
[21] Ibid. at 10.
[22] Ibid. at 69–71.
[23] Ibid. at 68.
[24] Ibid. at 64.
[25] Ibid. at 63.

because then the applier of the rule is actually free to make up new rules (via the exceptions) as he decides. There is thus no rule if it is understood that unformulated exceptions can be added to the general statement.

This tie of the existence of a single, individuated rule to its historical formulation, and the accompanying conceptual ban on unformulated exceptions, leads Schauer to his view that rules are always over- and under-inclusive. Since rules are individuated by their historical formulations, and because those formulations cannot be amended by supplying hitherto unformulated exceptions to meet the exigencies of the moment, rules will inevitably cover cases they shouldn't cover and not cover cases they should cover. Such judgements of over- and under-inclusiveness are not to be understood as moral judgements—only instrumental judgements about how perfectly a rule fits (yields decisions correct by the criteria of) its background justification.

Schauer's descriptive sociology yields what I shall call the 'social rules' concept of rules.[26] Since I wish to distinguish two other concepts of rules, approachable once (but only once) one leaves Schauer's sociology for moral theory, political theory, and jurisprudence, let us summarize Schauer's social rules concept of rules. We have identified ten features to Schauer's social rules concept:

1. *Existence conditions*: social rules do not exist *tout cour* but exist only relative to an agent and only when that agent entrenches that rule in his thought processes.
2. *Ontological status*: social rules are not abstract universals or entities of any kind; each such rule is a state within some agent's psychology, a state constituted by the giving of a subjective reason for action.
3. *Entrenchment*: a psychological process that a rule has to have to be a rule; once the process reaches the state of entrenchment, a rule achieves a 'life of its own' within some agent's psychology, meaning that the rule is a subjective reason for action for that agent.
4. *Background justification*: not the value that a rule serves, but the goal or desire of the rule-maker that he intends it to serve.
5. *Normative force*: the ability a rule must have to give an agent a subjective reason to act in conformity to the rule.
6. *Ruleness*: the constraint exercised on a given agent by a rule, measured by the divergence of what the rule demands from what the agent wants to do in the absence of the rule.

[26] The phrase 'social rule' in jurisprudence is most closely associated with Herbert Hart, who used it to distinguish 'social rules' (rules about which some members of a group had the internal attitude) from mere habits (behavioural regularities without those whose behaviour it is having the internal attitude). See Hart, *Concept*, above n. 4, at 55. See also Ch. 3 herein, § II.B.

7. *Continuous nature*: rules exist for an agent on a continuum; they do not simply either exist or not exist.
8. *Individuation conditions*: rules are individuated by their historical formulations, such that a semantically different formulation formulates a different rule.
9. *Unformulated exceptions*: to the extent a rule is subject in its applications to unformulated exceptions relieving a decision-maker from having to follow the (unexcepted) rule, a rule is not a rule.
10. *Over- and under-inclusiveness*: a rule is necessarily over- and under-inclusive with respect to attaining the rule-maker's goal that is that rule's background justification.

To say that Schauer is largely engaged in sociological description is not to disparage his work on rules, anymore than agreeing with Herbert Hart that his own book, *The Concept of Law*, was sociological would disparage that legal classic. Schauer and Hart have both given us valuable and detailed descriptions of that part of our current social practice that has to do with social rules. In particular Schauer's book supplies what Hart's book glosses over,[27] namely, how rule-appliers must treat the rules that they apply if there can be said to be a system of rules in operation in society. What merits clarification here, however, is what kind of work cannot be done—or even very well understood, when done by others—if one is armed only with the Hart/Schauer conception of rules as social rules.

Consider six debates in moral theory, political theory, and jurisprudence for illustration. The first is the well-known debate about the general nature of the demands morality makes upon us: are these demands in the form of rules addressed to each of us personally, saying things like, 'Don't you kill an innocent person even if your doing so would reduce the numbers of innocents killed by others?' Or are such demands in the form of a maximizing function such that the right thing to do is to minimize bad states of affairs by our actions irrespective of whether or not we or someone else directly causes such bad states of affairs? And if morality has the latter ('agent-neutral') kind of shape, are the states of affairs we are to maximize by our actions themselves states of conformity to rules like 'Don't kill', or are such states of affairs non-rule-conforming items such as happiness, pleasure, or preference-satisfaction? These are familiar questions with a long history of competing answers.[28] These debates cannot even be

[27] Hart deals with problems of rule application only in ch. 7 of *Concept*, above n. 4.

[28] For an introduction to the extensive literature on these topics, see M. Moore, 'Torture and the Balance of Evils', *Israel Law Review*, 23 (1989), 280–344, reprinted as ch. 17 of *Placing Blame: a General Theory of the Criminal Law* (Oxford: Oxford University Press, 1997). For what it is worth, I there defend the view that morality consists in part of a set of 'agent-relative' rules directed to each of us individually. For diverging views, see e.g. the collection of essays in Sam Scheffler (ed.), *Consequentialism and Its Critics* (Oxford: Oxford University Press, 1988).

understood, let alone solved, if one means by 'rules' the social rules that Schauer refers to with the word. For the moral rules at issue in these debates are not 'entrenched' vis-à-vis some 'background justifications'; rather, such rules (if the agent-relative, deontological theorists are right that such rules exist) are themselves right-making in the sense that acting in accordance with them is to do the right thing. Such moral rules, unlike the social artifacts to which Schauer refers, are not *means* to doing the right thing, decisional aids to being moral; conformity with such rules, if they exist, is an end in itself.

If we are to understand this long-standing debate in moral theory we need a different concept of rules than Schauer's social rules concept. Let me call the concept needed the real rules concept of rules, adopting the phrase 'real rules' from Schauer[29] but excising any disparaging connotations that the phrase may have for him. Real rules are not social artefacts of any kind. Their existence does not depend on anyone having a certain attitude towards them, or any group converging in their behaviours in any way. Such rules need not have an historical formulation in order to exist or in order to be individuated. Such rules exist whenever they are *true*, that is, whenever the entities and properties to which they refer exist. Such real rules are of course what we mean when we talk of moral laws. They are abstract entities, universals, in the same way as are scientific laws.

A useful expository device with which to lay out the real rules concept of rules are the ten aspects of rules that I used to clarify Schauer's social rules concept. A contrasting exposition of the real rules concept along these same ten dimensions would be:

1. *Existence conditions*: a real rule exists whenever it is true, namely, whenever the entities, qualities, and relations to which its terms refer, exist.
2. *Ontological status*: real rules are abstract universals, not acts, conventions, convergent behaviour, or shared mental states of historically situated persons.
3. *Entrenchment*: real rules are entrenched, not in the sense that any individual or group entrenches them within his/her/their own psychology, but rather, in the sense that such rules provide overriding reasons to rational and moral agents to act in conformity with them.
4. *Background justification*: conformity with such rules is an intrinsic good, so that, although such rules have a justification, that justification is *not* in terms of some further value by virtue of which the rules have value.
5. *Normative force*: the ability a rule must have to give all persons an objective reason to act in conformity with the rule.

[29] Schauer, *Playing*, above n. 2, at 64 n.19.

6. *Ruleness*: real rules are not, as such, guides for decision; they do not, thus, have a dimension of constraint of decision; nor do they have any dimension of 'degree of fit' with actions; they either apply, or don't apply, to any given action.
7. *Non-continuous nature*: rules either exist (are true) or they don't exist (are false); they do not 'more-or-less exist' any more than they 'more-or-less apply' to any given situation.
8. *Individuation conditions*: rules, being abstract universals, are individuated in whatever way such universals are individuated (no easy matter, but however this is done it is not affected by any social practice such as historical formulation).
9. *Unformulated exceptions*: a rule may (but need not) be subject to an indefinitely large number of exceptions that have never been formulated by anyone.[30]
10. *Over- and under-inclusiveness*: any rule that exists (is true) gets it exactly right; that is, since there will be an exception for any situation where the rule would yield the wrong decision, and since where there is no exception action in conformity with the rule is intrinsically right, real rules necessarily can neither be under-inclusive nor over-inclusive.

The debates between agent-relative versus agent-neutral, deontological versus utilitarian, moral theorists, are not about the existence of social rules. Such debates are about the existence of real rules. Of course, someone enamoured of the social rules concept of rules might deny the existence of real rules and even deny that *their* existence is really at issue in the above debates. Rather, they might say, although moral theorists often think they are debating the existence of real rules, what they are really debating (because all they can be debating) is the place of social rules within the moral conventions of our society.

Schauer appears more cautious than this. He sees that his enterprise of describing the operation of social rules is valuable (as it is) and does not need the justification that 'it is the only game in town' about rules. Thus, Schauer notes at one point that his 'account is about a set of problems not directly touching categorical and ultimate rules of a Kantian variety'.[31] Those who applaud Schauer's social rules analysis are not always so guarded in the claims they make for the analysis. Peggy Radin, for example, has urged that social rules are all the rules there are.[32] 'Rules depend essentially on social context', she urges us.[33] 'Only the fact of our seem-

[30] One might have a different view about there being unformulated exceptions to real rules, depending on how one thinks of moral dilemmas. For citation and discussion, Ch. 5 below.

[31] Schauer, *Playing*, above n. 2, at 86 n. 15.

[32] Margaret Jane Radin, 'Reconsidering the Rule of Law', *Boston University Law Review*, 69 (1989), 781–819.

[33] Ibid. at 797.

ingly "natural" agreement on what are instances of obeying rules permits us to say there are rules.'[34]

This is not the place for a frontal assault on the conventionalism about morals that such a view represents. It is sufficient here to note that the social rules concept cannot do the work Radin would demand of it. One cannot substitute the social rules concept for the real rules concept in the debates above mentioned and still have anything like the same debates. This is because such debates are not third person exercises in social description whereby the participants do not betray their own commitments; rather, such debates are attempts by committed individuals to state the general nature of their own commitments. Such debates cannot be about the place of social rules in the moral conventions of our society and retain the 'internal attitude' of the participants of such debates towards their subject matter.

Radin might think that she can escape this problem by identifying the objects of first person commitments (internal attitudes) to be social rules; then third person description would be first person commitment. There are limited occasions where such an identification is plausible (namely, for those social rules that solve co-ordination problems that everyone is obligated to solve). But as an across-the-board identification it is false to one of the basic facets of everyone's moral experience, Radin's included; we each sense the possibility that a diverging moral judgement by us about the right rule is correct even when it disagrees with the social rules of our society. As Radin notes, 'law and its institutions may indeed exhibit integrity or coherence . . . and yet be coherently wrong. A main task for nonfoundationalist theory is to find room for this kind of judgment.'[35] If we generalize a bit, we should say that any conventionalist theory of moral rules has to find room for non-conventional moral judgements.

This is not a proof of moral realism. It is an argument that an important debate about rules that we all have in our daily lives cannot be carried on with the social rules concept. Needed is a concept adapted to some first-person, non-descriptive, committed, internal point of view. The real rules concept is one such concept. Anti-realists about morality could propose others. Simon Blackburn, for example, sees clearly that no social rule concept can account for 'one of the essential possibilities for a moral thinker', namely, 'the thought that our own culture and way of life leads us to corrupted judgment'.[36] This rejection of the social rules concept does not leave a moral non-cognitivist like Blackburn with a real rule concept with which to ask questions about the correctness, say, of consequentialist moral theory. It does leave him with what he might call a 'quasi-real rules'

[34] Ibid. at 799. [35] Ibid. at 805, n. 85.

[36] S. Blackburn, 'Rule-Following and Moral Realism', in S. Holtzman and C. Leich (eds.), *Wittgenstein: To Follow a Rule*, above n. 3, at 171.

concept, a concept just like the real rules concept except we disavow the existence of objective reasons of morality in any sense other than as projections of our own individual (not social) creation.

Although there are serious problems with non-cognitivist accounts like Blackburn's, on this the realist and the non-cognitivist are agreed: no social rules concept can make sense of the practical debates about the general nature of moral norms.

A second debate about rules in moral reasoning that cannot be understood with a social rules concept of rules is the flourishing debate within utilitarian ethical theory between rule-utilitarians, on the one hand, and act-utilitarians, on the other. To be sure, some of that debate is about the optimal decision-procedures for the rational agent striving to maximize utility with her decisions. The issue framed in this form of the debate is whether utility is maximized by the agent calculating utility directly in each case, using rules only as epistemic aids ('rules of thumb'), or whether utility is maximized by pursuing utility indirectly through a two-step procedure, the first step of which is to calculate which rule maximizes utility and the second step of which is to apply the rule to individual cases without recalculating utility in each such case. For this issue, and thus this form of the debate, Schauer's social rules concept of rules is the appropriate concept.

There is another form of the debate, however, for which the social rules concept of rules is inappropriate. In this form, the debate is not about optimal decision-strategies (or institutional designs) for utilitarians. Rather, it is about the truth conditions of moral propositions. The debate is not, how can we individually reach the right decisions, nor even, how should we design institutions so as to maximize the numbers of right decisions they reach? Rather, it is, what are the right decisions we are trying to reach? When David Lyons, for example, argues that rule-utilitarianism collapses either into act-utilitarianism or into some deontological ethics,[37] he is not to be understood as talking about decision-procedures. Rather, Lyons is talking about the truth of certain moral propositions, specifically, whether the best result is that in conformity with that *rule* which is the best rule possible on utilitarian grounds, or whether the best result is that which itself is best on utilitarian grounds without regard to whether that result instantiates the best rule. Schauer recognizes that Lyons's concept of rules diverges from Schauer's social rules concept in such dimensions as ruleness, individuation conditions, unformulated exceptions, and over- or under-inclusiveness; for Lyons, rules are neither identical to, nor individuated by, their historical formulations; rules may have unformulated exceptions; and rules match perfectly the right decision. Schauer thinks

[37] David Lyons, *Forms and Limits of Utilitarianism* (Oxford: Oxford University Press, 1965).

that Lyons's sorts of rules may be 'rules only in form and not in effect'[38] because 'exclusion of these features of continuous malleability and unlimited specificity is necessary to the definition of the concept of a rule . . .'[39] On the contrary, what we should see is the poverty of the social rules concept of rules in making sense of the debate in which Lyons is engaged. Lyons is using what I have called the real rule concept of rules arguing that there is no such thing as a (real) rule-utilitarian ethical theory. This is a plausible (and by my lights, correct) argument to make if Lyons is using the real rules concept of rule-utilitarianism; it would be a ridiculous conceptual argument to make if one were using Schauer's social rules concept.

A third debate within moral and political theory also cannot be made sense of with Schauer's social rule concept of rules. Unlike the previous two debates, however, the real rules concept of rules is also not adequate to make sense of this debate. I refer to the debate about the impact of the exercise of authority upon our pre-existing moral obligations. There is a seemingly heterogeneous set of phenomena that can alter the moral obligations we would have had if such phenomena had not occurred. If a friend makes a request of us, if we promise to do something, take an oath to fulfil a role, consent that another do something, be commanded by one possessed of legitimate authority over us, we may have changed what would be obligatory for us to do or refrain from doing in the absence of such request, promise, etc. Joseph Raz helpfully labels all such phenomena the exercise of normative powers, because each such phenomenon is an instance of the limited ability we possess to change what morality requires of us.[40]

The debate within contemporary moral and political theory is this: in what way do normative powers change our antecedently existing moral obligations? This debate I examine in the next chapter. Joseph Raz centred much of his early writing on that question, elegantly detailing one view, that exercises of legitimate authority both give a new reason for action, and protect that new reason from competition with antecedently existing reasons by excluding the latter reasons from counting in determining the rightness of actions. An alternative view, argued for in the following chapter, concedes that the exercise of legitimate authority does create a new reason for action for the actors subject to such authority, but denies that such new reason is in any way protected from competition with antecedently existing reasons in determining the rightness of actions. A third view, held by Heidi Hurd, Larry Alexander, and Donald Regan amongst others,[41] denies that legitimate authority ever creates new rea-

[38] Schauer, *Playing*, above n. 2, at 83. [39] Ibid.

[40] J. Raz, 'Voluntary Obligations and Normative Powers', *Aristotelian Society Supplementary Volume*, 79 (1972), 79–102.

[41] H. Hurd, 'Sovereignty in Silence', *Yale Law Journal*, 99 (1990), 945–1028, at 1007–22; Hurd, 'Challenging Authority', *Yale Law Journal*, 100 (1991), 1611–77; Alexander, 'Law and

sons for action; rather, they assert, promises, commands, etc., create new reasons for belief about what are the true reasons for action that we have (and had before the exercise of authority). Utterances of authority then become epistemic guides to our antecedent obligations, but they do not change those obligations.

As before, who has the better of this argument is not our present concern. Rather, what we should see is that this debate is not about whether we should treat the utterances of authority as a social rule that we should defer to in our decisions. The debate is not about an optimal decision-procedure at all. Rather, the debate between Raz, myself, and others is a debate about the truth conditions of certain moral propositions. Is it true that the utterance of a legitimate authority becomes a new moral rule, giving actors subject to that authority a new reason to act in conformity with that rule, as Raz and I, but not Regan, Alexander, and Hurd, would assert? If so, is it true that such new moral rule makes right behaviour in conformity with it because it excludes antecedently existing reasons from counting any longer, as Raz but not I would hold? The rules whose existence and nature are in issue here are not Schauer's social rules giving actors *subjective* reasons for action, but some other kind of rules giving actors *objective* reasons for action.

On this Schauer appears to disagree, for he thinks that 'Raz's account of rules as exclusionary reasons is largely consistent' with Schauer's own conclusions with regard to the place of social rules in optimal decision strategies.[42] Yet Raz's account of rules as exclusionary reasons is neither 'largely consistent' nor largely inconsistent with Schauer's account of social rules; the two accounts simply have different subject matters. Raz is not talking about optimal decision strategies at all, and so is not talking about whether a social rule should be used to exclude from our consideration other items when he is talking about exclusionary reasons. Early in his career Raz noted that interpreting him to be talking about decision procedures would transform exclusionary (second-order) reasons into 'ordinary (first order) reasons not to consider the merits of the case (i.e. not to perform a certain mental act)'.[43] So interpreting Raz makes a hash of his distinction between antecedently existing (first-order) reasons for action, and exclusionary (second-order) reasons created by the exercise of legitimate authority—because second-order reasons get collapsed into first-order reasons 'not to perform a certain mental act'. Moreover, Raz urged, taken as a claim about psychological decision-procedures, the claim that rules give exclusionary reasons would be 'obviously wrong' because 'there is no reason to prevent a person . . . from going through the

Exclusionary Reasons', *Philosophical Topics*, 18 (1990), 5–22; D. Regan, 'Authority and Value', *Southern California Law Review*, 62 (1989), 995–1095, at 1001–40.

[42] Schauer, *Playing*, above n. 2, at 89.

[43] Raz, above n. 5, at 48.

[excluded] arguments to amuse himself or as an exercise, etc. . . .'[44] Raz has recently repeated these disavowals of any psychological, decision-procedure interpretation of his claim about authority,[45] in response to my own charge that despite himself he had on occasion unwittingly slipped into a decision-procedure discussion.[46]

Raz's opponents are not talking about the role of social rules in decision-procedures, either. My opposition to Raz's exclusionary reasons analysis of authority is mostly an opposition to thinking that exercises of legitimate authority ever give us new right-making rules that exclude (either from counting towards rightness, or from motivating us) antecedently existing, objective reasons we have for acting contrary to the rule. Even Hurd, Alexander, and Regan, who ultimately analyse authority in terms of optimal decision-procedures, argue against Raz's and my positions by denying that authoritative utterances create new reasons for action (new moral rules). At issue for everyone here is thus *not* the place of social rules in desirable decision-procedures, but rather, what rules determine that some decisions, but not others, are right.

I said earlier that the real rules concept of rules was also not adequate to explicate this debate about authority. This is because the rules at issue in this debate only partially have the character of real rules. Like real rules, rules that exist because of the exercise of legitimate authority give objective, not subjective, reasons for action. But unlike the real rules of morality, rules that come about because of a promise or a command have an historical existence; they exist only because at some point in time the actor promised, or was commanded, etc. Moreover, such rules have an historical formulation (in the speech act that constitutes the promise, the command, etc.). We thus need a third concept of rules if we are to understand the debate about authority.

Let us call this the 'authoritative rules' concept of rules. Utilizing our previously articulated ten dimensions of ruleness, an authoritative rule has the following characteristics:

1. *Existence conditions*: authoritative rules exist when but only when a normative power has been validly exercised by one in possession of it.
2. *Ontological status*: authoritative rules are the propositional contents of the speech-act constituting the exercise of a normative power.
3. *Entrenchment* (a feature that I but not Raz would deny that authoritative rules possess): authoritative rules give exclusionary reasons, that is reasons that disenfranchise other reasons (that before the exercise of authority were proper reasons for action) from being proper reasons on which to act.

[44] Ibid.
[45] J. Raz, 'Facing Up: A Reply', *Southern California Law Review*, 62 (1989), 1153–235, at 1157.
[46] See the following chapter.

4. *Background justification*: either the (subjectively) intended consequence an exerciser of legitimate authority intended to achieve with her promise, command, etc.,[47] or the (objective) value that can be served by the rule issued by a legitimate authority.[48]
5. *Normative force*: the ability of an authoritative rule to change (by exclusion or otherwise) the balance of objective reasons that determine the rightness of any action.
6. *Ruleness*: the constraint exercised on a given action, measured by the divergence of what the rule demands from what the real rules of morality would demand in the absence of any exercise of a normative power.
7. *Non-continuous nature*: authoritative rules exist if the real rules of morality create a normative power in a person; accordingly, if those real rules are non-continuous (see above), authoritative rules are non-continuous in the sense that they either exist or they don't.
8. *Individuation conditions*: authoritative rules are individuated by their precise historical formulations, so that a *syntactically* different formulation formulates a different rule.
9. *Unformulated exceptions*: to the extent a rule is subject in its applications to unformulated exceptions, the rule is not a rule.
10. *Over- and under-inclusiveness*: an authoritative rule may (but need not) be over- or under-inclusive with respect to its background justification, depending on whether or not that background justification is itself a real rule of morality with a content identical to the content of the authoritative rule.

Whether rules with the foregoing characteristics exist is the subject of the debate about authority, not whether social rules exist or play the roles in decision-making that Schauer describes.

A fourth debate also requires that one conceive of rules as authoritative rules and not as social rules. This is the debate in political theory about whether laws (or at least the laws in a democratic and reasonably just society) obligate citizen obedience. The question debated is whether laws can possess legitimate authority in at least my minimal sense: can laws create new reasons for action? The traditional answer was 'yes', but more recently there has arisen a chorus answering 'no'.[49] To understand this debate, one cannot equate 'laws' with 'social rules', for the question is not, 'Do laws give actors subjective reasons to act in conformity with them?' In legal systems that attach sanctions to their laws (as all do), to take the ques-

[47] As Joseph Raz believes. Raz, 'Authority, Law, and Morality', *The Monist*, 68 (1985), 295–324.

[48] As I argue, M. Moore, 'A Natural Law Theory of Interpretation', *Southern California Law Review*, 58 (1985), 277–398, at 338–58, 383–6.

[49] This is the position of Hurd, Alexander, and Regan, for example, above n. 41.

tion this way is to make the answer obvious. As Schauer observes, a fear of sanctions might still provide for most agents a reason for obeying the law *qua* law even if there is no moral obligation to obey the law.[50] When long-standing debates between intellectually well-armed opponents become this easy, it is probably because one has misunderstood what the debate was about. The question, 'Do laws obligate?', is not a question about whether laws are social rules giving actors subjective reasons to act in conformity with them. The question is the much more difficult—but much more interesting—question of whether laws are authoritative rules, i.e. do they give objective reasons to act in conformity with them just because they are rules created through a fair and just process such as democracy?

The fifth debate is one in which Schauer wishes to participate[51] and one to which his social rules concept of rules is at least one appropriate concept of rules. This is the debate in jurisprudence about the nature of law. Does law (that is a legal system) consist of a set of social rules in existence in some society? Herbert Hart famously answered that question affirmatively, and Schauer seeks to align himself with Hart with a legal theory he dubs 'presumptive positivism'. Yet the debate about the Hart/Schauer position requires more than the social rules concept of rules, for the claims of their opponents are precisely that law is not a set of social rules but rather, a subset of real moral rules (a pure natural law position), or, alternatively, a set of authoritative rules (which might be either a natural law or a legal positivist position).

Of course, if Hart and Schauer were obviously right in this debate, then the fact that others have opposed them could hardly vindicate the alternative concepts of rules for understanding the nature of law. Yet the Hart/Schauer view has a very well-charted difficulty with it: it seems to leave out the normativity of law. Hart himself reacted to the earlier views of Austin and Bentham by urging that their account of law—in terms of sanctions and habits of obedience—didn't adequately account for law's

[50] Schauer, *Playing*, above n. 2, at 123.

[51] In her essay in the symposium in which this chapter originally appeared, Ruth Gavison expressed some reservations about whether a general jurisprudence, such as that articulated by Herbert Hart, need include a theory of adjudication. See Gavison, 'Comment: Legal Theory and the Role of Rules', *Harvard Journal of Law and Public Policy*, 14 (1991), 727–70, at 744. If not, then Schauer's work is not related to the debate in general jurisprudence that I reference in the text, for Schauer's explicit aims are only within the theory of adjudication. Although there is a distinction between questions of general jurisprudence—when do we have law, in the sense of a legal system—and the questions asked by a theory of adjudication—how do and should judges reason—nonetheless I see Schauer's kind of enterprise to be a necessary accompaniment to Hart's kind of general jurisprudence. If one is going to analyse law as consisting of a certain hierarchical ordering of social rules (Hart), one has to at least show how such rules can attain the benefits claimed for them (predictability, etc.) by their power to constrain judicial decisions.

essential normativity. Following St Augustine, Hart thought that law must differ from the orders of a gunman by virtue of something other than mere generality. Law, Hart said, must *obligate* and not merely *oblige*, obedience. Yet notoriously, conceiving of law as social rules fails to give law any obligating force. If law must obligate to be law, then how can law merely be a collection of social rules and be law? Such social rules, when internalized by a society in the way Hart and Schauer describe, might well be *thought* to be law by those who internalize such rules. But unless the rules obligate—as only real rules and authoritative rules can do—then those participants in a system who think they have law would simply be mistaken.

So it is far from clear that Hart and Schauer are right in conceiving of law as made up of social rules, for both have to answer the nagging question of how such rules can be said to be obligatory. This is not to deny that both might well be right in their sociological enterprise of describing some society's (or even all societies') *concept* of law. This task of external jurisprudence may well succeed using only a concept of social rules. But such sociological enquiries do not foreclose a quite different (internal) jurisprudential enterprise, one that requires concepts of real, and of authoritative, rules.

The sixth and final debate that I wish to discuss is within that part of jurisprudence dealing not with the general nature of law but rather with the theory of adjudication (often called the theory of legal reasoning). Here, at least, Schauer's social rules concept may seem to be fully at home, for it is Schauer's explicit aim to discuss the role of rules in decision-making, including as a special case *judicial* decision-making (i.e. adjudication).

As I understand him, Schauer distinguishes five models of how social rules might operate in various decision-making environments. The first he calls 'particularism'.[52] On this model the decision-maker simply ignores the rule and decides on the basis of the background justification itself. The second model is particularism with an epistemic allowance for rules: the decision-maker treats the rule as a 'rule of thumb'—an 'indicator rule', or sometimes called a 'summary rule'—which is to be used, as all heuristics are used, as an aid to deciding.[53] Such heuristic devices are to be distinguished from rules that are themselves grounds for decision, that is, rules that are entrenched by the decision-maker in the sense that they are treated by him as themselves giving a reason for acting. The third model Schauer calls 'rule-sensitive particularism', of which I am supposed to be an exemplar.[54] A rule-sensitive particularist is a particularist because the grounds for his decision are the background justifications themselves, not some intermediate social rule; yet this fellow is 'rule-sensitive' because he

[52] Schauer, *Playing*, above n. 2, at 77. [53] Ibid. at 104–11. [54] Ibid. at 93–100.

includes in his calculation (of how well a decision serves its justification) the value of having a rule at all, and how much any decision by him flouting such a rule would disserve this value.

Schauer's fourth model he calls 'presumptive' rule-following.[55] A presumptive rule-follower generally assumes that he is precluded from deciding on the basis of the background justification for some rule; rather, he presumes he is to decide on the basis of the rule alone. He allows himself, however, a 'peek' at the background justification to see if this mightn't be a case where the presumption should be overcome. Since the presumption is not an epistemic one—it is not a mere heuristic but is instead a policy-based presumption that is to be given weight even if the decision-maker decides that the background justification would clearly be somewhat better served by a decision going against the rule—the overcoming of the presumption to decide against the rule should be a rarity for the presumptive rule-follower.

Schauer's fifth model is what he calls 'rule-based decision-making'.[56] On this model a decision-maker eschews entirely any resort to the background justification as a ground for his decision. Rather, he simply decides according to the rule, which is fully entrenched for him.

In the context of *judicial* decision-making, Schauer plumps for the fourth of these models, and calls this mode of judicial decision-making, 'presumptive positivism'. In his book Schauer defends presumptive positivism purely as a descriptive thesis: this is how our judges in fact decide cases. In his contribution to the symposium at which this chapter was first presented Schauer also defends presumptive positivism as a normative thesis: this is how our judges ought to decide cases, for allocation of power and other reasons.

In the course of his description of his five-part taxonomy, and in the course of his defence of presumptive positivism, Schauer makes many insightful, true, and helpful points. Again, however, I come neither to praise such points, nor even to bury some of their comrades. Rather, I seek to clarify what it is such points are about. To do this, let me focus on that part of Schauer's debate that I best understand, his debate against me as an example of that 'common mistake' known as rule-sensitive particularism.

In my work to which Schauer refers I do not defend rule-sensitive particularism as a decision-procedure that our judges either do or should use in their decisions. If I were to defend a decision-procedure, Schauer is correct to intuit that rule-sensitive particularism is one that I would probably favour. But in the work on which Schauer relies I was not defending any decision-procedure for judges, either descriptively or normatively.[57]

[55] Ibid. at 196–7.

[56] Ibid. at 78.

[57] As I say explicitly in Moore, 'A Natural Law Theory', above n. 48, at 396, n. 218.

Rather, I was describing what I took to be the right-making characteristics of judicial decisions, whether of the constitutional, statutory, or common law kind. About judicial decisions interpreting a statute or a constitutional text, I urged that the correct decision is one that gives the correct weight to four ingredients: antecedent ordinary meaning of the words of the text, antecedent legal meaning of the words of the text to the extent prior interpretations of that text by courts give such a distinctive legal meaning, the purpose (in the sense of value, not intention) the text should be seen to serve, and general justice considerations.[58] About judicial decisions under the common law, I urged that the correct decision is one that gives the correct weight (in terms of equality and other values) to the fact that prior litigants have been treated in a certain way in precedent cases, and correctly balances that moral freight of history with a judgement of what, if there were no such history, would be the best decision all things considered.[59]

Neither of these theories by me purported to be theories about what it is judges do or should consider when they make decisions. Rather, these were theories of what *are* the right decisions for judges to reach, however, they reach them. For example, some judges may do better—better even as judged by my theory of the right decision to reach under a statute—if they 'hunch' their decisions than they would do if they were to follow my four-part interpretive schema for statutes as a decision-procedure. What succeeds as a decision-procedure is an empirical question of psychology that could match any of Schauer's five models and still be compatible with my theories of interpretation and of precedent.

This is why I labelled my theories with the jurisprudential labels, 'natural law theory of interpretation' and 'natural law theory of precedent'. Such theories were metaphysical theories about the truth conditions of a certain type of proposition of law, namely, those singular propositions of law[60] that decide concrete cases. Schauer's own jurisprudential label—'presumptive positivism'—is misleading because he is not really debating my natural law theories of interpretation and of precedent. His is not a competing thesis about the truth conditions of singular propositions of law, nor is it a thesis about the nature of law at all.

This obliqueness of Schauer's 'presumptive positivism' to my own natural law theories relates to our three concepts of rules in the following way. If Schauer wishes to debate about how judges do and ought to reason their way to their decisions—and it is a perfectly worthwhile debate in

[58] See Moore, 'A Natural Law Theory', above n. 48.

[59] See M. Moore, 'Precedent, Induction, and Ethical Generalization', in L. Goldstein (ed.), *Precedent in Law* (Oxford: Oxford University Press, 1987).

[60] As I discussed in Ch. 3, a singular proposition of law is a proposition that is not universally generalized. 'All valid, non-holographic wills require two witnesses', is a general proposition of law; 'this will is valid', is a singular proposition of law.

which to engage—then the concept of rules as social rules is one appropriate concept to figure in such debates. If, however, Schauer wishes to engage me or others on the truth conditions of singular legal propositions, he has to abandon the social rules concept of rules. For my theories say in essence: statutes are authoritative rules, their authority deriving from certain rule-of-law values, which values then dictate the four-part theory of those statutes' interpretation, which interpretive theory then gives the truth conditions of singular propositions of statutory law; and common law rules are not authoritative rules, but are the real rules of morality as applied to the non-ideal situation of a society whose history diverges from perfect justice, which application gives the truth conditions of singular propositions of common law. Someone who disagrees with my theory of statutory interpretation might say: either statutes are not authoritative rules, or, alternatively, they are but for different reasons than those I defend, or, alternatively, the rule of law values that do give statutes the status of authoritative rules justify a different set of right-making characteristics than the four I defend. Likewise, someone who disagrees with my theory of precedent might say: either that common law rules are not real moral rules applied to the non-ideal world but are authoritative rules, or, alternatively, that common law rules may be the real rules of morality but that their application to the non-ideal situation (that is any society with any history) is quite different than I describe. Such disagreements, of course, *use* the concepts of real rules and of authoritative rules, as they must if they are to be about the truth conditions of (and not about the psychological recipe for discovering) legal propositions.

In closing, let me reiterate what I have said throughout this essay. It is not much of a criticism of Schauer's work on rules that it does not occupy the field of what is worth talking about about rules, particularly in light of the fact that what Schauer does talk about is a quite worthwhile subject. My remarks have been directed at pre-empting the thought that such work is a complete treatise on rules. Indeed, Schauer himself at times seems to succumb to the temptation so to regard his work, when he allows himself certain imperialistic construals of others' work on rules. Schauer's book will be a focal point for future discussion of how social rules work in decision-procedures in daily life and in the law. This essay is only a reminder that there is other worthwhile work to be done on rules, work that demands concepts of rules other than Schauer's social rules concept.

5
Authority, Law, and Razian Reasons

No chapter could summarize, let alone do justice to, the work of Joseph Raz taken as a whole. The corpus of Raz's work is simply too diverse in its subject matters, too rich in its insight, and too finely wrought in its detailed analyses for a comprehensive survey. Instead, I shall focus on one presupposition central to Raz's celebrated theories of authority and of law.[1] This presupposition has to do with the nature of practical rationality, and more specifically, with the kinds of reasons for action that authoritative legal norms give to rational actors. Raz presupposes that morality gives us 'exclusionary reasons' for acting under an authoritative norm. 'Exclusionary reasons' are second-order in that they give us reasons to discount other reasons in assessing an action's rightness.

Simply describing this presupposition is a complicated business, which is undertaken in Section II of this chapter. In the following introductory section, I shall confine myself to describing the theories of authority and of law to which this presupposition attaches.

[1] The relevant works are, in chronological order, J. Raz: *The Concept of a Legal System* (1st edn., Oxford: Oxford University Press, 1970) [hereinafter Raz, *Concept* 1st]; 'Voluntary Obligations and Normative Powers', *Aristotelian Society Supplementary Volume*, 46 (1972), 79–102, [hereinafter Raz, 'Voluntary Obligations']; 'Reasons, Requirements, and Practical Conflicts', in S. Korner (ed.), *Practical Reasoning* (New York: Oxford University Press, 1974) [hereinafter Raz, 'Reasons']; 'Reasons for Action, Decisions and Norms', in J. Raz (ed.), *Practical Reasoning* (Oxford: Oxford University Press, 1978) (reprinted in slightly edited form from *Mind*, 84 (1975), 481–99) [hereinafter Raz, 'Reasons for Action']; *Practical Reason and Norms* (Oxford: Oxford University Press, 1975) [hereinafter Raz, *Practical Reason*]; 'Promises and Obligations', in P. M. S. Hacker and J. Raz (eds.), *Law, Morality and Society* (Oxford: Oxford University Press, 1977) [hereinafter Raz, 'Promises']; 'Introduction', in J. Raz (ed.), *Practical Reasoning* (Oxford: Oxford University Press, 1978) [hereinafter Raz, 'Introduction']; *The Authority of Law* (Oxford: Oxford University Press, 1979) [hereinafter Raz, *Authority*]; *The Concept of a Legal System* (2nd edn., Oxford: Oxford University Press, 1980) [hereinafter Raz, *Concept* 2nd]; 'Authority and Consent', *Virginia Law Review*, 67 (1981), 103–31 [hereinafter Raz, 'Consent']; 'Hart on Moral Rights and Legal Duties', *Oxford Journal of Legal Studies*, 4 (1984), 123–11 [hereinafter Raz, 'Hart']; 'Legal Rights', *Oxford Journal of Legal Studies*, 4 (1984), 1–21, reprinted in J. Raz, *Ethics in the Public Domain* (Oxford: Oxford University Press, 1994) [hereinafter Raz, 'Legal Rights']; 'On the Nature of Rights', *Mind*, 93 (1984), 194–214 [hereinafter Raz, 'Rights']; 'Authority Law, and Morality', *The Monist*, 68 (1985), 295–324, reprinted in *Ethics in the Public Domain* (Oxford: Oxford University Press, 1994) [hereinafter Raz, 'Authority']; 'Authority and Justification', *Philosophy & Public Affairs*, 14 (1985), 3–29 [hereinafter Raz, 'Justification']; 'The Inner Logic of the Law', *Rechtstheorie*, 10 (1986), 101–17, reprinted in J. Raz, *Ethics in the Public Domain* (Oxford: Oxford University Press, 1994) [hereinafter Raz, 'Inner Logic']; *The Morality of Freedom* (Oxford: Oxford University Press,1986) [hereinafter Raz, *Freedom*].

I. INTRODUCTION: RAZ'S POLITICAL THEORY AND GENERAL JURISPRUDENCE

A. Raz's General Theory of Authority

Let us begin with Raz's theory of authority. Raz distinguishes between theoretical authority and practical authority.[2] This distinction parallels the ancient distinction between theoretical and practical reason. Theoretical reason tells us what we are justified in believing (it gives us 'reasons for belief') while practical reason tells us what we are justified in doing (it gives us 'reasons for action'). A theoretical authority, accordingly, is someone whose utterances give us reasons for believing that the propositions uttered are true. A practical authority is someone whose utterances give us reasons for acting in accordance with the propositions uttered.

Raz's interest lies in practical authority. He seeks a theory that can tell us when we are justified in treating another person's commands, wishes, and the like as reasons for us to act in accordance with those commands, wishes, etc. Raz's primary interest here lies in what he calls legitimate (practical) authority. Another person possesses legitimate authority over us when we are actually justified in treating their commands, wishes, and the like as reasons for our actions. Of secondary interest is the sociological concept of de facto authority, the authority one person possesses over another solely because the latter believes there are reasons to defer to the former. De facto authority is ascertained by a descriptive enterprise, whereas Raz is more concerned with the normative puzzle posed by the concept of legitimate practical authority.

The puzzle is simply this: how can it be rational (justifiable) to suspend one's own judgement about what, all things considered, one ought to do on some occasion and to defer to someone else's judgement about the matter? Why isn't practical authority always irrational and thus always illegitimate in its apparent requirement that we act against (or at least not judge for ourselves) what the balance of reasons indicates we should do?[3] Raz's answer is very attractive, given in terms of what he calls the 'service conception' of authority. As the name suggests, according to the service conception, authorities are legitimate to the extent that they serve us. Authorities serve us whenever they promulgate directives which, if we follow them, produce behaviour by us that better conforms to what we ought to do anyway (independently of any authoritative directive) than the behaviour which would result if we calculated directly what we ought to do. This is an attractive notion of legitimate authority because it meets the irrationality objection head-on: authority is legitimate only when it is rational not to act on those reasons that

[2] Raz, *Freedom*, above n. 1, at 29.

[3] Raz, *Authority*, above n. 1, at 3.

would otherwise (without the authority) make it rational for us to do something else.

The service conception of legitimate practical authority softens the line between theoretical and practical authority. If one grants that there is such a thing as knowledge about what, all things considered, one ought to do, then another person is a practical authority for us usually when he is also a theoretical authority (about one area of knowledge, namely, about where the balance of our reasons for action comes out). It is this greater knowledge of the reasons that antecedently bind us that often gives someone legitimate authority over what we should do.

On occasion, Raz may find authority legitimate because it serves us in ways other than as a superior calculator or motivator of what we already have reasons to do. We might rationally accept the authority of some institution, for example, because such an act of acceptance can be an act of identification that enhances our own sense of self-identity.[4] Such reasons are secondary for Raz, however, because they cannot alone justify an authority as legitimate. Only the service conception can do that.

B. Raz's Theory of Political Authority

Raz sees legitimate political authority—the authority of governments and of the laws that they issue—as an instance of his service conception of authority generally. Governments have legitimate practical authority only insofar as following their laws improves conformity by citizens with what they antecedently ought to do.[5] As Raz recognizes, this restrictive notion of when authority is legitimate 'invites a piecemeal approach to the questions of the authority of governments'.[6] That is, whether a government, an institution within it, or a law that it promulgates, has legitimate authority is not a question answered universally, once for all individuals. Rather, 'the extent of governmental authority varies from individual to individual, and is more limited than the authority governments claim for themselves in the case of most people'.[7]

Despite this fractionating of the question, there are a few general things Raz allows himself to say about how political authority is to be justified (i.e. be legitimate). First and most important, there is the function authoritative governments serve in promoting solutions to co-ordination problems. Because a government by its laws can render certain features of a co-ordination problem salient, and since all citizens have reason antecedently to seek the solution of co-ordination problems, we all have reasons to grant authority to laws attempting to co-ordinate the activity of many persons.[8] Second, the same can be said for the functions govern-

[4] Raz, *Freedom*, above n. 1, at 53–5. [5] Ibid. at 74. [6] Ibid. at 80. [7] Ibid.
[8] Ibid. at 75, 100.

ments serve in solving prisoners' dilemmas. Law has legitimate authority in such circumstances because it gives the guarantee of nearly universal compliance that allows each to do what, on balance, he ought to do without the law.[9] Third, certain governmental institutions at certain times on certain issues may have, compared to certain citizens, advantages of expertise, economy of effort, and immunity from the temptation or potential for blackmail, which might divert citizens from what, on balance, they ought to do.[10]

The service conception of authority generally, thus, gives some reason to think that governments sometimes have legitimate practical authority over their citizens. These service conception reasons can also be bolstered by secondary reasons justifying an authority as legitimate. In the case of governments, such secondary reasons are those that stem from 'consent of the governed'[11] and the respect for law[12] that some citizens may have acquired. To the extent that individuals do consent to their governments and do respect their laws, then those individuals, Raz admits, have secondary reasons to regard their governments as legitimate practical authorities. Raz cautions that these reasons justifying governmental authority as legitimate are only secondary reasons; like all secondary reasons, they are incapable of justifying governments as legitimate authorities except in conjunction with the service conception justifications given above.[13]

The combination of both the service conception of authority and secondary reasons provides a limited, context-specific justification of governments as legitimate authorities. Raz gives no carte blanche to any de facto political authority because he takes seriously the paradox of authority mentioned earlier (how can it be rational to defer to someone else's judgement rather than acting on one's own assessment of the balance of reasons?). The limited, context-sensitive kind of political authority is the most Raz sees as legitimate in light of this prima facie irrationality of all authority.

C. The Authority of Legal Texts For Citizens

Authority is usually thought of as an attribute possessed by persons (including the organized collections of persons that form governmental institutions). Yet, as Raz recognizes, to grant authority to someone is to grant authority to something which that person says, does, or thinks.

[9] Ibid. at 50–1.

[10] Ibid. at 75, 100.

[11] See generally Raz, *Freedom*, above n. 1, at 88–94; Raz, 'Consent', above n. 1 (discussing whether a person's consent to a government is alone sufficient to give that government legitimate authority).

[12] Raz, *Authority*, above n. 1, at 250–61; Raz, *Freedom*, above n. 1, at 94–9.

[13] Raz, *Freedom*, above n. 1, at 93.

Otherwise, there is no way that an authority can enter our practical reasoning, for she is not us; only a norm derived from her orders, wishes, exemplary behaviour, or general rules can enter our practical reasoning.

Thus, to say that a person possesses legitimate practical authority is to say that some text issued by her (or otherwise connectable to her) has such authority. Such text may be the propositional objects of her wishes; it may be the rules generalizable over her exemplary behaviour; it may be her specific commands, or her more general, standing orders. But some such text must have authority if a person is to have authority.[14] Correspondingly, to say that a government possesses legitimate authority over some matters is to say that its laws dealing with those matters have such authority.[15]

So for Raz, a tight, one-way implication holds by necessity between a government having authority and its laws having authority. A similarly tight conceptual connection holds for Raz between laws having authority over certain persons and those persons having an obligation to obey such laws. Raz defends at length the view that for a rule to have authority over someone it must obligate obedience by that person.[16] An authoritative rule does not merely give an actor subject to it an additional reason to do the act in question; it gives the actor that compelling kind of reason we call an obligation.

These two links (between the authority of a government and the authority of its laws, and between the authority of its laws and an obligation of obedience), when combined with Raz's limited, piecemeal justification of political authority, suggest a likewise limited, piecemeal approach to the question of citizens' obligations to obey the laws of their society. This is indeed where Raz comes out on this question: according to Raz,[17] citizens do not have any general obligation to obey the law. They may, of course, have obligations to do the acts various laws command, for just laws often command that which we already have an obligation to do. But Raz denies we have any general obligation to obey the law because it is the law.

This conclusion about citizen obligation is suggested by Raz's conclusions about when political authority is legitimate. For if the main way that we acquire an obligation to obey the law is by virtue of law's legitimate authority, and if the main way that law acquires legitimate authority is by virtue of its promulgation by a government with legitimate authority, then the piecemeal authority of government will translate into a piecemeal obligation of obedience by its citizens.

[14] Raz recognizes the general point of the text but is unnecessarily grudging in allowing the authority of a person to be transmitted to some text connected to the person. Rather than allowing wishes or exemplary behaviour of a person in authority to be the authoritative text, Raz allows that 'a person is an authority or has authority only if some of his utterances are authoritative' (ibid. at 28).

[15] Ibid. at 100.

[16] Ibid. at 23–37.

[17] Raz, *Authority*, above n. 1, at 233–49; Raz, *Freedom*, above n. 1, at 99–104.

The legitimate authority of government, it will be recalled, varies from person to person and from situation to situation, because people vary in how well they can calculate and act on their antecedent reasons for action. Governments have more authority over some types of situations, and over some types of persons, than over others. Citizens' obligation to obey the law varies accordingly.

Where Raz's secondary justifications for political authority[18] are operative—because a citizen has consented to his government's authority or because he has adopted a general attitude of respect for its laws—so too will be operative a secondary justification of a citizen's obligation to obey the law. Just as friends acquire obligations by assuming the relation of friend, so too, Raz holds, citizens can acquire general obligations to obey the law by acts of consent or acquisition of attitudes of respect. But since no one has an obligation either to consent to his government's authority or to adopt an attitude of respect for its laws, Raz's conclusion remains: there is no general obligation to obey the law any more than there is, in general, legitimate authority possessed by even the most just of governments.

D. The Authority of Legal Texts For Judges

One of the main consequences of calling something 'law' within some legal system has often been thought to be the prima facie obligation imposed on citizens to obey that thing. Raz, as we have seen, adopts a much more limited view of the matter, holding laws to be authoritative (and thus obligating) for citizens only in a piecemeal manner. The other main consequence of calling something 'law' within some legal system has been thought to be the obligation it imposes on the judges within that system to obey it (in the sense of applying it to the citizens that come before them).

Raz's legal and political philosophy does not dictate a similarly piecemeal and limited nature to the obligations of judges vis-à-vis the legal texts of their legal system. According to Raz, when there is a legal system and laws, 'the courts are bound to apply [them] regardless of their view of their merit . . . [L]egal systems consist of laws which the courts are bound to apply and are not at liberty to disregard whenever they find their application undesirable, all things considered'.[19]

Raz presents this as a conceptual truth about the concepts of law and legal system. If there are laws (legal texts) at all, there must be a legal system in which they can exist;[20] to have a legal system requires that there be institutions that perform the law-applying functions of courts;[21] and

[18] See text accompanying nn. 4, 11, and 12.

[19] Raz, *Authority*, above n. 1, at 113; Raz, *Practical Reason*, above n. 1, at 139.

[20] Raz, *Concept* 1st, above n. 1, at 16.

[21] Raz, *Authority*, above n. 1, at 105–11.

courts, to be courts, must at least be thought to be obligated to apply the laws of their legal system.

This conceptual claim (about law and the obligation of judges to follow it) is not of course a moral claim by Raz that judges are obligated to follow the laws of the legal system in which they are judges. But Raz would appear to make the parallel moral claim as well, at least for judges who voluntarily hold office in a legal system with relatively just laws. There are three relevant respects in which judges differ from citizens, each of which makes a difference regarding the obligation to obey the law.

First, when a judge applies the law to the cases before him, systemic benefits arise that would not be gained by citizens' compliance with the law. These systemic benefits do not depend on the content of the law—whether it is more or less just—but only depend on the authoritative law-appliers (judges) executing their office faithfully. Such benefits are called the 'rule of law values', which usually include in pride of place the enhancement of liberty made possible by predictable judicial application of the law.[22] Since such good states of affairs are obtainable only if judges decide cases by applying the law without generally assessing what, all things considered, would be best, each individual judge has reason to regard the laws of his system as possessing legitimate authority and thus as obligating of him as a judge.

Second, in a legal system with laws substantively just in their content, a judge has an additional reason to regard those laws as authoritative for his decisions. This is because everyone, judges and citizens alike, has an obligation to support just institutions.[23] This obligation to support just laws does not give rise to a general obligation to obey the laws on the part of citizens, Raz asserts, because 'it is a melodramatic exaggeration to suppose that every breach of law' by a citizen sets such a bad example that it will endanger the just system of laws everyone has an obligation to support.[24] Although Raz does not say so, presumably it is not nearly such an exaggeration to claim that judges cannot disregard the laws as they exercise their offices without demotivating by their example a large number of their fellow citizens to comply themselves. For citizens might well think that if even judges can be lawless in their official behaviour, what reason is there for ordinary citizens to be law-abiding? If this is so, then judges have a special obligation to obey the laws as they judge, an obligation admittedly dependent upon their sitting in a legal system the content of whose laws is relatively just.

Third, judges, unlike citizens, typically take an oath to obey the law, make a vow to do so, promise to do so, or undertake some combination of

[22] Raz, *Authority*, above n. 1, at 210–29.
[23] Suggested by Raz in ibid. at 237–42, 245–9; Raz, *Freedom*, above n. 1, at 101.
[24] Raz, *Freedom*, above n. 1, at 102.

all three actions. Raz recognizes that such a voluntary undertaking 'may impose a moral obligation to obey (e.g. when voluntarily undertaken prior to assuming an office of state which one is under no compulsion or great pressure to assume)'.[25] Such undertakings are instances of what Raz broadly calls 'normative powers', which are the powers we all possess to change our moral obligations by voluntary actions. When candidates for judicial office swear to perform the functions of that office, they have exercised their normative powers in ways that obligate them to perform those functions. Given Raz's earlier noted conceptual claim—that to perform the function of a judge is to grant legitimate authority to the laws of the relevant legal system—judicial oaths, promises, and vows obligate judges to apply the law to the exclusion of certain other considerations in the cases before them.

E. Raz's Concept of Law

Raz's general jurisprudence—his theory of law—can be partly stated in his familiar formula: it is the essence of law that it claim legitimate authority for itself.[26] 'No system', Raz tells us, 'is a system of law unless it includes a claim of legitimacy, of moral authority.'[27]

The animistic-sounding idea of law claiming something is unpacked by Raz along familiar Hartian lines. It is the behaviour and beliefs of judges within some purported legal system that is crucial in determining whether it is truly a legal system. The 'law's claims' are thus to be understood as the claims that 'the authentic representatives, the mouthpiece of the law'[28] claim on the law's behalf. As Raz puts it: 'Judges, if anyone, take the law as it claims it should be taken',[29] so it is their beliefs and behaviour that we should examine when we examine 'the law['s] claims for itself'.[30]

With this translation, Raz's general formula for law then includes the claim that there must be primary institutions of general norm-application to particular cases (i.e. courts) that claim legitimate authority on the behalf of those norms.

Exactly what it is that judges must believe in order to make this claim on the law's behalf is the subject of extensive discussion in Raz's jurisprudence, mostly in reaction to the here-diverging views of H. L. A. Hart. Hart has long thought that it is (conceptually) enough for law that the judges of some system accept the rule of recognition and the rules of law that that master rule validates; such acceptance for Hart does not betoken any belief by judges that the rules of their legal system are (morally) obligating on citizens. There would be law, according to Hart, even if judges accepted

[25] Raz, *Authority*, above n. 1, at 239.
[26] Ibid. at 28–33.
[27] Raz, 'Hart', above n. 1, at 131.
[28] Ibid.
[29] Ibid.
[30] Ibid.

the rules of their jurisdiction for any number of different considerations: 'calculations of long-term interest; disinterested interest in others; an unreflecting inherited or traditional attitude; or the mere wish to do as others do'.[31] Such different motives for individual judges accepting the law would only provide what Raz[32] and Hart[33] call a 'weak acceptance', namely, an acceptance that does not claim legitimate authority for that which is accepted.

Raz's theory of law requires a 'strong acceptance' by judges before they can be said to be operating in a system of law. Such strong acceptance claims moral legitimacy for the laws so accepted. This does not mean that the content of the law must be morally correct; it does mean, according to Raz, that judges must think that the rules of their system are supported by moral reasons. How else, Raz asks, could judges sincerely claim that the laws they enforce obligate citizens?[34]

Raz's views here have provided an elegant challenge to Hart's concept of law, for they require Hart to walk a delicate line between the familiar Austin/Bentham view that Hart rejects—the view that legal duty is not a normative concept, having to do only with sanctions and citizens' habits of obedience—and Raz's straightforward explication of the normativity of law in terms of its judicially claimed (and thus, usually, judicially believed) moral legitimacy. Such a line is not easy to find, for walking it commits Hart to describing a concept of the authority that law must possess to be law that does not presuppose legitimate authority. Raz has argued that there can be no such line to walk: although it is enough for there to be law that it possess de facto authority, for it to do so requires that citizens believe the law possesses legitimate authority which in turn usually requires judges to claim such authority.

Who is right in this debate about the kind of authority presupposed by our concept of law need not here detain us. For my purposes, what is important is what follows for Raz from his concept of law. What follows from this theory (that 'law claims legitimate authority') is the nature of reasons law gives for action. Like any legitimate practical authority (see above), the law necessarily purports to give to both citizens and judges special kinds of reasons that are to govern their actions. Such reasons purport to 'pre-empt' and 'exclude' other things a rational and moral actor would have considered if there were no law on the subject.[35] To put it colloquially, judges are to apply the law to the exclusion of many other

[31] H. Hart, *The Concept of Law* (Oxford: Oxford University Press, 1961), 198. Hart's unwavering adherence to this view is expressed in H. Hart, *Essays on Bentham* (Oxford: Oxford University Press, 1982), 255–68 [hereinafter Hart, *Essays*].

[32] Raz, *Authority*, above n. 1, at 155 n. 13.

[33] Hart, *Essays*, above n. 31, at 265.

[34] Raz, 'Hart', above n. 1, at 130.

[35] Raz's uniform view. Raz, *Authority*, above n. 1, at 113; Raz, *Freedom*, above n. 1, at 57–62; Raz, *Practical Reason*, above n. 1, at 143.

considerations as they decide cases; citizens are to follow the law rather than the dictates of their own conscience, whenever the demands of the two diverge.

Since Raz does not think that our concept of law presupposes that law must actually possess legitimate authority—only that it claim it—Raz does not, as we have seen, believe that citizens have even a prima facie obligation to regard the law as preempting or excluding their own conscience as they decide, all things considered, how to behave. There is, to repeat Raz's earlier conclusion, no general obligation to obey the law.

This chapter focuses on Raz's view about judicial obligation. Are judges always obligated in a just regime to grant the law its claim to possess legitimate authority and thus to treat it as preempting the consideration of other-than-law reasons? Are judges ever obligated to do this, even in the most just of regimes? My own answer to these questions is 'no'. My reasons for that answer are much more general than concerns exclusively focused on judicial obligation. Rather, my disagreement focuses on the view of moral reasons generally that Raz's concept of law and judicial obligation presupposes. For Raz's views about judicial obligation are but an instance of his more general views about moral obligation, namely, that morality is (objective) reason-giving; that the moral (and, indeed, rational) thing to do is always to act on the correct resolution of the conflict between those objective reasons; and that law, like promises, commands, and other exercises of normative powers, changes the very nature of the conflict between the objective reasons of morality. Although there is much here to agree with, my disagreement is with Raz's general view of normative powers and their influence on the conflicting reasons of morality. The next section addresses Raz's view on these topics.

II. RAZ'S UNDERLYING MORAL PHILOSOPHY

One of the virtues of Raz's writings is the very great depth they display. Raz has seen quite clearly that his political and jurisprudential theories of authority and law must be supported by a more general moral philosophy. Indeed, the theories of authority, political authority, citizen and judicial obligation, and law itself that we have just examined are conceived by Raz as special applications of a more general moral theory.

On this issue—of the continuity of political theory and jurisprudence with more general moral theory—Raz is much closer to Dworkin than he is to Hart. In understanding Raz's moral theory it is thus instructive to contrast him to Hart's here differing views. Hart's jurisprudence is separated by him from moral theory because he thinks he can explicate the normativity of law in ways not requiring recourse to the idea of moral obligation. Specifically, with regard to the legal obligation of judges, Hart appears to believe that a judge's legal obligation (to grant to the laws of his legal system the status of authoritative, and thus content-independent and pre-emptive, reasons for deciding) can be grounded in nothing stronger than judicial practice. Thus, Hart says:

> When a judge of an established legal system takes up his office he finds that though much is left to his discretion there is also a firmly settled practice of adjudication, according to which any judge of the system is required to apply in the decision of cases the laws identified by specific criteria or sources. This settled practice is acknowledged as determining the central duties of the office of a judge and not to follow the practice would be regarded as a breach of duty . . .[36]

Hart is clear that although a judge must be committed to following the rules of his legal system, a judge's 'view of the merits may be favourable or unfavourable, or simply absent, or, without dereliction of his duty as a judge, he may have formed no view of the moral merits'.[37]

For Hart, jurisprudence thus has an object worthy of study in its own right, legal obligation (conceived of as an obligation from a point of view, or a role-obligation). Hart is content to let jurisprudence be (in part) the study of the obligation one has in a legal role such as that of a judge. Hart's jurisprudence does not study how those role-playing considerations enter into a rational agent's overall calculation of what he ought to do. Here Raz differs fundamentally from Hart, for Raz's jurisprudence is firmly embedded in a larger moral theory aimed at telling us what, all things considered, we (including those of us who are judges) ought to do. Raz's jurisprudential views are, as Hart also recognizes, 'part of a comprehensive theory of practical reason'.[38] It is that comprehensive moral theory that in this section I aim to discuss.

A. Morality's Objective Reasons

1. *Raz's Analytical Moral Philosophy*

Raz for many years has been engaged in what might be called analytic moral philosophy. Such an enterprise does not seek to describe the nature of substantive values like liberty or equality, or virtues like courage or charity, or attributes like culpability or desert.[39] Rather, Raz has long been interested in what might be called the moral consequences of some aspect of a person, action, or institution being good, bad, just, unjust, etc.

The focus of Raz's moral analysis can perhaps best be seen by a legal analogy. In studying legal concepts it is common to regard them as Janus-

[36] Hart, *Essays*, above n. 31, at 158. [37] Ibid. at 159. [38] Ibid.

[39] Raz has more recently become interested in such substantive moral theory too. See Raz, *Freedom*, above n. 1; Raz, 'Principles of Equality', *Mind*, 87 (1978), 321–42.

faced; such concepts look both to the criteria of their correct application (for their meaning) and the legal consequences attached to their authoritative use (for their legal, perlocutionary effects). Alf Ross's old example was the concept of ownership, which looked both to criteria such as, 'acquired by adverse possession', and to consequences such as, 'can dispose of by will'.[40]

Moral concepts like justice and goodness share with legal concepts this Janus-faced nature. Moral concepts, of course, do not have authoritative usages nor are the perlocutionary effects of their use a matter of moral convention. Rather, it is the nature of moral qualities themselves that attaches certain consequences to the existence of such qualities.

The moral consequence of interest to Raz is the necessarily reason-giving nature of any moral quality. Raz shares with Richard Hare[41] and many others,[42] myself included,[43] the view that for a moral quality to exist implies that rational agents have a reason to act so as to further it (if it is good) or to retard it (if it is bad). As Raz puts it, 'it is a matter of logic that values are [I would say, 'give'] reasons . . .'[44] If an action is morally good or just, necessarily rational agents have a reason to perform it. Raz's view here is committed, in the late John Mackie's deprecating phrase, to the idea that moral qualities have 'have-to-be-doneness' built into them.[45]

It is crucial to be clear about what Raz is not saying here. The reasons which morality gives to all rational agents need not be subjective reasons that all persons share (or even share at some deep level below consciousness). Raz is not committed to any view of human nature that claims, for example, that everyone always has some motivational tendency to do what is just and right, no matter how suppressed or submerged that tendency might be. Raz's views here are not psychological at all. Rather, it is morality that is reason-giving even if some, most, or all of us are too blind, too weak, or too immoral to be moved by such reasons.

Raz's analytical moral philosophy aims to chart the structure—the systematic relations that hold—of this reason-giving nature of all moral qualities. This enterprise of Raz's might be met at the outset with the large objection that there are no such objective reasons of morality, as Hart has

[40] A. Ross, 'Tu-Tu', *Harvard Law Review*, 70 (1957), 812–25.

[41] R. M. Hare, *Freedom and Reason* (Oxford: Oxford University Press, 1963).

[42] See e.g. D. Richards, *A Theory of Reasons for Action* (Oxford: Oxford University Press, 1971).

[43] M. Moore, 'Moral Reality', *Wisconsin Law Review*, [1982], 1061–156, at 1094. See also Moore, 'Moral Reality Revisited', *Michigan Law Review*, 90 (1992), 2424–533.

[44] Raz, *Practical Reason*, above n. 1, at 25. As the quotation from Raz in the text suggests, he appears to believe that the reason-giving nature of moral qualities is all the nature that they possess. Whether Raz in fact adopts this Hare-like position does not matter for the present discussion.

[45] J. Mackie, *Ethics: Inventing Right and Wrong* (New York: Penguin Books, 1977), 15–49.

observed.[46] Raz himself has noted that the question of whether there are such objective reasons for action 'is the fundamental question of moral epistemology',[47] and that a currently 'fashionable position' is to deny their existence.[48]

Unfashionable as it may be, I am the last person to make such Humean objections to Raz's enterprise. I have elsewhere defended the view that morality gives objective reasons for action without necessarily subjectively motivating any segment of humanity.[49] Raz has on occasion been more cautious about his own meta-ethical stance: 'Nothing in [his introduction to his volume on practical reasoning] supports the view that there are, for example, moral values binding even on those who do not adopt them or that such values are reasons for action for those who reject them.'[50] At such cautious moments Raz clothes himself in the mantle of the sociologist of other people's moral judgements, his analytical moral philosophy being devoted to charting the structure assumed to exist by such other persons' judgements.[51]

Raz cannot afford this meta-ethical caution. He needs a notion of objective reasons for action to make sense of his enterprise of taking jurisprudence and political theory to be part of a theory of practical reason telling each of us what we ought, all things considered, to do. Moreover, even if Raz wished to limit his enterprise to a kind of analytic sociology of one kind of moral convention, by his own lights it is doubtful that he can so limit it. For Raz himself argues that when we study others' moral concepts, their own beliefs and conventions about the nature of their concepts cannot settle their true nature. We must do our own 'normative–explanatory' work on their concepts, and the result may well be concepts that they do not recognize as theirs.[52] By Raz's own analysis, thus, people may have reasons for action that they do not recognize as being a reason for them.

[46] Hart, *Essays*, above n. 31, at 159. The philosophers Hart has in mind are those descendants of David Hume, such as Gilbert Harman, who believe that the only reasons there are are subjective reasons; see G. Harman, *The Nature of Morality* (Oxford: Oxford University Press, 1977).

[47] Raz, 'Introduction', above n. 1, at 17.

[48] Ibid. at 15.

[49] Moore, 'Moral Reality', above n. 43, at 1094, 1120–2.

[50] Raz, 'Introduction', above n. 1, at 7.

[51] Ibid.

[52] Said by Raz specifically with regards to the concept of authority, rebutting the suggestion that someone can have de facto authority if others believe he has legitimate authority even when such beliefs use a concept of authority different than Raz's. Raz, *Freedom*, above n. 1, at 63; Raz, 'Authority', above n. 1, at 304. Raz evinces no unwillingness to impose his concept of authority on other persons' beliefs about who has authority. Similarly, he should impose his own notions of objective reasons on those conventions that may have differing concepts of objective reasons. I have elsewhere called this 'imperial intellectual history' (Ch. 6 herein), which is an enterprise that makes sense only when the concepts in question (here, objective reasons) refer to a reality independent of the conventions being studied.

2. Objective and Subjective Reasons for Action

Although Raz is (or should be) committed to the existence of moral qualities that give objective reasons for action, and although he is not charting the structure of our actual psychology when we reason practically, the moral theory (of objective reasons) ought to have some strong parallels with the psychological theory (of subjective reasons). It would be an odd and unfair morality that gave us objective reasons which we, because of our psychological equipment, could not incorporate into our practical reasoning processes.

Not surprisingly, therefore, when Raz gets down to charting the structure of objective reasons of morality, this structure parallels a familiar picture of our psychology. Thus, Raz distinguishes 'complete' moral reasons from 'parts' of moral reasons.[53] A complete reason is sufficient for any rational agent to have a reason to perform some action; parts of reasons do not, by themselves, give a reason to act.

Raz distinguishes two different kinds of parts of reasons: 'operative reasons' and 'auxiliary reasons'.[54] As Raz explains them: 'The operative reasons state valid goals. The auxiliary reasons state facts pointing to a way of realizing the goal.'[55] One complete reason will have one operative reason—that is how complete reasons are individuated—but may have many auxiliary reasons.[56]

This structure to objective moral reasons parallels exactly a familiar picture of the subjective reasons on which persons act.[57] On this familiar analysis, for an agent to have acted on a (subjective) reason R is for that agent:

1. To have desired (wished, wanted, intended, morally believed to be good, or otherwise have a 'pro attitude' towards) R;
2. To have believed that action A was a possible (likely or at least not impossible) means of achieving R; and
3. To have done action A because of the desire and belief in (1) and (2).

Note that the 'pro attitude' in the first premise is the subjective analogue to Raz's 'operative reasons' of objective morality, whereas the means–end belief in the second premise is the subjective analogue to Raz's 'auxiliary reasons' of objective morality.

[53] Raz, *Practical Reason*, above n. 1, at 22–5; Raz, 'Introduction', above n. 1, at 15.

[54] Raz, *Practical Reason*, above n. 1, at 33–5; Raz, 'Inner Logic', above n. 1, at 104; Raz, 'Introduction', above n. 1, at 15.

[55] Raz, 'Introduction', above n. 1, at 15.

[56] Ibid.

[57] See e.g. D. Davidson, *Essays on Actions and Events* (Oxford: Oxford University Press, 1980); D. Dennett, *Brainstorms* (Montgomery, Vt.: Bradford Books, 1978). I elaborate on this view of subjective reasons for action in M. Moore, *Law and Psychiatry: Rethinking the Relationship* (Cambridge: Cambridge University Press, 1984), 9–43.

To see how our practical reasoning capacities link up to the objective reasons of morality, we should make these objective/subjective analogues more precise. Objective reasons of morality have propositional content just as do the subjective reasons of our psychology (which Russell after all aptly called the 'propositional attitudes'). As Raz notes,[58] to say that there is a moral reason to help those in distress is to say that one ought (to help those in distress). Notice that if this operative reason of morality is to be acted on by a person, he will possess a desire or other pro attitude around a content that is identical to the content of the ought operator, thusly: X desires (help those in distress).[59] Similarly, to act on an auxiliary reason of morality will be to form a belief of identical content. For example, paralleling the objective fact (Y is in distress) and the further fact (if Y is helped by X, then X has helped those in distress), must be X's belief (Y is in distress) and X's belief (if Y is helped by X, then X has helped those in distress).

Thus, Raz's objective reasons have a structure that strictly parallels the structure of the subjective reasons on which persons act. If there were not such a parallel, allowing us to internalize the objective demands of morality, morality would be a kind of cruel hoax for us.

B. Conflict of Reasons I: Conflict Between First-Order Reasons

Raz finds deontic logic uninteresting because it only deals with single reasons and their implications for action,[60] whereas, Raz asserts, the fact about morality is that its objective reasons conflict in their demands. Raz thus could be seen as the Freud of moral theory: just as Freud thought that the basic fact about our psychology is our possession of conflicting mental states, so Raz believes that the basic fact about morality is the conflict of objective reasons with which it confronts us.

This insight about morality has made many sceptical about the existence of right answers to moral questions.[61] Although not defending a right-answer thesis for all moral dilemmas,[62] Raz nonetheless does not allow his insight about conflict to move him to scepticism about the existence of answers to many dilemmas. To support his partial right-answer thesis, Raz assumes that the objective reasons of morality have strength or weight

[58] Raz, *Practical Reason*, above n. 1, at 29.

[59] Explored further in Moore, *Law and Psychiatry*, above n. 57, at 12–14; see also B. Fay, 'Practical Reasoning, Rationality, and the Explanation of Intentional Action', *Journal for the Theory of Social Behavior*, 8 (1977), 77–101.

[60] Raz, 'Introduction', above n. 1, at 11.

[61] For a discussion of conflict in this context, see P. Foot, 'Moral Realism and Moral Dilemma', *Journal of Philosophy*, 80 (1983), 379–98; S. Guttenplan, 'Moral Realism and Moral Dilemmas', *Proceedings of the Aristotelian Society*, 80 (1980), 61–80.

[62] Raz, *Practical Reason*, above n. 1, at 27.

to them so that when they conflict it still makes sense to say that there is a correct balance of reasons favouring one action over another.[63] The component reasons that make up a conflict of reasons Raz calls prima facie reasons. Presumably every complete reason is a prima facie reason. The prima facie reason that wins over all competitors for the performance of some action Raz calls a conclusive reason.[64] A reason that would be conclusive in all possible worlds Raz calls an absolute reason. (These seem to be reminiscent of Kant's categorical imperatives, to be obeyed 'even though the Heavens may fall'.)

Raz's analytic moral philosophy will seem distinctly unsatisfying to those troubled by the sceptical implications supposedly arising from the existence of moral dilemmas, for Raz gives no algorithm for resolution of conflict. His only principle here is that one 'ought, all things considered, to do whatever one ought to do on the balance of reasons'.[65] Yet the sceptic's lack of satisfaction is misplaced. The tools with which to resolve practical conflicts of moral principle are themselves moral principles. To resolve a conflict between, say, liberty and equality on some particular issue is to discover the principle of each and the principles assigning weight to each. That substantive analysis is not part of Raz's analytic moral philosophy.

More pertinent than the sceptic's worries is my own worry whether the objective reasons of morality ever really do conflict. Raz nicely taxonomizes different ways in which reasons of morality certainly seem to conflict.[66] For our purposes consider only the most straightforward case, what Raz calls 'strict conflict': where reason R1 dictates that X do action A, and where reason R2 dictates that X not do action A.[67]

Raz distinguishes two ways in which such conflicts of reasons resolve themselves. One is where the weightiest reason(s) win. For example, the fact that I promised to meet a friend, which is a reason to meet him, is outweighed by my duty to help an injured stranger.[68] A less typical resolution is where one side to the conflict is subject to a cancelling condition, and the condition is in fact realized. For example, I am released from my promise to meet a friend by that friend.[69]

Notice that in the latter case we might well say that there was no real conflict of reasons, only an apparent conflict. A cancelled reason is not even a prima facie reason for action. Apparently unnoticed by Raz is the possibility that we might extend this last analysis to the former kind of conflict resolution as well. Perhaps all there ever is is an apparent conflict in the reasons given by morality; perhaps there is no real conflict because the content of operative reasons always contains unstated exceptions that,

[63] Ibid. at 25–8. [64] Ibid. at 27. [65] Ibid. at 36.
[66] Ibid. at 22–5, 180 n. 4; Raz, 'Reasons', above n. 1.
[67] Raz, *Practical Reason*, above n. 1, at 25. [68] Ibid. at 27. [69] Ibid.

when fully stated, reveal that one reason never conflicts with another in its demands.

Pursuing this line would be to use, and to use vigorously, Rawls's old distinction[70] between overriding a promise and finding exceptions to the (absolute) practice of promise-keeping. Rawls could allow himself to say that the 'promisor is bound because he promised: weighing the case on its merits is not open to him'[71] only because he also held that the moral reason (that we ought to keep our promises) is subject to numerous unstated exceptions.

Perhaps the objective reasons of morality, if the contents were ever completely formulated, would never conflict because in every case of apparent conflict there would be an exception in one reason allowing the other to prevail. I have at one time suggested this line on moral conflict,[72] and I still find it quite attractive. For one thing, such an approach does not require us to admit that there are conflicts in what we ought to do (i.e. between the 'ought' of a conclusive reason versus the 'ought' of a defeated or cancelled prima facie reason).[73] More important, only such a view on conflict gives particular moral judgements their due in the acquisition of moral knowledge; Raz's view that objective moral reasons can and do conflict, grants to the content of those reasons (which are often general standards) more weight than is due them. On my view, moral rules (which describe the content of objective reasons) are hostage to the particular decisions they imply no less than the laws of science are hostage to the particular observations they imply.[74] If this is so, then every case of apparent conflict between two or more moral rules should be treated as an occasion of discovery of an exception to one rule or another. Raz's view, by contrast, treats the content of such rules as fixed so that apparent conflict always betokens actual conflict.

[70] Rawls, 'Two Concepts of Rules', *Philosophical Review*, 64 (1955), 3–32. On this distinction, see M. Moore, 'Torture and the Balance of Evils', *Israel Law Review*, 23 (1989), 280–344, reprinted as chapter 17 of M. Moore, *Placing Blame: A General Theory of the Criminal Law* (Oxford: Oxford University Press, 1997).

[71] Rawls, above n. 70, at 16.

[72] Moore, 'Moral Reality', above n. 43, at 1151–2; Moore, 'Torture', above n. 70. For general discussion of this view (that experienced moral dilemmas evidence only apparent conflicts of moral reasons), see W. Sinnott-Armstrong, *Moral Dilemmas* (Oxford: Basil Blackwell, 1988), 92–5; Christopher W. Gowans (ed.), *Moral Dilemmas* (New York: Oxford University Press, 1987).

[73] Conflicts of 'oughts' may seem less idiomatic than conflicts between 'what we have reason to do' because of the closer connection of 'ought' to 'good reason'. See Whiteley, 'Review of Practical Reason and Norms', *Philosophical Quarterly*, 26 (1976), 287–8; see also Raz, *Practical Reason*, above n. 1, at 30.

[74] See M. Moore, 'Precedent, Induction, and Ethical Generalization', in L. Goldstein (ed.), *Precedent in Law* (Oxford: Oxford University Press, 1987) for further explication of this view; see also Moore, 'Moral Reality', above n. 43, at 1151–2.

On the other hand, Raz's view has a number of virtues. First, it keeps the structure of objective reasons close to the structure of subjective mental states. It certainly is not the case that the propositional objects of our beliefs and desires are subject to a host of unstated exceptions.[75] If the content of the objective reasons of morality are subject to such potentially infinite elaboration, then there seems to be less of a match between the subjective reasons that are a part of our psychology and the objective reasons given by morality.

Second, some, such as myself, argue that our subjective emotional experiences are evidence of (because typically caused by) objective moral features.[76] If this is generally so, there are three aspects to our experience of moral dilemmas that should give one pause: (*a*) we experience dilemmas as genuine conflicts of reasons; (*b*) even when we have decided a moral dilemma, and even when we are certain we have decided it correctly (i.e. we acted on the balance of reasons), we often feel emotions of remorse, regret, or even guilt at having acted against a prima facie moral reason; and (*c*) even if we do not experience such emotions of regret, remorse, and guilt at correctly resolved dilemmas, according to some theories of the virtues,[77] we would be more virtuous if we were to feel such emotions, and on some tests for the epistemic worth of the emotions,[78] virtuous emotions are also epistemically valuable emotions that may reveal truths about the underlying moral structure.

So an interesting issue is joined between Raz's and my own views on whether the objective reasons of morality ever really do conflict. Although there are rejoinders to the virtues of Raz's position, I shall not pursue them; if we were to resolve the issue in my favour, it would significantly affect the terms in which we could discuss that part of moral theory most directly relevant to Raz's political and legal theory. I prefer to discuss this part of Raz's moral theory in his own terms rather than altering those terms by this preliminary and very general objection. So let us assume that Raz is correct thus far: the objective reasons of morality do conflict and the rational thing to do when they conflict is to act on the balance of reasons.

[75] This, because the *de dicto* nature to the objects of mental states means that they have a kind of canonical text to them that cannot be susceptible to continued refinement. For an introduction to different ways in which such mental 'texts' are fixed, see D. Dennett, 'Beyond Belief', in *The Intentional Stance* (Cambridge, Mass.: MIT Press, 1987), and M. Moore, 'Intentions and Mens Rea', in R. Gavison (ed.), *Issues in Contemporary Legal Philosophy* (Oxford: Oxford University Press, 1987), reprinted as ch. 11 of *Placing Blame*, above n. 70.

[76] M. Moore, 'The Moral Worth of Retribution', in F. Schoeman (ed.), *Responsibility, Character, and the Emotions* (Cambridge: Cambridge University Press, 1987) reprinted as ch. 3 in *Placing Blame*, above n. 70 [hereinafter Moore, 'Moral Worth']; Moore, 'Moral Reality Revisited', above n. 43.

[77] H. Morris, 'Nonmoral Guilt', in F. Schoeman (ed.), *Responsibility, Character, and the Emotions* (Cambridge: Cambridge University Press, 1987).

[78] Namely, my own. See Moore, 'Moral Worth', above n. 76.

C. Conflict of Reasons II: Normative Powers and Second-Order Reasons

Raz's charting of the structure of the reason-giving aspects of moral qualities gets considerably more complicated with his introduction of the ideas of second-order reasons and second-order conflicts of reasons. Since this is also the part of moral theory most relevant to Raz's political and legal theories, we shall examine it with some care.

A second-order reason, as Raz defines it, 'is any reason to act for a reason or to refrain from acting for a reason'.[79] Such reasons are second-order because they are reasons for acting for reasons, whereas first-order reasons are simply reasons for acting. To conform to a second-order reason, in other words, it is not enough to do some specified action; rather, one must do the act for a certain reason.

Raz recognizes two types of second-order reasons, positive and negative.[80] A positive second-order reason is a reason to act for a certain reason. A negative second-order reason is a reason to refrain from acting for a certain reason. The latter are by far the most important for Raz's purposes, so he gives them a special name, exclusionary reasons.[81]

An example of a positive second-order reason would be where an actor has promised another to consider and act on certain reasons. For example, a father promises his son to base his decision about his son's birthday present, in part at least, on his son's desires. Since promises create reasons for acting where none existed before now, the father has a reason to purchase his son's present for the reason that his son wants it. Similarly, an example of an exclusionary reason may also be provided by a similar promise: the father promises not to base his decision on what the son's mother wants. Now the father has a reason not to purchase his son's present for the reason that the mother wants it. (Notice that, unlike positive second-order reasons, there are two ways for the father to conform to his exclusionary reason: either he may not buy any present at all (and thus does not buy one with the wrong motivation), or he may buy the present but not for the reason that the boy's mother wants it.) This lack of parallel between positive and negative second-order reasons is due to Raz's eschewal of an alternative conception of a negative second-order reason, namely, that such a reason gives us a prima facie reason not only to refrain from doing action A but also to refrain for the right reasons.[82]

[79] Raz, *Practical Reason*, above n. 1, at 39; see also Raz, *Freedom*, above n. 1, at 33; Raz, 'Reasons for Action', above n. 1, at 132.

[80] Raz, *Authority*, above n. 1, at 17.

[81] Raz, *Practical Reason*, above n. 1, at 39; Raz, 'Authority', above n. 1, at 17; Raz, 'Reasons for Action', above n. 1, at 132.

[82] More technically, the scope of the negation connective is ambiguous in English, between ought [not-(do A for reason R)], and ought [if do action A, then not (do A for reason

Raz holds that such second-order reasons give rise to a distinct kind of conflict between reasons, which I shall call a second-order conflict. A second-order conflict is a conflict between first-order reasons and second-order reasons. In such circumstances, Raz holds, conflict is not resolved by acting on a balance of reasons. Rather, second-order reasons have priority. An exclusionary reason defeats a first-order reason with which it is in conflict by excluding it from consideration and not by overriding or cancelling it, as is the case for first-order conflicts. Such exclusionary reasons deprive competing first-order reasons (if they are within the scope of the exclusion) of any weight whatsoever as the actor decides what he ought, all things considered, to do.

Raz's early work is rich in examples of exclusionary reasons defeating their first-order foes, not by outweighing them, but by depriving them of any weight. Raz has considered in detail how commands, promises, vows, oaths, authoritative rules (including laws), moral rules, social rules, decisions, and judgements about one's future incapacity to decide may each operate as exclusionary reasons.[83]

For reasons that will become apparent later, promises and authoritative commands and rules are Raz's best examples of items giving us exclusionary reasons. For promises, as well as commands and rules possessed of legitimate authority, actually change what it is morally right to do from what would have been the case in the absence of such commands, promises, or rules. Raz's distinctive claim is that such commands, rules, and promises change the moral landscape by excluding certain reasons urging non-compliance even though such reasons would have been good reasons not to do the complying act in the absence of the promise, command, or rule. Such a claim rejects an alternative description of how the moral landscape is changed by such commands, rules, and promises, namely, that these create new first-order reasons of great weight that usually but not invariably outweigh other first-order reasons with which they may occasionally conflict. While I will argue for this alternative description in the succeeding section of this chapter, at this juncture it is important just to see what distinctive claim Raz is making with his concept of exclusionary reasons.

If we pass over for the moment some deep ambiguities in Raz's concept of exclusionary reasons, we can move on to consider the more complex structures of second-order reasons that Raz builds with his exclusionary

R)]. One can satisfy the second obligation here either by not doing action A or, if one does it, not doing it for reason R. The first obligation could only be satisfied by refraining from doing action A and refraining from doing it for the right reason. Since Raz wishes to get at excluded reasons with his notion of 'exclusionary reason', he uses the phrase to label the second kind of obligation.

83 Raz, 'Promises', above n. 1; Raz, 'Reasons for Action', above n. 1, at 128–43; Raz, 'Voluntary Obligations', above n. 1.

reasons concepts. Raz notes that promises and authoritative rules and commands are more than merely second-order reasons that exclude certain first-order reasons from counting. These items are also themselves first-order reasons for acting in accordance with them. Because one ought to keep one's promises, and because one ought to obey the commands and laws of those possessed of legitimate authority over us, these items are not only excluding of contrary-inclining reasons but are also positively inclining of conforming behaviour. Raz appropriately dubs the combination of a first-order reason and an exclusionary reason a 'protected reason'—protected in the sense that as a first-order reason it enters the tournament field with most of its opponents disqualified from playing.[84]

With the concept of protected reasons established, Raz next introduces the fruitful notion of a normative power. Built by analogy on Hohfeldian legal powers (which are the ability to change the legal relations of (claim) rights and privileges), Raz's normative powers are the abilities we individually or collectively possess to change our moral universe. When we promise, Raz urges, we change what it is right to do by creating a protected reason for acting in conformity to the promise. When someone possessed of legitimate authority issues a command or a statute, she has changed what it is obligatory for us to do by creating a protected reason to behave in conformity with the command or statute. Although objective morality is not up to us to create, either individually or collectively, we nonetheless possess limited sovereignty to affect our obligations and rights through the exercise of normative powers.

Raz adds three more parts to this already complex structure of the reasons objective morality gives each rational agent. When one possessed of legitimate authority exercises that authority by issuing a rule, that rule will constitute not only a protected reason discussed above; it will also constitute a content-independent, dependent, and pre-emptive reason. Let us examine these three additional notions one at a time.

Early in his writings Raz introduced the notion of a 'content-independent' justification for a rule.[85] Such content-independent justifications justified the rule, not by showing that the actions the rule required were morally right, but rather, by showing that the rule was derived from one's own promise or from another person possessed of legitimate authority. A content-independent reason, accordingly, is just a first-order reason that has the status of a complete reason for action only because of its status as having been created by a promise or authoritative directive; it is not a first-order reason because the actions which it motivates are morally right (which would make it a content-dependent reason).[86] 'Content-

[84] Raz, *Authority*, above n. 1, at 18.

[85] Raz, 'Voluntary Obligations', above n. 1, at 95.

[86] Raz, *Freedom*, above n. 1, at 35–7.

independent' is simply Raz's (and Hart's) label for the kind of reason that promises and authoritative rules create by virtue of there being normative powers. All exercises of normative powers necessarily create content-independent reasons because such exercises create protected reasons.

The notion of 'dependent reasons' is a latecomer to the Razian family of reasons. A dependent reason is best construed as a kind of content-independent reason whose independence is in jeopardy. Raz's example is an arbitrator's decision on some matter of dispute between two persons.[87] Before the parties promised to be bound by the arbitrator's decision, and before he decides, there may well have been a balance of (first-order, usually content-dependent) reasons favouring one party or the other. Yet by the respective exercises of their normative powers, the parties and the arbitrator have created a new reason for action, one which is content-independent and protected. Yet unlike other content-independent reasons (such as requests, for example), the arbitrator's decision is a reason for action for the parties only because it itself depends on the balance of (first-order, content-dependent) reasons the parties faced to begin with. It is not, as Raz carefully notes,[88] that the arbitrator's decision is a reason for the parties only if he gets the balance of antecedent reasons right in his decision. If that were true, his decision would be without any force as a reason at all. Rather, his decision is dependent on the balance of antecedent reasons only in the weaker sense that it must be based on those reasons, however wrongly he adjudges their balance. Such dependence is the basis for the arbitrator's jurisdiction to create a new reason for action by his decision. In this sense his decision can both be dependent on antecedently existing reasons, and yet content-independent in the sense of not having its force as a reason depend on the force of those underlying, antecedently existing reasons.

Raz's third refinement is with his notion of 'pre-emptive' (occasionally 'peremptory') reasons.[89] A pre-emptive reason is a dependent (first-order) reason that is also an exclusionary (second-order) reason, and what is excluded are the antecedently existing reasons on which the dependent reason depends. In the example of the arbitrator, his decision is not only a first-order reason to act in accordance with the decision, it is also a second-order reason to exclude the original reasons the parties may have had to act in ways contrary to those required by the decision. Even though such original reasons might well be conclusive if balanced against their opponents (which opponents include the arbitrator's decision), such reasons no longer count in measuring the rightness of the parties' actions.

[87] Ibid. at 41; Raz, 'Authority', above n. 1, at 297.

[88] Raz, *Freedom*, above n. 1, at 41; Raz, 'Authority', above n. 1, at 297.

[89] See Raz, *Freedom*, above n. 1, at 57–62.

If we draw all of this together, we see that Raz's theories of legitimate authority and of law are built directly on his theory about the objective reasons morality gives us for action. A rule is a law only if issued by one possessed of de facto authority; persons or institutions possess de facto authority only if they claim legitimate authority; persons or institutions or the laws they issue actually possess legitimate authority for judges or citizens only if their commands or laws constitute protected and pre-emptive reasons for acting in conformity with such commands or laws; these commands or laws constitute protected reasons only if they constitute content-independent (first-order) reasons that are also exclusionary (second-order) reasons that exclude many potentially conflicting first-order reasons, and they constitute pre-emptive reasons only if they constitute (first-order) dependent reasons that are also (second-order) exclusionary reasons that specifically exclude the first-order reasons on which the dependent reasons depend.

This is an elegant structure, and before we move on to criticize some of its features and presuppositions we should pause to praise its elegance. Raz has truly integrated his jurisprudence and his political philosophy with his moral theory, conceiving the former as but a special application of the more general insights of the latter. Although complex in its detail, the whole is crisply specified and tightly unified. There is much to admire here.

D. The Ambiguity of Raz's Concept of Exclusionary Reasons

The linchpin of Raz's analysis of how promises, authoritative rules, and so on enter into the structure of moral reasons is his idea that such items give exclusionary reasons for action. I shall argue in this subsection that Raz is implicitly eliding three claims together here because there is an unnoticed double ambiguity in his concept of an exclusionary reason.

The first ambiguity is between exclusionary reasons as reasons that alter the relevance or bearing of reasons that otherwise exist within the content of morality, on the one hand, and reasons rational actors have to exclude certain reasons from their consideration as they are deciding what to do, on the other. It is one thing to claim that promise-making and other exercises of our normative powers actually change what it is right to do by excluding other reasons (that otherwise would have counted against doing the act promised) from counting at all; it is another thing to claim that a promisor, because of having promised to do some action, now has a reason to exclude certain reasons (that otherwise he would have weighed on the side opposed to do the act promised) from his deliberations about what to do. The former is a claim about how the exercise of normative powers actually changes what one ought to do by changing the structure of reasons morality makes relevant to any given action. The latter is a claim about how promise-making changes what one ought to consider as one decides what one ought to do. It is a claim about optimal decision-strategies for reaching correct moral decisions, whereas the former is a claim about the right-making characteristics of the actions decided upon. One can certainly make both kinds of claims with the concept of exclusionary reasons, but one need not do so, and in any case they remain distinct claims.[90]

At one point in his work Raz seems to eschew the second 'decision-strategy' interpretation of his exclusionary reasons claim. Raz accurately notes that the decision-strategy interpretation demotes exclusionary reasons from second-order reasons (not to act for certain first-order reasons) to mere first-order reasons not to do a certain act of deliberation. As Raz puts it, the decision-strategy interpretation would make exclusionary reasons 'ordinary (first-order) reasons not to consider the merits of the case (i.e. not to perform a certain mental act)'.[91] As a psychological claim, Raz finds it to be 'obviously wrong' because '[t]here is no reason to prevent a person . . . from going through the [excluded] arguments to amuse himself or as an exercise, etc., so long as he does not trust his judgement enough to act on it'.[92]

As I would understand this eschewal by Raz, he is only allowing an actor under an exclusionary reason to contemplate the excluded considerations; so long as they are not causally operative in the deliberations by which the actor makes such decisions, such an actor may idly contemplate such things. But Raz need not be here construed to be saying that an exclusionary reason is never meant by him to be a reason for excluding certain matters from consideration (the decision-strategy interpretation of 'exclusionary reason'). For such an eschewal would be hard to square with many of Raz's examples of exclusionary reasons. Consider, by way of example, Raz's discussion of decisions by an agent as constituting exclusionary reasons for that agent as she faces further choice:

Jill has made a rule to spend her holidays in France . . . Jill . . . faces many conflicting considerations but she has no intention to act on the balance of reasons. She has adopted a rule to spend her holidays in France and she did so precisely to spare herself the necessity of deciding every year what to do during the holidays. She adopted the rule in order not to have to act on the balance of reasons on each occasion. Having the rule is like having decided in advance what to do. When the

[90] Chaim Gans also notes this ambiguity in Raz's use of exclusionary reasons and sees the large impact the ambiguity has on Raz's claims. See Gans, 'Mandatory Rules and Exclusionary Reasons', *Philosophia*, 15 (1986), 373–94, at 390–2. The general distinction I rely upon here is the distinction between theories of truth—what makes an action right—and theories of discovery—how best can one discover that an action is right. For citations and discussion, see Ch. 10 herein.

[91] Raz, *Practical Reason*, above n. 1, at 48.

[92] Ibid.

holidays come she is not going to reconsider the matter. Her mind is already made up. Her rule is for her an exclusionary reason . . .[93]

Notice that Jill's earlier decision constitutes an exclusionary reason only in the sense that she now has reasons 'not . . . to reconsider the matter', i.e. not to go through any more psychological processes of decision-making. For reasons of time, effort, agony of indecision, incapacity for accurate subsequent judgement, and so on we each sometimes have reason not to consider alternatives further. Yet such general decisions to end or forego deliberation do not change what it is right for us to do or what objectively counts as a right-making characteristic of our actions. Unlike promises or rules issued by legitimate authority, our own decisions are not exercises of our normative powers. Long-term decisions may give us reasons not to engage in more deliberation about matters already decided. Such decisions may thus insulate us from criticism when we act on them rather than deliberating further. But such decisions cannot in any way alter the rightness or wrongness of our later actions in conformity with them. We do not have anything like this kind of sovereignty over morality.

Raz should thus sometimes be construed to be using 'exclusionary reasons' as the name of reasons we have not to consider certain reasons as we decide what to do. As often, however, Raz plainly has a non-decision-strategy notion of exclusionary reasons in mind. Promising and the issuing of authoritative rules, unlike mere decisions, are actions that change what it is obligatory for us to do. These actions do create exclusionary reasons in some sense more closely connected to the rightness of actions than are reasons not to consider reasons.

Here the second ambiguity enters. Raz's explicit definition of 'exclusionary reasons' gives one non-decision-strategy sense in which he uses the phrases, namely as a 'reason to refrain from acting for some reason'.[94] As an example, Raz considers 'the case of Colin who promised his wife that in all decisions affecting the education of his son he will act only for his son's interests . . .'[95] Such a promise, Raz urges, gives Colin a (positive) second-order reason to act with respect to his son's education for the reason that it is in his son's interests. Such a promise also gives Colin an exclusionary reason not to act for any other reasons than his son's interests when he acts with respect to his son's education.

I shall call this the motivational interpretation of 'exclusionary reasons', for in this interpretation, promises, commands and the like, change the structure of morality by changing the reasons (motives) for which we may act. Raz's example of Colin's promise is an example of this kind, although it is a very narrow example, dependent as it is upon the particular content

[93] Raz, 'Reasons for Action', above n. 1, at 140–1.
[94] Raz, *Practical Reason*, above n. 1, at 39. [95] Ibid.

of Colin's promise (not to act for certain reasons). Such examples cannot support any general thesis that promises as such give exclusionary reasons in this motivational sense.[96]

A more general example for Raz would be moral rules like the rule, 'One ought not to lie.'[97] On a Kantian view of the matter, such a norm is directed at our reasons as well as our actions. On this view, we need not only refrain from lying, but we must do so for the right reasons (such as reverence for the moral law) and not for excluded reasons (such as prudential calculations of self-interest).

Raz's explicit definition of 'exclusionary reasons', his special promising examples of them, and the alignment of both within the Kantian tradition in ethics should not blind us to a third interpretation of exclusionary reasons. On this interpretation, promises and authoritative rules actually change what counts as a right-making characteristic of an action. Promises not only create a new reason for acting in conformity with them (their first-order aspect); they also, according to this interpretation of Raz, exclude other reasons (that would have been reasons against action conforming to the promise) from counting. Let us call this the 'justificatory' interpretation of Raz's claim about exclusionary reasons, because on this interpretation, some of the objective reasons of morality are excluded from doing their normal justificatory work whenever there is an exclusionary reason.

Notice how different the justificatory interpretation is from the motivational interpretation of 'exclusionary reasons', even though both interpretations are about moral reasons and not simply about psychological decision-making procedures. On the motivational version, an exclusionary reason is part of morality's demands that we act or refrain from acting for the right reasons. On the justificatory interpretation, exclusionary reasons have nothing to do with demands that as we act we be motivated in certain ways but not others; rather, exclusionary reasons on this interpretation involve the right-making characteristics of actions. Nothing in this last view requires such right-making characteristics to be or not to be among our motives for action. It only requires that certain ordinarily right-making characteristics are excluded from being right-making characteristics on this occasion because of some promise, authoritative rule, and so on.

Some of Raz's remarks could be construed to eschew this last interpretation of 'exclusionary reasons' as well. Raz says, for example, that promises (giving exclusionary reasons) do not affect the balance of reasons for and against behaviour conforming to the promise that the actor had

[96] The narrow nature of Raz's examples here is also noted by Gans, above n. 90, at 392–4.

[97] Raz uses the example of morally valid rules as giving exclusionary reasons, in Raz, 'Reasons for Action', above n. 1, at 14–42, although he regards them as but one of three kinds of 'mandatory norms', all of which give exclusionary reasons.

before he promised; promises do not 'change whatever reasons there are'.[98] Yet such remarks should not be construed as an eschewal of the justificatory interpretation of 'exclusionary reasons'. For what Raz appears to mean by them is only that an exclusionary reason does not change the balance of first-order reasons as such; it pre-empts that balance from determining the rightness of an action by excluding certain of the first-order reasons making up that balance.[99]

In any case, however Raz's remarks are to be construed, some of his best examples of exclusionary reasons are most fruitfully unpacked with this justificatory interpretation. For promises and authoritative rules do not plausibly give us exclusionary reasons in the motivational sense. Unless the content of a promise or a law specifically obligates us to refrain from acting for certain reasons, as in Raz's special examples,[100] neither of these items concerns itself with the reasons that motivate conforming behaviour. When Congress passes a law requiring someone to register under the Selective Service System, that person has a new (first-order) reason for action he did not have before. Additionally, it is plausible that he also now has a second-order reason, namely, one that precludes the undesirability of a peace-time draft from counting in determining the rightness of his registering or omitting to register. What he does not now have is a second-order reason to register for some reasons but not for others. The law may obligate him to register, and it may create that obligation because the very passage of the law excludes from counting reasons such as the undesirability of a draft system. But the law does not concern itself with his reasons for registering. The enactment of the law, in other words, does not give one subject to its authority reasons not to act for certain reasons, the motivational interpretation of 'exclusionary reasons'.

There being three senses of 'exclusionary reasons' in Raz's work, I shall in succeeding sections of this chapter address each seriatim. Against the claim that promises, etc., give exclusionary reasons under the justificatory interpretation of that phrase, I shall urge a moral objection: legitimate

[98] Raz, *Practical Reason*, above n. 1, at 39. Such remarks appear to have misled some of Raz's commentators. Stephen Perry concludes that Raz's 'idea of acting in accordance with an exclusionary reason . . . does not depend on whether there ever could in fact be a justification for refusing to act on the balance of reasons' (Perry, 'Judicial Obligation, Precedent, and the Common Law', *Oxford Journal Legal Studies*, 7 (1987), 215–57, at 220).

[99] Raz analyses the exclusionary reasons given by authoritative orders in this way: 'You may see that on the balance of reasons one course of action is right and yet be justified in not following it. The order is a reason for doing what you were ordered regardless of the balance of reasons' (Raz, *Practical Reason*, above n. 1, at 38).

Perhaps a less paradoxical way of saying what Raz wishes to say here would be to say that the order may change the morality of a certain course of conduct ('A') so that what would have been right to do in the absence of the order is now not the right thing to do. What is changed by the order is not the intrinsic rightness of those aspects of A that generally make A the right course of conduct, but rather, the applicability of those aspects in justifying A or not A as the right course of conduct to do now.

[100] Ibid. at 39.

authorities cannot be construed to give us exclusionary reasons for action in this sense without making us too obeisant to such authorities. Against the claim that promises, etc., give exclusionary reasons under the motivational interpretation of that phrase, I shall urge that such a claim presupposes a psychological capacity that we do not possess, namely, a capacity to choose the reasons on which we act. Lacking such capacity, morality could not fairly obligate us to act on some reasons but not others. Against the decision-strategy interpretation, I shall urge that such an exclusionary reasons claim about judging severely impoverishes a judge's decisional resources if such reasons exclude as much as Raz says must be excluded by the role of judge. Indeed, since the unexcluded considerations are insufficient to decide any case whatsoever, Raz's exclusionary reasons claim, in this third sense, would require judges to make arbitrary decisions.

III. THE OBJECTION TO RAZ'S JUSTIFICATORY CLAIM

Under the interpretation of the phrase 'exclusionary reasons' here considered, Raz claims that morality sometimes gives us reasons not only to act or refrain from acting, but also reasons that disenfranchise certain reasons that would otherwise be relevant to the rightness of our actions. (It is this disenfranchising ability of exclusionary reasons that makes the first-order reasons conclusive, i.e. obligating.) My objection is a straightforward moral one: far from excluding certain reasons as being right-making characteristics of our actions, morality includes everything that is otherwise a valid and relevant reason within the overall balance of reasons that determine the rightness of our actions. Morality does this because the alternative is undue conformity with (supposedly reason-excluding) items like promises, orders, and authoritative rules.

Raz sees the alternative that poses this moral issue very clearly. He sees that we could conceive of commands, promises, and authoritative rules changing our moral obligations in two quite different ways. First, there is Raz's preferred conceptualization that such items constitute protected reasons for action (first-order reasons that exclude many or perhaps all of their competitors from conflicting with them). Alternatively, we could conceive of such items more simply as new first-order reasons of great (but not necessarily conclusive) weight. Under either conception, promises, valid laws, etc., change what is right for us to do; under either conception, such items will usually defeat competing reasons in determining what, all things considered, we ought to do; but, the two conceptions differ markedly in how promises, laws, and commands win out over other reasons for action.

In his explicit consideration of these two alternatives,[101] Raz only obliquely addresses the moral issue. For most of Raz's argument in favour of his exclusionary reason conceptualization is intended to show, not that it is morally right, but only that it is the conceptualization reflected in how most of us think about these moral issues. Thus, Raz makes two arguments. First, an actor's 'typical reaction' to acting in conformity to orders, promises, etc., is that she did not balance the reasons constituted by these items with other reasons inclining her to non-conforming behaviour; rather, she claims that her hands are tied so that she couldn't (shouldn't) consider conflicting first-order reasons.[102] Second, people generally are less conflicted, less equivocal, in their judgements of praise (or blame) when another gets it right (or wrong) in assessing a balance of first-order reasons, than they are in their judgements of another who acts under a valid order, law, or promise. From this Raz concludes that '[w]hen people react . . . with these "mixed" reactions . . . they provide the evidence required to ascribe to them belief in exclusionary reasons'.[103]

More to the point is to ask whether these two features of our moral practices evidence the structure of the objective reasons of morality that Raz envisions morality to possess. Raz's two features are in reality nothing more than the first and third person aspects of one feature, namely, the differentially greater feelings of unresolved and unresolvable conflict that accompany our resolutions of some moral dilemmas rather than others. Raz's first and third person aspects to his phenomenological claim are that for conflicts involving reasons derived from promises, commands, and laws (1) we feel the incommensurability of competing considerations when we are deciding these conflicts, and we feel conflicted after our decision, even if we are still convinced we chose correctly; and (2) when others face such conflicts, we are more equivocal in our judgements because we realize the incommensurability with which those others dealt. From this phenomenological claim, Raz infers the existence of a distinct kind of conflict, a second-order conflict, where a simple balance of reasons is not determinative of what one ought to do.

One question is whether Raz's phenomenological claims are true. Anyone who has taught or systematically thought through the ethics of some role—such as the role of a lawyer studied in professional ethics—has to grant some credence to Raz's phenomenological claims. The discussions of the ethics of a professional role do boringly repeat themselves in a familiar pattern whereby one juxtaposes the systemic justifications for a certain conception of a professional role with more ad hoc reasons for an individual stepping out of that role to avoid unjust results in a particular

[101] Raz, *Practical Reason*, at 40–5. [102] Ibid. at 42. [103] Ibid. at 45.

case. Captain Vere versus Jean Paul Sartre replayed endlessly with minor variation.

Yet it is also true that much of Raz's phenomenology is present in ordinary first-order conflicts as well. Sartre's famous example of a moral dilemma well illustrates how even conflicts not involving promises, orders, or laws can have an 'apples/oranges' feel to them as we decide them. The student who sought Sartre's advice was facing a conflict between two first-order reasons: that he ought to fight evil, in this instance, the Nazis, by joining the Free French outside of France; and that he ought to stay with his mother in France because she needed him.[104] Sartre correctly observes that the young man is torn between two seemingly incommensurable reasons, neither of which involve what Raz would call a second-order reason generating a second-order conflict.

Moreover, as noted earlier, once we have decided dilemmas such as that of Sartre's student, we may feel remorse, regret, and guilt even if we are certain we were right in what we decided. We are 'equivocal' and conflicted after the decision, even though it was only a resolution of a first-order conflict.

So Raz's phenomenological claim can only be one of degree: decisions involving reasons of promise, etc., have more of a conflicted feel to them—both as we are making such decisions and after we have made them—than ordinary moral dilemmas. Even so watered down, I doubt that the phenomenological claim is true.

A more plausible phenomenological claim for Raz to make would be the following. Granted, there are moral dilemmas not involving promises, etc., that generate the phenomenological features to which Raz adverts; even so, dilemmas that involve promises, etc., do regularly generate these features. Thus, while Raz's account of these phenomenological features (in terms of two kinds of conflict) is incomplete, it still may be good as far as it goes: that these features regularly accompany dilemmas involving promises, etc., is explained by there being two kinds of conflicts of moral reasons. Presumably, there will be other explanations, involving different typologies of conflict, for those other dilemmas that share these phenomenological features.[105]

Let us for purposes of argument take this more plausible phenomenological claim to be true. The next question is whether we cannot better account for such subjective experience with the alternative conception of

[104] J. P. Sartre, 'Existentialism is a Humanism', in G. Novak (ed.), *Existentialism Versus Marxism* (New York: Dell Publishing Co., 1966).

[105] For suggested taxonomies of the types of moral reasons that recurringly conflict see T. Nagel, 'The Fragmentation of Value', in *Mortal Questions* (Cambridge: Cambridge University Press, 1979) and E. J. Lemmon, 'Moral Dilemmas', *Philosophical Review*, 70 (1962), 139–58.

promises, laws, and commands, namely, that they provide only first-order reasons of great strength, and thus, that the only kind of conflict they generate is first-order conflict resolvable by the usual balance of reasons approach.

Richard Flathman, for one, argues just this point.[106] He argues that the alternative conception better accounts for these phenomenological features than does Raz's conception. On Raz's account, Flathman asserts, 'exclusionary reasons always prevail when in conflict with first-order reasons'.[107] From this it would follow, Flathman reasons, that ambivalence or dissonance on our part 'would be irrational and hence inexplicable' because we 'would know with entire certitude' that obeying an order, keeping a promise, or obeying the law, was the right thing to do.[108]

Unfortunately for Flathman, his inference that certitude must accompany decisions where there are exclusionary reasons is based on an extremely unsympathetic reading of Raz. For Raz can allow for lack of certainty about decisions of second-order conflicts in two ways: first, exclusionary reasons can have limited scope, so that they need not exclude everything else; there can remain plenty of unexcluded first-order reasons, conflict between which is of uncertain resolution. Second, (protected) exclusionary reasons even of unlimited scope (i.e. excluding all competing first-order reasons) may still conflict with other second-order reasons not to exclude this or that,[109] and such second-order conflict may be of uncertain resolution.

In any case, certitude is not the subjective experience from which Raz makes his evidentiary inference. Raz's phenomenological claim is that we experience ordinary reasons and promises, etc., as incommensurable, both as we are making such decisions and after we have made them.

The alternative conception's explanation of these features would be as follows. By Raz's own showing (see above), a first-order reason has a fixed content that does not possess as many unstated exceptions as there are potential conflicts with other first-order reasons. So all first-order conflicts will have an 'apples and oranges' feel to them as we decide them, and we will regret even the most clearly correct of such decisions, because even a correct decision will violate the content of a prima facie reason.

[106] R. Flathman, *The Practice of Political Authority* (Chicago: University of Chicago Press, 1980), 110–12.

[107] Ibid. at 112 (quoting Raz, *Practical Reason*, above n. 1, at 40).

[108] Flathman, above n. 106, at 112.

[109] Raz nowhere specifies what sort of anti-exclusionary reasons there might be to oppose exclusionary reasons. What he cannot say (without trivializing his first-order/second-order distinction) is that the anti-exclusionary reasons have the same force as the first-order reasons they seek to keep from exclusion. For if such anti-exclusionary reasons are just second-order proxies for such first-order reasons, then the first-order balance of reasons Raz says is displaced in the face of an exclusionary reason is in fact just duplicated at the second-order level.

What explains the typically large amount of subjective experience of this kind when promises, etc., are involved, is the large degree of difference that exists between systemic reasons and particular reasons. The reasons provided by promises, commands, and laws are reasons for us because of their systemic justifications. Such justifications appeal to the goods of some large, social system and how those goods are achieved only if, in general, people keep their promises and obey authoritative laws and commands. These justifications are different from reasons justified only by the good of one individual or small group of individuals, or the rights or other claims of justice of such an individual or group. There will be no easy measuring of the demands of the systemic reasons against the demands of particularistic reasons because there is no common metric. Even utilitarians—the moral theorists with the greatest ambitions to possess a common metric with which to assess the weight of moral reasons—experience an uncomfortable apples/oranges feeling about conflicts of this kind, some fleeing to 'rule-utilitarianism' to alleviate their discomfort.

Issue is thus joined on this argument by evidentiary inference from our subjective experience of moral conflict among Raz, Flathman, and myself. Rather than pursuing this line of argument further, let us shift to a more direct approach to ascertaining how morality stands with regard to second-order reasons. To do this we should ask Melville's implicit questions of Captain Vere in *Billy Budd*: is it ever morally right that competing moral reasons do not count in determining the rightness of an action and that the only reason that does count is some unexcluded reasons, such as the laws of courts-martial that prescribe a certain punishment for a certain action?

Much of the criticism directed to Raz's notion of exclusionary reasons has been on this point. D. S. Clarke, for example, assumes that 'there can surely be no justification for refusing to weigh [competing first-order reasons] against the reasons for following the rule . . .'[110] Unfortunately, most of this criticism is quite general. Clarke in the quoted language, for example, challenges Raz on rules in general, with no distinction between moral rules, rules issued by those with legitimate authority, and social rules.[111]

For such direct moral criticism in general, Raz has an adequate answer. There is nothing in his general theory of exclusionary reasons that commits him to Captain Vere's position in *Billy Budd*. Raz can allow for the protected reasons given by laws, promises, and commands to lose out to competing reasons in the two ways mentioned before with respect to Flathman: (1) exclusionary reasons have the dimension of scope, and Raz explicitly notes that promises, etc., rarely exclude all potentially

[110] D. S. Clarke, 'Exclusionary Reasons', *Mind*, 86 (1977), 252–5, at 254.

[111] Raz's three kinds of 'mandatory rules' in Raz, 'Reasons for Action', above n. 1, at 141–2.

conflicting first-order reasons.[112] There are almost always some types of unexcluded reasons, and sometimes at least, they may outweigh the prima facie reason represented by some particular promise, command, or law; (2) exclusionary reasons may conflict with other second-order reasons that oppose exclusion of some first-order reasons, and at least sometimes such opposing second-order reasons will outweigh the exclusionary reason given by some particular promise, command, or law.[113]

To test, therefore, the truth of the injunction that Raz believes himself to have discovered in the structure of morality's reasons, we need much more particular examples. More specifically, we need examples where the scope of the exclusionary reason given by the promise, etc., is specified, and where the existence and weight of conflicting (anti-exclusionary) second-order reasons is specified. Then we can see whether the moral thing is in accordance with the Razian view, to do the act whose rightness is determined by an artificial balance of reasons (artificial, because some seemingly good reasons count for nothing because excluded); or in opposition to the Razian view, to do the act whose rightness is determined by a balance of reasons with nothing excluded.

Although Raz makes some such specifications for orders and promises, our present focus is on the law and more particularly on the moral obligation imposed by the law on judges who voluntarily sit in reasonably just regimes. So let me construct two examples where this moral obligation is called in play to see whether Raz's recommendations for judicial behaviour square with what judges ought in reality to do.

Consider first the obligation of a common law judge when faced with the question of overruling a prior decision by the court on which he is now sitting. Assume that the judge possesses the legal power of overruling, and that the possession (and thus at least occasional exercise) of that power is morally justified. Can we flesh out a morally plausible description of when the judge ought to overrule if we use Raz's notions of exclusionary reasons?

Raz's account would have to go like this. Common law rules in this reasonably just regime possess legitimate authority for the system's judges. Therefore, each such rule constitutes a protected reason for the judge to decide in accordance with the rule whenever he faces what Raz calls a 'regulated dispute', a dispute covered by the rule in question.[114] Since there is and ought to be the power of overruling, Raz would have to say that the scope of the exclusionary reason provided by each common law rule is not unlimited; put another way, some kinds of first-order reasons that might incline the judge to decide contrary to the rule have to be unexcluded (oth-

[112] See Raz, *Practical Reason*, above n. 1, at 140.
[113] With the caveat mentioned above n. 109.
[114] Raz, *Authority*, above n. 1, at 181.

erwise there would be no power to overrule). On the other hand, if Raz's account is correct, the scope of the exclusionary reason cannot be empty, for that means that the judge simply decides whether to overrule based on the balance of all relevant reasons. Raz recognizes that his account commits him to saying that common law judges 'cannot change [precedents] whenever they consider that on the balance of reasons it would be better to do so. They may change them only for certain kinds of [unexcluded] reasons'.[115]

Raz has suggested a tentative list of first-order reasons not excluded by (the exclusionary reason aspect of) a common law rule: common law judges may overrule common law rules 'for being unjust, for iniquitous discrimination, [or] for being out of step with the court's conception of the body of laws to which they belong'.[116] Consider in isolation the last of these three unexcluded reasons for the moment. What sort of overruling would this unexcluded reason license? Something very much like the early Dworkin's implicit doctrine of overruling, which was that judges could not justify overruling decisions by direct repair to the 'background rights' of morality; rather, judges had to justify overruling by repairing only to such of those background rights as had sufficient 'institutional support' in the unquestioned law of their jurisdiction as to be supported by a 'legal principle'.[117]

Both Raz and I have criticized Dworkin on this point for the inherent conservatism of this restrictive notion of overruling. By not allowing any and all moral considerations to compete with the 'conservative principles' behind the doctrine of *stare decisis*, Dworkin's early theory would undesirably cramp the possible growth of the common law through overruling. For this reason, Dworkin's restricted doctrine of overruling was morally undesirable and did not represent a judge's true obligations in this respect.

Yet this same problem exists for Raz's more generous list of unexcluded first-order reasons that can count when a judge decides whether to overrule. I take 'iniquitous discrimination' and 'unjust' to be two kinds of wrongness that are not exhaustive. (If they are exhaustive of what it is wrong to do, then nothing is excluded by Raz's list.) So there must be other types of first-order reasons of morality that could be of great weight on some occasions of possible overruling that are nonetheless excluded from the judge's consideration by Raz's list. Thus, Raz's account suffers the same defect as Dworkin's, only to a lesser degree: some cases that a judge ought to overrule will not be overruled under Raz's account.[118]

[115] Raz, *Practical Reason*, above n. 1, at 140.

[116] Ibid. For a similar list, see Raz, *Authority*, above n. 1, at 114.

[117] R. Dworkin, 'Hard Cases', in *Taking Rights Seriously* (Cambridge, Mass.: Harvard University Press, 1978), 81.

[118] Stephen Perry comes to a similar conclusion regarding the possibility of fitting Raz's exclusionary reason account to the overruling powers of common law judges (although

Perhaps Raz now agrees that his own earlier views about overruling were too restrictive.[119] For Raz now holds that 'an improvement, however small it may be' in the common law, may be enough to justify overruling, so long as the judge is certain that the change is an improvement.[120] Raz's idea of an 'improvement' seems not to restrict the reasons that make the rule better. So long as the overruling judge takes 'notice of the possible bad effects of the very process of changing the law on the social and economic activities dependent on it',[121] and so long as courts do not feel themselves 'free to overrule . . . whenever they wish',[122] any overall improvement seems to justify overruling for Raz.

This is a much more preferable view about when a judge ought to overrule. But it cannot be squared with Raz's earlier argued-for exclusionary reason status for common law rules. What Raz has more recently said about overruling can only be said if we regard common law rules as unprotected first-order reasons. The judicial obligation is to overrule whenever the balance of all reasons (including the reasons inclining against overruling given by the rule-of-law values) makes it right to do so.

If the (rule-of-law and other) reasons that cut against overruling are often of great weight, then the great bulk of the time judges ought not to overrule. This insight might tempt one to seek a kind of temporal accommodation between the 'exclusionary reason' and the 'balance of all reasons' approaches to overruling, namely, that most of the time a judge can treat common law rules as fully exclusionary reasons (that is, as reasons to exclude all other first-order reasons) even if once in a while he will have to not so treat them and balance all reasons to see if the rule shall continue to be part of the law.

At the level of the objective reasons of morality that define what a judge's obligations are, no such temporal accommodation is possible. If the moral argument just concluded is correct, then common law rules should be followed by judges in their decisions only if, on the balance of all reasons, that is desirable. The most such temporal accommodation can be is a recommended decision-strategy to judges: if one can identify in advance types of rules that are most invulnerable to overruling, then there is reason to spend less time considering the question of overruling rules of such types. Such subjective rules of thumb for good decisional strategies

Perry's critique is based on the descriptive, not the moral, inadequacy of Raz's account). Perry, above n. 98, at 243–8. Perry's own account of overruling—in terms of which common law rules do not exclude but discount the weight of antecedently existing first-order reasons— itself is subject to my moral objection; to discount the weight of reasons counting in favour of overruling is to refrain from desirable overrulings.

[119] See Raz, *Authority*, above n. 1, at 190 n.15 (modification and expansion of Raz's earlier views on overruling).

[120] Ibid. at 191. [121] Ibid. [122] Ibid. at 190.

do not change in the least the moral fact that overrulings are correct or incorrect solely depending on the balance of all reasons.

My second example is drawn from statutory interpretation. This is a topic on which Raz has not written extensively, but enough of Raz's views of interpretation are evident that we can use them to flesh out my second moral thought experiment.

If statutes possess legitimate authority for judges within the relevant legal system, then on Raz's account these statutes give judges protected reasons for deciding cases in conformity with the statutes. As with common law rules, Raz recognizes that statutory law is not complete in the sense that it does not cover all disputes that courts must decide. Statutory law has 'gaps', either because of vagueness or other indeterminacy of language and legislative intention, or because of conflict between statutes.[123]

As with common law rules, let us restrict our gaze to 'regulated disputes', that is, a dispute covered by some statute and not covered by any other statute that provides for conflicting legal remedies. Precisely how a statute covers a dispute is no more crucial here than it was for how a precedent covers a later case. Raz argues that all that is necessary for a statute to possess legitimate authority (and thus be a protected reason for judges) is that its content be confined to what the enacting legislature 'can be said to have held or to have presented itself as holding'.[124] Raz appears to recognize three theories of statutory interpretation that would satisfy this requirement: to take the statute's meaning to be the plain meaning of the language used in the statute; to find such statutory meaning only in the intentions of the enacting legislature (its statutory language being then regarded 'merely as presumptive evidence of its intentions'); or to take a statute's meaning to be a function of both plain meaning and legislative intention, constructing an artificial re-creation of what the legislature 'can be said to have held'.[125] Raz himself appears to favour the last of these three possibilities:

> To establish the content of the statute all one need do is to establish that the enactment took place, and what it says. To do this one needs little more than knowledge of English (including technical legal English), and of the events which took place in Parliament on a few occasions.[126]

So, for Raz, the content of a statute (that is protected from competition with other first-order reasons) is a function of (1) the established meanings of the words that appear within it, and (2) the intentions with which such words were written by the legislature that enacted the statute.

This gives us the content of the first-order, prima facie reason that a statute represents. Unfortunately Raz is not similarly explicit about the

[123] Raz, *Authority*, above n. 1, at 72–5.
[124] Raz, 'Authority', above n. 1, at 313.
[125] Raz, *Authority*, above n. 1, at 72 n. 17.
[126] Raz, 'Authority', above n. 1, at 306.

second-order, exclusionary aspect of a statutory reason. For unlike his discussion of common law rules, Raz's discussion of statutes does not specify the scope of the reasons excluded by a statutory reason.

A possible position for Raz would be to say that statutory reasons are exclusionary reasons of unlimited scope, that is, judges ought to exclude all first-order reasons other than the reason given by a statute's plain meaning plus intention as they decide cases regulated by such statutes. An argument for this position might be that judges have, and ought to have, no power to overrule statutes as they can overrule common law rules, and therefore when the statute covers the situation all competing considerations are excluded.

There is a name for this approach in the literature on statutory interpretation; it is called the plain meaning rule.[127] (In Raz's variation, we might call this the plain meaning cum intention rule.) The problem with any such approach to statutory interpretation has been repeated many times:[128] if all other considerations are excluded so that judges are never justified in overruling plain meaning cum intentions, then undesirable (unjust, absurd, or downright silly) interpretations result. For example, a federal statute makes it a crime to interfere with, obstruct, or delay the passage of the US mails; the stated intent behind the statute is to speed passage of the US mails; a federal mail carrier is arrested while he is carrying the mails, and this results in a literal interfering with, obstructing, and delaying of the passage of some US mail; yet the state sheriff who arrests the carrier claims that his act of arrest does not violate the federal statute because the carrier was wanted for murder, and the apprehension of wanted murderers is a greater good than the harm of slightly slower mail.[129]

Even though the plain meaning of the statutory language, and the intention behind it, seem to require conviction of the state sheriff, such an interpretation would be morally wrong. As the US Supreme Court held in this famous case: 'All laws should receive a sensible construction. General terms should be so limited in their application as not to lead to injustice, oppression, or an absurd consequence.'[130] Put in the language of Razian reasons, the scope of the reasons excluded by a statute's plain meaning cum intention cannot be unlimited; first-order reasons of preventing injustice, oppression, or other absurdity must remain unexcluded so that on

127 See generally Arthur Murphy, 'Old Maxims Never Die: The "Plain-Meaning Rule" and Statutory Interpretation in the "Modern" Federal Courts', *Columbia Law Review*, 75 (1975), 1299–317 (arguing that the 'plain-meaning rule obstructs the development of more useful methods of statutory interpretation').

128 See e.g. L. Fuller, 'Positivism and Fidelity to Law—A Reply to Professor Hart', *Harvard Law Review*, 71 (1958) 630–72, at 661–9; see also M. Moore, 'The Semantics of Judging', *Southern California Law Review*, 54 (1981), 151–295, at 273–81 (developing Fuller's argument that judges must have the power to overrule plain meaning).

129 *United States v. Kirby*, 74 U.S. (7 Wallace) 482 (1869).

130 Ibid. at 486.

occasion they can justify overruling the first-order reason given by plain meaning cum intention.

Accordingly, we should give Raz's theory of interpretation a second reading. Paralleling our stipulations about the common law judge, suppose Raz agrees: judges both do and ought to have the legal power to 'overrule' a statute's plain meaning cum intention and to substitute a different meaning for that statute, and that sometimes judges are obligated to exercise this power. In order to frame our moral thought experiment, Raz now needs to specify what are the unexcluded (first-order) reasons outside the scope of a statute's (second-order) exclusionary reasons. Since judges are sometimes obligated to overrule a statute's plain meaning cum intention in their interpretations, the scope of the exclusionary reason given by a statute cannot be unlimited; put another way, there must be some unexcluded first-order reasons that can count against following plain meaning cum intention on some occasions (else there would be in reality no power to overrule plain meaning cum intention).

What is the scope of first-order reasons excluded by a statute's plain meaning cum intention? Former Chief Justice Warren Burger once articulated a highly restrictive list of unexcluded reasons, so let us start with him. According to Burger, it is only those reasons that the legislature (the one that drafted the statute) intended to be unexcluded that determine the rightness of overruling the plain meaning cum intention of the statute.[131]

The moral objection to excluding this much from the justification of when it is proper to overrule plain meaning cum intention is the same as the objection to Dworkin's highly restrictive list of unexcluded reasons for common law overruling. In both cases, highly desirable overrulings will be prevented, because many reasons that justify such overrulings are excluded from counting. Congress can hardly anticipate when a literal application of its words or intentions will lead to an absurd or unjust result (for if it does, it will either frame new statutory language or create legislative history to deal with the problem). So in the case of statutes, giving such a large scope to excluded reasons would result in a large number of highly undesirable interpretations.

A much more lenient list of non-excluded reasons was once given by the US Supreme Court: Judges may consider as an unexcluded reason for overruling the moral absurdity to which a plain meaning interpretation would lead if the absurdity is large. As the Court put it, judges may 'override the literal terms of a statute only under rare and exceptional circumstances . . . [T]o justify a departure from the letter of the law upon that

[131] *Tennessee Valley Authority v. Hill*, 437 U.S. 153, 187 n.33 (1978) ('[T]here must be something to make plain the intent of Congress that the letter of the statute is not to prevail.') (quoting *Crooks v. Harrelson*, 282 U.S. 55, 60 (1930)); see generally Moore, above n. 128, at 280 n. 281.

ground, the absurdity must be so gross as to shock the general moral or common sense'.[132] Yet this much more desirable list seems to exclude nothing, for any type of moral absurdity can count, if its weight as a reason is great enough.

This list is a much more desirable description of a judge's obligation to overrule the plain meaning cum intention of statutes precisely because it does not exclude any reason from overruling the first-order reason constituted by the statute. For that reason, such a list, even though much more desirable, is not compatible with Raz's exclusionary reasons account of judicial obligation. For what the Court says in *Crooks* is this: overrule whenever, on the balance of all reasons, you ought to—with the caveat that, since there are usually good reasons (of predictability, legislative supremacy, etc.) not to overrule the seemingly obvious import of statutory language, it will require weighty reasons in favour of overruling in order to tip the balance that way. This practice is preferable to any that Raz's exclusionary reasons account can recommend precisely for the reason that Raz's account in any form prevents some desirable overrulings.

As with precedent and overruling, so with statutes and overruling of their plain meaning cum intention, it may be tempting to find some temporal accommodation between Raz's 'exclusionary reasons' account and my 'balance of all reasons' account. The ordinary, run-of-the-mill cases do not, it might be thought, call for a balance of all reasons to determine whether the plain meaning cum intention should be overruled; rather, the ordinary cases require only an application of that meaning, justified by the exclusion of competing considerations. Only extraordinary cases, to finish the thought, call for Moore's 'balance of reasons' approach, for it is only in those cases that the question of overruling even arises.

Ruth Gavison, for example, appears to seek this kind of accommodation when she criticizes my account of overruling plain meaning as being 'a misleading claim from the practical point of view'.[133] More specifically, she states:

> It is true, logically, that whenever judges 'apply' the ordinary language of a statute . . . they make a judgement that no moral or other reasons suggest that they should do otherwise. Nonetheless, saying that in such cases judges indeed applied the norm to cases is justified. These cases are easy ones.[134]

As I understand Gavison's point, it is a psychological ('practical') point about how judges ought to approach their task of interpreting statutes. If they can type cases where the reasons behind an 'ordinary meaning' read-

[132] *Crooks v. Harrelson*, 282 U.S. 55, 60 (1930).

[133] R. Gavison, 'The Implications of Jurisprudential Theories for Judicial Election, Selection and Accountability', *Southern California Law Review*, 61 (1988), 1617–62, at 1633.

[134] Ibid.

ing are unlikely to be outweighed by countervailing reasons favouring overruling, then they may treat the ordinary meaning as if it gave exclusionary reasons. In reality, however (Gavison's 'logically'), what makes an overruling correct or incorrect is whether, considering all reasons, the right balance of reasons was reached. This, again, is not to find a place for Ratz's exclusionary reasons within morality's objective reasons; rather, only a place for certain subjective reasons for not considering certain items as the decisional strategy most likely to bring about the right action by a judge.

If common law and statutes are exhaustive of the law of some jurisdiction, then the two examples just considered are sufficient to demonstrate a quite general point: by Raz's analysis of legitimate authority it is morally undesirable to conceive of law as possessed of legitimate authority. By the analysis given above, no common law or statutory rule constitutes a protected reason for judges to follow it.

This point, in turn, should lead to another. Since (as Raz admits) our concept of law influences our concept of authority as much as the other way around, we should reject the conclusion that law does not possess legitimate authority for judges voluntarily sitting in a just legal system. Rather, we should use the above insight to say that the concept of legitimate authority ought not to be analysed in terms of protected reasons. Rather, authoritative norms, law included, should be seen as giving first-order reasons for conforming behaviour; these first-order reasons may well be of great weight, but they should not be seen as accompanied by an exclusionary reason that protects them against overruling in light of certain non-legal considerations.

Indeed, the moral argument provided by these two examples can be extended beyond law and other authoritative norms to include promises and commands. Morality never gives us reasons that exclude morally compelling considerations from counting to determine the rightness of keeping some promise or following some order. Morality never does this because nothing can be excluded in the balance of the objective reasons of morality without leading to moral error. The reasons provided by laws possessed of legitimate authority, promises, or commands can only be first-order reasons, often of great weight in the balance of reasons that determine the rightness of our behaviour. Whenever they are additionally considered to be (second-order) exclusionary reasons, their weight gets exaggerated and moral error results. Although such moral error will not often be the case because the great weight of authoritative laws, promises, or legitimate orders as reasons means they will usually win anyway, whenever it is the case, Raz's account of our obligations is morally inferior to the alternative (first-order only) conception.

IV. THE OBJECTION TO RAZ'S MOTIVATIONAL CLAIM

Raz's explicit definition of 'exclusionary reasons', as we have seen, is not the justificatory interpretation. Rather, it is the motivational interpretation, according to which an exclusionary reason is a reason morality gives each rational agent to exclude certain reasons from their motivations as they act. On this interpretation, Raz's claim is that rules possessed of legitimate authority give those subject to that authority reason not to be motivated by rule-excluded reasons. It is this motivational version of Raz's claim that I want to examine here.

To begin with, notice that if one rejects Raz's justificatory claim, one undercuts the plausibility of the motivational claim. To see this, imagine that in the absence of any authoritative rule there is a prima facie reason of morality R to do action A. Now imagine that there is a rule possessed of legitimate authority whose content gives reasons not to do A to all actors subject to the rule's authority. For example, there is reason to give surplus food to the homeless in some city, but a city ordinance prohibits the distribution of such food by anyone other than a governmentally licensed agency. If one rejects Raz's justificatory claim about such a rule, then R, which was a prima facie reason to do A before the rule was passed, remains a prima facie reason to do A after the rule was passed; all the rule did was add a new (first-order) reason to the balance of reasons, and R has to compete with that new reason.

If all this is true of how things stand with morality's objective reasons after an authoritative rule is issued, then why would morality contain an injunction to actors subject to the rule not to use R as the motive with which they act? R counted as a good reason for action before the rule was passed, and it still counts as a good reason after the rule is in place; how then could morality forbid actors to be motivated by R as they did A? If R was and is a good reason in morality, a reason that still counts in determining the rightfulness of doing A, how does R become an impermissible motivation with which to do A?

Even if one did not reject Raz's justificatory claim about the effect of authoritative rules on the structure of morality's reasons, the motivational claim remains very implausible for the examples with which we are here most concerned: authoritative rules. The ordinance just imagined, for example, can plausibly be supposed to give citizens a new (first-order) reason not to do A. But why would such an ordinance also give citizens a new (second-order) reason not to do A for reason R? Those in authority who issue rules are concerned about conforming behaviour; rarely are they concerned with the motives with which citizens conform their behaviour to the rules.

Raz's earlier-mentioned example of Colin's promise[135] does give an instance whereby the promisor has an obligation not to act for certain reasons because he promised not to act for certain reasons. Similar examples could be constructed for authoritative rules, wherein the content of the rule is explicitly about an actor's motives rather than his behaviour. For example, a statute is passed making it unlawful to invoke criminal process for motives of revenge or private gain. Yet as was pointed out earlier,[136] almost all authoritative rules, like almost all promises, do not have a content concerning itself with citizens' motivations; rather their content is about behaviour alone, as in the rule, 'Don't kill.' Indeed my own reading of Raz confirms an observation made earlier by Chaim Gans.[137] Raz nowhere gives examples of exclusionary reasons (in the motivational sense) that do not depend on the special content of a promise or a rule (namely a content directed to motives rather than actions). This severely undercuts Raz's claim that he has given an analysis (with his concept of exclusionary reasons) of how rules and promises *as such* affect our reasons for action.

So without going further, we have sufficient reason to reject Raz's motivational claim with respect to authoritative rules. Still, since Raz makes the motivational claim explicitly for many items besides authoritative rules (decisions, valid moral rules, social rules, etc.), and since there is a strong tradition in ethics with which Raz aligns himself when he makes such broader claims, I shall present a third and more general objection to Raz's motivational claim.

A. 'Ought Implies Can' Applied to Raz's Motivational Claim

It is often and correctly observed that our obligations presuppose that we can either perform, or refrain from performing, those actions covered by such obligations. Although this is sometimes thought to be a formal principle, it is in fact a substantive moral principle. Because morality ought not to make demands on us (obligate us) in ways that are unfair, it must contain an 'ought implies can' principle.

There has been a long-standing debate in moral philosophy about the meaning of the 'ought implies can' principle, particularly focusing on the sense of 'can' as used in the principle. There are two mistakes to be avoided. The first is to give too strong a reading to the principle. In the strong sense of 'can', the principle would commit us to a libertarian metaphysics, in the sense of 'libertarian' that is opposed to 'determinist'. Yet compatibilists about the free will issue, such as myself, have long urged

[135] See above text accompanying n. 95.

[136] See above text accompanying n. 96.

[137] Gans, above n. 90, at 392–4.

that the principle does not so commit us.[138] The 'can' in the principle does not refer to anything as strong as contra-causal freedom to act; a simple ability to act will suffice to satisfy the principle. Following Herbert Hart's lead,[139] I have analysed that ability into a capacity to act in requisite ways coupled with a fair opportunity to so act.[140] Such capacities and opportunities may be present even for choices and actions that are fully determined by causes external to the will of the actor.

The opposite mistake is to give 'can' too weak a reading. One might think if we do some acts of type A on some occasions, that is enough to show that we can do acts of type A. This mistake as applied to Raz's motivational claim is the following: if we do on occasion act for certain reasons but not others, then we can act for certain reasons but not others. Yet any such weak behavioural reading of 'can' leaves out the element of control that gives the 'ought implies can' principle all of its plausibility. Notice that in this weak sense of 'can', a broken clock can tell the correct time—because on some occasions (twice every twenty-four hours) it does tell the correct time. Left out by this weak sense of 'can' is the general ability (capacity plus opportunity) of a clock to control the match between the correct time and the times shown on its face. The same critical omission would be present if one were to use this weak sense of 'can' in the 'ought implies can' principle. It is not true that people can act for some reasons but not others if they have no ability to control their motives for acting, in the only sense of 'can' relevant to the principle.

If we apply the principle so construed to Raz's claim that we have obligations to have certain reasons but not others as the motives with which we act, we have a problem. As James Brown observed some years ago, 'clearly there are at least difficulties in the way of accepting that it is within an agent's power, on a particular occasion, to determine which motive will be the one which moves him to action . . .'[141] If this is so, how can it be the case that morality obligates us to act on some reasons but not others?

There are only two responses open to Raz here. One, he could do what Brown did when faced with this impasse, which was to deny that the ought/can principle is part of morality. Or two, Raz could hold on to the ought/can principle but deny that we lack the ability to choose the reasons for which we act. This latter tack would commit Raz to developing a (psychological) account of the (subjective) reasons on which we act that makes it plausible that our motives are included amongst the items that we can will.

138 M. Moore, 'Causation and the Excuses', *California Law Review*, 73 (1985), 1091–149, at 1139–48, reprinted as ch. 12 in *Placing Blame*, above n. 70.

139 H. Hart, *Punishment and Responsibility* (Oxford: Oxford University Press, 1968).

140 Moore, 'Causation', above n. 138, at 1148–9.

141 J. Brown, 'Moral Theory and the Ought-Can Principle', *Mind*, 86 (1977), 206–23, at 210.

In this subsection I explore briefly what might be said for the first strategy, and in the succeeding subjection I explore what Raz would have to say to use the second strategy. The results of both analyses will be that neither strategy is viable, from which it follows that morality does not contain any norms giving us any reasons to act for certain reasons but not others.

The most promising route to defending the view that morality need not contain the ought/can principle, to my mind, is the following. The content of 'ought' statements are given by descriptions of the actions that are right or wrong to do. Our present formulation of such descriptions, I argued earlier, are inherently incomplete because there are many unanticipated situations of conflict between norms where an actor will be justified in violating one or more of them ('violate' them, that is, as those norms are formulated without such exceptions). Such exceptions, however—and here is the crux of the argument—do not contain the excuses. Even though there are moral principles that determine when an actor is excused and therefore not culpable, such principles (unlike principles of justification, which are just other conflicting moral norms about actions) are not part of the norms of obligation. Excuses, it is often said, relieve an actor of culpability for violating a moral norm; they do not make the action he did right. The action is still wrong when done by an excused actor because the action still falls under a moral norm that contains no exception for such excuses.

Therefore, one might continue, there is no unfairness in a morality that does not contain the ought/can principle. Such a morality can say to individuals: 'You ought to do A even if you lack the ability to do A; but of course, you will not be blameworthy for your (inevitable) failure to do A if you lacked the ability to do A because in that event you will be excused.'

This is in fact a pretty good description thus far of morality. Yet does it help extricate Raz from his difficulty? Imagine a norm that obligated us to do some type of action A, and that A was a type of action that no person ever had, or is likely in the foreseeable future to have, the ability to perform. For example, 'All persons ought to make causation work backwards through time whenever they can do so to save an innocent life.' There is a universal excuse to our daily violations of such a norm because none of us has the ability to exert causal influence backwards through time. Does it make sense to think that morality contains such a norm, when all creatures to whom it applies are universally excused for its violation?

To be untroubled by norms requiring actions that no one can perform would be like a hard determinist who nonetheless proclaims his moral realism about the norms of obligation. As in: 'Yes, culpability (including absence of excuse amongst its requirements) requires contra-causal freedom, and yes, no rational creature possesses contra-causal freedom, but since such lack of freedom only has to do with excuses, what does its lack have to do with the existence of the norms of obligation? There are such objective moral norms, giving each of us reasons to act on them, even if none of us can ever act on them.'

I take this to be an absurd position because it makes the norms of obligation irrelevant to our actual behaviour. (It severs, that is, the connection between the objective reasons morality gives us to act and the subjective reasons on which we do act.) Although such a morality escapes the unfairness objection—because no one can be blamed—by the same token such a morality would be useless to us. I take that uselessness to be reason enough to reject this route to saving Raz's second-order reasons. Some of us, some of the time at least, have to be able to choose the reasons for which we act if morality can contain the injunction to act for some reasons but not for others.

B. Can We Will the Reasons on Which We Act?

Whether we can make certain reasons be our reasons for performing some action depends on a theory about subjective reasons for action. More specifically, it depends on a part of such a theory that I have hitherto ignored in my brief comments about subjective reasons in this chapter, namely, what the relation must be between our beliefs and desires, on the one hand, and our actions, on the other.

That there must be some such relation should be obvious. At the very least, there has to be a 'rationalizing' relation between a belief/desire set and an action for that belief/desire set to have been my reason for doing some action. As I have elsewhere analysed this rationalizing relation:[142]

1. Actor X desires that the state of affairs described by q obtain;
2. X believes that in situation s, if he performs the action described by p, then q will obtain; and X believes that he is in situation s;
3. X does p.

The rationalizing relation between action p and X's desire that q obtain is that both p and q enter into the content of X's means/end belief in the requisite way, namely, p in the antecedent clause and q in the consequent clause. Such a rationalizing relation must hold or else X cannot be said to be acting for a reason (nor could he be said to be rational).

It should also be obvious that this rationalizing relation between belief/desire sets and actions is not enough to determine the reasons on which we act. Imagine that I want very much to offend you; I believe that if I blow smoke in your face, then you will be offended by me; and I blow smoke in your face. We yet do not know whether I blew smoke in your

[142] M. Moore, 'The Nature of Psychoanalytic Explanation', in L. Laudan (ed.), *Mind And Medicine: Pittsburgh Series in the Philosophy and History of Science*, 8 (Berkeley: University of California Press, 1983), 5, 11–14.

face for the reason that I wanted to offend you. All of the above may be true of me and yet I blow smoke in your face for an entirely different reason. For example, you are in danger standing where you are, and I, knowing that you will move out of danger if I blow smoke in your face, cause you to move by blowing the smoke.

Whether saving you or offending you is the motive with which I blew smoke in your face cannot be settled by looking for the requisite rationalizing relations; both belief/desire sets stand in that relation to the action in question. Moreover, it simply is not true that every rationalizing belief/desire set that we ever possess is at least a 'mixed motive' for our actions, else psychoanalysis, history, and literary criticism become much too easy. There are (in Ernst Jones's early and useful coinage[143]) 'rationalizations', that is, belief/desire sets that we possess that exhibit the actions one performs as rational but that were not the real reasons on which we acted.

So some other relation is needed between our mental states and our actions if the former are to be our reasons for performing the latter. The consensus in the contemporary philosophy of mind about the nature of this additional relation is that it is a causal relation. Of all the belief/desire sets that we possess that rationalize a particular action we have performed, the set(s) that caused us to so act was (were) our reason(s) for so acting. That is why psychoanalysis, history, and interpretation of novels are such difficult activities. In each, we must discern which of the rationalizing belief/desire sets that could have caused some action, did in fact cause it.

If the causal theory of (subjective) reasons for action is correct, then it follows that we cannot choose the reasons on which we act. On the causal account of reasons, we cannot make something be our motive for the same reason that we cannot manufacture a causal relation between solar flares and cancer. In both cases, whether there are such causal relations is a question of scientific fact over which we have no control.

We can tell ourselves stories about what our reasons are or were for some action, and we can (and often do) even pretend that we can know such things with certainty because we can just make it be true that our reasons are this rather than that. But simple mistakes, or those motivated mistakes we call self-deception, are as common as they are precisely because one cannot make it be true that our reasons are one rather than the other.

Notice that our inability to choose the reasons on which we act is not presented as some corollary of the hard determinist thesis that we cannot choose which actions to perform. I assume that we have already answered the hard determinist with our earlier mentioned compatibilism: in the relevant (compatibilist) sense of 'can', we can choose our actions. My point

143 E. Jones, 'Rationalization in Everyday Life', *Journal of Abnormal Psychology*, 3 (1908), 161–9.

here is that, in the exact same (compatibilist) sense of 'can', we cannot choose which of our belief/desire sets will be the reasons on which we act. Reasons are not among the possible objects of our willing, even though the actions for which they are reasons are.

Some further clarifications are doubtlessly in order. It is commonplace in the philosophy of action to distinguish between basic and complex descriptions of actions.[144] A basic act is a kind of act I do by simply willing it, not by doing some other action. Moving my finger, for example, usually describes a basic action because I do not do something else in order to do it.[145] A complex act, by contrast, is a kind of act I do only by doing some other act. 'Killing someone', for example, is always a complex description because we cannot simply will the death of another; we can cause such a death but only by doing some other act, such as moving a finger that pulls a trigger that . . . etc.

What the causal account of our subjective reasons makes implausible is that we can will the reasons on which we act as a basic (mental) act. A defender of Raz and Kant might respond that, even so, we can indirectly cause ourselves to be motivated by one reason rather than another, and that our ability to perform such complex (mental) action is all that is required for morality fairly to demand of us that we act on some reasons but not others. Consider the following possibilities:

1. The causal account of reasons for action does not rule out the possibility that, sometimes at least, we can will desires into and out of existence. Harry Frankfurt has persuasively argued that persons characteristically have some of this ability, which he calls the ability to form second-order wants (i.e. wants to have, or not have, certain wants).[146] Much earlier, Bertrand Russell presupposed such an ability when he recommended a route to happiness alternative to satisfying the desires that you presently possess—namely, will away the desires that you clearly will not be able to satisfy.

2. The causal account of reasons for action does not rule out the possibility that, sometimes at least, we can even will beliefs into or out of existence. While this is never as easy as William James made it seem—if believing determinism to be true leads to unpalatable consequences for

[144] See Moore, *Law and Psychiatry*, above n. 57, at 68–9.

[145] True, many other things must happen in order for me to move my finger, such as certain synaptic firing patterns must take place, certain impulses must be sent down the nerves, certain muscles must contract; but I do not do any of these except in the sense that I move my finger and these events are thereby brought about.

[146] H. Frankfurt, 'Freedom of the Will and the Concept of a Person', *Journal of Philosophy*, 68 (1971), 5–20; Frankfurt's 'second-order desires' theory of the person is further developed in H. Frankfurt, 'Identification and Wholeheartedness', in F. Schoeman (ed.), *Responsibility, Character, and the Emotions* (Cambridge: Cambridge University Press, 1987).

you, then just will it out of your beliefs[147]—more recent work gives plausibility to the notion that persons can will changes of belief in themselves.[148]

3. Neither does the causal account of reasons for action deny that, sometimes at least, we can arrange the circumstances in which an action can be performed just so that the only possible reason for which we could have done the action, if we do it, would be some one desire.[149] In the smoke example, if we wanted to make sure that our contemplated act of blowing smoke in another's face was not done to offend him, we could make prior arrangements with him so that any smoke coming his way from us is to be taken by him as a warning. Then we will know that he cannot be offended by the smoke, and thus, unless we are irrational, when we do blow smoke at him we cannot be trying to offend him rather than warn him.

Each of these three capacities to cause ourselves to have certain reasons does not give us the ability simply to will there to be a relation between certain of our belief/desire sets and our actions any more than the ability to complexly cause a wiggling of one's ears (done by moving them with one's hand) gives one the ability to simply will the ears to move. Rather, each of these three abilities would only allow us to choose our reasons in the sense that we can do other things by virtue of which, when we do action A, it will be more likely to have been for some reasons and not others. Such 'furniture arranging' may be done by eliminating competing desires; it may be done by eliminating the means/end beliefs needed for certain desires to be reasons for a certain act; it may be done by arranging exterior circumstances such that only one desire can be satisfied by a given action.

4. A fourth ability that we possess is not incompatible with a causal account of reasons for action. Within limits, we can choose what it is we will consider and deliberate about when we are trying to decide what to do. We do have some ability to arrange this bit of mental furniture too, and it is plausible to think that this bit of arranging has some effect on which reasons it is that end up motivating us to do or refrain from doing the action. Again, however, such an ability is not an ability to simply will some belief/desire set to be the reason for which we act; it is a complex causing of our being caused to act by a certain reason, with no guarantee at all of success.

[147] W. James, *The Will to Believe* (New York: Longmans, Green and Co., 1898), 147.

[148] See Barbara Winters, 'Acquiring Beliefs at Will', *Philosophy Research Archives*, 4 (1978), 433–5; Winters, 'Believing at Will', *Journal of Philosophy*, 76 (1979), 243–56. Richard Wollheim accurately attributes to Freud the belief that we can will belief-eliminating forgetfulness (belief-eliminating at the conscious level at least). R. Wollheim, *Sigmund Freud* (London: Fontana, 1971), 82–3. For my scepticism about this, see Moore, above n. 57, at 318–19.

[149] I owe this example to Herbert Morris.

Why cannot Raz simply adjust his idea of second-order reasons so that, he might say, morality gives us reasons to do certain actions (like confining our attention to certain things but not others, changing certain desires, certain beliefs, or certain features of the situation in which the action might take place), that will make it more likely that when we act, we will act for some reasons and not others? Raz rather too quickly rejects this suggestion on the grounds that it would make exclusionary reasons 'ordinary (first-order) reasons not to consider the merits of the case (i.e. not to perform a certain mental act)'.[150] Yet Raz might use the suggestion to contend, not that the exclusionary reasons of morality are such reasons to perform certain mental acts, but that we have such (first-order) reasons to perform such mental acts because that is the only way we can approach our (second-order) obligation not to act on certain reasons.

So construed, Raz's defence to my psychological objection would concede that we cannot choose the reasons on which we act as a basic act while contending that we have enough ability to indirectly cause the reasons on which we act so that morality can contain exclusionary reasons without violating the ought/can principle. I am doubtful that we have such indirect causal power, for despite my four earlier concessions I think it rare that we can will desires or beliefs into or out of existence, rarer still that we can do so in order to affect a particular decision, rare that we can arrange the circumstances of action such that only one likely consequence of our action can have been the object of our reason for doing it, and rare that we can direct our motivation by channelling the directions of our conscious deliberations. Of course, by its nature such an issue is difficult to resolve with a knock-down argument either way. So I shall leave it.

Supposing that I am correct on our lack of any significant ability to change our reasons if those reasons are construed to be causes of our actions, then in order to say that we choose our reasons at all, Raz must reject the causal account of subjective reasons for action that is incompatible with such ability, and he must substitute for that account his own account of a relation between rationalizing belief/desire sets and actions that makes it plausible that we have greater control over our reasons than the causal account allows. Raz is not unaware of a body of philosophical literature that undertakes both of these tasks, since he cites much of it at one point in his work.[151] Raz assumes, however, that the issue is 'of too little relevance' to his concerns of charting the structure of the objective reasons of morality, related as the issue is only to the nature of the subjective reasons on which we act. [152] If I am correct so far in the argument of this part of the paper, Raz cannot afford the luxury of this assumption.

[150] Raz, *Practical Reason*, above n. 1, at 48.
[151] Ibid. at 21, 179–80 n. 2.
[152] Ibid. at 21.

Raz must undertake the two tasks just mentioned. Both of these tasks are difficult. (1) How does one resuscitate the now difficult-to-motivate arguments of Ryle, Peters, Melden, Winch, MacIntyre, Louch, and others, that 'reasons cannot be causes'?[153] Donald Davidson's 1963 demolition[154] of the five leading arguments of that literature seems difficult to answer. (2) How does one make out a positive account of the relation of reasons to actions, something like Richard Taylor's metaphysics of 'agent-causation'[155] or Tony Flew's metaphysics of 'inclining causation',[156] each of which purport to allow actors to create a unique kind of causal relation between themselves and their actions? Such accounts may well allow actors the power to directly create (i.e. to will) a kind of relation between their mental states and their acts, but the accounts themselves posit an ad hoc notion of causation that is very hard to justify.

These tasks are thus not easy to sustain. Since Raz has not undertaken them, I will not give the detailed rebutting arguments I would give to support my doubts about the possibilities for success here. If the Ryle/Taylor view of the nature of our subjective reasons is the foundation for Raz's motivational claim, as I have tried in this section to show that it is, then that claim rests on very shaky psychological foundations that are in need of shoring up.

V. AN OBJECTION TO RAZ'S DECISION-STRATEGY CLAIM

The third interpretation of Raz's claim (that rules give exclusionary reasons to those subject to the rule's authority) is the decision-strategy interpretation, namely, the claim that such persons should not allow the 'excluded' considerations to enter their deliberations about what to do. This is, as we have seen, a claim about psychological processes to be used in reaching correct moral decisions; it is not a claim about certain items being excluded from counting towards the correctness of some decision (the justificatory interpretation), nor is it a claim about certain items being impermissible motivations with which an otherwise permissible act may be done (the motivational claim).

Although there are three distinct claims being made by Raz with his concept of exclusionary reasons, they are related closely enough that if my

[153] For the citations and a discussion of these works see Moore, above n. 138, at 1124 n. 95.

[154] Davidson, 'Actions, Reasons and Causes', *Journal of Philosophy*, 60 (1963), 685–700, reprinted in D. Davidson, *Essays on Actions and Events* (Oxford: Oxford University Press, 1980) (the latter collection containing further anti anti-causal accounts of reasons).

[155] R. Taylor, *Action and Purpose* (Englewood Cliffs, NJ: Prentice-Hall, 1966).

[156] Anthony Flew's dualistic causal views were put forward in support of my own compatibilist metaphysics, in Flew, 'Psychiatry, Law and Responsibility', *Philosophical Quarterly*, 35 (1985), 425–32, at 430–1. For my response, see Moore, 'Causation', above n. 138, at 1120–1.

objections to the first two claims succeed, then that is sufficient to reject the third claim as well. To explain: suppose I am right that no otherwise good reason ever has its justifying power stripped from it by being excluded by an authoritative rule; suppose I am also right that no otherwise laudable motivation for an action is ever transformed into an impermissible motivation by the action falling under an authoritative rule; then how could it ever be rational and moral for an actor to exclude from his considerations those very same (right-making and motivating) reasons? In other words, (1) if the justice of some rule does count in justifying some action under that rule as right, why would an actor ever adopt a decision strategy that excluded considerations of the justice of the rule from his deliberations? (2) If the justice of some rule is a permissible and laudable motive with which to motivate one's action under that rule, why would an actor ever adopt a decision strategy that excluded consideration of the justice of the rule from his deliberations? As a general decision strategy, excluding such things only makes sense if those things are similarly excluded either from counting as right-making characteristics or from being permissible motivations.

Thus, Raz's decision-strategy claim is hostage to either his justificatory claim or his motivational claim being true. If the objections presented thus far convince us that neither the justificatory nor the motivational claim can be made out, then the decision-strategy claim fails as well.[157]

Apart from this rather blunderbuss objection to Raz's decision-strategy claim, there is a finer-grained and independent objection to be made. This objection applies to Raz's specific application of his decision-strategy claim to the decision strategies of judges.

My general argument structure in this section begins by noting that Raz's psychological claim about decisions under authoritative rules, as

[157] As a limited claim—about desirable decision procedures only for certain narrow areas—the psychological claim can be plausibly made independently of the justificatory or motivational claims. Thus, as I noted earlier, above text accompanying nn. 122–3, if judges could identify in advance types of common law rules where overruling was so unlikely to be desirable that even considering the question was more costly than not overruling the few cases within that class, then judges had reason to exclude considerations urging overruling from their deliberations in those cases. Similarly, I noted earlier, above text accompanying nn. 133–4, that if judges could identify in advance types of statutes where overruling of the statute's plain meaning was so unlikely to be desirable that even considering the question was more costly than not abandoning the few plain meanings that ought to be abandoned, then judges had reason to exclude considerations urging overruling plain meaning from their deliberations in those cases. Similarly, if judges could identify in advance types of considerations that do count in making the overruling of plain meaning or common law rules desirable in fact but which are for them distorting considerations—they characteristically overweight them for one reason or another so that if they consider them at all they get more cases wrong than otherwise—then judges have reason to exclude such considerations from their deliberations. But these require special showings, showings that cannot plausibly be made for statutes or common law rules (let alone for the class of authoritative rules) across the board.

Raz himself fleshes it out for common law rules and statutes, excludes just the things that a judge needs in order to be able to conform his decisions to the rules. The result is that a judge cannot simply 'follow the rules'; nor, by hypothesis, can he supplement the rule with the excluded considerations; by necessity, therefore, since he must decide, on Raz's account he must decide without recourse to reason, not just in hard cases but in all cases.

If this conclusion is as unpalatable as I believe it is, then one of the premises that leads to it must be rejected. I would reject Raz's theory that obligates judges to exclude from their deliberations competing and dependent first-order reasons. Raz, no doubt, would reject the premise that judges cannot simply follow the rules (in at least some cases) if his decision-strategy claim is correct. Since this last is where issue is joined, this section is devoted to its examination. I do so, first, in the context of common law reasoning, and second, in the context of statutory interpretation.

A. The Ratio of Precedent Cases as Giving Judges Reasons to Exclude Other Considerations From Their Deliberations

In our prior discussion of Raz's theory of precedent in Section III, we made do with an unspecified notion of what a common law rule was and gave Raz his assumption that there were 'regulated' common law disputes, i.e. disputes where a binding common law rule was applicable. We did this in order to focus the discussion on overruling. Now let us take back the assumption, and ask how a common law rule gets extracted from a precedent case so that it can 'regulate' future disputes.

Raz's account, although complicated, is attractive in that it reflects many common sense things we say and think about the law made by judges. Raz implicitly distinguishes three levels of influence that a precedent case may have on the decision of future cases:

1. The precedent case has a *ratio decidendi*, or holding, that is authoritative (although subject to overruling as above discussed) for subsequent judges;[158]
2. There is a narrower rule of law for which the precedent case may come to stand if subsequent courts exercise their powers to distinguish the precedent case from their own; on Raz's view, such distinguishing can only narrow the holding by eliminating some precedent fact as inessential, but a court may not broaden the rule in the guise of distinguishing;[159]
3. There is a much broader rule of law with which the precedent case may come to be associated if subsequent judges exercise their powers to

[158] Raz, *Authority*, above n. 1, at 184. [159] Ibid. at 183–9.

extend the rule by analogical reasoning; such analogical reasoning should seek a rule that is as broad as was the value that justified the holding of the precedent case, for in this way analogical reasoning diminishes the undesirable conflict of values within a system of law.[160]

Raz clearly distinguishes questions of judicial law-making, power, and obligation, on the one hand, from the question of what is the law, on the other. The only thing that is the common law is the first item on this list, the holding of the case. The narrower or broader rules for which the precedent case may come to stand are not part of the common law unless and until some court narrows or extends the holdings in these ways.

Answering the question of what the common law is does not, for Raz, answer the question of what are a judge's powers and obligations to change the common law. Judges have the legal power to distinguish or analogically extend a precedent case. Moreover, Raz holds, judges have legal obligations to exercise those legal powers in certain ways and not others. (Raz calls such powers coupled with an obligation 'directed powers'.[161]) When engaged in the act of distinguishing, judges have a legal duty 'to adopt only that modification which will best improve the rule'.[162] More generally, Raz notes that whenever courts have the power to change the common law, they have a legal duty to 'adopt those rules which they judge best'.[163] The narrower or broader rules that subsequent judges have a legal duty to adopt, however, are not part of the law until so adopted; before that law-making act, they are for Raz only moral rules at best.

None of the three judicial obligations that Raz describes—to follow a precedent decision's holding, to narrow it by distinguishing it when appropriate, or to broaden it by analogical reasoning when appropriate—can be accounted for in terms of exclusionary reasons. This is seen most easily with regard to the second and third of these obligations, so I shall initially focus on them. Suppose, with Raz, we regard the ratio of a precedent case as constituting a pre-emptive and protected reason for deciding future cases in conformity with that ratio. This obviously cannot mean that judges should so regard the ratio when they are distinguishing or extending it by analogy, for to carry out their obligations here judges must not exclude any moral considerations. As Raz recognizes, judges should seek

160 Raz, *Authority*, above n. 1, at 201–6.

161 Raz, 'Inner Logic', above n. 1.

162 Raz, *Authority*, above n. 1, at 187.

163 Ibid. at 197. I put aside Raz's statement that 'there is no point in saying that judges are legally obliged to use analogical arguments', ibid. at 206, because such a view seems inconsistent with Raz's general views about legal duties to exercise directed powers in certain ways. There are good reasons for judges sometimes to make analogical arguments, just as there are good reasons for judges sometimes to distinguish prior cases; in neither case does Raz think that those reasons are themselves part of the law, or that the rules towards which they lead judges are part of the law. See Raz, 'Inner Logic', above n. 1. If there is nonetheless a legal duty vis-à-vis distinguishing, there should also be one about analogical argument.

the best rule when they distinguish, and they should seek the rule that best describes 'the same purpose or value which justifies the original rule [ratio] on which the analogy is based' when they reason by analogy.[164] These considerations cannot be excluded, so Raz must think that the ratio of prior decisions does not create a pre-emptive and protected reason whenever a judge is engaged in the tasks of distinguishing or extending a precedent case's ratio.

This thought by Raz is not inconsistent with Raz's description of the judicial duty to extend a precedent, for in such cases the dispute is an 'unregulated' one (outside the ratio of the precedent case) and so the ratio need not operate as an exclusionary reason. Yet Raz cannot avoid inconsistency for the activity of distinguishing, for by hypothesis the present case before a judge is within the ratio of a precedent case; how could distinguishing cases be possible at all if a judge must exclude from his deliberations just the moral ideas he needs to justify his narrowing of the precedent court's ratio?

There seem only two escape routes for Raz if he is to maintain his exclusionary reasons account of ratios in the face of the admitted power of common law judges to distinguish. First, he could adopt Stephen Perry's suggestion[165] that the ratio of the precedent case is the reason behind the stated rule of the precedent case, not the rule itself. Thus, the subsequent, distinguishing judge is not deciding a case that is within the real ratio of the precedent case and thus is not bound with its exclusionary force. This has the unhappy consequence that judges never (really) do have the power to narrow a precedent case's ratio by distinguishing, because the narrower rule was really always the ratio all along. Second, and more plausibly, Raz might specify a limited scope to the exclusionary reasons provided by a precedent case's ratio, so that distinguishing, like overruling, would be based only on limited (because unexcluded) considerations. The problem with this possible response of Raz's is that it undesirably constricts the power of judges to distinguish: precedent cases they ought to distinguish they won't because they will have excluded the very considerations that would have led them to distinguish.[166] I conclude that Raz's exclusionary reason account cannot be squared with a judge's legal obligation to distinguish a prior case, even on Raz's own description of that obligation.

Turning to a judge's legal duty to extend by analogy the ratio of a precedent case, Raz's exclusionary reasons account of that ratio places a heavy burden on Raz's theory of what the ratios of precedent cases are. For ratios

[164] Raz, *Authority*, above n. 1, at 204.

[165] Perry, 'Judicial Obligation', above n. 98, at 236–7.

[166] My argument here is strictly analogous to the moral argument made earlier, above text accompanying nn. 115–23, against Raz's exclusionary reasons account of overruling.

must be clear enough that judges in subsequent cases can know when they are to regard their case as governed by the pre-emptive and protected reason of some earlier ratio, and when they are free to make balance of reasons kinds of judgements in giving due deference to past decisions as they extend by analogy their ratios.

Raz adopts a version of the 'classical theory' of the ratio: '[e]ssentially the ratio is the reason(s) by which the court justifies its decision' in its written opinion.[167] Since 'courts may be and often are a little careless in formulating' their *ratio decidendi*, 'it is unreasonable to attribute great weight to the actual formulation of the rule in the hands of the court'.[168] Rather, the ratio is the stated rationale or justification for the stated holding, not the stated holding itself.

Raz thus seeks to avoid the rigidity that marks most versions of the classical theory of precedent, tied as they are to the explicit language used by the deciding court as it states its holding. Raz also seeks to avoid the well-known problem of specifying the level of generality of the ratio of precedent cases.[169] Whatever the generality of the language used by the deciding court in stating the reason is the generality to be used by subsequent courts when they seek to find the earlier ratio.[170]

I have elsewhere expressed some disagreement with Raz's view of the ratio of precedent cases,[171] but let me put those objections aside. Our question here is, if this is the ratio, can it be a pre-emptive and protected reason for subsequent judges? One minor problem in saying that it can stem from the pre-emptive part of Raz's thesis: the ratio of a precedent case is a dependent reason (for the deciding judge) which will exclude (for subsequent judges) the reasons on which it depends. That means subsequent judges are not to count the value (first-order prima facie reason) that justified the precedent court's stated rationale. Yet once we distinguish, as does Raz, a court's stated rule from its stated reason behind its rule and find the ratio only in the latter, there seems little left to be pre-empted by a precedent case's ratio. To avoid such an empty pre-emption, Raz must think that the reasons some subsequent judge may think justify the stated rule of some precedent case may not be the reason stated in the precedent court's opinion. What is pre-empted, Raz might say, are the reasons discovered by subsequent judges, not the reasons stated by the precedent judge. Raz can (and seemingly must) say this, but saying it does not square easily with what Raz elsewhere says are the defining characteristics of a

167 Raz, *Authority*, above n. 1, at 184.
168 Ibid. at 188.
169 See e.g. Moore, 'Precedent', above n. 74.
170 '[A]ll the court's reasons of whatever generality are part of the ratio' (Raz, *Authority*, above n. 1, at 184 n. 9).
171 Moore, 'Precedent', above n. 74.

pre-emptive reason, namely, that what are pre-empted are just those reasons on which the prior decisions depended.

A second criticism is more substantive than simply a demand for consistency. This stems from Raz's understandable desire to have a theory of a precedent decision's ratio that allows subsequent judges considerable leeway in reformulating that ratio in different ways. After all, common law rules do not seem to have a canonical wording in the way that statutes do, and Raz's earlier quoted warnings about exact wording are responsive to this feature of our legal practice.

This leeway for redescription by subsequent judges lands Raz in the midst of the familiar generality problem about ratios. Since there are many equally authoritative but nonsynonymous descriptions of the reasons a court used in its decision, how are subsequent judges to pick one as that decision's ratio? The usual answer is in terms of the value(s) that justified the stated reasons, so that judges are enjoined to use the value that justifies the reasons stated by the deciding judge in order to justify an appropriate description of the stated reason. But this is just the answer that Raz's pre-emptive reasons account precludes.

It is possible that Raz wishes to eschew any leeway for redescription of a prior court's ratio by subsequent judges. If so, he escapes the generality problem by granting authority to all and only the descriptions used by the deciding judge in stating his reasons. Apart from other features making this an unattractive theory of precedent,[172] this would make common law rules very much like statutes, in that both would have a canonical formulation. Since I argue immediately below that statutes cannot be regarded as giving judges pre-emptive and protected reasons without reducing judges to arbitrariness, the same conclusion would hold for common law rules, on this last view of them. I shall accordingly turn to the problems with regarding statutes as pre-emptive and protected reasons.

B. The Plain Meaning cum Intention of Statutes as Giving Judges Reasons to Exclude Other Considerations from their Deliberations

As we have seen, Raz has not worked out a theory of interpretation for statutes in the detail that he has worked out a theory of precedent. This is because Raz thinks that his theory of authority and law 'by itself does not dictate any one rule of interpretation, [but] is compatible with several'.[173]

[172] See J. Stone, *Legal System and Lawyers' Reasoning* (Stanford: Stanford University Press, 1964). Stone accurately characterizes this view of ratio as reducing the content of the common law to a kind of 'lottery' in word selection by judges who, unlike legislators, do not carefully craft the exact wordings of their stated rules or reasons. Raz too scornfully puts aside Julius Stone's point here (*Authority*, above n. 1, at 184–5 n. 11).

[173] Raz, 'Authority', above n. 1, at 317.

Still, the major contours of Raz's theory of interpretation are visible and have been sketched earlier in Section III: we are to treat legislation as a communication from someone in authority, and therefore we should attribute meanings to that person as we would an ordinary person, even though the 'person' in question is a multi-membered institution. The only thing essential to Raz's theory of interpretation of statutes is that such interpretations must be 'the view of the relevant legal institution'.[174]

To make the required attribution of a 'view' to a legislature, Raz, as we have seen, allows only two ingredients: the plain meaning of the words used in a statute and the intentions of the legislature in using those words. Such plain meaning cum intention is what provides the content of the first-order prima facie reasons that statutes give to judges, and all moral values are to be excluded by the second-order reasons that is also given by such content to statutes. As Raz puts the latter point: 'such attributions [of the legislature's views] can only be based on factual considerations. Moral argument can establish what legal institutions should have said or should have held but not what they did say or hold.'[175]

The problem for Raz's exclusionary reason account of a statute's authority is that it excludes just the materials a judge needs to make a fully reason-based interpretation of any statute. For plain meaning and legislative intention are inadequate materials for the application of any statute to any case.

Consider first plain meaning. My objection in Section III was that a plain meaning approach to interpreting statutes was morally deficient because it did not allow for the overruling of plain meaning by purpose, and that such overrulings are morally desirable features of any legal system.[176] My point here is different: plain meanings cannot guide judicial interpretations of statutes by themselves or in conjunction with legislative intentions, and thus Raz's injunction to judges to exclude moral considerations from their deliberations is an injunction to render reason-less judgements.

I have elsewhere dealt in detail with the problems with a plain meaning approach to interpretation,[177] so only a summary need be given here. The linguistic problems stem from the fact that natural languages are riddled with vagueness, open texture, ambiguity, and metaphorical usages,[178] and the language used in statutes is no exception. Raz's recognition of this linguistic fact is the same as Hart's; he concedes that there is an inevitable indeterminacy in statutes such that some cases will be hard cases where the judge must use his discretion, but he balances that concession with the

[174] Raz, 'Authority', above n. 1, at 316. [175] Ibid

[176] See above text accompanying nn. 123–34.

[177] Moore, 'Semantics of Judging', above n. 128; Moore, 'A Natural Law Theory of Interpretation', *Southern California Law Review*, 58 (1985), 277–398.

[178] For a discussion of these attributes of language use see Moore, 'Semantics of Judging', above n. 128, at 181–202.

claim that there will also be easy cases where the statutory language is not vague, open-textured, ambiguous, etc., as applied to the case at hand.[179]

Yet this answer is insufficient, for two reasons. In the first place, in any complex legal system there will be a number of legal standards potentially applicable to any case and those standards will attach legal consequences that are inconsistent with one another.[180] Consider that old stalking horse of American jurisprudence, *Riggs v. Palmer*,[181] the case of the grandson who murdered his grandfather in order to hasten his inheritance. One of the grounds the New York Court of Appeals used to justify not following the plain meaning of the New York Decedents Law was that that statute's plain meaning conflicted with a legal principle, namely, that one should not profit by his own wrong.[182] When the law of a jurisdiction has principles as vague as this, even if there are some cases within the 'core' of included instances of some statutory predicate, those cases will very likely be within the 'penumbra' of some contrary-inclining legal standard. The problem here is not that there is no ordering principle between the two legal standards (although that is also a problem); rather, the problem is that the nonvagueness of some statute as applied to some case is no guarantee at all of there being a similar absence of vagueness in all other legal standards that could bear on that case.

The second difficulty with Raz's 'hard cases/easy cases' answer to the problem posed by vagueness, etc., is that the answer does not specify what gives any predicate in a natural language a 'core' of easy applications. As Herbert Hart once recognized about his own notion of core applications, 'it is a matter of some difficulty to give any exhaustive account of what makes a "clear case" clear or makes a general rule obviously and uniquely applicable to a particular case.'[183] Hart's own answer was in terms of a 'standard instances' or 'paradigm case' theory of meaning, according to which the standard instances from which a predicate took its meaning constituted the core of easy applications of such predicate.[184] Neither this, however, nor alternative criterial or criteriological theories of meaning, are up to the task of specifying a core of easy applications.[185] This leaves

[179] Raz, *Authority*, above n. 1, at 73; H. L. A. Hart, 'Positivism and the Separation of Law and Morals', *Harvard Law Review*, 71 (1958), 593–629.

[180] See Moore, 'Semantics of Judging', above n. 128, at 198–9, 272.

[181] 115 N.Y. 506, 22 N.E. 188 (1889).

[182] One need not rely on the early Dworkin to think that such principles are part of the law. In some jurisdictions, such principles have been enacted by the legislature. See e.g. *California Civil Code* § 3517 (West 1970 and Supp. 1989).

[183] H. L. A. Hart, 'Problems in the Philosophy of Law', in Paul Edwards (ed.), *Encyclopedia of Philosophy*, vi, 264–76 (New York: MacMillan, 1967), reprinted in Hart, *Essays in Jurisprudence and Philosophy* (Oxford: Oxford University Press, 1983), at 106.

[184] See Hart, 'Positivism', above n. 179.

[185] For a detailed discussion of all such theories of meaning and why they cannot provide sense to the idea of there being a core of easy applications see Moore, 'Semantics of Judging', above n. 128.

Raz with the task of articulating some theory of meaning that can make sense of the notion that words have a core of easy applications.[186]

The usual response to the indeterminacy of interpretation created by vagueness, ambiguity, etc., is to urge that such indeterminacy be resolved by judges through use of the purpose or value that a statute may be thought to serve. 'Purposive interpretation' is, indeed, pretty much a staple of post-Legal Realist American legal education. Yet this standard answer is not available to the Razian judge, who is to exclude such values in his interpretive process. Raz's pre-emption thesis regarding authority enjoins the judge to exclude the values that led the legislature to write the rule that it did, and to simply apply the rule. By the argument just given, if judges do exclude such values from their deliberations, they have no choice but to be arbitrary as they seek to resolve problems of vagueness, ambiguity, and the like.

It may be that Raz believes that his inclusion of legislative intention alleviates his linguistic difficulties here. Yet if we pay close attention to what legislative intention can be, such an ingredient can be of no help whatsoever in making a case easy to decide under some statute.

Raz holds that a legislature's intention is a function of the intention of the legislators within it. As Raz puts it, '[e]very attribution of an intention to the law is based on an attribution of a real intention to a real person in authority or exerting influence over authority.'[187] Real people may have two different kinds of intentions when they speak: they intend to achieve some further consequence by their act of speaking, and they intend to mean something by the language they have chosen.[188] We might respectively call these their 'perlocutionary' and their 'locutionary' intentions, respectively.

A speaker's perlocutionary intent is the value he hopes to achieve by speaking. It is his reason for speaking. Accordingly, Raz's pre-emption thesis about authoritative utterances precludes an interpreter of such speech from having recourse to this value. It is a pre-empted or excluded reason that is not to be considered by him.

That leaves the speaker's locutionary intentions. The problem with relying on these intentions in the interpretation of a speaker's utterance are: (1) Most speakers do not have the mental experiences on which the content of such intentions depend; they do not picture paradigmatic exemplars, or recite definitions, of the words they employ. (2) When speakers do have such mental experience, they do not have a Humpty-Dumpty-like intention that the words employed be assigned meaning based on such exemplars or definitions; rather, they may think such exemplars or definitions

186 My own suggestions in this regard are set forth in ibid., at 281–92.

187 Raz, 'Authority', above n. 1, at 318.

188 See Moore, 'A Natural Law Theory', above n. 177, at 338–9.

to be accurate but they realize they could be inaccurate because the meaning of the words they employ is not up to any individual speaker. (3) Even if speakers do have such intentions, an interpreter cannot infer any further intentions about the case before the interpreter; because I intend to eat the salad in front of me, and because the salad in front of me is (unbeknownst to me) your salad, does not mean you can infer that I intend to eat your salad. (4) Neither can an interpreter use a speaker's intended exemplars as the basis for reasoning by analogy without smuggling in (via the criterion of relevant similarity) just what he was to keep out, namely, the value served by the rule.[189]

Alternative to these separate problems for the use of perlocutionary and locutionary intentions of a speaker in interpreting his utterance are the problems that reliance on either such intentions face when it is a legislative utterance that is being interpreted. These are the familiar but unanswered problems of how one constructs an intention out of the diverse intentions of legislators.[190]

The upshot of this is that plain meaning plus legislative intention is insufficient as a tool for statutory interpretation, for this combination by itself cannot guide a judge to a decision in any case whatsoever. If judges are enjoined to exclude from their deliberative processes the values that are needed to supplement a judge's linguistic knowledge, then they are enjoined to be arbitrary.

VI. CONCLUSION: RAZ'S POLITICAL THEORY AND JURISPRUDENCE WITHOUT SECOND-ORDER REASONS

Despite the length of the foregoing chapter, I have criticized only one aspect of Joseph Raz's thought, namely, his analysis of authoritative rules in terms of exclusionary reasons. I have developed three interpretations of just what claim might be made with a conception of exclusionary reasons, and I have given an argument against each interpretation: first, that it would be morally undesirable for the enactment of authoritative rules to have the effect of excluding other moral reasons from counting in determining the rightness of actions done under authoritative rules; second, that it would be unfair for morality to give us reasons not to be motivated by certain reasons as we act, unfair in light of our limited capacity to choose the reasons on which we act; and third, that if authoritative rules exclude from a judge's deliberative processes as much as Raz says they

[189] These arguments are more fully spelled out in ibid. 340–4, and in M. Moore, 'Originalist Theories of Constitutional Interpretation', *Cornell Law Review*, 73 (1988), 364–70.

[190] For a discussion of the problems of intent see Moore, 'Semantics of Judging', above n. 128, at 265–70.

exclude and leave judges with as little to work with as Raz says they do, then such rules require reason-less judgement by our judges.

These reasons are sufficient to convince me that an alternative account of how authoritative rules fit in with our general theory of practical reason must be available. Such an authoritative account makes the rightness of action done under an authoritative norm always depend on the balance of all reasons, with none excluded. Such an account has a place for the normative power possessed by those in legitimate authority, but such power is conceived of in terms of the creation of new first-order reasons for action of great weight, not in terms of second-order protected and pre-emptive reasons. Such an account would not eliminate Raz's attractive service conception of authority, although it modifies it by a matter of degree; legitimate authorities are owed somewhat less deference when the rightness of behaviour in conformity to their directives is always determined by a balance of all reasons rather than by a restricted balance of reasons.

On the alternative account of authoritative rules there is no claim that such rules generally give us (second-order) reasons to exclude certain motives as well as (first-order) reasons to do or refrain from doing certain actions. Only if the content of some rule is explicitly directed to motivations rather than actions does such a rule give us an 'exclusionary reason' in this sense—and even then the authority of a rule is tarnished, because of the unfair demand it places on us to exercise a capacity (choosing our motives) that we do not possess.

On the alternative account of authoritative rules, there is also only limited room for any exclusion of otherwise relevant considerations from an actor's deliberative processes. As has been adverted to from time to time in the body of this chapter, it may sometimes be a rational decision strategy for us to banish certain thoughts from our minds as we deliberate about what to do. We may have reason to use this strategy when we know we have an undue craving for certain items, and we wish to counteract the psychological influence of such craving on our decisions. There is no reason why a similar strategy might not sometimes be appropriate vis-à-vis authoritative rules. But there is no reason to think that authoritative rules as such give the actors subject to their authority a reason to exclude otherwise relevant considerations. On the contrary, there is every reason not to banish too much from our deliberative processes, or else we leave our decisional resources impoverished as we try to act under an authoritative rule. And, again, when the exclusion strategy is a good one, the rightness of the decisions that it produces are not right because the considerations we sought to banish have no weight morally speaking; rather, that rightness is determined with such considerations counting for whatever they are worth.

For these reasons, I conclude that in none of the three senses of the phrase are exclusionary reasons given to actors subject to authoritative rules. Such rules add new reasons to an actor's balance of reasons, but the reasons added are first-order reasons only.

Raz's theories of citizen obligation, judicial obligation, and of law are changed little by the alternative conception of legitimate authority. Raz's piecemeal justification of citizens' obligation of obedience to the law, his non-piecemeal justification of judicial obligations in a just legal system, and his theory of law as a system of norms claiming legitimate authority are changed only insofar as the concept of legitimate authority is changed. The elimination of the concept of second-order reasons from the concept of legitimate authority eliminates second-order reasons from the explication of these ideas too. But otherwise they remain unchanged.

It would thus be a mistake to see my conclusions as a frontal assault on Raz's elegantly linked theories. Tightly related as they are, Raz's theories of law, authority, and citizen and judicial obligation do change together if I am correct in my argument. But the relations between such theories do not change at all.

Part II
Legal Scepticism

6

The Need for a Theory of Legal Theories: Assessing Pragmatic Instrumentalism

According to the central thesis of Robert Summers's *Instrumentalism and American Legal Theory,*[1] the collection of ideas Summers labels 'pragmatic instrumentalism' forms America's only indigenous legal theory. Summers's further thesis is that pragmatic instrumentalism qualifies as a legal theory comparable to three more established competitors: natural law theory, analytical positivism, and historical jurisprudence.

In this chapter on Summers's book, I shall seek to accomplish four tasks: first, to describe the subject of the book—pragmatic instrumentalism—and to describe in more detail Summers's aims and theses regarding his study of pragmatic instrumentalism; second, to raise certain questions about the methodology Summers uses to achieve his aims; third, to suggest how another theorist might have alternatively conceived the enterprise Summers has undertaken in this book; and fourth, to assess Summers's overall thesis that pragmatic instrumentalism is one of four great traditions in legal theory.

I. PRAGMATIC INSTRUMENTALISM AND THE AIMS OF SUMMERS'S BOOK

'Pragmatic instrumentalism' is Summers's label for a collection of ideas about law to which an influential group of early twentieth-century American legal theorists subscribed. From the beginning, Summers is admirably clear about what and whose ideas he has in mind. Generally speaking, pragmatic instrumentalism combines pragmatism in philosophy with sociological jurisprudence and Legal Realism in legal theory. More specifically, Summers has in mind the beliefs of John Dewey in philosophy, and John Chipman Gray, Oliver Wendell Holmes, Jr., Roscoe Pound, Walter Wheeler Cook, Joseph Walter Bingham, W. Underhill Moore, Herman Oliphant, Jerome Frank, Karl N. Llewellyn, and Felix S. Cohen in legal theory.[2]

Summers has organized the beliefs of these theorists into four parts in his book: one on the elements of law; a second on what I would call core issues in contemporary legal theory (theories of precedent, of interpretation, of

[1] R. Summers, *Instrumentalism and American Legal Theory* (Ithaca, NY: Cornell University Press, 1982).

[2] Ibid. at 23.

validity of norms, of change of law, and of the separation of law and morals); a third on the implementation and general functioning of law in our legal system; and a fourth on the efficacy of law and how one judges the success of laws. To understand more precisely what Summers means by 'pragmatic instrumentalism', it may be helpful to restructure this four-part organization into three.[3] First, there are ideas about law that belong to legal theory proper; second, there are ideas about how law and legal institutions should be studied in the social sciences, i.e. ideas about the sociology of law. And third, there are more general philosophical ideas that underlie both the legal theory and the social science approaches to law. Summers's pragmatic instrumentalism, I think, is best viewed as a combination of a legal theory, a sociology of law, and certain general philosophical positions presupposed by both the legal theory and the legal sociology.

The questions of legal theory Summers believes the pragmatic instrumentalists addressed all relate to what is commonly called today a 'theory of adjudication'. This is a theory about how judges decide and ought to decide cases. Within the theory of adjudication Summers discusses the legal positivist and predictivist theories of the pragmatic instrumentalists regarding the validity of legal standards;[4] Summers also discusses the American Legal Realist theory of precedent which advocates looking at what the precedent court did on the facts before it and not at what it said.[5] Summers briefly examines the famous Legal Realist pooh-poohings of logic and plain meaning in legal interpretation.[6] He then analyses the well-known predilection of the Legal Realists for legal reform and the accompanying theory about change in law and the desirability of such change.[7] Finally, Summers discusses the legal positivist tendencies of Holmes, Gray, and others to regard law as having no essential connection to morals in adjudication.[8]

The second set of questions Summers believes the pragmatic instrumentalists addressed concerns the sociological study of law. Here Summers discusses the instrumentalist view about law, namely, that law is essentially a means to certain social goals; Summers also attempts to map the means–goal structure of our legal system.[9] Similarly, Summers analyses structural questions about the legal means available to implement social goals,[10] the nature of the legal personnel who implement social goals,[11] and theories about the roles of force and coercion in the law.[12] Finally, Summers includes in this sociological study of law and

[3] It will become clear from the subsequent discussion that this reorganization of Summers's presentation is not neutral concerning certain matters about which there is doubtless some disagreement between Summers and myself.

[4] See Summers, *Instrumentalism*, above n. 1, chs. 4, 5, respectively.

[5] Ibid. at 147–53.

[6] Ibid. at 153–6.

[7] Ibid. at 83–100.

[8] Ibid. at 176–90.

[9] Ibid. at 60–80.

[10] Ibid. at 193–208.

[11] Ibid. at 209–23.

[12] Ibid. at 224–35.

legal institutions efficacy questions, asking what it means to judge the efficacy of laws and of law, and how one measures it.[13]

The more general philosophical ideas underlying the legal theory and legal sociology just described might be classified collectively as 'pragmatism'. In various parts of the book Summers usefully subdivides these ideas into more discrete packages. First there is a theory of value shared by the thinkers in question.[14] Summers accurately describes this theory of value as both utilitarian in that it seeks to maximize the preferences of the citizens and conventionalist in that it takes the existing wants of citizens as simply more or less intense preferences to be tallied up when the utilitarian calculation is being made. Such utilitarian/conventionalism, Summers rightly stresses, 'largely obliterates the intuitively sound distinction between the wants and interests that citizens in fact pursue and those that they ought to pursue'.[15] It reduces morals to a summing of arbitrary (if shared) desires.

Second, the pragmatic instrumentalists defended a theory of meaning that Summers describes as functionalism. This theory holds that the meaning of any word is a function of the consequences of its utterance in certain contexts.[16] The pragmatic instrumentalists thought functionalism applied to both legal words such as domicile (the meaning of which one understands when one comprehends the legal consequences attached to its authoritative use) and to words of ordinary speech such as glass (the meaning of which one understands when one comprehends the perlocutionary speech acts it is conventionally used to perform).[17]

Three other sets of ideas are linked with the theories of value and of meaning of the pragmatic instrumentalists: a general epistemological and

[13] Ibid. at 239–67. [14] Ibid. at 41–59.

[15] Ibid. at 50 (emphasis in original).

[16] Summers defines functionalism a bit differently than do I. For Summers, functionalism 'holds that the true significance of any term lies in its likely consequences'. Ibid. at 32. The meaning of the word 'glass' for Summers's functionalist would be in terms of the dispositional tendency glass has to break under certain circumstances. The difference between us lies in the kinds of consequences to which a functionalist looks as he seeks the meaning of a word: my functionalist looks to the consequences of uttering 'glass'; Summers's functionalist looks to the consequence of hitting glass (namely, it breaks). Summers may well be closer to the historical functionalism of Felix Cohen (see M. Golding, 'Realism and Functionalism in the Legal Thought of Felix S. Cohen', *Cornell Law Review*, 66 (1981), 1032–57, at 1051–2, for an exposition of Cohen's like confusion of operationism with functionalism); yet I choose to characterize functionalism in a way more amenable to contemporary speech-act theory.

[17] 'Perlocutionary speech act' is a term of art borrowed from the philosophy of language. Speaking is a kind of acting, an insight that generates the phrase 'speech act'. J. L. Austin divided speech acts into various kinds, one of which was 'perlocutionary'. A perlocutionary speech act for Austin was an act that included the consequences of speaking in the description of the speech act itself, e.g.: 'He quieted the mob with his speech' (J. L. Austin, *How to Do Things with Words* (Oxford: Oxford University Press, 1960)). To understand the meaning of the word 'glass', according to functionalism, would be to understand the consequences one could cause by uttering that word in various contexts.

metaphysical position known as pragmatism;[18] a political programme that was progressive and reformist;[19] and an empiricism that revered observable facts above both theoretical entities and moral qualities.[20]

Pragmatic instrumentalism, then, should be seen as a wide-ranging set of beliefs primarily encompassing legal theory and the sociology of law but secondarily encompassing more general positions in philosophy. Pragmatic instrumentalism thus becomes something like a Weltanschauung for Summers, a world view that not only includes beliefs on a wide variety of topics but which also coalesces those beliefs into a system or theory.

Although Summers does not make it a major theme in the book, he does present this cluster of ideas as the middle term in a historical dialectic. He briefly sketches an opposing Weltanschauung of the late nineteenth century, consisting of a conservative political programme, legal formalism in legal theory, Social Darwinism, laissez-faire economics, and a natural law theory of ethics. Summers presents pragmatic instrumentalism as a reaction to this conservative nineteenth-century vision, and then goes on to trace the twentieth-century reaction to pragmatic instrumentalism itself. We are thus to see pragmatic instrumentalism as a kind of way station, a reaction to the excesses of the dominant ideology that preceded it, but a reaction which in turn had excesses of its own that have spawned a new reaction from critics such as H. L. A. Hart, Lon Fuller, John Dickinson, Hans Kelsen, Morris Cohen, and, of course, Summers himself in this book.[21]

In presenting this overview of a wide-ranging set of ideas, Summers enunciates two distinct aims. His 'primary aim' is to further 'the exploration of the instrumental and pragmatic facets of legal phenomena . . .'[22] Summers thus intends the book to be a substantive contribution to legal theory; he intends to use the pragmatic instrumentalists not as objects of historical study but as springboards for his own thoughts on legal theory. Because Summers clearly shows throughout the book that he agrees with much of pragmatic instrumentalism, this springboard is prima facie an appropriate one for him.

Summers's secondary aim in the book is historical.[23] He wishes to display the beliefs of a set of people in a way that may be unfamiliar to us; he hopes to demonstrate a coherence and unity among them that escaped their critics and sometimes even themselves. Summers aims to reconstruct the world view of the pragmatic instrumentalists and, in doing so, to

[18] Summers, *Instrumentalism*, above n. 1, at 31–2.
[19] See ibid. at 29.
[20] See ibid. at 33, 54–6.
[21] Summers names each of these critics (save himself) as the relevant critics he considers as part of the reaction to pragmatic instrumentalism. See ibid. at 38.
[22] Ibid. at 12.
[23] Ibid.

defend both the hidden unity of their disparate beliefs and the partial correctness of some of those beliefs. This is, in other words, a rehabilitative intervention by Summers on behalf of a group of thinkers he feels have been undervalued as legal theoreticians.

Summers seeks to achieve both the legal-theoretic and historical aims of the book by defending what I take to be the book's central theses: first, a philosophical thesis that the cluster of ideas he has described about law, values, social science, and so forth, pass some minimum threshold of coherence so that they constitute a relatively unified theory of law; second, a historical thesis that the influential thinkers Summers names held enough of the beliefs he has described so that they fairly can be called pragmatic instrumentalists and their influence on legal thought can be attributed to pragmatic instrumentalism; and third, an evaluative thesis that pragmatic instrumentalism is a good legal theory—at least as good as the traditional theories about law (analytic positivism, natural law theory, and historical jurisprudence) that Summers regards as the hitherto recognized 'big three' of legal theory—and, in any event, good enough to form an important part of any future synthesis of legal theories that may emerge.[24]

II. METHODOLOGICAL QUERIES

It is helpful to follow Summers's own division of legal-theoretic and historical aims and to raise questions corresponding to each. I shall deal first with Summers's primary aim of advancing our understanding of legal theory, using pragmatic instrumentalism as a springboard for his own thoughts.

There is nothing wrong with using the ideas of others as a springboard from which to launch one's own thoughts. It is a common heuristic and persuasive device to present one's own views as the revised, corrected, more balanced or more sophisticated version of ideas advanced by others. Summers's choice of the pragmatic instrumentalists as his vehicle for this purpose is problematic, however. First, the choice led him to emphasize what the pragmatic instrumentalists emphasized as important to legal theory. Thus much of the work in the book that is original asks questions about the sociological study of law and legal institutions for the simple reason that such things interested the pragmatic instrumentalists. Both Summers and the pragmatic instrumentalists assume that the sociological study of law is relevant to legal theory. Although Summers's book may

[24] See ibid. at 281 (predicting that 'the perfect general theory about law and its use' will include parts of the three traditional legal theories and pragmatic instrumentalism).

advance the sociological study of law, it leaves this basic assumption unsupported.

The core issues of legal theory concern theories of adjudication, legislation, and citizenship. These theories are both descriptive and normative, telling us how judges, legislators, and citizens do and should perform their roles. Whether describing or prescribing, such theories focus on the legitimacy of the conduct and decisions of the occupants of legal roles. For example, a legal theorist focusing on the legislative role either may prescribe the correct limits to which a legislator should seek to legislate conventional morals or may describe the limits thought by legislators in certain systems to be legitimate.

These questions of legitimacy are distinct from the kinds of questions Summers addresses in chapters 2, 8, 9, 10, 11, and 12. These chapters raise questions properly described as part of a sociology of law: questions about the various implementive devices for furthering social goals available in our legal system, about the efficacy of laws and how to measure their efficacy, and so forth. There is nothing wrong with such sociological questions about law. Summers fails to demonstrate, however, that answering these questions will aid in answering the questions traditionally posed by legal theory.

Summers is not unaware of this objection. In his concluding chapter he helpfully summarizes the sociological questions that interest him [25] and recognizes that one might object that 'the questions of pragmatic instrumentalist theory are too "empirical" or too "sociological" '[26] to qualify as part of a legal theory. Summers's response is that legal theory must adopt a sociological approach because of the nature of law itself:

> Law, after all, is not religion, not physics, and not just an applied social science. Law is law. We have to know what it is. We have to understand its methods and uses. And we have to consider what it ought to be. Thus, in matters of method, legal theory must be something more than analytic philosophy, something more than moral theory, and something more than descriptive sociology. Indeed, it must be all of these, yet at the same time more than the sum of its parts. Law has a kind of autonomy of its own.[27]

If I am right in my own view of the nature of legal theory, Summers's response is unhelpful. All inquiries about law may well involve some factual questions, but such a reminder does not answer the objection that legal-theoretic inquiries do not require the particular facts that interest Summers qua sociologist.

Even if one rejects my view of legal theory as hopelessly parochial, Summers needs to develop his own theory about what legal theories should embody. It will not do to assume that we all know what law is and

[25] See Summers, *Instrumentalism*, above n. 1, at 269.
[26] Ibid. at 270.
[27] Ibid. at 271.

thus assume that understanding how 'it' is used must be part of anything that could be called legal theory. Legal philosophy, like all philosophy, cannot take its subject matter for granted. A legal philosopher must develop a theory of what he is philosophizing about. That might or might not include some of the things that interest Summers. We can assess that case only when it is made. For my own part, much of Summers's sociological work leaves the impression of being an answer to a question that is not asked by any properly focused legal theory.

Elsewhere Summers identifies three themes shared by his sociological questions: (1) 'that law is a complex interacting set of means and goals which expresses conceptions of value';[28] (2) that '[l]aw must be brought into being by humans, and thereafter identified, interpreted and applied or modified by them';[29] and (3) that law is 'something for use and in use in daily life'.[30] Such vague generalities may apply to the wide range of sociological questions that interest Summers and they may characterize Summers's answers to such sociological questions. They are not a substitute for a theory about the proper concerns of legal theory. Such themes compare poorly with the unified concerns that animate, for example, H. L. A. Hart's theory of law,[31] Ronald Dworkin's theory of adjudication,[32] or Neil MacCormick's theory of legal reasoning.[33] However much Summers advances our understanding of various aspects of law, he has not advanced something recognizable as legal theory.

Summers's choice of the pragmatic instrumentalists as the springboard to further his own views of legal theory presents a second problem: the mushiness of the theses with which Summers is bound to work. Pursuing this heuristic strategy, Summers must begin his discussions with 'theories' or 'theses' that are, in reality, hardly that. Rather, they are either maxims, slogans, or battle cries of the old Legal Realist assault on legal formalism, or loosely formulated social science generalizations. For example, Summers begins chapter 2 by examining Karl Llewellyn's slogan that we must 'view law as means to ends; as only means to ends'.[34] Summers then uses this slogan as a springboard into his own discussion of the goal-structures endemic to law. Not surprisingly, Llewellyn's maxim hardly directs Summers's thought here, which is much more indebted to Lon Fuller than to any of the instrumentalists. Similarly, Summers begins chapter 3 with another maxim from Llewellyn, that '[s]ociety is in flux, so law needs re-examination'.[35] Small wonder that this reduces Summers's

[28] Ibid. at 270. [29] Ibid. [30] Ibid.

[31] H. L. A. Hart. *The Concept of Law* (Oxford: Oxford University Press, 1961).

[32] R. Dworkin, *Taking Rights Seriously* (Cambridge, Mass.: Harvard University Press, 1978), chs. 2–4.

[33] N. MacCormick, *Legal Reasoning and Legal Theory* (Oxford: Oxford University Press, 1978).

[34] Summers, *Instrumentalism*, above n. 1, at 60. [35] Ibid. at 83.

own contribution to the palliative that 'these thinkers went too far'.[36] Although these thinkers did go 'too far' here as in many other places, correcting their reformist zeal hardly furthers our own understanding of a theory of change in law, the nominal topic of this chapter. Or consider the instrumentalist 'thesis' that begins chapter 9: 'Instrumentalists tended to emphasize the importance of "social engineers"—of personnel, particularly judges—in a functioning legal order.'[37] Summers promulgates a corrective that is as hopelessly bland and vague as this instrumentalist 'thesis': 'In sum, both legal forms (precepts, structures, processes, techniques) and the factor of personnel are of vital import in the functioning of a legal system. And so, too, is the interaction between them.'[38] Surely Summers would not tell us that we need both law and legal personnel to have a functioning legal system if he were not trying to correct the instrumentalists' misplaced emphasis on personnel.

Finally, consider what Summers calls the '"direct action" thesis in instrumentalist writings'.[39] This 'thesis' proclaims that 'the actions of officials are overwhelmingly direct rather than indirect'.[40] This thesis launches Summers into a taxonomy of all the ways the law achieves its various ends by indirect means, concluding that 'it cannot be assumed that in our own system the means on which we rely are overwhelmingly direct'.[41]

In each of these instances Summers's discussion begins with a slogan, or a generalization that is so vague that any qualification of it will be at most a matter of emphasis. With enemies like these, a theory has little hope of gaining friends.

One might raise other queries about Summers's work in the sociology of law that have little to do with Summers's choice of the pragmatic instrumentalists as his springboard for further discussion. In particular, it is striking in reading the sociological chapters (chapter 2, and chapters 8 to 12) how many taxonomies Summers either presents or calls for. Summers apparently considers these taxonomies necessary to a full-fledged legal theory. My own taxonomy of Summers's taxonomies includes:

1. An 'inventory of the main types of goals that law may serve in a modern society',[42] such as preserving order or promoting health.
2. A taxonomy of goal levels that inform particular legal precepts (immediate goals, intermediate goals, ultimate goals).[43]
3. A taxonomy of the 'basic types of relationships between goals and the means of their realization through law' (external, constitutive, and intrinsic).[44]

36 Summers, *Instrumentalism*, above n. 1, at 97.
37 Ibid. at 209.
38 Ibid. at 215.
39 Ibid. at 230–1.
40 Ibid. at 230.
41 Ibid. at 235.
42 Ibid. at 64.
43 See ibid.
44 Ibid. at 69.

4. An 'inventory of law's implementive resources'.[45]
5. A subinventory of implementive 'technique designs' (including private-arranging, grievance-remedial, distributive, regulatory, and penal).[46]
6. A subinventory of implementive devices.[47]
7. An inventory of the legal tasks 'that personnel of various kinds must regularly perform within a going legal system'.[48]
8. An inventory (explicitly adopted from Bentham) of direct and indirect means of implementing legal goals.[49]
9. 'A typology of five basic types of uses of law.'[50]
10. An 'inventory of general factors that may operate to limit the effectiveness of a use of law'.[51]

Summers himself anticipates one objection to this armchair social science, namely, that it is done in the armchair rather than in the field with empirical data.[52] Summers properly rejects any such across-the-board criticism of his sociological method. There is nothing illegitimate about theoretically-oriented social scientists creating taxonomies of variables that can be studied. Intelligent empirical research in social science surely requires such preliminary categorization of what one is studying.

Although a blanket objection to Summers's sociology by taxonomy is inappropriate, his book does not clearly demonstrate the usefulness of some of the taxonomies it provides, even if they were to be continued and elaborated according to Summers's proposals. Some of these lists strike one as 'philosophy by distinction', a legal zoology whose purpose is not always clear. In this category, for example, I would place the inventory of the main types of goals that law may serve in a modern society.[53] It is true, as Summers notes in defence of this taxonomy,[54] that rational basis review of statutes under the equal protection clause requires a court to keep in mind the intelligible goals that a law may serve. Yet such knowledge of values is part of our cultural heritage.[55] Our ability to apply that cultural heritage in understanding particular laws probably exceeds our ability to develop an explicit taxonomy of all such values. If this is so, it is doubtful that the general taxonomy could aid us in deciding particular cases under the equal protection clause.

Summers offers more compelling justifications for other of his taxonomies. In supporting his inventory of legal tasks,[56] for example,

[45] Ibid. at 200.
[46] Ibid. at 199–200.
[47] See ibid. at 196.
[48] Ibid. at 209.
[49] See ibid. at 231–2.
[50] Ibid. at 259.
[51] Ibid. at 261.
[52] Ibid. at 266.
[53] See above n. 42 and accompanying text.
[54] Ibid. at 66.
[55] For a discussion concerning the intelligibility of values, see A. J. Watt, 'The Intelligibility of Wants', *Mind*, 81 (1972), 553–61.
[56] See above n. 48 and accompanying text.

Summers urges that '[i]t would open up avenues of fruitful reflection on the basis of which general factors of inefficacy might be independently identified' and that 'it would provide a set of functional categories around which the various general factors that limit the effectiveness of law could be organized'.[57] Summers hopes that his inventory of legal tasks will aid in organizing his inventory of ineffectiveness factors in the use of law. He further hopes that such knowledge can then be related to his typology of the basic uses of law to form further generalizations about when law is ineffective.[58] Summers may be a bit optimistic here, for we might be sceptical about whether such large or universal generalizations exist about law's inefficacy. Nonetheless, the taxonomies Summers here creates have the provisional justification of all such categorizations in social science: if the categories are necessary in order to frame fruitful generalizations, then they are justified.

Such heuristic and hypothesis-generating justifications do not accompany all of Summers's taxonomies, unfortunately. Too often throughout the book Summers presents his taxonomies in the same way as did Bentham (whom Summers greatly admires); he presents these taxonomies without indicating their intended uses. At times Summers gives the impression that he may share Bentham's view that taxonomies inevitably generate worthwhile understanding and can be spun out without great worry about their exact purpose. Unfortunately this is not the case. If a theorist is going to lead us through some labyrinth of distinctions, we need some advance reason for taking the journey.

Turning to Summers's historical aims, the most obvious query concerns the nature of pragmatic instrumentalism: to what extent is pragmatic instrumentalism a historical phenomenon (as opposed to construction of a theory that Summers is willing to advance). As discussed earlier, Summers does nothing illegitimate in constructing his own legal theory over the abandoned ruins of Legal Realism, sociological jurisprudence, and pragmatism. But to satisfy his historical ambitions, and not just his legal-theoretic ambitions, Summers must convince us of more than the philosophical thesis about the logical coherence of the various ideas he has set forth. In defending the philosophical thesis, Summers need only show that certain ideas (ideas in the sense of timeless propositions) stand in certain logical relations to one another. The ideas must be free from contradiction and must be coherent.[59] To defend his historical thesis and thereby satisfy his historical ambitions, however, Summers must show that certain

[57] Summers, *Instrumentalism*, above n. 1, at 262–3. [58] Ibid.

[59] Exactly what sort of a relation 'coherence' may name is a matter of dispute in philosophy. See e.g. M. Williams, *Groundless Belief* (Oxford: Oxford University Press, 1977), 104–5. By 'coherence' I mean some relation stronger than consistency and weaker than mutual entailment.

historical persons actually had these ideas (ideas in the sense of beliefs, mental states that exist at a time in history) and that these ideas influenced one another (influence here meaning a causal relation between belief states and not merely a logical relation between the contents of such beliefs).

By separating his historical from his legal-theoretic aims, Summers shows that he recognizes these two distinct tasks. He has also thought about what he must do to convince us that pragmatic instrumentalism constitutes a historical phenomenon. Unlike some contemporary legal theorists interested in intellectual history, Summers names the thinkers whose work he discusses, gives a bibliography of their relevant works, and copiously quotes them as he constructs his historical thesis. He attends carefully to what the instrumentalists said as the best evidence of what they believed, and alertly notes differences among the thinkers he is considering whenever they disagreed in their relevant beliefs.

These methodological virtues of Summers's work would be too obvious to praise if it were not so common in contemporary legal scholarship to slight them. Critical legal studies scholars, for example, commonly referee a tournament between ideas without making it clear exactly what the ideas are, or who supposedly adhered to them. When pressed with historical counter-examples, such scholars will respond that their work is not intellectual history, but rather an attempt to show logical relationships between ideas as timeless propositions. When pressed with logical arguments about the incoherence of grouping certain ideas, these scholars can claim immunity because they are seeking a pure history of ideas, arguing that any logical incoherence reflects the contradictions in the thought of the historical subjects of study, not the faulty analytic abilities of the historian. When pressed that these two responses are inconsistent, these scholars offer a third. They claim that the ideas they discuss are neither contemporaneous belief states in causal relations with other belief states, nor are the ideas timeless propositions logically related to other propositions. Rather, these scholars bid us see the critical enterprise as involving unique entities with unique relationships with one another, entities and relations that we can only glimpse but not really comprehend because of our own historical limitations.[60]

In such a climate of legal scholarship, it is thus no small praise to say that Summers rigorously pursues the task of recreating historical beliefs in the persons he names, and that his results are thorough and honest.

Despite Summers's thorough exposition, some queries remain having to do with the book's historical thesis that pragmatic instrumentalism was the legal theory held by the influential persons Summers names. Summers

[60] As a once prominent example, see R. Unger, *Knowledge and Politics* (New York: Free Press, 1975) 12–16.

easily brushes aside one such query early in the book:[61] the objection that the thinkers in question did not call themselves 'pragmatic instrumentalists' nor did they see some of the similarities (of a pragmatic and instrumentalist sort) that lead Summers to so name them. Of course, Summers, as any historian, is entitled to divine similarities among the beliefs of his subjects that they themselves did not see, and he is equally free to name the resulting collection of beliefs in any way that reasonably describes the similarities so discovered.

A related query about Summers's historical thesis merits more serious attention. First, as Summers himself carefully points out, not all of the writers in question held all of the views Summers considers definitive of pragmatic instrumentalism. Second, many of the views these thinkers did share were unfinished: without further elaboration we would not think these ideas complete enough to constitute a theory.[62] Third, the thinkers in question often did not think of themselves as propounding a theory of law as such, however much they may have thought of themselves as propounding the more particular views from which Summers extracts the theory of law he calls pragmatic instrumentalism. These three points together might raise doubts as to whether Summers can truthfully attribute pragmatic instrumentalism to the persons he names.

As Summers himself notes, such considerations force him (even qua intellectual historian) to do some rational reconstruction of the views of his historical subjects.[63] Such reconstruction should not be limited to finding hidden similarities among stated views, and giving a new name to the aggregate of beliefs so related. The reconstruction must also include a weeding out of the unimportant ideas in those being studied; a fleshing out of incompletely developed ideas; and even an outright exclusion of some thinkers' ideas on those subjects where consistency (among the ideas of one thinker, or among thinkers) demands it. The query that arises at this point is whether this kind of intellectual history by rational reconstruction truly differs from the legal-theoretic aim of Summers, i.e. the advancement of what he believes to be the right legal theory.

This last query is only a query, and not a conclusive objection to Summers's reconstructivist intellectual history. For Summers's attempted systematization of the beliefs of the pragmatic instrumentalists may be a history of their ideas, and not necessarily a defence of his own. Even if Summers ultimately ends up with a total set of beliefs that none of the thinkers in question would avow as his own, he may yet legitimately claim

[61] Summers, *Instrumentalism*, above n. 1, at 20–2.

[62] Summers himself concedes that there is 'some substance to this objection' (ibid. at 273). This problem is discussed at length in the next section of this essay, which uses the incompleteness of the instrumentalists' theory of adjudication as an example.

[63] Ibid. at 25.

that such beliefs were that thinker's beliefs, in the sense that such beliefs represent the best reconstruction possible of the total set of that thinker's beliefs. We all engage in this kind of reconstructivist belief attribution when we say such things as 'she says she opposes all abortions on moral grounds, but she really does not'—when we know that she does not because we know she has other, more general beliefs that imply the opposite of her stated position on abortion.[64]

The upshot is that Summers will have made out his historical thesis if indeed the system of beliefs he attributes to the pragmatic instrumentalists is the best reconstruction of the whole of their known beliefs. That is a large question requiring detailed consideration of alternative reconstructions. Without having made such comparisons, my own impression is that Summers has made a persuasive case for his theory of their beliefs.

My complaint about Summers's historical method is quite different than the just discussed fear that he has put his own views in the mouths of his historical subjects. Rather, on one crucial point Summers needed to step away from the views of his subjects and to impose his own ideas. That point concerns the nature of legal theory itself. This point is crucial both to Summers's efforts to establish his historical thesis that these persons actually held the pragmatic instrumentalist legal theory and his evaluative thesis that pragmatic instrumentalism is a good legal theory. Summers should have developed his own theory about what a legal theory is. Unfortunately he chose to adopt his subjects' views on that topic as his organizing principle.

Admittedly, there are two differing views on how to do intellectual history, one that I shall call 'modest' history and the other that I shall call 'imperial' history. A modest intellectual historian will attempt to follow faithfully his subjects' own second-order beliefs about the character of their first-order beliefs. If the historian is composing a history of medieval religious beliefs, for example, he will organize his discussion around his subjects' own second-order beliefs about their first-order religious beliefs. A modest historian, in other words, will use his subjects' concept of religion to organize and limit his discussion. In contrast, an imperial historian will use his own concept of religion in order to organize and limit his discussion of the religious beliefs of his historical subjects. He will regard their beliefs about what constitutes a religion as just another belief to be taken into account; he will not regard those beliefs as having any special status and will not feel constrained to adopt his subjects' concept of religion as his polestar.

Summers, who is suitably imperial when it comes to reconstructing the first-order beliefs of his subjects, becomes unfortunately modest when it

[64] For a defence of the general necessity of this kind of holistic approach to belief attribution, see D. Davidson, *Essays on Actions and Events* (Oxford: Oxford University Press, 1980).

comes to imposing his own concept of what a legal theory should be. Rather, as Summers admits, the 'entire book is organized around the themes that interested the American pragmatic instrumentalists'.[65]

Some may think that Summers must be modest on this point if he is to do intellectual history at all.[66] Under this view, Summers and his audience could not gain a true understanding of the pragmatic instrumentalist legal theory unless Summers adopts those theorists' own concept of what a legal theory is. We could not place ourselves within their system of thought, could not empathize with their views, unless we were modest intellectual historians.[67]

This defence of Summers's modesty (and it is not Summers's defence) is surely overstated. We can impose our views of what a legal theory should be on legal theorists of an earlier time, and the result will still be a history of their ideas—organized in ways they might find alien, but a history of their ideas nonetheless. What imperial historians lose in empathetic understanding of another set of ideas they more than gain by relating those ideas to contemporary concerns. If religious beliefs interest us, our interest will relate to our idea of what religion is; if legal theory interests us, our interest will relate to our idea of what legal theory should be. A modest history of such beliefs relegates them to a scrapbook of historical curiosities. An imperial history of such beliefs relates them to our own concerns and enables the ideas to speak to us in a way that we can understand. Imperial history reorganizes the beliefs of historical subjects in a way that allows them to compete with contemporary ideas. In that sense imperial history takes the beliefs of historical subjects more seriously than does modest history, even though imperial history ignores one of the central beliefs of its subjects.

If Summers had articulated his own view of what a legal theory should contain and had organized his discussion by his own categories, we would be able to understand the pragmatic instrumentalists in a way that would make their theory come alive for us. We would know more readily their thoughts on each of the crucial issues of contemporary legal theory. We would even know if these thinkers had no thoughts on certain subjects because they did not think that these subjects were an important part of legal theory. We would then be able to judge the correctness of Summers's historical thesis that these influential people had a legal theory called pragmatic instrumentalism; we could also judge Summers's evaluative thesis that these people had a good legal theory. Without imposing our

[65] Summers, *Instrumentalism*, above n. 1, at 12.

[66] See e.g. the well-known argument (along these Weberian and Wittgensteinian lines) in P. Winch, *The Idea of a Social Science* (London: Routledge and Kegan-Paul, 1958).

[67] For a sympathetic contemporary summary of such views, see G. von Wright, *Explanation and Understanding* (Ithaca, NY: Cornell University Press, 1971).

own ideas of what a legal theory is onto the beliefs of the pragmatic instrumentalists, it is difficult to see how we could judge either of these theses.

It is possible that Summers believes that the pragmatic instrumentalists held the right views about what a legal theory should be; in that case his book should be seen as educating us to such a view of legal theory so that we can properly make the historical and evaluative judgements. However, this is not Summers's apparent position. Rather, Summers urges that 'we must not assume that there is, within the field of legal theory, a widely accepted convention governing what can count as a sufficiently unitary general theory'.[68] Rather than taking this state of affairs as an invitation to develop his own concept of a legal theory and then organize his discussion of pragmatic instrumentalism around it, Summers contents himself with the modest historical position that allows his subjects' beliefs to organize his discussion.

III. PRAGMATIC INSTRUMENTALISM AND THE THEORY OF ADJUDICATION

In this section, I shall attempt the always dangerous task of following my own advice, which means I shall attempt to use my own notions of what legal theory should be to organize my discussion of both pragmatic instrumentalism and Summers's response to it. Rather than attempting to articulate a complete legal theory, I focus on what I earlier called the theory of adjudication. Several reasons support this limitation to the analysis. First, selection of some subtheory within legal theory makes the discussion more manageable. Second, this chapter has largely ignored this particular part of legal theory despite the extensive attention devoted to it in part two of Summers's book. Finally, this subtheory tests the validity of my point about the desirability of imperial history, because Summers does discuss much of what I discuss herein; thus a reader of this review and of Summers's book can more easily assess whether imposing a theory of adjudication onto the pragmatic instrumentalists, and forcing them to answer our questions, is preferable to Summers's modest historical approach.

A theory of adjudication answers the questions of how judges decide cases and how they ought to decide cases.[69] It is thus a theory of judicial reasoning. As such it should contain a number of subtheories within it: (1) a theory of law proper that tells judges what standards their office obligates them to consider when they decide cases; (2) a theory about facts and about descriptions of facts that legitimates the use of some descriptions,

[68] Summers, *Instrumentalism*, above n. 1, at 270.

[69] For purposes of this abbreviated discussion, I ignore the functional division of labour present in a jury system such as ours.

but not others, of 'what happened' within the legal decisional process; (3) a theory of interpretation legitimating only some interpretive premises in a judge's attempt to apply the law to the facts; and (4) a theory about logic and the place of logic in legal reasoning.

A theory of adjudication should contain each of these subtheories, at a minimum, because every judicial decision necessarily requires a judge to ascertain the relevant law, to find the facts of the case, to connect the law to the facts via the meanings of the terms employed in the law, and to use logic to justify deductively the result reached. A formalist or value-free theory of adjudication, for example, would contain: (1) some version of a legal positivist theory that maintains that there exists an exclusively factual (value-free) test of law with which to pedigree the decisional standards a judge is obligated to consider; (2) some theory that urges that our perception and description of factual matters is uncontaminated by value judgements; (3) either some 'plain meaning' theory of interpretation, according to which the meaning of legal predicates exists in the conventions of ordinary or legal usage, or some intentionalist theory of interpretation, according to which the relevant intentions can be discovered and applied in a value-free manner; and (4) some theory of logic and of its place in legal reasoning that sees logic as universal and value-free.

Because of the wild implausibility of thinking that adjudication can be value-free in the way just sketched, any theory of adjudication needs a fifth subtheory: a theory of value. Such a theory should answer three questions: (1) whether there are right answers to moral questions; (2) whether judges should incorporate such right answers in their legal decisions, or whether they should use the conventional morals of their time and place instead; and (3) regardless of whether judges use conventional or real morals, just where it is in the processes of legal reasoning that the deciding judge should use knowledge of values.

With this thumbnail sketch of what a fully articulated theory of adjudication should contain, we can ask whether the pragmatic instrumentalists formulated anything that could reasonably be called a theory of adjudication. We shall consider first, as Summers does in detail,[70] their theory of law proper.

Summers accurately sees a 'deep ambivalence in the instrumentalists' position on standards of legal validity'.[71] The ambivalence Summers notes is between the traditional legal positivist view that there is a factual test for all valid legal standards, and the legal realist view, originating with Holmes, that valid law consists of predictions of what courts will do in particular cases. Many legal theorists would also agree with Summers's detailed criticisms of both the traditional legal positivist view[72] and the

[70] Summers, *Instrumentalism*, above n. 1, chs. 4, 5.
[71] Ibid. at 116.
[72] Ibid. at 102–11.

legal realist or predictivist view.[73] But what a more imperial historian might have said here is that the instrumentalists were bound to be deeply ambivalent and deeply wrong because they never even saw the right question to ask. If we impose our ideas of what a theory of adjudication requires, we should perceive the need for a subtheory—a theory of law proper—that allows a judge to ascertain the valid legal standards with which to make his decision. The predictivism of American legal realism simply cannot provide an answer to that question because, as Summers[74] and many other legal theorists have noted,[75] a judge's prediction of his own decision can hardly provide him with a standard with which to justify deciding one way or the other. Judges may on occasion predict their own decisions, but even to have something to predict they must also decide them.

Admittedly this criticism imposes our question on the pragmatic instrumentalists' answer. But we care about our question precisely because the best theory of adjudication we can devise mandates that we ask and answer the question of how one finds out what the valid legal standards are. The instrumentalists' failure to answer this question properly may well be due to the fact that predictivism came from concerns oblique to the development of a theory of law; nevertheless, we must force their answer to be an answer to our question if we are to understand to what extent they had a good theory of adjudication, or even a theory of adjudication at all.

In our system, a theory of law proper must include a theory of precedent. Despite Bentham's well-known protestations,[76] common law rules form an important part of the standards we call law. Accordingly, we need some theory about how judges and lawyers should discover authoritative formulations of common law rules.

The instrumentalists had a well-known answer to this question: a deciding judge should attach precedential significance to what the preceding court did on the facts before it, and no significance to what it said.[77] Summers recognizes this as the instrumentalist theory of precedent,[78] but curiously fails to criticize the weaknesses of the 'what was done' theory of precedent. Even contemporary instrumentalists such as Felix Cohen recognized that the 'what was done' theory of precedent was woefully

[73] Ibid. at 121–35.

[74] Ibid. at 132.

[75] See e.g. F. Cohen, 'The Problems of a Functional Jurisprudence', *Modern Law Review*, 1 (1937), 5–26, at 17.

[76] A. W. B. Simpson nicely summarizes Bentham's distaste for the common law in 'The Common Law and Legal Theory', in A. Simpson (ed.), *Oxford Essays in Jurisprudence*, Second Series (Oxford: Oxford University Press, 1972), 77.

[77] See H. Oliphant, 'A Return to *Stare Decisis*', *American Bar Association Journal*, 14 (1928), 71–6, 107, 159–63.

[78] Summers, *Instrumentalism*, above n. 1, at 147–9.

incomplete.[79] Given his aims of assessing instrumentalist legal theory, Summers should have pursued Cohen's point and demonstrated that the deficiencies could or could not be remedied. This would not require Summers to impose our question on the instrumentalists—because our question about formulating common law rules was approximately their question—but would simply require Summers to assess the adequacy of the instrumentalist answer in light of more contemporary discussions of precedent.[80]

Summers curiously omits entirely any discussion about the second subtheory of a comprehensive theory of adjudication, a theory about facts. This omission would be unusual for an imperial historian of ideas because such a theory is necessary in a complete theory of adjudication. Such an omission is curious even for a modest historian of ideas because on this topic some of the instrumentalists asked exactly the questions that needed to be asked. Jerome Frank, for example, proclaimed himself to be a 'fact sceptic', meaning that he doubted the ability of legal fact-finders even to approximate the truth about past facts in adjudication.[81] Similarly, Walter Wheeler Cook wrote of the multiplicity of descriptions of facts and the consequent impossibility of sorting out those descriptions in the ways contemplated by the rules of pleading and evidence; Cook thought that one could not just 'state the facts' in either pleading or in testimony without presupposing some of the opinions of the pleader or the witnesses.[82]

Such concerns about facts and factual descriptions in adjudication did not predominate in instrumentalist literature.[83] Yet those concerns existed and deserve coverage in an assessment of pragmatic instrumentalism as a theory of adjudication because concerns about facts are a legitimate part of any full-fledged theory of adjudication. In this instance, imposing our own question (how can we pedigree some factual descriptions but not others in adjudication) onto the instrumentalists might allow us to see that it was their question too.

The theory of interpretation is the third pertinent subtheory. Summers barely mentions this theory.[84] The lack of emphasis is not justified. Even a modest historian of instrumentalist literature has to consider the major

[79] See F. Cohen, 'The Ethical Basis of Legal Criticism', *Yale Law Journal*, 41 (1931), 201–20, at 205–19.

[80] Julius Stone, for example, has pursued Felix Cohen's criticism of the Legal Realist theory of precedent in J. Stone, *Legal Systems and Lawyers' Reasonings* (Stanford: Stanford University Press, 1964), ch. 7.

[81] Jerome Frank, *Law and the Modern Mind* (New York: Coward–McCann, 1949), pp. xi–xix.

[82] See Walter Wheeler Cook, 'Facts and Statements of Fact', *University of Chicago Law Review*, 4 (1937), 233–46.

[83] For a survey of the concern about facts of the Legal Realists and others, see K. Twining, 'Taking Facts Seriously', *Journal of Legal Education*, 34 (1984), 22–42.

[84] Summers, *Instrumentalism*, above n. 1, at 153–4, 189–90.

source of instrumentalist scepticism about the ability of courts to conduct value-free adjudication: the scepticism of rules proclaimed by Frank and many others, a scepticism about the ability of courts to find value-free meaning to the words appearing in legal rules. Moreover, a more imperial historian would see that Pound, Frank, Llewellyn, and others correctly devoted their attention to this issue. The theory of interpretation is crucial in assessing the degree to which values enter into legal reasoning.[85]

In fairness, Summers urges that 'interpretation and construction may overlap with the application of standards of validity. There can be no sharp line between these'.[86] Summers may thus think that having spent so much time discussing the instrumentalists' theories of validity he need not duplicate the discussion by an equally extended critique of the instrumentalist theory of interpretation.

I suspect that Summers is correct about the unimportance of this distinction under the modest view of intellectual history. The instrumentalists probably did not draw any clear line between the question of how a judge validates certain standards as law and the question of how a judge interprets those standards. For a more imperial historian, however, there should be an important distinction between validating some standards as authoritative and interpreting the standards already validated as authoritative. The distinction is as basic as that between the syntax and the semantics of natural languages. A language's syntax tells us what strings of symbols form meaningful sentences; the language's semantics interpret those strings of symbols. A theory of law is thus a kind of legal syntax and tells us what authoritative strings of symbols judges must consider; a theory of interpretation is a kind of legal semantics and tells us how to interpret the authoritative strings of symbols.

If we impose this distinction on the instrumentalist literature, we can see that the instrumentalists were interested in giving antiformalist answers to both questions. We can see this even if they did not clearly perceive the distinction between the two questions. But we gain such an ability to assess the adequacy of the instrumentalist theory of interpretation only if we impose on them one of our distinctions.

If we do impose this syntax–semantics distinction onto the instrumentalists and examine their theory of interpretation more closely than does Summers, we find that the instrumentalists largely failed to articulate a theory of interpretation. Summers accurately explains that Pound and others condemned the 'mechanical jurisprudence' of interpreting statutes by their 'plain meaning' without considering the purposes that might

[85] See M. Moore, 'The Semantics of Judging', *Southern California Law Review*, 54 (1981), 151–295.

[86] Summers, *Instrumentalism*, above n. 1, at 110.

plausibly have motivated the enactment of those statutes.[87] Yet nothing in instrumentalist literature matches the Hart–Fuller debate[88] and its progeny in describing how a good theory of interpretation should blend ordinary meaning, purpose, and moral knowledge. Rather, the instrumentalist literature often ended in a kind of very implausible functionalism that ignored any pre-existing meaning (ordinary or otherwise) of legal standards, and instead assigned such standards a meaning in light of the desirable consequences attainable by that assignment.

The fourth subtheory, a necessary part of any complete theory of adjudication, is a theory about logic and its place in legal reasoning. A theory of logic in this context might address three subjects: first, the nature of logic itself—whether it is simply a set of inference patterns adopted by convention, or whether the logics of Aristotle and of Gottlob Frege should be seen as progressively better theories of something that exists independently of human convention, namely, logical truth; second, whether legal reasoning uses any distinctive logic; and third, the extent to which logic is involved in legal reasoning.

Summers again devotes limited space to these issues. He briefly considers Dewey's attempt to develop a 'logic of inquiry' that differed from the traditional logic of demonstration, a logic the instrumentalists thought useful in investigating the likely effects of legal policies.[89] Summers also discusses some of the more famous instrumentalist attacks on 'too much logic' in legal reasoning,[90] rightly concluding that logic was the wrong whipping boy for the evils the instrumentalists had in mind. These two topics are all that is said about logic in legal reasoning.

Summers gives limited attention to this important topic in legal theory presumably because the instrumentalists themselves had little of value to say about it. As Summers notes, 'most of these thinkers . . . were not highly conscious of the precise canons of deduction or of the content of the phrase "logically entailed" as it is utilized within the abstract discipline of formal logic'.[91] Yet in assessing the completeness of the instrumentalists' theory of adjudication this is a failing that needs to be stressed. That they had no theory about logic or of its place in legal reasoning is an important omission. Here again their idea of the necessary components of legal theory simply bypassed crucial issues. When we apply our ideas about the issues that a subtheory of logic should address to the work of the instrumentalists, we find that they failed to contribute much to the theory.

[87] See ibid. at 154, 190.

[88] H. L. A. Hart, 'Positivism and the Separation of Law and Morals', *Harvard Law Review*, 71 (1958), 593–629; L. Fuller, 'Positivism and Fidelity to Law—A Reply to Professor Hart', *Harvard Law Review*, 71 (1958), 630–72.

[89] Summers, *Instrumentalism*, above n. 1, at 34.

[90] See ibid. at 154–5.

[91] Ibid. at 155.

The fifth and last subtheory of the theory of adjudication is a theory of value. Here Summers does what he elsewhere avoids: he relies on his own theory about what a legal theory must include to organize his discussion. Summers believes (as do I) that 'any general theory of law that fails to address issues of value is fundamentally incomplete',[92] and therefore he devotes a chapter to reconstructing the instrumentalists' theory of value, something that did not truly interest those thinkers.

The reconstruction of an instrumentalist theory of value forms one of the best chapters in the book. Summers addresses each of the three issues I earlier identified as part of a theory of value in this context[93] and describes the instrumentalists' ideas about each issue. First, the instrumentalists' meta-ethical stance tended towards scepticism. Summers qualifies this unlikeable attitude: 'Extreme scepticism about value is not an essential or natural corollary of any of the general directions of instrumentalist thought. Nor can it be said that such scepticism was widely shared.'[94] This last statement is hard to square with Holmes's or Frank's well-known, trenchant scepticism about values; Summers's first statement quoted does not give due weight to the sceptical implications of pragmatism as a general epistemological position. Still, Summers correctly indicates that the instrumentalists at least wavered in their scepticism, particularly when they had to espouse a substantive ethical theory.

In discussing the second issue earlier distinguished as part of a theory of value[95]—whether judges should incorporate right answers to moral questions in their decisions or instead use the conventional morals of their time and place—Summers accurately describes the instrumentalists as favouring conventional values over true values. Scepticism certainly generated some of this conventionalism: if no true values existed, conventional values are the only values that could be used in adjudication. Certainly Holmes's scepticism generated his conventionalism as the quotes on which Summers relies clearly illustrate.[96] In other instances, the preference for conventionalist values stemmed from majoritarian considerations: the majority, as represented by their conventional morals, have the right to be wrong. However conventionalism was motivated, Summers accurately assesses instrumentalist value theory as thoroughly conventional and thus opposed to any form of natural law adjudication.

[92] Ibid. at 41.

[93] See text at nn. 70–1, above.

[94] Summers, *Instrumentalism*, above n. 1, at 52.

[95] See text at nn. 70–1, above.

[96] e.g. Holmes declared: '"I am so sceptical as to our knowledge about the goodness or badness of laws that I have no practical crit[erion] except what the crowd wants."' Summers, *Instrumentalism*, above n. 1, at 46 (quoting M. Howe (ed.), *Holmes–Pollock Letters*, i (Cambridge, Mass.: Harvard University Press, 1941), 163; see also M. Moore, 'Moral Reality', *Wisconsin Law Review* [1982], 1061–156, and Moore, 'Moral Reality Revisited', *Michigan Law Review*, 90 (1992), 2424–533 (further elaborating moral scepticism of Holmes and other legal theorists).

The weak link of the chapter on value theory is Summers's treatment of the third issue necessarily addressed by a complete theory of adjudication—the ways in which knowledge of values (conventional or real) combines with knowledge of other things such as the meanings of words, brute or institutional facts, to form an overall theory of adjudication.[97] Summers does identify the nature of the substantive ethical theory held by the instrumentalists—utilitarianism. His conclusion that instrumentalist policy analyses are usually instances of utilitarian reasoning is persuasive. Summers identifies less clearly how these utilitarian values combine with other things to produce an overall theory of adjudication.

Summers's inability to state precisely how values enter a theory of adjudication may reflect the instrumentalists' confusion on this issue. To proclaim, for example, that values enter into all legal interpretations, as the instrumentalists frequently declared, should not deny a role to other items, such as the ordinary meanings of the words appearing in the rules to be interpreted.[98] Yet the instrumentalists were notably weak in specifying the role of such formalist ingredients in adjudication. Frank and the early Llewellyn sometimes seem to argue that legal decisions are nothing but value judgements, that the existence of legal rules makes no difference to legal decision-making except in the rhetoric employed after the fact to rationalize a decision reached on other grounds. The instrumentalists' neglect of this important part of constructing a positive theory of adjudication provides no reason that Summers should gloss over that failure, a failure as judged from our perspective on what an adequate theory of adjudication must include.

When channelled in each of these ways the instrumentalist literature can answer the questions of contemporary legal theory. If rechannelled in these ways, can it be said that the instrumentalists produced a theory of adjudication? In particular, is Summers correct in his claim that pragmatic instrumentalism is 'a full-fledged and distinctive jurisprudential tradition'?[99] Of course, the instrumentalists had a full-fledged jurisprudential theory in the sense that they had something to say on each of the major subparts of an overall theory of adjudication. Yet surely quality is relevant here. Even when welded together to form a comprehensive theory, their disparate ideas do not add up to a complete and cohesive theory. Most of the instrumentalists were not philosophers. With the exception of Dewey and Felix Cohen, they knew little of logic, ethics, epistemology, or the phi-

[97] Nevertheless, Summers's discussion in other chapters (chs. 4–7) does contain some suggestions regarding this question of mixing morals with other ingredients in a complete theory of adjudication.

[98] I argue for this at some length in M. Moore, 'A Natural Law Theory of Interpretation', *Southern California Law Review*, 58 (1985), 277–398.

[99] Summers, *Instrumentalism*, above n. 1, at 14.

losophy of language—areas of philosophy that could have helped them formulate the various subtheories necessary to a full-fledged theory of adjudication. As Summers concedes, some of the instrumentalists were so antiphilosophical that they proudly proclaimed their lack of even a philosophy of law.[100] It is thus not surprising that the theory of adjudication that results from piecing together their views is philosophically unsophisticated. In addition, most of the instrumentalist insights about adjudication are to be found in their attacks on formalist modes of legal reasoning. Their positive theory is accordingly quite sketchy, because developing a positive theory was not their primary concern.

Given both of these factors, and applying our own theory about what a theory of adjudication should contain, it is difficult to agree with Summers's view that the instrumentalists propounded a new and important type of legal theory. I will concede that I have only tested the case for them having propounded such a theory by examining that subpart of legal theory known as jurisprudence, or the theory of adjudication. Still, the test seems a fair one, for these issues in adjudication greatly concern both Summers and the instrumentalists; if the instrumentalists failed to propound much of a theory here, they have failed where Summers must claim they have succeeded if he is to support his thesis that pragmatic instrumentalism represents a major type of legal theory worthy of our respect.

IV. CONCLUSION

To a certain extent, Summers's philosophical thesis is accurate: the various views Summers discusses can be systematized into a unified legal theory. Indeed, the last section outlines the way in which I would unify the various views of the instrumentalists into a recognizable theory of adjudication. Two points should be kept in mind, however. First, one must be rather charitable in one's requirements of completeness to concede that the instrumentalists even had a 'full-fledged' theory of adjudication. Second, Summers has a broader ambition here than merely to show that the instrumentalists had a theory of adjudication; he wishes to demonstrate the hidden unity of all of the instrumentalists' views he discusses in his book, including those in legal sociology as well as those in legal theory. As I have argued, lumping these two things together necessarily results in something that is rather lumpy. For there is no common question to which the legal theory and the legal sociology provide the links of a unified answer. The questions asked in legal theory concerning the legitimacy of reasoning in certain ways are different from the questions asked in

[100] Ibid. at 273.

sociology regarding, for example, the efficacy of laws. Summers's attempt to unify the instrumentalists' views with three broad themes[101] does not, as Summers believes, 'provide as much unity as is usually found in general theories of law'.[102] Such thematic similarity in answers to different questions cannot provide the unity needed for anything to be called a theory of law. The needed unity must be provided by asking the same question about the same thing.

Regarding Summers's historical thesis, I have little disagreement with his assessment that the theorists he names held the views he ascribes to them. If one allows Summers the freedom to engage in a 'rational reconstruction' of the instrumentalists' combined views—and one should allow any intellectual historian such a course—Summers's attributions of their beliefs seem accurate and informative. Summers's additional historical point, that the ideas of the pragmatic instrumentalists heavily influenced our contemporary legal theory,[103] also seems undeniable. However, that part of Summers's historical claim characterizing their system of beliefs as a legal theory is more problematic; without applying some theory regarding what a legal theory must include, it is difficult to assess whether the totality of the instrumentalists' views about law amounts to a legal theory, much less *the* legal theory of the period.

This last point hinders Summers's evaluative thesis as well. Summers makes the general evaluative claim that pragmatic instrumentalism is a good legal theory. He also makes two more specific evaluative claims: first, that pragmatic instrumentalism is as good a theory as analytical positivism, natural law theory, or historical jurisprudence; and second, that it is good enough to contribute to any final synthesis of the various types of legal theory.

Assessing these evaluative claims is difficult because Summers does not give us much guidance on what for him constitutes a type of legal theory. Summers does tell us that '[a] general type of legal theory is to be characterized mainly by the objects of its focus, and the questions it addresses'.[104] Thus natural law theory qualifies as a major type of legal theory because it studies 'the nature of human beings and the human condition, with their implications for legal ordering';[105] historical jurisprudence qualifies because it examines 'the general modes, forms and sources of legal change and development over time and in different places';[106] and analytic positivism qualifies because it investigates 'the nature and varieties of legal norms, their status as law, their hierarchical ordering, and the analytic relations within and between these and other fundamental legal notions'.[107] Similarly, Summers urges, pragmatic instrumentalism quali-

[101] See above text accompanying nn. 28–30.
[102] Summers, *Instrumentalism*, above n. 1, at 270.
[103] See ibid. at 274–8.
[104] Ibid. at 268.
[105] Ibid.
[106] Ibid.
[107] Ibid.

fies as a major type of legal theory because the 'instrumental and pragmatic facets of law qualify as important objects of theoretical study'.[108]

I do not think that Summers can be this tolerant of what qualifies as a type of legal theory and retain significance for his specific evaluative claims. Using Summers's criterion, any approach that studied any general facet of law would qualify as a type of legal theory. For example, comparativists and anthropologists could have a distinct 'theory of law' because they study comparative facets of legal phenomena. This tolerant reading of what comprises a type of theory also makes it difficult to see how the four major theories about law could be combined in the way Summers envisions. He believes that 'the perfect general theory about law . . . will partake of the best in all four of the great traditions'.[109] It is puzzling how any such unification of disciplines that study different things could occur. It is also unclear how Summers can believe both that pragmatic instrumentalism is a major type of legal theory because it studies something quite different than do the other three types of legal theories, and that pragmatic instrumentalism can nonetheless be combined with the other major types of legal theory into an amalgamated theory about some one subject.

A less tolerant view of what constitutes a type of legal theory would individuate types not by their subject matters but rather by their differing views on the nature of the same subject matter. Different types of legal theory must genuinely compete with each other about the nature of some aspect of law. A natural law theory of adjudication, for example, should be seen as a genuine competitor with a positivist theory of adjudication, because both concern the same thing even though they each give different answers as to the nature of that thing. Since the theory of adjudication (of any type) is a large part of any general legal theory, natural law and positivism should be seen as major types of legal theory.

According to this criterion, pragmatic instrumentalism could qualify as a major type of legal theory only if it is about the same thing as are other major types of legal theory and only if it gives distinctive answers about the nature of that thing. Using the theory of adjudication as an example, one might consider pragmatic instrumentalism a type of theory, depending on how one resolves the issues raised in the third section of this chapter. I believe that the instrumentalists lacked the necessary detail and philosophical sophistication to qualify the amalgam of their views as a distinct theory of adjudication. One can make this judgement (or Summers's opposite judgement) only by analysing the beliefs of the instrumentalists under one's own theory about what a theory of adjudication must include. Using my own theory in this regard, I do not think

[108] Ibid. [109] Ibid. at 281.

pragmatic instrumentalists worthy of the exalted position to which Summers's book would elevate them. In the absence of any other theory about what such theories must contain, that leaves me with the old Scottish verdict on Summers's evaluative claims: 'not proven'.

Part III

Natural Law

7
Legal Principles Revisited

I. INTRODUCTION

In a recent article[1] Larry Alexander and Ken Kress have returned us to a perennial question of jurisprudence, which is the role of principles in legal reasoning. They rightly remind us, and nicely detail, how Ronald Dworkin's treatment of principles is foundational of modern treatments of the topic. Dworkin's persuasiveness here is due to the fact that he recapitulated in his own idiom a position familiar to all lawyers, familiar because of their practice[2] and because of earlier descriptions of that practice by such staples of American jurisprudence as Cardozo, Warren and Brandeis, Levi, Wechsler, Langdell, Cohen, Bingham, and Fuller.[3]

I shall follow Alexander and Kress in their focus on Dworkin's treatment of legal principles, because Dworkin's treatment was systematic and even in places elegant, as well as because Dworkin has stated the problem for our generation in the way that C. C. Langdell, Morris Cohen, Edward Levi, and Lon Fuller did for theirs. Although Alexander and Kress do an able presentation of Dworkin on legal principles,[4] I shall begin by giving my own reconstruction of Dworkin's treatment of legal principles. Doing so will be justified if it pinpoints where Alexander and Kress's criticisms fit into Dworkin's scheme.

[1] Larry Alexander and Ken Kress, 'Against Legal Principles', in A. Marmor (ed.), *Law And Interpretation* (Oxford: Oxford University Press, 1995), reprinted in the *Iowa Law Review*, 82 (1997), 739–86.

[2] Ibid. at 287–92.

[3] In chronological order, Christopher Columbus Langdell, *Summary of the Law of Contracts* (2nd edn., Boston: Little, Brown, 1880); Samuel Warren and Louis Brandeis, 'The Right of Privacy', *Harvard Law Review*, 4 (1890), 193–220; Morris Cohen, 'The Place of Logic in the Law', *Harvard Law Review*, 29 (1912), 622–39; Joseph Bingham, 'What is the Law?', *Michigan Law Review*, 11 (1912), 1–25; Bingham, 'The Nature of Legal Rights and Duties', *Michigan Law Review*, 12 (1913), 1–26; Benjamin Cardozo, *The Judicial Process* (New Haven: Yale University Press, 1923); Edward Levi, *An Introduction to Legal Reasoning* (Chicago: University of Chicago Press, 1949); Lon Fuller, 'Purpose and Natural Law', *Natural Law Forum*, 3 (1958), 68–76; Herbert Wechsler, 'Toward Neutral Principles of Constitutional Law', *Harvard Law Review*, 73 (1959), 1–35.

[4] Alexander and Kress, 'Against Legal Principles', above n. 1, at 280–5.

II. DWORKIN'S PRINCIPLES

Dworkin's jurisprudence from 1963 to 1978[5] was an 'internal' jurisprudence in the sense that it addressed participants within our legal system (particularly judges) and either described how they did practise law or recommended to them how they ought to practise law. This was in marked contrast to H. L. A. Hart's 'external' jurisprudence, which distanced itself from any legal system's law practice and asked a general question of social science, namely, what sort of a social practice is law?[6] Dworkin's internal jurisprudence also asks a 'what is law?' question, but it asks it from a practical standpoint: from the standpoint of a judge within this legal system, or of a lawyer who must argue to such a judge, what are those standards that the role of a legal professional obligates one to follow in his decisions? Whatever those standards are, let us call them 'law' in this internal sense of the word.[7]

As Hart noted in the debate with Fuller that set the agenda for Anglo-American jurisprudence these past forty years,[8] we can debate either what concept of law we do employ or what concept of law we ought to deploy. The first is a question of descriptive jurisprudence, seeking a lexical definition of law teased out of the linguistic or other practices of legal professionals or others.[9] The second is a normative question, first isolating what values law should serve and then seeking a stipulative definition of a concept of law to serve those values.[10]

[5] The legal philosopher I discuss may be something of a fictional creature, one I happen to call, 'Dworkin'. He is the person who believes the best that can be made of the writings of an actual philosopher also named Dworkin during the period 1963 through 1978. The actual beliefs of the real Ronald Dworkin, except insofar as they are verbatim the text of these writings, will thus be beside the point. I have chosen 1978 as my cut-off point for text because, like Joseph Raz ('Dworkin: A New Link in the Chain', *California Law Review*, 74 (1986), 1103–19), I see significant enough changes in the writings of the real Ronald Dworkin that I am loathe to attribute all such beliefs to just one person, even a fictional one. Cf. Larry Alexander and Michael Bayles, 'Hercules or Proteus: The Many Theses of Ronald Dworkin', *Social Theory and Practice*, 5 (1980), 267–303.

[6] H. L. A. Hart, *The Concept of Law* (Oxford: Oxford University Press, 1961). For a comparison of Hart's project with that of Dworkin, see Chs. 2 and 3, above.

[7] As Dworkin nicely puts it, this internal question of what is law is not an academic puzzle to be taken out of the cupboard on rainy days, but an eminently practical question on which all lawyers must take some position. Dworkin, 'The Model of Rules', *University of Chicago Law Review*, 35 (1967), 14–54.

[8] H. L. A. Hart, 'Positivism and the Separation of Law and Morals', *Harvard Law Review*, 71 (1958), 593–629.

[9] Hart was careful not to limit his data to the linguistic usage of the word, 'law'. He saw himself to be, in part, a sociologist, looking at legal practices to ascertain the concept of law implicit in them. Hart, *Concept*, above n. 6, at 17.

[10] I here exclude a non-moral but also non-descriptive task Hart saw for jurisprudence, namely, telling us what concept of law we *ought* to employ for reasons of good theory construction in social science. See Ch. 2, above.

Dworkin's conclusion that the law consists of legal principles should be seen as an exercise of internal jurisprudence that is sometimes descriptive of the concept of law implicit in our legal practices and that is sometimes normative in its recommendations about the concept of law we should employ in our legal practices. As it happens, in Dworkin's world as in Candide's, the concept of law in which both sorts of internal jurisprudence result is the same, but that is no reason not to separate these two quite separate arguments for it.[11]

To argue for a concept of law as a constellation of principles, Dworkin believed he had to answer affirmatively four questions:

1. Is there a logical difference between principles and rules?
2. Do lawyers and judges (ought they) resort to such principles in their arguments and decisions of disputed law cases?
3. Do lawyers treat such principles (ought they to be regarded) as part of the law and thus binding on all legal professionals, or are they only moral principles whose use by judges is discretionary?
4. Is it impossible for there to be a purely factual (i.e. non-evaluative) pedigree, such as Hart's rule of recognition, showing such principles to be valid law?

Since Dworkin answered all four questions affirmatively (including both the descriptive and normative versions of questions 2 and 3), he concluded that legal positivism could not account for something it had to account for if it were to be an adequate internal jurisprudence, namely, the legal principles we rightly use in our practice of law. From here, Dworkin went on to argue that law is better seen, not as a set of individuated rules emanating from an historical source, but holistically, as a constellation of principles owing their status as law as much to their moral correctness as to their historical, institutional basis.

In order to see where Alexander and Kress get off Dworkin's boat, let me describe in greater detail the intellectual strokes Dworkin used to move this boat along. In answer to his first question, Dworkin sought a 'logical difference' between principles and rules in terms of two dimensions: rules are all or nothing in their application, principles are not; principles have weight, rules do not.[12] Alexander and Kress rightly collapse

[11] My fictional Dworkin thus does not take the interpretive turn taken by the actual Dworkin of the 1980s. See Ronald Dworkin, *Law's Empire* (Cambridge, Mass.: Harvard University Press, 1986). See also Ch. 10 below for a discussion of the real Dworkin's interpretive turn. I put aside the interpretive turn here because it would claim that both descriptive and normative jurisprudence should be combined into an 'interpretive jurisprudence' that is at once descriptive and normative. For reasons given at length in Ch. 10, this is not a good idea.

[12] Dworkin, 'Model of Rules', above n. 7, at 25–8.

these into one dimension. They then, however, add another: rules are canonically formulated, principles are not.[13]

There was once a cottage industry within jurisprudence arguing both sides of Dworkin's first question.[14] The debate is bootless in the present context, and neither Dworkin, nor Alexander and Kress, needed to take a position on it. Compare a like debate in post-World War II philosophy of science, about the difference between observation statements and theoretical statements. Much ink was spent arguing (against the logical positivists) that there was no logical difference between those two types of statements.[15] Yet on non-logical positivistic views of scientific explanation, where one refuses to distinguish real (empirical) entities, from instrumental (theoretical) entities, one can make do with a vague-by-degree continuum: some statements are closer to sensory experience than others, in the sense of 'closer' having to do with inferential distance from perceptual reports.

About rule and principle in the philosophy of law we can be as relaxed. By whatever theory, concept, or intuitions about law one has, start with the obvious stuff (statutes, perhaps?) and call that rules. Principles are the unobvious stuff, the hidden law, if it exists.[16] If one's intuitions about obvious law are fleshed out with enacted law, then one can say, with Alexander and Kress, that 'principles must arise from the legal materials' and they 'cannot be enacted'.[17] Principles cannot be enacted because if they were, they would be obvious law, and thus not principles.

One does not want to say that principles have weight whereas rules are all or nothing, nor does one want to say that rules have a canonical formulation and principles do not—and particularly one does not want to say *both* of these things, as do Alexander and Kress.[18] For this is to make principles merely epistemic; on this view they are heuristic devices to finding one's way to truth. They themselves do not describe the truth; they are rather, evidence of the truth, to be weighed when they conflict with other evidence. Preferable is Kant's way of looking at principles: it is inconceivable that they could conflict, and thus need 'weighing' against one another, because each principle either has lexical priority over another or, more often, exceptions making way for the other.[19] It is this last possibil-

[13] Alexander and Kress, 'Against Legal Principles', above n. 1, at 280–1.

[14] See e.g. 'Special Issue: Legal Philosophy', *Yale Law Journal*, 81 (1972) 799–1053.

[15] Frederick Suppe, *The Structure of Scientific Theories* (2nd edn., Urbana: University of Illinois Press, 1977), 80–6.

[16] This is pretty much where I interpret the historical Dworkin to have ended up, with his distinctions between concepts (the obvious stuff) and conceptions (the unobvious and thus disputed stuff), and between pre-interpretive data (the obvious stuff) and interpretations (the unobvious stuff). See R. Dworkin, *Law's Empire*, above n. 11, at 65–6.

[17] Alexander and Kress, 'Against Legal Principles', above n. 1, at 281 n. 6.

[18] Ibid. at 281.

[19] This Kantian view of moral standards is briefly described in Ch. 5.

ity, of an indefinitely large number of exceptions to any plausible moral principle, that prevents one from thinking it very likely that principles have canonical formulations. One might well think the same of moral rules, however, and on precisely the same ground.

About the only structural ('logical') difference between rules and principles is one that stems from the relationship that is said to exist between them. Rules are said to 'instantiate', 'exemplify', or 'illustrate' principles. Principles are said to 'establish', 'imply', 'incorporate', or 'embody' rules.[20] What all of these words signify is that principles (together with other premises) logically imply, but are not implied by, rules.[21] The reason such a relationship exists between rules and principles is because the latter are said to *justify* the former, which is done by showing how the obvious law (of rules) follows from some good described by the unobvious law (of principles).

The structural feature that emerges from this is that principles must be semantically more general than rules. Such generality is necessary if principles are to imply the rules, and not vice-versa.[22] But this vague-by-degree distinction in semantic generality is all one can or should say about the structural differences between the obvious law of rules and the unobvious law of principles.

Turning to Dworkin's second question, consider first the descriptive branch. Alexander and Kress agree with Dworkin that Anglo-American judges do make reference to general principles that are not part of the obvious law when they decide cases, at least the hard ones. Dworkin[23] used *Riggs*[24] and *Henningson*,[25] Alexander and Kress[26] use *MacPherson*,[27] but the point is the same: judges, and the lawyers who argue to them, purport to discern general standards 'arising from' obviously legal materials, and they use such general standards to decide cases where the obvious law has run out.

Alexander and Kress diverge from Dworkin on the normative version of this second question, however. Dworkin's argument for why judges *should* use general standards that are not obviously part of the law can be

[20] These metaphors have been culled from the work of Rolf Sartorius and Ronald Dworkin. For the culling, see Ch. 8, below.

[21] I shall discuss momentarily, text below at nn. 81–5, why this must be taken to be the relationship asserted here.

[22] Parallel to this relationship in law between principles and rules is the relationship in science between experimental laws and scientific theories. For a discussion of this relationship, as well as of the difficulties in making more precise the idea of semantic generality, see Ernst Nagel, *The Structure of Science* (New York: Random House, 1961), 37–42.

[23] Dworkin, 'Model of Rules', above n. 7, at 23–9.

[24] *Riggs v. Palmer*, 115 N.Y. 506, 22 N.E. 188 (1889).

[25] *Henningson v. Bloomfield Motors*, 32 N.J. 358, 161 A. 2d. 69 (1960).

[26] Alexander and Kress, 'Against Legal Principles', above n. 1, at 289–90.

[27] *MacPherson v. Buick Motor Company*, 217 N.Y. 382, 111 N.E. 1050 (1916).

divided into three strands, corresponding to three kinds of cases. Take first the argument about what I shall call 'truly hard cases', cases where the obvious law has run out in the sense that no obviously legal standard has any bearing on the facts of the case. Here, anything beats flipping coins, so even a legal positivist like Hart would argue that judges should make reasoned judgements of value.[28] Yet Dworkin wanted judges to make a certain kind of reasoned judgement of value, namely, one that is general enough to imply as much obvious legal stuff as possible.

Why is this kind of generalizing effort by judges good? I put aside Dworkin's later answer in terms of integrity.[29] I agree with Alexander, Kress, and Waldron[30] that Dworkin's renaming of equality as 'integrity', analogizing a legal system to a single person, and linking the integrity of the former to some communitarian ideal, is both less clear and less cogent than staying with equality as an intrinsic good justifying the deciding of cases as a matter of principle.

Equality is also the value that justifies judges in resorting to principled value judgements when they decide my second category of cases, what I shall call 'hard cases that look easy'. What the latter cases are like can be seen by noting that Dworkin's examples of hard cases were not in any obvious way hard.[31] In *Riggs*, the New York Decedents Law (a set of statutes) was clear in giving the property to whomever the testator's will designated, in this case, Elmer, the murderous grandson. In *Henningson*, New Jersey's obvious (statutory and common) law on implied warranties was also clear. These were easy cases under the obvious law. They became hard cases only because the courts discovered unobvious law, certain general principles, which conflicted with obvious law and made such cases hard.[32]

This is where Dworkin's equality-based argument shows its teeth. For the same demand for principled generality is operative here, only what it now demands is that some obvious law be put aside in the name of a general principle that is so good and so embedded in other obvious law that it must be followed, even here. The obvious law put aside may be the plain meaning of statutory language[33] or it may be the stated holding of precedent cases.[34] It may even be the actual holding of precedent

[28] Hart, 'Positivism', above n. 8, at 614.

[29] Dworkin, *Law's Empire*, above n. 11.

[30] Alexander and Kress, 'Against Legal Principles', above n. 1, at 310–26.

[31] A point seen clearly by many contemporary commentators on Dworkin. See e.g. Theodore Benditt, *Law as Rule and Principle* (Stanford: Stanford University Press, 1976), at 74–82.

[32] It is in this sense that Holmes's famous aphorism—'hard cases make bad law'—is to be understood. I discuss such hard cases at length in Moore, 'The Semantics of Judging', *Southern California Law Review*, 54 (1981), 151–295.

[33] See ibid. at 246–7.

[34] M. Moore, 'Precedent, Induction, and Ethical Generalization', in L. Goldstein (ed.), *Precedent in Law* (Oxford: Oxford University Press, 1987).

cases.[35] In any case, the good of equal treatment of the similarly situated demands that such seeming obvious law be stripped of its status as law, for only in this way can equality be served.

There is a third class of cases to be considered here. Let me call them 'truly easy cases'.[36] These are cases easily covered by the obvious law, *and* there is no principle derived in the requisite way speaking against such obvious application of obvious law. Even here Dworkin finds a place for his principles. Dworkin imagines a thoughtful judge confronting such a truly easy case. Being thoughtful, such a judge asks: but why is this statutory, common law, or constitutional rule binding on me as a judge (i.e. why is it law in the internal sense)? Her answer will likely be a matter of principle: because of the principle of legislative supremacy (for statutes), of *stare decisis* (for case law), and of constitutional supremacy (for constitutions).[37] And to justify these principles, in turn, Dworkin told us, will take the thoughtful judge deep into her entire basket of principles of political morality. Dworkin can be interpreted to have had a kind of 'Crossing the Rubicon' picture here, so that once a judge sees that to justify her obligation to follow obvious law she has to resort to some unobvious law, she has crossed the only line worth holding onto and she may as well let in *all* of her principles of political morality.[38] In fact, Dworkin was not nearly as sloppy as this. The way substantive principles get used by judges in truly easy cases depends on the way such principles get used in cases that are hard but looked easy. The law even in truly easy cases is not just a function of the obvious law, even as backed up by the principles of legislative supremacy, *stare decisis*, and constitutional supremacy. Rather, the law is still a balance between these last 'conservative' principles and the substantive principles that urge overruling of old cases, overruling of plain meanings, and the like. Even in truly easy cases, therefore, the law is still a complex balance of a constellation of principles even if the balance is easily in favour of the obvious law.[39]

Let me come to Dworkin's third question, raising whether the principles judges both do and should use in their decision of these three kinds of cases, are *legal* principles. Given Dworkin's internal sort of jurisprudence, this is equivalent to asking whether use of such principles is (legally)

[35] Ibid. at 201.

[36] I used to call these 'easy, easy cases'. See Moore, 'Semantics of Judging', above n. 32, at 279.

[37] The argument is fleetingly raised in Dworkin, 'Model of Rules', above n. 7, at 20–2. It only comes into its own in R. Dworkin, 'Hard Cases', *Harvard Law Review*, 88 (1975), 1057–109, at 1083–93.

[38] Bertrand Russell's kind of argument for why we should let properties into our ontology: since we have to let in some universals anyway, namely relations, we might as well let all properties in as well. Bertrand Russell, *The Problems of Philosophy* (New York: Henry Holt and Co., 1912).

[39] Dworkin, 'Model of Rules', above n. 7, at 22.

discretionary or (legally) obligatory with judges. (The parenthetical qualifiers, because if Dworkin has adequately answered the normative branch of the second question, then he has shown use of such principles to be *morally* obligatory on judges.)[40]

To the descriptive version of this third question, Dworkin made a kind of transcendental deduction from legal practice. The deduction began with an observation about 'the rights thesis':[41] even in the hardest cases, litigants do not come before judges as supplicants of judicial favour; they come, and are treated, as claimants of pre-existing legal rights. This is true even in truly hard cases, where there is no obvious law; therefore, there must be some unobvious law of a general sort generating the right to win a truly hard case. It is equally true of hard cases that look easy—for the 'plain meaning' of a statute is not, and never was, the law. The 'spirit' or 'deeper principle' is and was the law. Likewise, a prior holding of an older case now for the first time overruled is not now, and never was, the law, but only erroneous evidence of the true rule of law discovered for the first time in this case. The rights thesis also held for truly easy cases, but it did so only because the legal right seemingly generated by some bit of obvious law alone is in fact generated by the general principles justifying why judges are legally obligated to follow the obvious law in truly easy cases, balanced against the reasons that may exist not to so follow the obvious law. Our practice of the 'rights thesis', and its corollary, 'the right answer thesis',[42] thus presupposes that the principles judges resort to in these three kinds of cases are as much part of the law as are more obvious sources of law like statutes.

I call this a 'transcendental deduction' by Dworkin because it has a kind of Kantian formality to it: we engage in a certain practice, the condition for the possibility of our practising the practice is that something else be the case, therefore we must treat that something else as being the case because we can't imagine practising our practice any differently.[43] It is thus some-

[40] It might also be tempting to think that no *separate* normative argument need here be given, in addition to the normative argument given to answer the normative version of the second question. After all, if judges are morally obligated to use principles to resolve all three kinds of cases, this is an obligation that comes to them *qua* judges, that is, as part and parcel of the judicial role. It must therefore be a *legal* obligation of judges, because legal obligations are just moral obligations with respect to a legal rule. And if such principles are *legally* obligatory on judges, that they are *law* in the internal sense Dworkin's internal sort of jurisprudence uses.

Although such an argument is available, I prefer to put less weight on the single specification of law's function in terms of judicial obligation. Rather, a richer functional characterization of law in terms of the values law serves if it so obligates judges, is available.

[41] Dworkin, 'Hard Cases', above n. 37, at 1063.

[42] R. Dworkin, 'Is There No Right Answer?', *New York University Law Review*, 53 (1978), 1–32. I discuss the right-answer thesis in detail in Ch. 8, below.

[43] For Kant's version of this, see Lewis White Beck, *A Commentary on Kant's Critique of Practical Reason* (Chicago: University of Chicago Press, 1960).

what out of bounds to object that such arguments seem bootstrapping, because that is their essential nature;[44] only, they make virtue out of vice by denying that there is any choice about it.

Dworkin's argument for why we cannot give up the ways we practise law that demand the rights thesis, was cast in terms of retroactivity and the separation of powers.[45] The idea was that if we failed to practise law in the ways that presupposed the truth of the rights thesis, then we would be admitting to litigants that judges created new legal rights for them at trial, which rights would apply retroactively to the occurrence of those events that gave rise to their lawsuit. Such admission would also at the same time give up our legal theory that judges don't make the law, they only apply the law that is already laid down.

Alexander and Kress take these arguments to be normative arguments, particularly in their assumption that retroactivity is bad because it is unfair: retroactively applicable law unfairly surprises litigants who justifiably relied on the old version of the law.[46] Yet it is doubtful whether Dworkin was ever using retroactivity in this way, because the unobvious law (that could tell litigants what their legal rights were in hard cases) was for Dworkin just that, unobvious. Dworkin thought that it took a mythical judge of Herculean powers to see such law, so the justification for resort to such law can hardly have been to prevent unfair surprise.

Dworkin was making a very formal point here, about how much of our legal practices we would have to change if we abandoned the rights thesis. That judicial decisions are never retroactive applications of new law, but only discovery of old (even if unobvious) law, was thought by Dworkin to be a deep part of our thinking about law that we would find difficult if not impossible to give up.[47]

Coming to the normative version of Dworkin's third question, why *should* we regard the principles judges use in deciding cases to be legal, and not merely moral, principles? Of course, if we really couldn't think of practising overruling prospectively, or of going with plain meaning even against a statute's purpose, or of admitting that judges invent new legal rights in truly hard cases, or that judges *morally* justify their *legal* obligation to follow statutory or common law rules in truly easy cases, then

[44] As Justice Arabian of the California Supreme Court said in one of my seminars for judges: 'Legal rights are not like planets; they exist if our practices demand they do.'

[45] Dworkin, 'Model of Rules', above n. 7, at 31–45; Dworkin, above n. 37, at 1061–2.

[46] Alexander and Kress, above n. 1, at 296. This normative identification of retroactivity with the upsetting of reliance is surprising in that Kress in his earlier work is sensitive to the point. See K. Kress, 'Legal Reasoning and Coherence Theories: Dworkin's Rights Thesis, Retroactivity, and the Linear Order of Decisions', *California Law Review*, 72 (1984), 369–402, at 398–400.

[47] Even the formal point is subject to Kress's earlier argument based on what he calls the 'ripple effect'. See Kress, 'Legal Reasoning', above n. 46.

Dworkin could have used his 'transcendental deduction' normatively as well as descriptively. What we *must* do, we not only do, but we ought to do too (or least, it cannot be the case that we ought not to do it). Yet the Legal Realists taught us how easy it is to think in these alternative ways, and to change our legal practices accordingly.

The normative argument that Dworkin needed here is again best put in terms of equality. As we saw, Dworkin's argument (about why judges should resort to general principles drawn from legal materials to decide their three kinds of cases) in answer to the second question was in terms of *equal* legal treatment for present litigants with that given past litigants or to be given to future litigants. Now suppose one viewed law as what I have called a functional kind, i.e. something whose identity is bound up with its function (or what Fuller used to say, 'what it is good for'[48]). If one then held equality to be *the* distinctive value served by law, that would be reason enough to call those principles that serve this value *legal* principles.

If we interpret Dworkin to make him the best he can be, this is a fair reading of his argument here. For equality is just the kind of value Dworkin seeks with his unhelpful, 'integrity': equality is a value in its own right, and thus can be the distinctive value of law; and yet equality also involves one in using all values (because it takes all of morality to say when one case is relevantly like another), and thus broadens the reach of law into all of morality. This, as I have elsewhere argued, is the classical natural lawyer's strategy, from Aquinas to Finnis, Fuller, and Dworkin.[49]

Non-natural lawyers (i.e. legal positivists) can also avail themselves of this functionalist argument for why the principles that are rightly used to decide all three kind of cases are part of the law. Suppose, for example, one's theory of law's essential functions was more Benthamite: law exists only insofar as there is predictability of sanctions, for the values law serves are liberty and fairness, both of which demand that citizens can know (and thus, not be unfairly surprised) when public force will follow upon their actions.[50] Or suppose one's theory of law's essential function was more Fullerian: law exists only insofar as there is the efficient guidance of behaviour by clear, non-contradictory, public, prospective, etc., standards.[51]

With these theories of law's essential function, one could also argue that the general principles judges rightly use to decide cases are part of the law, because such principles serve the essential function(s) characteristic of law. Consider the claims made for deep and systematizing principles by Langdell and Morris Cohen: such principles make the law more knowable, even when the principles cover the same ground as the more obvious

[48] Discussed in Ch. 9, following.

[49] Ibid.

[50] For a convincing exposition of Bentham's concern with notice, see Gerald Postema, *Bentham and the Common Law Tradition* (Oxford: Oxford University Press, 1986).

[51] Lon Fuller, *The Morality of Law* (2nd edn., New Haven: Yale University Press, 1969).

(but much more complicated) legal materials from which they are drawn;[52] and such principles make the law much more extendable, so that the law truly becomes a seamless web that never runs out.[53] In both these ways, predictability of legal sanctions is enhanced, and the efficient guidance of behaviour by standards is enhanced, if judges are obligated to resort to such principles in their decisions. Serving such essential functions of law, such principles ought to be regarded *as law*, on this functionalist view of the matter.

I come, finally, to Dworkin's fourth question: why cannot there be a rule of recognition, a factual pedigree or test by historical sources, for such legal principles? True, because such principles are non-obvious law, the test cannot be as obvious as for obvious law. No legislature or court enacted such standards, or constitutional convention voted on them. Yet why cannot one make up a kind of recursion scheme as Rolf Sartorius once imagined,[54] whereby one logically derives legal principles from the obvious law? One may schematize Sartorius's idea in terms of the following rule of recognition:

$$L(p) \equiv [(\text{Stat.}(p) \text{ or } \text{Case}(p) \text{ or } \text{Const.}(p)) \text{ or } ((\text{Stat.}(q) \text{ or } \text{Case}(q) \text{ or } \text{Const.}(q)) \text{ and } (p \supset q))]$$

In English: The law provides some proposition p if and only if either a statute, case holding, or constitutional text says p, or such obvious sources say something else, q, and q is implied by p. The first disjunct on the right-hand side of the biconditional gives the rule of recognition for the obvious law, and the second, the rule of recognition for the unobvious law.

Dworkin's argument against this sort of deep legal positivism—the kind that matched him stride for stride in the use of legal principles to validate the rights thesis and the right answer thesis—was never very satisfactory. In his initial essay he only anticipated Hart's less deep positivism, a positivism that admitted that principles should be used to decide truly hard cases but denied these were *legal* principles. Thus, Dworkin urged that no rule of recognition could be formulated for such principles, because:

1. Their validity depended on professional acceptance, not on a single source.[55]
2. Their number and complexity outran the ability of any rule (of recognition) to generate them.[56]

[52] Langdell, *Summary*, above n. 3, at 52; Cohen, 'Place of Logic', above n. 3, at 622.
[53] Langdell, *Summary*, above n. 3, at 52; Cohen, 'Place of Logic', above n. 3, at 630.
[54] Rolf Sartorius, *Individual Conduct and Social Norms* 37 (Encino, Calif.: Dickenson Publishing, 1975).
[55] Dworkin, 'Model of Rules', above n. 7, at 23.
[56] Ibid.

3. The infinite gradations of their weight outran the ability of any rule (of recognition) to generate them.[57]
4. To allow principles to validate rules, as well as rules validate principles, would introduce a 'note of validity into the chord of acceptance', i.e. it would depart from Hart's linear kind of positivism that began with an *accepted* rule of recognition from whence all *valid* legal rules sprang.[58]

None of these arguments go any distance towards answering the kind of deep positivism of a Sartorius, a Langdell, or a Posner, although I shall not delay us by detailing why here. Potentially more interesting were the arguments Dworkin later deployed specifically against Sartorius's kind of deep positivism:

5. Nothing can *justify* legal rules but principles of moral content, and there is no rule of recognition for critical morality (as opposed to formal principles of a purely descriptive or explanatory kind that might be extracted from legal materials).[59]
6. Unuttered, unknown principles cannot be validated by a source-oriented rule of recognition, yet such principles are rightly regarded (when discovered) as having always been a part of our law.[60]

Yet neither of these arguments work either. Consider the examples provided by Langdell's deep principle of contract law (contracts require a meeting of minds) and by Posner's deep principle of tort law (a tort is inefficient behaviour by one person who causes injury to another who was not more inefficient in his behaviour).[61] The claim made by both Langdell and Posner for their principles was a Sartorius-style claim. Such principles were derived, they claimed, purely formally by seeing what general principle logically implied the many cases and the rules announced in them.

Such principles need never have been uttered, or even thought of, by those laying down the obvious legal sources from which such principles are drawn. This is quite possible, for there is nothing in a Sartorius-enriched rule of recognition requiring, e.g., that judges see the logical relationship between the principle of efficiency and the cases they were deciding. Such a logical relationship can exist no matter what they thought.

Similarly, such principles need not have any moral content (although both in fact do) to do the justificatory work demanded of them. If Langdell was right in the two claims he made for his principle—it rendered a mass of rules more easily knowable, and it extended the reach of the law to cases

[57] Dworkin, 'Model of Rules', above n. 7, at 23.
[58] Ibid.
[59] R. Dworkin, 'Social Rules and Legal Theory', *Yale Law Journal*, 81 (1972), 855–90, at 857.
[60] Ibid. at 877.
[61] Richard Posner, 'A Theory of Negligence', *Journal of Legal Studies*, 1 (1973), 29–96.

not covered by the rules—and if such knowability and determinateness are valuable, then such principles *justify* judges in deciding in accordance with them. The value of such principles need not lie in the goodness of the content, but rather, in their ability to further some good functions of law.

Better arguments for why legal principles must have a moral content, and thus cannot be pedigreed by any factual (or factual cum logical) test, are these. The first is a possibility argument based on the underdetermination of theory by any finite set of more particular data.[62] There are an infinite number of theories that fit the obvious law, in Sartorius's sense of 'fit' captured by his version of a rule of recognition. The choice of one of these cannot be purely a matter of fact and logic, as the deep legal positivist claims. It is true of course that data underdetermines theory in science too, yet we do not think of scientific theories as having a moral content because of this. Yet internal theories (principles) serve a justificatory function in the law that they do not serve in science; such theories in law give judges reasons to decide new cases in light of them. Judges can thus conform new data to their theories, in a way that scientists cannot make new experiments conform to theirs. Underdetermination is thus much more of a problem for a purely formal derivation of principles in law than it is in science.[63]

Second, in addition to this possibility argument there is a more straightforwardly moral argument. The moral argument is that we get a morally better legal system if we sacrifice some degrees of logical fit for some degrees of moral goodness in the content of the theory being fitted to the obvious law.[64] Posner, for example, does this when he acknowledges that the all or nothing contributory negligence rule of American tort law does not follow from his principle of efficiency, but he retains the principle despite such lack of fit.[65]

With these two arguments in place, one might then conclude that the general principles judges both do and should use in deciding all three kinds of cases are not only rightly regarded as part of the law that obligates them in their role as judges, but also and necessarily such principles have a moral content to them. That is the conclusion against which I wish to put Alexander and Kress's arguments.

[62] See M. Moore, 'Causation and the Excuses', *California Law Review*, 73 (1985), 1091–149, at 1094, for this use of Duhem's underdetermination thesis.

[63] Even in science, where experiments can narrow (but never eliminate) the possibilities of acceptable theory, underdetermination presents a long-noticed problem giving rise to non-moral but perhaps aesthetic virtues of theory construction. See e.g. Paul Thagard, *Conceptual Revolutions* (Princeton: Princeton University Press, 1992).

[64] Implicit in Dworkin, above n. 37, at 1057. Rather remarkably, Dworkin only announces the conclusion of this argument, but never makes the normative argument for that conclusion. For a beginning in that direction, see M. Moore, 'A Theory of Criminal Law Theories', in D. Friedmann (ed.), *Tel Aviv University Studies in Law*, 10 (1990), 115–85.

[65] Posner, 'Negligence', above n. 61, at 39–40.

III. ALEXANDER AND KRESS'S UN-PRINCIPLED ARGUMENTS

I think it is fair to construe Alexander and Kress as joining Dworkin in a quest for an internal jurisprudence. Even though the central argument they make could be made against use of legal principles by judges in any legal system, they nonetheless focus on law as it binds judges within our legal system. They, like Dworkin, take 'law' in its internal sense to be that which binds judges in their role as judges. Thus, if judges cannot or should not make use of things called legal principles in justifying results in particular cases, then in the only sense Alexander and Kress care about legal principles do not exist.[66]

Alexander and Kress also do not take issue with the descriptive version of Dworkin's internal jurisprudence, at least not on the face of what they say.[67] That is, Alexander and Kress do not dispute that judges do make reference to what they think of as legal principles as they decide cases, or that the way we practise constitutional and statutory interpretation and precedent in the Anglo-American legal system presupposes the truth of the rights thesis and the right answer thesis, which themselves presuppose the existence of legal principles of sufficient richness to cover all cases.

Theirs is a normative disagreement with Dworkin, a disagreement focused on the normative version of his argument in answer to his second and third questions. With respect to the second question Alexander and Kress argue that equality cannot justify to judges the use of general principles extracted from the obvious law in the way that Dworkin (let alone Sartorius, Posner, or Langdell) would recommend. Such extracted principles, they tell us, are either correct moral principles—in which event it is their moral correctness that enjoins judges to use them, *not* their extraction from the obvious law—or incorrect moral principles, which have no force both because they are morally incorrect and because there is no value of equality that can justify the continuation of moral mistakes. With respect to the third question, Alexander and Kress urge that all judges ought to

[66] Alexander and Kress, 'Against Legal Principles', above n. 1, at 303 n. 96.

[67] The equivocation, because they seem to be tempted by a flat metaphysical denial that legal principles exist even if the ways in which we practised law demanded that they do. Ibid. For a clearer example of this kind of descriptive scepticism, see Mark Temin, 'Toward an Account of the Truth of Propositions of Law', *University of Cincinnati Law Review*, 49 (1980), 341–61. By not addressing the descriptive version of Dworkin's claim here, Alexander and Kress fail to undermine a compelling feature of Dworkin's account, and that is the seamlessness of the law that it depicts. When contrasted with views that say that judges do two quite different things when they decide cases (follow the obvious law *or* resort to non-legal morality), or that say that statutes or case holdings have determinate domains (e.g. Frank Easterbrook, 'Statutes' Domains', *University of Chicago Law Review*, 50 (1983), 533), Dworkin's seamless web view of law and univocal mode of judicial reasoning look very attractive and familiar.

employ in deciding cases are correct moral principles, as applied so as to take into account in the appropriate way the inevitable fact that the obvious law bequeathed to us by the past is far from ideal. That taking into account of a non-ideal legal past, they tell us, does not itself demand a set of principles that are distinctively legal principles, which principles would describe how this adjustment is to proceed. Thus, the only *law* there is is obvious law, because the principles that decide my three classes of cases are only moral principles, not themselves part of the law. Both of these considerations lead them to their conclusion that legal principles do not exist.

A. Alexander and Kress on the Second Question

It is crucial to their first argument getting off the ground that legal principles not be construed to be a subset of moral principles,[68] so let me address that presupposition of theirs before coming to the argument that presupposes it. A natural reading of Dworkin's four-step argument for principles is to think that legal principles are in content a subset of moral principles, a subset marked by the institutional support such principles have received in a given legal system. Such an interpretation of legal principles would hamstring Alexander and Kress's first argument, because then: the supposed emptiness of equality as a value would not remove the moral force of legal principles (because they would have the force of their moral content); and such principles would not be superfluous, because *as a set* they would dictate outcomes in cases different than that the *complete* set of moral principles would yield.

Alexander and Kress are entitled to their presupposition. To see this, ask of this natural interpretation of Dworkin the kind of question Herbert Hart actually directed to Dworkin[69] (no less than to Fuller[70]): what about evil legal regimes? If the obvious law from which legal principles partly spring is bad law, how can Dworkinian principles, any more than Fullerian purposes, be good? Putting even the best face on very bad law can still result in far from ideal principles (or Fullerian purposes). Legal principles in all real world (i.e. non-utopian) cases will thus be non-ideal versions of moral principle (what Alexander and Kress prefer to call incorrect moral principles), that is, principles that dictate results at some remove from the

[68] As they recognize: 'Against Legal Principles', above n. 1, at 293–4 n. 74.

[69] Hart, 'Reply', in R. Gavison (ed.), *Issues in Contemporary Legal Philosophy* (Oxford: Oxford University Press, 1987); H. L. A. Hart, *The Concept of Law* (2nd edn., Oxford: Oxford University Press, 1994), at 203.

[70] Hart, above n. 8 at 613; H. L. A. Hart, 'Book Review Fuller: The Morality of Law', *Harvard Law Review*, 78 (1965), 1281–96, at 1288.

[71] I put aside Fuller's incredible faith that coherence has an inevitable affinity with goodness. Fuller, 'Fidelity to Law—A Reply to Professor Hart', *Harvard Law Review*, 71 (1958),

results required by correct moral principles.[71]

This is what sets up the central contention in Alexander and Kress's first argument. Once a principle diverges, however slightly, from what would be morally ideal, there is no value served by following such a defective principle. Following the ideal moral principle would always be better, and there is no value served by following the defective principle that can make up for this obvious deficit.

This joins issue between Dworkin and Alexander and Kress on the value of equality. Equality seems to justify following a less than ideal principle that accurately describes how others have been treated or will be treated, so Alexander and Kress have to show us that this is an illusion.

Alexander's previous mode of argument here was a kind of frontal assault on the value of equality.[72] To see how the argument gets started, imagine a claim of what I shall call purely formal equality. Suppose I am distributing a benefit that not all can have, and I announce only to myself that I am giving the benefit to the first recipient because she has red hair. Suppose further that hair colour on no conceivable theory has anything to do with justified receipt of such a benefit. My criterion of decision, in other words, is morally arbitrary. When a second redhead comes along, but I deny him the benefit, does he have any claim stemming from the fact that another person received the benefit because she was red-headed? That I might publicly *announce* the redhead criterion, so that people rely on it, is not the question. That my psychoanalyst can criticize me, either for irrationality in not generalizing my first decision at all, or for self-deception about what it was, or for changing my mind, is also by the by. Does equality in any way give the second person a reason to complain about not getting the benefit?

If you agree with me that the answer must be no, then there is no such thing as a purely formal equality. Put in a different way, no good whatsoever is served by treating cases alike that are similar to each other only in morally arbitrary ways such as hair colour.[73] Thus, for equal treatment to be of value, the cases to be *treated* alike must *be* alike in morally relevant respects.

Critics of equality as a value usually, like Alexander, seize upon this fea-

630–72, at 636. Although the historical Dworkin himself early on castigated Fuller for this faith (R. Dworkin, 'The Elusive Morality of Law', *Villanova Law Review*, 10 (1965), 631–9; Dworkin, 'Philosophy, Morality, and Law—Observations Prompted by Professor Fuller's Novel Claim', *University of Pennsylvania Law Review*, 113 (1965), 668–90), Dworkin himself has proved remarkably optimistic that a cohered extension of past legal material yields just his vision of how things should be.

[72] Lawrence Alexander, 'Constrained by Precedent', *Southern California Law Review*, 63 (1989), 1–64, at 9–13.

[73] Argued for in Moore, 'Precedent', above n. 34, at 185–7.

[74] The best known are Peter Westen, 'The Empty Idea of Equality', *Harvard Law Review*, 95 (1982), 537–96; Joseph Raz, *The Morality of Freedom* (Oxford: Oxford University Press, 1986).

ture of equality.[74] They note, quite accurately, that to know what are and what are not morally relevant respects that could justify unlike treatment requires nothing less than knowledge of all the values there are. Any difference between cases could make a difference in the treatment they deserve, and it is nothing less than all of morality that can tell us whether this is one of those factual differences that makes a moral difference.

To finish the objection: once we apply all of morality in deciding on the merits whether some difference should make a difference, we will already have answered our question about whether someone deserves a certain treatment *without regard to equality*. If you have a right to speak freely in a certain situation, and I claim that therefore I do too, there are only two possibilities: my case is relevantly like yours, or it is not. If it is relevantly like yours, that will only be because I too have the substantive right to free speech. Having such a substantive right, I have no need of a claim of equality. Alternatively, if my case is relevantly different than yours, that will only be because I lack the substantive right to speak freely in my circumstances. Again, it is the contours of the substantive right doing all the work, leaving none for equality to do as a separate value.

This is not yet Alexander's argument against equality, for he sees clearly the flaw in the argument. If equality ever matters, he rightly argues, it matters when the first decision is morally incorrect.[75] It is when the first person was given the right, but wrongly so, that the second person has any claim truly based in equality. Alexander gives the example of the rock concert that he allows his daughter to go to at age 14 but subsequently realizes that this was a mistaken judgement on his part.[76] When his son reaches 14, Alexander has to decide whether his son has any claim of equality to like treatment. If the son has such a claim, even if he doesn't get to go because it would be such a mistake that the badness of his going outweighs the badness of denying equal treatment, then equality has independent moral life.

Alexander's earlier argument against equality was simply to deny that his son, or people like him, have *any* claim that arises out of mistaken treatment by other people. His son should really complain, Alexander argues, if he let him go to the rock concert against his (Alexander's) own best judgement.[77]

Put this bluntly, this has been a hard argument for Alexander to sustain. After all, most people's intuitions are the other way. Punish one criminal a certain amount for a certain crime, then a second criminal guilty of a like crime is usually thought to have strong equality claim to be punished no more severely, even conceding that the first punishment was too light. In simply pitting his intuitions against the common ones, Alexander was

[75] Alexander, 'Constrained by Precedent', above n. 72, at 9–13. [76] Ibid. at 5–7.
[77] Ibid.

thus very much swimming upstream.

In their present article Alexander and Kress seek to reach the same conclusion about equality, but with a subtler line of attack. What, they now ask, can be the determiner of relevant sameness or difference between cases if a prior decision was morally incorrect? A legal principle, perhaps, on the model of a kind of second best moral principle: this makes sons like daughters for rock concerts, but does not make the family dog like a daughter for purposes of attending rock concerts. Yet, they ask, how is such a non-ideal moral principle to be drawn? Why not include the family dog as well as the son for purposes of like treatment here? Because there is a big difference between a dog and a son, you say, more than the difference between a son and a daughter? How can there be any *morally relevant* difference between them, because on morally correct principles none of them have any right to go to the rock concert? In all respects relevant to such a right, they are all the same.[78]

Another way of putting this same point is to say that morality is completely silent about morally relevant respects for projecting a morally mistaken decision into the future. Morality only provides relevant respects for correct decisions, but for them, equality has no work to do. But any respect claimed to be relevant on some basis other than morality's will reduce equality's claim to that of pure formal equality, which is no claim at all. Thus, if Langdell and Posner were right that their principles were purely formal principles, derived logically from cases some of which were mistaken, there could be no claim that following such principles (i.e. allowing such principles to determine relevant similarities deserving of like treatment) furthered anything but pure formal equality, which is of no value. And to the extent that Dworkin is right that part of the pedigree for his principles is a formal fit with decisions some of which are mistaken, he is subject to the same remonstrance. Indeed, anyone purporting to follow any principle that diverges to any extent from morally correct principles cannot justify this on equality grounds, for to the extent his non-ideal principle matches the ideal moral principle equality has no work to do and to the extent his non-ideal principle does not match the ideal moral principle the 'equality' generated by like treatment under this principle is only the purely formal equality having no value whatsoever. One is thus driven, Alexander and Kress conclude, to the view that equality has nothing to work with in projecting mistaken decisions into the future. The morally relevant is of no help, and the morally arbitrary is of no value. Equality dies of unemployment.

If equality does not justify diverging from the morally ideal (by follow-

[78] This is my own reworking of the argument they make, Alexander and Kress, 'Against Legal Principles', above n. 1, at 301–7.

ing non-ideal legal principles), why do so? Alexander and Kress put this incrementally: for any legal principle diverging from an ideal moral principle, why not confine the past to the past and go with the ideal moral principle?[79] They are somewhat unclear as to *how* confined they intend the obvious legal materials of the past to be. They seem to have in mind past decisions in particular cases, and seem to suggest that such decisions 'be confined to their facts', as lawyers often put it. For statutes or other canonical rules, perhaps the confining is to the plain meaning of such statutes, or perhaps to the prior applications of such statutes. But none of this matters to their thesis. However confined may be the obvious legal materials, all a present judge ever needs is those materials, and correct moral principles. He has no reason to construct a third thing, legal principles.

There are two ways to go after this argument of Alexander and Kress. One is to find some value other than equality that justifies the continuation of moral error in past legal materials into the future via the construction of legal principles. The other is to dispute their rejection of equality as a value. I shall pursue both avenues.

As to the first, our prior discussion suggests the line of march here. Suppose one thought, like Langdell and Morris Cohen, that the function served by legal principles was primarily the notice function.[80] Legal principles better illuminate areas of law already covered by obvious legal materials, and such principles also cover new ground so that that which was unknowable because indeterminate is now knowable because determinate. Then the values justifying judges projecting past errors into the future via the construction of legal principles are the values of liberty and fairness. In such a case, the emptiness of equality would be beside the point in the normative argument for use of legal principles by judges.

It is far from obvious that legal principles constructed in the manner urged by Dworkin—or by Cohen, Langdell, Posner, or Sartorius, for that matter—do increase notice to citizens or to their lawyers of the legal consequences that will follow on their behaviour. To see, let us separate the abbreviatory or heuristic function of principles from the creative or extending function.

Part of the notice claim, as made by Langdell and Cohen, is that legal principles are more graspable, more memorable, and more easily applicable than the more numerous, more complicated legal rules, and the cases from which such rules are derived. I call this the heuristic function of legal principles, but also the abbreviatory function because legal principles so conceived do not add coverage to existing legal materials. They merely abbreviate those materials in a way that is heuristically useful.

There have been strictly abbreviatory conceptions of legal principles in

[79] Ibid. at 305. [80] Text at nn. 51–3, above,

legal theory, as there were such conceptions of theories in science. In both cases, what made the legal principles or scientific theories strictly abbreviatory was the reductionist definitions of the terms used in the legal principles or scientific theories.[81] Take Alf Ross's analysis of the legal concept of ownership.[82] On Ross's view, the two-place predicate, 'x owns y', has as its meaning *two* biconditionals: it is equivalent to what Ross called 'conditioning facts', such as the fact that x was the original possessor of y, x was given y, x bought y, etc.—in short, the facts made relevant by legal rules specifying the conditions under which original or derivative title were acquired. 'X owns y' is also equivalent, Ross thought, to the legal consequences we usually call 'the incidents of ownership', consequences like, that x may possess y, x may exclude others from possessing y, x may transfer y, etc.

On this view, the statement, 'x owns y', is strictly abbreviatory of a large set of rules that could be specified without mention of ownership. Such rules would connect individual conditioning facts to individual legal consequences in an 'if . . . then . . .' form. The content of such numerous rules would be the same as the statement, 'x owns y', but the usability of such mass of rules would be considerably less.

If legal principles were abbreviatory of a mass of legal rules in the way Ross's analysis suggests, then their value as heuristics would be assured. Yet legal principles don't look like Ross's analyses, and it is important to see why. 'Efficiency' in Posner's principle of efficiency, 'meeting of the minds' in Langdell's principle of contract formation, to say nothing of 'profit from his own wrong' in Dworkin's favourite example of a legal principle, do not have their meaning given in terms of two sets of necessary and sufficient conditions, and it is doubtful that even ownership, as we actually use it in our legal system, does either.[83] This is, I think, intuitive just on its face, but one can also see why this has to be so.

Suppose the terms of such legal principles could be reductively defined in the way Ross suggests. Then the legal principle in which such terms are used would not only imply the rules from which it was derived; such principle would also be implied by such rules. Let 'P' represent such principle, and let '$R_1, R_2 \ldots R_n$' represent the rules from which it is derived. Then:

(1) '$R_1, R_2 \ldots R_n$' $\supset$ P

Yet legal principles are also supposed to cover new ground, that is, decide cases not decidable on the basis of the rules from which they are derived.

[81] In law, Alf Ross, 'Tu-Tu', *Harvard Law Review*, 70 (1957), 812–25. In science, operational definition of theoretical terms, as in P. W. Bridgeman, *The Logic of Modern Physics* (New York: Macmillan, 1927).

[82] Ross, 'Tu-Tu', above n. 81.

[83] On the latter point, see Moore, 'Semantics of Judging', above n. 32, at 232–42.

Let 'R_{n+1}' represent the new rule that decides such cases. What legal principles are supposed to do is allow us to derive R_{n+1} from P, thusly:

(2) $P \supset R_{n+1}$

But (1) and (2) yield:

(3) $R_1, R_2 \ldots R_n \supset R_{n+1}$

What this tells us is that a legal principle whose terms are reductively defined can decide no case not already decidable by the obvious law.[84] Thus, truly abbreviatory legal principles that might serve the heuristic function cannot serve the creative or extending function.

It is clear from looking at principles like Posner's, Langdell's, and Dworkin's, that the legal principles proposed are intended to serve the creative/extending function. That is, after all, required by the idea Alexander and Kress find so problematic about legal principles, namely, their projection of past error into the future. Yet this robs legal principles of the most obvious way (i.e. as mere abbreviations) in which they could serve the heuristic function.

Still, even non-abbreviatory, truly extending principles might increase the knowability of law in the way that Langdell suggests. It depends on the obviousness of the (non-reductive) semantic rules giving meaning to the terms such principles employ. Dworkin's 'profit from his own wrong' does not look very promising here, nor does Langdell's 'meeting of the minds'. As Morris Cohen argued in detail, it takes acceptance of Langdell's postulated and non-obvious meanings to get from his principle to the new rules he derived from it, such as the rule that an unaccepted offer cannot survive the death of the offeror, that an offer cannot be irrevocable, or that a mailed acceptance of an offer was effective only upon receipt but that a mailed revocation of an offer was effective upon dispatch.[85] On the other hand, Posner's principle of efficiency looks more promising, because 'efficiency' looks better defined. Although factually hard to calculate, semantically the concept of efficiency looks clear enough in terms of minimizing the sum of accident and safety costs, in part because the idea of a cost is intuitively clear.

We thus end up with a shaky but not impossible case for legal principles in terms of their ability to give better notice than the rules from which they were derived. How plausible this sort of case can be for projecting past errors into the future all depends on the content of the principles being

[84] The same holds for reductive analyses in science: being able to derive a theory from an experimental law eliminates the power of the theory to generate new predictions and laws. See Suppe, *Structure of Scientific Theories*, above n. 15, at 11, 18–21.

[85] Cohen, 'Place of Logic', above n. 3, at 635–6.

proposed. I shall thus leave this question unresolved, and turn to the other issue raised by Alexander and Kress analysis, the value of equality.

The back of the Alexander and Kress argument against equality can be broken the moment one gets rid of their all-or-nothing presupposition about equality.[86] That is, they assume that equal treatment is either demanded (because two cases are alike in all morally relevant respects) or it is not (because there is some morally relevant difference between the cases). For them, there cannot be matters of degree so that some pairs of cases are *more* relevantly similar than others (meaning that equal treatment is *more* demanded between such pairs of cases than between the *less* similar pairs).

Recall Larry's largest dog, whose name is Karl. My sense is that Karl is less like Larry's daughter, Jenny, than David and Jonathan (Larry's sons) are like Jenny for purposes of assessing their moral right to go to a rock concert at age 14 (age 2, presumably, in dog years). Thus, equality is *more* denied when Larry's sons don't get to go, when his daughter did, than when the family pooch is denied the right to go. I say this, conceding that none of them, Jenny included, ever had the substantive right to go to a rock concert at age 14. The mistake Larry made in letting her go carries more of equality's force to his sons than to his dogs. Indeed, there are doubtlessly some relevant differences between the sons: so one of them probably has a stronger claim based in equality than the other (this, to avoid the worry that dogs have no rights at all).

Alexander and Kress have to deny sense to this scalar picture of equality. They admit that morality specifies the relevant respects in which cases must be similar enough to merit equal treatment (anyone who believes in the existence of *any* logically general standards has to admit this).[87] But they deny that morality also specifies degrees of closeness between cases, so that two cases can be more (morally relevantly) similar than two other cases even though no such cases are similar enough to merit the same treatment.

This is not just a 'bright-line' picture of equality. Theirs also has to be a bright-line picture of all moral standards. Someone with characteristics A, B, and C has a certain moral entitlement; anyone who lacks any of these attributes below a certain degree does not. And it does not matter how much of A, B, or C one may be possessed of if one is below the cut-off point for the entitlement, nor does it matter if one lacks A, B, *and* C, or just one of them—one is in no sense *closer* to having the entitlement. So far as moral

[86] Which Dworkin implicitly does in his talk about the 'gravitational force' of past cases. Dworkin, *Taking Rights Seriously* (Cambridge, Mass.: Harvard University Press, 1978), at 110–13, 118–19.

[87] This, because equality on their minimalist analysis is nothing but the logical generality of moral standards, standards that apply to *all* members of a given class.

mistakes go, on their view, there is nothing to be said about the degree of mistake. Mad dogs and Englishmen, sons, daughters, and family pooch—since none of them have a right to hear the Sex Pistols, letting any of them go is equally a mistake.

Yet it seems clear to me that morality is not unconcerned about the degree to which we may be mistaken on some particular matter. Some mistakes are worse than others, because some situations are closer (to the situation demanded by some moral rule) than others.[88] Yet if we can grade the seriousness of mistakes by the degree to which the cases about which we make them fail to possess the factual characteristics demanded by the relevant moral norm, then we can also grade by degrees the strength of equality's demands. Closer cases more demand like treatment than more removed cases, even though none of such cases meet the criterion justifying such treatment to begin with. Such a scalar equality, built on such a scalar morality, is not at all nonsensical or impossible. Indeed, it seems to be precisely the picture of morality most of us share.

Alexander has one more arrow to draw from his quiver of arguments against equality, and that is to concede (*arguendo*, to be sure) that equality is a scalar value but to deny that it is scalar in the way it would have to be to avoid reducing itself to absurdity. Surely, Alexander has argued in previous work,[89] the degrees of closeness between pairs of cases cannot be measured by their simple spatio-temporal removes from one another. Yet unless they are so measured, this commits equality buffs like me to enquiring after the treatment of cavemen and Indonesians when I ask what equality demands in a contemporary American law case. For the spatio-temporally distant treatments of cavemen and Indonesians press just as strongly as the treatment rendered in yesterday's West Reporter system.

Since Alexander's conclusion is indeed too absurd to embrace, I reject the premise that generates it. Equality is scalar in just the way that Alexander rejects. With regard to time, equality is like radium: its force decays simply in proportion to time elapsing. Long past cases, or cases we can predict in the distant future, are much less (morally) close to a present case than are yesterday's and tomorrow's decisions. What matters in measuring degree of moral closeness includes time in addition to the kind of partial possession of morally relevant attributes earlier discussed.

This purely temporal dimension to degrees of moral closeness between cases explains an often noticed feature about equality. At some point we

[88] I explore one example of morality's concern with the degree of moral mistakenness in Moore, 'Torture and the Balance of Evils', *Israel Law Review*, 23 (1989), 280–344, at 313–14. There I argue that the degree to which an action is wrong affects the level of good consequences that may justify the doing of such an action, even to an agent-relative moralist like myself.

[89] Alexander, 'Constrained by Precedent', above n. 72, at 9–13.

commonly think we have paid the respect due to a past, mistaken decision. At some point, equality's force is spent enough that the desirability of making the right decision outweighs the now weakened demand of equality. For academics, tenure is a familiar example of this balance. Most of us will admit that we have participated in tenure decisions that were mistaken. If the mistake was to deny tenure when it should have been granted, the gravity of the mistake outweighs any equality claim right from the start, so that we do not deny tenure to other meritorious individuals just so that the first has no complaint. If the mistake was to grant tenure when it should have been denied, the seriousness of the mistake may be outweighed initially by the demand of equality: the next person who comes along, if possessed of no greater (but no lesser) desert for tenure, probably gets it. Yet at some point, the force of the old mistake will become spent enough, that a candidate no more undeserving than the original will nonetheless be denied tenure. And rightly so, if equality is scalar over time.

Of course, if decisions on tenure have to be made often, so that an erroneous decision generates another which generates another, etc., a mistake may never 'tire' in the manner contemplated. Instead, it may become embedded by recapitulation. But if such a chain of mistaken decisions can be foreseen before it becomes such a chain, that shows the mistake to be so serious that the badness of perpetuating it a second time (and foreseeably a third, a fourth, etc.) may well outweigh the demand(s) of equality. This doesn't show equality to be without value; only, how complicated may be the calculations of when the value is overcome.

One might well think space to differ from time when it comes to measuring how close one situation is to another for purposes of assessing the strength of equality's demand for similar treatment. Spatial distance as such seems morally irrelevant. Such literal distance may be a crude proxy, however, for something else that is not morally irrelevant. I refer to those relationships, some voluntary, others not, that so deeply affect our rights and obligations. These tend to dissipate with distance, so that the dear are often literally the near to us. Since the degree of moral closeness that determines the strength of equality's claim depends on all of morality, these moral differences will make a difference for equality. There will likely be morally relevant differences between US citizens and Indonesians for purposes of a court assessing the strength of the demand for equal treatment, and the difference may easily be of such magnitude that how Indonesians are treated on a certain issue can for all practical purposes be ignored.

Equality thus is not empty, nor is it weak as it applies to morally close cases. It is thus a better candidate than liberty and fairness for the value that justifies judges in projecting those mistakes into the future that are embedded in obvious legal materials.

B. Alexander and Kress on the Third Question

That gets us to the normative version of Dworkin's third question. The question is why the principles that describe the extent to which past mistakes in obvious legal materials are to be projected into the future, should be thought of as *legal* principles. Alexander and Kress put it this way: grant that there might be some values like liberty, fairness, or equality justifying judges in continuing to diverge from what would be morally ideal in the absence of past mistakes. That is, grant that judges for these reasons should project past mistakes into the future. Yet still, all such judges need are the obvious legal materials containing such past mistakes, and correct moral principles (including the principles of liberty, fairness, equality, or whatever). There is no need, and no room, for *legal* principles too.[90]

There is a sense in which what Alexander and Kress here have to say is true, and it is this sense that gives their argument whatever plausibility it may possess. At the level of basic building blocks, all a judge needs is indeed the obvious law and morality. But given the scalar nature of equality—a value here conceded by Alexander and Kress to be a meaningful part of that morality[91]—there will be some description of how close (morally) a present case has to be to a past, mistaken bit of obvious law before it is close enough that the goodness of equal treatment wins out over the badness of the mistake. That description of closeness will necessarily have a content that will be generalized into a legal principle (that is, any other case that is also that close should also be treated that way). Such legal principle, being a kind of second best, non-ideal, or incorrect moral principle will both describe the degree of closeness and prescribe to a judge to decide in a way that projects past errors that far and no further.

At this juncture, one might interpose that this only argues that there are such non-ideal *moral* principles, not that they should be regarded as part of the law. The objection is correct, but the argument to get around it is easy to complete: if the legal philosopher I invented that I have been calling 'Dworkin' is correct, the unique value served by law is the furtherance of equality.[92] Any standard that serves that value through obligating judges to apply that standard, thus should be called law, in the functionalist, internalist sense of the word that we should care about.

IV. CONCLUSION

This completes my case for thinking, contra Alexander and Kress, that there are legal principles. Since I agree with Dworkin's fourth thesis (that

[90] Alexander and Kress, 'Against Legal Principles', above n. 1, at 326–7.
[91] Ibid. at 326.
[92] Text at nn. 47–9 above.

there can be no purely factual pedigree showing such principles to be part of the law) this commits me to a kind of natural law position. At least for those standards that are part of the law but not part of the obvious law, they are law in part because they are morally good—not ideally good perhaps, but good enough for government work, given the mistakes in past institutional history from which they were drawn.

8

Metaphysics, Epistemology, and Legal Theory

In this chapter I shall continue my discussion of Ronald Dworkin's theory of adjudication.[1] More specifically, I discuss two theses that can fairly be attributed to Dworkin. The first is what I shall call the 'conventionalist thesis'. The conventionalist thesis holds that the truth of a proposition lies in its fit with those explicit or implicit agreements in belief or attitude that one may call conventions. The second thesis is what I shall call the 'right-answer thesis', which holds that (on Dworkin's theory of how judges ought to reason) there will always be a right answer to disputed cases at law, no matter how 'hard' the case or 'undemonstrable' the conclusion.

In Section I,[2] I describe in greater detail the conventionalist thesis and lay out why I believe Dworkin holds it with regard to propositions about morality, literature, and law. In Section II, I then describe the right-answer thesis in greater detail, and examine Dworkin's arguments for it. In the course of this exegesis, I point out the tensions I think exist between the two theses.

Section III lays out Dworkin's attempt to avoid taking any metaphysical position, be it conventionalist, realist, or sceptical. Finding this avoidance strategy of Dworkin's to be unavailing, I conclude with my own belief about how the tension is to be resolved. We should reject the conventionalist thesis in favour of a metaphysical realism that is not only consistent with the right-answer thesis but would demand that such a thesis be true.

[1] See R. Dworkin: *A Matter of Principle* (Cambridge, Mass.: Harvard University Press, 1985) [hereinafter Dworkin, *Principle*]; *Taking Rights Seriously* (Cambridge, Mass.: Harvard University Press, 1977) [hereinafter, Dworkin, *Rights*]; 'A Reply to Critics', in *Taking Rights Seriously* Appendix, above [hereinafter Dworkin, 'Critics']; 'A Reply by Ronald Dworkin', in M. Cohen (ed.), *Ronald Dworkin and Contemporary Jurisprudence* (Oxford: Oxford University Press, 1984) [hereinafter Dworkin, 'Reply']; 'Judicial Discretion', *Journal of Philosophy*, 60 (1963), 624–38 [hereinafter Dworkin, 'Discretion']; 'Law's Ambitions For Itself', *Virginia Law Review*, 71 (1985), 173–87 [hereinafter Dworkin, 'Ambitions']; '"Natural" Law Revisited', *University of Florida Law Review*, 34 (1982), 165–88 [hereinafter Dworkin, 'Natural Law']. Dworkin has continued to work out his theory of adjudication in *Law's Empire* (Cambridge, Mass.: Harvard University Press, 1986) [hereinafter Dworkin, *Empire*], which appeared in print after this chapter was originally written.

[2] The three divisions of this chapter correspond to the main themes of chapters Six, Five, and Seven, respectively, of Dworkin, *Principle*, above n. 1.

I. THE CONVENTIONALIST THESIS

A. What Is Conventionalism?

We need a more exact statement of the conventionalist thesis in general before we seek to find it in Dworkin's writings about literature, law, and morality. Because conventionalism is a species of anti-realism, we would do well to define realism first.

Realism is: (1) a theory of truth, according to which 'is true' is defined so as to satisfy Tarski's convention T, and according to which there must be something in the external world by virtue of which any proposition p or its negation is true (the correspondence theory of truth);[3] (2) a theory of logic such that the logical connectives are given their usual (truth-functional) definitions in terms of truth tables (the classical theory of logic); (3) a theory of meaning for statements such that the meaning of any statement is the set of conditions under which an assertion of that statement would be true (the truth conditional theory of meaning); and (4) a theory of reference for singular terms and predicates such that no exhaustive list of descriptions can be specified that authoritatively fixes the reference or extension of singular terms or predicates (the causal theory of reference).[4] While 'realism' is often taken to be the name of only the correspondence theory of truth, I prefer the expanded definition of realism in this context because it encompasses other beliefs (about logic, meaning, and reference) that a realist about truth should hold.

These four theories characterize what might be called a realist's metaphysics. A realist, like anyone else, also needs an epistemology, or what I would call a theory of justification. While there are a wide variety of theories of justification (both foundational and non-foundational) that are consistent with realism, the one thing a realist must deny is that the conditions under which a rational agent is justified in believing or asserting some proposition to be true are the same as the conditions under which the proposition is true. A realist must deny, in other words, any identification of her theory of justification with her theory of truth. For what is distinctive about realism is the belief that propositions can be true even if we, at present, have no rational grounds for believing or asserting that they are true.

[3] See M. Dummett, *Truth and Other Enigmas* (Cambridge, Mass.: Harvard University Press, 1980) 14; H. Putnam, *Meaning and the Moral Sciences* (Cambridge: Cambridge University Press, 1978), 30. In Ch. 10 I give a more ontological, less semantic, definition of realism.

[4] See S. Kripke, *Naming and Necessity* (2nd edn., Cambridge, Mass.: Harvard University Press, 1980) (defending a causal theory of reference); H. Putnam, *Mind, Language and Reality* (Cambridge: Cambridge University Press, 1975), 215–71 (defending a causal theory of reference).

Conventionalism is a kind of anti-realism.[5] About truth, an anti-realist may or may not deny the adequacy of Tarski's convention T for any truth definition, but he will certainly deny that there is something in the external world by virtue of which any proposition p or its negation is true. An anti-realist will define truth in terms of justification: whatever it is that justifies a rational agent in believing some proposition p or its negation to be true, is all that 'is true' means.

A conventionalist is an anti-realist who ties the justification (and thus the truth) of some proposition p to the shared acceptance of some other proposition(s) q. A foundationalist-conventionalist might assert, for example, that q is some general proposition on which everyone (or everyone who counts) agrees, and that p follows deductively from q; or such a conventionalist might assert that q is some singular proposition describing some perceptual experience from which p can be derived by a combination of analytic truths and inductive inference. More relevant for purposes of understanding Dworkin, a non-foundationalist in epistemology who is also a conventionalist in his metaphysics will think that what justifies a rational agent in believing some proposition p to be true is that p 'fits' (coheres) better with q than does not-p, where q represents those propositions (of both greater and lesser generality) on which the relevant population agrees.

In addition to defining truth in terms of justification, and justification in terms of convention, a conventionalist will shift his theories of logic and of meaning to accommodate his reconstrual of 'is true'. His theory of logic now will not be the classical theory, but will be an intuitionist theory whereby one does not define the logical connectives in terms of (realist) truth but rather, in terms of warranted (justified) assertibility (conventional truth). A conventionalist will deny all truth conditions theories of the meaning of statements and replace it with some variation of the idea of 'assertion conditions' or 'verification conditions' for statements. He will also deny the causal theory of reference and think that the meaning of singular terms and of predicates is determined by the usage of those terms by some linguistic community ('meaning is use'). From such usage one will extract the sense of singular terms or of predicates, which will be given in terms of criteria (in either the strong sense that will generate an analytic truth or in Wittgenstein's weaker 'criteriological' sense) or, in the case of

[5] My use of the term 'conventionalism' is to be distinguished from one of Dworkin's recent usages where he calls a legal positivist theory of adjudication by this name. Dworkin, 'Natural Law', above n. 1, at 178. Most recently, Dworkin uses 'conventionalism' to name a legal positivist theory of adjudication that is 'interpretive' rather than 'semantic' in its foundation. Dworkin, *Empire*, above n. 1, at 94–5, 114–17. Legal positivism is a species of conventionalism, but I intend by the word to name the metaphysical notion, not any derivative notions in legal theory.

predicates, in terms of paradigmatic experiences conventionally clumped together and associated with certain symbols.[6]

B. Dworkin's Conventionalism

The choice between realism and conventionalism is not an all-or-nothing choice that we must each make about all areas of thought. It is possible that different sorts of phenomena call for different metaphysics. At least, it requires an argument to show the contrary, as I have tried to do with moral realism and scientific realism.[7] We, therefore, should not seek to abstract from Dworkin's work some general metaphysical position. Rather, we should allow Dworkin his own divisions and follow his thought in the areas of morality, literature, and law.

Before we do so, there is one general observation to be made and that is about Dworkin's epistemology, not his metaphysics. With an apparent nod to Quine, Dworkin accepts a non-foundationalist theory of justification as an adequate general view of knowledge.[8] One of Dworkin's central tenets is that justification in law, ethics, aesthetics, and science is a matter of coherence and not a matter of finding indubitable first premises.

1. *Dworkin's Conventionalist Ethics*

The kind of moral realism that I have elsewhere defended is an instance of the realism sketched above.[9] That is, a moral realist will believe: that moral propositions are true in virtue of their correspondence to things in the world like justice; that classical logic applies to such propositions; that the meaning of such propositions lies in the conditions under which they are true, in the correspondence sense of 'true'; and that the meaning of words like 'justice' is guided by the nature of the thing (justice) to which the word refers. Conventionalism is likewise the denial of these theories and the substitution of its own notions of truth, logic, meaning, and reference. Conventionalists about morals differ considerably, however, in their selection of various aspects of that agreement in attitude, belief, judgment or action that constitutes a social convention. Lord Devlin, for example, is a conventionalist who takes popular morality pretty much as he finds it, so that if people share a belief that homosexuality is wrong, then so it is.[10]

[6] For an exposition of these conceptualist semantic theories, see M. Moore, 'The Semantics of Judging', *Southern California Law Review*, 54 (1981), 151–295, at 170–9, 202–46, 281–92.

[7] See M. Moore, 'Moral Reality', *Wisconsin Law Review*, [1982], 1061–156. See generally Dummett, *Truth*, above n. 3, at pp. xxxi, 145–65.

[8] See Dworkin, *Principle*, above n. 1, at 169.

[9] See Moore, 'Moral Reality', above n. 7. See also M. Moore, 'Moral Reality Revisited', *Michigan Law Review*, 90 (1992), 2424–533.

[10] See generally P. Devlin, *The Enforcement of Morals* (Oxford: Oxford University Press, 1965), 1–25.

The constructivism of Rawls is a much more sophisticated conventionalism, applying as it does a coherence justificatory theory to popular judgements so that the answer as to what morality requires on a particular topic cannot be reduced to a survey type question; rather, only a deep systemization of popular morality can yield an answer.[11]

Dworkin is a conventionalist about the morals a judge should use to find right answers: when a judge is reasoning in Dworkin's recommended way he should take 'the community's moral traditions into account, at least as these are captured in the whole institutional record that it is his office to interpret'.[12] It is not the second of these factors—the embedding of certain values but not others in institutions—that necessarily marks Dworkin as a kind of conventionalist here. For what the relevant institutional record is, and how values are to be seen as embedded within it, must themselves be matters of political theory and Dworkin could argue that judges ought to employ the right political theory, and not merely the community political theory, in answering these questions. The first such feature does unambiguously mark Dworkin as a conventionalist, however, because Dworkin's idea of community morality is, as the name suggests, necessarily conventionalist in character.

Dworkin's 'community morality' cannot be equated with Lord Devlin's kind of 'surface conventionalism'.[13] Rather, Dworkin, like Rawls, is a deep conventionalist:

> [T]he community's morality . . . is not some sum or combination or function of the competing claims of its members; it is rather what each of the competing claims claims to be. When Hercules relies upon his own conception of dignity . . . he is still relying on his own sense of what the community's morality provides.[14]

In other words, it is because members of a community make important the concept of dignity that Hercules (or any other member of that community) can and must develop his own deeper conception (theory) of dignity. When he does develop such a deeper theory, Hercules is giving 'his philosophical opinions about what the community's concepts require'.[15]

This is a subtle and much more appealing conventionalism than Devlin's but it is still a conventionalism in its appeal to a community's shared beliefs as the source of moral concepts. Compare this with the realist's account, that it is reality that causes us to develop concepts adequate

[11] See J. Rawls, *A Theory of Justice* (Cambridge, Mass.: Harvard University Press, 1971), §§ 4, 9, 87. Whatever may have been Rawls's original intent in the *Theory* book, the conventionalist nature of his 'constructivist' views is laid bare in his Dewey Lectures. See Rawls, 'Kantian Constructivism in Moral Theory', *Journal of Philosophy*, 77 (1980), 515–72; see also his 'Justice as Fairness: Political not Metaphysical', *Philosophy & Public Affairs*, 14 (1985), 223–51.

[12] Dworkin, *Rights*, above n. 1, at 125–6.

[13] Ibid. at 126, 248–55.

[14] Ibid. at 128–9.

[15] Ibid. at 129.

to describe it. Because there are lemons, we have a concept 'lemon'; and because there is injustice in this world, we have a concept with which to name it.

Dworkin gives two reasons justifying why a judge should or must look to the community's morality. The first reason does not derive from any metaphysical views of Dworkin; rather, his argument for conventionalism here is a moral one. Dworkin concedes that in personal decisions we might follow what we take to be the right moral views and not simply those of our community (no matter how deeply reconstructed).[16] But judges engaged in adjudication, Dworkin argues, do not have the job of showing 'which principles are best independently of history'.[17] The judge's job is to submerge certain intuitions she may have about what is right in particular cases because: (*a*) a judge should act in accordance with a consistent and coherent programme 'that can be made public and followed until changed';[18] and (*b*) that programme should accommodate the community's common convictions, with no claim to being a description of an objective moral universe, so that citizens and others will not be tempted to object that the judge's judgements were based on a false observation about objective morality.[19]

Neither of these is, to my mind, a compelling argument. The first depends upon the mistaken idea that a moral realist will be more inclined to follow troublesome intuitions (because of her realist idea that such intuitions must correspond to reality) than will Dworkin's conventionalist moralist who, having no moral reality to account to, must throw out such intuitions if he cannot fit them in with his best theory of a social concept.[20] This has to be mistaken for those realists and conventionalists who are coherentists in their theories of justification. There should be no difference in the procedures of either of them when facing what Quine calls a 'recalcitrant experience',[21] namely, a particular intuition that seems inconsistent with settled beliefs. In particular, the realist-coherentist does not treat any troublesome intuition as a veridical read-off of reality that she cannot change, any more than the conventionalist-coherentist will treat the fact that he shares an intuition with others as a given that he cannot change. A realist may hold onto the troublesome intuition despite her inability to fit it in with her theory, and one might characterize this as having 'faith' in

[16] Dworkin, *Rights*, above n. 1, at 163; see also Dworkin, 'Reply', above n. 1, at 279.

[17] Dworkin, 'Reply', above n. 1, at 279.

[18] Dworkin, *Rights*, above n. 1, at 162.

[19] Ibid. at 163. For a good exposition of the trouble Dworkin gets himself into by making these arguments on behalf of his constructivist meta-ethics, while trying to hang onto his right-answer thesis, see M. B. E. Smith, 'Rights, Right Answers, and the Constructive Model of Morality', *Social Theory & Practice*, 5 (1980), 409–26.

[20] Dworkin, *Rights*, above n. 1, at 161–2; Dworkin, 'Reply', above n. 1, at 278.

[21] W. Quine, 'Two Dogmas of Empiricism', in *From a Logical Point of View* (2nd rev. edn., Cambridge, Mass.: Harvard University Press, 1980), 44.

future discovery.[22] Yet a conventionalist may do this too, thinking that there may be a way of reconciling the opposing beliefs even though he cannot see how it is done. In this latter case, we might characterize this faith as a kind of 'waiting for his Hercules'.

There may yet seem to be one difference between a realist and a conventionalist here, and that stems from the need a realist has to explain away those intuitions that she discards from the continued elaboration of her theory. If she is to discard hallucinatory experiences (either visual or moral), she needs an explanation for why she has them (that also explains along the way why the beliefs that they produce are false). If the conventionalist does not have such an explanatory burden—because he can take his intuitions, if shared, as arbitrary posits without need of explanation—then he might not be as reluctant to give up a troublesome intuition as is the realist. Yet the conventionalist has an equivalent burden here, despite what Dworkin says about the conventionalist's supposed ability to ignore troublesome intuitions in order better to serve his theory.[23] As Dworkin himself might put it, the conventionalist about morals has to have a theory of mistakes with which he can justify his discarding of certain widely shared intuitions.[24] Part of that theory, for example, will show that certain experiences such as racial prejudice, envy and pity, although widely shared, give rise to judgements that cannot be reconciled with the deep theory of the community's moral sensibility, considered as a whole, and so must be discarded.[25] Dworkin's deep conventionalist cannot, thus, regard shared intuitions as simply arbitrary posits that he may discard without further theorizing. Facing such a justificatory burden, the conventionalist should be no less (and no more) reluctant than any realist to discard certain particular intuitions.

The second moral argument for conventionalism stated above is also unconvincing. Dworkin's conflict-minimization defence of conventionalism may be possible for the shallow conventionalism of Lord Devlin, at least on issues less controversial than abortion or the death penalty. But surely Dworkin's deep conventionalism will invite disagreement as much as any realism, for, as Dworkin recognizes, a judge's best theory or conception of any abstract concept like dignity need not square very much with competing conceptions of that concept.[26] Perhaps the tone of the disagreement will be less destructive when it is about the best conception of some concept of justice that is widely shared (rather than about what justice is); yet, as Dworkin recognizes, developing deep theories of shared concepts does not often display the 'self-conscious air of sociological inquiry' that makes debate dispassionate, because the participants tend to value the concepts about which they are arguing.[27]

[22] Dworkin, *Rights*, above n. 1, at 161.
[23] See ibid. at 165.
[24] See ibid. at 118–23.
[25] Ibid. at 248–55.
[26] Ibid. at 126.
[27] Ibid. at 128.

Neither of these arguments of political morality provide much reason for judges to be conventionalists about the morality that enters legal reasoning. While one can muster other moral arguments to this conclusion—from democracy in particular—these, too, as I have argued elsewhere, are not persuasive.[28] Further, whatever persuasive power such supplemental arguments may possess is greater for Devlin's shallow conventionalism than it is for Dworkin's deeper version.

The second reason a judge should look to the community's morals is because, if Dworkin is right, the judge has no real choice. Dworkin's argument here is metaphysical rather than moral. Although it is far from clear (because of Dworkin's attempt to avoid the issue), I think that Dworkin also believes that conventionalism is the correct metaphysical posture to assume about morality and moral reasoning. If so, then for Dworkin, morality as such (and necessarily the morality judges may properly use in adjudication) is a matter of social convention.

We should examine Dworkin's metaphysical conventionalism about morals in two stages, negative and positive. Dworkin's negative point is his explicit rejection of realism about morals. Dworkin tells us that the realists' correspondence theory of truth is, for moral statements:

> [A] mysterious and highly blurred idea of 'real' truth, which they express only in metaphors, and which I doubt can be expressed in any other way. They can say that a proposition is 'really' true only if it accurately describes facts that are 'out there', or part of 'the fabric of the universe', or 'locked into' an 'independent reality' or something of that sort.[29]

As all the scare quotes indicate, Dworkin rejects such a realist notion of truth for moral propositions. We create 'incomprehensible metaphors', Dworkin thinks, whenever we claim 'that the injustice of slavery is part of the furniture of the universe, that it is really "out there" in some way'.[30]

There is nothing mysterious about the moral realist's theory of truth here; it is the same theory of truth as that employed by the scientific realist about the propositions of science. Dworkin's questioning of the realist account of truth as correspondence must thus be based, not on the relation of correspondence, but on an ontological objection to there being anything to which moral statements may correspond.

In voicing this apparent ontological objection, Dworkin has a picture of what moral reality would have to be like if moral realism were true.[31] It

[28] See M. Moore, 'A Natural Law Theory of Interpretation', *Southern California Law Review*, 58 (1985), 277–398, at 388–96.

[29] Dworkin, 'Reply', above n. 1, at 277.

[30] Dworkin, *Principle*, above n. 1, at 172; see also Dworkin, *Empire*, above n. 1, at 83 (Dworkin finds it 'absurd' to claim 'that moral values are "out there" or can be proved').

[31] See Dworkin, *Rights*, above n. 1, at 160 (discussing moral realism, misleadingly called 'the natural model', only in terms of this special realm picture of moral reality).

is the two-worlds picture of non-naturalism, wherein we are to think of special, indefinable moral properties like goodness. These special ('non-natural') properties call upon us to conceive of special, sui generis relations existing between them and natural properties. Such odd properties and relations further call upon us to think that persons, in addition to their sensory equipment, have a special mode of perceiving these properties, the faculty of intuition. Finding all of this a wildly incomprehensible picture—with its queer entities, sui generis relations, and extravagant epistemological pretensions—Dworkin rejects moral realism as such.

Although there have been moral realists (even some named Moore) who conceived of moral reality in this fantastic way, I and most other contemporary moral realists with whom I am familiar do not. Culpability, for example, is a property that persons sometimes possess when they cause harm to others. Believing this does not commit one to inventing a special realm in which culpability exists, or to conceiving it as having indefinable relations to the natural properties of voluntariness and intentionality, or to discovering it by intuition. Culpability is inferred from voluntariness and intentionality, much as those properties are inferred from various behavioural, phenomenal, and physiological clues. We cannot see culpability; but then, we cannot see intentionality either.

Admittedly, deeper philosophical questions than these need to be plumbed in order to answer adequately Dworkin's queerness fears here. This I have attempted to do elsewhere.[32] The only point to be made here is that Dworkin is hardly entitled to his rather blithe assumption that moral realism is necessarily a kind of fantastic non-naturalism. Dworkin might consider more seriously the naturalist's version of moral realism, which at one point Dworkin acknowledges as the view 'that our beliefs about slavery are forced upon us by physical properties of objects, as our beliefs that fire engines are red might be said to be forced on us by such properties'.[33] Dworkin's only reason for rejecting this alternative is that 'almost no one' who thinks of themselves as a moral realist subscribes to such naturalism. Yet, there are a few such strange philosophers, myself included.[34] And besides, what does the scarcity of our number have to do with the correctness of our views? The correctness of realism can hardly be tested by its popularity—at least, not unless one assumes from the start that conventionalism is true.

[32] See Moore, 'Moral Reality', above n. 7, and 'Moral Reality Revisited', above n. 9.

[33] Dworkin, 'Reply', above n. 1, at 277.

[34] See Moore, 'Moral Reality', above n. 7, and 'Moral Reality Revisited', above, n. 9; see also N. Sturgeon, 'Moral Explanations', in David Copp and David Zimmerman (eds)., *Morality, Reason and Truth* (Totawa, NJ: Rowman and Allanheld, 1984), 49.

Dworkin's anti-realism about morality does not commit him to scepticism.[35] Rather, Dworkin's positive point is to suppose that 'there are moral facts, which are not simply physical facts or facts about the thoughts or attitudes of people'.[36] What Dworkin means by this, however, is not that there are what he calls 'transcendent' or 'Platonic' moral facts;[37] rather, 'moral . . . judgements have the sense and force they do just because they figure in a collective human enterprise' and for that reason 'such judgements cannot have a "real" sense and a "real" truth value which transcend that enterprise and somehow take hold of the "real" world'.[38]

Dworkin's argument is the common ground on which he is a conventionalist about literature and law as well as morals, so I shall consider it only preliminarily here. Dworkin urges us to see all three of these areas of knowledge as activities in which people engage. Like any other intelligently directed activity, the making of moral judgements will have certain presuppositions about how the activity is to be done. From the outside we can see that people performing such actions as praising and blaming one another are constructing the conventions by virtue of which praise and blame are appropriate. The actors doing the praising and blaming need not see it that way, although they might. In any case, we theorists can step back and see that moral judgements have the sense they do because they are made as a part of this shared activity, and thus cannot have a sense that describes a reality 'out there' waiting to be discovered by these actors.

Dworkin says as much about morality. He thus prefers Rawlsian constructivism over any form of moral realism.[39] He thus analogizes morality to literature, where Dworkin is explicitly constructivist in this way.[40] Such constructivism marks Dworkin as a conventionalist about morals because it forces him to assert that 'is true', as used about moral statements, only means: warrantedly assertible within the practices constitutive of our moral life.[41] Such conventionalism about the truth of moral judgements will carry with it the rest of a conventionalist's beliefs about the appropriate theories of logic, meaning, and reference for this area of discourse. About the meaning of moral claims like 'slavery is wrong', for example, Dworkin explicitly urges the conventionalist position that 'the practices of interpretation and morality give these claims all the meaning they need or could have'.[42]

[35] See Dworkin, *Empire*, above n. 1, at 78–86; Dworkin, *Principle*, above n. 1, at 175–7; Dworkin, 'Natural Law', above n. 1, at 173–8; Dworkin, 'Reply', above n. 1, at 279.

[36] Dworkin, *Principle*, above n. 1, at 138.

[37] Ibid.

[38] Ibid. at 174.

[39] See Dworkin, *Rights*, above n. 1, at 159–68.

[40] See Dworkin, *Principle*, above n. 1, at 167–77.

[41] Dworkin, 'Reply', above n. 1, at 278.

[42] Dworkin, *Empire*, above n. 1, at 83.

2. Dworkin's Conventionalism About Literature

Dworkin believes that a fruitful way of understanding both morality and law is through an understanding of the interpretive practices of literary critics. Such critics make interpretive claims: about characters in a novel or play, such as, 'Hamlet really loved his mother'; about events not related by the author but which make better sense of the events which are related by the author; and about the general sense, meaning, theme, or point of a work of art.

Dworkin surely appeals to very widespread intuitions when he denies any realist interpretation of these interpretive claims. A realist interpretation of 'Hamlet loved his mother' seemingly requires there to be a Hamlet, a mother of Hamlet, and a relation of love from the first to the second.[43] Yet these singular terms fail to refer to any real persons, so that if we must assign a truth value to statements claiming there to be a relation between such persons, such statements seem everywhere and always to be false. If realism requires literary interpretation to be biography or history (and false biography or history to boot), then realism is a bad interpretation of such interpretive claims.

Dworkin's positive account of how we are to take interpretive claims in literature comes in two parts. First of all, there is the dimension of fit with what the author said: 'Hamlet loved his mother' is warrantably assertible if that proposition provides a better fit than its negation with Shakespeare's text. Such an interpretive proposition fits better with the text if such proposition is either part of a theory that explains why Hamlet did what he did in the play better than any other theory, or follows from such a theory.[44] As Dworkin puts it, this account assumes that 'there are facts of narrative consistency' that are not moral facts or empirical ('hard') facts.[45] Such facts are of two kinds: facts about the identity of the play, which require that it (the play) be identified as 'Hamlet' by a canonical text; and facts about the relations between propositions expressed in the text, propositions that express the general theory of what the play is about, and propositions that, although not in the text, complete the story that is in the text in a way that follows from the theory of the play.[46] (For ease of future reference, let us call these respectively 'identity facts' and 'coherence facts'.) To speak of there being facts of narrative consistency in no way erodes Dworkin's anti-realism here. Such facts are not things that could be referred to in interpretive statements, because such facts are about those interpretive statements (the text, the theory, or the extension of text the theory makes possible) and the relations between them.

[43] Dworkin, *Principle*, above n. 1, at 142; ibid. at 136; Dworkin, 'Reply', above n. 1, at 276.

[44] Dworkin, *Principle*, above n. 1, at 136.

[45] Ibid. at 138.

[46] Ibid. at 150–1.

The second dimension Dworkin uses in assessing interpretive claims is that of artistic value. An interpretive claim should attempt to show which way of reading 'Hamlet' reveals the play as the best work of art.[47] This dimension, obviously, requires a theory of what literature ought to be about, a theory of artistic value.[48] Such a theory of artistic value may have a moral cast to it—witness Mathew Arnold or John Gardner—but even if it does not, there is clearly an evaluative claim being made here.

Dworkin's general account of interpretive claims in literature is quite attractive. It is a helpful bulwark against all those (and there are many) who wish to say that literary interpretation is essentially unprincipled and arbitrary. In addition, insofar as we can divide the justification for interpretive claims into two dimensions—a point on which Dworkin is understandably cautious[49]—Dworkin's conventionalism about the dimension of fit is appropriate. If it makes sense to talk of a separable dimension of fit (Dworkin's 'formal features'), then claims that are justified in this way alone can be true only in the sense of being, warrantedly assertible in light of a text that is accepted as authoritative.

We should be more troubled by Dworkin's views about artistic value. Dworkin seems to be an anti-realist in aesthetics as in ethics because of his vehement denials that he holds any 'silly metaphysical theory of interpretation, according to which meanings [of works of art] are "just there" in the universe'.[50] Realistic interpretation of aesthetic statements is more than silly to Dworkin. It makes nonsense of those statements: 'we can make sense of interpretive claims . . . only if we stop treating them as doomed attempts to report ontologically independent meanings scattered among the furniture of the universe.'[51] I infer from this anti-realism about interpretive claims that Dworkin must be an anti-realist about one of the two dimensions of such interpretive claims: artistic value. For if there were aesthetic values (out there with the furniture, so to speak), a realistic interpretation of interpretive claims would make sense. This, I think, is exactly the case in legal interpretation as well, despite it, too, having a conventional dimension.

Dworkin's arguments for his anti-realism about artistic value and thus, interpretive claims, are two. His explicit argument against realism here has three premises to it: (1) the correctness of a realist interpretation of interpretive claims is a question of semantics, that is, it turns on the sense of interpretive claims; (2) the sense of interpretive claims turns on what the people who made them believe they meant by them; and (3) the people who make interpretive claims—at least those with tenure in respectable English departments—do not believe they meant to be asserting a corre-

[47] Dworkin, *Principle*, above n. 1, at 149. [48] Ibid. at 151.
[49] Dworkin, 'Natural Law', above n. 1, at 172.
[50] Dworkin, *Principle*, above n. 1, at 167. [51] Ibid. at 168.

spondence between states of the world and their judgements.[52] Although Dworkin finds this argument 'decisive', I find it a surprising argument given Dworkin's well-known penchant for not granting people any authority over their own deepest beliefs. The argument's second premise grants to literary critics an authority over their ontological commitments and their theory of truth that no speaker or set of speakers ever has. If speakers had this authority over their own deepest presuppositions, how could it ever be paradoxical for the Cretan to say, 'All of my statements are false'? We have a liar's paradox only because what a speaker believes (even when she explicitly asserts her belief) can be contradicted by what she presupposes.

Dworkin surely wants to repair to his second argument here, which is to deny that there is a meaningful question to ask about aesthetic values being out there because such a question is 'external' to the practice of literary criticism.[53] I do not think that this argument succeeds, but I shall defer discussion of it (as of its moral cousin) until Section IV, since it is part and parcel of Dworkin's general defence of his supposedly ametaphysical stance about law, literature, and morals.

What if one were a realist about aesthetic values? Given the heavily conventionalist cast to the dimension of fit, could one be a realist about interpretive claims? If so, would such realism in literature require some 'ghostly biography' view of fiction? I think the answer to these questions is 'yes' for realism, 'no' for the need for ghostly referents. I am very unclear, however, whether realism is the correct view to take about aesthetic value, so I shall pursue these questions no further.

C. Dworkin's Conventionalism about Law

1. *How Law Is and Is Not Like Literature*

One of Dworkin's central analogies is that of law to literature. As Dworkin says at one point, he wishes 'to use literary interpretation as a model for the central method of legal analysis'.[54] Such an analogy can hold only if 'the central method of legal analysis' is interpretive in character, for it is interpretive claims in literary criticism to which Dworkin wishes to make his analogy.

Dworkin assumes, but does not defend, the idea that legal reasoning is interpretive in character. It is hard to get a handle on this question because Dworkin does not make clear what he means by 'interpretation'. Dworkin does say that interpretation is an enterprise 'in which participants extend a discipline into the future by re-examining its past', and that this characterization of interpretation is broad enough to include much of 'literary

[52] Ibid. at 167. [53] Ibid. at 171–4. [54] Ibid. at 158.

criticism, history, philosophy, and many other activities'.[55] Yet, in this sense, why is not all of social and natural science interpretive, as Richard Rorty and a long tradition of 'hermeneuts' have argued?

A narrower idea of interpretation is needed if it is to capture the salient features that make at least some legal reasoning similar to literary interpretation. Such a narrower idea of interpretation should focus on the idea of an authoritative text. An interpretive activity is one in which the participants justify their decisions about what to do or believe by reference to a text that they regard as authoritative. What the text is will be a matter of the tests they employ to ascertain it. Freud's test for the text (manifest content) of dreams was the patient's statements upon awakening, no matter how repetitious and inconsistent.[56] Theologians and literary critics employ differing tests for what is included in their respective texts.[57] Such tests are justified not by their conventional acceptance, but rather by a theory of why they should be taken as authoritative for the activity in question. Freud thought his therapeutic aims were best furthered by construing the texts of dreams as consisting of all waking statements, because he thought that differing versions of a dream presented clues to those sensitive parts of the dream most important to a therapeutic interpretation.

Science and ethics are by this criterion not interpretive activities because decisions, at least for scientific and moral realists, are not justified by their conformity to texts. To be sure, there are laws and rules in such disciplines, but except for pre-Baconians in science and religious persons in ethics, the 'authority' of these laws and rules depends upon their correspondence to how things are in the external world. In science and ethics no one has the authority of a novelist, a prophet, a dreamer, or a legislator to dictate the general standards that others ought to interpret.

By this criterion, law is only sometimes an interpretive discipline. When reasoning from statutes and (written) constitutions, lawyers justify their decisions and arguments by reference to authoritative texts. There are tests

[55] Dworkin, 'Natural Law', above n. 1, at 166. Most recently, Dworkin has despaired of giving any definition of the concept of interpretation, 'for if a community uses interpretive concepts at all, the concept of interpretation itself will be one of them: a theory of interpretation is an interpretation of the higher order practice of using interpretive concepts' (Dworkin, *Empire*, above n. 1, at 49). Yet Dworkin, by his own interpretive theory, should at least be able to give us the concept of interpretation around which we build competing conceptions.

[56] M. Moore, *Law and Psychiatry: Rethinking the Relationship* (Cambridge: Cambridge University Press, 1984), at 282–5.

[57] See generally R. Garet, 'Comparative Normative Hermeneutics: Scripture, Literature, Constitution', *Southern California Law Review*, 58 (1985), 35–134. Dworkin arguably adopts the idea of an authoritative text as the sine qua non of his own narrower idea of interpretation. See Dworkin, *Empire*, above n. 1, at 65–6, where Dworkin talks of there being a pre-interpretive stage to creative interpretation, in which the interpreter identifies the rules and standards that are to be interpreted.

for such texts, and behind such tests there are normative theories as to why such texts are authoritative quite apart from any goodness in the decisions that such texts may imply. Reasoning from precedent, however, does not seem to fit this at all, for there seems to be no text to the common law.

The most obvious candidate for a common law text is the written opinions of judges. According to the classical theory of precedent, the law that emanates from any one case is found in the stated holding of the deciding court, in its description of those facts deemed material to its decision, or in its stated reasons for deciding as it did. Dworkin can, however, ill afford to adopt any version of the classical theory of precedent. Not only is such a theory inaccurate in its description of our practices, but it also does not square well with one of the main values on the basis of which we justify a doctrine of precedent to begin with: the value of equality.[58] Dworkin himself acknowledges this, realizing that cases possess a 'gravitational force' that extends well beyond (and sometimes well within) the statements of holding, facts or reasons to be found within judicial opinions.[59] Put my way, equality gives each decided case a projection class of other cases that only by accident will bear any relation to the class of cases covered by the language used in the deciding court's written opinion.

Dworkin, thus, should focus on what the earlier judge did, and not on what she said as she was doing it, in order to say what law arises out of precedent. Adopting this Legal Realist theory of precedent means that common law reasoning is not an interpretive activity, for the decisions in particular cases are not a text in any meaningful sense of the word. Common law reasoning, construed in Dworkin's non-classical way, is more fruitfully analogized to the non-interpretive reasoning of ethics and science, wherein one must also abstract more general propositions from particular decisions or observations. Such general propositions, as noted earlier, do not constitute an authoritative text by which future decisions or observational beliefs are to be justified by a process of interpretation.

It is tempting to attribute to Dworkin some intuitive appreciation of this bifurcation of legal reasoning into interpretive and non-interpretive parts, despite his attempt to gloss all of legal reasoning as 'interpretive'. When Dworkin discusses a judge's obligation to theorize the uncontroversial institutional history of his legal system, he does so in two different ways. Dworkin speaks of theorizing in common law reasoning in terms of finding principles that underlie or are embedded in past decisions.[60] By contrast, he speaks of theorizing in statutory or constitutional contexts in terms of finding either conceptions (theories) of concepts to be found in

[58] M. Moore, 'Precedent, Induction, and Ethical Generalization', in L. Goldstein (ed.), *Precedent in Law* (Oxford: Oxford University Press, 1987).

[59] See Dworkin, *Rights*, above n. 1, at 110–13, 118–19.

[60] See ibid. at 22–8, 115–16.

the relevant texts[61] or (in language Dworkin regards as being equivalent) concrete intentions that are derived from the theories of the more abstract intentions which themselves may be attributed to the authors of those texts.[62] Dworkin implicitly recognizes that statutory or constitutional reasoning proceeds by interpreting concepts or abstract intentions that a relevant text makes authoritative, while common law reasoning proceeds by generalizing over particular, concrete decisions that are authoritative.

In any case, whether or not Dworkin recognizes this distinction, he should. Accordingly, I shall organize my discussion of Dworkin's conventionalism about law into two parts: interpretive reasoning and common law reasoning.

2. *Dworkin's Conventionalism About Interpretive Claims in Law*

It might be thought that interpretive claims in law are necessarily conventionalist, given that the concepts (or abstract intentions) being interpreted are the objects of such efforts only because they appear in statutory or constitutional texts. In other words, one might think that because the concepts are authoritatively laid down in some bit of institutional history, any claims about them must be conventionalist in character. Yet, it is one of the lasting contributions of Dworkin's early work to show why this need not be so. A thoughtful judge cannot take a text and its concepts to be authoritative, just because it (or a rule of recognition recognizing it) is accepted by other officials as authoritative. Rather, she must justify to herself why and to what degree such a text should be authoritative in terms of a political theory about constitution- and statute-making.[63] Such values will stand behind her interpretive activity, and, thus, her interpretive activity can not be justified by its conformity to some social convention.

Despite this, Dworkin is a conventionalist about interpretive claims in law. One reason for this lies in Dworkin's conventionalism about the moral values that justify to a judge why she has the duty to interpret statutory and constitutional texts. Despite his attempt to distance himself from Hart's conventionalism about judicial duty,[64] Dworkin himself concedes that 'it may be that judicial duty is a case of conventional morality', because it may be justified by common judicial practice.[65]

More fundamentally, Dworkin is a conventionalist about interpretive claims in law because of his concept/conception idea of interpretation. Recall that for Dworkin, legal interpretation proceeds by developing conceptions (theories) of textually authoritative concepts (abstract intentions

[61] See Dworkin, *Rights*, above n. 1, at 134–5.
[62] See Dworkin, *Principle*, above n. 1, at 49.
[63] Dworkin, *Rights*, above n. 1, at 36–8, 60–1, 106–10.
[64] See ibid. at 48–58.
[65] Ibid. at 58. See generally Les Green, 'Authority and Convention', *Philosophical Quarterly*, 35 (1985), 329–46.

or purposes) and that from such conceptions more particular propositions can be inferred which will be sufficient to decide disputed cases.[66] Judges are invited to develop theories of concepts like dignity either by the intent of the drafters that such theories be developed by judges,[67] or by the use of 'essentially contested concepts' in legal texts,[68] or by judges' general duties to develop coherent theories of law.[69]

In developing such a conception or theory, Dworkin tells us that a judge, like the literary critic, will have to pay attention both to formal features (abstract meaning of the concept or previous interpretations of it by courts) and to the values that could justify such a theory as a good conception of the concept.[70] Because Dworkin is a conventionalist about values, he is a conventionalist about interpretive claims in law no less than in literature. Because the values judges should use in adjudication are the community's values, and because Dworkin is himself a deep conventionalist (constructivist) about community morality, interpretive claims in law for him are necessarily conventionalist in character.

Because it is crucial to our later assessment of whether Dworkin's conventionalism is consistent with his right-answer thesis, we need to explore further what his concept/conception interpretive theory amounts to. How are we to understand a conventionalist's invitation to judges to develop deep theories (conceptions) of moral concepts like privacy, dignity or justice? Of what are such theories theories? The realist's idea of theorizing a concept we understand. Justice refers to a kind of thing in the world; our use of such a word shows it to possess the kind of 'semantic depth'[71] that is possessed by words naming natural kinds. Because of this usage, the extension of 'is just' is fixed, not by some agreement (no matter how deeply reconstrued), but by the nature of the thing to which 'justice' refers, and such nature can only be given by better and better theories of what justice is.

What is the conventionalist's comparable account of what it is we are theorizing about when we construct theories of justice? Inviting a theory of a concept, while acknowledging that the concept does not refer, sounds dangerously like inviting theories of the concepts of witches and winged horses. The conventionalist can only respond, as Dworkin does, that justice refers to 'an institution we interpret . . . [which] has a history'. Justice, in other words, is not a thing in the world; it is a set of judgements by people about what is just. The most general of those judgements on which people agree—their concept of justice—will be 'the plateau from which

66 See Dworkin, *Empire*, above n. 1, at 70–2; Dworkin, *Principle*, above n. 1 at 49; Dworkin, *Rights*, above n. 1, at 134–5.

67 Dworkin, *Rights*, above n. 1, at 136.

68 Ibid. at 103.

69 Ibid. at 160–1; Dworkin, *Empire*, above n. 1, at 176–275; Dworkin, 'Reply', above n. 1, at 279.

70 See Dworkin, *Principle*, above n. 1, at 160–2.

71 M. Platts, *Ways of Meaning* (London: Routledge and Kegan Paul, 1979), 249.

arguments about justice largely proceed'. Philosophers may seek to 'define the "concept" of justice for their community', but even if they fail, we as members of that community 'share a pre-interpretive sense of the rough boundaries of the practice [of justice] on which our imagination must be trained'.[72]

If one cuts through the concept/conception rhetoric, Dworkin essentially answers the ontological question by repairing to his 'facts of narrative consistency.' The only facts to which Rawlsian constructivist theories of justice are committed, are these relational facts about the maximally-coherent, organizational structure of shared judgements. One conception of justice is better than another, on this view, not because it better describes what justice is, but because it better systematizes what basic judgements we share about our concept of justice.

3. Dworkin's Conventionalism about Non-Interpretive Claims in Law

Dworkin's interpretation of non-interpretive claims in common law is also conventionalist in character for the same kinds of reasons as were just discussed: it is conventional morals that justify a judge's obligation to fit her decision in with old cases;[73] and it is the reconstructed, community's morality that provides the background rights to which the judge repairs when she leaves the dimension of fit for the dimension of value.[74]

There is one aspect of Dworkin's treatment of non-interpretive claims in law that merits separate attention, and that is his notion of 'fit'. What is it for one principle (theory) to fit better with prior decisions than another? Dworkin's general statement of this relation is not satisfactory. 'The dimensions of fit suppose that one political theory is pro tanto a better justification than another if, roughly speaking, someone who held that theory would, in its service, enact more of what is settled than someone who held the other.'[75] With respect, this gives us about as much of an idea as to what constitutes 'fit' as would a definition of 'death' where to be dead is to be buried by someone. Surely we are entitled to ask what it was about the relation (or the corpse) that led someone to enact more settled law with it (or bury it), and this further something will tell us more of what 'fit' (or 'death') means.

What we need to know is why someone in the service of a theory would make certain decisions rather than others. What is the relation between the statements setting forth the theory (Dworkin's principles) and the statements describing past decisions, that will justify the present judge in deciding one way rather than another? Dworkin has only characterized

[72] All quotations from Dworkin, *Empire*, above n. 1, at 73–5.
[73] Dworkin, *Rights*, above n. 1, at 48–58.
[74] Ibid. at 115–23; Dworkin, *Principle*, above n. 1, at 143.
[75] Dworkin, *Principle*, above n. 1, at 143.

this relation in metaphors: principles 'underlie' common law decisions;[76] they are 'embedded' in them;[77] principles are 'implicit in' or may be 'inferred by analogy from' a set of decisions;[78] or they are 'exemplified by' those decisions.[79] Yet none of these hints are more than vaguely suggestive.

Dworkin equivocates on a feature of his theory that will prove crucial if we are to assess the plausibility of his right-answer thesis. Dworkin needs some determinate notion of fit if we are to make sense of, not only the relation of legal principle to legal rules, but also the relation between legal and moral concepts and their conceptions (theories). Given Dworkin's general coherentism about justification, it is tempting to read him as adopting some general views about the relations that must exist if statements in any field are to cohere with one another. At a minimum, such cohering statements must be consistent in the sense that their conjunction neither constitutes nor implies a contradiction.[80] Yet this is surely only a necessary condition of coherence, not a sufficient condition. Coherence theories about knowledge, in general, have always held that something more than mere consistency was required for a set of statements to cohere with one another.[81]

Rolf Sartorius, whose version of legal positivism also requires him to have a concept of fit, urges that the standards that describe the decisions in particular areas (common law rules) 'imply', 'incorporate', or 'establish' the principles (theory) that may be used to decide novel cases in law.[82] Yet if the established rules imply principles, and principles are to imply new rules and decisions, the transitivity of 'implies' guarantees that principles can yield answers in no cases that did not have answers without mention of such principles.[83]

Nonetheless, it seems to me that Sartorius is on the right track with his explicit analogy to theory construction in science.[84] Yet, rather than conceiving of the relation as implication of principles by rules and cases, we should see the relation as the converse, namely, principles imply the rules that decide cases, but not vice-versa. As Ernst Nagel points out about

[76] Dworkin, *Rights*, above n. 1, at 115.
[77] Ibid.
[78] Dworkin, *Critics*, above n. 1, at 340.
[79] Dworkin, *Rights*, above n. 1, at 118.
[80] Cf. ibid. at 119; N. MacCormick, 'Dworkin As Pre-Benthamite', in M. Cohen (ed.), *Ronald Dworkin and Contemporary Jurisprudence* (Oxford: Oxford University Press, 1984), 182, 189.
[81] M. Williams, *Groundless Belief* (Oxford: Oxford University Press, 1977), 105.
[82] See R. Sartorius, *Individual Conduct and Social Norms* (Encino, Calif.: Dickenson Publishing, 1975), 192.
[83] M. Moore, 'Causation and Excuses', *California Law Review*, 73 (1985), 1091–149, at 1100–1.
[84] See Sartorius, above n. 82, at 184–6.

scientific theories and their relation to scientific laws, so conceiving of the relation does not trivialize the predictive power of theories.[85]

Dworkin, it is true, has eschewed any scientific analogies for his idea of the relation of principles to decisions.[86] Yet as I understand that eschewal, Dworkin thinks that the analogy to science is broken only because of his second dimension to common law reasoning, the dimension of political morality. For the dimension of fit alone, Dworkin appears to agree that the analogy to science is apt, so that principles that fit common law decisions will be those more general statements that imply, but are not implied by, the statements of those more particular decisions. Notice that Dworkin can accept this analogy of the coherence relation in law to that in science, without for a moment believing—as Dworkin does not[87]—that moral, legal or aesthetic facts are implied by the 'hard facts' of science.

II. THE RIGHT-ANSWER THESIS

Despite his conventionalism about the truth of propositions in ethics, literature, and law, Dworkin thinks that there are right answers to the hard questions in all three fields. The shared beliefs in all three fields are rich enough in their details that all questions that have arisen and will arise will have answers that are correct, even if such answers cannot be demonstrated to those who share the initial beliefs. Given Dworkin's conventionalism, I find this wildly implausible. It would be like thinking that a novel could have a text of sufficient density of detail that all questions one could ask of any historical person could be asked and answered about some fictional character in the novel.

Again, however, Dworkin's arguments are too well-considered to admit of such blunderbuss assaults, so I shall first construe in greater detail his right-answer thesis and then address whether any plausible argument can be made for it if one starts with Dworkin's conventionalist metaphysics.

A. What Is the Thesis?

Dworkin is a bit cagey about the degree to which he is committed to there being right answers in hard cases. He waffles on five essential items: (1) the degree to which he is committed to there being a right answer in all cases; (2) the degree to which he is committed to there being some positive argument for the thesis, and not just the absence of any good argument against it; (3) what the positive right-answer thesis is, in light of Dworkin's

85 E. Nagel, *The Structure of Science* (New York: Random House, 1961), 33–4.
86 See Dworkin, 'Critics', above n. 1, at 341.
87 See Dworkin, *Principle*, above n. 1, at 139.

two versions of the negative, 'no-right-answer' thesis; (4) the sense of 'right answer' he intends, given his eschewal of any realist notions (like correspondence) that give a straightforward interpretation of what makes a right answer right; and (5) the sense in which a right answer can or cannot be 'demonstrated' to be the right answer.

1. Consider the first query in light of Dworkin's remarks about right answers to interpretive claims in literature. According to Dworkin, if literary critics follow his two-dimensional interpretive procedure, there will be an answer to all but 'very boring questions no one would wish to ask'[88] about characters in novels. There will be answers to questions like, 'Did David Copperfield have a homosexual affair with Stearforth?' even if there will be no answers to questions like, 'Did David have type-A blood?' These last questions will be boring in the sense that they will have no bearing on anything that could interest us about the novel, *David Copperfield*. They do not bear on anything that Dickens asserted or presupposed,[89] and they do not make the novel better or worse as a work of art.

We should not allow Dworkin's 'boring' epithet to mask how many questions there will be about *David Copperfield* to which there will be no right answer, even within the confines of Dworkinian interpretive practice. Think of all the questions you could ask about a real person, and how few of them would make any difference in an interpretation of *David Copperfield*. As Dworkin himself writes, 'the fact that a boy had the specific characteristics Dickens described . . . can have little bearing' on any 'feature that is randomly distributed throughout a [real] population', so that for questions about all such features, 'it is more likely that the question[s] will have no right answer'.[90] Numerous as they are, Dworkin is right that such questions are boring in the context of literary criticism—for in that enterprise, we care about David Copperfield only as a Dickens creation. Given these interests, of course, questions irrelevant to Dickens's Copperfield are boring and beside the point.

Yet what possible reason is there to think that our interests in law are similarly restricted to the fictional creation of some text? Fact, as the saying goes, is richer than fiction. Real life disputes between persons will not be boring to us (or to them) just because the issues raised bear no relation to the text of the law. If there are as many questions without unique solutions in law as there are about the character of a novel, then Dworkin's right-answer thesis becomes very weak.

Not surprisingly, in light of the foregoing, Dworkin holds a stronger version of the right-answer thesis for law. In law, 'such cases [having no right answer], if they exist at all, must be extremely rare in the United States and Great Britain'.[91] Although Dworkin does not make it explicit,

[88] Ibid. at 130. [89] Ibid. at 143. [90] Ibid.

[91] Ibid. at 144; see also Dworkin, 'Critics', above n. 1, at 334.

the differences between law and literature are twofold: (1) a novel has a less dense text with which to work than does the body of law of a mature legal system that deals with a wide range of conduct of its citizens;[92] and (2) the value dimension of interpretive claims in law is deontological (a theory of rights), so that, unlike maximizing theories of value, '[t]here seems to be no room here for the ordinary idea of a tie'.[93]

Surely, the first of these alleged differences is suspect. Science is very rich in general standards, so that in its present stage of development its laws and theories purport to cover all possible events in the world. Yet no one since the rise of empiricism has believed that the present laws and theories of science in fact are adequate to resolve all questions that will continue to arise. For right answers in science, we need new, particular data (experiments) because the existing 'text', rich as it is, isn't nearly rich enough.

I tend to agree with Dworkin's second argument although, as discussed below, I do not understand how a conventionalist about morals can make the argument. In any case, one should construe Dworkin to hold a strong right-answer thesis about law: there is a right answer in all disputed cases at law, any exceptions being de minimis and forgettable.

2. Dworkin is leery about committing himself to any positive argument for the right-answer thesis. He recognizes that he presupposes the thesis in his argument that judges have a duty to find right answers even in the hardest of cases, but he refuses to make any positive argument on behalf of the thesis.[94] Dworkin will avail himself of only two sorts of arguments here: first, he will advance arguments why the general arguments offered by others against the right-answer thesis are no good;[95] second, he will make particular arguments about why a particular answer on some legal issue is better than competing answers.[96]

I shall, in this part, examine only Dworkin's arguments of the first sort, testing them for their consistency with Dworkin's conventionalism. The second sort of argument I shall consider in Section IV, where I conclude that the existence of such particular arguments constitutes a general, positive argument for the right-answer thesis that is true but cannot be made by any anti-realist.

3. Because Dworkin will make explicit, general arguments only against the 'no-right-answer' thesis, and not in favour of the 'right-answer' thesis, it is difficult to say what the right-answer thesis means for Dworkin. Fortunately, we get considerable help in this exegetical task from

92 Dworkin, *Principle*, above n. 1, at 143; Dworkin, *Rights*, above n. 1, at 286.
93 Dworkin, *Principle*, above n. 1, at 144.
94 See Dworkin, 'Reply', above n. 1, at 280.
95 Dworkin, *Principle*, above n. 1, at 119–45.
96 Ibid. at 171–7; Dworkin, *Rights*, above n. 1, at 283–90; Dworkin, 'Critics', above n. 1, at 332.

Dworkin's two versions of the 'no-right-answer' thesis. The two versions are: (1) the version that denies that legal concepts (like 'valid' and 'invalid' as applied to contracts) exhaust the logical space, which denial would allow that 'this contract is neither valid nor invalid' is a possible statement; (2) the version that can concede that 'valid' and 'invalid' are contradictories and not mere contraries of one another, yet denies that statements using such concepts in hard cases have any truth value because certain presuppositions of such statements (availability of non-vague text, non-controversy, etc.) are not met.[97] Prima facie, Dworkin's right-answer thesis correspondingly is: (1) a thesis about legal concepts, namely, that they and their apparent contradictories do exhaust the logical space; and (2) a thesis about legal statements, namely, that they are always true or false, either because the alleged presuppositions of such statements are not in fact presupposed, or because such presuppositions are met, or because of an insistence that propositions whose presuppositions are not met have the truth value, 'false'.

I do not find this two-part division of the right-answer thesis to be helpful, for it is the second version which goes to the heart of the matter. I would put it this way: law cases are decided by singular propositions, that is, propositions in which some terms are singular terms (terms that refer to some particular person, entity, event or state). An example is: 'This contract is invalid.' Such propositions decide cases because, unlike the universally quantified statements that are laws, they assert that the contract in this case possesses an attribute (invalidity) that gives rise to a legal remedy. Let p be any such singular proposition about any case whatsoever. The right-answer thesis is that for all p's, p is either true or false (the principle of bivalence) and for all p's, if p is not false, then it is true.[98]

Dworkin's thesis dealing with legal concepts should be seen, not as a competing version of the right-answer thesis, but as an attempt to state a presupposition of the right-answer thesis. That is, one might think that for bivalence and stability to hold for legal propositions like p, the general predicates within p must be paired with contradictories (and not mere contraries) somewhere in the legal lexicon. In Dworkin's language, 'valid' and 'invalid', for example, must, when applied to contracts, 'exhaust the logical space'.[99] Yet this does not have to be true for bivalence and stability to hold for legal propositions; if contracts can be 'inchoate' (Dworkin's marginal possibility—'voidable' might be a more realistic possibility) as well as valid or invalid, the proposition, 'this contract is inchoate' will have a truth value. What Dworkin is really driving at with his misnamed

[97] Dworkin, *Principle*, above n. 1, at 119–22.

[98] This is what Dummett calls the principle of stability (Dummett, *Truth*, above n. 3, at p. xix).

[99] Dworkin, *Principle*, above n. 1, at 121.

'"bivalence thesis" about dispositive concepts'[100] is this: no matter how the logical space is divided by legal concepts (contradictory pairs, triads, etc.), (1) all possible fact patterns that could occur in any legal case will be captured by one such concept; (2) such patterns will not be captured by any other such concept; and (3) all such concepts are (in the Hohfeldian language Dworkin adopts) 'dispositive'.[101] That is, once it is determined that some fact pattern fits within the concept, then there is a legal remedy attached to such finding so that those litigants with 'inchoate' or voidable contracts are not left in legal limbo.[102]

It is helpful to draw out this aspect of the right-answer thesis, not because it is a competing version of the thesis, but because anyone like Dworkin who holds the thesis must also defend the foregoing three propositions about legal concepts. The right-answer thesis itself, however, is that bivalence and stability hold for any singular proposition needed to decide any legal case whatsoever.

Such a version of the right-answer thesis is consistent with Dworkin's earlier and well-known arguments for the rights thesis[103] and for the absence of any judicial discretion.[104] As Dworkin himself recognizes, these earlier arguments 'suppose that there is often [always?] a single right answer to complex questions of law and political morality',[105] and the thesis just described seems to be exactly this supposition.

4. Saying this, unfortunately, does not get rid of all the puzzles. So far, we only know that the right-answer thesis is committed to legal propositions always having a truth value. Yet what is it that determines a legal proposition's truth value to be 'true', i.e. what makes a right answer right? For a realist, an answer is right when it corresponds to a complex moral fact (which in law includes the institutional facts that further moral facts make important). That account of a right answer will hardly do for a conventionalist such as Dworkin, however. Rather, Dworkin is committed to saying that 'facts of narrative consistency' make a right answer right; whenever an answer best fits the past decisions or statutes, and whenever

[100] Dworkin, *Principle*, above n. 1, at 120.

[101] Ibid. at 119–20.

[102] Perhaps it helps to formalize this. Let p represent the proposition that this contract is valid, q the proposition that this contract is voidable, r the proposition that this contract is invalid. (~p will be, 'It is not the case that this contract is valid'; ~q will be, 'It is not the case that this contract is voidable'; and ~r will be, 'It is not the case that this contract is invalid'.) Let s, t, and v be propositions describing various legal consequences. Then all Dworkin needs in the way of a 'bivalence thesis' about concepts in order to maintain bivalence and stability about propositions is:

(1) $p \vee q \vee r$ (the exhaustion thesis);

and (2) $[p \supset \sim (q \vee r)] \cdot [q \supset \sim (p \vee r)] \cdot [r \supset \sim (p \vee q)]$ (the exclusivity thesis);

and (3) $(p \supset s). (q \supset t). (r \supset v)$ (the disposition thesis).

Despite its misleading connotations, I shall continue to use Dworkin's terminology in the text, referring to the conjunction of these three theses as 'the bivalence thesis about concepts'.

[103] See Dworkin, *Rights*, above n. 1, at 82–90.

[104] See ibid. at 31–9.

[105] Ibid. at 279.

that answer also best fits the political theory that itself best fits the shared moral judgements of the community, then that answer is correct.[106] (This is in line with the general conventionalist programme of substituting 'warranted assertibility' for 'true'.)

Just as Dworkin avoids saying anything very determinate about what it means for legal principles to fit legal rules (as discussed above), so he wants to avoid saying much about what 'fit' or 'facts of narrative consistency' more generally might mean. At many points, Dworkin explicitly grants the participants in the legal system the final say on what 'fit' and 'narrative consistency' might be. According to this view it is an 'illusion' to suppose 'that facts about narrative consistency are part of the external world' in any normal sense;[107] rather, '[w]hatever sense statements about narrative consistency may have, they are given that sense by the enterprise that trains participants to make and respond to such statements'.[108] This seems to mean that we should not expect from Dworkin any characterization of what 'fit' comes to, since that relation is a matter of consensual agreement by the participants within the system and they might construct an enterprise in which they might agree about anything at all counting as 'fit'.

Dworkin can ill-afford this nonchalance about what relation 'fit' might be.[109] He needs to say what the relation is so that we can assess the plausibility of his right-answer thesis. For if he relegates this question to the practices of the participants in the legal system, those individuals obviously would not agree. In the face of such disagreement, Dworkin's judge obviously has to develop his own idea about what 'fit' is,[110] but so does Dworkin if we are to get a handle on what his right-answer thesis means.

For this reason, we must generally construe Dworkin to have a theory of what 'fit' is: it is based on the one-way logical relation of implication between propositions such that a statement of a principle (p) fits a statement of a decision or rule (q) whenever p implies q. (Likewise, q fits p whenever p implies q.) More than this needs to be said about 'fit', just as it does in science; but in both cases, what else is said[111] builds on and is not inconsistent with 'fit' as one-way implication.

5. Construing Dworkin's 'facts of narrative consistency' so that fit is built upon a logical relation between propositions leaves us with one more interpretive hurdle about what Dworkin means by a right answer. An answer can be correct, Dworkin asserts, even if it cannot be demonstrated to be the right answer.[112] By 'demonstrate' Dworkin means 'backed by

106 Dworkin, *Principle*, above n. 1, at 137–43. 107 Ibid. at 141. 108 Ibid.

109 See e.g. ibid. at 153; Dworkin, *Rights*, above n. 1, at 282–3.

110 See Dworkin, *Empire*, above n. 1, at 256–7; Dworkin, 'Natural Law', above n. 1, at 170.

111 See e.g. P. Thagard, 'The Best Explanation: Criteria for Theory Choice', *Journal of Philosophy*, 75 (1978), 76–92 (simplicity, consilience, analogy).

112 See e.g. Dworkin, *Principle*, above n. 1, at 140, 142.

arguments such that anyone who understood the language in which the proposition is formed must assent to its truth or stand convicted of irrationality'.[113] The problem is this: if 'fit' is the determinate, logical notion I have just explicated, why doesn't the right-answer thesis commit Dworkin to a 'demonstrability thesis' too? That is, let r be the proposition that decides a hard case. Let p be the principle that best fits both previous cases and the normative theory that itself best fits community judgements of morality. Then r will be the right answer (rather than not-r), if p implies r. Yet surely this last relation can be demonstrated, in the sense that a logical deduction can be given.

If Dworkin has the determinate notion of fit that I think he must have, then in the sense just explicated he must maintain a demonstrability thesis. To a perfectly rational person with full information, answers like r, if they are right answers because of best fit, are demonstrable. This need not cause Dworkin grief, however, because he only needs to deny a demonstrability thesis in the context of arguing against those who take the fact of disagreement in hard cases to mean that there could not be a right answer for those cases.[114] Those people need a much stronger demonstrability thesis, namely, one that holds that continued disagreement between persons with imperfect rationality and incomplete information betokens the lack of any right answer to the issue about which they are disagreeing. Dworkin could and should deny this demonstrability thesis.

Dworkin, however, appears to deny even my weaker demonstrability thesis. At one point, he construes the demonstrability thesis to hold 'that no proposition can be true unless the means exist, at least in principle, to demonstrate its truth through arguments to everyone who understands the language and is rational',[115] and the thesis in that form he denies. Such a denial makes a shambles of what a right answer could be for Dworkin. Unlike the realist, Dworkin cannot say that an answer is right because it corresponds to a moral fact. Dworkin's conventionalism commits him to the view that an answer is right when it is demonstrable, in principle (i.e. demonstrable to any being with perfect rationality and full information), from the theory that itself is demonstrable from the conventions that constitute both the moral and the institutional facts that a Dworkinian judge is to consider. I should have thought that Hercules, indeed, was invented by Dworkin to be just the person who could demonstrate whatever right answers there can be, even if the rest of us have to muddle along with demonstrations somewhat less perfect.

In the 'No Right Answer' essay, Dworkin is more cautious, because he construes the demonstrability thesis (whose truth he denies) to be the thesis that, 'if a proposition cannot be demonstrated to be true, after all the

113 Ibid. at 137. 114 See Dworkin, *Rights*, above n. 1, at 281.
115 See Dworkin, 'Natural Law', above n. 1, at 175.

hard facts that might be relevant to its truth are either known or stipulated, then it cannot be true'.[116] Since 'hard facts' are only physical facts (including behavioural and mental facts but excluding Dworkin's 'facts of narrative consistency'),[117] Dworkin can be interpreted to be denying only what he should deny, a strong demonstrability thesis. Even better is a third formulation of the demonstrability thesis he wishes to deny: 'no important aesthetic claim can be "demonstrated" to be true or false; no argument can be produced for any interpretation which we can be sure will commend itself to everyone, or even everyone with experience and training in the appropriate form of art.'[118] This is all Dworkin needs to deny to get around any argument from disagreement. Denying this also allows him to affirm the weak demonstrability thesis that he needs to even have a right-answer thesis to defend.

B. Dworkin's Conventionalism and the Right-Answer Thesis

1. *Dworkin's Arguments for the Bivalence of Legal Concepts*

a. The Argument from Legal Practice

As we have seen, one prerequisite for legal statements to satisfy bivalence and stability principles is for legal concepts to: (1) exhaust the 'logical space' in which any case could arise; (2) be exclusive of one another; and (3) dispose of all cases by attaching legal consequences to all possibilities. Dworkin's central positive argument about legal concepts satisfying these theses is simply an observation about how our (Anglo-American) legal system is carried on. About the exhaustion and exclusivity points, for example, he notes that 'lawyers do seem to treat "not valid" as the negation of "valid"'.[119] About the remedies point, he observes that our legal concepts are dispositive, so that we use legal concepts 'not simply to report in a neutral way that certain events . . . have occurred, but as an argument in itself that certain legal consequences . . . follow from these facts'.[120]

Although Dworkin also engages in minor skirmishing with some (not very well-armed) proponents of Dworkin's first version of the 'no-right-answer' thesis,[121] he plainly feels secure with this descriptive point. After all, the question is one of semantics—'about the meaning of legal concepts'—and Dworkin therefore finds it 'natural to support the claim by some appeal to a linguistic practice that is decisive'.[122] If evidence of the linguistic practices of lawyers were not 'decisive', how else, asks Dworkin, are we to proceed to answer this semantic question?[123]

116 Dworkin, *Principle,* above n. 1, at 137. 117 Ibid. 118 Ibid. at 153.
119 Ibid. at 123. 120 Ibid. at 124. 121 Ibid. at 123–7. 122 Ibid. at 123.
123 Ibid. Compare Dworkin, *Empire,* above n. 1, at 31–46, where Dworkin is much less enamoured of conventionalist semantics, at least about the concept of law itself.

There is a puzzle here that Dworkin's conventionalism about semantics leads him to ignore. Recall Dummett's well-worn example of whether 'brave' or 'not brave' have any application to a person who is now dead and who never faced an occasion on which his courage was tested.[124] In adverting to this example,[125] one might urge with Dworkin that the question—of whether 'brave' and 'not brave' are contradictories or contraries of one another, or do not negate each other at all—is decisively settled by the facts of ordinary usage. If such usage contains no intermediate category with which to describe unverified and unverifiable instances of bravery or cowardice, then 'brave' and 'not brave' are contradictories of one another. Yet, at the very least, this conventional feature of our English usage itself cries out for explanation. Why should people have come to talk this way rather than the other?

A conventionalist who reduces 'truth' to 'warranted assertibility', 'meaning' to 'assertion conditions', and 'reference' to 'whatever satisfies sense', has no answer to this question. Indeed, he may not even see the question. On his view people just adopt a bivalent semantics about 'bravery.' As David Papineau has recently observed, this is possible but very unlikely:

> If we did not expect that there was some underlying state for the verification conditions of 'brave' and 'not brave' to get right eventually, then why should we think that their verification conditions will ever be guaranteed not to apply simultaneously? Why should 'not bravery' ever establish the impossibility of 'bravery' unless it were that it had come to mean the absence of what made people 'brave'?[126]

Bivalent semantics is plausible for language users who suppose:

> that there is some kind of underlying state, such as a certain physiological structure, such that our 'eventual' use of 'brave' will make it apply to just those individuals who have that state, and our 'eventual' use of 'not brave' will make it apply to just those individuals who lack that state.[127]

Without such realist suppositions, however, why would lawyers or anyone else have developed the bivalent linguistic practices Dworkin relies upon?

It is thus possible, but unresolvably puzzling on conventionalist assumptions, to think that a bivalent semantics for legal concepts developed as it has. Moreover, if we put explanatory puzzles aside, what justification can a conventionalist like Dworkin give for continued use of such concepts in law? There is an article of faith involved in using such a seman-

124 See Dummett, *Truth*, above n. 3, at 14–16.
125 Dworkin, *Principle*, above n. 1, at 121.
126 D. Papineau, *Theory and Meaning* (Oxford: Oxford University Press, 1979), 184.
127 Ibid. at 182.

tics, namely, that eventually we will know enough (about bravery or about promises and religion) to show how to resolve what we previously thought were hard cases (quiet lives or Sunday contracts). The realist justifies his bivalent semantics by sharing the language-users' faith that there is an underlying reality out there whose 'hidden nature'[128] is determinative of truth values one way or the other in cases we presently cannot resolve. It is the rightness of promises being kept, except when made in conditions insulting to religious aspirations, that justifies lawyers in using their concepts in a way that makes any given contract either valid or not valid, sacrilegious or not sacrilegious. Without such (moral) realist suppositions, what possible justification is there for lawyers to continue to play a language game whose terms have a bivalent semantics? Without such suppositions, the linguistic features to which Dworkin adverts look like an unjustified mythology adopted by a profession for either self-serving or illusory ends.

b. The Argument Against Vagueness

Dworkin supplements his positive argument from lawyerly usage with a rebuttal of an obvious objection to the idea that legal concepts 'exhaust the logical space', namely the objection from vagueness.[129] If legal concepts are vague, and if there is no legal remedy attached to their 'penumbral' applications, then Dworkin could not make out his 'bivalence thesis' about legal concepts, and thus could not make out the bivalence and stability theses for legal statements.[130]

In one of the answers Dworkin gives to the vagueness objection, he contradicts his own narrower version of the bivalence thesis for legal concepts. For Dworkin speculates that one might hold the position that 'if a statute uses vague language it must be taken to have changed the legal status quo ante only to the extent justified by the indisputable core of the language employed'.[131] This suggestion amounts to an admission by Dworkin that our legal concepts might be such that there are contracts that are core-valid, contracts that are core-invalid, and contracts that are penumbrally neither. This is a harmless inconsistency for Dworkin, however, because by stipulating that we have a legal remedy attached to penumbral cases—either the remedy attached to 'valid' or the one attached to 'invalid', whichever represents the status quo—Dworkin resuscitates the only version of the 'bivalence thesis' about legal concepts

[128] Putnam, *Mind, Language and Reality*, above n. 4.

[129] See Dworkin, *Principle*, above n. 1, at 128–31.

[130] In the text, I have ignored what I take to be Dworkin's misallocation of the vagueness question to the bivalence and stability theses about legal statements. See ibid. at 129–30. Instead I treat the question as one about Dworkin's 'bivalence thesis' about legal concepts.

[131] Ibid. at 129.

that he need defend, namely, the three theses of exhaustion, exclusivity and disposition set forth earlier.[132]

In any event, this is not Dworkin's main response to the vagueness objection.[133] Dworkin's non-throw-away response to the vagueness objection is that his theory about interpretive claims in law 'will provide an answer to the question of what happens to the law when some institution has used vague language'.[134] As applied to statutes, Dworkin's theory, he reminds us, is that 'the impact of the statute on the law is determined by asking which interpretation, of the different interpretations admitted by the abstract meaning of the term, best advances the set of principles and policies that provides the best political justification for the statute at the time it was passed'.[135]

Actually, Dworkin cannot decide which way he wishes to put this response: either as a denial that words like 'sacrilegious' are vague when used in a statute,[136] or as an assertion that, although such words are vague, such vagueness can nonetheless be remedied by some theory of interpretation, his own included.[137] Since I take the latter version only to be an arguendo concession so as to allow in other theories of interpretation besides Dworkin's, I construe him to prefer to put the matter the first way when discussing his own theory of interpretation.

So construed, Dworkin's denial of vagueness is a puzzling argument for a conventionalist. Dworkin says that a term like 'sacrilegious' is (when used by a legislature in a statute) not vague, but rather a concept that admits of different conceptions.[138] This as we have seen is one of Dworkin's terminologies for describing the theorizing a language-user must do if he is to apply a word or phrase. A realist can easily make this argument, because vagueness is a conventional feature of the use of language. A realist will say that 'justice' is not vague in its meaning (even if it is in its use), because the meaning of 'justice' is given by the best theory of the nature of justice.[139] Yet, what does a conventionalist (for whom meaning is use) say that renders intelligible the conclusion that 'sacrilegious' is not vague?

Dworkin says that his conventionalist will develop a theory (conception) that renders the concept not vague; but what is Dworkin's theory a

[132] See above n. 102.

[133] Although Dworkin is extraordinarily tenacious in hanging onto it in the face of persuasive criticism of this response by Raz. (See Dworkin, *Principle*, above n. 1, at 129–30, 405 n. 3 for Dworkin's apparent response.) Raz's point is that 'core' and 'penumbra' are themselves vague notions so that what is in the one or the other will often have no determinate answer. This means that Dworkin's conservative rule would only reduce but not eliminate vagueness. J. Raz, 'Legal Reasons, Sources, and Gaps', in *The Authority of Law* (Oxford: Oxford University Press, 1979), 73–4.

[134] Dworkin, *Principle*, above n. 1, at 130.

[135] Ibid. at 129.

[136] See ibid. at 128.

[137] See ibid. at 128–9.

[138] Ibid.

[139] See e.g. Moore, 'Moral Reality', above n. 7, at 1149–52.

theory of, if it is not about the nature of things like the fairness of keeping one's promises? Dworkin's answer here has to be that his deep theory of 'sacrilegious' is about the 'facts of narrative consistency', which as we recall are of two kinds in legal interpretation: facts about the formal features of legal institutions (here, the 'abstract meaning' of the term);[140] and facts about the community's background morality (here, the 'best political justification' for a statute of this kind).[141] Yet, these facts of narrative consistency, being a coherence of linguistic conventions in the one case and moral conventions in the other, would seem to perpetuate vagueness, not eliminate it. That there is some unifying coherence to linguistic conventions about the use of a word like 'sacrilegious' is a fact plausibly denied by Wittgensteinians and other criteriologists.[142] Yet, is not criteriological analysis as applicable to moral conventions as to linguistic conventions? Why should there be any greater coherence in what people believe about sacrilegious contracts (and related matters) than what they say about them?

Dworkin appears to believe that he can always scamper ahead of any series of objections of this kind. So what, he asks, if the attitudes of the public (out of which community morality is constructed) are themselves indeterminate? Our deep theory will render them determinate, on this and every other question that could be asked.[143] And if the vagueness-critic continues to harp on the indeterminacies of various parts of the deep theory as it is articulated, Dworkin will respond with the injunction, 'more theory'!

This call for an indefinitely lengthy elaboration of theory about the meanings of words makes sense to a realist, for the potential data with which to verify such theories is also indefinitely large. Yet a conventionalist like Dworkin is stuck with those (large but finite) agreements in attitude that constitute the linguistic or moral conventions of a community. One can cry 'more theory', but one will sooner or later run out of anything about which to have a theory.

2. *Dworkin's Arguments for the Bivalence of Legal Propositions*

a. The Argument Against the Objection from Legal Positivism

The two objections Dworkin here considers are what he calls the objection from positivism and the objection from controversy. The positivist objection to the right-answer thesis stems from the plausibility of saying, for any positivist interpretation of some modal operator L, e.g. 'the sovereign commands that . . .', neither L(p) nor L(~p) for some singular propositions of law. For there are many propositions that the sovereign has not

[140] Dworkin, *Principle*, above n. 1, at 129. [141] Ibid.

[142] Moore, 'Semantics of Judging', above n. 6, at 218–21.

[143] Dworkin, *Principle*, above n. 1, at 130–1.

commanded one way or the other, so that if the truth of all legal propositions depends on such commands, many propositions needed to decide hard cases will be neither true nor false.

Dworkin's response to this objection has framed an elegant challenge to legal positivist theorists. If legal propositions are held by the positivist to be identical in meaning to those propositions restated within the scope of some positivist operator—'this contract is valid' means, 'the sovereign has commanded that this contract is valid', for example—then Dworkin's 'simple-minded argument against positivism'[144] shows that there is a right answer in every case.[145] Since such a conclusion is understandably an anathema for most positivists, the monkey is on their back to come up either with some relation between p and L(p) that is not truth-functional equivalence, or some interpretation of the legal terms in p that shows that apparent contradictories ('valid', 'invalid') are not related to one another in the way they appear to be.

Dworkin's challenge to the legal positivist has spawned a variety of interesting moves.[146] Rather than assessing whether such moves are themselves plausible, I wish to keep the argument focused on Dworkin, for it seems to me the insight behind the simple-minded argument puts the monkey on Dworkin's back as much as on the back of the positivist. Let B represent the operator, 'Most people believe that . . .', and p represent the propositions believed. Reductive (Dworkin's term is 'semantic') conventionalism is committed to reducing statements about the world to statements about what most people believe, or: (1) $B(p) \equiv p$. Yet by the same moves that Dworkin uses against the positivist, from (1) and an equally plausible statement, (2) $B(\sim p) \equiv \sim p$, it is derivable that $\sim B(p) \equiv B(\sim p)$ (if it is not the case that most people believe a proposition, then it is the case that they believe the negation of that proposition, and vice versa). This conclusion says that there is a community belief one way or the other on every conceivable proposition about the world!

144 Ibid. at 132–3, 405–6 n. 4.

145 Dworkin's *reductio* against the reductionist positivist is:

(1) $L(p) \equiv p$

(2) $L(\sim p) \equiv \sim p$

Ibid. (1) and (2) are what such a positivist seems committed to, given his reduction of legal propositions like p to statements about what a sovereign has commanded, a rule of recognition provides for, etc. Yet from (1), it follows that:

(3) $\sim L(p) \equiv \sim p$

From (2) and (3), therefore:

(4) $L(\sim p) \equiv \sim L(p)$

(4) is the right answer thesis, for it says that if the sovereign has not commanded p (where p is any legal proposition whatsoever), then the sovereign has commanded ~p, and vice versa.

146 See Raz, *The Authority of Law*, above n. 133, at 53–77.

One might think that Dworkin could embrace this conclusion, taking the argument to show why a community's morality contains within it a shared belief about every conceivable act, institution or state; the fact that community morality is so complete is what allows there to be right answers in hard cases. Dworkin can ill-afford to take this line, however, because doing so entails giving up any connection between his and the ordinary meaning of 'believe'. Beliefs are intentional states that do indeed take propositions as objects,[147] yet we should hesitate to say that the truth of B(p) is in any way connected to the truth of p. We—even a majority of us—believe all sorts of false propositions. Yet, what then is the relation that a more sophisticated conventionalist will posit to exist between p and B(p)? To be a conventionalist at all, he has to think there is some intimate relation. My suspicion is that if Dworkin explored this question a bit, he would find himself tempted by some of the same manoeuvres that Raz and other positivists have used to defend positivism against this kind of attack. Certainly the central intuition that moves the positivist about law would move Dworkin about beliefs. What propositions are believed by some person or group depends on some fact about him or them (a sources thesis, as Raz puts it), and it is wildly implausible to think that that mental or behavioural fact has occurred with respect to all conceivable propositions.

A conventionalist might respond to this by saying that the realist, no less than the conventionalist, needs an account of the relations between statements about beliefs and statements about propositions believed. After all, the conventionalist might say, surely there is some connection, even for a realist between first-person avowals of belief ('I believe slavery is unjust') and the proposition believed ('slavery is unjust'). Yet, a realist has an acceptable account here because she has a truth-conditions semantics that allows her to distinguish the meaning of a statement from the illocutionary force with which it may be uttered on most occasions of its usage.[148] The realist can allow there to be a connection between B(p) and p of conventional force, namely, the speaker who utters 'I believe that slavery is unjust' and is sincere, is committed to uttering 'slavery is unjust', and vice-versa. Yet, because force is divorced from meaning for the realist, there is nothing in this pragmatic connection of B(p) and p to tempt the realist to anything like a truth-functional relation existing between them. For the conventionalist, however, who does not have a viable distinction between 'assertion conditions relating to meaning' and 'assertion conditions relating to force',[149] the systematic connection in usage between B(p)

[147] M. Moore, 'Intentions and Mens Rea', in R. Gavison (ed.), *Issues in Contemporary Legal Philosophy: The Influence of H. L. A. Hart* (Oxford: Oxford University Press, 1987).

[148] Platts, *Ways of Meaning*, above n. 71, at 50.

[149] B. Mates, 'On The Verification of Statements About Ordinary Language', in V. Chappell (ed.), *Ordinary Language* (Oxford: Oxford University Press, 1964), 71–2.

and p forces him to articulate some semantic connection. If it is not identity of meaning (and thus a truth-functional equivalence leading to the absurdity that a community has a belief about every conceivable proposition), then what is the relation?

b. The Argument Against the Objection from Controversy

Dworkin lastly considers what he calls the objection from controversy. This objection is that there can be no right answer to some disputed question of law whenever reasonable lawyers disagree about what the answer is, and reasonable lawyers disagree a lot in hard cases.[150] An analogous objection can be made about literature[151] and morality.[152] Against a shallow conventionalist like Devlin, this objection would be a knockdown winner, for if the truth of 'abortion is wrong' and of 'abortion is not wrong' depends on what most people feel about that subject, neither statement has any truth value because there is no consistent feeling shared by most people. Against a deep conventionalist like Dworkin, however, the objection has little bite. There is no reason whatsoever to believe that 'most people' always know the deepest presuppositions of their own beliefs, so that some disagreement about those deep presuppositions is to be expected.

Actual disagreement, however, is not what Dworkin really wants to discuss here. What he really wants to show is that for legal statements (and for the concepts within them) there need not be any tests an answer must demonstrably satisfy in order to be a right answer. Dworkin considers this point when he discusses what he oddly calls 'the argument from realism'.[153] As the objection would be put by the 'realist' sceptic: 'If we look to the actual tests the law provides for claims about the validity of contracts, we see that in fact there is sometimes no right answer to the question of whether these tests are met in a particular case.'[154] Such a sceptic is hardly a philosophical realist, since he says just the opposite of what a realist would say about the connection between testability and truth.

A philosophical realist would have a ready response to this sceptic: on realist semantics, running out of tests is not to run out of meaning. We may not know whether some person is dead or not because our present tests for death derive from past experience, and such a person may present a situation we have never seen before. But since 'death' takes its meaning from the best theory there is on the nature of death, running out of tests does not leave the realist thinking there is no right answer to such cases.[155]

[150] Dworkin, *Principle*, above n. 1, at 137.
[151] Ibid. at 175–6.
[152] Dworkin, 'Natural Law', above n. 1, at 175.
[153] See Dworkin, *Principle*, above n. 1, at 127.
[154] Ibid.
[155] Moore, 'A Natural Law Theory', above n. 28, at 291–301, 322–8.

Given Dworkin's conventionalism, what should be his answer to this sceptic? Most plausibly he should do what MacCormick at one time suggested for him,[156] which is to articulate what the tests for legal concepts are such that they do not run out of determinateness in the face of novel applications. Yet Dworkin has never done this, defending instead the idea that there need be no tests that an answer must satisfy if it is to be correct.[157] In making this move, however, Dworkin renders himself unintelligible on what a right answer is. Consider morality: we can understand the shallow conventionalist who says that an answer is right when a large majority of people agree on it; similarly, we can understand the realist who says that an answer is right when it corresponds to moral reality; and we can even understand the deep conventionalist who, accepting the weak demonstrability thesis, says that an answer is right when it can be demonstrated (by Hercules, if no one else) to follow from a theory that itself can be demonstrated to derive from the community's shared concepts and paradigm judgements. There is no fourth possibility here for the deep conventionalist who rejects even the weak demonstrability thesis.

This is why I earlier construed Dworkin, despite what he says in places, to be the deep conventionalist who does accept the weak demonstrability thesis.[158] Yet so construed, Dworkin can hardly think that there will be right answers to all hard cases in morality, law or literature; his data base (shared judgements) simply is not rich enough.

Consider this last point in two parts, corresponding to the two steps a deep conventionalist must take once he has ascertained the community's shared judgements. He must first abstract from such judgements a theory that fits[159] the judgements. Yet, if fit is based on one-way implication as it is in science, then the Duhemian thesis (about the under-determination of theory by any finite set of data) states that there are an infinite number of theories that equally well fit the data, even if there are also a larger number (also infinite) of theories that do not fit the data.[160] No right answer on morality can come from an infinite choice of moral theories.

Dworkin might well respond to the under-determination point by saying that 'fit' includes more than one way implication, namely, the aesthetic notions of scope, simplicity, and analogy. These are used in science to answer Duhem,[161] so why may not moralists, lawyers, and literary critics use them as well? One problem with this response is that it is not clear whether adding the aesthetic virtues of theory-construction in science

[156] See MacCormick, 'Dworkin as the Pre-Benthamite', above n. 80, at 189–90.
[157] See above text accompanying nn. 106–10.
[158] See above nn. 112–18 and accompanying text.
[159] See above nn. 99–105 and accompanying text.
[160] See generally Quine, *From a Logical Point of View*, above n. 21, at 21.
[161] See e.g. Thagard, 'Criteria for Theory Choice', above n. 111.

allows any finite set of data to uniquely determine theory, nor is it clear that non-question-begging analyses can be given of 'simplicity' and the other aesthetic notions.

Another problem is even more basic: what is it that would justify a moralist (or a judge) in using these aesthetic criteria to select the theories that will yield determinate implications from the community's morality? Dworkin, as we have seen, favours moral arguments to justify theorizing the community's morality. Yet what justifies looking to simpler, or broader, or more analogous, theories? Such theories are more architecturally splendid, but how can the aesthetics of a theory justify it over those uglier competitors who imply the data just as well? Put another way, why should we care about a deep theory of the community's morality if it is *the* deep theory only because of its beauty?[162]

A moral realist has an answer here, just as does the scientific realist in the case of science. It is part of her moral (or scientific) theory as to how things are that the universe is simpler, or broader, or more analogous, in structure. 'God doesn't play dice with the universe' is an animistic way of putting this non-pluralist view of how things stand. The realist sees the aesthetic virtues, not as restrictions she might arbitrarily stipulate in order to narrow her choice of theories, but as theories about when theories are true.[163] The realist thus has a reason to rely on such virtues. Not being in the business of theorizing the community's moral judgements, she needn't worry that no theory can claim the mantle of being *the* theory of the community's morality.

Second, suppose one could derive from a community's moral judgements some one general theory, for example, of dignity or privacy. The conventionalist about morality then has to apply that theory to his hard case or moral dilemma. Here he faces the problem we have discussed before: how can such a conventionalist hope to think that his theory will decide all cases when its terms fail to refer to anything whose (indefinitely rich) nature guides meaning? A 'theory' for a conventionalist is a set of general statements containing a set of general terms. Yet no conventionalist semantics—where the general terms do not have their meaning fixed by the nature of the kind referred to—has a prayer of yielding right answers

[162] Dworkin's recent attempt to justify theorizing the shared concepts of our community's morality in terms of the values of integrity and fraternity does not answer this puzzle. See Dworkin, *Empire*, above n. 1, at 176–216. For Dworkin nowhere connects the aesthetic virtues of theory construction to the values of integrity and fraternity and thus does not address the under-determination problem raised by his continued call for more theory. Furthermore, even if Dworkin were to make this connection, these 'values' turn out to be just two more conventionally accepted moral concepts about which we must theorize, presenting yet again under-determination problems.

[163] Alan Musgrave, 'Realism Versus Constructive Empiricism', in *Images of Science* (Chicago: University of Chicago Press, 1985), 202–4; see N. Daniels, 'Wide Reflective Equilibrium and Theory Acceptance in Ethics', *Journal of Philosophy*, 76 (1979), 256–79.

in all cases.[164] Fact, as J. L. Austin once amended the saying, is richer than diction[165]—at least, richer than Austin's (and Dworkin's) conventionalist diction.

Nor does it help to consider as part of a 'theory' the more particular judgements from which it was derived. These will yield arguments by analogy, but analogies only hold by virtue of properties made relevant by some theory, and we are back staring at general words.

My own conclusion about all of this is that there is no way for Dworkin to hang on to both his conventionalist and his right-answer theses. It is obvious to me which he should hang on to and which he should give up, although anyone with legal positivist inclinations will doubtlessly think just the opposite.

III. DWORKIN'S SUPPOSEDLY AMETAPHYSICAL STANCE

Dworkin's response to the foregoing charge of inconsistency is easily anticipated from what he has written. Dworkin would like to deny that he is a conventionalist, deny he is a realist, deny he is a sceptic—and indeed, support all such denials by denying that there is a question to be asked about these three metaphysical positions to which there could be any sensible, general answer.[166] He thus thinks he is off one horn of his inconsistency, leaving him free to assert (or at least to deny others' denials of) the 'right-answer' thesis.

Although I do not think that this avoidance strategy can work, we need to examine it in order to understand why Dworkin believes he can assert the theories he has about law, literature, and morality and yet hold onto a right-answer thesis about all such areas. Working our way through these arguments of Dworkin's will also suggest where we should go if we wish to salvage both the 'right-answer' thesis and much of Dworkin's interpretive theory. I shall begin with Dworkin's arguments against scepticism.

A. Dworkin's Rebuttal of Scepticism

Dworkin's arsenal of arguments has within it two main weapons to be used against a sceptic who denies that claims in law, literature, or morality can be true or false. The first is the distinction between external and internal criticism. An external critic purports to stand outside the

[164] Moore, 'Semantics of Judging', above n. 6.

[165] J. L. Austin, 'A Plea For Excuses', in H. Morris (ed.), *Freedom and Responsibility* (Stanford: Stanford University Press, 1961), at 15.

[166] See Dworkin, *Empire*, above n. 1, at 76–86, 266–71; Dworkin, *Principle*, above n. 1, at 171–2.

enterprises he is criticizing and (if he is a sceptic) condemns the whole thing, root and branch. An internal critic, on the other hand, is someone who operates within the ground rules of the enterprise but who nonetheless criticizes the game as she is playing it.

The way philosophers for generations have used this distinction against the sceptic is to construe him to be an external critic and then to deny the possibility of external criticism. Quine used this distinction to argue against there being any external point of view from which Carnap's Language Schema L could be viewed and from which Carnap could discover those sentences made true by the conventions of L (analytic truths).[167] I have recently employed the argument against would-be sceptics about the justification of induction.[168] It seems to me that Quine and Davidson are persuasive in their arguments that there is no theory-less place outside of all science from which to ask such basic questions about scientific methods.[169] Only if we allow ourselves to rely on most of our scientific beliefs can we question some of those beliefs at any one time. Even though we can question each of them at some time, we cannot do so all at once.

Dworkin wishes to use this kind of argument against would-be sceptics about law, literature, and morality, recognizing that the philosophy of science has been the paradigmatic use of the argument in philosophy.[170] Unfortunately for Dworkin, the 'external' label does not capture all would-be sceptics about law, literature, or morality. Indeed, it is increasingly recognized that sceptics in science can reformulate their scepticism in a way that does not presuppose a point of view external to all science.[171] About the old riddle of induction, for example, an internal sceptic might say that, even granting the truth of all our scientific laws and theories, there is still no reason to believe we are justified in projecting from past cases to the future.

To answer the internal sceptic we need a second distinction, one between (using Rescher's terms) wholesale and retail criticism.[172] The general form of the strategy against the sceptic is the same as before: her internal scepticism about induction, for example, is construed to be wholesale criticism, and, it is then argued, only retail criticism is possible. For exam-

[167] See Quine, *From a Logical Point of View*, above n. 21, at 32–7.

[168] Moore, 'Precedent', above n. 58.

[169] See D. Davidson, 'On the Very Idea of a Conceptual Scheme', in Michael Krausz and Jack Meiland (eds.), *Relativism: Cognitive and Moral* (Notre Dame: University of Notre Dame Press, 1982).

[170] Dworkin, *Principle*, above n. 1, at 169.

[171] See B. Stroud, *The Significance of Philosophical Scepticism* (Berkeley: University of California Press, 1984), 209–54. See generally H. Kornblith (ed.), *Naturalizing Epistemology* (Dordrecht: Reidel, 1985) (for a collection of essays defending or criticizing a scepticism that does not presuppose a point of view external to all science).

[172] N. Rescher, *Induction* (Oxford: Blackwell, 1980), 208–9.

ple, I have argued that the sceptic about induction is typically a wholesale sceptic in his (Humean) demand that some general methodology ('warranted inductive inference', for example), or some supreme principle of science ('the principle of the uniformity of nature') or some general form of all scientific judgements (universally quantified) be justified on pain of the scientific enterprise collapsing.[173] What is wrong with such wholesale demands is that they presuppose that there is some general characteristic of science, separate from all scientific laws and theories, and they demand that it be justified. Yet, what is the 'principle of the uniformity of nature', for example, but the conjunction of all the laws and theories of science? Nature is not so uniform that everything is like everything else in every respect. To argue for such a purported, supreme general principle is to argue for all those more particular laws and theories, and once they are justified there is nothing else left over to be justified as a supreme principle of science.

Such arguments (collapsing the very general items the sceptic wants justified) force the sceptic to be sceptical 'at retail', that is, about individual laws and theories. And here, it is impossible to maintain scepticism about the ideal gas theory, for example, unless one is willing to deal with the exact sort of evidence with which scientists deal. Put another way, at this level of (internal) retail criticism, there is no room for a purely philosophical scepticism.

Although Dworkin at various points confuses the second of these distinctions with the first—assuming at these times that any internal criticism is necessarily retail[174]—he does also use the retail/wholesale distinction against would-be sceptics in law, literature, and morality.[175] What I shall next examine is the sense it makes to employ the external/internal and wholesale/retail strategies outside the confines where I think such strategies make a very good case against scepticism, namely, in science.

1. On Being 'External' to the Practices of Law, Literature, and Morality

The success of the 'relegation-to-the-(non-existent)-external' strategy in science trades on the difficulty the sceptic or anyone else has in thinking intelligibly about an Archimedean point outside all science by which to judge science itself. Yet, when we move to literary criticism, law and even morality, the external point of view about such fields does not seem so inconceivable. Might one not question the customary practices in any such fields, not from no point of view to be sure, but from the point of view of science? We certainly do not think that external criticism of astrology, phrenology, religion, hermeneutics-style psychoanalysis, or sociobiology—to name five

[173] Moore, 'Precedent', above n. 58.

[174] Dworkin, 'Reply', above n. 1, at 280.

[175] See Dworkin, *Empire*, above n. 1, at 79, 267–75; Dworkin, *Principle*, above n. 1, at 175.

suspect enterprises—is misplaced, just because many people engage in practices presupposing astrological truths, religious truths, and the like. What is it that insulates law, literature, and morality from the external criticism of science? Why cannot one say of the latter enterprises what I would say of the former, that the entities, states, or relations presupposed by the respective practices do not, in general, exist?

Dworkin is genuinely troubled by this question, as evidenced by the evolution of five different arguments in his work on this issue. One argument, suggested but never developed, is a kind of transcendental deduction about the deepest aspects of our legal practices:

> It may be that the supposition that one side may be right and the other wrong [in a hard case] is cemented into our habits of thought at a level so deep that we cannot coherently deny that supposition, no matter how sceptical or hard-headed we wish to be in such matters.[176]

Yet, it is only in morality that this kind of transcendental idealism has much of a chance, and even there the undeniability of our moral beliefs in toto would stem from their connection to features of our personhood that we could not conceivably deny (our theoretical and practical reason), not to deep features of those moral beliefs themselves.

Another argument that Dworkin has pursued is what I shall call the irrelevance argument. Here Dworkin admits that from some point of view external to law or literature (or chess), one might well question whether some entire enterprise made any sense at all as practised by its participants; still, Dworkin urges, such external criticism would be irrelevant once one began refereeing chess matches, writing literary criticism, or deciding hard cases.[177] For in doing these things, the sceptic must throw off her scepticism about the practice and make claims like anyone else within the practice. True, she might urge radical reform of our interpretive practices in law and literature, but even in doing this she would be making competing claims about how best to carry on the practice.[178] Even these last claims would presuppose special truth conditions for the practice that would not allow external criticism of the practice.[179]

The irrelevance argument, however, is no more than a *tu quoque* argument against the sceptic. It does not deny him a point of view from which to be sceptical (the external point of view) because there is nothing that forces him to play these games. Dworkin thus needs to advance a more radical argument against the external sceptic if he is to join issue with the armchair variety.

176 Dworkin, *Rights*, above n. 1, at 290.

177 Dworkin: *Empire*, above n. 1, at 82–3; *Principle*, above n. 1, at 176; *Rights*, above n. 1, at 282, 283–4; 'Natural Law', above n. 1, at 175–7.

178 Dworkin: *Principle*, above n. 1, at 134–7; *Rights*, above n. 1, at 288.

179 Dworkin, *Rights*, above n. 1, at 289.

Third, Dworkin urges that the only external argument about morality that we need to take very seriously depends on the weak version of the demonstrability thesis.[180] This thesis, Dworkin urges, cannot itself be demonstrated (verificationism unverified and all that), so we may also bypass its purported disqualification of morality as having right answers. Yet, this argument of Dworkin's is surely too short to do justice to the serious claims put forward by philosophically sophisticated moral sceptics. Sceptics such as Gilbert Harman or John Mackie have pressed external arguments about morality that in no obvious way depend on undemonstrated demonstrability theses.[181] A sampling: necessarily motivating moral entities are 'queer' in the sense that they do not square with our normal views (science) about what exists; the best explanation of our moral experience as a whole makes no ontological commitments to moral reality; and the failure in convergence in moral beliefs evidences a lack of anything objective to be agreed upon, whereas convergence in science evidences a reality causing such convergence.[182] Although I believe that such external criticisms of morality are wrong,[183] that is a matter requiring detailed argument,[184] not 'external/internal' wand-waving.

Dworkin's fourth and fifth arguments appear to be his present resting place in his quest to deny the sceptic an (external) point of view from which to be sceptical. We have encountered Dworkin's fourth argument before in limited form: it is Dworkin's tolerant view about what 'fit' might be, granting each enterprise autonomy in deciding what is to count as 'fit'. Dworkin applies a like 'ban on imports' to notions of validity,[185] objectivity,[186] independence from convention,[187] and even truth,[188] meaning and reality,[189] holding that it is wrong to assume that the propositions central to any public enterprise must be judged by the standards of science.[190] Rather, we should 'proceed more empirically',[191] by ascertaining what counts as a good reason within each such enterprise and judging the objectivity of its practice accordingly.

I do not think that we can be nearly this eclectic about basic notions like truth and reality and understand ourselves or our 'public enterprises'.

180 See Dworkin, 'Natural Law', above n. 1, at 175.

181 See G. Harman, *The Nature of Morality* (Oxford: Oxford University Press, 1977); J. Mackie, *Ethics: Inventing Right and Wrong* (New York: Penguin Books, 1972).

182 See Harman, *Nature of Morality*, above n. 181, at 3–23; Mackie, *Ethics*, above n. 181, at 36–42.

183 See Moore, 'Moral Reality', above n. 7, and 'Moral Reality Revisited', above n. 9.

184 As will be found in the essays in T. Honderich, *Morality and Objectivity* (London: Routledge and Kegan Paul, 1985). More recently, Dworkin has recognized that he cannot accuse external sceptics about morality of philosophical naivety, since such sceptics press arguments not so easily disposed of. See Dworkin, *Empire*, above n. 1, at 80.

185 See Dworkin, *Principle*, above n. 1, at 153.

186 See ibid. at 162.

187 See ibid. at 174.

188 See Dworkin, 'Reply', above n. 1, at 277.

189 See Dworkin, *Rights*, above n. 1, at 174.

190 Ibid. at 153.

191 Ibid.

Religions often say that their standards of justification and truth are different from those of science and that faith alone can justify religious truths. Protracted and detailed disputes within various religious traditions give ample evidence of the degree to which practitioners within these various traditions believe they are disputing something resolvable and significant. Yet, surely there is nothing in this to tempt us to eschew making those external criticisms of such practices that could show (by our normal, science-based notions of truth and justification) that all of some traditions' religious propositions are both unwarranted and false, or that all the entities, states or relations that the traditions posit do not exist. If we could not apply our science-derived notions of truth, justification, and reality to such enterprises, how would we understand them?

Dworkin's granting of autonomy over truth, objectivity, meaning, and reality to each public enterprise is reminiscent of the categorical distinctions employed by a generation of post-Rylean, ordinary language philosophers, and more than one generation of *verstehen*, *Geisteswissenschaften* types, since in each case the result is to insulate a category of discourse from the external criticism of science. I think, on the contrary, that we have to live in one world if we are not going to license every complex, coherent and publicly practised fairy tale that comes along.[192]

Dworkin's fifth argument is subject to the same objection because it, too, is built on the dangerous premise that any public enterprise can be self-certifying by its own autonomous standards of truth, meaning, and justification. Dworkin sweepingly denies that 'any skeptical argument about morality can be other than a moral argument, or skeptical argument about law other than a legal argument, or skeptical argument about interpretation other than an interpretive argument'.[193] External skepticism about such practices is 'a fake because the distinction that might give it meaning, the distinction between substantive arguments within and skeptical arguments about social practices, is itself a fake'.[194] Such statements make Dworkin look even more like someone in the Weber–Wittgenstein tradition.[195]

This fifth argument of Dworkin's, that denies an external point of view by denying that there is any distinction between external and internal

[192] See A. Grunbaum, *The Foundations of Psychoanalysis* (Berkeley: University of California Press, 1984), 1–94; Moore, *Law and Psychiatry*, above n. 56, at 18–26, 172–5, 271–80, and 'Moral Reality Revisited', above n. 9. See also Ch. 10, below.

[193] Dworkin, *Principle*, above n. 1, at 174.

[194] Ibid.

[195] See e.g. P. Winch, *The Idea of a Social Science and its Relation to Philosophy* (London: Routledge, 1958) (notoriously arguing for the autonomy of the social sciences on the ground that no external understanding of a social practice is possible). For recent expressions of Dworkin's presupposition of 1950s style linguistic dualism, see Dworkin, *Empire*, above n. 1, at 51, 64, 419–20 n. 2, 422 n. 14, wherein Dworkin repeats such Winchian slogans as 'the interpretation of social practices and works of art is essentially connected with purposes rather than mere causes' and that a social scientist must 'join the practices he proposes to understand'.

points of view, is also based on his view of the autonomy of public enterprises. Ultimately, this autonomy is itself based on Dworkin's semantic notion that the sense of moral or aesthetic or interpretive judgements is fixed by their role within their respective collective human enterprises, and because of this, 'such judgements cannot have a "real" sense and a "real" truth value which transcend that enterprise and somehow take hold of the "real" world'.[196] Thus, ultimately, it is Dworkin's conventionalist semantics which undoes him here, allowing Pegasus to fly whenever enough people talk about him enough in a systematic way.

2. *Wholesale, Internal Criticisms*

Dworkin's second strategy against the sceptic is to reduce any remaining sceptical arguments into internal, retail arguments. Retail arguments are particular arguments within an enterprise to the effect that, in some particular case, there is no right answer. One might, for example, be sceptical about there being any uniquely correct answer for a group of emotional distress cases in tort law,[197] or one might be sceptical about some particular proposition, such as whether Hamlet loved Ophelia.[198] In such cases, one might speak of 'ties', either in the sense that there is no factor in text or theory that makes any answer matter, or in the sense that the considerations of text or theory that do bear on the question are of equal weight on either side.

There is nothing to prevent the sceptic from summing her retail arguments from particular cases into a kind of general argument. Yet, if she does this, it seems Dworkin is right to think that the sceptic's claim 'is so implausible that it can be set aside at once'.[199] It is just not true of our attitudes about most particular claims we make about Hamlet, slavery, or privity of contract, that the opposite claim is equally plausible to us.

What Dworkin wants to deny the sceptic is a different kind of general argument, one that proceeds by a wholesale rejection of certain general presuppositions of the enterprise itself. Against the sceptic about induction in science, as we saw, this strategy might work because we may plausibly dissolve the general features of science to be justified at wholesale (methodology, supreme principles, general form of scientific judgements) into more particular, retail claims. Dworkin does not consider this possibility, however, because he thinks that wholesale ('global') arguments, because they are internal arguments, must be substantively moral, interpretive, or legal arguments. A wholesale argument about morality, as Dworkin understands it, must employ 'what the author takes to be the

196 Dworkin, *Principle*, above n. 1, at 174.
197 Dworkin, 'Natural Law', above n. 1, at 176.
198 Ibid.; Dworkin, *Principle*, above n. 1, at 175; Dworkin, 'Natural Law', above n. 1, at 174.
199 Dworkin, *Rights*, above n. 1, at 287.

best conception of morality in service of a wholesale internally skeptical position.'[200] Because Dworkin 'cannot think of any plausible arguments for global internal scepticism about political morality',[201] he would deflect the sceptic away from wholesale to retail criticism.

Sometimes, Dworkin inconsistently abandons this restrictive view of what wholesale arguments can be available to an internal sceptic.[202] Sometimes he grants sense to the internal sceptic's claim that judgements in literature and morality are too 'unstructured and disconnected' to generate the facts of narrative consistency Dworkin needs for his right-answer thesis.[203] Dworkin even allows the sceptical argument from disagreement to be made internally,[204] so long as it takes the form of asserting that the point of morality or literature is agreement, not correspondence to some objective reality. Yet, with these concessions (proper, it seems to me), why isn't the door open to allow in many of the sceptical claims that Dworkin wants to consider either 'illegitimately wholesale' or 'external'? Take Mackie's sceptical arguments about morality based on the alleged queerness of motivating qualities and the supposed lack of convergence in moral beliefs. If Mackie is right, as here I believe he is, in his express assertion that our practice of morality uses truth, justification, and meaning no differently than those concepts are used in science and everyday 'descriptive' discourse, then these criticisms of morality on queerness and non-convergence grounds are internal criticisms. After all, such scepticism takes a position on the point of morality—to describe how things are—no less than does the lack-of-agreement scepticism of Stanley Fish that Dworkin allows as internal criticism.[205]

Or imagine the moral sceptic who urges that certain presuppositions of our moral practices are not met by our own psychology: we are too weak-willed and self-deceived for morality as we conceive it to have any application, for example. Such scepticism is not subject to either of Dworkin's anti-sceptic weapons: such scepticism is internal because it takes morality as it is and shows an inconsistency in it; and although such scepticism is wholesale, there is no way to rule it out as illegitimate so long as such scepticism is correct in its assertion that there is a general psychological presupposition of our practices that is false.

There is a wholesale objection to be made to some forms of scepticism about morality and law, but I do not think that Dworkin has his finger on it. If we repair to the successful use of the retail strategy against the sceptic about induction, we can see that such a strategy should also work against any sceptics in law or morality who demand justification of some

[200] Dworkin, 'Natural Law', above n. 1, at 177.
[201] Ibid.
[202] See e.g. Dworkin, *Empire*, above n. 1, at 267–71; Dworkin, *Principle*, above n. 1, at 175.
[203] Cf. Dworkin, *Principle*, above n. 1, at 169–70.
[204] See ibid. at 175–6.
[205] See ibid.

allegedly general practice that we, in fact, do not practise. I have recently urged this strategy against moral sceptics who demand justification of a supreme principle of morality (that the form of our moral judgements is universalized) and against sceptics in law who demand justification of a supreme principle of *stare decisis* (that common law decisions be universalized into common law rules).[206] But to use the strategy in this way, one must show that the scepticism in question misconceives what in our practices needs justifying. This Dworkin has not done, and, as noted above, cannot do for many prominent forms of scepticism.

B. Dworkin's Scepticism about Realism

Dworkin urges that the arguments he has advanced against the sceptic are also arguments against the necessity, or even the possibility, of any metaphysics or epistemology for legal theorists. As Dworkin at one point puts his ametaphysical advice to moral, legal, and literary theorists: 'We should stick to our knitting.'[207]

This could be taken as a bit of practical advice to those who wish to make any contribution to literary criticism, moral theory, or jurisprudence, building on the irrelevance objection against external scepticism earlier discussed. But Dworkin has a much more metaphysical point to make himself: any metaphysics, realist or sceptical, is done from a point of view external to the enterprises of literature, law, and morality. The realist's kind of external support, Dworkin thinks, is no more possible than is the sceptic's kind of external attack. As Dworkin sees it, the realist and the sceptic have nothing to debate because both purport to stand outside the practices that they discuss.

This is, as indicated earlier, a plausible position to take about the laws and theories of science. How can one speak from some theory-less stance that we cannot even imagine? But for the reasons stated earlier in connection with Dworkin's argument against the sceptic, this is not a plausible move to make with respect to the practices of literature, law or morality. For here, the 'external point of view' is our normal scientific point of view, and on any naturalist theory of morality (and thus law on a natural law theory), morality has to compete in the one world of natural fact in which we live. If we put aside the 'special realm' picture that non-naturalism bequeaths to us about morality, then moral entities and qualities must exist and moral propositions must be meaningful, true and justified, in the same senses of the words 'exist', 'true', 'meaningful', and 'justified', as we use when we say that intentions, numbers, kinetic energy, and the rest of the normal furnishings of the world exist and that propositions about

[206] Moore, 'Precedent', above n. 58.

[207] Dworkin, *Principle*, above n. 1, at 172.

them are meaningful, true and justified. The alternative is to insulate moral, legal, and literary beliefs and practices from the test they must meet if they deserve to survive in our continued articulation of the ontology to which we commit ourselves by our theories.

In any case, none of Dworkin's five arguments against the sceptic taking the external point of view fare any better against the realist taking this scientific point of view about morality, law, and literature. Indeed, the last two arguments ultimately depend on Dworkin's own conventionalist metaphysics, according to which it is the conventional practices of a collective human enterprise that give the propositions used within that enterprise the sense (conventional meaning) that they have and that governs what 'true', 'valid', 'independent', and 'objective' mean when applied to such propositions.[208] There is no more reason for the realist than the sceptic to accept this conventionalism of Dworkin's. In particular, there is nothing in the internal/external distinction that can allow Dworkin to claim that his conventionalism is not just a metaphysics competing with the realist's and the sceptic's—illustrating again the old (philosophical) folk wisdom that those who proclaim the death of metaphysics are inevitably touting their own metaphysics.

Furthermore, even if Dworkin could make out his 'elimination-of-the-external' argument against the realist, the realist could reproduce most of her arguments for realism internal to the enterprises in question. Putnam, for example, being convinced that metaphysical realism about science was inconceivably external to all theory, moved some years ago to his well-known 'internal realism'.[209] Many other scientific realists (not Putnam) have urged that realism about science is, when (properly) viewed as a question internal to science, just another scientific hypothesis: if the best explanation for certain of our experiences requires that there be intentions, armchairs, or numbers, then we have good reason to believe realism about such entities.[210] A similar move would seem to be open to the moral realist/natural lawyer against whom Dworkin is arguing. If external (scientific) discussions of morality are inconceivable, beside the point, or in some other way ruled out, then why is internal moral realism not the natural alternative? Why cannot we take the ontological commitments of our moral theories as seriously as we do those commitments of our scientific theories (again, once we allow the one to be sealed off from criticism by the other)?

[208] See e.g. ibid. at 153 (discussing art); 162 (discussing literature); 174 (discussing morality); Dworkin, 'Reply', above n. 1, at 277.

[209] See H. Putnam, *Meaning and the Moral Sciences* (Cambridge: Cambridge University Press, 1978), 123–38; see also B. Ellis, 'What Science Aims To Do', in *Images of Sciences*, above n. 163, at 48–74.

[210] G. Harman, *Thought* (Princeton: Princeton University Press, 1972); see also R. Boyd, 'Lex Orandi est Lex Credendi', in *Images of Science*, above n. 163, at 3–34.

Dworkin can perhaps be construed as urging the retail strategy against the internal moral realist here, insofar as Dworkin's realist opponent always gets stuck defending the difference between realism and scepticism in terms of a difference between saying 'slavery is unjust' and saying, 'slavery is really unjust'.[211] Yet, an internal realist could defend his realism retail and not wholesale, the same way that he does in science: although his beliefs face reality en masse, those beliefs making ontological commitments should not be defended generally. The internal realist in science need defend only that kinetic energy exists, electrons exist, and only in the summation of those claims defend a more general commitment to theoretical entities as such. *Mutatis mutandis* for the internal realist about morals.

Indeed, it is arguable that Dworkin himself is this kind of internal realist about morals. For Dworkin does suppose that 'there are moral facts, which are not simply physical facts or facts about the thoughts or attitudes of people'.[212] By such a supposition, Dworkin does not mean 'transcendent' (external?) moral facts. He only means that 'a particular social institution like slavery might be unjust, not because people think it unjust, or have conventions according to which it is unjust . . . but just because slavery is unjust'.[213]

My only disagreement with such an internal, retail, moral realist is that voiced before: unlike science, morality (and literature and law) can and must be judged externally. The only alternative is to live in many worlds whose comparative rationality cannot be discussed. There is thus no intelligible position called 'internal realism' about morality. The upshot is that Dworkin's realism, to the extent he is a realist at all, can only be 'external'.

Finally, using a *tu quoque* strategy Dworkin has used against MacCormick,[214] and which is in fact a well-worn strategy of realists against sceptics:[215] How does Dworkin regard his own arguments? Are they just 'true-within-the enterprise' for morality, literature, or law? If so, how does Dworkin make his cross-disciplinary, three-way comparison? He needs some external notion of 'true', 'justified', and 'objective', in order to speak meaningfully of how law and morality are like literature. In any case, surely Dworkin, like the rest of us about our own theories, thinks of his theory of legal interpretation as correct *tout cour*, and not just as 'correct within the concept of law as we have conventionally practiced it'. Dworkin should abandon his supposedly insulated, internal realism, leaving him to defend the right-answer thesis on the only grounds on which it can be defended, namely, (external) moral realism and its accompanying natural law theory of legal reasoning.

[211] See Dworkin, *Empire*, above n. 1, at 80–1, and *Principle*, above n. 1, at 172.
[212] Ibid. at 138. [213] Ibid. [214] See Dworkin, 'Reply', above n. 1, at 279–80.
[215] Moore, 'A Natural Law Theory', above n. 28, at 309–13.

9

Law as a Functional Kind

Natural law has for a long time had a bad press. It is supposed to be the sort of spooky stuff that Bentham derided when he hooted at natural rights as not being just simple nonsense, but 'nonsense on stilts'.[1] Oliver Wendell Holmes's own brand of ethical scepticism and legal positivism led him to characterize the natural law as a 'brooding omnipresence in the sky',[2] sort of like the northern lights apparently, but without the lights. The prevalence of such views has for some time made it the case that 'to be found guilty of adherence to natural law theories is a kind of social disgrace'.[3]

Recently the experience of announcing a natural law view has become a little less like removing one's hat and revealing one's antennae for all to see. This greater acceptance is partly due to the increased acceptance of moral realism within philosophy.[4] Since a natural lawyer about law is also (necessarily) a moral realist about morality, this greater acceptance of the moral metaphysics of natural law has removed some of the 'spookiness' attitude toward natural law theories. But part of this reaction to natural law remains even for those cured of metaphysical naivety about morality. To such persons, the natural lawyers' assertion that a necessary connection exists between law and morality seems obviously false even if not metaphysically outrageous. It is this latter rejection of natural law—the rejection of the thesis that law and morality are necessarily connected—that I wish to examine here.

The jurisprudence that interests me is that natural law jurisprudence which grew up after World War II and which may be seen as being in part a reaction to the atrocities done by the Nazis in the name of German law. Post-World War II natural law jurisprudence argues for the relational thesis distinctive of natural law on the following basis: (1) general jurisprudence studies the nature of law in general; (2) the essence of law in general is to be found in law's functions (or ends), not in its distinctive structures (or means); (3) such function of law is . . . [some value that is both a true moral value and can be served by law uniquely so that that value can be

[1] Jeremy Bentham, *Anarchical Fallacies*, in *Works* (Edinburgh: W. Tait, 1843), ii, 501.

[2] *Southern Pacific Ry. v. Jensen*, 244 U.S. 205, 222 (1916).

[3] H. Voegelin, 'Kelsen's Pure Theory of Law', *Political Science Quarterly*, 42 (1927), 268–76, at 269.

[4] Bill Lycan reports that he found himself 'preaching to the choir' in a recent defence of moral realism, contrary to the more typical reaction in the past that regarded moral facts as 'right up there with Cartesian egos, moxibustion, and the Easter Bunny. . . .' (William Lycan, *Judgement and Justification* (Cambridge: Cambridge University Press, 1988), 198).

said to be law's distinctive end]; (4) given the end of law and given human limitations in achieving that end, the structural attributes law must possess to fulfil its function include the possession by law of legitimate practical authority obligating citizen obedience; (5) law can possess legitimate practical authority obligating citizen obedience only if in content it is not too unjust; therefore, (6) for something to be law at all it must necessarily not be unjust, the natural lawyer's conclusion.

Such an argument obviously opens up large areas where much must be said even to be clear, let alone convincing. I shall proceed in the following way. Beginning at the end of the foregoing argument, I shall first examine the conclusion (6). In the first part of the chapter I thus clarify what I understand a natural law theory of law to assert. In Section II I turn to the beginning of the argument (1), examining the presuppositions about the nature of jurisprudence contained in the idea that jurisprudence studies law in general. In Section III, I examine the idea of functional attributions, taking the functional organization of the human body as my point of departure, and seek to show how jurisprudence is best carried on in functionalist terms (2). Section IV constitutes a preliminary view of the difficulties attendant on marrying a functionalist methodology in jurisprudence to the natural law thesis. In this section I describe the tension that exists between giving law a functional characterization (3), on the one hand, and discovering amongst law's structural features that authoritativeness of its norms that make unjust 'laws' no laws at all (4) (5). In this chapter I shall not undertake the further tasks of defending my own view of the end of law, nor of arguing for a structural realization of some such end of law that includes as one of law's features that it obligate obedience. My chapter is thus preliminary and expository, not itself a defence of a natural law view.

I. WHAT IS A NATURAL LAW THEORY OF LAW?

As I shall use the phrase, a 'natural law theory' contains two distinct theses: (1) there are objective moral truths; and (2) the truth of any legal proposition necessarily depends, at least in part, on the truth of some corresponding moral proposition(s). The first I shall call the moral realist thesis, and the second, the relational thesis.

It is the relational thesis that interests me in this article, and so I shall not outline how one might defend the moral realist thesis.[5] What does need saying here, however, is how often 'natural law' is used to label the moral

[5] A defence of the moral realist thesis may be found in M. Moore, 'Moral Reality', *Wisconsin Law Review* [1982], 1061–156; Moore, 'Moral Reality Revisited', *Michigan Law Review*, 90 (1992), 2424–533.

realist thesis by itself.[6] There are four related usages of 'natural law' of this sort that require mention just to dispel confusion.

One is as a synonym for moral realism itself. Lawyers often use the phrase 'natural law' to refer to any 'objectivist' meta-ethical position. Such generic meta-ethical objectivism is more precisely known as moral realism. A 'natural lawyer' in this broadest meta-ethical sense holds that the truth of any moral proposition lies in its correspondence with a mind- and convention-independent moral reality. 'Natural law' in this sense is committed to two meta-ethical theses: (*a*) moral qualities such as justice exist (the existential condition); and (*b*) such qualities are mind- and convention-independent (that is, their existence does not depend on what any individual or group thinks—the independence condition).[7]

Sometimes 'natural law' is used by lawyers and others to refer to a particular species of moral realism. One such more particular usage of the phrase can be seen by attending to the distinction between 'naturalists' and 'non-naturalists' in ethical philosophy. A non-naturalist believes that there are mind- and convention-independent moral qualities to which true moral propositions correspond, but believes that these qualities are 'non-natural', that is, they do not exist in the natural world. Such qualities may be related in various ways to natural ones, or they may not, but in any case they are not identical to those natural qualities nor are the expressions referring to such non-natural qualities equivalent to or synonymous with expressions referring to natural qualities. Moreover, existing as they do in a non-natural realm, such non-natural qualities must be known in some supra-sensible way, which usually leads theorists of this stripe to posit a special faculty of intuition (leading to a common epistemic label for this metaphysical position, 'intuitionism').[8]

A naturalist believes none of these things. Rather, he believes that moral qualities such as culpability do not exist in any realm different than the natural realm in which such properties as causation and intentionality exist. Moral qualities are simply natural qualities of a certain kind, just as intentionality is a natural quality of a certain kind (that is, a quality of mind). With this distinction in mind, 'natural law' can be seen as sometimes being used to refer to that kind of meta-ethics that is naturalist, rather than non-naturalist, in its realist metaphysics.[9]

[6] See e.g. the many papers discussing 'natural law' in Sidney Hook (ed.), *Law and Philosophy* (New York: New York University Press, 1963), where what is discussed is some variant of moral realism.

[7] These two theses—of existence and independence—are distinctive of realism in any domain, be it morality, psychology, mathematics, etc. See Ch. 10, below.

[8] The *locus classicus* of non-naturalist realism is G. E. Moore's *Principia Ethica* (Cambridge: Cambridge University Press, 1903).

[9] It is this sense of 'natural law'—as naturalist realism—that generates the much overblown discussion in twentieth-century ethics of the 'naturalistic fallacy'. For a discussion, see Moore, 'Moral Reality', above n. 5.

Sometimes a further refinement is intended by the usage of 'natural law'. Sometimes the phrase refers to a particular kind of naturalistic moral realism, namely, one finding moral qualities to be identical to or supervenient upon only one kind of natural facts, the facts of human nature. This is the 'wired in' view of natural law, holding that there is a universal and discrete human nature, and that the nature of that human nature determines what is morally right. The human nature referred to here may be teleological, so that it is cast as the natural function of mankind; or it may be a more contemporary anthropology, using only non-teleological descriptions of universal human traits. In addition, such human nature may be thought to possess epistemic power within each human being, so that each has a natural access to moral truth; or it may be thought to possess motivational power within each human being, so that each can not only see the good but has some natural inclinations to pursue it. We might call any and all of these variations, 'human nature naturalism'.[10]

A fourth exclusively meta-ethical usage of 'natural law' is to refer to that species of naturalistic moral realism associated with many religious traditions.[11] On this view, the nature of moral qualities like goodness is given by their having been commanded by God. This is a naturalist realist view because it asserts the (human) mind- and convention-independent existence of moral qualities and because it makes them depend on the natural fact of divine command.

These four meta-ethical senses of 'natural law' are worth mentioning only because the phrase is so often taken to be used in those senses. Yet the natural law theory of law I defend is committed only to the first of these senses of natural law—the moral realist sense—and not to naturalism, human nature naturalism, or religious naturalism. One can be as atheistic and as non-naturalist in one's metaphysics as one pleases and still be a natural lawyer in my sense. (For this reason some have suggested that a better label for my kind of view would be the 'moral law theory of law', but for reasons I shall mention later the traditional label is best.)

It bears the emphasis of repetition that subscription to 'natural law' in any of the meta-ethical senses of the phrase is insufficient to be a natural lawyer in my sense. The natural law that interests lawyers asserts not only the meta-ethical thesis of moral realism but also the relational thesis. One could thus be a 'natural lawyer' in the meta-ethical sense of being a moral

[10] Perhaps the best reason to dispense with the label, 'natural law', is the assumption that a natural lawyer is committed to human nature naturalism in her meta-ethics. Because some natural lawyers such as Aristotle and Aquinas were committed to human nature naturalism makes the confusion understandable but no less a confusion.

[11] See e.g. Kai Nielsen, 'The Myth of Natural Law', in S. Hook (ed.), *Law and Philosophy*, above n. 6, at 129 ('If there is no God . . . the classical natural law theory is absurd . . .'). I dispute this conclusion of Nielsen's at length in M. Moore, 'Good Without God', in Robert George (ed.), *Natural Law, Liberalism, and Morality* (Oxford: Oxford University Press, 1996).

realist yet not be a natural lawyer in legal theory. This would be the combined view that there are mind- and convention-independent moral truths but that such truths are irrelevant to the truth conditions of legal propositions. Legal positivists often hold just this combination of views.[12]

A moral realist view is thus not sufficient to be a natural lawyer. Some have argued that it is not even necessary.[13] Such people argue that natural law does not require that the truth conditions of legal propositions depend on moral truth but only on there being certain moral *beliefs* conventionally accepted in the society whose law it is. One might think, for example, that the truth of the singular legal proposition, 'This segregated school system violates the Equal Protection Clause of the Fourteenth Amendment', depends on a moral belief of most Americans (namely, a belief that segregated schools are immoral because they are violative of each person's moral right to equality).

There is nothing incoherent about this view; my only point here is that it is not a natural law view. For given its conventionalism about the morals to which law relates, such a view is really a kind of legal positivism: What is legally required does not depend on what is morally right, but only upon a certain kind of social fact, namely, whether a group of people have the requisite moral beliefs. That segregated schools are wrong is a moral fact; that most Americans now believe that they are wrong is a social fact, which this kind of legal positivist would add to facts about Supreme Court utterances in order to have a value-free theory of law. Such a positivist is

[12] As Herbert Hart noted in his classic description of legal positivism. Hart, 'Positivism and the Separation of Law and Morality', *Harvard Law Review*, 71 (1958), 593–629. Legal positivism, as Hart points out, is a legal theory; it is not committed to non-cognitivism in meta-ethics nor, indeed, to any meta-ethical position. Still, as Hart did not point out, one motive for seeking a 'pure' theory of law—that is, a theory holding law to be uncontaminated by morality—is the fear that morality is irrational and that law cannot be scientific if it is tied to morality. Kelsen and Holmes both were partly motivated to their legal positivism by this fear.

[13] See e.g. Theodore Benditt, *Law as Rule and Principle* (Stanford: Stanford University Press, 1978), who argues for what he calls 'natural law' based on there being a necessary connection between law and conventional morality. Ronald Dworkin has throughout his career flirted with conventionalism about the morality to which law is related. See Dworkin, 'Philosophy, Morality, and Law—Observations Prompted by Professor Fuller's Novel Claim', *University of Pennsylvania Law Review*, 113 (1965), 668–90, at 688–90; Dworkin, *Taking Rights Seriously* (Cambridge, Mass.: Harvard University Press, 1978), 95, 125–6, 129, 134–5, 159–66; Dworkin, *Law's Empire* (Cambridge, Mass: Harvard University Press, 1986), 73. I and many others have noted this conventionalism before. See Ch. 8 above; M. Moore, 'A Natural Law Theory of Interpretation', *Southern California Law Review*, 58 (1985), 277–398, at 298–300; L. Alexander, 'The Empire Strikes Back', *Law and Philosophy*, 6 (1987), 419–38; H. Hurd, 'Relativistic Jurisprudence: Scepticism Founded on Confusion', *Southern California Law Review*, 61 (1988), 1417–1509, at 1458–9; J. Finnis, 'On Reason and Authority in *Law's Empire*', *Law and Philosophy*, 6 (1987), 357–80. To the extent Dworkin is a conventionalist about the morality to which law is related, he is not a natural lawyer, despite his own occasional self-labelling in these terms. (Dworkin, '"Natural" Law Revisited', *University of Florida Law Review*, 34 (1982), 165–88.)

as much a natural lawyer's opponent as is the more traditional kind who seeks to keep even shared moral beliefs out of his theory of law.

Having said what a theory of natural law is not, it is time to say what it is. The relational thesis distinctive of a natural law theory of law asserts that there is some necessary connection between law and morality. In clarifying this thesis we need to say more about the two things being related—law, morality—and then about the relation asserted to exist between them.

Take law first. Clarity demands that we distinguish two dimensions of generality of law. The first can be seen by referring to Herbert Hart's fruitful distinctions about law in his 1958 debate with Lon Fuller.[14] In the context of discussing the *law* from which morality is separated (according to legal positivism), Hart distinguished: (*a*) *law*, in the sense of legal system, from (*b*) *laws*, in the sense of the individual statutes or common law rules that may exist in a legal system, from (*c*) the *law of a case*, in the sense of that singular proposition of law that decides a particular case.

The distinction between laws and the law of a case can be seen in terms of the (logical) generality of the legal proposition involved. When we use the word 'laws', we refer to those standards describable by what I shall call general legal propositions. There is commonly a legal rule, for example, that a non-holographic will must be subscribed to by at least two witnesses in order to be valid. A general legal proposition is one which asserts the content of such a rule, thus: 'All non-holographic wills must be subscribed to by at least two witnesses to be valid.' A singular legal proposition, by way of contrast, picks out a discrete individual, event, or state of affairs, and predicates of it some legal attribute. For example: 'This will (referring to a particular document executed by a particular testator) is valid.' The difference between the two kinds of legal propositions is a matter of logical form. A general proposition uses universal quantifiers (for example, 'all wills') while a singular proposition singles out (by use of definite referring expressions) one particular thing in the world for legal characterization. In the example given, 'this will' picks out one particular thing in the world.

Judges need singular legal propositions in order to decide cases. In a will contest, what decides the case is the truth of singular propositions such as, 'this will is valid' or, 'this will is invalid'. The truth of certain general legal propositions has a bearing on the truth of such singular legal propositions; but it is the truth of the latter that decides particular cases because it is only the latter kind of propositions that refer to the particular party or transaction before the courts in individual cases. I thus call the law expressed by such singular legal propositions the 'law of the case'.

[14] Hart, 'Positivism', above n. 12, at 600–1. The distinctions in the text are not quite the way Hart described them.

Law is a yet more general notion than laws. Here, one's concern is about the conditions that must be present before law as such is present. The questions, 'When is there law?', or 'Does this society have law?', or 'When do we have the Rule of Law?', are invariably questions about when there is a legal system.[15] I shall accordingly call the systemic notion *law*.

A second dimension of generality has to do with the distinction between general and particular jurisprudence.[16] General jurisprudence studies law (laws, laws of cases) in the abstract, without regard to any particular legal system. General jurisprudence is thus often described as 'external' because the phenomena with which it deals, and the viewpoint from which it deals with them, are external to any particular legal system, including the one in which the observer lives. Particular jurisprudence is in this sense internal, for it studies law (laws, laws of cases) as those phenomena occur within some one particular legal system and from the vantage point of actors (lawyers, judges, citizens) within that legal system. Particular jurisprudence is thus a culture-bound enterprise while general jurisprudence is not.

One asserting or denying a connection between law and morality must specify with what generality he is talking about law in each of these dimensions of generality. The natural law jurisprudence that I wish here to examine primarily asserts the connection of morality to law to exist at the most general level of each of these two dimensions. That is, such jurisprudence talks about the connection of morals to the existence conditions of law as such, and not, for example, to the American legal system. Moreover, this primary focus is on law in the sense of legal system, not laws or the singular laws of particular cases. The primary relational thesis of the theory is that the truth conditions of the statement, 'law exists', includes the truth conditions of certain corresponding moral propositions.

I say that this is the *primary* relational thesis of the theory because there are secondary relational theses, namely: (*a*) the truth conditions of the statement, 'X is a law', include the truth conditions of the corresponding moral statement, 'X is just', and (*b*) the truth conditions of the statement, 'X is the law of some case', include the truth conditions of the corresponding moral statement, 'X is just'. These are secondary relational *theses* to the primary thesis, and not mere corollaries, because there are independent arguments establishing the truth of (*a*) and (*b*) that give them a meaning broader than they would have as corollaries alone. Nonetheless, these are

[15] So argued in Joseph Raz, *The Concept of a Legal System* (Oxford: Oxford University Press, 2nd edn., 1980).

[16] There are often several distinctions elided together under the labels 'general jurisprudence' and 'particular jurisprudence'. See e.g. J. W. Harris, *Legal Philosophies* (London: Butterworths, 1980), 4, where Harris has the distinction turn on the generality of the concepts analysed and not on the culture-free/culture-bound nature of the enterprise.

secondary relational theses because they are partly corollaries of the primary thesis: since the existence of laws of cases and of laws presupposes that there is a legal system to which such laws of cases and laws belong, the moral existence conditions of law will also be among the moral existence conditions for laws and laws of cases.

There is also of course a like trickle-down effect from a natural law *general* jurisprudence to a natural law *particular* jurisprudence. If law as such can exist only if certain moral criteria are satisfied, then law in America exists only when such criteria are satisfied too. Such particular relational theses are thus *secondary* theses too. They are *theses*, not mere corollaries, because in many legal systems there are additional ways that morality enters the existence conditions for laws and laws of cases that are peculiar to that legal system. In America, for example, the existence of judicial review and of a value-laden, written Constitution results in much 'natural law' constitutional law. These particular connections heavily colour how morality is related to law in the American legal system in ways not following from the general connection of morality to law. Nonetheless, the natural law jurisprudence discussed in this article focuses on the general connection between law as such and morality, not the particular jurisprudence of specific cultures.[17]

Turning now to the nature of the thing, morality, to which law is related by natural law theory, less needs to be said. Nothing here needs to be said regarding the metaphysical status of the morality to which law is related—that question is already dealt with by the moral realist thesis of natural law theory. Rather, the question is what boundaries there are to morality so that the relational thesis can be made more precise.

This is a more difficult question than it may appear. If moral facts are as factual as any other fact—which, crudely put, is what the moral realist thesis asserts—how do they differ from other facts, such as the fact that an action was motivated by a desire to see another suffer? Is this less a moral fact than the fact that the action was sadistic in its motivation? Less than the fact that the action was cruel? Less than the fact that the action was wrong? Which of these are moral properties of the action, and which are properties of a non-moral kind? Non-naturalist moral realism has an easy answer (easy to state, at least, although hard to analyse) to this query: the moral properties are the non-natural ones. For those of us who are naturalist realists, however, that easy answer is unavailable. For naturalist realism, moral properties are either type-identical to natural properties, or they supervene upon them. Neither possibility gives rise to any clear answer to our 'moral borders' question.[18]

[17] The exception again is Dworkin, who apparently eschews general jurisprudence. See text at nn. 27–9, below.

[18] See Moore, 'Moral Realism', above n. 5.

A tempting answer may be in terms of the illocutionary act-potential of the words used to refer to moral properties. This speech-act criterion works like this: words that in their typical use not only describe a property but express an evaluation of the object possessing it are evaluative words, and the properties they refer to are moral properties.

This is close, but too tied to conventional features of language use—change the illocutionary act potential of a word, and thereby effect a change in morality? I doubt it. Better is to focus on the prescriptive element of evaluations: a moral property not only gives us a reason to believe that it exists, like any other property; a moral property also has 'has-to-be-doneness' built into it in the sense that its existence gives rational actors a reason to act (to pursue it if it is good, retard it if it is bad). A moral property gives rational actors an objective reason to act.

Saying this may not seem to resolve our 'borders' problem about morality. Objective reasons to act can be self-regarding or other-regarding, prudential or non-prudential, reasons of autonomy or reasons of deontology, agent-neutral reasons or agent-relative reasons. Are all these to count as *moral* reasons, and thus, the properties that give rise to them to count as *moral* properties? By the notion of morality that interests me here, the answer is yes. The morality to which law is necessarily related of course includes properties like justice and injustice, equality, right and wrong, entities like right and duties—the properties and entities that give obligation-reasons, reasons of deontology, or morality in its narrowest sense. Yet I also mean to include non-obligation-imposing properties such as the virtues, which give each of us reasons to pursue them even if not obligating us to do so. Further, we should include properties giving us only prudential reasons to promote and retard them—properties like painfulness, our own as well as others.

We need a notion of morality that is as broad as practical rationality itself because that poses the interesting question to a natural law theory of law. Is some norm law despite its not being a dictate of practical rationality, or can a norm be law only if in content it conforms to the dictates of practical rationality for the persons that the norm purports to bind? That I take to be the interesting question of debate between legal positivism and natural law, and a sense of 'morality' narrower than 'practical reasonableness' only distorts that debate.

Broad as it is, this sense of morality is narrow enough to exclude the purely subjective and instrumental 'oughts' that Lon Fuller's critics were so fond of throwing up at him as *reductios*. It does not include the 'ought' of Hart's murderous poisoner who, on learning of the failure of his poison, says, 'I ought to have given her a second dose.'[19] Such 'oughts' are wholly

[19] H. L. A. Hart, 'Book Review—*The Morality of Law*', *Harvard Law Review*, 78 (1965), 1281–96, at 1286.

instrumental; they are means to the satisfaction of the subjective desires of an evil person; such a person has no *objective* reason to have given his intended victim a second dose, not even an objective reason of prudence.[20] Such oughts, accordingly, are not part of the morality to which law is related.

Our third and last clarification of the relational thesis of natural law was to describe the relation asserted to exist between law and morality. There are three possible relations that a natural law theorist might think exist here. The strongest is to assert an identity in legal and moral properties and thus an equivalence in legal and moral propositions. If 'slavery is unjust' is true, then 'slavery is legally prohibited' is true too, on this view. Such a view makes the justness of a norm *sufficient* for that norm's status as law.

This is a very strong or pure view of the relation between law and morality, for it makes law depend on nothing other than morality. Statutes can at most be evidence of laws, court decisions, only evidence of the law of the cases decided, constitutions, only evidence of the foundations of a legal system. Although Cicero, Blackstone, and other natural law thinkers on occasion said such things, and although such a strong version of natural law would be required to describe the prosecutions at Nuremberg as prosecutions under non-retroactive *law*, this is not the view post-World War II natural law jurisprudence has defended.

A much weaker view would make law (laws, laws of cases) always depend on morality, in the sense that the morality or immorality of a norm would always be *relevant* to its legal status. But this weak natural law view would not assert that the justness of a norm—say one prohibiting criminal conduct—was *sufficient* to constitute that norm into a law, nor would this view even assert that the justness of a norm was *necessary* for that norm's legal status. Rather the justness of a norm would only be 'criteriologically' relevant.[21]

My own view of the relation is stronger than this. My view is Augustine's view, that the justness of a norm is *necessary* to its status as law, but that law and morality are not identical. Just because some action is immoral and just because a norm prohibiting that action would be just, does not mean that action is illegal. This 'less-than pure' natural law view leaves room to include institutional history—facts like legislatures passing statutes, courts deciding cases—as relevant to a norm's legal status. On the

[20] The attentive reader will have noticed that I not only presuppose that each of us has reasons to act that we in no sense subjectively desire—'objective reasons'—but that satisfaction of desire is not itself among the objective reasons of practical reasonableness. For defence of both points, see Tom Nagel, *The View From Nowhere* (Oxford: Oxford University Press, 1985), 169–71.

[21] On criteriological theories generally, see M. Moore, 'The Semantics of Judging', *Southern California Law Review*, 54 (1981), 151–295, at 214–21.

other hand, my Augustinian view rejects the weak or criteriological view of the relation. The Augustinian view has a bite to it lacking in the weaker view, for on the Augustinian view the justness of a norm is *necessary* to its status as law. Or, to use Augustine's much-quoted language, an unjust law is no law at all.[22] Similarly, an unjust court decision is not the law of the case so decided, an unjust political system, not a legal system at all. These are strong enough conclusions to be counter-intuitive to many.

There is one last clarificatory hurdle to be cleared before getting on to the argument, and that concerns the nature of the *necessity* claimed here. It is sometimes said that there may well be an accidentally 'necessary' relation between law and morality, but that such accidental 'necessity' is not what the natural lawyer needs. He needs, it is further said, that it be *analytically* necessary—part of the meaning of 'law'—that law be connected to morality in the way just specified.

There is a grain of truth to this charge, so let me extract it before throwing the rest away. The legitimate point is that natural law as a legal theory cannot be established by doing particular jurisprudence alone. This is true even if the particular jurisprudence that is done is done for all the cultures there are or have been in the world. Suppose every legal culture has (or had) the following characteristics: for every plausible moral argument there is a plausible constitutional law argument, and vice-versa; there is judicial review, so that every statute or case decision is subject to being overturned if contrary to the constitutional law (which is by hypothesis the same in content as morality). In such circumstances, it could be said of each culture that an unjust law is not a law of the system and that an unjust decision does not determine the law of the case decided. Even so, the natural lawyer's relational thesis would not have been made out, because it would not have been shown that law (or laws and laws of cases) itself is connected to morality in the requisite way. One has to do general jurisprudence in order to make out the natural lawyer's relational thesis (or its opposite, the legal positivist's thesis of the separation of law and morals).

Some sense of 'necessity' is thus involved in saying that, *necessarily*, law cannot be too unjust and still be law, and 'accidental necessity' is no kind

[22] Augustine, *De Libero Arbitrio*, I. v. 11. There is an ambiguity that affects considerably just how strong this Augustinian view is. The ambiguity turns on whether we count only the unjustness of the content of a purported legal norm when we are assessing its legal validity, or we count also other considerations of morality (such as the unfairness of surprising reliance on the norm, the injustice caused by the encouragement of lawlessness by civil disobedience by others, etc.) when we ask, is this norm unjust? The latter view can be much weaker than the former, depending on how much weight is attached to the secondary moral considerations that might make a norm unjust-in-content nevertheless overall just. Aquinas appeared to have adopted the second, weaker view, as would I. A. C. Pegis (ed.), *Basic Writings of Saint Thomas Aquinas* (New York: Random House, 1945), ii. 795 (*Summa Theologica*, I–II, Q. 96, Art. 4); J. Ross, 'Justice Is Reasonableness: Aquinas on Human Law and Morality', *The Monist*, 58 (1974), 86–103, at 103.

of necessity at all. Such 'accidental necessity' is based on what is sometimes called an accidental generalization. An accidental generalization is a generalization that is true of a finite sample size of things but that is not necessarily true because of the nature of the kind of things making up the sample. 'All American lawyers are under seven feet tall' is, as far as I know, true about the hundreds of thousands of American lawyers that exist. Yet the generalization is not necessarily true because it does not answer correctly the crucial counterfactual question, 'If someone were over seven feet tall, would he not be a lawyer?' There is, in short, no necessary connection between size and being a lawyer, only an accidental connection. Similarly, to observe that all legal systems we have seen invalidate laws that are contrary to morality does not support the counterfactual (would there be law without this connection to morality?) needed to apply the generalization to all legal systems that could exist, and not just those that have existed.

So some sense of necessity is required. *Analytic* necessity, however, is not what the natural lawyer needs to establish, because few if any words have a meaning supporting analytic relations.[23] 'A bachelor is an unmarried man' may be an analytically necessary truth, but I would hardly defend 'an unjust norm is not law' as having the same nature.

Saul Kripke's notion of 'metaphysically necessary' is the sense of necessity needed by the natural lawyer here.[24] Unlike the semantic notion of analytic necessity, a metaphysically necessary truth is a truth only dependent on how the world is and not upon the conventions of human language use. 'Water is H_2O' is (as far as we know) a metaphysically necessary truth because something wouldn't be water if it weren't H_2O. Put another way, one atom of oxygen bound to two of hydrogen gives the essential nature of water. Such essence is *not* fixed by what English speakers mean when they say or think to themselves, 'water'. Such an essence is to be found in the nature of the kind of thing that water is. We have theories about such essential natures, but theories can be wrong; definitions (analytic truths), which purport to fix such essences by conventional stipulation, could not be wrong.

A natural lawyer should say that the essence of law is such that it includes justice, among other things. *Necessarily*, that is, if some system, norm, or decision is unjust, it is not *legal*. Not as a matter of conventional usage of the word 'law' (analytic necessity); not as a matter of universal social practices (accidental necessity); but as a matter of the nature of one of the things that exists in the world, namely, law.

23 See Moore, 'Semantics', above n. 21.

24 Saul Kripke, *Naming and Necessity* (Cambridge, Mass.: Harvard University Press, 2nd edn., 1980).

II. THE STRUCTURE OF GENERAL JURISPRUDENCE: FOUR JURISPRUDENTIAL DEBATES

A. The (Im)Possibility of General Jurisprudence

Before getting to the nature of, and justification for, functionalist general jurisprudence, we need to deal with certain debates about jurisprudence more generally. The first is the debate whether general jurisprudence in any form is possible. The argument is that an historically situated human observer (i.e. any of us) cannot get external to her own legal culture in order to think about (either descriptively or normatively) 'law in general'. The most such an observer can do, this view continues, is to interpret one's own legal culture, and one will only mislead oneself and others if one parades the results of such internal interpretation as if it were an external description or evaluation of something more general than, say, *American* law.

Ronald Dworkin's recent work is imperialistic against general jurisprudence in this way.[25] Dworkin's 'you can't be doing anything different than I'm doing, which is particular jurisprudence' claim is based mostly on epistemological scepticism but partly on the positive claim that law is an interpretive concept (that demands therefore an interpretation of *a* culture's legal system).

Against general epistemological scepticism, little will be said here.[26] The positive claim is jurisprudentially more interesting. An interpretive concept for Dworkin is a concept towards which we take the 'interpretive attitude'.[27] The interpretive attitude, in turn, is mainly marked by regarding some practice as authoritative for one's decisions in the sense that there is some point or value served by making one's decisions depend on interpretations of some authoritative practice (or 'text').[28] The point or value justifying judges in taking the interpretive attitude towards statutes, for example, might plausibly be thought to be the furtherance of democracy (assuming that the statutes in question issue from a democratic legislature).

The problem with this positive claim lies in its justification of the interpretive attitude for legal theorists as well as for judges, for there is an important disanalogy between the reasoning of judges and the reasoning

[25] Dworkin, *Law's Empire*, above n. 13; R. Dworkin, 'Legal Theory and the Problem of Sense', in R. Gavison (ed.), *Issues in Contemporary Legal Philosophy* (Oxford: Oxford University Press, 1987). I discuss this aspect of Dworkin's thought in Chs. 3, 8, and 10.

[26] But see Chs. 3, 8, and 10.

[27] Dworkin, *Law's Empire*, above n. 13, at 47.

[28] Ibid. See below, § IV, where I give an alternative interpretation of Dworkin's interpretivism that makes it (to my mind, at least) much more plausible but at the cost of reducing it to functionalist general jurisprudence.

of legal theorists. It is just not very plausible to think that jurisprudence is interpretive in the way that much of the legal reasoning done by judges when they decide cases is interpretive, for what is distinctive about interpretive reasoning is the authority granted to some text as one decides particular cases. And what authority is possessed by the practices of Anglo-American judges for me as a legal theorist? When I seek to articulate the best way for judges to justify their decisions, how are those judicial practices in any way authoritative for me, as a kind of text that I must respect? Granted, there are persuasive normative arguments making certain texts authoritative for *judges* when they decide cases; but what are the analogous arguments making those judges' practices authoritative for me when I seek to articulate the best theory of how judging should be done? Why should I care if none of them, all of them, or some of them, for example, actually look for the psychological intentions of the framers in applying the United States Constitution? No matter what the practices of American judges might be in this regard, I would argue (and have argued) that the framers' intentions are irrelevant to both the right answer, and the right way to justify what is the right answer, in constitutional cases.

Of course, one can target normative arguments at particular audiences, and when one does so it is often a good rhetorical strategy not to bend too much the practices of your targeted audience as you seek to persuade them to mend their ways. Perhaps the authoritativeness of Anglo-American legal practice for Dworkin comes to no more than that. But such considerations have to do with the pragmatics of presentation of a theory of legal reasoning, not with there being some intrinsic mandate that jurisprudence be limited to interpreting some culture's legal practices. Such pragmatic considerations hardly require some kind of 'interpretive' jurisprudence that is limited in its ambitions to providing interpretations of some one legal culture's practices; such considerations only constitute a practical limitation on how one presents general jurisprudence to certain audiences.

Alternatively, perhaps the point only is that general jurisprudence must be worked out not only in the ideal case but also as applied to the less-than-ideal world. To be practical, general jurisprudence must take into account certain features of existing legal cultures because those features themselves are morally relevant. It matters, for example, to what degree a legislature or a constitutional convention is truly democratic because such representativeness affects the degree of respect to which legislative or constitutional enactments are entitled.

Yet this defence of interpretivist and therefore particularist jurisprudence is ill-conceived because it in no way defends the authoritativeness of some culture's legal practices for a legal theorist. The only point this argument establishes is that when general jurisprudence is applied to some culture it must take into account the features of that culture that make a difference. The point is the same as that to be made to an observer generally: when describing or evaluating the practice of slavery in Athens, take into account whatever features of Athenian culture (limited alternative economic opportunities?) as are relevant. In neither case does such context-sensitive application of one's moral or scientific theory mandate the authoritativeness of any set of practices, legal or otherwise.

B. Descriptive Versus Normative General Jurisprudence

General jurisprudence is often divided between descriptive jurisprudence and normative jurisprudence. A descriptive jurisprudence seeks to describe law and in so doing employs a concept of law that such jurisprudence does not create. A normative jurisprudence, by contrast, does not seek to employ a concept of law already formed but rather, to stipulate a meaning to 'law' that we ought hitherto to employ. The first seeks to tell us what law (or our concept of law) *is*, whereas the other seeks to tell us how law *ought* to be conceived.

Normative jurisprudence most typically gives moral reasons why we ought to conceive of law in one way or another. Legal positivist conceptions of law, for example, are often accused of making persons who accept them too obeisant to legal authority; natural law conceptions are accused of breeding both reactionaries and anarchists.[29] In either case, the reason given to adopt a concept of law is a moral one. Normative reasons can also be of a non-moral kind, however. Instrumentalists about theoretical terms in social science take there to be no reality dictating how such terms are to be used; rather, we must create a concept like law to suit our explanatory/predictive purposes. Following this instrumentalist perspective out in jurisprudence will result in a normative jurisprudence, for such jurisprudence will purport to tell us how we *ought* to conceive of law, even though the reasons backing the 'ought' are of a non-moral kind.[30]

Both kinds of normative jurisprudence should be put aside as being incapable of answering the legal positivist/natural law debate.[31] The nat-

[29] The arguments of Lon Fuller and Herbert Hart, respectively, in L. Fuller, 'Positivism and Fidelity to Law—A Reply to Professor Hart', *Harvard Law Review*, 71 (1958), 630–72; Hart, 'Positivism', above n. 12. See generally P. Soper, 'Choosing a Legal Theory on Moral Grounds', in J. Coleman and E. F. Paul (eds.), *Philosophy and Law* (London: Basil Blackwell, 1987).

[30] Hart suggests such a social-science-construct approach to jurisprudence in various places in *The Concept of Law* (Oxford: Oxford University Press, 1961), but he does not apparently follow the method in the book. I discuss this briefly in Ch. 2.

[31] As also noted by John Finnis, *Natural Law and Natural Rights* (Oxford: Oxford University Press, 1980), 24–5. See also Philip Soper, *A Theory of Law* (Cambridge, Mass: Harvard University Press, 1984), where at 171 n. 13, Soper urges that 'one must take care not to confuse the question of what is important about law with the question of what is important in

ural lawyer asserts that there is a necessary connection between law and morality, and neither kind of normative jurisprudence can support or rebut that claim. To give moral reasons for *inducing* belief in the natural law theses is not to give reasons to believe those theses. Put another way: the good or bad consequences of someone believing some proposition to be true have nothing to do with the truth of the proposition. The question the natural lawyer poses is whether or not natural law is true. He is not concerned with whether our believing such theses to be true will have good or bad consequences. The latter calculation may affect to whom he tells his natural law theory, but it cannot affect whether he believes the theory to be true.

Theory-building reasons of social science likewise cannot answer the natural lawyer's question. Even if we *ought* to adopt a certain concept of law for, say, increased-predictability-of-judicial-decisions reasons, that cannot effect whether and how law *is* related to morality. For our newly defined construct—let us call it 'schmaw'—does not refer to law; it in fact (on instrumentalist views of scientific theories) doesn't refer to anything at all. Schmaw does not exist, but the term 'schmaw' is a logical place-holder in some predictive calculi of social science. How law is related to anything is untouched by the success of social scientists in framing some construct like 'schmaw'.

So ours is a quest in descriptive general jurisprudence. I next shall consider how this enterprise is best carried on.

C. Describing Law versus Describing A Social Concept of Law

Most often descriptive general jurisprudence adopts a conventionalist theory of meaning in its quest to analyse law.[32] A conventionalist about meaning believes that words like 'tiger', 'gold', 'malice', and 'law' refer to their respective things in the world only via a conceptual intermediary. That is, what determines what the word 'gold' refers to—gold—is our *concept* of gold. There are thus three things, on this view of meaning: gold, 'gold', and "gold" (double quotes used for concepts, single quotes for words).

Most often a concept takes the form of a list of criteria for a thing to be gold,[33] e.g. 'yellow, precious, malleable, metal'. Anything that satisfies

deciding whether to classify something as law'. Despite this warning, Soper himself appears to mix normative arguments about how we ought to classify law (ibid. at 158–60) with his nominally non-normative, essentialist search for the nature of law (ibid. at 25).

[32] On conventionalist theories of meaning, see Moore, 'Natural Law', above n. 13, at 291–301.

[33] Alternatively, some think that a concept is conventionally fixed by paradigmatic examples. See e.g. W. B. Gallie, 'Essentially Contested Concepts', *Proceedings of the Aristotelian Society*, 56 (1956), 167–98. Arguably, Herbert Hart shared this 'paradigm case' view of concepts. See Hart, 'Positivism', above n. 12, 607–8, where Hart discusses 'standard instances';

such a list must (analytically must) be gold, and anything lacking these properties must not be gold.

On this view of meaning general jurisprudence becomes a study of 'the *concept* of law' or 'the *concept* of a legal system'—to paraphrase the titles of the best-known books of this genre.[34] For on this view of meaning one studies the nature of the thing, law, by studying our concept of law (remembering that law is whatever our concept of law fixes it as). In rejecting the claim that natural law theory's relational thesis is an analytic truth I have already implicitly rejected this approach to jurisprudence. It is now time to make this rejection explicit.

The alternative theory of meaning under which I shall proceed asserts that our concepts do not determine the reference of terms like 'gold' or 'law'. Rather, the theory is one of 'direct reference' whereby 'law' refers to law without some third thing intervening. The meaning of 'law', on this theory, is given by the nature of the thing referred to—law—and not by some concept of law that fixes (by linguistic convention, or 'analytic necessity') what can be law.

The theory of direct reference has been defended elsewhere at length with respect to natural kind terms like 'gold' or 'tiger'.[35] Whether such a theory of meaning properly applies to artifactual words like 'pencil', 'lawyer', or 'law' is more controversial, for such kinds of things are often thought to lack any natural essence that can guide the meaning of such terms.[36] What is included in the class of such things, one might think, is wholly a matter of our conventions, conventions that can be fully stated as *concepts* (lists of properties) of pencil, law, etc.

Often those who adopt the conventionalist line on words like 'law' confuse two different ways in which conventions might be relevant to the meaning of 'law'. Such persons often confuse conventions being part of the nature of a thing, on the one hand, with our linguistic conventions

see also Hart, 'Ascription of Responsibility and Rights', *Proceedings of the Aristotelian Society*, 49 (1949), 171–94, where Hart thought it 'absurd' to seek criterial definitions of legal concepts. Nonetheless, Hart's own theory of law in *The Concept of Law* is statable as a definition of law (in terms of two individually necessary, jointly sufficient conditions, general citizen obedience of the primary rules and adoption of the internal attitude by officials towards the secondary rule of recognition). On this, see P. Hacker, 'Hart's Philosophy of Law', in P. Hacker and J. Raz (eds.), *Law, Morality and Society* (Oxford: Oxford University Press, 1977).

[34] Hart, *Concept*, above n. 30; Raz, *The Concept of a Legal System*, above n. 15.

[35] Moore, 'Natural Law', above n. 13, 'Semantics', above n. 21.

[36] See e.g. S. Munzer, 'Realistic Limits on Realist Interpretation', *Southern California Law Review*, 58 (1985), 459–75; S. Schwartz, 'Putnam on Artifacts', *Philosophical Review*, 87 (1978), 566–74; D. Patterson, 'Realist Semantics and Legal Theory', *Canadian Journal of Law and Jurisprudence*, 2 (1989), 175–9. Compare Hilary Putnam, *Mind, Language, and Reality* (Cambridge: Cambridge University Press, 1975), 242–5; Moore, 'Semantics', above n. 21, at 217–18; Moore, 'Natural Law', above n. 13, at 300–1; D. Brink, 'Semantics and Legal Interpretation (Further Thoughts)', *Canadian Journal of Law and Jurisprudence*, 2 (1989), 181–91; Leo Katz, *Bad Acts and Guilty Minds* (Chicago: University of Chicago Press, 1987), 82–96.

(concepts) fixing that nature as a matter of analytic necessity, on the other. Take the phrase, 'co-ordination solution' as it is used by game theorists. A co-ordination solution is a convention that forms around some salient feature of a co-ordination problem. But that does not mean that the kind of thing that can be a co-ordination solution is fixed by our linguistic conventions (concepts) about the correct use of the phrase, 'co-ordination solution'. We study the nature of co-ordination solutions as a matter of better or worse theory; we do not study them only by attending to the concept of co-ordination solution in use in our language.

My own view is that the only things whose nature is fixed by our concepts are 'things' that do not exist—Pegasus, the twentieth-century kings of France, and the like. There are no things referred to by such terms, so such words' meaning can only be given by their concepts. Pencils, law, co-ordination solutions, etc., do exist and thus can have a nature that gives the meaning of their respective words.

I accordingly shall not seek to tease out a concept of law. General jurisprudence should eschew such conceptual analysis in favour of studying the phenomenon itself, law.

D. Law as a Nominal versus Functional Kind

The immediately foregoing remarks will seem more controversial than they are until it is realized what has been left open by them. Specifically, the possibility they leave open is that law is a nominal kind. A natural kind is a thing that exists in nature as a kind without human contrivance. Natural kinds have a nature that makes them kinds even if no human makes use of that nature or even discovers or labels it. A nominal kind, by contrast does not exist as a kind in nature, although its particular specimens may exist. Indeed, a nominal kind is *nominal* in the sense that as a kind its only nature is given by the common label attached to its various specimens.

Consider Figueroa Street, the North–South street in Los Angeles often listed as the longest municipal street in the world. Figueroa streetness is a good candidate for being a nominal kind not just because it was created by man (or at least a related species, Angelenos) but because there is no nature to Figueroa streetness that determines whether any given bit of asphalt or concrete is or is not part of it. Whether some bit of asphalt partakes of Figueroa streetness wholly depends on human convention: how were the Los Angeles maps and street signs posted?

If law were a nominal kind like Figueroa streetness then there would be no unified nature to seek in descriptive general jurisprudence. General jurisprudence would become the study of whatever was *called* 'law' by native speakers of English as they observed their own and others' societies. The attempt would be to distil universal characteristics possessed by all things so labelled.

I implicitly rejected this sociological conception of general jurisprudence when I rejected 'accidental necessity' as the kind of necessity needed by the natural lawyer. Let me now make the rejection more explicit and more defensible. In the first place, I doubt that there is a conceivable enterprise called general jurisprudence if law were a nominal kind like Figueroa streetness. For all that unifies the bits of pavement that together form Figueroa Street is the symbol, 'Figueroa Street', attached to each bit. When we change cultures and change language, we give up the unifying symbol. 'Law' is not a word in French or German; of course, 'droit' and 'Recht' are, but how could one say that these mean what we mean by 'law' when there is no *nature* to law that *droit* and *Recht* share? General jurisprudence could only be a language-specific study, so that there would be an English general jurisprudence, a French general jurisprudence, etc.

One might agree with this last point and simply give up on general jurisprudence on the ground that it, indeed, has no subject matter, law being a nominal kind without a nature susceptible of cross-cultural study. One is thus not forced by this argument to view law as other than a nominal kind.

More conclusive argument against thinking that law is only a nominal kind may be found if we repair to other artifactual terms. Consider the term, 'mower'. The Seventh Circuit Court of Appeals in the United States had to consider recently whether a haybine that both cut the hay and conditioned it was a mower within the meaning of a statutory exemption of 'one mower' for a farmer in bankruptcy. As Frank Easterbrook noted, haybines are not *called* 'mowers'; they are called 'haybines'. If mower were a nominal kind, this linguistic fact should have been the end of the case. Yet the court correctly decided that the symbol attached to haybines was not determinative because mowers had a nature:

> [N]either is it appropriate to say that the statute concerns only machines called 'mowers.' . . . 'mower' is not limited to the thing called a mower today, or even the thing called a mower in 1935. A statutory word of description does not designate a particular item . . . but a class of things that share some important feature.[37]

As Easterbrook concluded, in order to apply the statutory word, 'mower', he had to discover 'what a mower *is* . . .'[38]

What is the nature of a mower, if 'mowerness' is not merely a nominal kind? It is not very plausible to think that mowers have some essential structural features, features without which they would not be mowers. Technological advances have changed the structural features of mowers considerably, and will continue to do so—and will not those instruments

[37] *In re Erickson*, 815 F.2d 1091, 1092 (7th Cir. 1987). [38] Ibid. at 1093.

for the mowing of hay still be *mowers*? An affirmative answer suggests that the essence of mowerness is given by function and not by structure. Anything that mows hay is a mower, whatever its structural features turn out to be. (Think of the common answer to the question, 'Do you have a dishwasher?', given by pointing to one's children and saying, 'I have two of them.')

I call kinds like mowers functional kinds. Unlike nominal kinds, items making up a functional kind have a nature that they share that is richer than the 'nature' of merely sharing a common name in some language. Unlike natural kinds the nature that such items share is a function and not a structure. A stomach, for example, could have a silicon-based chemistry and be cubical in shape (rather than carbon-based and roundish) and still be a stomach because it performs the first-stage processing of nutrients distinctive of stomachs.

Whether law is a functional kind is not obvious. One cannot simply say that law is created by *purposive* human activity and that therefore law is 'purposive' (i.e. a functional kind), as Lon Fuller used to do.[39] This glosses all the interesting questions. I shall accordingly examine the question (of what kind of kind law is) in two stages: first, we need to be clear how functions are attributed to parts of systems and how systems themselves are assigned functions, and to illustrate this I shall talk about the functional organization of the human body. Second, we need to apply this analysis to legal systems and see what sense we can make of the idea that legal systems serve a function.

III. FUNCTIONALIST JURISPRUDENCE

A. Health and the Functions of the Human Body

'The function of the human heart (or the heart's beating) is the circulation of blood.'[40] This seems to be a true statement, but my enquiry is into what we mean when we assign such a function to body parts or processes. Most

[39] Fuller consistently elided 'purpose' in the sense of mental state with 'purpose' in the sense of function in his rush to conclude that law is purposive. See e.g. L. Fuller, 'Human Purpose and Natural Law', *Natural Law Forum*, 3 (1958), 68–76. Because of this and like confusions, Hart's jurisprudential epitaph for Fuller was accurate (if a bit brutal): 'The author [Fuller] has all his life been in love with the notion of purpose and this passion, like any other, can both inspire and blind a man . . . I wish that the high romance would settle down to some cooler form of regard. When this happens, the author's many readers will feel the drop in temperature; but they will be amply compensated by an increase in light' (Hart, 'Book Review', above n. 19, at 1296).

[40] This example, and the analysis that follows, are presented in greater detail in Michael Moore, *Law and Psychiatry: Rethinking the Relationship* (Cambridge: Cambridge University Press, 1984), 26–32.

obviously, we at least mean that one of the things the heart does—one of the consequences of its beating—is that the blood circulates. Whatever else we mean, we do mean to assert this much when we discover functions of things.

Often this is all that function statements are taken to assert. Joe Raz, for example, in his discussion of the functions of law, means only to discuss the *effects* of law.[41] The function of a thing for Raz just is its effects, which he taxonomizes as being either direct or indirect. More generally, social scientists often use function language in this limited way, saying for example that the *function* of certain ceremonial dances in certain tribes is the relaxation of group anxieties; all they apparently mean is that such dances have such effects. Similarly, much of the current research into the function of sleep is purely an empirical research into the *effects* of sleep—does it sweep away unnecessary memories of the day (Hughlings Jackson), allow us to dream and thus to discharge drive energies (Freud), prevent or combat fatigue (Claparede, Coriat), or even 'knit up the ravelled sleeve of care' (Shakespeare)?[42]

Such usages of 'function' are misleading, because all we have done when we isolate the effects of something else is to discover *possible* functions for that thing. The function it actually has will be one of those consequences, but it will not be all of them.

In the heart example, we cannot simply mean that one of the effects of one of the heart's activities is that blood circulates when we give that as the heart's function. For hearts do many things—they occupy space in the chest cavity, put upward pressure on the peristaltic gut for example—and even when we focus on their beating activity to the exclusion of others, that beating has many consequences besides the circulation of blood. Such beating produces noise in the chest cavity, for example.

None of these other consequences are the function of the heart, so we must mean something more determinate when we say that its function is to circulate the blood. Similarly, when we discover the functions of sleep, we will not have simply catalogued all the effects sleep in fact causes. (Otherwise, we should include as a possible function of sleeping the maintenance of the mattress industry, the provision of opportunities for nighttime burglaries, etc.)

One temptation may be to think that of all the consequences of an activity like sleeping or heart-beating, we honour as its function only those consequences the designer had in mind when he made such things. This solution leads very quickly to the teleological argument for God's exis-

[41] J. Raz, 'The Functions of Law', in Raz, *The Authority of Law* (Oxford: Oxford University Press, 1979).

[42] These and other theories as to the function of sleep are explored in Ernest Hartmann, *The Functions of Sleep* (New Haven: Yale University Press, 1973).

tence, for with hearts and human bodies there is no *human* designer to have intended some effect; so if a designer's intention is needed in order for a function to exist, and if hearts and sleep have functions, then there must be a Grand Designer.

Those of us who are not theists reject such a conclusion and therefore must reject the premise that leads to it (namely, that functions are the intended effects of a system's designer). Another temptation may be to think that the function of something is the consequence either actually brought about, or intended to be brought about, by the average human user of that thing. The function of a hammer is to drive nails because that is the usual intention with which it is used, on this view. While such conventionalist ascriptions of function may be all that is meant on some occasions for artefacts like hammers, this can't be what we mean about hearts and sleep; for neither the beating of our hearts nor our sleeping are acts we will and thus are not done by us to achieve further intentions. The function of sleep thus cannot be the consequence we typically intend to achieve by going to sleep.

My answer to our problem is different from the preceding two answers, relying on designers' or users' intentions. To find an activity's function, we sort through all the consequences of that activity in light of an hypothesis both about there being some larger system in which the activity occurs and about that system having an overall goal. The heart's beating and sleeping are both activities within (or of) the system we call the human body. We think such a system itself has a function or goal, namely, physical health. Such a system-wide goal is aided by some consequences of a heart's beating and by some consequences of sleeping, and not by others. We call the former the function of the heart or of sleep.

This selection amongst the consequences of sleep or of the heart's beating is thus in part guided by a further causal judgement: not only must the circulation of blood be caused by the heart's beating, but the circulation of blood must itself cause maintenance of that state of the system that is its goal (here, health). But this is only part of the story about discovering what is the function of what. Also needed of course is some way of picking out what is the overall goal of the system.

Finding the goal of the human body cannot itself use the same strategy we just detailed in selecting the function of sleep or of hearts. The finding of ever-larger systems, with ever-larger goals, has to stop somewhere. There are two leading possibilities for how we discover the overall goals of some system: we either find that the system naturally tends to maintain itself in some state of equilibrium despite widely disequilibriating conditions; or we discover that of all the human goods there are some but not others that either are or can be served by the system in question. The first is a value-free enterprise while the second is value-laden.

With regard to the first of these possibilities, there are cybernetic mechanisms with feedback loops that maintain various natural or man-made systems in certain states. We call such states homeostatic states. The subsystem of the human body that maintains constant inner body temperature despite widely varying environments is one example. One can study such systems and meaningfully index what one learns around the maintenance of this naturally occurring end state. The function of dilating capillaries in the skin would then be said to be the ridding of inner body heat, the function of perspiration, the same, etc. In no sense does this kind of function assignment require an evaluation by the investigator. Both the discovery of a goal for the system, and the discovery of the causal contribution of each part of the system to its attainment of its goal, are matters of hard, scientific fact.

Most of the time, however, this is not how we assign functions. Most of the time we are evaluating something as good when we say what it is good *for* (i.e. what its function is). In such cases we consult our list of all the good things there are and ask, which of these, if any, does/can this system promote? Physical health is on just about everyone's list of goods ('when you have your health, you have . . .' etc.). Physical health is the good that the human body can contribute—it can't contribute justice or liberty or economic well-being—so physical health is the goal of the human body.[43] When we attribute functions to body parts or processes based on their causal contributions to physical health, we are positively evaluating such parts and processes. 'The heart's beating is good for circulation which is good for physical health, and physical health is good', is the evaluation that lies behind the innocent statement, 'The function of the heart is to circulate blood.'

The evaluative nature of such goal attribution is easily missed in the case of physical health because there is such widespread agreement on health's desirability. Freedom from death, distress, or disability—the 'three D's' typical in definitions of negative health—are seen to be good by

[43] See Moore, *Law and Psychiatry*, above n. 40, 190–4. Chris Boorse has long disagreed with me on this. See Boorse, 'On the Distinction Between Disease and Illness', *Philosophy and Public Affairs*, 5 (1975), 49–68; Boorse, 'Wright on Functions', *Philosophical Review*, 85 (1976), 70–86; Boorse, 'What a Theory of Mental Health Should Be', *Journal of Theory of Social Behaviour*, 6 (1976), 61–84; Boorse, 'Health as a Theoretical Concept', *Philosophy of Science*, 44 (1977), 542–73. One can only settle the long-standing debate between myself and Boorse on the basis for function assignments on a piecemeal basis. About function assignments within physical medicine, Boorse's and my own method largely overlap in the functions they assign body parts because the health we value is by-and-large the health our bodies normally tend to achieve anyway, given aeons of natural selection. Still, the overlap is not perfect: we value capacities that make obesity dysfunctional even though there is no natural tendency to maintain *healthy* (i.e. not dysfunctional) weight; indeed, the body's natural tendency to store energy in the form of fat we find to be quite dysfunctional and thus unhealthy.

just about everybody.[44] Move to mental health, however, and the disagreement becomes larger, particularly about the level of mental capacities that are healthy to have. Since mental health guides the functional organization of the mind just as physical health guides the functional organization of the body, disagreement about the goodness of various ideas of mental health makes more evident the normative nature of mental function attributions.

Let me now draw this together in a way that can be applied to functional jurisprudence. Suppose we are ignorant of modern medicine or biology, but we have a sense that perhaps the human body is a functional system. The steps we should take as we test our intuition should go like this.

1. We isolate some parts or processes that we are relatively certain are parts or processes of the system. These are provisional hunches only, because we know that if we are right about the system as a whole—it is a functional kind, a kind whose essence is given by its function and not by its structure—we could be wrong about any particular structure actually belonging to the system. In the example I have been using, we start with the heart and sleeping as a part or activity of the human body.

2. We isolate the effects of the activities of the heart, or the effects of the activity of sleeping. This is our list of possible functions for each of these parts or activities.

3. We ascertain of all the human goods which one or ones could be served by the human body. Physical health being such a good, we hypothesize that physical health is the goal of the body, i.e. what the body is good for.

4. In light of such hypothesis about the goal of the human body, we discover which of the various activities of the heart, and which of the various effects of sleep, themselves causally contribute to the maintenance of the body in the state of health. These activities and effects are the functions of the heart and of sleep.

5. We continue the same four-step analysis both from the 'bottom-up' and from the 'top-down'. The bottom-up strategy picks other parts or processes we are relatively sure belong to the human body and probes their effects for any contribution to health. Such a procedure may modify what we think physical health to be. The top-down strategy begins with our increasingly well-defined notion of health and looks for parts or processes that must exist if the overall goal of health is to be maintained. Such a procedure may throw out certain parts of the body that are not

[44] This definition of health will be found in Robert Spitzer and Jean Endicott, 'Medical and Mental Disorder: Proposed Definition and Criteria', in R. Spitzer and R. Klein (eds.), *Critical Issues in Psychiatric Diagnosis* (New York: Raven Press, 1978). My own fine-tuning of the definition is in Moore, 'Definition of Mental Illness', in *Critical Issues*, above; and in *Law and Psychiatry*, above n. 40, at 210–16.

essential in that they perform no function (e.g. 'love-handles', the bits of waist fat that serve no function but which we nonetheless label in (humorously) functional terms).

At the end of our multiply iterated four-step procedure we will have written a comprehensive medical textbook on the human body. The overall system will be subdivided, not by structural principles, but by functional ones, so that we will have major subsystems such as the 'limbic system', the 'reticular system', etc. Such subsystems will themselves be divided into sub-subsystems, etc., so that eventually each essential (structural) feature will have its (functional) place in the teleological organization of the body. Such a textbook is a book in applied ethics because it asserts (or more often, presupposes) the goodness of health and then charts in detail the unique ability of the human body to realize that good. The same, I shall now argue, is true of jurisprudence textbooks when properly written, except that both the good the legal system obtains, and the means of its attainment, are of course quite different than the function and structure of the human body.

B. Law as a Functional Kind

As Phil Soper has noted, 'in the case of the concept of a legal system, most modern theorists agree that it is function that provides the clue to the latent principle [essence]'.[45] Suppose we share the intuition that law (legal systems) is a functional kind. Functionalist jurisprudence, rightly conceived, should play out that intuition in the five steps just outlined.

1. What are, provisionally at least, features of law? There is no poverty of suggestions in this regard. We might plausibly think that law is marked by coercive sanctions and the habit of obedience that such sanctions induce in people.[46] Alternatively, we may fasten onto the idea that law regulates its own creation,[47] or that law is marked by the existence of a special secondary rule that legitimates all other rules as rules of law.[48] We may think that 'law has authority', and mean by that: either that law is actually morally obligating,[49] or that law is *regarded* by its citizens and/or judges as obligating,[50] or that from the point of view of the legal professional law is obligating.[51] Yet again, we may fasten onto those features often called the

[45] Soper, *A Theory of Law*, above n. 31, at 170, n. 9. See also P. Soper, 'Legal Theory and the Problem of Definition', *University of Chicago Law Review*, 50 (1983), 1170–200, at 1187 n. 62.

[46] John Austin's and Jeremy Bentham's view. For a modern discussion of each, see Hart, *Concept*, above n., 18–76, and Hart, *Essays on Bentham* (Oxford: Clarendon Press, 1982), 127–43.

[47] Kelsen's slogan. Hans Kelsen, *General Theory of Law and State* (Cambridge, Mass.: Harvard University Press, 1949), 124, 126, 132, 198, 354.

[48] Hart, *Concept*, above n. 30.

[49] Finnis, *Natural Law*, above n. 31.

[50] Soper, *A Theory of Law*, above n. 31.

[51] Raz, *The Authority of Law*, above n. 41.

rule of law features—characteristics such as general, prospective, public, clear, stable, consistent rules that only command the possible and which officials apply when they adjudicate citizens' claims.[52] Others have thought that law is marked by formal features, such as the continuity of legal entities over time, the treating of past acts as having authority now, the gapless nature of law, or its ability to generate an authoritative rule without there being some other rule authorizing it,[53] whereas still others think that law is most uniquely marked by its justification of present state coercion by past political decisions or by its inherently controversial nature.[54]

Each of these have been presented as being features of law as such. Each is plausible enough that it could be selected as the place to begin in seeking the function law serves and the structures needed to realize that function. For ease of illustration, let us pick a simple feature, that a legal system is marked by its citizens at least believing that its norms have legitimate practical authority over them.

2. We now need to isolate the typical effects of such (provisionally) structural feature of law. We might suppose, for example, that the effects of citizen belief in the authoritativeness of law include: (*a*) it makes citizens less willing to think for themselves in moral matters; (*b*) it frees citizen time for more leisure activities; (*c*) it increases rebelliousness in children, who by virtue of such widespread belief must revolt against the law as well as against parents in order to develop into autonomous adults; (*d*) it allows the solution of co-ordination problems because the perceived authoritativeness of laws will make them salient features of any co-ordination problem faced by citizens. This list, could of course be drawn out considerably even from this one feature of law.

3. In order to say what the function is of law being believed to be authoritative, we next need some hypothesis about the general goal of law. As with structural features of law, again, there is no dearth of plausible suggestions here. Law, it has been suggested, has as its goal: the subjecting of human conduct to the guidance of rules;[55] the enhancement of the liberty and autonomy of persons through the opportunities for choice law can create when it has predictable legal sanctions;[56] the promotion of the common good, which on one conception of it, is that way of realizing

[52] Lon Fuller, *The Morality of Law* (New Haven: Yale University Press, 2nd edn., 1969).

[53] Finnis's five formal features of law in *Natural Law*, above n. 31, at 268–70.

[54] Dworkin's 'concept' of law in *Law's Empire*, above n. 13.

[55] Fuller, *Morality of Law*, above n. 52.

[56] F. A. Hayek, *The Road to Serfdom* (London: Routledge and Kegan Paul, 1944), 54. This is also most clearly the value that makes best sense of Fuller's eight desiderata for law. See Finnis, *Natural Law*, above n. 31, at 272; Hart, 'Book Review', above n. 12, at 1291; M. J. Radin, 'Reconsidering the Rule of Law', *Boston University Law Review*, 69 (1989), 781–819; and D. A. Gianella, 'Thoughts on the Symposium: The Morality of Law', *Villanova Law Review*, 10 (1965), 676–8, for reconstructions of Fuller along these lines.

substantive human goods made possible by life in a community;[57] the maximization of the common good in another sense, namely the aggregative sense that aggregates the preferences of citizens into a social welfare function;[58] promote the common good in yet another sense, namely, the goods of individuals which as individuals each has in common with other individuals;[59] the enhancement of simple survival for individuals;[60] attaining integrity in government, a desirable mode of government's achieving substantively good results through comprehensive, coherent, and equality-respecting means;[61] the maintenance of peace and order;[62] the peaceable settlement of disputes between citizens;[63] social control not by actual obligation or by force but by prima facie obligation.[64]

To get a handle on such a list requires nothing less than a full theory of the good and the right. One has to know, that is, what is objectively good and one has to know the permissible means of reaching it through action. Then one can decide which of this list are goods and thus which could be what a legal system is good for.

John Finnis's comprehensive *Natural Law and Natural Rights* illustrates this insight nicely. In the early chapters Finnis lays out his view of the seven good things and the nine conditions of practicable reasonableness that constrain any moral person's attainment of those seven good things. Finnis needs such a fully described moral theory in order to pick out the distinctive goal of law, which Finnis urges to be the 'common good'. The common good as Finnis conceives it is 'a set of conditions which enables the members of a community to attain for themselves reasonable objectives, or to realize reasonably for themselves the value(s), for the sake of which they have reason to collaborate with each other . . .'[65] The common good is thus not for Finnis the good each individual has which is the same as the good of everyone else. Although Finnis is a moral realist, his view of morality allows there to be different answers to how persons should lead their lives that are equally good. The law, as Finnis sees it, is uniquely situated to co-ordinate these different visions of the good life allowing each to realize his/her own vision.

[57] Finnis, *Natural Law*, above n. 31. Arguably Fuller too had some co-ordinative goal in mind for law when he said that law provides 'firm base lines for human interaction'. (*Morality of Law*, above n. 52, 209, 210, 223, 229), that it enables men to collaborate effectively (*Anatomy of Law*, Westport, Conn.: Greenwood Press, 1968, 6), and that it allows for that 'collaborative articulation of purpose' (Fuller, 'A Rejoinder to Professor Nagel', *Natural Law Forum*, 3 (1958), 83–104) Fuller thought essential to moral insight.

[58] Richard Wasserstrom, *The Judicial Decision* (Stanford: Stanford University Press, 1961), 10–11.

[59] One of Finnis's senses, although not his main one, in *Natural Law*, above n. 31, at 155.

[60] Hart, *Concept*, above n. 30, at 188.

[61] Dworkin, *Law's Empire*, above n. 13.

[62] e.g. Hobbes, *Leviathan* (Oxford: Clarendon Press, 1909).

[63] Karl Llewellyn, *The Bramble Bush* (New York: Oceana Publications, 1930), 12.

[64] Soper, *A Theory of Law*, above n. 31.

[65] Finnis, *Natural Law*, above n. 31, at 155.

Consider, by contrast, Lon Fuller's once held view that legal theorists did not have to develop a full theory of the good and the right in order to ascertain the unique good of law. Fuller purported to discover an 'internal morality of law' that allowed him to ground his famous eight structural features (publicity, generality, etc.) as being necessary to law.[66] Yet the goal that Fuller's truncated morality produced was the colourless, neutral goal of subjecting human conduct to guidance by rules. As many of Fuller's contemporary critics pointed out,[67] there is nothing intrinsically good about that goal. By itself, guiding persons by rules cannot be the goal of law because by itself, guiding persons by rules is not a good.

Suppose one has a full theory of the good and the right. And suppose that one has enough of an idea of the structural characteristics of a legal system to sort through that full moral theory and to isolate which good(s) are those uniquely achievable through law. One then could hypothesize which of the suggested goals of law is in fact its goal.

For illustration, let me continue with Finnis, since his system is so completely worked out. Finnis argues that the common good is a good—it consists in: (1) the good of co-ordinating conflicting individual goods for mutual benefit, (2) the good of co-ordinating individual goods when doing so has intrinsic merit (as in play), and (3) the good of co-ordinating when that realizes the goods of friendship and love.[68] Finnis further argues that this threefold common good is the unique good law can achieve and thus is law's goal.

4. Armed with a view of the goal of law, one can then isolate which of the effects of certain features of law are those features' functions. In Finnis's case, this would be to pick the consequence, co-ordination, as the function served by law being believed to be authoritative by its citizens. Such co-ordination, and not citizen obeisance or children's patterns of rebelliousness, would be the function served because such co-ordination itself causes the common good to be realized.

5. Having a provisional theory of the goal of a legal system and the functional and formal features of some parts of such a system, functionalist jurisprudence then repeats steps 1–4 for each plausible part of a legal system, asking in each case whether such a part could perform a function in the attainment of the goal of law. Working from the bottom up is to start with a feature such as coercive sanctions and ask whether this feature is a necessary part of law (necessary in the sense of necessary to attain the goal

[66] Fuller, *Morality of Law*, above n. 52.

[67] Hart, 'Book Review', above n. 19; Dworkin, 'Professor Fuller's Novel Claim', above n. 13; Dworkin, 'The Elusive Morality of Law', *Villanova Law Review*, 10 (1965), 631–9; Marshall Cohen, 'Law, Morality, and Purpose', *Villanova Law Review*, 10 (1965), 640–54. For a contemporary expression of this criticism, see Radin, 'Reconsidering The Rule of Law', above n. 56.

[68] Finnis, *Natural Law*, above n. 31, 139–47.

of law). Sanctions, for example, are not an obviously necessary feature of law if the goal of law is the common good in Finnis's sense, because co-ordination problems do not require sanctions for their solution.[69] Working from the top down is to start with the goal of the legal system and seek to discover what structures one would need in order to realize such a goal. Herbert Hart, for example, once speculated that a goal of the legal system on which everyone could agree was survival and that from such a goal one could infer that law would have to have a 'minimum content' of criminal prohibitions and property entitlements.[70]

IV. FUNCTIONALIST JURISPRUDENCE AND NATURAL LAW

We now should ask whether the enterprise just described will inevitably result in a natural law theory. In exploring this question I shall along the way explore other doubts about the enterprise.

One broadside objection would deny that functionalist jurisprudence carried on along the lines outlined above *could* yield a natural law result. The argument is that in functionalist jurisprudence there can be no *necessary* connection of law to morals because no structural features are necessarily law. Herbert Hart voiced a moderate form of this objection in his consideration of 'natural law with a minimum content'.[71] Hart correctly noted that even conceding arguendo that survival is good and that survival is a goal of the legal system, it still requires assumptions about human nature to generate conclusions about the shape of law. Hart's example: if we each had an armoured exterior rendering us invulnerable to physical attacks by our fellows, the criminal prohibitions needed would be quite different than those needed by us quite vulnerable persons.

Marshall Cohen once put Hart's point more bluntly. In objecting to defining law by whatever structural features that maximally realize the goal of law, Cohen objected that 'Means are not logically entailed by ends.'[72] Cohen's example: political office is often obtained through the means of party service, military glory, and intellectual eminence; yet no one would define 'political office' in terms of these typical means of obtaining it.[73]

Both Hart and Cohen mistake the necessity claimed by natural law (or by any sensible theory of law). They thought that to give the nature of law

[69] On this, see Leslie Green, 'Law, Co-ordination, and the Common Good', *Oxford Journal of Legal Studies*, 3 (1983), 299–324. Compare J. Finnis, 'Law as Co-ordination', *Ratio Juris*, 2 (1989), 97–104.

[70] Hart, *Concept*, above n. 30, 189–95; Hart, 'Positivism', above n. 12, at 622–3.

[71] Ibid.

[72] Cohen, 'Law, Morality, and Purpose', above n. 67, at 623, n. 19.

[73] Ibid. at 649.

was to produce an analytic definition (concept) of 'law' so that law's structural features (including its relation to morality, if any) would be analytically necessary features of law. As I argued before, this is a mistake. Legal theorists doing general jurisprudence only need point to a metaphysical necessity about the nature of law. And while Hart is certainly right that functionalists need to plug in certain assumptions about human nature, these human nature claims are (if true) metaphysical necessities too. *Given* these (metaphysically necessary) truths about human nature, and *given* the (metaphysically necessary) truths about morality that make some goal of law good, then law (metaphysically) must have certain structural features. Such non-analytic necessity about law's structural features is enough for any legal theorist, natural lawyer or otherwise.[74]

A second objection to functionalist jurisprudence focuses on the dependence of any structural feature being a feature of *law* on the selection of an ultimate goal for law. The idea is that even if familiar criminal prohibitions are necessary to preserve survival, that does not make such prohibitions necessary to law as such.[75] But this objection forgets what it is functionalist jurisprudence claims about the goal of law: the claim is that law's essence is given by that goal, not by any structural feature. Therefore any structural feature necessary to attain law's goal *is* law in any sense that the functionalist need defend. The only way this essentialist claim of the functionalist can be forgotten is by focusing on examples like Hart's, where a goal is picked for law (survival) only because of widespread agreement on its desirability[76] and not because such a good is the good law can uniquely achieve.

This raises a third objection to functionalist jurisprudence: there is no universal agreement on an end for law.[77] This objection can be put aside quickly. The last thing a moral realist means by objectivity is universal agreement. Moral realism is not the doctrine that certain values, such as the value of law, are universally agreed upon. Rather, it is the claim that such values exist and that their existence does not depend on what we or any group of people think. Agreement about the ends of law is not to be expected, but neither is the issue of agreement relevant. In this context it is a red herring.

[74] The assumptions about human nature that must be made in order for functionalist jurisprudence to yield determinate answers about law's structural features is what inclines me to retain the otherwise misleading label, 'natural law theory of law'. Human nature enters here, in the determination of what is instrumentally necessary for the attainment of law's good; human nature does not enter in to determine what is intrinsically good.

[75] For such an objection, see Kai Nielson, 'The Myth of Natural Law', in Hook (ed.), *Law and Philosophy*, above n. 6, at 136–8.

[76] Both Hart and Nielson explicitly discuss such goals as survival because of their popularity, not because of their plausibility as distinctively legal goals. See ibid. at 136–7; Hart, *Concept*, above n. 30, at 187–8.

[77] Hart, 'Positivism', above n. 12, at 623.

A fourth and more serious objection about functionalist jurisprudence would be the objection that it just assumes that law serves a goal (that is, that law is a functional kind). Not only is this unsupported, but as a natural law theory it is question-begging because functionalists assume from the start that law must serve some good. No surprise that they then end up with a theory of law asserting that law is necessarily connected to morality (i.e. to something good).[78]

There are two aspects to this objection that need separating. One is a circularity charge to functionalist jurisprudence as such, independent of whether such jurisprudence reaches a natural law conclusion; the other is the question-begging charge directed against functionalist jurisprudence insofar as it purports to yield a natural law conclusion. As I now propose to show, to answer the circularity charge will be to answer the question-begging charge as well.

The circularity part of the objection can be fleshed out like this. A functionalist about law starts with some feature he takes to be a feature of a legal system (call it feature 'X'), and then seeks X's function. Yet he can't know whether X is or is not a feature of law without knowing the goal of law, for the goal determines what is functionally necessary to its realization (i.e. is law). On the other hand, he cannot know the goal of law—nor even whether law has a goal—until he knows which of all the goods there are is the good that law can uniquely serve, but to know this he has first to know what law's structural features are.

Strange as it may sound to say it, the circularity of functionalist jurisprudence is not a defect of that mode of analysis but a virtue. For if the epistemic credentials claimed by the analysis were any stronger than they are, they would have to be false. As it is, such credentials are exactly analogous to those obtaining anywhere where one claims to know anything.

Consider our knowledge of the existence of a natural kind like gold, together with our knowledge of the kind's essential nature (gold's atomic structure) and of its instances (pieces of gold). How might one come to know whether there is in the world some kind of thing that we can call gold, what its nature was, or what its instances were, if he began in ignorance on all these matters? He might come across some initial examples, say some bits of iron pyrites (fool's gold). He might later come across many other individual bits of yellow, metallic stuff, and decide to label the whole class, 'gold'. This at the moment is a highly provisional hypothesis, because he is hypothesizing that all the members of the class of things that he has encountered share some essential nature even though he doesn't

[78] I am indebted to Stephen Morse for seeing this objection clearly. See Frederick Olafson, 'Essence and Concept in Natural Law Theory', in Hook (ed.), *Law and Philosophy*, above n. 6, at 237, for an apparent form of the objection.

know what it is. He could be wrong about this, as the case of jade illustrates; but he provisionally thinks that there is a kind, gold.

He next seeks to discover gold's essential nature, and develops various theories. Such theories are constructed in light of everything else that he knows (say, about other elements of the periodic table) and in light of such theories' ability to include as gold the instances of the stuff he has so far encountered.

Suppose eventually he reaches our theory of gold, that it is an element with such and such atomic structure. He will then turn that theory back onto the examples that suggested it to see whether or not they are truly instances of gold. As I have posed this little story, it turns out that his initial examples are not instances of gold at all.

There is no natural stopping point in this process any more than there is a natural starting point. Theories of the nature of a kind, hypotheses that there is a kind, hypotheses about what are the instances of a kind, are just that, theories and hypotheses. They are always subject to improvement and even replacement. At any point in time the most one gets is a kind of 'reflective equilibrium'—which is enough certainty to justify worrying about something else.

Consider another illustration of this non-foundationalist epistemology, the currently fashionable 'interpretivism'. In Dworkin's hands, for example, interpretivism begins by focusing on some 'pre-interpretive data'.[79] Such data is pre-interpretive in the sense that one hypothesizes that this data is part of the law before one has (by interpretation) justified that claim. Dworkin's example in jurisprudence: start with the idea that law is inherently controversial at a theoretical level.[80] Next, one seeks the point or value of law, which Dworkin calls our interpretation or *conception* of law. For Dworkin, this is integrity. Then, one applies back onto the data that generated it, this theory of law's point to justify what are and are not features of law. This results for Dworkin in a general description of law's structural features, what Dworkin calls our *concept* of law: law is marked by its use of political decisions made in the past to justify present state

[79] Dworkin, *Law's Empire*, above n. 13, at 65–6. My interpretation of Dworkin's interpretivism is alternative to that earlier given. Earlier, I took Dworkin to be claiming that jurisprudence is interpretive in the sense that there was some authoritative text for legal theorists whose theories therefore were interpretations of that text. Now, I construe Dworkin to be eschewing the need for any text; such 'interpretivism' proceeds rather by seeking a 'point' or value to the existence of law (not a point or value to regarding some legal practices as authoritative for theorists—true interpretion). The difference is that such textless 'interpretivism' just is functionalist general jurisprudence under a quite misleading label, for like the functionalist Dworkin seeks a goal for law and lets that goal guide what structural features are part of law.

[80] Ibid. at pp. vii, 3–15. See esp. 13: '[L]aw is a social phenomenon. But its . . . function . . . depend[s] on one special feature of its structure. Legal practice, unlike many other social phenomena, is *argumentative*.'

coercion.[81] With such more complete picture of law's structural features, Dworkin then more fully justifies his 'interpretation' (or 'conception') of law's point or function: law as integrity is the conception of law making law's structural features (given by our 'concept' of law) the best they can be.

Thus, even those who began their jurisprudential careers sceptical of functionalist jurisprudence[82] have ended up doing such jurisprudence, however unwittingly. The reasons for this are twofold: first, knowledge of any kind, natural or functional, will be non-foundationalist ('circular') in the way indicated. Second, law's nature as a functional kind forces those who would study it to do so in the functionalist way. Law does seem to be good for something more than it seems to have a structural essence, and playing out this intuition in the way indicated is to verify or falsify this intuition.

Does this beg any questions about natural law? Only in the sense that a physical scientist 'begs' questions about the relation of gold to atomic structure by his theory that that is the nature of gold—which is to say, not at all. The theory that law is a kind and that its nature is given by such-and-such a goal is just that, a theory, falsifiable as is the atomic theory of gold. It is not a foundational assumption about law's nature that begs the question, 'Is law related to morality?' True, if law is a functional kind then necessarily law serves some good and thus, necessarily, law is in that way related to morality. But this is a discovery, not a posit, of functionalist jurisprudence.

I have saved the best objection for last. This is the opposite of the question-begging objection just considered. Now the objection is that functionalist jurisprudence cannot result in a natural law theory. An observation of Ruth Gavison's begins this objection: 'It is true that a description of a thing that is defined by its function must affirm that it has some minimal capacity to perform the function, but such functional attributions are morally evaluative only if the function itself has a determinate moral value. Nothing will be called a knife if it could not cut; yet knives are not inherently good or bad.'[83]

Lon Fuller's functionalist jurisprudence well illustrates this pitfall. Early in his career[84] Fuller likened a legal system to a steam engine in that both were functional kinds; this, he thought, meant that there could be no clear separation of the questions, 'Is X a steam engine?' and 'Is X a good steam

[81] Dworkin, *Law's Empire*, above n. 13, at 93, 110.

[82] R. Dworkin, 'Does Law Have a Function? A Comment on the Two-Level Theory of Decision', *Yale Law Journal*, 74 (1965), 640–51. In this criticism of Dick Wasserstrom's functionalist jurisprudence, the early Dworkin regarded 'the assumption of a fundamental social goal as chimerical, even as a legislative standard'. Ibid. at 648.

[83] R. Gavison, 'Natural Law, Positivism, and the Limits of Jurisprudence: A Modern Round', *Yale Law Journal*, 91 (1982), 1250–85, at 1266–7.

[84] L. Fuller, *The Law in Quest of Itself* (Boston: Beacon Press, 1940), 10–11.

engine?', for the reason that Gavison references: to be a steam engine at all is to perform the function of steam engines to some degree. Gavison's point is that the goodness of a good steam engine need not be moral goodness but only an instrumental goodness. One can, as earlier noted, be a *good* poisoner in the instrumental sense of 'good'.

Fuller's functional jurisprudence was peculiarly open to this charge, because much of the time Fuller proclaimed that the overall goal of law as simply the subjecting of human conduct to the guidance and control of general rules.[85] This by itself is not very plausibly thought to be among the things that are intrinsically good. If such an instrumental good were the only thing law was good for, then like a knife or a steam engine such an instrument can equally well be used for good or for evil.[86] Yet it is not difficult to think of intrinsic goods that are plausibly served by those aspects of law (generality, prospectivity, publicity, etc.) on which Fuller focused. Liberty and autonomy come most easily to mind, for Fuller's rule of law virtues allow citizens more predictability of when law will sanction their behaviour and such increased predictability enhances planning ability and hence liberty and autonomy. Alternatively, such features may plausibly be supposed to serve the good of co-ordination and collaboration.[87]

Liberty, autonomy, and the common good (in the co-ordinative sense) are genuine moral goods. If these are the goals of law, then for a system to be a *legal* system there must be some moral goodness in these dimensions. This by itself would support a weak version of the natural law relational thesis, for what would be said is that the existence of a legal system in part depends on its moral worth (in the dimensions of liberty, autonomy, and the common good).

This would be a weak version of the natural law relational thesis because the goods of morality other than those that are the goals of law are not related to the existence conditions for a legal system. It is thus still possible that a legal system exists (because it is sufficiently promotive of law's distinctive goods) and yet that it is patently unjust. As Hart observed, systems can be highly respective of individual liberty (assuming *arguendo* that is the good at which law aims) and still possessed of great iniquity in every other dimension of morality.[88]

[85] Fuller, *Morality of Law*, above n. 52, at 53, 107, 115, 122, 130, 146, 150, 162.

[86] The first of the two main criticisms commonly levelled at Fuller's functionalist jurisprudence. See Hart, 'Book Review', above n. 19; Dworkin, 'Professor Fuller's Novel Claim', above n. 13; Cohen, 'Law, Morality, and Purpose', above n. 67.

[87] Finnis so appropriates Fuller's eight desiderata of law. *Natural Law*, above n. 31, at 270–3.

[88] Hart, *Concept*, above n. 30, at 202; 'Book Review', above n. 19, at 1287. See also Kenneth Stern, 'Either-or or Neither-Nor', in Hook (ed.), *Law and Philosophy*, above, 249–50, where Stern urges that the best mousetrap is not necessarily one that is best in trapping mice (a mousetrap's function); rather, the best mousetrap may be one that is pretty good at catching mice *and* that serves other values best, e.g. one with a safety catch that prevents human harm.

There is thus something of a dilemma facing any functionalist jurisprudence that has a natural law theory as its conclusion. On the one hand, functional jurisprudence seeks some distinctive end that law serves. The very idea that law is a functional kind depends on there being some such good that law can uniquely serve. That is what allows the functionalist to define law by its (functional) ends, and not by its (structural) means. Law cannot have as its distinctive good, 'all things that are good', without ceasing to be a functional kind.

Yet the natural law conclusion sought by functionalist jurisprudence seems to demand that law have as its goal nothing less than all the goods there are. For short of such a comprehensive goal for law, law seems 'compatible with great iniquity'.

Lon Fuller's mode of confronting this dilemma was highly problematic. Fuller assumed that any system that promoted law's goal had to promote all other goods as well. As Fuller put it throughout his work,[89] his was the faith that if you do things the right way (i.e. seek law's goal, its 'internal morality'), you'll end up doing the right things. That requires a stronger faith in the interconnectedness (within human nature) of the various motivations to promote all the goods there are than I can sustain.[90]

A better mode of confronting this dilemma is to seek some goal for law that does have connections to all the goods there are and yet is not simply, 'all the goods there are'. This is Finnis's strategy insofar as he assigns law the goal of the common good, which is not another of the seven good things Finnis thinks there are; yet the common good consists in the seven goods insofar as we can obtain them through co-ordination and community. Dworkin's implicit response to the dilemma is the same. He posits a goal of law, integrity, which is not one of the four political goods there are (distributive justice, fairness, procedural fairness, fraternity). Integrity is thus distinct, a separate end distinctively law's; yet integrity is connected to all legitimate political aims (the above four goods). Integrity purports to be both intrinsically good and the good uniquely served by law, and yet it purports to be linked to all goods such that its denial denies them as well.

Whether these responses by Finnis and Dworkin to the dilemma fare any better than Fuller's I shall leave to another occasion. Important here is to see that some such resolution is necessary if a functionalist jurisprudence is going to lead to a natural law theory of law.

[89] L. Fuller, 'What the Law Schools Can Contribute to the Making of Lawyers', *Journal of Legal Education*, 1 (1948), 189–204, at 204; Fuller, 'Fidelity to Law', above n. 29, at 636, 643, 661; Fuller, 'A Reply to Professors Cohen and Dworkin', *Villanova Law Review*, 10 (1965), 655–66, at 661–6. Fuller, *Morality of Law*, above n. 52, at 152–86, 223–4.

[90] This was the second major criticism of Fuller's functionalist jurisprudence: even if law's 'internal morality' (law's goal) was intrinsically good, one could achieve that moral good without necessarily achieving any other goods (Fuller's 'external morality of law'). For a limited resuscitation of Fuller on this point, see Finnis, *Natural Law*, above n. 31, at 273–6.

I shall close with a few remarks on how functionalist general jurisprudence may also generate a natural law theory of *laws* and of *laws of cases*. Suppose the functionalist–natural lawyer has made her case about law. That is, it is shown that law has a distinctive goal, that goal is intrinsically good, and that good can be realized only if all other goods are also realized to some degree. An unjust system will in that case not be a legal system.

This natural law conclusion about legal systems will have a trickle-down effect on laws and laws of cases. If the unjustness of a society precludes it from having a legal system, then that unjustness will also preclude it from having any laws or laws of cases. No law, no laws and no case-laws. As much Fuller would have had the post-World War II German courts decide; they should invalidate the Nazi informer statutes, not on the ground that such statutes were themselves unjust, but on the ground that there was no legal system in place in Nazi Germany. The same would be true for the judgements of Nazi courts: they should not be given *res judicata* effect because such judgements could not represent the laws of the cases purportedly decided by them if there was no legal system.

To this limited extent the functionalist who has made out his natural law theory about law has also made it out about laws and laws of cases. Yet natural law theory typically is more ambitious than this for laws and laws of cases. About laws, the natural lawyer's relational thesis is that the degree of *their* injustice (not the overall injustice of the legal system of which they are a part) determines their status as laws. The functionalist thus needs some argument about laws that is independent of the argument about law if he is to establish his secondary relational thesis about laws.

About laws, the crucial issue between legal positivist and natural law theories is whether laws necessarily obligate to be laws. If the answer is 'yes', as Augustine asserted, then laws must be relatively just to be laws—for only morality can obligate. If the answer is 'no', as Bentham proclaimed, then it is perfectly possible that unjust norms can both fail to obligate and yet be laws.

The functionalist in jurisprudence who wishes to defend the natural law theses about laws must thus show that laws necessarily obligate. This showing can be made by a functionalist only by showing that the end of law is served by laws obligating obedience to their terms by citizens and judges. The function of law, in other words, must be such that law's structure possesses this feature.

Consider Finnis's end for law for purposes of illustration. If law exists in order to promote the co-ordination of the differing goods of individuals (the 'common good'), then laws may be thought to need acceptance by citizens as authoritative (obligating) in order to serve their co-ordinating function. For laws that are believed to be obligating are strongly salient features of any co-ordination problem and thus can serve as such a problem's solution. Finnis, however, needs to show more than this to make out his natural law thesis about laws. Laws need to *be* obligating—not just believed to be obligating by citizens—in order for the natural law relational thesis to be true. And this structural feature does not seem necessary for laws to serve their co-ordinating function. To make it necessary, Finnis would have to argue that citizens will not maintain their belief in the obligating character of laws unless they believe that the laws are just, and they will not maintain any long-term belief that the laws are just unless those laws *are* just.

There are problems with this chain of reasoning. Why do laws need to be accepted as authoritative by citizens in order to have the salience needed to solve co-ordination problems—couldn't sanction-backed rules that are not believed to be obligating be equally salient? Also, asserting that long-term beliefs in justice are supportable only if the objects of belief *are* just, is to assert a strong causal thesis about moral qualities, namely, they inevitably cause belief. Although a moral realist should think that moral qualities do cause belief, it is not very plausible to assert it so strongly; there can be (and are) numerous factors that cause people to hold false beliefs about morality permanently.

Finnis appears to believe that he can sidestep a defence of these troublesome points by adverting to his notion of 'central' or 'focal' meaning.[91] The central case of 'law' for Finnis is seen only from the internal point of view of an actor asking, 'How does *that* (some norm that purports to be a law) affect my obligations?' The necessary obligatoriness of laws to be laws stems from the conceptual primacy of the question asked from such internal point of view, for Finnis. Yet whatever the merits of this defence of the natural lawyer's crucial structural claim about laws, it is not a defence based on functionalist grounds. This is not a defence proceeding *from* law's co-ordinating function *to* law's obligatory nature; rather, this defence abandons functionalist jurisprudence for a direct argument that the essence of law (law's 'focal meaning' or 'central case') lies in its obligating character.

Whatever the problems Finnis would have in defending the natural law thesis at the level of laws, I mention it for illustration only. Consider now the thesis at the level of the laws of cases. The laws of cases can have two different sources: one, in authoritative general rules or other standards, such as statutes; or two, in the reasoning by analogy from prior particulars that are regarded as having been authoritatively decided. The first source requires interpretive legal reasoning in order to discover the law of some

[91] Personal communication, 7 Jan. 1990. On 'focal meaning', see Finnis, *Natural Law*, above n. 31, ch. 1.

case, and the second source requires non-interpretive (or common law) reasoning in order to discover the law of some case.[92] Let me consider each type of case-law separately.

With regard to interpretive case-law, Lon Fuller famously argued for 'purposive interpretation' in his 1958 debate with Herbert Hart.[93] Statutes, Fuller argued, should be interpreted by their purposes, so that a fully operational truck mounted on a pedestal as a war memorial in a park should not be considered a vehicle for purposes of a statute forbidding vehicles in the park—no matter how much such a truck was a standard instance of the word 'vehicle' in ordinary English. Hart responded that a legislature's purpose could be evil and that purposive interpretation was no guarantor of the justness of the law of the case that resulted. Could not Nazi judges have interpreted Nazi statutes regarding the Jews in a way that furthered the purposes of such statutes?[94]

If the natural lawyer has made out his relational thesis at the level of laws, then the answer to Hart's question must be no. If laws must be obligating to be laws, and if they must be just to be obligating, then the purpose that guides interpretation of such laws cannot be evil. Imagine a statute motivated exclusively by an immoral purpose. For example, the legislature requires margarine-makers to dye their product red solely because butter-makers do not want competition with their product. Suppose that dyeing margarine red in fact causes a real good to be achieved, perhaps the prevention of its consumption by those deathly allergic to it. Purposive interpretation of such a statute would then not be guided by the purpose (motive) of the legislature that passed the statute. Rather, such interpretation would ignore that psychological question altogether and engage in moral reasoning: how can the moral good that is the purpose (function) of the statute best be served?[95] The law of the case that results from this latter kind of purposive interpretation will be dependent upon morality in just the way the natural lawyer asserts. If the judgement of a case is unjust, it is not the law of that case, but a judicial mistake.

Now consider common law reasoning. Here we cannot rely on the necessary justice of laws to argue for the necessary justice of laws of cases, because there are no laws in common law reasoning. (There is law, but no laws.) Instead, the natural law argument here proceeds from the goal of common law reasoning, which is equality. (One must of course have some overall goal to law that makes equality the goal of this kind of laws of

[92] I defend the view that statutory reasoning is interpretive in Moore, 'Natural Law Theory of Interpretation', above, and I defend the view that common law reasoning is non-interpretive in Moore, 'Precedent, Induction, and Ethical Generalization', in L. Goldstein (ed.), *Precedent in Law* (Oxford: Oxford University Press, 1987).

[93] Fuller, 'Fidelity to Law', above n. 29.

[94] Hart, 'Positivism', above n. 12.

[95] I argue for *this* kind of purposive interpretation in 'Semantics', above n. 21, and in 'Natural Law Theory of Interpretation', above n. 13.

cases, but I leave that to the side for now.) Equality requires that like cases be treated alike, the requirement of formal justice. How one determines the likeness that morally entitles litigants to like treatment is the crucial question. I have elsewhere argued that equality is an intelligible good only if one judges likeness as including all and only morally relevant features.[96] If this is so, then the law of a common law case depends on all of morality, for only all of morality can answer the question of relevant likeness. This does not mean that the decisions of past cases have no bearing on the content of the common law; only that the directions of like treatment such cases demand are determined by a moral judgement about relevant similarity. This is enough to make out the natural law thesis for this kind of law of the case.

[96] Moore, 'Precedent', above n. 92.

Part IV

Interpretivist Jurisprudence

10

The Interpretive Turn in Modern Theory: A Turn for the Worse?

> When someone starts talking about 'interpretation', reach for your gun.
>
> Michael Devitt, 1988[1]

> One [philosopher] characterized Derrida as 'the sort of philosopher who gives bullshit a bad name'. We cannot, of course, exclude the possibility that this may be an expression of praise in the deconstructionist vocabulary.
>
> John Searle, 1983[2]

This chapter was originally dedicated to my late friend John Kaplan, whose criticism of interpretivism was even more succinct than that of Michael Devitt or John Searle (to say nothing of the criticism that follows herein).[3]

There is a debate that most legal academics and social scientists (and not a few philosophers) wish to ignore, despite its wide-ranging implications for each of their respective disciplines. This is the metaphysical controversy between philosophical realists, who emphasize the world's independence from our concepts and language, and antirealists, who deny that the 'furniture of the universe' exists in any way independent of us. Such a debate, abstract though it is, directly influences the activity of all disciplines. In law, for example, those badly misnamed 'Legal Realists' have changed significantly the way we now theorize about and practise law. Indeed, the Legal Realists have so thoroughly applied their brand of philosophical antirealism to legal entities and qualities that it is difficult for us post-Realist generations even to understand what a metaphysical realist about law could believe.[4]

[1] Quoted in William Lycan, *Judgement and Justification* (Cambridge: Cambridge University Press, 1988), at 195 n. 7.

[2] John R. Searle, 'The Word Turned Upside Down' (Book Review), *New York Review of Books*, 27 Oct. 1983, at 74, 78 n. 3.

[3] See John Kaplan and Robert Weisberg, *Criminal Law: Cases and Materials* (Boston: Little, Brown, 1986), at p. v.

[4] So that terminology does not get in the way, we should be clear at the start that the unfortunately called 'Legal Realists' were not metaphysical realists about law and legal entities. Far from it. As Jerome Frank himself admitted, it was a blunder on his part to employ the label 'Legal Realism' 'because, among other things, "realism" in philosophic discourse has an accepted meaning wholly unrelated to the views of the so-called "legal realists"' (Jerome Frank, *Law and the Modern Mind*, ix (6th printing, Garden City, NY: Doubleday, 1963)

My aim in this article is not to undo the effects of philosophical antirealism in law or in any other discipline. Although I do think that the influence of such philosophical antirealism has usually been unfortunate, my topic is more preliminary: I aim only to rescue the debate itself from the criticisms of those who proclaim it either meaningless or irrelevant to any practical concern. More specifically, my target is 'interpretivism', my label for a view that denies either sense or practical significance to any metaphysics (be it realist, idealist, or sceptical) because of some supposed need for 'interpretation'.[5] These 'interpretivists', inspired by hermeneutic approaches to the human sciences and pragmatism in philosophy, have not sought to defend any metaphysical position. Rather, interpretivists think they can avoid taking any position in the metaphysical debate between realism, on the one hand, and idealism and scepticism, on the other, by their supposed discovery that knowledge is 'interpretive'.

My aim is to show that metaphysics has been prematurely interred. The metaphysical debate over realism is both meaningful and relevant to practical concerns, in law as elsewhere. I seek to defend these conclusions in the following way. In the first section of this article, I reconstruct the meta-

(originally published 1930)). As I discuss below, most Legal Realists were metaphysical antirealists (of the sceptical kind) about law and legal entities. See text accompanying nn. 37–42 below. I have adopted the following convention to keep our terminology clear: 'Legal Realism' refers to the metaphysically sceptical views of legal theorists like Jerome Frank, Karl Llewellyn, Max Radin, etc.; 'legal realism' refers to the metaphysically realist views about law and legal entities that others and I have recently defended. For a sketch of Legal Realism, see text accompanying nn. 37–42 below; for a sketch of legal realism, see text accompanying nn. 30–4 below.

[5] 'Interpretation' and therefore 'interpretivism' are much interpreted words, so we also need some terminological preliminaries for them. We need first to put aside the following familiar usages of 'interpretation': (1) as the code word for restraint in the exercise of judicial review in American constitutional theory, see Michael S. Moore, 'A Natural Law Theory of Interpretation', *Southern California Law Review*, 58 (1985), 277–398, at 279 n. 1 (discussing the 'interpretive' versus 'non-interpretive' debate in constitutional law); (2) as a synonym for one particular kind of judicial restraint in constitutional law, searching for framers' intent, see e.g. Walter Benn-Michaels, 'Response to Perry and Simon', *Southern California Law Review*, 58 (1985), 673–81; (3) as referring to the activity that judges must do only in hard cases, where it is commonly said that 'interpretation' (i.e. giving a legal word some general meaning) must precede 'application' (i.e. determining whether the word covers some case's particulars), see e.g. n. 313 below (Justice Brandeis's usage); Annette Barnes, *On Interpretation* (Oxford: Basil Blackwell, 1988), 7–41 (ordinary language analysis of 'interpretation' limiting the word to discovery of non-obvious meanings); (4) as the name for the activity of applying a general legal predicate to the factual particulars of cases, see Moore, 'A Natural Law Theory of Interpretation', above, at 283 (my own usage in that article).

All such distinctively legal usages are not nearly broad enough for present purposes. 'Interpretivism', as I shall employ the word, names a general philosophical position proclaiming the senselessness and/or irrelevance of metaphysics to the practice of some discipline, because that discipline's proper method has supposedly been discovered to be interpretation. 'Interpretation', in turn, shall name the activity one does to find the meaning of some text or text-analogue. One should not define the genus, 'interpretation' much more precisely than this because the body of this article deals with three kinds of interpretivism, each of which operates with its own species of interpretation.

physical debate that interpretivism seeks to avoid and show the connections between metaphysical positions (realism, idealism, and scepticism), on the one hand, and legal theory and practice, on the other. The remaining sections engage the interpretivists on their own terrain. I distinguish and address three variants of interpretivism: (1) 'pragmatic' interpretivism, associated with Richard Rorty and Stanley Fish; (2) 'dualist' interpretivism, found both in Continental philosophy and in the 'ordinary language' strand of Anglo-American philosophy; and (3) 'modest' interpretivism, as exemplified in legal theory by Ronald Dworkin.

No version of interpretivism, I conclude, can make good its claim to have escaped from metaphysics. The interpretive turn has only obscured the metaphysical presuppositions of our thought, in law as elsewhere. The result is not a successful escape from doing metaphysics, as interpretivists believe; it is rather only metaphysics done unselfconsciously and badly.

I. THE METAPHYSICAL DEBATE ABOUT REALISM AND ITS IMPACT ON LEGAL THEORY

A. What Is Metaphysics?

Before we get to the metaphysical debate between realists and antirealists, we need to be clear about what metaphysics itself is.[6] In a narrow sense of

[6] I also explore the view of metaphysics developed in this chapter in Ch. 8 and in Michael S. Moore, 'Moral Reality Revisited', *Michigan Law Review*, 90 (1992), 2424–533 [hereinafter, Moore, 'Moral Realism']. My view of what metaphysics is is not uncontroversial. More traditional conceptions of metaphysics: (1) make it a foundational study that must be undertaken first to enable understanding of more particular matters; (2) make it a universal study that applies to *being* as such and not to the existence of particular classes of entities; (3) make it an incorrigible study through which certainty can be found; or (4) make it a distinct study that is not continuous with science. For these traditional views of metaphysics, see Roger Hancock, 'History of Metaphysics', in P. Edwards (ed.), *The Encyclopedia of Philosophy*, v (New York: Macmillan, 1967), 289; W. H. Walsh, 'Nature of Metaphysics', in ibid. at 300; see also Archie Bahm, *Metaphysics: An Introduction* (New York: Barnes and Noble, 1974), 3–7; David Hamlyn, *Metaphysics* (Cambridge: Cambridge University Press, 1984), 1–10; Richard Taylor, *Metaphysics* (Englewood Cliffs, NJ: Prentice-Hall, 2nd edn., 1974), 1–9.

My own view of metaphysics shares none of these features. I take it principally to be the study of ontology, of what exists (and secondarily a study of the corollaries of ontological commitment, namely, what must also be said about truth, logic, meaning, and reference). Such a study makes no claims that we must settle existential questions first, that there is anything useful to be discovered about 'being qua being', that existential claims can or must be known with certainty, or that metaphysics studies the existence of some class of entities in any way distinct from the way the relevant science studies the existence of those entities. For this more contemporary view of metaphysics, see Simon Blackburn, *Spreading the Word* (Oxford: Oxford University Press, 1984), 3–8, 145–80; Michael Devitt, *Realism and Truth* (Cambridge: Cambridge University Press, 1984), 35; Michael Devitt and Kim Sterelny, *Language and Reality* (Cambridge, Mass.: MIT Press, 1987); Michael Dummett, *Truth and Other* the phrase, a metaphysical theory is: (1) an ontology, that is a theory of what there is. When someone says that there are tables, chairs, electrons, intentions, legal rights, and moral qualities, she betrays a part of her ontological commitments. Were she to say that such things would exist even if neither she nor any other mind recognized them, then she would have revealed more of her ontological theory, namely, whether existence for her is mind independent or not.[7] I use the word 'metaphysics' in a broader sense, to include not just ontology but also (2) a theory of truth, (3) a theory of logic, (4) a theory about the meaning of sentences, and (5) a theory about the meaning of the words used in sentences.

A theory of truth attempts to say something about what the predicate 'is true' means. Does it mean 'correspondence with the world', or does it mean 'coherence with other things that some individual or some community antecedently accepts'? A theory of truth is thus distinct from ontology: the latter discusses only what there is; but the former examines the relation between what there is and the sentences we use to describe what there is; a relation named by the predicate 'is true'.[8]

A theory of logic, among other things, takes a position on whether the principles of bivalence and stability are true. According to the bivalence principle, for all propositions p, p is either true or false. According to the stability principle, for all propositions p, if p is not false, then it is true.[9] Classical logic adheres to both of these principles. Various schemes of non-classical logic do not. Thus, and most important for my purposes, classical logic, unlike non-classical logic, requires commitment to a 'right answer' thesis. That is, for any area of discourse to which we apply classical logic,

Enigmas (Cambridge, Mass.: Harvard University Press, 1978), pp. ix–li, 1–24, 145–65, 215–47; Rom Harre, *Varieties of Realism* (New York: Blackwell, 1986); Mark Platts, *Ways of Meaning* (London: Routledge and Kegan Paul, 1979), and 'Introduction', in M. Platts (ed.), *Reference, Truth and Reality* (Boston: Routledge and Kegan Paul, 1980), 1–18; Hilary Putnam, *The Many Faces of Realism* (Cambridge: Cambridge University Press, 1987), *Mind, Language, and Reality* (Cambridge: Cambridge University Press, 1975), *Meaning and the Moral Sciences* (Cambridge: Cambridge University Press, 1978), 123–40, *Realism and Reason* (Cambridge: Cambridge University Press, 1983), and *Reason, Truth, and History* (Cambridge: Cambridge University Press, 1981); Crispin Wright, *Realism, Meaning and Truth* (New York: Blackwell, 1987). Not all of these theorists agree on which of the metaphysical theories of ontology, truth, logic, meaning, or reference has priority, although each sees the theories as interrelated.

[7] For subtleties connected with the idea that mental states, legal rights, and moral qualities could be mind independent, see Moore, 'Moral Realism', above n. 6, at 16–19; cf. Geoffrey Sayre-McCord, 'The Many Moral Realisms', *Southern Journal of Philosophy*, 24 (Supp. 1986), 1–22 (questioning how mental states, moral qualities, or legal rights could be mind and convention independent); Elliott Sober, 'Realism and Independence', *Nous*, 16 (1982), 369–85.

[8] For discussions of differing theories of truth, see Blackburn, above n. 6, at 224–60; Devitt, above n. 6, at 25–33; Dummett, above n. 6, at 1–24; Platts, *Ways of Meaning*, above n. 6, at 9–42. Although some, like Michael Dummett, would make the theory of truth central to metaphysics, I prefer Michael Devitt's separation of a theory of truth from a theory of ontology and emphasis on the latter as central to metaphysics. See Devitt, *Realism and Truth*, above n. 6, at 34–46.

[9] I am here adopting Dummett's terminology. See Dummett, *Truth*, above n. 6, at p. xix.

there is in principle a 'right answer' to every meaningful question because every meaningful sentence is either true or false and not both.

Metaphysics in the broader sense I intend also includes a semantic theory about the meaning of sentences.[10] Such a theory takes a position on the meaning of 'meaning'. One such position, for example, is the truth-conditional theory of meaning, according to which any sentence's meaning is the set of conditions under which that sentence is (or would be) true. Other theories more leniently allow any conditions relevant to verifying (or falsifying) the sentence to be part of its meaning. Still more lenient theories consider all conditions of acceptable or appropriate utterance of a sentence to count as part of its meaning.[11]

Finally, a complete metaphysics must also take some position on the meaning of those sentence components we call words and phrases.[12] One might think, for example, that a general predicate like 'is a tiger' is applied to things in the world (mostly tigers, presumably) by a kind of checklist procedure: First, one examines the usage of native speakers to extract the criteria for the correct use of 'tiger', such as 'striped, carnivorous, Asian, cat'; and then one applies the checklist to objects in the world to see if they can be called 'tigers'. An alternative theory of word meaning, often called the 'causal' theory, holds that the existence of 'natural kinds', or sets of objects in the world that share certain essential properties, causes us to refer to those objects by a common name. While the 'checklist' theory begins with a fact about our linguistic practice—that speakers in a linguistic community happen to associate the word 'tiger' with certain properties that tigers are stereotypically thought to possess—the causal theory begins with a fact about the world: there are natural kinds, such as tigers, whose essential nature causes us to refer to them by a common name. The checklist theory takes linguistic usage to fix the meaning of a word, while the causal theory does not; rather, it takes the meaning of a word to be fixed by the nature of the thing referred to. Such nature is not a fact of usage but a fact about objects in the world.[13]

[10] As Dummett says, 'the theory of meaning underlies metaphysics' (ibid., at p. xl). Dummett actually overemphasizes the theory of meaning's centrality to metaphysics, virtually defining metaphysical positions by their adherence to truth-conditional versus verification-conditional theories of meaning. See ibid., at pp. xxi–xxii. It is preferable, however, to define metaphysical positions by their theories of ontology, recognizing that such theories will have implications for their theories of meaning. For this latter approach, see Devitt, *Realism and Truth*, above n. 6.

[11] On each of these theories of meaning, see Dummett, *Truth*, above n. 6, at pp. xxi–xxii; Platts, *Ways of Meaning*, above n. 6, at 53–67.

[12] This is because the meaning of sentences must be in some important sense a function of the meaning of the words that make them up. See Devitt and Sterelny, *Language and Reality*, above n. 6, at 17–19.

[13] For the causal theory and its contrast to definitional theories of meaning, see Putnam, *Mind, Language and Reality*, above n. 6, at 139–52, 196–271. For summary and citation of the large secondary literature on this topic, see Moore, 'A Natural Law Theory', above n. 5, at

Other philosophical theories are often confused with the metaphysics just defined. These theories can be called, in a broad sense, 'epistemology'. Epistemology is not concerned with what there is, but rather with how we know what there is.[14]

Pride of place among epistemological theories belongs to the theory of justification, sometimes called the theory of rationality, or epistemology proper.[15] Such a theory takes a position on what, in general, justifies us in believing a proposition to be true. Is it, for example, that the proposition in question coheres better than does its negation with other propositions[16] we antecedently accept as true? Or is it that the proposition follows deductively from some self-evidently true proposition? Or perhaps it follows 'inductively' from some veridical sensory reports. All of these are theories of justification, for they purport to tell us when we are justified in believing some proposition to be true. (Again, they do not tell us what it means for some proposition to be true; that question belongs to the domain of metaphysical theories.)

Such theories of justification are often confused with metaphysical theories, particularly with the theory of truth. Often, for example, it is said that if one accepts a coherence (or non-foundationalist[17]) theory of justifi-

291–301; Michael S. Moore, the 'Semantics of Judging', *Southern California Law Review*, 54 (1981), 151–295, at 167–80.

[14] No matter what one's metaphysics, one needs to distinguish between epistemology and the metaphysics mentioned in the text. This is because every epistemologist wishes at some point to connect his theory of when it is rational to believe some proposition p with the world given that p is true. To make such connections requires that we distinguish, at least initially, our theory of justified belief (epistemology) from our theories of truth and ontology (metaphysics). See e.g. Richard Foley, *The Theory of Epistemic Rationality* (Cambridge, Mass.: Harvard University Press, 1987), 155–73 (distinguishing truth from epistemic rationality in order to assert the contingent connection between the two); Lycan, *Judgement and Justification*, above n. 1 (coherentist epistemology linked to realist metaphysics); David Papineau, *Reality and Representation* (New York: Blackwell, 1987), pp. x, 1–3 (distinguishing thought from reality with epistemology as the theory showing the relationship between the two); Nicholas Rescher, *Methodological Pragmatism* (New York: New York University Press, 1977), 81–98 (coherentist epistemology linked to idealist metaphysics); Peter Unger, *Ignorance* (Oxford: Oxford University Press, 1975), 272–3 (separating truth from rational belief in order to deny that truth exists).

[15] See e.g. Keith Lehrer, *Knowledge* (Oxford: Clarendon Press, 1974) (articulating and defending a theory of knowledge and justification).

[16] I use 'proposition' throughout interchangeably with 'sentence', intending no distinctions between them. Although propositions are often distinguished from the sentences that express them, we need not enter that debate here.

[17] As I explore in my discussion of Rorty, see text accompanying nn. 94–103 below, a non-foundationalist epistemology gives up the old Cartesian dream of finding some secure foundation on which knowledge can be built. Instead, a rational agent is justified in believing some proposition p only because p coheres better with everything else the agent believes than does not-p. Since this is true for each of an agent's beliefs, there are literally no 'foundations' (beliefs whose truth can be taken as given) from which justification proceeds. Rather, each belief supports every other belief. For the classic expositions on this view of justification, see Gilbert Harman, *Thought* (Princeton: Princeton University Press, 1972); W. V. O. Quine, *Word and Object* (Cambridge, Mass.: MIT Press, 1960); M. White, *Towards Reunion in Philosophy* (Cambridge, Mass.: Harvard University Press, 1956).

cation one must also accept a coherence theory of truth. Yet that isn't true at all. Some persons, myself included, argue that it makes perfectly good sense to say both: (1) that to be justified in believing some proposition p to be true is to find p more coherent with the totality of one's other beliefs than not-p, and (2) that what 'p is true' means is not coherence with one's other beliefs. Such a position of course has to be argued for, but so does its opposite. Keeping the theory of justification provisionally distinct from the theory of truth allows one to consider the position on its merits instead of discarding it without argument.

A second epistemological theory is the theory of discovery.[18] Such a theory does not tell us when we are justified in believing some proposition to be true; rather, it tells us how to attain such a state of knowledge when we start in ignorance. A theory of discovery is quite literally a theory about how we are to discover those states we call knowledge, that is, justified true beliefs.[19] Such a theory, like the theory of justification, is quite distinct from any theory of what 'true' means, what sentences or words mean, and the like. Such a theory only tells you how to get from A to B, once you have decided where B is.

A third theory sometimes regarded as 'epistemological' in a broad sense is a theory of understanding. Such a theory addresses the question of what it is to understand a sentence. Is to understand a sentence s only to possess a belief that s is true or false? Or does understanding require that one have justification for believing that s is true or false? Or does understanding s require some more involvement with the states of affairs in the world to which the terms in s refer, some emotional investment, significant experience, or empathetic identification?[20]

The theory of understanding, like the theories of justification and discovery, is not metaphysical. Asking what there is is a different question from asking what state one has to be in to understand what there is. To be sure, metaphysicians such as Michael Dummett argue that the truth conditions of some sentence s must be identified with the conditions under which the human mind can grasp or understand s.[21] But Dummett and his opponents can debate this controversial point only if they first distinguish, at least provisionally, between truth and understanding.

[18] For classic separations of the theory of discovery from the theory of justification in science, see Hans Reichenbach, *Experience and Prediction* (Chicago: University of Chicago Press, 1938), 4–5; Israel Scheffler, *Science and Subjectivity* (Indianapolis: Bobbs-Merrill, 1967), 68–73.

[19] I ignore the Gettier problems for this traditional account of knowledge. See Edmund Gettier, 'Is Justified True Belief Knowledge?', *Analysis*, 23 (1963), 121–7.

[20] See e.g. Georg von Wright, *Explanation and Understanding* (Ithaca, NY: Cornell University Press, 1971).

[21] Dummett assumes that the metaphysical puzzle of realism/antirealism is the same as whether we can understand evidence-transcendent truth conditions. Dummett, *Truth*, above n. 6, at 153–65, 358–9. But see Devitt, *Realism and Truth*, above n. 6, at 204–20 (arguing that the metaphysical puzzle is distinct from the psychological question of what we can grasp).

B. The Realist/Antirealist Debate

A metaphysical realist about some class of entities—say, real numbers in mathematics—is a person who holds certain particular versions of each of the metaphysical theories mentioned above. First, his ontology maintains both: (1) that the entities in question exist, and (2) that their existence is independent of any individual's mind or any community's conventions.[22] Put simply, there are numbers; and their existence does not depend on us. Second, a realist will hold a correspondence theory of truth, according to which the meaning of 'is true' is given by the correspondence of some sentence s to some mind and convention-independent state of affairs.[23] For example, 'is true' in the sentence, '4 is greater than 2 is true', means that there is a state of affairs such that: there is a number 4; there is a number 2; there is a relation, 'greater than'; the number 4 stands in the relation of 'greater than' to the number 2; and the sentence, '4 is greater than 2', corresponds to that state of affairs.

All realists will adhere to this realist ontology and correspondence theory of truth. A full-blooded realist will also adhere to the classical theory of logic, according to which bivalence and stability hold. I say 'full-blooded' realist because there are paler, less robust cousins who properly call themselves realists but who think that reality comes with gaps. John Finnis, for example, is a realist about moral entities and qualities yet believes that we can 'run out' of moral reality.[24] Finnis accordingly rejects the principles of bivalence and stability for moral assertions, for to 'run out' of moral reality is to admit that there are sentences about morality that are neither true nor false.

The metaphysical realist I shall discuss, however, is the full-blooded kind, the one who adheres to the classical theory of logic in those domains for which she is a realist. Such a full-blooded realist, furthermore, will hold a truth-conditional theory of the meaning of sentences. Because the realist sees sentences as corresponding to states of affairs in the world, her semantics will ignore all forms of deviant utterance that do not have to do with inaccurate representation of how things are.[25] For example, the utter-

[22] See Devitt, *Realism and Truth*, above n. 6, at 11–21.

[23] On the role of correspondence–truth in characterizing realism, see Putnam, *Meaning and the Moral Sciences*, above n. 6, at 1–38. To my mind, Putnam, like Dummett, overemphasizes truth at the expense of ontology in his characterization of realism. Cf. Devitt, *Realism and Truth*, above n. 6, at 34–46 (separation of truth from ontology in characterizing realism).

[24] John Finnis, *Natural Law and Natural Rights* (Oxford: Oxford University Press, 1980), 284–6. Dummett would not classify Finnis as a realist about moral qualities because Dummett includes adherence to classical logic (bivalence) in his definition of realism. Dummett, above n. 6. Yet many are properly sceptical that adherence to classical logic can displace ontology as realism's hallmark. See e.g. Wright, *Realism, Meaning and Truth*, above n. 6, at 8–9.

[25] On the gap between semantics and pragmatics created by a truth-conditional theory of meaning, see Platts, *Ways of Meaning*, above n. 6, at 68–94.

ance, 'I am in pain', is usually appropriate only when the speaker is aware that he is in pain; yet such a condition (of awareness) is not part of the truth conditions of the sentence (for there are unfelt pains) so that the meaning of the sentence does not include the condition of its appropriate utterance. Finally, the full-blooded realist subscribes to a causal theory of meaning for words like 'tiger', 'polio', or 'water'. The realist reverses the checklist theory of meaning by saying that the existence of natural kinds causes us to ascribe to them a common name and that the meaning of such words is given by the nature of the kind. The realist does not think that a term's meaning is given by the checklist of properties conventionally associated with the term in some linguistic community, nor does she think that to investigate whether a certain kind exists is a matter of seeing whether anything in the world answers to that checklist of properties. Rather, she begins with the natural kind as it is found in the world, arguing that the term's meaning comes from the natural kind's essential nature as it exists in the world. For realism, then, a theory of meaning investigates not a term's conventional uses in linguistic practice but the nature of the objects the term denotes.[26]

Again, less robust forms of realism do not adopt this theory about the meaning of natural-kind terms. In fact, a nominalist does not believe in natural kinds. For the nominalist, only particulars such as this dog or that dog exist; there is no such thing as doghood. Although nominalism and realism are in this sense opposed, in another sense a nominalist may nonetheless be a kind of realist: she may assert that her preferred class of entities—particulars—both exists and is independent of us. Still, she is not the full-blooded realist who opposes not only idealism but also nominalism.[27]

A realist, like anyone else, also needs some position on the epistemological theories mentioned earlier. Yet what is distinctive about realism does not lie in epistemology. Within the theory of justification, for example, the realist may adopt some foundational theory of knowledge, one according to which a belief is justified if and only if it follows deductively from some self-evidently true propositions. Alternatively, the realist can hold some more contemporary non-foundational theory of knowledge, according to which a belief is justified if it forms part of the best total account of all of our beliefs.[28] The one thing in epistemology that a realist must deny is that the conditions under which a rational agent is justified

[26] See text accompanying n. 13 above.

[27] See Dummett, *Truth*, above n. 6, at 147 (recognizing that nominalists can be in some sense realists). My 'full-blooded' realism is more like the scientific realism that Bas von Fraasen opposes in *The Scientific Image* (Oxford: Clarendon Press, 1980).

[28] On foundational versus non-foundational epistemologies, see generally Michael Williams, *Groundless Belief* (Oxford: Oxford University Press, 1977). See also nn. 14–15 above.

in believing some sentence to be true are necessarily the same as the conditions under which the sentence is true. A realist must resist, in other words, the identification of truth with justified belief, for one of realism's distinctive tenets is that a sentence can be true (correspond to how things are) even if we have and can have no rational grounds for believing it to be true.

A realist must likewise resist any identification of her theory of discovery or understanding with her metaphysical theories of truth or ontology. The realist is committed to the possibility that there are truths that are neither discoverable nor even comprehensible to the human mind. Accordingly, the realist must separate the conditions of understanding or discovery from truth conditions, even when the truths she is considering are both discoverable and understandable.

Those who straightforwardly disagree with realists are often called antirealists. Corresponding to the two essential tenets of realist ontology are two kinds of antirealists: (1) those who deny the existence of some class of entities, such as real numbers, and (2) those who grant the existence of such entities but deny their independence from our minds or our conventions. The first kind of antirealist is a sceptic; the second is an idealist.[29] The idealist can be either a subjectivist or a conventionalist. In either case, the idealist asserts that the entities in question exist only as ideas—either as the ideas of each of us (subjectivism), or as those shared ideas we call social conventions (conventionalism).

The form of antirealism most appealing to lawyers is conventionalism. A conventionalist, like any antirealist, denies much of what the realist asserts in each of the five metaphysical theories mentioned earlier. In addition, social convention does the work for the conventionalist that convention-independent reality does for the realist.

Thus, the conventionalist about real numbers, for example, will assert: (1) that they exist, but only as constructions within a system of conventional symbol manipulation called 'mathematics'; (2) that 'is true' in the sentence, '4 is greater than 2 is true', means that mathematical conventions can justify belief in that sentence and warrant its assertion; (3) that logic preserves not the truth of sentences but the warranted (justified) assertability of sentences, and that there can be many sentences about real numbers that are not warrantedly assertable and whose negations are not warrantedly assertable (because we run out of conventions with which to deal with all possible situations); (4) that the meaning of sentences like '4 is greater than 2' is not to be found in the conditions under which the sentence is true, but rather, in the conditions under which the sentence could be rationally believed or

[29] For this taxonomy of realism's opponents, see Wright, *Realism, Meaning and Truth*, above n. 6, at 2, and Moore, 'Moral Realism', above n. 6.

warrantedly asserted; and (5) that the meaning of predicates like 'is greater than' is given by the mathematical conventions that govern that phrase's correct usage, not by any essential nature of the relation itself.

Issue is thus joined between the realist and the conventionalist at all five levels. Notice, however, that the opposed metaphysical positions just sketched need not be held across the board for all entities. One might be a realist about natural science and psychology, for example, but a conventionalist about mathematics, morality, and law. Indeed, a typical world view is realistic about the common sense world of tables, chairs, and tigers, realistic about theoretical entities in science such as electrons, kinetic energy, or gravitational force, realistic about states of mind such as intention, desire, or belief, and yet conventional about moral or legal entities such as rights, duties, or virtues. We now need to sketch how this metaphysical debate plays out specifically within law.

C. Realism Versus Antirealism in Law and Legal Theory

We need a portrait of the metaphysical realist about law—a 'legal realist', if I may reappropriate an old phrase[30]—before we contrast her to the legal conventionalist and other antirealists. A general characterization of the legal realist is that she asserts the realist line on all five of the metaphysical theories over the domain of legal entities. Although such a general definition is accurate, we can better understand the ontological commitments distinctive of legal realism if we approach them in three stages. (These stages are heuristic only, representing what I take to be the best discovery route to understanding legal realism.)

To begin with, the legal realist as I shall define her is both a scientific and moral realist. That is, without regard to the law, she takes the metaphysically realist line on many entities or qualities such as electrons, intentions, justice, or kindness. Such an individual thus believes, first, that things like causal relations, intentions, and moral turpitude exist in a way not dependent on what we or anyone else thinks about them; second, that truth about such entities is a matter of correspondence between sentences and the way things are; third, that there is a right answer to all scientific queries and moral dilemmas; fourth, that the meaning of sentences about such entities is just the conditions under which such sentences are true; and fifth, that the meaning of words like 'causation', 'intention', and 'culpability' is given by the nature of the things to which such words refer and not merely by conventional English usage.

The first stage of legal realism is reached by simply applying such scientific and moral realism to the propositions, words, and entities in the

[30] See n. 4 above.

laws the legal realist happens to find in her legal system. Consider how this first-level realist might analyse certain examples from the American legal system. (1) Some legal rules refer to what the realist calls 'natural kinds'. Tort liability or criminal sanctions, for instance, usually presuppose that a defendant's acts caused a person's injury. Similarly, particular rules might prohibit the importation of python skins, regulate the rate that may be charged for certain amounts of electricity, or allow organs to be transplanted only when the donor is dead at the time of removal. (2) Other laws refer to those particular natural kinds we categorize as mental kinds. Contractual, tort, or criminal liability, for example, often turns on what some defendant intended; various particular rules allow a tort plaintiff to recover for pain and suffering, hold a defendant responsible for what he knew or believed, and require that a defendant will a movement of his body before that movement can be considered his action. (3) Still other laws refer to what I have called 'moral kinds'. Such laws, for example require a petitioner for citizenship to have good moral character before she may be granted citizenship, allow deportation of any aliens convicted of crimes involving moral turpitude, grant custody of children to that parent in a divorce proceeding who will maximize the best interest of the child, imply into all contracts a promise of good faith and fair dealing by each party, and guarantee due process, equal protection of the laws, and freedom from unreasonable searches and seizures to each citizen.

Our embryonic (i.e. first-stage) legal realist will rely on her scientific and moral realism when applying these terms to particular cases. These metaphysical views will thus lead her to practise law in quite a distinctive way. When statutes use such terms, she will understand judges to be directed to apply them in light of the best theories they can muster about the nature of the things to which the terms refer. This generates two very distinctive features for the legal realist's theory of statutory interpretation. First, even when there are legal, linguistic, or moral conventions that purport to define such terms, and even when such conventions clearly seem to cover some case, judges are not to base their interpretations on them. In the realist view, such conventions are but provisional theories or heuristics about the nature of the things referred to, to be put aside whenever a better theory about the true nature of the things demands that they do so. Second, the meaning of statutory terms will not run out—such statutes will not have a 'penumbra' of uncertain application—even though legal, linguistic, and moral conventions will have no clear application to many cases. Although conventions run out—novel cases may present situations quite unlike those covered by conventional definitions—reality does not run out. And it is reality, not convention, that fixes the meaning of terms like 'intend', 'cause', or 'culpability'.

Realism has similar implications for constitutional interpretation. A moral realist will take his predecessors in American history—Madison, Hamilton, and the other Lockean framers—to have been realists and to have written the Bill of Rights intending to refer to the moral rights persons possess. Indeed, the framers were so confident that such rights existed independent of positive law or convention that they hesitated to write them down at all and, once having referred to certain enumerated rights, went on to allow for additional, unenumerated rights. One who shares the framers' moral realism will not interpret the Bill of Rights according to 'framers' intent', 'original understanding', or the 'evolving standards of decency that mark the progress of a maturing society'.[31] Rather, she will develop a theory about what punishments are cruel, when speech is truly free, and what other rights persons possess, and interpret the Constitution in light of that theory. Moral realism tells her that conventional exemplars or definitions of free speech, for example—whether those exemplars be traced to the framers, their original audience, or current consensus—may miss slightly or entirely the true nature of that liberty.

The moral and scientific realism of the embryonic legal realist will also directly influence her understanding of common law precedent. Her theory of precedent will reject all conventions in that theory's central task of extracting general rules from prior case decisions. Rather, her theory of precedent will decide whether one case is like another (and thus, because of equality, deserving of like treatment) by generalizing over all morally relevant features, features as to which moral, linguistic, or legal conventions are provisional but often inaccurate guides.

Thus, even at this first stage, our proto-realist already practises law in a distinctive way. Yet, she is not yet a full-fledged legal realist because her metaphysical theories have not yet produced any distinctively legal commitments. Hypothesize, therefore, a second level of sophistication for a legal realist. The realist discovers here that the legal system may generate its own concepts and terms, which do not appear to refer to any natural or moral kinds.

An example may be 'malice' in American homicide law. This law provides that if a killing is performed with malice, then it is murder; if without malice, then it is manslaughter, some lesser crime, or no crime at all. So used, 'malice' is usually thought to be a term of art. It does not name any single mental state, such as ill will or bad motive, and thus does not name a natural kind. Nor is such a term commonly thought to name a moral kind, unnoticed until the common law lawyers stumbled across it

[31] The latter is Earl Warren's famous phrase for contemporary conventions in *Trop v. Dulles*, 356 U.S. 86, 101 (1958).

years ago.[32] Interpretation of such a term thus differs from interpretation of words such as 'cause', 'intention', or 'culpability', where the kinds in question exist independently of the law. A legal realist thus cannot straightforwardly use her scientific and moral realism to unpack the meaning of such terms.

Many have sought, therefore, to interpret these peculiarly legal terms as mere abbreviations for the names of diverse natural or moral kinds. 'Malice', for example, is often analysed as having four disjuncts: intentional and unprovoked killing, intentional and unprovoked infliction of grievous bodily harm resulting in death, killing in the course of a felony, and reckless killing where the recklessness expresses extreme indifference to the value of human life. An abbreviationist about 'malice' will think that these four disjuncts give a criterial definition of 'malice': any killing that is one of these four kinds must be malicious, and any killing that is not one of these four kinds cannot be malicious. There is, in short, nothing about the nature of malice—the thing—that can guide interpretation because this conventional definition exhausts its meaning.

My second-level realist will not accept this abbreviationist account of theoretical terms in law. She will see that such terms are not mere abbreviations for the names of diverse natural kinds, for such terms are not invented simply to serve the function of abbreviated reference. Returning to the 'malice' example, common law judges invented the term to name the difference between killings deserving the most serious punishment (murder) and killings deserving significantly less punishment (manslaughter). By attaching sharply different legal consequences to two kinds of culpable killings, such judges (and later, legislatures) created the need for some state that marks the difference. The four-part definition just described above was built up as a theory of the nature of that state. Such a theory is not a criterial definition of 'malice', for like any theory, it is not 'true by convention'. Rather, if it is true, it is true because it corresponds to the true nature of malice.

This seems to commit the legal realist to the existence of 'legal kinds', for malice (in the legal sense) is not a natural or a moral kind. It is a state needed within a legal system that creates two very different punishments for culpable killings. Malice thus arises from and depends upon the structure of sanctions within a legal code.

[32] In an earlier discussion of 'malice', as used in Anglo-American homicide law, I treat the term as the name of a moral kind. See Moore, 'A Natural Law Theory', above n. 5, at 332–8. Whether 'malice' names a natural clumping of culpability with respect to causing the death of another (i.e. it is a moral kind existing independently of the law), or it names an artificial clumping of culpability necessitated only by our legal system's distinctive sanctions for two kinds of homicide (i.e. it is a functional kind), need not be decided here. We may assume it is the latter in order to illustrate the nature of the functional kinds created by law. (I owe this reminder of my previous treatment of 'malice' to Heidi Hurd, who tells me that I was at least once right about the nature of malice.)

My second-level legal realist is thus committed to something named 'malice' that is neither a natural nor a moral kind. Rather than calling this a 'legal kind', however, I prefer the label 'functional kind'. The legal realist view of 'malice' is no different from the general realist understanding of terms like 'lawyer', 'knife', 'vehicle', or 'paper-weight': all these terms refer to kinds of things whose essence is not given by their structure but by their function.[33]

Consider, for example, the word 'stomach'. Suppose we came across a person, otherwise healthy, who has an item in her abdominal cavity that performs the task of first-stage food processing in the way ordinary stomachs do for the rest of us. This item, however, is cubical in shape and made of silicon, not roundish and made of carbon-based soft tissues. Does she have a stomach? If 'stomach' is a functional word, as I believe it is, then such an individual has a stomach because she has a subsystem that performs the function constitutive of stomachs—even though her stomach differs widely from ours in its physical structure.

To find the essence (i.e. function) of a functional kind like stomach, one must know the end towards which the item in question contributes. For stomachs, that end is the physical health of the human body. When we have determined such an end, we then need to gather some information about causal connections, namely, about what sorts of processes contribute to the maximal attainment of that end. Since health is partly characterized by survival, and since digesting food is causally necessary for the human body's survival, we discover that, of all the things that stomachs do—they make sounds, occupy space, use up blood, etc.—one thing and one thing alone is their function, namely, digesting food. Anything that performs that function in the human body will be a stomach, for it performs the essential function of stomachs.

Finding the essence of a functional kind, then, requires us to apply two kinds of knowledge: first, our knowledge about the end served by the kind, and second, our knowledge about the causal relations that exist so that that end is in fact served by the item performing its function. If one is a realist about values and about causal relations, one should also be a realist about functional kinds, for belief in their existence is no more than an application of one's moral and scientific realism.

Malice is a functional kind whose essence is discovered in a manner analogous to that of a stomach's. In the case of a legal kind like malice, we need not engage in a factual inquiry about the various consequences of a killing being malicious in order to know where to start in seeking malice's function. This contrasts with items like stomachs, where we must engage

[33] For a (decidedly non-metaphysical) introduction to functional words, see R. M. Hare, *The Language of Morals* (Oxford: Oxford University Press, 1952), 100; A. W. Cragg, 'Functional Words, Facts, and Values', *Canadian Journal of Philosophy*, 6 (1976), 77–94, at 85.

in such inquiry (into the consequences of stomachs' activities) before we can honour one such consequence as its function. The law artificially fixes the distinctive consequence of a killing being malicious for us when it fixes the punishment for malicious killing at a certain level.

The nature of all artificial legal terms is fixed by the legal consequences attached to them. Thus, the nature of malice is: whatever makes one properly liable for the punishment fixed for murder. We know more about this nature when we know more about the end the punishment itself is supposed to bring about. If retribution is the correct theory of punishment, then the end served by a malicious killer suffering a murderer's punishment is retributive justice (namely, the morally culpable receiving their just deserts). Knowing this to be the ultimate end served here, we also know more about the nature of malice: it is constituted by whatever attributes of mind or person makes one deserve the punishment fixed for murder.

Not only will our second-level legal realist think that there are right answers to what legal terms of art like 'malice' mean, answers given by the nature of malice and not by conventional definitions or exemplars, she will also think that where there are no legal terms of art there will still be right answers. For example, there is no legal word that names the state that distinguishes the first-degree murderer who deserves the death penalty from the first-degree murderer who deserves life imprisonment without possibility of parole. Yet a legal realist at this second level will think that this nameless state exists and that the judge's decision as to whether or not a first-degree murderer is in this state determines the correct sentence.

A third-level legal realist will not confine her realism to questions about her own or any other single legal system. She will move from 'particular jurisprudence' to 'general jurisprudence' and apply her realism to law as such, not merely to the laws of any particular legal system. My third-level legal realist will say that 'law' itself names a functional kind and that general jurisprudence, rightly conceived, should study the nature of that kind.

Such a view demands that the legal realist specify the ends of law. What are the distinctive goals that law and a legal system serve? A familiar answer would be in terms of the rule-of-law virtues: law serves the goals of liberty (because of the predictability made possible by a legal system), equality (because like cases get treated alike in a legal system), substantive fairness (because the legitimate expectations of citizens are protected from disruption), procedural fairness (all get a chance to participate in adjudication), utility (legal systems' deference to the past does not leave decisionmakers always reinventing the wheel), and so forth.

What sort of thing will maximally satisfy the rightly ordered set of some such values? Law, a thing that has just such a functional essence. And about the structure of that functionally defined thing we can say a great deal, knowing what we do of human nature. General jurisprudence, so conceived, is the attempt to specify the details of that structure in light of one's best theory of law's functional essence.

I have gone into the legal realists' beliefs in such detail because they are so rarely encountered in contemporary jurisprudence. Indeed, forms of metaphysical conventionalism (Legal Positivism) and of metaphysical scepticism (Legal Realism) have so dominated the jurisprudential landscape in this century that it is easy to forget the realist metaphysical tradition to which they were reactions. To further revive the debate, let me briefly paint the more familiar, opposing views of the conventionalist and the sceptic.

A metaphysical conventionalist about law will usually also be a conventionalist about morality and a somewhat inconsistent conventionalist about some of the entities of common sense and theoretical science. This combined conventionalism will lead her to say, at the first level, that there is no convention-independent nature to things like 'good moral character', 'due process', or 'moral turpitude'. These are just nominal kinds whose 'nature' is fully given by the moral conventions in place in some society. Further, such a conventionalist might say the same about some or all of the entities of science, such as intention, causation, death, or gravitational force. The reference of such terms, she will think, is given only by the public rules of some Wittgensteinian language game (for intention), the Humean habits of mind induced by observation of constantly conjoined events (for causation), the legal conventions in place at the time (for death), or the scientific conventions that allow theoretical terms to abbreviate a complicated range of observable phenomena (for gravitational force).

This combined conventionalism will affect how the legal conventionalist practises law. As with the legal realist, one can more easily understand legal conventionalism by approaching what the conventionalist believes in three stages. At the first stage, the conventionalist simply applies her conventionalism about science and morality to the terms used in the laws of her particular legal system. She will thus interpret statutes and constitutional texts as if there were a 'core' of clear applications of the relevant conventions and a 'penumbra' where the conventions run out.[34] She will practise precedent in the same way that conventionalists about science practise induction: she will look for categories that are 'entrenched' or 'embedded' in the conventions of the discipline and generalize prior case holdings from such categories.[35]

[34] See e.g. H. L. A. Hart, 'Positivism and the Separation of Law and Morals', *Harvard Law Review*, 71 (1958), 593–629, at 606–11.

[35] See e.g. Nelson Goodman, *Fact, Fiction, and Forecast* (3rd edn., Indianapolis: Bobbs-Merrill, 1973), 22–3 (for science); Frederick Schauer, 'Precedent', *Stanford Law Review*, 39 (1987), 571–605 (for law).

At the second stage, the legal conventionalist will deny that there are functional kinds in any sense different than nominal kinds. What is a 'vehicle', for example, will not be given by some essential function, but rather by conventionally accepted exemplars or definitions of 'vehicle'.[36] Similarly, terms of art in law, like 'malice', have their meaning exhausted by legal conventions like the four-part definition given earlier.

At the third stage, the legal conventionalist will practise general jurisprudence quite differently from the legal realist. She will write books about our shared concepts of law or the legal system.[37] Her method will be 'conceptual analysis', in which one extracts a concept of law from both ordinary language analysis of the linguistic conventions governing the use of the word 'law' and from a sociology that describes the conventional legal practices of some or all legal systems. Such conventions will exhaust her subject, leaving no room for reflection about the nature of the thing, law.

We can describe the legal antirealist of the sceptical kind even more briefly, for such a sceptic simply denies what both the legal realist and the legal conventionalist assert. Neither natural, moral, nor functional kinds exist for the sceptic; and the conventions relied upon by the conventionalist to define such kinds are completely indeterminate. Thinking this, the sceptic finds both legal texts (statutes, constitutions) and prior case decisions woefully indeterminate. Her judge 'interprets' legal texts by finding what she wants in them—for neither nature nor convention binds her interpretive efforts, the words of legal texts becoming mere chameleons in her hands.[38] Because past cases exemplify an infinite number of rules, any choice of rules can be consistent with precedent—so long as one denies, as does the sceptic, that there are any natural kinds or conventional categories that would limit the rules he might choose.[39]

Since functional kinds do not exist for a sceptic, and since conventional definitions are woefully indeterminate, terms of legal theory are especially suspect.[40] If the sceptic cannot convince legislatures and judges to cease using words like 'malice', then he will define them 'functionally', i.e. let them stand for their legal consequences.[41] Then, at least, judges will stare at the consequences of using such words in their decisions and decide (as

[36] See e.g. Stephen R. Munzer, 'Realistic Limits on Realist Interpretation', *Southern California Law Review*, 58 (1985), 459–75, at 467.

[37] See e.g. H. L. A. Hart, *The Concept of Law* (Oxford: Oxford University Press, 1961); Joseph Raz, *The Concept of a Legal System* (Oxford: Oxford University Press, 1970).

[38] See the discussion of rule scepticism in Hart, *Concept*, above n. 37, at 121–51.

[39] See Felix Cohen, 'The Ethical Basis of Legal Criticism', *Yale Law Journal*, 41 (1931), 201–20.

[40] See the discussion and citations in Moore, 'Semantics of Judging', above n. 13, at 227–8.

[41] On Legal Realists' functional definitions, see discussion and citations in Moore, 'A Natural Law Theory', above n. 5, at 302–3.

a matter of consequential calculation) whether to say a killing was 'with malice' or not.

General jurisprudence is not a possible enterprise for the sceptic, for it lacks a subject matter. Law (in general) and the legal system (in general) lack a context in which some sense could be made of them. The sceptic therefore recommends doing something else, such as behavioural social science.[42]

The debate between realists and their two kinds of antirealist foes in law, Legal Positivists and Legal Realists, is thus a wide-ranging debate. Beginning with disagreement over the most basic assumptions about science and morality, the debate influences the theory and practice of law and even determines what sort of activity thinking about law can be.

My own positions in this debate are no secret. I have defended realism in science, specifically with respect to the causal relation,[43] natural kinds,[44] intentions,[45] and mental states in general.[46] I have also defended realism about culpability,[47] desert,[48] and moral qualities generally.[49] I have tried to show how such scientific and moral realism generates the legal realist's theories of statutory interpretation,[50] constitutional interpretation,[51] and

[42] On the antiphilosophical and antijurisprudential nature of Legal Realism, see Ch. 6, above.

[43] Michael S. Moore, 'Thomson's Preliminaries About Causation and Rights', *Chicago-Kent Law Review*, 63 (1987), 497–521, reprinted as ch. 7 of M. Moore, *Placing Blame: A General Theory of the Criminal Law* (Oxford: Oxford University Press, 1997); Moore, 'Causation and Responsibility', *Social Philosophy and Policy*, 16 (1999), 1–51.

[44] Moore, 'A Natural Law Theory', above n. 5, at 291–301, 'Semantics of Judging', above n. 13, at 204–7.

[45] Michael S. Moore, 'Intentions and Mens Rea', in R. Gavison (ed.), *Issues in Contemporary Legal Philosophy* (Oxford: Oxford University Press, 1987), reprinted as ch. 11 in *Placing Blame*, above n. 43.

[46] Michael S. Moore, *Law and Psychiatry: Rethinking the Relationship* (Cambridge: Cambridge University Press, 1984), 9–112; Michael S. Moore, 'Mind, Brain, and Unconscious', in P. Clark and C. Wright (eds.), *Mind, Psychoanalysis, and Science* (Oxford: Basil Blackwell, 1988), 141; Michael S. Moore, 'The Moral and Metaphysical Basis of the Criminal Law', in J. Pennock and J. Chapman (eds.), *Criminal Justice: Nomos XXVII* (New York: New York University Press, 1985), 11.

[47] Moore, *Law and Psychiatry*, above n. 46, at 44–90.

[48] Michael S. Moore, 'The Moral Worth of Retribution', in F. Schoeman (ed.), *Responsibility, Character, and the Emotions*, (Cambridge: Cambridge University Press, 1987), reprinted as ch. 4 of *Placing Blame*, above n. 43.

[49] Moore, 'Moral Realism', above n. 6; Michael S. Moore, 'Moral Reality', *Wisconsin Law Review* [1982], 1061–156.

[50] Moore, 'A Natural Law Theory', above n. 5, 'Semantics of Judging', above n. 13; text accompanying nn. 30–1 above.

[51] Michael S. Moore, 'The Exportability of the Madisonian Compromise', in F. Cameron (ed.), *The Influence of the U.S. Constitution in Pacific Nations* (Kapalua, Hawaii: Kapalua Pacific Center, 1988); Moore, 'A Natural Law Theory', above n. 5; Michael S. Moore, 'The Written Constitution and Interpretivism', *Harvard. Journal of Law & Public Policy*, 12 (1989), 3–14; Michael S. Moore, 'The Constitution As Hard Law', *Constitutional Commentary*, 6 (1989), 51–67; Michael S. Moore, 'Do We Have an Unwritten Constitution?', *Southern California Law Review*, 63 (1989), 107–39; text accompanying n. 31 above.

precedent.[52] Finally, I have sought to show how functions are assigned to parts of natural and social systems,[53] how functional kinds can be derived from them,[54] how terms like 'malice' have a functional essence,[55] and how law itself is a functional kind.[56] My task in what follows is not to defend again these realist conclusions on the merits. Rather, it is to preserve the meaningfulness of the debate with either sceptical or conventional anti-realists, for the significance of the debate itself has been challenged by that loose assemblage of philosophers, social scientists, and lawyers who think of themselves as 'interpretivists'.

D. The Interpretivist Rejection of Realist (or Any Other) Metaphysics

It has become fashionable in contemporary philosophy and legal theory to say that the realism/antirealism debate can and should be avoided. Sometimes the point is put as a modest normative recommendation: we ought to stop talking at such an abstract level because we can do more good with more practical and concrete issues. More often, however, critics buttress this normative recommendation with a necessity claim: the realism/antirealism debate cannot be solved because the debate itself is misconceived. Realism and antirealism, the argument goes, are both extremes that one should avoid because each seeks a kind of unattainable metaphysical knowledge.

This kind of end run is a plausible enough strategy in the face of a protracted debate. It is always at least refreshing, and sometimes even promising, to attempt to recast the issues of an old debate that by its terms seems insoluble. Kantians, logical positivists, ordinary language philosophers, and pragmatists have attempted this manoeuvre for decades, issuing regular pronouncements on the death of all metaphysics, whether realist or idealist.[57] The most recent fashion for this manoeuvre is 'interpretivism'. An interpretivist is someone who claims not to have a metaphysics or an epistemology because, she thinks, she does not need

[52] Michael S. Moore, 'Precedent, Induction, and Ethical Generalization', in L. Goldstein (ed.), *Precedent in Law* (Oxford: Oxford University Press, 1987), 183; text accompanying nn. 31–2 above.

[53] Moore, *Law and Psychiatry*, above n. 46, at 26–32; Michael S. Moore, 'The Nature of Psychoanalytic Explanation', in L. Laudan (ed.), *Mind and Medicine*, Pittsburgh Series in the History and the Philosophy of Science, v (Berkeley: University of California Press, 1983), 36–40.

[54] Moore, above n. 5, at 301 n. 44.

[55] Ibid. at 332–8.

[56] Michael S. Moore, 'Law as a Functional Kind', in R. George (ed.), *Natural Law Theories* (Oxford: Oxford University Press, 1992), reprinted as Chapter 9 above.

[57] For a brief history, see Hancock, 'History of Metaphysics', above n. 6, at 297–9. The metaphysics-avoidance techniques of logical positivism and ordinary language philosophy are described in Richard Rorty's detailed Introduction, in R. Rorty (ed.), *The Linguistic Turn* (Chicago: University of Chicago Press, 1967), 1–39.

them for the activity in which she wishes to engage, namely, interpretation.[58]

As I suggested earlier, interpretivism comes in three sizes: very ambitious, ambitious, and modest. A very ambitious ('pragmatist') interpretivist thinks that all knowledge is interpretive in character—physics as much as sociology. Such a claim is grounded in a view of knowledge and truth within which their existence depends upon some situated human observer (who thus must 'interpret' to know anything). A merely ambitious ('dualist') interpretivist, in contrast, thinks that knowledge of the humanities and the social sciences is interpretive, even if the natural sciences are not interpretive. This less ambitious claim is grounded in one of two views. Either the phenomena with which the human sciences deal (human behaviour) are themselves possessed of meaning, and thus require interpretation to be understood, or the language used in the human sciences is categorically different from the language used in the natural sciences, making it senseless (a 'category mistake') to attempt to do anything other than that which the categories of the human sciences demand—interpretation.

Finally, a modest interpretivist is modest in the scope she claims for her interpretive methods: interpretation is the method appropriate to certain specific activities, such as understanding a dream, a novel, or a statute; it is not a method appropriate to all knowledge, to all knowledge in the human sciences, nor even to all the activities carried on in a discipline. This form of interpretivism is also refreshingly modest in any claims to be grounded in anything, be it knowledge and truth, the meaningful nature of human behaviour, or the categories of social scientific understanding. On the contrary, interpretation under this view is an activity that (like eating or running or writing law review articles) demands a justification or value for it to make sense.

Legal theoreticians have used each of these three kinds of interpretivism to reach their antimetaphysical conclusions about how legal theory ought to be carried on. Very ambitious or pragmatic interpretivism is the weapon of choice for many 'critical legal studies' types.[59] Theorists as

58 On interpretivism generally, see n. 5 above.

59 See e.g. Mark Kelman, *A Guide to Critical Legal Studies* (Cambridge, Mass.: Harvard University Press, 1987), 14 ('The search for "objective truth" is misguided; consensus within a viable community is all we mean by the truth of ethical propositions, just as it is all we mean when we say that a reading of a literary text is a true or sensible one.'); James Boyle, 'The Politics of Reason', *University of Pennsylvania Law Review*, 133 (1985), 685–780, at 778 ('what we need is makeshift work surfaces, not Platonic tables'); Gerald E. Frug, 'The Ideology of Bureaucracy in American Law', *Harvard Law Review*, 97 (1984), 1276–388; Robert W. Gordon, 'Historicism in Legal Scholarship', *Yale Law Journal*, 90 (1981), 1017–56; Mark Kelman, 'Interpretive Construction in the Substantive Criminal Law', *Stanford Law Review*, 33 (1981), 591–673; Joseph William Singer, 'The Player and the Cards: Nihilism and Legal Theory', *Yale Law Journal*, 94 (1984), 1–70; John Stick, 'Can Nihilism Be Pragmatic?', *Harvard Law Review*,

diverse as Stanley Fish,[60] Sanford Levinson,[61] and at incautious moments, David A. J. Richards,[62] also subscribe to this view that all knowledge is interpretive and shape their views of legal knowledge accordingly. Ambitious or dualist interpretivists include Owen Fiss,[63] the late Robert Cover,[64] and Jim White.[65] The legal theorist who most prominently uses a modest interpretivism to defend his antimetaphysical stance is Ronald Dworkin,[66] although others have not been slow to jump on this particular interpretivist bandwagon.[67]

My aim in this chapter is not so much to show that these interpretivists are wrong in their particular arguments, but rather to show that the arguments themselves do not raise the interpretivist above the field of fray. He is but another metaphysician who touts his own brand of metaphysics (usually idealist in character). Interpretivism is not a way of escaping the metaphysical issues debated by realists, idealists, and sceptics about the nature of mind, morality, causal relations, or law. Rather, interpretivism is but a form of idealism—a participant in the debate, not a conscientious objector to it.

Because the arguments that support the three different kinds of interpretivism are distinct, I shall treat each version separately. In doing so, I shall wander far from legal theory to get at the interpretivist views themselves, not their applications to legal theory. I do this because legal theory has been a borrower here, and it is best to go back to the philosophical positions it has borrowed from.

100 (1986), 332–401 (correcting Singer for not understanding Rorty's pragmatic interpretivism, which Stick himself appears to adopt).

60 See nn. 139–66 below and accompanying text.

61 Sanford Levinson, 'Law as Literature', *Texas Law Review*, 60 (1982), 373–403.

62 David A. J. Richards, 'Interpretation and Historiography', *Southern California Law Review*, 58 (1985), 489–549, at 522–4: 'The most arresting feature of such [postpositivistic] philosophy of science is its focus away from a timeless scientific method neutrally operating on simple facts to a historically self-conscious philosophy of science that takes seriously Polanyi's emphasis on the intuitive practices of scientific communities. . . . [I]t requires a historically self-conscious interpretation of the practices of scientific communities that cannot be sharply demarcated from the larger cultural communities of art, philosophy, and religion in which they are embedded. . . . [T]he example of science strikes home the conviction that thinking of current practices ahistorically may distort their interpretive complexity and disfigure the very reality and sense of these practices and their connections to broader cultural ideas. Interpretation in law is . . . interpretively complex in this way.'

63 Owen M. Fiss, 'Objectivity and Interpretation', *Stanford Law Review*, 34 (1982), 739–63.

64 Robert Cover, 'Foreword: Nomos and Narrative', *Harvard Law Review*, 97 (1983), 4–306.

65 James Boyd White, 'Law as Language', *Texas Law Review*, 60 (1982), 415–45.

66 Ronald Dworkin, *Law's Empire* (Cambridge, Mass.: Harvard University Press, 1986).

67 See e.g. Richard H. Fallon, Jr., 'A Constructivist-Coherence Theory of Constitutional Interpretation', *Harvard Law Review*, 100 (1987), 1189–286.

II. ALL KNOWLEDGE AS INTERPRETIVE: PRAGMATIST HERMENEUTICS

A. Richard Rorty's Pragmatist Interpretivism

One of the clearest exponents of pragmatist interpretivism is Richard Rorty.[68] Rorty's work has also strongly influenced other theorists in law, literature, and philosophy.[69] For both of these reasons I shall use him as my main stalking horse in this section.

Perhaps the place to start is with Rorty's interpretivist conclusion. Rorty urges us to move beyond realism and idealism and to do without 'an "objective" theory about the real nature of reality or knowledge or language'.[70] We don't need, and shouldn't want, philosophy of this kind. Under my sense of 'metaphysical', Rorty urges us not to have any of the theories that make up a metaphysical world view. We should, first, eschew 'metaphysics' in the narrow sense—i.e. as ontology, or a theory of what there is. A properly pragmatic philosopher 'does not think of himself as *any* kind of a metaphysician, because he does not *understand* the notion of "there being—out there"'.[71] Not only does such a philosopher not adopt a realist view of ontology, he does not adopt an idealist view either: '[S]ince he regards all vocabularies as tools for accomplishing purposes and none as representations of how things really are, he cannot possibly claim that "Xs really are Ys"', even if the Ys are ideas or conventions.[72]

Similarly, Rorty urges us to have no theory of truth. '[T]ruth is not the sort of thing which has an essence.'[73] Truth, accordingly, 'is not the sort of thing one should expect to have a philosophically interesting theory about'.[74] The only theory of truth that is possible is a disquotational theory in which 'is true' attached to some sentence s says no more than s by itself says.[75] Such a theory is not helpful to anything we should care about; it is harmless enough in providing rhetorical pats on the back to successful inquiries but dangerous if taken to have any depth or substance.[76]

[68] See Richard Rorty, *Consequences of Pragmatism* (Minneapolis: University of Minnesota Press, 1982), and *Philosophy and the Mirror of Nature* (Princeton: Princeton University Press, 1979).

[69] See e.g. Levinson, 'Law as Literature', above n. 61; Singer, 'Nihilism and Legal Theory', above n. 59; Stick, 'Can Nihilism be Pragmatic?', above n. 59; text accompanying nn. 139–96 below (Fish).

[70] Rorty, *Consequences*, above n. 68, at 156.

[71] Ibid. at p. xxviii.

[72] Ibid. at p. xlvi n. 31.

[73] Ibid. at 162.

[74] Ibid. at p. xiii.

[75] Ibid. at p. xxiv. The 'disquotational theory of truth' is sometimes called the redundancy theory because it makes the predicate, 'is true', strictly redundant to the sentence to which it attaches. To use Tarski's famous example: '"[S]now is white is true" is equivalent to the quoted sentence, "snow is white". The truth predicate, under this analysis, adds nothing to the sentence to which it is attached. In such a case, to talk of truth is only a way of talking about sentences rather than talking about the world. This is, as any metaphysician should recognize, an "anemic notion of truth"' (Devitt, *Realism and Truth*, above n. 6, at 29).

[76] Rorty, *Consequences*, above n. 68, at p. xvii.

We can also do quite nicely, Rorty thinks, without any theory of the meaning of sentences or any theory about reference or, for that matter, anything called a philosophy of language. We should hold a language-game view of language, according to which language use is a game whose goal is not to map the world but to continue the conversation. Words and statements relate to the world only 'by being counters used in games of assertion and denial, where any game can be played as long as there are conventions to tell one what moves to make'.[77] On such a view of language, referential 'questions about "ties with the world" do not arise';[78] we can therefore dispense with anything called a 'theory of reference': '[W]hatever semantics (or "philosophy of language") may be good for, it will not tell you anything about "how words relate to the world"—for there is nothing *general* to be said. On this view, the notion of "reference" . . . is pointless, a philosopher's invention.'[79] Rather than seeking a theory of reference or a theory of meaning, we should rest content with descriptions of the conventions followed by some linguistic community in some area of their discourse, conventions that make some assertions 'warranted' and others not.

Rorty similarly would find no sense to a metaphysical debate about the nature of logic. The only things logic studies are the 'inferences we habitually accept',[80] so what sense would there be to looking for a nature to this aspect of our language games any more than any other?

Rorty thus wants to avoid all the metaphysical questions raised in the last section. It is not, he tells us, that he has his own theories of ontology, truth, reference, meaning, or logic; rather, it is that he 'would simply like to change the subject'.[81] Rorty extends this conversational recommendation from metaphysics to epistemology. He does not think that it is any more fruitful to seek or to have a general theory of knowledge, be it foundational or non-foundational, than it is to have a general metaphysical theory. Knowledge, rationality, and rational justification are no more possessed of an essence than is truth.[82] We are thus equally unable to have any general theory of them: '[T]here is no wholesale, epistemological way to direct, or criticize, or underwrite, the course of inquiry.'[83] Epistemology is only a matter of local constraints—that is, conventions that mark one language game off from another: '[T]here are no constraints on inquiry save conversational ones—no wholesale constraints derived from the nature of the objects, or of the mind, or of language, but only those retail

[77] Rorty, *Consequences*, above n. 68, at 119. [78] Ibid. at 114.

[79] Ibid. at 127.

[80] Rorty, *Mirror*, above n. 68, at 321 (paraphrasing Goodman, *Fact, Fiction and Forecast*, above n. 35, at 67). As Rorty here makes clear, he views logic as simply another 'practice [that] has continued long enough [so that] the conventions which make it possible—and which permit a consensus on how to divide it into parts—are relatively easy to isolate' (ibid.).

[81] Rorty, *Consequences*, above n. 68, at p. xiv. [82] Ibid. at 162. [83] Ibid.

constraints provided by the remarks of our fellow-inquirers.'[84] Such constraints 'are in no sense "inevitable" ones discoverable by "reflection upon the logic of inquiry". They are just the facts about what a given society, or profession, or other group, takes to be good grounds for assertions of a certain sort.'[85]

Rorty's anti-epistemological stance extends to the theory of understanding. Rorty is as much against there being any general ('wholesale') theory of human understanding as he is against there being such a theory of justification. There is no hope, Rorty thinks, for those in the tradition of the sciences of spirit who would seek to replace epistemology, with its general categories of knowledge and explanation, with hermeneutics and its general categories of understanding and interpretation.[86]

Rorty is thus different from the dualistic interpretivists that I shall consider in the next section. One might legitimately ask how Rorty's pragmatist conclusions are interpretivist at all. Part of the answer lies in the conclusion common to pragmatism and interpretivism, namely, that metaphysics and epistemology are not possible human activities. As Rorty puts it about his brand of interpretivism: 'Hermeneutics does not need a new epistemological paradigm, any more than liberal political thought requires a new paradigm of sovereignty. Hermeneutics, rather, is what we get when we are no longer epistemological.'[87] Rorty goes on to claim: 'Hermeneutics is not "another way of knowing"—"understanding" as opposed to (predictive) "explanation". It [along with pragmatism] is better seen as another way of coping.'[88]

Rorty's pragmatism and other forms of interpretivism thus agree on what physicists, sociologists, lawyers, psychoanalysts, and literary critics do instead of 'seeking knowledge': they all interpret a social practice (albeit different ones). The point of such interpretations is not to get at the true nature of something. The point, rather, is to 'keep the conversation going'[89] so that we can achieve the agreements that form new practices (or we achieve at least that fruitful disagreement from which new agreements are possible).[90] Interpretivism and pragmatism share the view that agreement is all there is to attain with conversation, that interpreting those agreements is all there is to do, realizing that each interpretation is itself an offer of a new agreement as much as an interpretation of an old agreement.

Such is the very ambitious interpretivist stance exemplified by Rorty. The question, however, is what reason Rorty gives us to adopt this stance. What reason do we have to stop talking of competing metaphysical and epistemological theories in favour of conversing about our conversations? One answer that interpretivists might give would be that there is no

[84] Ibid. at 165.
[85] Rorty, *Mirror*, above n. 68, at 385.
[86] Ibid. at 343–56, 380–5.
[87] Ibid. at 325; see also ibid. at 315.
[88] Ibid. at 356.
[89] Ibid. at 377.
[90] Ibid. at 318.

'reason', no 'argument', as to why we should adopt their concerns—nothing, that is, that would count as a reason or an argument by our (implicitly metaphysical) lights. Rorty attributes such a response to Derrida, who has no 'interesting arguments' to make to us because he is 'not working by the same rules' of argumentation as we are.[91] Richard Bernstein attributes the same response to Gadamer: 'Gadamer does not simply state the theses that he seeks to defend, and argue for them in the usual manner of analytic philosophers. He proceeds in what, from an analytic perspective, looks like indirect, oblique, "suggestive" discourse—by interpreting, questioning, and conversing with texts.'[92]

The suggestion is that to defend the interpretive turn in our conversation we should use interpretive methods, not didactic arguments. Thus, we might expect what we in fact receive from Bernstein—long exegeses of Kuhn, Feyerabend, Wittgenstein, Geertz, Gadamer, Winch, Habermas, Derrida, Heidegger, Nietzsche, Hegel, etc. The 'argument' of such textual exegeses is the interpretive observation that our culture is moving towards different conversational topics than realism versus idealism in metaphysics and foundationalism versus non-foundationalism in epistemology. Such exegeses are of course not an argument as we might understand 'argument', but the interpretivist might claim that she is changing what an argument should be thought to be.

To pursue this suggestion would be to end any conversation, at least with me. Fortunately Rorty does not similarly disdain giving reasons for his interpretive turn.[93] Although Rorty himself makes no effort to organize these reasons, as I read him he deploys essentially two arguments to urge us beyond metaphysics and epistemology.

First and foremost is the argument that stems from Rorty's antifoundationalism in epistemology. Throughout his work Rorty rehearses the now-standard theses of his Quinean position: (1) There are no 'starting points' from which beliefs may be justified.[94] This is the familiar observation that there are no privileged beliefs that we may use as foundations for erecting our other beliefs.[95] Neither of the empiricist candidates for such beliefs—neither the naive realist's observational statements in object language, nor the phenomenalist's sense datum reports—turns out to have that foundational character. Nor are the rationalist's 'self-evident' starting points

[91] Rorty, *Consequences*, above n. 68, at 98.

[92] Richard J. Bernstein, *Beyond Objectivism and Relativism* (Oxford: Blackwell, 1983), 114.

[93] At least, Rorty does not always disdain giving reasons for why we should change the topic of our conversations. But see text accompanying nn. 131–4 below.

[94] Rorty, *Consequences*, above n. 68, at pp. xx, 166, 170.

[95] See generally, W. V. O. Quine, *From A Logical Point of View* (4th edn., Cambridge, Mass.: Harvard University Press, 1980); see also Harman, *Thought*, above n. 17; Lehrer, *Knowledge*, above n. 15; Rescher, *Pragmatism*, above n. 14; White, *Towards Reunion*, above n. 17; Williams, *Groundless Belief*, above n. 28.

sufficiently 'indubitable' to provide an absolute foundation for knowledge. (2) Furthermore, no statements are guaranteed to be true by the very meanings of the terms comprising such statements—what philosophers call 'analytic truths'.[96] Such truths, if they existed, would preserve the certainty of the foundationalist's starting points by licensing inferences that were equally certain (because analytically true).[97] (3) All observation is theory laden in the sense that all seeing is 'seeing as', or seeing under a description: '[W]e shall not see reality plain, unmasked, naked to our gaze.'[98] If observation statements are 'theory-laden', they cannot ground the theories with which they are laden. (4) Relatedly, there is no distinction in kind between theoretical statements and observation statements: all such statements are theoretical.[99] (5) Hence, justification is inescapably holistic: since no belief faces reality by itself, but only en masse with all of its fellows (to paraphrase Quine),[100] justification of one belief is supported by, and in turn supports, innumerable others. All beliefs are thus interdependent; a recalcitrant experience requires changes that reverberate throughout our belief system.[101] (6) Finally, this holistic view implies that for any finite set of data there are an infinite number of theories that fit that data equally well.[102] Or, as Rorty more colourfully puts it: '[S]uggested constraints, necessities, and principles are as plentiful as blackberries.'[103]

Rorty derives two conclusions from this antifoundationalism, one epistemological and the other metaphysical. He concludes, first, that epistemology as most philosophers practise it is misconceived because there can be no such thing as a general theory of justification (or of discovery or understanding, for that matter). One might legitimately wonder how Rorty can reach this epistemological position when he accepts the essential tenets of a now-standard, very general theory of epistemological justification, the coherence theory.

To answer this challenge Rorty must begin by denying that he too has this general theory of justification. True, Rorty may say that a belief's justification is a matter of coherence with other beliefs and not (always) a deductive or inductive inference from some foundational 'seeing' of reality; but what Rorty has to mean by 'coherence' is something completely

[96] Rorty, *Consequences*, above n. 68, at p. xviii. A standard example of a supposed analytic truth is the statement, 'A bachelor is an unmarried man.' The classic attacks on analyticity relied on by Rorty are Quine's. See Quine, *From a Logical Point of View*, above n. 95, and *Word and Object*, above n. 17.

[97] Particularly good at showing the certainty-preserving use to which foundationalist philosophers once put analyticity is Harman, *Thought*, above n. 17, at 7–15.

[98] Rorty, *Consequences*, above n. 68, at 154.

[99] Ibid. at p. xviii.

[100] See Rorty, *Mirror*, above n. 68, at 319.

[101] Rorty, *Consequences*, above n. 68, at 28.

[102] This is the familiar Duhemian thesis that Quine did so much to revive. See Quine, *Word and Object*, above n. 17.

[103] Rorty, *Consequences*, above n. 68, at 169.

context dependent.[104] Coherence theorists in epistemology have a notoriously difficult time of finding some general relation between propositions that is stronger than mere consistency (freedom from contradiction) yet weaker than entailment. Nonetheless, coherence theorists seek such a relation because it is distinctive of what they think justifies belief in any proposition.[105] Rorty differs from such theorists in denying that there is any single relation called 'coherence'. Rather, what it is for one proposition to cohere with another depends on the inquiry's context. What qualifies as a good justification will thus vary from context to context.

Rorty makes this crucial move via a distinction he draws between 'wholesale' and 'retail' justifications. Retail justifications are the justification we give within what Kuhn calls 'normal science'.[106] Justifications for believing, e.g. that Jones intends to get a haircut at noon, that water is composed of hydrogen and oxygen atoms, or that 'Hamlet' is a play about indecision, are retail justifications in that they give 'detailed, concrete reasons which have brought one to one's present view' on such matters.[107] Wholesale justifications, by contrast, are more ambitious. If we had them, they would underwrite our retail justifications by showing, wholesale, what counts as a good justification for any belief. Rorty's antiepistemological conclusion is that there are no wholesale justifications: '[T]here are no constraints on inquiry save conversational ones—no wholesale constraints derived from the nature of the objects, or of the mind, or of language, but only those retail constraints provided by the remarks of our fellow-inquirers.'[108]

Such a view grants autonomy to each area of discourse when practised by some linguistic community. There being no wholesale notion of justification by which to judge the adequacy of the (retail) justifications offered within such practices, each area of discourse is autonomous in judging what will count as a justification.

Rorty welcomes this conclusion because it is part and parcel of his general rejection of philosophy's traditional self-image as 'arbiter of culture'. According to Rorty, the epistemologist simply has nothing special to offer in the way of retail justification. If, he claims, we reject the notion that philosophy has privileged access to the very foundations of knowledge—special insights into the nature of objects in general, or the nature of mind or language in general—and if philosophy cannot even give a general characterization of justification in terms of 'coherence' or some other uni-

[104] One wishes he would say so clearly someplace. An example of a sympathetic philosopher who does say so clearly is Hilary Putnam, who in his current incarnation has urged that 'our notion of coherence has proved to be extremely topic relative' (Putnam, *Realism and Reason*, above n. 6, at 301).

[105] See e.g. Williams, *Groundless Belief*, above n. 28, at 104–5.

[106] See Rorty, *Consequences*, above n. 68, at 165.

[107] Ibid.

[108] Ibid.

tary relation between beliefs, then we have no reason to think that epistemology has anything important to say about actual inquiry. Each community of discourse and inquiry is 'autonomous' in the sense that its standards of validity, its accepted procedures, and its established truths arise internally from the 'conversations' among fellow inquirers. Traditional epistemology thus becomes irrelevant to the conduct of any inquiry.

Rorty also seeks to draw his antimetaphysical conclusion from his antifoundationalism. Here Rorty relies on a second distinction, this time between 'internal' and 'external' criticism. Internal criticism evaluates a statement according to its consistency with other statements accepted within the relevant linguistic community. It claims to use no standard to criticize the participants within a practice other than the standards accepted by the participants themselves or by a community to which the observer belongs. External criticism, by contrast, ignores the practices of any community and critiques beliefs or behaviours by some external standard that the participants may or may not accept. The validity of these external standards does not depend upon their acceptance by any community of either subjects or observers.[109]

As suggested above, Rorty's version of antifoundationalism leads him to reject the notion that philosophy has a privileged position from which it can judge the culture in which it is situated; it occupies no 'Archimedean point from which to survey culture'.[110] Furthermore, Rorty claims, no discipline can occupy such a position. Its standards, he suggests, are always internal, always situated in a determinate cultural, historical and linguistic context that we cannot simply think away. 'It is impossible', Rorty tells us, 'to step outside our skins—the traditions, linguistic and other, within which we do our thinking and self-criticism—and compare ourselves with something absolute.'[111] Rorty rejects, apparently even as an ideal, C. S. Peirce's notion of an ideal theory that would give us 'an all-embracing ahistorical context in which every other species and discourse could be assigned its proper place and rank'.[112] The only available criticisms are

[109] Rorty appears to have adopted this distinction from Putnam (*Mirror*, above n. 68, at 294–9). For Putnam's discussion, see generally Putnam, *Realism and Reason*, above n. 6. Putnam's external/internal distinction, however, was between assertions made relative to an ideal theory and assertions made relative to no theory but only to the world as it is. Putnam called the latter point of view external because it purports to judge from a viewpoint external to all theory, even that of an ideally rational person with complete information. 'Internal' for Putnam did not mean, 'internal to some set of present practices' (as it does for Rorty), but only, 'internal to the practices we would have if we were ideally rational and possessed of full information'. See ibid. at 125. For a discussion of Putnam's kind of internal/external distinction, see Brian Ellis, 'What Science Aims to Do', in P. Churchland and C. Hooker (eds.), *Images of Science* (Chicago: University of Chicago Press, 1985), 48, 67–73.

[110] Rorty, *Mirror*, above n. 68, at 150.

[111] Rorty, *Consequences*, above n. 68, at p. xix.

[112] Ibid.

internal criticisms, for the only kinds of truth any of us possess are those 'provided by current practice (by, e.g., the best moral and scientific thought of the day)'.[113]

The appeal of this 'impossibility-of-the-external' argument is straightforward enough: how indeed can we step outside our own beliefs and stare at an unmediated reality? The absolute unknowability of any Kantian 'thing-in-itself' or of any Peircean 'God-like knowledge of ideal theory' may seem to make either of these kinds of metaphysical knowledge impossible to attain.

Rorty's second argument, which does not stem directly from his antifoundationalism, is what I shall call his verificationist argument.[114] It is based on the insight that, as the sceptic reminds us, the evidence with which we verify a proposition is always less than the proposition evidenced. For example, the behavioural clues from which we infer the existence of mental states in others—facial expression, 'body language', or explicit statements, for example—don't ever present a knockdown case for another having a certain mental state, or, indeed, for him having any mental states. Likewise, the particular instances that support an inductive inference are less than the instances we take the proposition to cover. That is the very meaning of 'induction'. Similarly, the phenomenal clues we each use to infer the existence of objects like tables and chairs do not guarantee us of the existence of those objects, nor even of the external world they constitute.[115] In each case there is what Nelson Goodman calls a gap between evidence and the things a metaphysician would say are evidenced by the evidence.[116]

Rorty sees epistemology and metaphysics as an attempt to cross this uncrossable gap between evidence and things evidenced. As he puts it: '[E]pistemology is the attempt to see the patterns of justification within normal discourse as more than just such patterns. It is the attempt to see them as hooked on to something which demands moral commitment—Reality, Truth, Objectivity, Reason.'[117] The verificationist, by contrast, gives up this attempt and adopts what Kripke calls a 'sceptical solution': since the gap cannot be crossed, the verificationist gives up the metaphysical notion of something evidenced that is in any sense independent of the

[113] Rorty, *Mirror*, above n. 68, at 374.

[114] I use the term 'verificationist' because the insight prompting this argument is the same as the insight that prompted the verificationists' well-known slogan that the meaning of a statement is its method of verification. See e.g. A. J. Ayer, *Philosophy in the Twentieth Century* (New York: Random House, 1982), 80–1.

[115] See Harman, *Thought*, above n. 17, at 3–6 (discussing each of these three well-worn problems posed by the sceptic).

[116] Nelson Goodman, *Ways of Worldmaking* (Hassocks, England: Harvester Press, 1978).

[117] Rorty, *Mirror*, above n. 68, at 385.

evidence for it.[118] Kripke's example is the Humean 'solution' to the gap problem about causation. Causation for Hume was not evidenced by the regular concurrence of classes of events; it was constituted by such regularity. There was thus for Hume no gap between what we can observe—one class of events regularly following another—and that which we usually take such observations to evidence, a causal relation between singular events. Similarly, the behaviourist in psychology does not cross the gap between behaviour and mind but eliminates it by reducing talk about mental states to talk about behaviour. Or consider the antimetaphysical view of induction, which denies that there is anything called inductive inference; such inference, according to this view, is only the habitual practice of scientists. Likewise, the phenomenalist rejects a metaphysics of objects in external reality for a view that treats objects as mere constructions out of sense impressions.

Rorty also adopts a sceptical solution to the gap problem by reducing truth to evidence across the board: ' "[O]bjective truth" is no more and no less than the best idea we currently have about how to explain what is going on.'[119] If that is all there is or can be to objective truth (and to reality, ideal justification, and like notions), then of course epistemology and metaphysics are impossible. The crucial premise of this second argument is the premise that makes such verificationism the only alternative to outright scepticism in the face of the perceived gap between evidence and things evidenced.

We now need to assess whether Rorty's arguments are sufficient to induce us to move our conversation beyond metaphysics and epistemology. We should first ask, as good 'internal' critics, from what point of view Rorty himself can make his arguments. To employ one of his own distinctions, is Rorty's critique external to the practices of philosophers in the realist metaphysical tradition? If so, is it external only to realist metaphysical practices but not to the practices of idealist philosophers? Or is it external to all metaphysical practices, realist, idealist, or sceptical? Or should we see Rorty's critique as internal to the practices of realist philosophers, showing the inconsistencies in their own views but promoting no view itself? I shall pursue these possibilities as I seek to show not that Rorty's two arguments are wrong, but only that they do not differentiate him from the garden variety idealist metaphysician.

Consider Rorty as a critic external to the practices of realist or Platonic philosophers. There seem to be three possibilities for the viewpoint from which one could make such external criticism: he is arguing from the practices of (1) idealist metaphysicians; (2) some sceptical metaphysics that is

118 Saul A. Kripke, *Wittgenstein on Rules and Private Language* (Cambridge, Mass.: Harvard University Press, 1982), at 66–8.

119 Rorty, *Mirror*, above n. 68, at 385.

neither idealist nor realist; or (3) non-metaphysical philosophers, i.e. his is a 'view from nowhere'.[120]

None of these three possibilities can be palatable to Rorty. The first two place him explicitly in metaphysical camps (idealism, scepticism) that his interpretivism seeks to avoid; the third presupposes that realism is true, because it presupposes that Rorty's two arguments can be 'just true' and not just 'true relative to the practices of certain metaphysical philosophers'.

Rorty explicitly seeks to avoid this old ploy of the realist metaphysician.[121] Rorty recognizes that interpretivists (he calls them 'edifying philosophers') 'have to decry the very notion of having a view, while avoiding having a view about having views'.[122] Rorty finds this to be 'an awkward, but not impossible position'.[123] Presumably, then, we should not view Rorty as making his two arguments from a standpoint external to the practices of realist metaphysicians. That seems to leave only two possibilities. On one hand, he may be making arguments internal to the practices of realist philosophers, conceding arguendo much of their viewpoint in order to show the impossibility of the rest of it. Or, on the other hand, he may not be making arguments at all, either internal or external—like Gadamer and Derrida, he may only be 'participating in a conversation rather than contributing to an inquiry', 'saying things' rather than 'saying how things are'.[124] I shall explore each possibility in turn.

First, consider Rorty as internal critic of metaphysical philosophy. So construed, Rorty can neither assert nor presuppose any metaphysical view himself; he can only point to inconsistencies in the metaphysical views of others. Yet how do we make out Rorty's arguments from non-foundationalism and verificationism as arguments proceeding from some inconsistency in the practices of realist or idealist metaphysicians? On their face, Rorty's two arguments do not display a contradiction in the practices of either idealist or realist metaphysicians. Indeed, idealists have made each of his two argu-

[120] I adopt the title of Nagel's book. Thomas Nagel, *The View from Nowhere* (New York: Oxford University Press, 1986).

[121] I once advanced this inconsistency ploy against Rorty and his legal admirers. See Moore, 'A Natural Law Theory', above n. 5, at 310–11. Hilary Putnam states the general form of the objection: 'That (total) relativism is inconsistent is a truism among philosophers. After all, is it not obviously contradictory to hold a point of view while at the same time holding that no point of view is more justified or right than any other? . . . [I]f all is relative, then the relative is relative too' 'Reason, Truth and History', above n. 6, at 119–20). Bernard Williams also finds Rorty's interpretivism to be 'self-defeating: If the story he tells were true, then there would be no perspective from which he could express it in this way' (Bernard Williams, *Ethics and The Limits of Philosophy* (Cambridge, Mass.: Harvard University Press, 1985), 137).

[122] Rorty, *Mirror*, above n. 68, at 371.

[123] Ibid.

[124] This seems to be Rorty's own preferred answer to his query of how he may 'decry the very notion of having a view, while avoiding having a view about having views'. See text accompanying n. 122 above.

ments for centuries, not to establish the impossibility of metaphysics per se, but the falsity of realist metaphysics. Thus, Rorty seems to be but a closet idealist, no matter what his protestations to the contrary.

Consider Rorty's main argument, which stems from the contemporary critique of foundationalism in epistemology. As we have seen, Rorty thinks that a non-foundationalist epistemology is incompatible with a realist metaphysics, because in the former view we cannot get external to our own collective belief systems. He thinks, therefore, that a refutation of foundationalism is a refutation of realism. Yet this is the same basic argument that contemporary sceptical or idealist metaphysicians employ against realist metaphysics.[125] Moreover, as Rorty himself recognizes, this is the very same argument that those he calls 'technical realists' believe they have answered.[126] The technical realists not only argue that metaphysical realism is consistent with non-foundationalism; they argue that non-foundationalism requires metaphysical realism as the best explanation available for why we believe what we do. 'Truth as correspondence', they argue, is an explanatory term in the same way that 'gene' is explanatory. This means that the reference relation between words and things is also a real relation and thus that correspondence and reference must themselves be explained in physicalist terms, just as Tarski's theory of truth and the causal theory of reference purport to do.[127] Rorty disagrees. He denies that 'there is any interesting notion called "reference" in addition to the commonsense notion of "talking about".[128] He denies that the correspondence theory of truth is explanatory: '[W]hen realists . . . argue that Tarski's account of truth is merely a placeholder, like Mendel's account of "gene", . . . pragmatists reply . . . that "true" . . . is not an explanatory notion.'[129] 'What', Rorty continues, 'is the microstructure of "corresponding"?'[130]

Again, it is not the burden of this article to show that Rorty is wrong in his antifoundationalist argument against realism (although I believe he is; the best argument for realism is the argument of the 'technical realists', although I would call it by its more standard names in philosophy, 'naturalized epistemology' and 'naturalized metaphysics'). My point here is more limited: Rorty's supposed 'internal critique' does not show some embarrassing inconsistency in the practices of realist metaphysicians. Rather, he tries to show that realism is false using the exact same arguments

[125] See Devitt, *Realism and Truth*, above n. 6, at 125–223 (a very nice survey of the arguments of Kuhn, Feyerabend, Von Fraassen, Davidson, Dummett, and the latest Putnam).

[126] Rorty, *Consequences*, above n. 68, at p. xxiii.

[127] The mid-1970s Putnam, for example, engages in this kind of argument. Putnam, *Meaning and the Moral Sciences*, above n. 6, at 1–45; see also Devitt, *Realism and Truth*, above n. 6, at 61–9; Papineau, *Reality and Representation*, above n. 14, at 151–8; Richard N. Boyd, 'Lex Orandi est Lex Credendi', in *Images of Science*, above n. 109, at 3–34, and 'Scientific Realism and Naturalistic Epistemology', *Philosophy of Science Archives*, 2 (1980), 613.

[128] Rorty, *Consequences*, above n. 68, at 129. [129] Ibid. at p. xxv. [130] Ibid.

as the idealist metaphysician. One hardly shows the senselessness of some debate, in this case, that between metaphysicians, by participating in one well-defined side of it.

This leaves Rorty with the other possibility, that he is not making an 'argument'—as we would recognize it—at all. Finding metaphysical presuppositions 'too abstract to argue against', Rorty mostly seems to favour construing himself as 'merely try[ing] to show how things look if they are not made'.[131] In these moods, Rorty presents his 'arguments' as mere pictures of our intellectual life that we may find more attractive than the picture bequeathed to us by traditional philosophy:

> The question of what propositions to assert, which pictures to look at, what narratives to listen to and comment on and retell, are all questions about what will help us get what we want (or about what we should want). The question of whether the pragmatist view of truth—that it is not a profitable topic—is itself true is thus a question about whether a post-philosophical [i.e. nonmetaphysical] culture is a good thing to try for.[132]

And lest the language of 'should want' and 'good' seem to betray realist metaphysical commitments, Rorty cautions us that when and if we do produce these 'new and better ways of talking and acting', we will have done so only 'in the sense that they come to seem clearly better than their [metaphysical] predecessors'.[133] Such choices are 'not going to be resolved by any sudden new discovery of how things really are'. Rather, they 'will be decided . . . only by a slow and painful choice between alternative self-images'.[134]

When someone reaches this position we know that we are reaching the end of our conversation with him. Telling us we must choose and that some choices will seem better than others, without giving any reasons why we should choose one way or the other or why the 'seeming-better' should be taken to *be* better, does not engage us. Such suggestions are empty in the way that non-cognitivist and existential ethics were always empty. For what it is worth, here in the realm of the non-cognitivist, Rorty's world does not seem better to me. It seems a barren place in which all arguments are made only by pulling oneself out of deep existential nausea, itself possible only by a bad-faith forgetfulness that all arguments are rhetorical substitutes for the bullets one either does not possess or is unwilling to use.

Even Rorty cannot live in this world. As he wrote to Sandy Levinson, one of his legal admirers:

> I confess that I tremble at the thought of Barthian readings in law schools . . . I suspect that civilization reposes on a lot of people who take the normal practices of the

131 Rorty, *Consequences*, above n. 68, at 111.
132 Ibid. at p. xliii.
133 Ibid. at p. xxxvii.
134 Ibid. at p. xliv.

discipline with full 'realistic' seriousness. However, I should like to think that a pragmatist's understanding of knowledge and community would be, in the end, compatible with normal inquiry—the practitioners of such inquiry reserving their irony for after-hours.[135]

I gather from this that Rorty's pragmatic interpretivism, like Hume's scepticism, should be put aside at the fireside of daily living. What better confession of Sartrean bad faith?

Responding perhaps to this fear, Rorty's 'non-argumentative' interpretivism will allow him 'just one' argument. The interpretivist's 'only argument for thinking that these intuitions and vocabularies [i.e. metaphysical ones] should be eradicated is that the intellectual tradition to which they belong has not paid off, is more trouble than it is worth, has become an incubus'.[136] Rorty's 'one argument' is designed to allow us to choose whether to continue our metaphysical conversation, or to go Rorty's interpretivist route:

I do not think one can decide between Hegel and Plato save by meditating on the past efforts of the philosophical tradition to escape from time and history. One can see these efforts as worthwhile, getting better, worth continuing. Or one can see them as doomed and perverse. I do not know what would count as a noncircular metaphysical or epistemological or semantical argument for seeing them in either way. So I think that the decision has to be made simply by reading the history of philosophy and drawing a moral.[137]

The moral that we are supposed to draw is that the Platonic tradition has failed for two thousand years. On correspondence truth, for example, Rorty thinks that 'many centuries of attempts to explain what "correspondence" is have failed'.[138] So what reason could we have for thinking it will now succeed in the hands of the technical realists and the naturalizing epistemologists?

It is hard to know, given Rorty's ultimately non-argumentative stance, whether we are to take this as an argument or not. If we are, then it is the same antifoundationalist argument against the technical realist that we considered before and is subject to the same rejoinder. Issue is again joined between the realist, on the one hand, and the idealist, sceptic, and the interpretivist, on the other. The realists don't think that Plato (or the rest of us footnotes to Plato) failed. That of course remains to be seen, but the only way to see it is to work through the realist/antirealist arguments about the explanatory role of correspondence truth and the like. Rorty's meta-induction from the history of philosophy depends on the antirealist

135 Quoted in Levinson, 'Law as Literature', above n. 61, at 401 n. 117.
136 Rorty, *Consequences*, above n. 68, at p. xxxvii.
137 Ibid. at 174.
138 Ibid. at p. xxvi.

being right on the merits of his metaphysical arguments, for that is the only way of knowing that 'Plato' (i.e. metaphysical realism) has failed.

If this 'meta-induction' is not an argument by Rorty—just more words in lieu of bullets—then we have reached the end of our conversation with him. While there are certainly non-rational modes of persuasion, if that is what Rorty is ultimately up to, we should respond in kind, not with further argument.

B. Stanley Fish's Atheoretical Interpretivism

Although quoting and relying on Rorty extensively, Stanley Fish has arrived at his own distinctive brand of pragmatic interpretivism. To begin at the end, Fish, like Rorty, believes that he has moved beyond metaphysics and epistemology. Thus, Fish too claims the high ground in the debate between realists and antirealists, which is to say, ground so elevated above the debate that we can see it as fruitless and senseless, much ado about nothing.

Thus, Fish admonishes me (as a representative metaphysician) that '[n]o matter how intriguing the choice between conventionalist and realist theories may be on a meta-critical level, it has no role whatsoever to play on the level of practical action'.[139] We don't have to choose between realism and my usual stalking horse in metaphysics, conventionalism, because, Fish assures us, neither the realist nor the conventionalist is 'a theorist of any kind'[140] when interpreting a legal text. An interpreter 'will see what he sees independently of whether his theory of knowledge (should he have one) is realist or conventionalist'.[141] Fish concludes: '[Y]ou don't use your account of knowing [both epistemology and metaphysics, for Fish] in order to "do" knowing.'[142]

Fish's general point here is that epistemological and metaphysical theories are empty of real-world consequences. Fish criticizes even other interpretivists for failing to see the emptiness of any kind of metaphysical or epistemological theory, antirealist as well as realist. Thus, for example, Fish castigates Mark Kelman (whom I would classify as a very ambitious interpretivist) for criticizing liberal legal doctrines on the grounds that they rest on unexamined 'interpretive constructs'.[143] This, Fish says, 'is to fall into the characteristically left error of assuming that an [epistemological] insight into the source of our convictions (they come from culture, not from God) will render them less compelling'.[144] More generally, Fish

[139] Stanley Fish, 'Dennis Martinez and the Uses of Theory', *Yale Law Journal*, 96 (1987), 1773–800, at 1782–3.

[140] Ibid. at 1783.

[141] Ibid.

[142] Ibid. at 1784.

[143] Mark Kelman, 'Interpretive Construction in the Substantive Criminal Law', *Stanford Law Review*, 33 (1981), 591–673.

[144] Fish, 'Dennis Martinez', above n. 139, at 1796.

indicts all those Critical Legal Studies types who are also very ambitious interpretivists of the epistemological crime of ' "anti-foundationalist theory hope", the hope that because we now know that our foundations are interpretive rather than natural (given by God or nature), we will regard them with suspicion and shake ourselves loose from their influence'.[145] Such hope is a crime for Fish because it concedes to metaphysical and epistemological theories practical consequences that they do not and cannot possess:

> [A]ny such hope rests on the possibility of surveying our interpretive foundations from a vantage point that was not itself interpretive; and the impossibility of doing that is the first tenet of anti-foundationalist thought. It follows then that anti-foundationalist thought cannot have the consequences that many hope that it will have.[146]

In a similar vein Fish accuses other very ambitious interpretivists, such as Sanford Levinson,[147] of taking epistemology and metaphysics too seriously. Their mistake is thus the same as Kelman's, although for them this mistake leads to antifoundationalist theory despair rather than hope. Such despair, Fish urges, is as unwarranted as Kelman's hope; both give an undeserved credence to metaphysics and epistemology. In particular, Levinson's kind of 'theory despair' assumes there could be such a thing as metaphysically grounded knowledge and is despairing only because it compares the knowledge we do possess to such grounded knowledge. A Fish-like interpretivist despairs no more than he hopes because metaphysically grounded knowledge is so incoherent as an idea that it cannot even serve as a standard of comparison:

> It is not simply that supra-contextual facts [of the metaphysician] are unavailable to us, but that the very notion of a supra-contextual fact makes no sense since something that had no relation to the concerns of a particular human situation would not be a fact and therefore could not be known by a human agent. What that something might be, God only knows. The irony is that the state which is for Levinson the precondition of true knowledge—the state of being above all situations and therefore of being in none at all—is the state in which the very idea of knowledge is incoherent.[148]

Fish also criticizes less ambitious interpretivists on the ground that they are too 'metaphysical'. Owen Fiss,[149] for example, is an ambitious interpretivist (believing that the human sciences are uniquely interpretive in

[145] Ibid. at n. 60 (criticizing Duncan Kennedy and Robert Gordon); see also Stanley Fish, 'Anti-Professionalism', *Cardozo Law Review*, 7 (1986), 645–77, at 656–61.

[146] Fish, 'Dennis Martinez', above n. 139, at 1796 n. 60.

[147] See Levinson, 'Law as Literature', above n. 61.

[148] Stanley Fish, 'Interpretation and the Pluralist Vision', *Texas Law Review*, 60 (1982), 495–505, at 497.

[149] See Fiss, 'Objectivity and Interpretation', above n. 63.

their methods) whom Fish criticizes on just this ground. In general terms, Fiss is like Fish in seeking an interpretive theory that is neither wholly objective nor wholly subjective.[150] Fiss thinks he finds such a theory in the 'disciplining rules' of interpretive communities.[151] Such rules might be the professional rules that govern lawyers' behaviour, for example.[152] Although the rules that lawyers interpret ('the law') may be indeterminate, the rules that discipline their interpretive effort may not be, which is how Fiss defends what he calls the 'objectivity' of interpretation.

To Fish, both this problem and its solution smell fishy. According to him, there is no real problem of 'subjective' or 'nihilistic' interpretation: '[N]ihilism is impossible; one simply cannot "exalt the . . . subjective dimension of interpretation" or drain text of meaning, and it is unnecessary to combat something that is not possible.'[153] So much for Fiss's problem. Moreover, Fiss's solution, stated in terms of disciplinary rules that provide constraints on interpretation, is also too metaphysical for Fish: '[A] so-called "disciplining rule" cannot be said to act as a constraint on interpretation because it is (in whatever form has been specified for it) the product of an interpretation.'[154] For Fish, both Fiss's problem and his solution stem from the same mistake: Fiss's interpretivism is not sufficiently purged of metaphysics. Fiss presupposes an external stance in even questioning interpretation's objectivity, and he similarly takes an external stance when he seeks to guarantee interpretation's objectivity with 'just there' disciplining rules that are miraculously free of the need for interpretation.

Finally, Fish has repeatedly chided Ronald Dworkin, a fellow interpretivist whom Fish very much resembles, for not seeing clearly enough interpretivism's antimetaphysical and anti-epistemological implications.[155] Fish accuses Dworkin 'of a general failure to understand the nature of interpretation'.[156] This nature is something Fish has described before: '[I]t is neither the case that interpretation is constrained by what is obviously and unproblematically "there", nor the case that interpreters . . . are free to read into a text whatever they like.'[157] Dworkin, according to Fish, 'com-

[150] See Fiss, 'Objectivity and Interpretation', above n. 63 at 739.

[151] Ibid. at 744.

[152] Ibid. at 745.

[153] Stanley Fish, 'Fish v. Fiss', *Stanford Law Review*, 36 (1984), 1325–47, at 1346 (quoting Fiss, 'Objectivity and Interpretation', above n. 63, at 746).

[154] Ibid. at 1327.

[155] Fish's anti-Dworkin campaign begins in Stanley Fish, 'Working on the Chain Gang: Interpretation in the Law and in Literary Criticism', *Critical Inquiry*, 9 (1982), 201–16, reprinted in *Texas Law Review*, 60 (1982), 551–67, and W. Mitchell (ed.), *The Politics of Interpretation* (Chicago: University of Chicago Press, 1983), 271. It continues in Fish, 'Dennis Martinez', above n. 139, and rests at Stanley Fish, 'Still Wrong After All These Years', *Law & Philosophy*, 6 (1987), 401–18.

[156] Fish, 'Working on the Chain Gang', above n. 155, at 281.

[157] Ibid.

mits himself to the very alternatives he sets out to avoid',[158] simply by theorizing about interpretation at all. Interpretation is a doing for Fish, a practice. Theorizing about interpretation distorts it by reintroducing the very metaphysics that the interpretive move sought to avoid. A true interpretivist, for Fish, just engages in the activity of interpretation. To theorize about how to interpret, or with what to limit or constrain the interpreter's freedom, is already to buy into the metaphysical/epistemological programme from which interpretivism was to save us.

Fish thus presents himself as the true upholder of the interpretivists' antimetaphysical faith, and he aims much of his writing (when he is not criticizing metaphysicians like me) at keeping his fellow interpretivists from unwittingly straying into the serpentine windings of metaphysics.

What arguments does Fish give for his antimetaphysical fetish? Throughout his work, Fish appears to rely on a two-step argument. The first step is Fish's psychological claim that action is always guided by tacit knowledge, not by the application of general rules, principles, or theories. Fish here takes as his point of departure Thomas Kuhn's description of how scientific laws enter into scientific reasoning:

> Taken by itself, the verbal statement of the law . . . is virtually impotent. Present it to a contemporary student of physics, who knows the words and can do all the problems but now employs different means. Then imagine what the words, though all well known, can have said to a man who did not know even the problems. For him the generalization could begin to function only when he learned . . . something, prior to the law, about the situations that nature does and does not present. That sort of learning is not acquired by exclusively verbal means. Rather it comes as one is given words together with concrete examples of how they function in use [nature and words are learned together]. . . . To borrow . . . Michael Polanyi's phrase, what results from this process is 'tacit knowledge' which is learned by doing science rather than by acquiring rules for doing it.[159]

Fish repeatedly makes this psychological claim about the priority of tacit knowledge over conscious application of rules throughout his works. He claims, for example, that the inventors of a satisfactory synthetic-bristle paint brush did not follow any general recipe in reaching their insight; rather, they simply realized one day that a paint brush is in many ways like a pump and therefore could be subjected to hydraulic analysis.[160] Fish also claims that a baseball pitcher who knows how to pitch 'literally carries it in his bones';[161] he does not apply a rule, theory, or algorithm when

[158] Ibid. at 278–9.

[159] Fish, 'Fish v. Fiss', above n. 153, at 1331–2 (quoting Thomas S. Kuhn, *The Structure of Scientific Revolutions* (2nd edn., Chicago: University of Chicago Press, 1970), 191).

[160] Fish, 'Dennis Martinez', above n. 139, at 1775–7 (citing Donald Schon, 'Generative Metaphor', in A. Ortony (ed.), *Metaphor and Thought* (New York: Cambridge University Press, 1979), 254).

[161] Ibid. at 1774.

he pitches. Similarly, basketball coaching is not a matter of giving the player recipes or rules for good playing. Good basketball playing applies 'a kind of knowledge that informs rules rather than follows from them'.[162] Likewise, linguistics errs insofar as it attempts to discover rules of linguistic competence that any speaker must possess. According to Fish, any such rules 'will be rules only within the silent or deep context that allowed them to emerge and become describable. Rather than being distinct from circumstantial (and therefore variable) conditions, linguistic knowledge is unthinkable apart from these circumstances. Linguistic knowledge is contextual rather than abstract'.[163] Finally, judges are not and cannot be guided by theories of judging; rather, their judging skill is a matter of tacit knowledge of the practices in which their judging is embedded: 'The internalized "know how" or knowledge of "the ropes" that practice brings is sufficient unto the day and no theoretical apparatus is needed to do what practice is already doing, that is providing the embedded agent with a sense of relevancies, obligation, directions for action, criteria, etc.'[164]

Fish thus has a very broad psychological claim that he wishes to defend: all activities that we do are not, and cannot be, guided by any theories (by which he means, rules, recipes, algorithms, and the like). Fish specifically applies this psychological claim to metaphysical and epistemological theories, too. If no theories are needed or possible for scientific discovery, good baseball pitching, successful basketball coaching, competent use of one's native tongue, or judging, then it follows that epistemological or metaphysical theories are not necessary or possible for such activities either. Specifically, a judge 'is not a theorist of any kind, at least when he is in the process of deciding' cases.[165] Rather,

> [a]t that moment he is listening to arguments with an ear already informed by a sense of what is and is not evidence, and of what, in the field of evidence, is weighty and conclusive. To be sure, any sense of the evidentiary will have its source in . . . some conventional system of assumptions . . . but the decisionmaker is not using that system (or any other); rather it is what he sees with . . . and he will see what he sees independently of whether his theory of knowledge (should he have one) is realist or conventionalist.[166]

Grant for the moment the truth of Fish's psychological claim. A standard rejoinder is that psychological truths cut no epistemological ice. Put more exactly, Fish's psychological claim is prima facie a claim made within the theory of discovery, not the theory of justification. It is a claim about how one discovers how to pitch, coach, judge, speak, or make scientific discoveries. Fish's discovery recipe is to 'hunch' ('trust the Force?')

[162] Fish, 'Fish v. Fiss', above n. 153, at 1330.
[163] Stanley Fish, 'Consequences', *Critical Inquiry*, 11 (1985), 433–58, at 438.
[164] Fish, 'Dennis Martinez', above n. 139, at 1790. [165] Ibid. at 1783. [166] Ibid.

based on one's tacit knowledge. Whatever its plausibility as an answer to the question of how one should go about discovering truths, this is not a very plausible answer to questions of justification, truth, or ontology. As is often pointed out in the philosophy of science and in ethics, recipes for discovery are not necessarily justifications showing such discoveries to be true;[167] still less are such recipes to be regarded as theories of what there is, what 'true' means, or what a sentence or word means. A good recipe for discovery of the solution to a difficult mathematical proof, for example, is sometimes to think about something other than the puzzle itself. When the solution comes to me, however, I cannot justify my belief that it is the solution by pointing out that I thought about something else. Rather, the justification lies elsewhere, namely, in the other truths of mathematics and logic and their implications for this problem.

Sometimes it seems that Fish's psychological claim about discovery is his only support for his antimetaphysical stance. For example, from the psychological observation that 'facts can only be known by persons, and persons are always situated in some institutional context', he moves immediately to his antimetaphysical conclusion: 'therefore facts are always context relative.'[168] When Fish's chain of inference from psychology—how we discover something—to ontology—how things are—is this abbreviated, he is simply confusing theories. To be more than yet another example of this familiar confusion, Fish's argument needs a second step.

Such a second step should assert: (1) the collapse of metaphysical theories of ontology, truth, logic, and meaning into a theory of justification, and (2) the further collapse of a theory of justification into a theory of discovery. Then the (psychological) conditions for discovery will also be the justification conditions for rational belief, will also be the truth conditions for the proposition believed. Then Fish wouldn't be confused, but profound.

Yet what is Fish's argument for this crucial equation of discovery conditions with justification conditions with truth conditions? Fish's only apparent argument here is to deny sense to any notions of justification or truth that are not just discovery recipes. As Fish says, paraphrasing Thompson Clark's own brand of scepticism: '[T]heories which seek to answer "philosophical" questions about what is "really" legitimate (or true, or known) undercut themselves. They demand answers that are entirely detached from practical constraints; and yet it is only from within a constrained

[167] See n. 18 above. Notice that the distinction between theories of discovery and theories of justification enjoys robust good health in antifoundationalist as well as foundationalist epistemologies. 'Take a cold shower' may be a good recipe for discovering that some proposition p is true. For a non-foundationalist, however, what justifies rational belief in p is not that a cold shower was taken, but that p coheres better with one's other beliefs than does p's negation.

[168] Fish, 'Pluralist Vision', above n. 148, at 497.

practice that asking the questions makes any sense.'[169] As Fish elsewhere puts it, it makes no sense to speak of there being 'a [foundational] knowledge above beliefs'.[170] 'One wonders . . . where one would have to be in order to have access to such knowledge,'[171] Fish speculates. He answers:

> [N]owhere; that is, we would not be in a particular or limited situation . . . informed by interests and concerns in relation to which something could be a fact that someone might know . . . [T]he very notion of a supra-contextual fact makes no sense since something that had no relation to the concerns of a particular human situation would not be a fact . . . [T]he state of being above all situations and therefore of being in none at all . . . is the state in which the very idea of knowledge is incoherent.[172]

Fish thus denies that justification or truth could be anything but the methods we use within a practice to discover 'truths' (i.e. truths relative to that practice) and bases his denial on the familiar denial of an external vantage point from which alternative notions of truth or justification could make sense.

We should ask of Fish's 'denial of the external' argument the same question we asked of Rorty's identical argument: from what viewpoint, context, or situation is Fish making his confident pronouncements about what is possible, what there is, and what makes sense? Fish does not seem to be taking Rorty's ultimately non-argumentative stance,[173] so it is tempting to construe Fish in the same way I alternatively construed Rorty, namely, to be making arguments internal to his metaphysician opponents' practices and then showing how their assertions contradict their presuppositions. But Fish is not after a contradiction in my or any other metaphysician's practices. He wants to show us that the world is such that our presuppositions cannot be met: the external point of view, or 'view from nowhere' of the realist metaphysician,[174] is not a vantage point from which we can gain knowledge. Fish's argument thus seems to be 'external criticism': he deems it a fact, not simply a problem of inconsistency in his opponents' practices, that the view from nowhere is not a possible viewpoint.

So Fish looks very much like he is doing the external metaphysics he so deplores: deplore everyone else's metaphysics from your own privileged glance at how things really are (namely, that there really is no way for anyone to say how things really are). Fish, like Rorty, is not unaware of this danger. Fish sees that his own 'anti-foundationalism cannot itself (without contradiction) be made into a foundation'[175] and attempts to sidestep the difficulty as follows:

[169] Fish, 'Dennis Martinez', above n. 139, at 1788 n. 43 (citing Thompson Clark, 'The Legacy of Scepticism', *Journal of Philosophy*, 69 (1972), 754–69).

[170] Fish, 'Pluralist Vision', above n. 148, at 497.

[171] Ibid.

[172] Ibid.

[173] But see text accompanying nn. 178–82 below.

[174] See n. 120 above.

[175] Fish, 'Dennis Martinez', above n. 139, at 1796 n. 60.

The thesis of anti-foundationalism is not that there are no foundations, but that whatever is taken to be foundational has to be established in the course of argument and debate and does not exist to the side of argument and debate. This thesis includes itself within its own scope, not in any self-contradictory sense, but in the sense that it too must make its way in the face of counterexamples and purportedly 'irrefutable' evidence. To put it another way, the assertion that everything is in principle challengeable does not in and of itself constitute a challenge to any assertion.[176]

In making this response (specifically to my earlier challenge to interpretivists to see if they could state their interpretivism in a way free of their own metaphysics), Fish is undone by his failure to attend to the difference between metaphysics and epistemology. Fish's statements could and should be agreed to by all non-foundationalists in epistemology, myself included. Non-foundationalists in epistemology concede that there are no incorrigible sense perceptions, analytic truths, or self-evidently true propositions that could serve as the objects of foundational beliefs. No belief, therefore, is immune to falsification. And Fish is right: to say this is not to say that all beliefs, including the one just stated, are false.

Yet Fish's interpretivism is not merely a defence of coherence (or non-foundational) epistemology. He also wants to show the senselessness of metaphysics—the senselessness of theories of ontology, truth, logic, meaning, and reference mentioned earlier. To show this without contradiction, it is not enough for Fish to avoid having any foundational belief. He also needs to avoid using the very notions of truth and existence whose sense he wishes to deny. How, then, can Fish claim that it is true that 'philosophical' questions about what is 'really . . . true' make no sense?[177] How can Fish claim that it is a fact that 'something that had no relation to the concerns of a particular human situation would not be a fact'.[178] In making such claims about truth and ontology, Fish seems to be using the very notions whose sense he is denying. To do so is contradictory.

To save himself from contradiction, ultimately Fish has to adopt the same non-argumentative stance that Rorty too adopts in the face of a like objection. Rather than seeing Fish as self-contradictory in doing metaphysics while proclaiming the senselessness of all metaphysics, perhaps Fish should be seen as making 'arguments', stating 'truths', or discovering 'facts', in a sense wholly relative to his own practices. Fish has recognized that there is a practice called 'the rhetorical practice of talking theory'[179] and, more generally, that 'theory . . . is itself a form of practice'.[180] Perhaps Fish's claims about truth and justification always being relative to a

176 Ibid. at 1784 n. 28. 177 Ibid. at 1788 n. 43.
178 Fish, 'Pluralist Vision', above n. 148, at 497.
179 Fish, 'Dennis Martinez', above n. 139, at 1791.
180 Fish, 'Consequences', above n. 163, at 452.

context, about facts being facts only as relative to human ends, are not as metaphysical as they seem; Fish is only engaging in his own brand of theory practice.

This interpretation of Fish's antimetaphysical claims reduces Fish from a metaphysician to a rhetorician, as he himself recognizes. His theory, under this interpretation, is 'no more (or less) than a kind of talk; it would be precisely the kind of talk one was advised to engage in when presenting one's decision' to some group who shares the practice and thus the rhetoric.[181] In short, Fish's interpretivism (within this rhetorical interpretation of it) is not an argument 'from nowhere' establishing the impossibility of arguments from nowhere, but 'a pragmatic strategy by means of which decisions are successfully inserted into a field of practice that requires of its decisions that they be filled with certain forms of talk, in this case with theory talk'.[182] Fish is thus not giving us a justification for abandoning metaphysics, only presentational strategies to be used to get others to abandon metaphysics if that is what we want.

I refrain from making the obvious rejoinder to this form of Fish interpretivism (namely, that Fish needs to pursue a different rhetorical strategy with me or with anyone who doesn't already want to get rid of metaphysics). Rather, I prefer to make a less obvious point against Fish here, one that is internal to his own theory-practice: consider how inconsistent this 'theory as a practice' point is with Fish's own psychological claim about practices, that is, that we never apply rules, algorithms, general recipes, or theories to the doing of a practice. If 'talking theory' is a practice—a rhetorical strategy for getting what we want, just like baseball pitching—then it too should be divorced from Fish's (or anyone else's) theorizing about how to carry on that practice. Recall that Fish's psychology postulates a divorce between all doings and theories about how doings should be done. If theorizing is just another doing, how (under Fish's psychology) can Fish tell us anything useful about how this doing is to be done?

I conclude that under none of the various interpretations of Fish's second step does Fish have a defensible argument. Yet without such a second step his overall argument collapses into a purely psychological claim about the best discovery route for practitioners of various disciplines to get at the truth. As such, even if the claim were true, it could not establish what Fish wants to establish with it. Metaphysical and epistemological theories would still be the theories by which we establish what are good literary or legal interpretations, even if those who practised in such fields as literary criticism or law did not use such theories as the routes to discover such truths. In my own case, my heavily metaphysical theory of

[181] Fish, 'Dennis Martinez', above n. 139, at 1791. [182] Ibid.

legal interpretation[183] would still be the standard for judging whether particular interpretations by judges or other scholars were correct or not, even if (granting Fish's psychological claim) I should not expect judges to use my theory as a decision procedure.[184]

We should turn from considering the relevance of Fish's psychological claim to considering its correctness. Even if it were relevant to his antimetaphysical conclusion, Fish's claim is wildly implausible as a general description of our psychology as we act. Consider one of his examples, the activity of judging.

We might divide the psychological process of deciding legal disputes into two stages. Call the first the 'tentative decision' stage, in which the judge reaches her initial inclination to decide a case one way rather than another. Call the second the opinion-writing stage, in which the judge then justifies to herself why the tentative decision she has reached is the right one. Fish's psychological claim about judging has to be that theorizing about how each of these judging phases ought to be done can have no impact on how judges actually do either of them.

About the first stage of judging, Fish's claim is reminiscent of those Legal Realist judges who confessed to 'hunching' their decisions rather than deducing them from the law.[185] Admittedly, the 'hunch' theory seems plausible at the tentative decision stage of judging. Let us therefore concede arguendo that the conscious phenomenology of judging is as they say: judges just hunch their tentative decisions. But surely no adequate psychology of decision-making should end with such conscious phenomenological descriptions. For even if the decision-maker experiences her decision as produced by 'tacit knowledge' whose source seems mysterious, that knowledge does not come from nowhere. Tacit knowledge (about judging, at least) is learned, just as the tacit knowledge exercised in playing the piano is learned. That knowledge comes from practice that is itself guided by a theory of how to play the piano well. Just because an accomplished piano player is someone whose laboriously acquired routines have receded from consciousness does not mean that his skills were always there, 'in his bones', so to speak. Theory's impact upon intuitive skills such as piano playing or the hunching of legal decisions may well precede in time later exercises of those skills; such effect of theory is still an effect, even on skills as intuitive as piano playing.

[183] See Moore, 'A Natural Law Theory', above n. 5.

[184] See ibid. at 396 n. 218, where I explicitly disavow any intent to give judges a psychological recipe for reaching decisions.

[185] See e.g. Joseph C. Hutcheson, Jr., 'The Judgment Intuitive', *Cornell Law Quarterly*, 14 (1929), 274–88. The Legal Realists thought such confessionals belay any significant role for logic in legal reasoning. For an accurate diagnosis of why such confessionals were irrelevant to using logic in justifying legal decisions, see Neil MacCormick, *Legal Reasoning and Legal Theory* (Oxford: Oxford University Press, 1978), 15–16.

Now let me take back the arguendo concession. Isn't it just dogmatic for Fish to equate judging, even in this first stage, with the exercise of physical skills like piano playing or pitching? Sometimes the phenomenology may be as Fish describes: the decision just comes to a judge. Just as often, however, the phenomenology of judging is not like piano playing at all. Judges think about how they should judge as they judge and direct their thoughts accordingly. They may consider, for example, whether it is proper to consider 'Framers' intent' in constitutional interpretation and, concluding one way or the other, decide accordingly. Indeed, we place judges in our pantheon of great judges in part because of such theorizing abilities, not only their great hunching capacities.

In the second stage of judging, Fish's psychological claim is not even prima facie plausible. Opinion writing is not an atheoretical activity. As they write opinions, judges think about and apply their theories of how to find the holdings of precedential cases, how to interpret statutes, what weight to give to industry customs. After all, in writing opinions judges are consciously seeking to state reasons justifying their decision as the right one.

Fish implicitly concedes as much about the opinion-writing stage. When writing opinions, according to Fish, judges

> are engaging in the practice of self-presentation . . . which is not the same thing (why on earth should it be?) as offering an account of how they actually did it . . . [Opinion writing] is not a mechanism by which decisions are generated, but the complex of rhetorical gestures to which one has recourse when a decision, already made, must be put into presentable form.[186]

Fish thus concedes the influence of theory and legal principle on opinion writing but seeks to make opinion writing a practice wholly separate from that of reaching a tentative decision. Fish slides from a correct observation—that giving justifying reasons in an opinion is not the same thing as describing the motivating reasons for an initial decision—to the incorrect conclusion that opinion writing is therefore mere rationalization of a decision already made on other grounds. In fact, however, judges sometimes change their tentative decisions precisely because they cannot find reasons that will produce a plausible opinion. As judges say at such times, 'The opinion just wouldn't write.'

Fish's basic psychological claim is thus not only irrelevant to his antimetaphysical conclusion; it also has the lack of grace to be false, and pretty obviously so. In closing, let me point to a third failing of Fish's psychological claim: it too presupposes a good deal of just the kind of metaphysics from which Fish's interpretivism was to save us.

[186] Fish, 'Dennis Martinez', above n. 139, at 1790.

One can see this by examining Fish's response to my objection that decisions consciously experienced as hunches may nonetheless be the products of theory-guided learning.[187] In discussing how one learns intuitively exercised skills like baseball batting or basketball shooting, Fish acknowledges that '[l]istening to theory talk may be part of the experience of becoming a practitioner' but then denies that any understanding of the theory listened to generates the tacit knowledge of how to bat or shoot.[188] Rather, such tacit knowledge is acquired independently of understanding and applying such theory talk (even though done contemporaneously with it). The baseball batter acquires such tacit knowledge in 'a trial-and-error attempt to match an example (e.g. Ted Williams' swing)';[189] a basketball coach points novice players to examples of good basketball shooting;[190] a scientific inventor sees 'painting as similar to pumping' without seeing what properties painting and pumping share.[191] All such use of theory talk—to nudge novices to learn their respective skills by paying attention to exemplars—Fish calls 'local hermeneutics'. In each case, 'the practitioner is being told, "In a situation like this here are some of the things you can do," where it is left to the agent to determine whether or not he has encountered a situation "like this" and which of the possible courses of action is relevant.'[192]

Fish is thus a nominalist about what the mind can grasp: it can grasp particulars, not (initially, at least) universals. Further, Fish must think, as Quine once speculated, that our minds have 'innate similarity spacings' in them,[193] for Fish believes that we can 'just see' similarity between particulars without seeing (and perhaps without there being) any of the universals that such particulars share as properties.

This is a possible metaphysics of mind, although not one that my 'full-blooded realism'[194] accepts. My only point here is that it is a metaphysical view, the kind Fish says he does not have. Fish thus illustrates again how impossible it is to avoid having any metaphysical views. Not only does he wax metaphysical in making out his 'impossibility of metaphysics' claim, [195] he also uses his metaphysics when he gets down to telling us how he thinks our minds work. Both lapses into metaphysics illustrate the lesson I was trying to teach in the article to which Fish has responded:[196] we are

[187] See text accompanying n. 185 above.

[188] Fish, 'Dennis Martinez', above n. 139, at 1775 n. 3.

[189] Ibid.

[190] See Fish, 'Fish v. Fiss', above n. 153, at 1329–30.

[191] Fish, 'Dennis Martinez', above n. 1398 at 1776.

[192] Fish, 'Consequences', above n. 163, at 434.

[193] W. V. O. Quine, 'Natural Kinds', in *Ontological Relativity and Other Essays* (New York: Columbia University Press, 1969), 114.

[194] See text accompanying nn. 26–7 above.

[195] See text accompanying nn. 176–8 above.

[196] See Moore, 'A Natural Law Theory', above n. 5, at 309–13.

all metaphysicians, both in our daily life judgements (e.g. about how the mind works) and in our occasional attempts to show that metaphysics is impossible. Fish's work is thus an exemplar from which we should draw (again) this lesson.

III. ALL KNOWLEDGE IN THE HUMAN SCIENCES AS INTERPRETIVE: PSYCHOANALYSIS AND DUALISTIC INTERPRETIVISM

Hermeneutics did not begin with claims as ambitious as those of Rorty and Fish, claims that seek to reorient our notions of metaphysics and epistemology across the board, for all discourses. There is a less ambitious form of interpretivism that claims as its domain the human sciences only, leaving the natural sciences to be accounted for in non-interpretivist terms.[197] The general idea is that the sciences of human behaviour are special. They deal with a special kind of data, one possessed of meaning and self-understanding, an attribute lacked by stones, chemicals, and other objects studied by the natural sciences. Such special data demand that we ask different questions, seek a different kind of understanding, and use a different method than the predictive/explanatory calculus of the natural sciences. Such a distinctive science is called 'hermeneutics', based on the Greek root meaning 'to interpret'.

Like Rorty's and Fish's interpretivist views, however, this less ambitious, or dualist hermeneutics, hopes to transcend metaphysics and epistemology, at least in the human sciences. If those sciences are not concerned with explaining or predicting phenomena, not concerned with accurate descriptions of things, not concerned with knowledge but with understanding, then metaphysical questions are as out of place as are the physical questions asked by a natural science approach to human behaviour. If one wants to understand a dream's meaning, for example, and not to explain what caused it to occur, asking questions like 'Did the wish the dream interpretation has revealed really exist, and did it cause the dream?' is as out of place as asking whether, in literary interpretation, David Copperfield really exists (in some fictional realm, presumably). A dualist interpretivist believes either that one cannot assign sense to such metaphysical questions or that, for non-explanatory activities like interpretation, such questions (even if meaningful) serve no purpose because they are irrelevant to the task of interpretation.

[197] For accessible introductions to the history of hermeneutics, see Josef Bleicher, *Contemporary Hermeneutics* (London: Routledge and Kegan Paul, 1980), 9–26; Wright, above n. 20, at 1–7; see also the very clear 'hermeneutics for lawyers' introduction in David Hoy, 'Interpreting the Law', *Southern California Law Review*, 58 (1985), 135–76.

Similarly, epistemological questions may seem out of place. Epistemology studies the justifications which transform the beliefs of a person into the knowledge of a rational being. Yet under this view of hermeneutics, the human sciences are not concerned with knowledge; they seek understanding, something distinct from the knowledge sought by the natural sciences. Moreover, understanding the meaning of some phenomena is often likened to understanding one's own mental states—you have strong intuitions about when you have such understanding, but justification of those intuitions seems out of place. ('How do you know?', as the ordinary language philosophers were so fond of pointing out, is an odd thing to say to someone who says, 'I am in pain.') Accordingly, there may seem to be no need for a general theory of justified belief (epistemology), justification itself being irrelevant to understanding.

The interpretivism I consider here I regard as an ambitious interpretivism, even if not as ambitious as that of Rorty and Fish, for two reasons: first, it is ambitious in the scope of its claim as to when interpretive methods are justified, which is for all the human sciences; second, it is ambitious in its claim that the activity of interpretation is warranted by the very phenomena it studies, that is, phenomena with meaning. This latter claim is that the only thing the human sciences can do is understand such phenomena by interpreting them, so that there is no choice (requiring justification) but to engage in interpretation. The world, if you will, provides all the warrant that is required for interpretation as an activity.

I shall explore several variations of this ambitious hermeneutics of the human sciences, concluding in the fourth and final section that this hermeneutics must become much more modest in both the scope and the groundedness it claims for interpretation if it is to be as free of metaphysics as it claims. To make the discussion more concrete, I shall focus on one of the human sciences, psychoanalysis, as my example. I do this in part because the hermeneutic literature is as well developed here as anywhere;[198] in part because psychoanalysis is often taken to represent both the human sciences and the natural sciences in its clinical and its metapsychological theories, respectively; and in part because (heeding Wittgenstein's caution against having an insufficient diet of examples in philosophy) psychoanalysis is not literary criticism, the favourite hermeneutic-activity example of so much recent legal theory discussion.[199]

[198] Indeed, psychoanalysis has become the model through which to understand hermeneutics for recent theorists like Habermas and Ricoeur. See Bleicher, *Contemporary Hermeneutics*, above n. 197, at 156, 227–8.

[199] See generally Dworkin, *Law's Empire*, above n. 66; Mitchell, *The Politics of Interpretation*, above n. 155; Abraham, 'Statutory Interpretation and Literary Theory', *Rutgers Law Review*, 32 (1980), 676–94; Walter Benn-Michaels, 'Against Formalism', *Poetics Today*, 1 (1979), 23–34; 'Symposium: Law and Literature', *Texas Law Review*, 60 (1982), 373; Stephen C. Yeazell,

A. Metaphysically Dualist Interpretivism

The interpretive turn in psychoanalysis has been motivated in part by the desire of some psychoanalytic theorists to insulate their discipline from the standards of criticism appropriate to the natural sciences.[200] In fact, there is something of a salvage operation going on here, throwing out part of the theory, the metapsychology, in order to save the rest, the clinical theory.[201] The idea is that the mechanistic Freud of the metapsychologies sought natural-science style explanations for phenomena like dreams, while the hermeneutic Freud sought only to interpret dreams, to find their meaning. Given the doubtful scientific validity of Freud's metapsychological explanations, the move is to save the clinical theory from a like fate of disconfirmation by proclaiming that it is not an explanatory science at all, but a hermeneutic art. It therefore can only be judged internally, by its own standards of what counts as a good interpretation; it cannot be judged by the external standards of natural science. Metaphysics, like metapsychology, goes by the board under this view of the clinical theory.

My first interpretation of this interpretive turn in clinical psychoanalysis is that it aligns itself in the classical hermeneutical tradition of Dilthey,[202] carried on into the twentieth century by Emilio Betti and others.[203] For our purposes only two aspects of this tradition require mention. The first is the 'special realm' claim made to justify interpretation as the

'Convention, Fiction, and Law', *New Literary History*, 13 (1981), 89–102. As Tom Grey has pointed out, literature is not the obvious hermeneutic analogy for law because only under some versions does literary criticism have a theory of authority for its texts. Thomas C. Grey, 'Constitution as Scripture', *Stanford Law Review*, 37 (1984), 1–25. Of the law and literature comparativists, only Ron Garet seems to have seen this point clearly, for he restricts his analysis to Gardner's kind of 'moral fiction' criticism. Ronald R. Garet, 'Comparative Normative Hermeneutics', *Southern California Law Review*, 58 (1985), 35–134.

[200] For an early and influential critique of psychoanalytic theory in the philosophy of science, see Ernest Nagel, 'Methodological Issues in Psychoanalytic Theory', in S. Hook (ed.), *Psychoanalysis, Scientific Method, and Philosophy* (New York: New York University Press, 1959). For the more recent collections of essays in the philosophy of science, see L. Laudan (ed.), *Mind and Medicine, Explanation in Psychiatry and the Biomedical Sciences* (Berkeley: University of California Press, 1983); *Mind, Psychoanalysis, and Science*, above n. 46.

[201] See Adolf Grunbaum, *The Foundations of Psychoanalysis* (Berkeley: University of California Press, 1984), 1–94 (discussing much of the literature of the clinical theory salvagers); see also Morris N. Eagle, *Recent Developments in Psychoanalysis* (New York: McGraw-Hill, 1984), 147–81; Moore, *Law and Psychiatry*, above n. 46 (both also discussing this literature).

[202] Wilhelm Dilthey, *Gesammelte Schriften* (2nd edn., Leipzig and Berlin: Teubner, 1927). For discussion of Dilthey and his predecessors in 19th-century, hermeneutics, see Bleicher, above n. 197, at 11–26.

[203] Emilio Betti, 'Hermeneutics as the General Methodology of the Geisteswissenschaften', in Bleicher, *Contemporary Hermeneutics*, above n. 197, at 51–94. For other contemporary hermeneuts in the Diltheian tradition, see Robin George Collingwood, *The Idea of History* (2nd edn., Oxford: Clarendon Press, 1967); see also Paul Rabinow and William Sullivan, 'The Interpreting Turn', in P. Rabinow and W. Sullivan (eds)., *Interpretive Social Science* (Berkeley: University of California Press, 1979).

method peculiarly appropriate to the human sciences. This is the claim that meaningful phenomena exist in a different way, on a different level, than the meaningless phenomena that are the subject of the natural sciences. As Betti puts it, the meaningful 'belongs to a level fundamentally different from the physical',[204] requiring its own goal (understanding, not knowledge) and its own method (interpretation, not explanation). The second claim is that interpretations in social science, although different than explanations in natural science, are no less objective, no less capable of being true or false. Although 'objectivity means something quite different in the Geisteswissenschaften compared with the natural sciences',[205] nonetheless understandings and interpretations in the former can be correct or incorrect depending upon whether they 'correspond fully to the meaning underlying the text as an objectivation of mind'.[206]

I call this a metaphysically dualist kind of ambitious interpretivism because the Diltheian tradition quite explicitly embraces a dualist metaphysical view in order to justify its turn towards interpretation. The metaphysical claim that grounds interpretation is that minds (and mind-dependent entities like texts and human actions) exist in a way different from stones, avalanches, and brains in that minds are meaningful and stones are not.[207] This last claim is metaphysical because it itself is not presented as an interpretation but as a true description of the essence of mind and mind-dependent entities.[208]

A closer look at the interpretive turn in psychoanalysis reveals that it too is often metaphysically dualist in its justification of the claim that clinical psychoanalysis, being interpretive in character, can be sealed off from the external criticism of natural science. Habermas, for example, tells us that patients in psychoanalysis are the ones who must validate interpretations because only they have privileged access to the subjective meanings that are to be interpreted. This dependence of interpretation on patient validation renders clinical psychoanalysis methodologically distinct from the natural sciences, where intersubjective validation methods are possible.[209] More recently, Atwood and Stolorow would justify separating clinical psychoanalysis from normal science on similar grounds:

A science is defined by its domain of inquiry . . . [P]sychoanalysis seeks to illuminate phenomena that emerge within a specific psychological field constituted by the intersection of two subjectivities—that of the patient and that of the analyst

[204] Betti, 'Hermeneutics', above n. 203, at 53. [205] Ibid. at 63. [206] Ibid. at 79.

[207] The metaphysical dualist position is usually associated with Descartes. The modern classic description and critique of Cartesian dualism is in Gilbert Ryle, *The Concept of Mind* (London: Hutcheson, 1949).

[208] Rorty clearly perceives this and criticizes the Diltheian tradition on just this ground: *Consequences*, above n. 68, at 191–210.

[209] Jurgen Habermas, *Knowledge and Human Interests* (Boston: Beacon Press, 1971), 261–6; see also Grunbaum, *Foundations of Psychoanalysis*, above n. 201, at 21–43.

. . . [P]sychoanalysis is pictured here as a science of the intersubjective, focused on the interplay between the differently organized subjective worlds of the observer and the observed. The observational stance is always one within, rather than outside, the intersubjective field . . . being observed, a fact that guarantees the centrality of introspection and empathy as the methods of observation.[210]

Similarly, the late Heinz Kohut[211] has argued that the clinical theory must be formulated in concepts that are 'experience near' because it is subjective experience (of the self) that is the data of psychoanalysis. This, for Kohut, too, results in 'empathetic understanding' being the observation mode in clinical psychoanalysis, as distinguished from the natural sciences.[212]

Other hermeneutic psychoanalysts focus on intentionality as the mark of clinical psychoanalysis. Thus, the late George Klein argued: 'The central objective of psychoanalytic clinical explanation is the reading of intentionality; behavior, experience, testimony are studied for meaning in this sense.'[213] Since such a position 'requires a clear-cut stand on the relation of "mind" to "body"',[214] Klein too was led to argue that meaning is metaphysically distinct from physical objects: '[P]rinciples of meaning perceivable in the psychoanalytic situation are on a level which is not deducible from a physiological schema, no matter what the physiological model.'[215]

Finally, consider Roy Schafer's turn to hermeneutics for the philosophical basis of his 'action-language' conceptualization of clinical psychoanalysis.[216] According to the hermeneutic Schafer (as opposed to the ordinary language philosopher Schafer examined later[217]), what makes clinical psychoanalysis 'an interpretive discipline whose practitioners aim to develop a particular kind of systematic account of human action'[218] is the existence of objects that are created by narratives and the 'narrative structures' that guide narratives.

[210] George E. Atwood and Robert D. Stolorow, *Structures of Subjectivity* (Hillsdale, NJ: Analytic Press, 1984), 41.

[211] See Heinz Kohut, *The Analysis of Self* (New York: International Universities Press, 1971), and *The Restoration of the Self* (New York: International Universities Press, 1977).

[212] See Eagle, *Recent Developments in Psychoanalysis*, above n. 201, at 150–2. Similar thoughts are expressed by Barnaby B. Barratt, 'Freud's Psychology as Interpretation', *Psychoanalysis & Contemporary Science*, 5 (1976), 443, 467–8 ('psychoanalysis cannot be objectivistic because there can be no defined demarcation between its epistemological subject and object'); by H. J. Home, 'The Concept of Mind', *International Journal of Psycho-Analysis*, 47 (1966), 42–9; and by Ricoeur, insofar as he eschews the observational method of normal science for the special validation of empathy in therapy, see Grunbaum, *Foundations of Psychoanalysis*, above n. 201, at 43–69.

[213] George S. Klein, *Psychoanalytic Theory* (New York: International Universities Press, 1976), 26.

[214] Ibid. at 61.

[215] Ibid.

[216] Roy Schafer, 'Narration in the Psychoanalytic Dialogue', *Critical Inquiry*, 7 (1980), 29–53.

[217] See text accompanying nn. 267–70 below.

[218] Schafer, 'Narration', above n. 216, at 29.

We are forever telling stories about others. These others, too, may be viewed as figures or other selves constituted by narrative actions. Other people are constructed in the telling about them; more exactly, we narrate others just as we narrate selves. The other person, like the self, is not something one has or encounters as such, but an existence one tells.[219]

Since narration as an activity frees us from any ontological constraints, supposedly even Schafer's favoured 'action-language' conceptualization of the clinical theory is not based on any metaphysics of personal agency, but rather on a choice of narrative structure: 'Choosing action as the suitable narrative language allows the analyst to begin to retell many inability narrations as disclaimings of action. . . . In analytic narration, one is not governed by the ordinary conventions.'[220]

Preferable to such metaphysical evasions as Schafer's is Paul Ricoeur's forthright admission that the interpretive turn in psychoanalysis rests on metaphysical foundations. Ricoeur has consistently maintained that the psychic is 'a region of being distinct from the region of nature'[221] and that 'psychoanalysis deals with psychic reality and not with material reality'.[222]

Whether stated up front or not, it should be plain as day that the 'special data' claim is based on a dualistic metaphysics that is idealist when it comes to the human sciences. Subjective experience with its epistemic claims of privileged access and empathy, the intentionality of mental states, and the irreducibility (to causation) of personal agency are the three features of mind and mind-dependent entities (texts) that defenders of metaphysical dualism have relied on for centuries. This form of interpretivism thus cannot license any antimetaphysical conclusions. Not only is the Diltheian tradition in clinical psychoanalysis metaphysical in its justification of its interpretive methods, as just discussed; the interpretive method is justifies is also metaphysical, adopting an idealist theory of truth as to when interpretations are correct, when understanding is achieved.[223] Accordingly, if any other discipline (such as law) were to mimic this version of the interpretive turn in psychoanalysis, it could hardly do so under the illusion that it was getting away from metaphysics. Moreover, the metaphysics this kind of interpretive turn buys into is very problematic, suffering as it does not only the problems of both realism (about the physical world) and idealism (about minds), but also the problem of relating two such different realms of being.[224]

219 Ibid. at 35.

220 Ibid. At 47.

221 Paul Ricoeur, *Freud and Philosophy* (New Haven: Yale University Press, 1970), 363.

222 Paul Ricoeur, *Hermeneutics and the Human Sciences* (New York: Cambridge University Press, 1981), 251.

223 See nn. 205–6 above and accompanying text.

224 I briefly explore problems for metaphysical dualism in Michael S. Moore, 'Causation and the Excuses', *California Law Review*, 73 (1985), 1091–149, at 1121–4, reprinted as ch. 12 of *Placing Blame*, above n. 43.

B. The Interpretivism of 'Philosophical Hermeneutics'

Many psychoanalytic interpretivists wish to retain the clinical theory's insulation from science's external criticism yet do not wish to purchase this insulation with the Diltheian tradition's dualism and idealism. One of psychoanalysis's more clear-headed theorists, B. B. Rubinstein, noted that in referring to aspects of a separate mental realm, it is doubtful that 'many psychoanalysts who . . . speak as if they used the high-level theoretical terms are willing to accept the dualistic implications of their usage'.[225]

Such theorists have two seemingly less metaphysical routes open to them through which they might justify their view of the clinical theory as beyond the criticism of natural science. One such route is that of 'semantic ascent', the method of ordinary language philosophy explored in the following subsection. The other, explored in this section, is what is sometimes called 'philosophical' (or 'existential' or 'phenomenological') hermeneutics.[226]

Philosophical hermeneutics radically rejects all metaphysical positions as I have defined them. Martin Heidegger's lifetime project was to show how realism, idealism, and scepticism—indeed, the entire metaphysical debate since Plato and Aristotle—must be left behind us,[227] for such a debate was insufficiently fundamental. In Heidegger's language, it has been only ontic, not ontological. That is, the debate has been only about individual things and the individual qualities and relations they possess—in Heidegger's language, about 'beings'. Fundamental ontology, by contrast, deals with the 'being of beings', usually denoted, 'Being'. All of our 'ontic' scribblings and scratchings—what I have been calling metaphysics

[225] Benjamin B. Rubinstein, 'Psychoanalytic Theory and the Mind-Body Problem', in N. Greenfield and W. Lewis (eds.), *Psychoanalysis and Current Biological Thought* (Madison: University of Wisconsin Press, 1965), 45.

[226] The labels vary according to the development stage emphasized. The interpretivism of Martin Heidegger, Hans-Georg Gadamer and, to some extent, Habermas and Ricoeur, began in phenomenology, was influenced by existentialism, and yet is best referred to by the more neutral 'philosophical'. See Bleicher, *Contemporary Hermeneutics*, above n. 197, at 9–127 (discussing the history of this form of interpretivism).

Although Heidegger is clearly a very ambitious interpretivist about all knowledge and not merely an ambitious interpretivist about the human sciences, I consider his brand of interpretivism here mainly because Gadamer, the main actor in this tradition, is not as ambitious in his interpretivism. See ibid. at 109, 120 (interpreting Gadamer to distinguish between the Geisteswissenschaften and natural science on the basis that the former has an object of study with a historical character while the latter studies an object with its own autonomous laws of development).

[227] Of Heidegger's many works, *Sein und Zeit* (Berlin, 1926) is central. Its 6th edn. translation is *Being and Time*, trans. J. Macquarrie and E. Robinson (New York: Harper and Row, 1962).

and epistemology—are only our interpretations of Being, interpretations that misconceive their object.[228]

How one understands (properly interprets) Being is not an easy question to answer. We get glimpses, Heidegger tells us, in our daily life where our prereflective understanding is already in play.[229] This understanding is prelinguistic, as it must be, since our subject-predicate grammar inevitably channels our thought toward beings, rather than Being. We also get glimpses in the pre-Socratic Greek philosophers' work that was not contaminated by the Western philosophy metaphysical debate.[230] Basically, however, Being will seem incomprehensible to us, given that we will try to understand it verbally, which would make it into an object referred to by a concept—just the metaphysics of beings that Heidegger wishes to leave behind.

One of my persistent objections is also appropriate here: this seems to be an extraordinarily metaphysical ('Metaphysical?') way to write off all metaphysics.[231] Yet let me pass it by, for Heideggerians would undoubtedly deflect it by saying that Heidegger's 'fundamental ontology' seems metaphysical to me only because talk of Being means the speaker already is making ontological commitments to a thing (namely, the thinghood of all things). Being, they might say, cannot be understood verbally; to approach it, we must rely on our preverbal knowledge of it.

I wish to pursue a different objection, one which will become apparent once we see how Heidegger's project gets realized in Gadamer's form of interpretivism.[232] Two aspects of Gadamer's interpretivism merit attention here, both due directly to Gadamer's Heideggerian understanding of understanding. One is the proper reliance by all interpreters on their 'prejudices'. All understanding, Gadamer holds, is built on our own pre-judgements, or prejudices. Gadamer sees himself as attempting

> to restore to its rightful place a positive concept of prejudice that was driven out of our linguistic usage by the French and English Enlightenments. . . . Prejudices are not necessarily unjustified and erroneous, so that they inevitably distort the truth. In fact, the historicity of our existence entails that prejudices . . . constitute the

[228] For explications of Heidegger along these lines, see Bleicher, *Contemporary Hermeneutics*, above n. 197, at 98–103; John Llewelyn, *Beyond Metaphysics* (Atlantic Highlands, NJ: Humanities Press, 1985), 3–29, 173–84; Rorty, *Consequences*, above n. 68, at 37–59.

[229] See Llewelyn, *Beyond Metaphysics*, above n. 228, at 4.

[230] Martin Heidegger, *An Introduction to Metaphysics*, trans. R. Mannheim (Garden City, NY: Doubleday, 1961).

[231] This is ultimately Rorty's objection to Heidegger as well, despite Rorty's and Heidegger's affinity in writing off metaphysics and epistemology. See Rorty, *Consequences*, above n. 68, at 42, 52–4.

[232] Hans-Georg Gadamer, *Truth and Method* (London: Sheed and Ward, 1975). Two Gadamer exegeses relating him to Heidegger are: Bleicher, above n. 197, at 97, 108–27, and Llewelyn, above n. 228, at 99–126.

initial directedness of our whole ability to experience. Prejudices . . . are simply conditions whereby we experience something—whereby what we encounter says something to us.[233]

Prejudice—the knowledge we bring to an interpretive question—is what makes interpretations possible because it allows us to invest what we are interpreting with meaning.

This sounds highly subjectivist, but actually Gadamer is much more a conventionalist (if one may be pardoned for using these ontic terms). Gadamer recognizes that we wish to distinguish between legitimate and arbitrary prejudices; he does so by reinforcing some prejudices but not others with tradition: 'Understanding is not to be thought of so much as an action of one's subjectivity, but as the placing of oneself within a tradition, in which past and present are constantly fused.'[234]

The second point follows from this view of prejudice's role in interpretation and understanding. There is, for Gadamer, no question to be asked about the validity (correctness, truth) of an interpretation if that question seeks an interpretation's correspondence to something other than the interpreter's prejudices. Gadamer explicitly rejects the Diltheian tradition, inasmuch as the latter makes the correctness of an interpretation turn on its correspondence with the ideas that prompted the text being interpreted. For Gadamer, interpretation is a dialogue between the interpreter (with his prejudices) and the text.[235]

This was Heidegger's own position about the question of validity in interpretation. As described by Ricoeur:

With Heidegger's radical manner of questioning [about Being], the problems that initiated our investigation not only remain unresolved but are lost from sight. . . . How can the conflict of rival interpretations be arbitrated? These problems are not properly considered in a fundamental hermeneutics, and this by design: this hermeneutics is intended not to resolve them but to dissolve them.[236]

Gadamer too refuses to have a theory about when an interpretation is correct, when a proper understanding has been reached. He sees himself alongside Heidegger, raising more basic questions about the possibility of understanding as such.[237]

233 Hans-Georg Gadamer, 'The Universality of the Hermeneutical Problem', in Bleicher, *Contemporary Hermeneutics*, above n. 197, at 128, 133.

234 Gadamer, *Truth and Method*, above n. 232, at 258.

235 For the relation between Gadamer and the Diltheian tradition, see Bleicher, *Contemporary Hermeneutics*, above n. 197, at 122–3; see also Llewelyn, *Beyond Metaphysics*, above n. 228, at 107; Hoy, 'Interpreting the Law', above n. 197, at 137–41.

236 Paul Ricoeur, *The Conflict of Interpretation* (Evanston: Northwestern University Press, 1974), 10.

237 See Llewelyn, *Beyond Metaphysics*, above n. 228 at 114–24.

My objection is a familiar one, voiced as it has been within hermeneutics by theorists as diverse as Betti,[238] Apel,[239] and Ricoeur:[240] whatever the merits of the Heidegger/Gadamer problematic about Being, the resulting interpretivism is empty of implications for interpretation's practice in law, psychoanalysis, or elsewhere. It has nothing to say about when an interpretation of a dream or a statute is a good one. As Ricoeur puts it, discussing Heidegger: '[H]e gives us no way to show in what sense historical understanding . . . is derived from this primordial understanding [of Being].'[241]

This objection gathers force when we consider how Gadamer's 'interpretation as dialogic process' has worked out in psychoanalysis. Many of the same psychoanalytic theorists we discussed in the earlier section have attempted to incorporate dialogue and self-understanding into their theories of interpretation in psychoanalysis. They flounder on the question that Heidegger and Gadamer refuse to answer, the question of validity.

Barrett, for example, criticizes Ricoeur for his 'failure to elaborate any clear standards by which hermeneutic propositions might be validated'.[242] Barrett, himself a devotee of the critical theorists of the Frankfurt school,[243] treats Ricoeur as a philosophical hermeneut who does not even see 'the necessity of establishing criteria by which rival interpretations within psychoanalysis might be adjudicated'.[244] Barrett then gives his own criterion for an interpretation's validity in psychoanalysis:

> Although [the patient's] nonadoption of an interpretation does not constitute refutation, an interpretation is valid if successfully adopted, that is, it leads to further valid interpretations, to increased self-understanding, and to the continuation of self-formative processes. In a certain sense, interpretations are adjudicated by the subject to whom they pertain, and thus meaning is created when subject and analyst mutually agree about the lucidity of a particular narrative . . . an interpretation is valid if it is consistent with the facts and if it implies an advance in critical self-understanding which motivates the continuation of self-formative processes which had been arrested; a good interpretation contributes to the task of consciousness, that is, the creation of authentic discourse. This is not the public standard of 'cure' but the personal, intersubjective criterion of insight and the appropriation of meaning. In sum, interpretations are adopted for their emancipatory value.[245]

[238] Betti, 'Hermeneutics', above n. 203, at 51, 73–84.

[239] For the relationship between Apel and Gadamer, see Bleicher, *Contemporary Hermeneutics*, above n. 197, at 147.

[240] Ricoeur, *Conflict*, above n. 236, at 10.

[241] Ibid. Like Ricoeur, Rorty also objects that unless Heidegger can connect his fundamental ontology of Being with real-life problems, all we get is 'an all too empty and formal, though often emotionally charged and mystically religious, thinking of absolute unity' (*Consequences*, above n. 68, at 48).

[242] Barratt, 'Freud's Psychology', above n. 212, at 458.

[243] Ibid. at 445 n. 3.

[244] Ibid. at 462.

[245] Ibid. at 463.

Despite the apparent embarrassment of riches in Barrett's criteria of validity, I take this to be a non-answer to the question of when an interpretation in psychoanalysis is correct. The patient's adoption is mentioned, only to be dropped in favour of successful adoption. Success, in turn, is partly defined circularly, in terms of valid interpretation. More promising is the definition of success in terms of increased self-understanding and unblocking of self-formative processes. Yet these notions are themselves not to be understood in the sense that there was a pre-existing self, whose nature was to be grasped by a correct interpretation; rather, meaning and authentic discourse are created by a good interpretation. In this sense a good interpretation continues the conversation, with no apparent standard of what the conversation has to be about to be correct.

Barrett is not idiosyncratic. Others also assert subjectivist and dialogic 'criteria of validity' in psychoanalysis, including Robert Steele,[246] Roy Schafer, [247] and, more recently, Atwood and Stolorow.[248]

None of the criteria they offer answers the question of validity any better than Gadamer's philosophical hermeneutics. How could they, when each, like Gadamer, thinks of interpretation as a kind of conversation that is not about anything whose nature can be used as a check on accuracy? Philosophical hermeneutics cannot be the brand of interpretivism that any theoretician should want for her discipline—on pain of losing any discipline at all.

C. Linguistically Dualist Interpretivism

The second form of explicitly antimetaphysical, ambitious interpretivism that has found favour in psychoanalysis is based on the insights about language found in ordinary language philosophy. An entire generation of 'ordinary language' philosophers purported to discover a fundamental sundering in our speech about ourselves, a sundering sometimes called 'linguistic dualism'.[249] I do not have the space to describe in any detail

[246] Robert Steele, 'Psychoanalysis and Hermeneutics', *International Review of Psycho-Analysis*, 6 (1979), 389–416, at 405.

[247] Schafer, 'Narration', above n. 216, at 50–1.

[248] Atwood and Stolorow, *Structures of Subjectivity*, above n. 210, at 100–1.

[249] Charles Landesman, 'The New Dualism in the Philosophy of Mind', *Review of Metaphysics*, 19 (1965), 329–45, at 330; Richard J. Bernstein, *Praxis and Action* (Philadelphia: University of Pennsylvania Press, 1971), 230–304. One can distinguish at least eight variants of Ryle's general point, see generally Ryle, *Concept of Mind*, above n. 207, that there is a category difference between 'mind talk' and 'body talk', each of which seeks to articulate one or more distinctive features of 'mind talk': (1) Roderick Chisholm's view that mental state words take Intentional objects, but physical state words do not, Roderick M. Chisholm, *Perceiving* (Ithaca, NY: Cornell University Press, 1957), 168–73; (2) the view (heavily influenced by the later Wittgenstein) that the language of human action differs in kind with the

each of these doctrines of categorical difference, let alone critique them. Instead, I shall focus on the most general and influential account of the categorical difference between mental and physical concepts, that of Gilbert Ryle.

Ryle originated the general notion that there was a categorical difference between mind talk and body talk and illustrated that difference by focusing on the usage of the word, 'exist'. Ryle thought he detected an ambiguity in the word 'exist'.[250] 'Exist', he thought, is like 'rising', in that it has different senses. It would be nonsense to say in a single sentence that tides, hopes, and the average age of death were rising; that would be to elide three meanings of the word into one usage.[251] Similarly, Ryle thought, one could not meaningfully say that physical causes of behaviour and mental causes of behaviour both exist, because 'exist' means something different when predicated of physical things than it does when predicated of mental things.[252] Ryle thought he could detect such an ambiguity in 'exist', not by looking to the differing natures of the things for which existence is predicated, but simply by looking at how the word 'exist' is used in ordinary speech.[253] There were, Ryle noted, different questions one could appropriately ask about 'mental', as opposed to 'physical', things.

Ryle's point was emphatically not to say that there are two kinds of existence—that would be the kind of metaphysical dualism that he so

concepts of physical causation, A. I. Melden, *Free Action* (London: Routledge and Kegan Paul, 1961), 90; Norman Malcolm, 'The Conceivability of Mechanism', *Philosophical Review*, 77 (1968), 45–72, at 47–9; see also G. E. M. Anscombe, *Intention* (2nd edn., Ithaca, NY: Cornell University Press, 1963), 18–25; A. C. MacIntyre, *The Unconscious* (London: Routledge and Kegan Paul, 1958); R. S. Peters, *The Concept of Motivation* (London: Routledge and Kegan Paul, 1958); Peter Winch, *The Idea of a Social Science* (London: Routledge and Kegan Paul, 1958); (3) the view that talk of reasons is evaluative discourse, whereas talk of physical events is merely descriptive, A. R. Louch, *Explanation and Human Action* (Berkeley: University of California Press, 1966); (4) the view that use of mental words in the first person expresses one's mental states but does not describe anything, Ludwig Wittgenstein, *Philosophical Investigations* (Oxford: Basil Blackwell, 1958), 89–90; (5) the view that first-person, present-tense use of mental words is only proper if questions of justification (how one knows, what observations or inferences one has made, etc.) are ruled out, Anscombe, *Intention*, above at 57–60; Norman Malcolm, 'Behaviourism as a Philosophy of Psychology', in T. Wann (ed.), *Behaviorism and Phenomenology* (Chicago: University of Chicago Press, 1964), 141, 149–52; (6) the view that action and mental state concepts logically depend upon the concept of rules and rule-following, while physical concepts do not, Winch, *Idea*, above, at 24–39; A. I. Melden, 'Action', *Philosophical Review*, 65 (1956), 523, 538–41; (7) the view that mental state concepts are not used (appearances to the contrary notwithstanding) to explain human actions but only to redescribe them, while other concepts may be used in genuinely explanatory sentences, MacIntyre, *The Unconscious*, above, at 72; Melden, 'Action', above at 90; and (8) the once-held view of Ryle's one-time student, Daniel Dennett, that mental talk is 'fused' (i.e. is used only in highly limited contexts—for example, the word 'dint') while body talk is not, D. C. Dennett, *Content and Consciousness* (London: Routledge, 1969), 3–18.

250 See generally Ryle, *Concept of Mind*, above n. 207.

251 Ibid. at 23.

252 Ibid. at 22.

253 Ibid. at 22–3.

elegantly attacked. Rather, Ryle saw himself as having no metaphysics, arguing at the level of language alone. From the ordinary usage of the word 'exist', one can detect an ambiguity in its 'meaning', where 'meaning' is construed as 'systematic connections with other words'. Armed with this view of the meaning of 'exist', Ryle thought he could avoid taking any metaphysical position about the relation of mind to body. For one cannot meaningfully assert that both minds and bodies exist (dualism) or that only one or the other existed (idealism, physicalism). With this view of the meaning of 'exist', all of the traditional metaphysical positions about mind and body become senseless.[254]

A generation of ordinary language philosophers followed Ryle's lead and began charting the systematic relations they saw in the ordinary usage of mental terms like 'wanting', 'feeling', 'believing', 'intending', etc. All of these states could be said to exist in the same sense of 'exist' because they are all systematically linked together in ordinary usage. Terms, however, like 'force', 'field', and 'velocity', which are not part of the same pattern of ordinary English usage, cannot share the sense of 'exist' proper to mental terms; physical terms belong in a different category.

It should be no surprise that this view came to be known as linguistic dualism, since it explicitly rejected metaphysical dualism while claiming nonetheless that language was sundered by a categorical divide. Those who crossed this divide to raise questions external to one discourse or the other were convicted of the ordinary language philosopher crime of making a 'category mistake', and one form of employment for philosophers was to reformulate the sayings of the uninitiated to correct that error. Freud and other psychoanalysts in particular were chided for their sloppiness in talking of 'motive-forces', as one example, or for seeking ties to physiology and drive states.[255]

The payoffs in psychoanalysis from Ryle's doctrine of category difference have been the same as the payoffs from adopting the Diltheian tradition's version of interpretivism: if one but adds to Ryle's notions the ideas that mind talk is interpretive talk (not explanatory talk), and that clinical theory in psychoanalysis is full of mind talk whereas physical science (including psychoanalysis's own metapsychology) is not, then one has all the justification one needs to conceive of the clinical theory as an interpretive enterprise insulated from the external criticisms of natural science. Even better, this kind of justification, unlike that offered by the Diltheian tradition, is itself free of any metaphysical presuppositions. If it could be pulled off, psychoanalysts would be justified in developing their own

[254] See generally Ryle, *Concept of Mind*, above n. 207, at 22–3.

[255] See e.g. Anthony Flew, 'Motives and the Unconscious', in H. Feigl and M. Scriven (eds.), *The Foundations of Science and the Concepts of Psychoanalysis and Psychology* (Minneapolis: University of Minnesota Press, 1956), 172.

interpretive discipline (clinical psychoanalysis), to be judged by its own autonomous standards and not by the (ultimately metaphysical) questions of truth, ontology, and reference of natural-science-style discourse.

As I understand it, this is the general strategy of theorists like Paul Ricoeur,[256] George Klein,[257] Merton Gill,[258] Ilham Dilman,[259] and Roy Schafer.[260] These theorists take the distinction between clinical theory and metapsychology to be between two different 'logical planes'[261] or two different 'types of discourse'.[262] The language of clinical theory is the language of mind, meaning, and the humanities, while the language of metapsychology is the language of physical events, mechanisms, and natural science. Given that these are two different categories of discourse, the two theories have nothing to do with each other but are interpretations (or explanations, as the case may be) sufficient unto themselves in their respective realms of discourse.

Consider two more concrete examples of this strategy in psychoanalysis. In the first, Ilham Dilman attempts to separate the clinical notion of a mental state being unconscious from the metapsychological (and ultimately, physicalistic) notion that the brain is functionally organized such that there is a 'system Ucs', to use Freud's term.[263] Dilman bases his argument for this categorical separation on the general epistemic thesis of Freud's clinical theory. Freud's early clinical ideal of 'making the unconscious conscious' is only attained by the recapture through memory (rather than by an inference from evidence) of what was previously unconscious. Dilman founds two arguments on this clinical ideal. First, it is a kind of category mistake to think that one could have such privileged access to a theoretical entity, as one would if the pretheoretical unconscious were also the System Ucs of Freud's topographical theory. As Dilman puts it:

> [O]ne cannot talk of seeing an electron (not even as a possibility one might wish to speculate about) without sinning against logic; for if the concept of an electron is theoretical . . . then seeing cannot have a place in statements in which the concept

[256] Ricoeur, *Freud and Philosophy*, above n. 221, at 358–75.

[257] Klein, *Psychoanalytic Theory*, above n. 213, at 1–3.

[258] Merton M. Gill, 'Metapsychology Is Not Psychology', in M. Gill and P. Holzman (eds.), *Psychology Versus Metapsychology* (New York: International Universities Press, 1976), 71, 71–5.

[259] Ilham Dilman, 'Is the Unconscious a Theoretical Construct?', *Monist*, 56 (1972), 313–42, 'The Unconscious', *Mind*, 68 (1959), 446–73, and 'Intentions and the Unconscious', in *Mind, Psychoanalysis, and Science*, above n. 46, at 169.

[260] Roy Schafer, *A New Language for Psychoanalysis* (New Haven: Yale University Press, 1976), 9–15.

[261] George S. Klein, 'Freud's Two Theories of Sexuality', in *Psychology Versus Metapsychology*, above n. 258, at 16.

[262] Gill, 'Metapsychology', above n. 258, at 71.

[263] See Moore, 'Mind, Brain, and Unconscious', above n. 46 (arguing for this conceptualization of Freud's 'system Ucs').

of an electron has a place. . . . So while we can talk of observing the effects of electrons, the expression 'seeing an electron' is at best a misleading locution. The same would be the case of 'making the unconscious conscious' if the concept of the unconscious were a theoretical concept.[264]

Dilman also grounds his second argument on the privileged access we each have to the contents of our own, clinically recoverable unconscious. Such privileged access gives rise to an asymmetry in verification modes of first and third person statements about our mental states, unconscious included.[265] Dilman argues that treating the unconscious as a theoretical entity would do away with this asymmetry for unconscious mental states, because then even first person statements would be verified only by inference from a theory and not directly from awareness:

My main objection to the view that the unconscious is a theoretical construct has been that it does not recognize the difference between a person's recognition of his own unconscious feelings and desires and another person's recognition of them. It hinders a proper appreciation of what is involved in what is unconscious becoming conscious.[266]

Both of these arguments lead Dilman to conclude that 'unconscious', as the word is used in clinical psychoanalysis 'logically' (i.e. on pain of committing 'category mistakes') cannot refer to anything in the physical world. This kind of argument can be constructed no matter what one takes to be the touchstone of mind talk.

Roy Schafer, my second example, fastens upon those aspects of language characteristic of our talk about personal agency as such a touchstone.[267] Two linguistic arguments, Schafer thinks, warrant his conclusion that the 'nonaction' language of science cannot touch his 'action' language about mind. First, he argues that the normal matrix of discourse in which we use words that truly refer to things (science) is inappropriate to mental words. About 'anger', Schafer asks (in a manner reminiscent of Ryle):

The vocabulary of anger thus depends on the legitimacy of assuming or referring to an inside and an outside—but, I ask . . . again, inside or outside of what? Where? Is anger anywhere? . . . The questions are unanswerable, of course, because they cannot be asked in a logical inquiry. Anger is not the kind of word about which such questions may be asked.[268]

[264] Dilman, 'The Unconscious', above n. 259, at 455.

[265] This asymmetry in verification modes between first and third person usages of mind words is one of the differences philosophers have used to mark the 'categorical divide' between mental talk and physical talk. See e.g. Malcolm, 'Behaviorism as a Philosophy of Psychology', above n. 249.

[266] Dilman, 'Is the Unconscious a Theoretical Construct?', above n. 259, at 339.

[267] Schafer, *A New Language*, above n. 260.

[268] Ibid. at 165.

From this feature of usage Schafer concludes that 'anger' and (by parallel argument) 'the unconscious' do not refer to any entities, that we must regard them only as properties of certain entities, namely, actions.[269]

Second, Schafer argues, it is possible to tell from usage all there is to know about the reference of 'angry action' or 'unconscious action'. These phrases cannot refer to anything unknown to their competent speakers. Specifically, such phrases cannot refer to neurotransmitter alterations in the brain (for anger), or to a functional organization of the brain (for unconscious), for these are unknown to ordinary speakers. Schafer blatantly makes Ryle's ordinary language philosophy assumption that the rules of ordinary usage can fix the reference of the words used, so that if ordinary speakers don't know the deep theory of the emotions or of the unconscious, then the words they employ cannot refer to such things.

Yet what justifies thinking that the usage patterns adverted to by Ryle, Dilman, or Schafer can limit what is referred to by mental words or by the words of any other category of discourse? As Roderick Anscombe concludes in his generally perceptive review of Schafer's work, 'Questions about how best to conceptualize the unconscious have more to do with fact than with language.'[270] Anscombe has his finger on the basic problem with this ordinary language version of psychoanalytic interpretivism. The ordinary language philosophy that followed upon the work of Ryle and the later Wittgenstein took as its slogan that 'meaning was use'. In other words, one could find out about the meaning of words in natural languages simply by looking at how native speakers used the words. One discovered the 'logic' of each expression by doing such 'conceptual analysis', without for a moment thinking that such conceptual analysis was hostage to the world because of the reference of the expressions used.

For ordinary language philosophy, a mental concept like intention was to be analysed in terms of its analytic or pragmatic relations with other mental state concepts, such as belief and desire. The ordinary language analysts were content to discover such relations of sense and pragmatic implication, building in this way a matrix of systematically connected concepts. They never asked, 'To what does the word "intention" refer? And does it (can it) refer to the same kind of thing as can be found in physiology?' They felt justified in ignoring these questions of reference and identity because one knew all there was to know about intentions (the things) when one knew all there was to know about how 'intention' (the word) was used.[271]

269 Ibid. at 169.

270 Roderick Anscombe, 'Referring to the Unconscious', *International Journal of Psycho-Analysis*, 62 (1981), 225–41, at 233.

271 One of the clearest examples of this 'preclusion of the material mode' by semantic ascent to the 'linguistic mode' (as the ordinary language philosophers used to put it), is Norman Malcolm, *Dreaming* (London: Routledge, 1959). Malcolm accurately surveys our

Simply to state this assumption of ordinary language philosophy is pretty much to refute it. Do we really think that the usage patterns that form the large clumps Ryle called categories can justify us in suspending questions of reference and identity? As an admittedly not very sympathetic thought experiment,[272] suppose we place ourselves back in ancient Babylon at just the time the Babylonian astronomers were discovering that the star that appeared in the morning ('The Morning Star') and the star that appeared in the evening ('The Evening Star') were one and the same thing, the planet Venus. One can imagine a Babylonian ordinary language philosopher 'disproving' the astronomer's claim in the following way. He (the philosopher) has not been looking at stars but at language use. He has observed the phrases, 'Evening Star' and 'Morning Star' in all of their ordinary uses, and from such observation it is clear that the phrases appear in different categories of discourse (evening talk and morning talk). Accordingly, the phrases cannot refer to the same thing. Otherwise (by Leibniz's law) the expressions would be equivalent, which their differing use shows they manifestly are not. Indeed, it is absurd—a category mistake—even to speak of the Evening Star and the Morning Star existing in the same sense of 'exist' since the latter word appears in different categories of discourse.

The problem with this view of meaning, and with its accompanying doctrine of categorical differences, is that systematic connections in the ordinary usage of certain words purport to render nonsensical questions of reference and identity that seem to make perfectly good sense. How can the fact that ordinary people built up a set of systematic usages for the phrase 'evening star' and another set for the phrase 'morning star' preclude us from asking whether those phrases purport to refer to something, whether the things to which they refer exist, and whether these things are in reality one and the same thing? To be sure, if something in the patterns of usage showed us that the phrases did not refer, all well

ordinary usage of the word 'dreaming', concluding that the only criterion for its correct use in ordinary speech is that we have waking remembrances. Malcolm then concludes that the dream research begun in the 1950s—in terms of rapid eye movements and EEG patterns—could not be about dreaming, for what dreaming was was fixed by how 'dreaming' was used in ordinary speech. For discussion and the corrective, see Putnam, *Mind, Language and Reality*, above n. 6, at 304–24.

[272] I have not always been so unsympathetic. I cut my philosophical teeth in the ordinary language philosophy movement and once had a great deal more sympathy for its tenets. Fortunately, most of my ordinary language style writings were never published, the exception being 'Legal Conceptions of Mental Illness', written and delivered in 1976 but not published until later, in B. Brody and T. Engelhardt (eds.), *Mental Illness: Law and Public Policy* (Dordrecht: Reidel, 1980), 25. Undoubtedly, no critic is as unsympathetic as a reformed true believer.

and good.[273] Then the facts of usage could constitute an argument why the questions of reference and identity can be put aside. Then 'conceptual analysis' is the only possible activity for finding the meaning of such words.

Yet nothing in simple usage patterns can show this. Without such a demonstration, we should take ordinary usage at face value—'intention' refers to the various mental states of intention—and then ask what sort of things those are. We cannot be foreclosed from discovering that intentions really are, e.g. brain states of a certain type, by facts about how people have used 'intention', any more than a Babylonian astronomer can be foreclosed from showing that the Evening Star is the very same thing as the Morning Star by the linguistic fact that the phrases were, until then, used in totally separate discourses.

These considerations apply with full force to Ryle's own example of a category mistake using the word 'exist'. How could one detect an ambiguity in the word, let alone that kind of 'big ambiguity' that is a category difference, simply by looking to usage? We normally detect ambiguities in our word use by looking to the world to see how many classes of things are referred to by a common symbol. We do not think words are

273 The kind of argument Ryle and Company needed could not, of course, start with the position that there are no things referred to by mental words—that is just a physicalist metaphysical position from which (among other things) linguistic dualism was to save us. Rather, they need a linguistic argument, showing how words like 'intention' do not occur in referential position in the sentences containing them.

Emotivism in ethical philosophy provides one example of this kind of linguistic argument. Emotivism (crudely characterized) translated seemingly descriptive statements, such as 'That action was unjust', into expressions of disapproval: 'That action—ugh!' 'Unjust', used in such a speech act, is not used referentially. Similarly, Herbert Hart once argued that concepts of human action were not used to describe events but to ascribe responsibility to persons for events. H. L. A. Hart, 'The Ascription of Responsibility and Rights', *Proceedings of the Aristotelian Society*, 49 (1949), 171–94. Also, Wittgenstein once urged, first person mental statements like 'I am in pain' really perform the same role as 'ouch'—signalling one's pain but not describing it—so that 'pain' need not be taken as any more referential than 'ouch'. Wittgenstein, above n. 249, at 89.

All such views have long been discredited in the philosophy of language for the same reasons that have led to the demise of emotivist and prescriptivist analyses of ethical expressions; they all presuppose a speech-act semantics that has never materialized. More specifically, their crucial assumption was that an expression's typical use for performing certain illocutionary or perlocutionary speech acts—express pain or emotion, ascribe responsibility—could be taken by itself as sufficient grounds for treating these expressions as not referring to anything. They assumed that an expression could only do one 'job', so that if one were, for example, ascribing, one could not also be describing. Such an assumption seems plainly false as a test of reference and description, see e.g. Peter Geach, *Logic Matters* (Berkeley: University of California Press, 1980), 250–4, and has come to be known as the 'speech act fallacy'. William Lycan, 'Moral Facts and Moral Knowledge', *Southern Journal of Philosophy*, 24 (Supp. 1986), 79–94, at 83. There is nothing that prevents words from both asserting something to be the case and expressing emotion, ascribing responsibility, etc. This dual function can even be their typical, or most ordinary usage, as with 'murder' in, 'You are a murderer.'

ambiguous simply because they may typically get used in several different contexts.[274]

I conclude that ordinary language philosophy cannot keep its promise of a metaphysics-free justification for a metaphysics-free interpretivism in psychoanalysis. It offers nothing that can keep psychoanalytic interpretivists off the horns of a dilemma: either they adopt the heavily metaphysical programme of the Diltheian tradition, or they give up the claim that the interpretivism of psychoanalysis's clinical theory is in any way immune to answering the metaphysical questions of truth, reference, and ontology that any (explanatory) science must answer.

D. Beginning Again: Towards a Modest Psychoanalytic Interpretivism

The results of our excursion into psychoanalytic interpretivism and the various philosophies that underlie it have so far been largely negative. We have examined three forms of psychoanalytic interpretivism that theorists in other disciplines like law would do well to avoid. We now should inquire whether we might draw some more positive lesson from the philosophical attempts to make sense of what may remain a stubborn intuition, namely, that in some sense psychoanalysis is an interpretive discipline.

In a paper on the nature of explanation in psychoanalysis written over two decades ago, I dismissed out of hand 'hermeneutic' accounts of psychoanalytic explanation.[275] Adolf Grunbaum not only adopted this dismissal of hermeneutic approaches to psychoanalysis in his fine book;[276] he detailed why it was justified in ways that overlap with many of the arguments I have made earlier in this part.[277] Insofar as both of us were concerned with Freud's explanatory accounts, what we said was and is true.

Yet we both ignored the possibility of what I shall now call 'modest psychoanalytic interpretivism'. This view concedes that all the theorizing Freud did, in the clinical theory as well as the metapsychology, was intended as explanation and should be judged as such. But psychoanalysis, as Freud was so fond of reminding his audiences, is not only a theory, it is also a therapy. A modest interpretive claim about psychoanalysis

[274] For this argument explicitly directed against Ryle, see Quine, *Word and Object*, above n. 17, at 131. For a general discussion of ambiguity, see Moore, 'Semantics of Judging', above n. 13, at 181–8.

[275] Moore, 'The Nature of Psychoanalytic Explanation', in *Mind and Medicine*, above, n. 199, at 5–58 (given originally as part of the Eighteenth Annual Lecture Series in the Philosophy of Science, University of Pittsburgh, 1977–8, first published in *Psychoanalysis and Contemporary Thought*, iii (1980), 459–543, and revised and republished in light of Adolf Grunbaum's detailed comments).

[276] Grunbaum, *Foundations of Psychoanalysis*, above n. 201, at 57, 60, 75, 82–3.

[277] Ibid. at 1–94.

would be that interpreting a patient's symptom, slip of the tongue, or dream in therapy is a distinct activity from explaining (by one's theory) why that symptom, slip, or dream occurred.

Notice how modest is the claim made by this version of psychoanalytic interpretivism. Psychoanalytic therapy's distinctiveness is based on the dominant activity engaged in during therapy. This is not a distinction between 'mind' and 'nature' or 'meaningful' and 'non-meaningful' phenomena. Modest interpretivism makes no claims for any of the metaphysical or categorical differences between interpretation and explanation that we surveyed in this part's previous sections. Unlike these more ambitious hermeneutics, the modest form makes no claim that human behaviour must be understood in a special way (first person experience, third person empathy), that the data of the discipline is different (meaning, intentionality), or that the language used is categorically different. Rather, the basic justification for distinguishing therapy's interpretive activity from theorizing's explanatory activity is that the activities are different. No more philosophical heavy weather can be made of this point than of the equally profound observation that running and eating are different activities with different criteria for good execution.

What makes the activity of psychoanalytic therapy not only non-explanatory but interpretive is the focus of both analyst and analysand on a kind of text. With dreams, for example, that text is what Freud called the dream's 'manifest content', the content the dreamer remembers upon awakening. Analysis seeks to interpret such a text and extract from it what Freud called the dream's 'latent meaning'.

For some of us, at least, theorizing (and explanatory activities generally) comes with its justification on its sleeve: seeking the truth is prima facie a justified activity to engage in. Others may prefer justifications that are more pragmatic than truth for truth's sake, such as controlling nature. In any case, no such justifications are available to non-explanatory activities like interpreting a dream in psychoanalytic therapy. Like eating, running, and other non-explanatory activities, doing therapeutic dream interpretation requires some justifying point or goal; no non-explanatory activity can claim the mantle of truth-seeking as its justification without ceasing to be non-explanatory.

When the non-explanatory activity in question is an interpretive one, with its necessary focus on some text as the object of interpretation, this demand for justification translates into a demand for some reason why the text in question merits attention. In psychoanalytic therapy, why is it worth anyone's time to interpret the patient's symptoms, dreams, etc.?

More broadly, any modestly interpretive activity, inside or outside of psychoanalysis, only makes sense when those who participate in it have some answer to the question, 'What makes a certain text authoritative?'

Modestly interpretive activities presuppose some theory that justifies why particular decisions are warranted by some pre-existing text. In law, we sometimes call this a theory of authority. For example, our democratic political theory is partly what makes a statutory text authoritative for a judge in particular decisions. In theology, one needs some theory about a text—e.g. the Bible—that justifies paying attention to it when moral decisions are made. That theory may specify, for example, divine origins or inspiration for the text. In literary criticism, the critic has to justify why he and his readers should pay attention to the text of some play or novel as they make various decisions in their lives. One answer might be in terms of certain authors' moral authority, their ability to educate morally using fictive variations in a way more didactic methods cannot.[278]

A dream's manifest content is not authoritative in the same way as a statute (enacted by the popular will), a religious text (enacted by God's will), or a literary text (written by one with moral wisdom). What makes this manifest content authoritative for us when engaged in psychoanalytic therapy? The answer, it seems to me, lies in the therapeutic goal that justifies therapy at all: some interpretations can make a patient better. The goal of clinical psychoanalysis as a therapy (not as a theory) gives the activity of interpreting dreams and symptoms its point. Without such a therapeutic aim, there would be no point to interpreting dreams and symptoms (although there would be a point, of course, to explaining them). And with no point to the interpretive enterprise, there would be neither (*a*) a basis for preferring one text to another nor (*b*) a basis for judging one interpretation to be better than another. With acknowledgment of such a therapeutic goal, by contrast, (*a*) there is a basis for preferring one text to another as authoritative—Freud, for example, regarded all of a patient's stated remembrances of a dream as part of its manifest content for explicitly therapeutic reasons;[279] and (*b*) there is a basis for judging whether an interpretation is a good one or not, namely, does it cure (or help to cure) the patient?

The separateness of such (modestly) interpretive activity from explanation is easily missed because of Freud's insistence on what might be called the 'Socratic therapy thesis'.[280] Freud thought that a symptom's interpretation would be effective in removing the symptom only if the interpreta-

[278] This is to adopt Garet's theory about the point of literature according to critics such as John Gardner and Matthew Arnold, that it is to instruct us morally. See Garet, 'Comparative Normative Hermeneutics', above n. 199, at 37–40.

[279] For citations and discussions, see Moore, 'The Nature of Psychoanalytic Explanation', above n. 275, at 8 (*Psychoanalysis and Contemporary Thought*, iii, at 463).

[280] I discuss this thesis briefly as part of my exegesis of the clinical theory in Michael S. Moore, 'Psychoanalysis and the Mind–Body Problem' (Charles Phelps Taft Lectures in Philosophy, University of Cincinnati, April 1986) (unpublished manuscript); see also Grunbaum, *Foundations of Psychoanalysis*, above n. 201, at 127–72.

tion reproduced the repressed mental state causing the symptom to start with. Successful therapy depended on 'making the unconscious conscious', to use one of Freud's famous formulations of the psychoanalytic clinical ideal, or on transforming what was id into ego, to use the other. In this view, successful therapy requires the patient to become conscious of his symptom's origin. This thesis means that good interpretations will also be good explanations, however distinct the activities of interpretation and explanation may be.

Claims similar to Freud's Socratic therapy thesis have also been made in other disciplines where interpretive activity often takes place. In law, one form of judicial conservatism claims that a good interpretation of a legal text recaptures the intention with which the enacting legislature or constitutional convention created that text. In literature, the claim is still sometimes made that the only legitimate interpretation of a literary text captures the intentions with which the author wrote the text. Similarly, in theology, one might argue that God's intentions motivated some holy text and that a good theological interpretation corresponds to these intentions. In each case the claim is that a good interpretation of a text is also a good explanation for why that text came into being. Such claims, here as in psychoanalysis, thus obscure the distinction between interpretation and explanation by making the goodness of the first dependent on the truth of the second.

The easiest way to remove the blinders put on by Freud's Socratic therapy thesis, and by like theses in other disciplines, is to consider other claims regarding how best to achieve the various goals of various interpretive activities. Consider as examples two other accounts of psychoanalytic interpretation that do not obscure the sharp distinction between explanation and interpretation. Wittgenstein gave the first in criticizing Freud's Socratic therapy thesis:

> If I take any one of the dream reports . . . which Freud gives, I can by the use of free association arrive at the same results as those he reaches in his analysis—although it was not my dream. And the association will proceed through my own experiences and so on.
>
> The fact is that whenever you are preoccupied with something, with some trouble or with some problem which is a big thing in your life—as sex is, for instance—then no matter what you start from, the association will lead finally and inevitably back to the same theme. Freud remarks on how, after the analysis of it, the dream appears so very logical. And of course it does. You could start with any of the objects on this table—which certainly are not put there through your dream activity—and you could find that they all could be connected in a pattern like that; and the pattern would be logical in the same way.
>
> One may be able to discover certain things about oneself by this sort of free association but it does not explain why the dream occurred.[281]

[281] Ludwig Wittgenstein, ed. C. Barrett, *Lectures and Conversations on Aesthetics, Psychology and Religious Belief* (Berkeley: University of California Press, 1966), 50–1.

Someone concerned not with explanation, only with therapy, might regard Wittgenstein's remarks not as a criticism but rather as a therapeutically justified interpretive strategy alternative to Freud's. Within this strategy, an interpretation would succeed therapeutically because it gets at what is bothering someone, even if that had nothing to do with producing the patient's dreams or symptoms.

Some hermeneuts, such as Robert Steele, take an interpretive stance even more distant from Freud's.[282] Steele rejects not only Freud's view that a good interpretation must recapture the states that caused the dream or symptom but also Wittgenstein's suggestion that an interpretation must at least describe mental states the person really has. As Steele bluntly puts it:

> [T]he meaning of a dream does not reside in some prior latent dream, but in the manifest dream and the analysand's associations to it. Interpretation creates a coherent meaning, one that analyst and analysand can agree on. . . . The interpretation of dreams, parapraxes, and symptoms is aimed at facilitating the incorporation of these fragments with the life of the analysand.[283]

As Steele elsewhere puts it, psychoanalytic 'interpretation does not reveal something real';[284] rather, good interpretations are those 'that help make the past intelligible'.[285]

Construed purely as interpretive strategies aimed at therapeutic success, neither Wittgenstein's nor Steele's interpretive theories have anything to do with explanation. Nor, viewed as interpretive theories, is there anything suspect about the Wittgensteinian or Steelean variations. Whether one prefers Freud to Steele here depends on the facts of successful therapy, and it is quite possible that comfortable and coherent fairy tales are more therapeutic than Socratic wisdom. If so, one can see very clearly the separation between interpretation in psychoanalytic therapy and explanation in psychoanalytic theory.

The foregoing is the most sense I can make of the intuitions that interpretive activities are distinct from explanatory activities and that psychoanalysis as a discipline is engaged, at least in part, in interpretive activity. Much to the surprise of my former self,[286] I find that I too am an interpretivist about psychoanalytic therapy, in this modest sense. Seeing this also allows one to glimpse the possibility of equally modest interpretivisms about some of the activities of other disciplines such as theology, literary criticism, and law. Wherever there is a point to engaging in the non-explanatory activity of paying attention to some text when one is deciding what to do—whenever, in other words, some text possesses

[282] See Steele, 'Psychoanalysis and Hermeneutics', above n. 246.
[283] Ibid. at 400–1.
[284] Ibid. at 405.
[285] Ibid. at 406.
[286] See text accompanying nn. 275–7 above.

legitimate authority for us[287]—then interpretation as an activity can be justified.[288]

This modest interpretivism's legitimacy, however, should not for a moment lead us to think that we have at last hit on an interpretivist justification for putting aside metaphysics and epistemology. Nothing could be further from the truth. Interpretation is an activity distinct from explanation and as such makes no use of the categories that demand a metaphysics—truth, reference, reality. But interpretation does not compete with explanation, despite the claims of all the more ambitious interpretivisms we have explored. The moment we wish to understand (seek the truth of, gain knowledge of) anything, we must cease interpretation and do something else, namely, explanation. This follows from clarity about how modest is our interpretivism about psychoanalytic therapy. As an activity, interpretation in therapy is justified because it makes patients better; it is not justified in any more ambitious way (such as the Diltheian claim that it gets at a special kind of truth in a special kind of way).

Suppose as therapists we wished to understand why certain interpretations succeeded in therapy as well as they do. Now we must cease interpreting anything and begin explaining why saying such-and-such caused the improvement we observed.

Even in Steele's version of what makes for a good interpretation, if meaning-giving fairy tales are therapeutic, that fact is itself not a meaning-giving fairy tale (good interpretation) but a true explanation. Such a fact is itself to be judged by the normal theories of science, no matter how out of place such theories might be in the practice of interpretive therapy itself.

This means that the moment clinical psychoanalysts seek to explain their clinical successes, they, like all fellow seekers of truth, must ask after the reference of their terms, whether the entities to which they purport to refer exist, whether their statements are true in the sense of corresponding to the things that really exist, what sort of justification they have for their beliefs, etc. These are, of course, just the sort of questions that demand that they have a metaphysics and an epistemology, however implicit.

Can clinical psychoanalysts refuse to leave their clinics and practise their interpretive methods uninterrupted by the clamour of external criticism? They can, of course, in the same sense that an ostrich can refuse to look at the world. But none of them do,[289] and for very good reason:

[287] See text following n. 277 above.

[288] For clarity, it may be helpful to list some of the disciplines that do not include interpretive activities. History and ethics are two that come to mind, since more ambitious interpretivists take both to contain interpretive activities. There are no plausible candidates for authoritative texts in either history or ethics, which is why a modest interpretivist should not consider these disciplines to be interpretive in character.

[289] See Moore, 'Mind–Body Problem', above n. 280 (construing the clinical theory contexts as confined neither to a therapy nor even to explanations of therapeutic efficacy); see also

Without seeking explanations they could not know whether or not they were achieving the whole point of their interpretive practice. How would they know whether a particular interpretation produced an improvement in a patient without an accurate description of that patient's condition and a causal explanation of how she got into it? How would they know whether Freud, or Wittgenstein, or Steele is right about what kind of interpretations produce therapeutic outcomes? They cannot answer such questions by repairing to their interpretive strategy because such questions are not part of the therapeutic practice that gives that strategy its point. Imagine a 'validation' of a therapeutic technique that consisted of the declaration: 'It is therapeutic for me as a theorist so to explain the successes of my therapeutic technique.'

Thus, nothing in a modest interpretivism about psychoanalytic therapy can justify an ametaphysical stance by psychoanalytic therapists in theorizing about their therapy. Moreover, even a Fish-like therapist, who refuses to acknowledge that theory is necessary to justify and guide good therapy,[290] may get ensnared in the basic philosophical questions I have called metaphysical and epistemological. Notice that if clinical psychoanalysts adopt Freud's strategy—the Socratic therapy thesis—then their own interpretive strategy demands that they ask and answer metaphysical and epistemological questions as they practise their interpretive activity. If interpretations are therapeutic only if they give true explanations, then clinical psychoanalysts ask questions of reference, truth, existence, and justification even within their interpretive practice. The very point of that practice—cure—demands that they seek the truth, that is, the real wishes that caused the symptom.

Habermas, for one, recognizes that his buying into Freud's version of clinical interpretation lands the Habermasian analyst squarely in the land of explanations: 'The What, the semantic content of a systematically distorted manifestation, cannot be "understood" if it is not possible at the same time to "explain" the Why, the origin of the symptomatic scene with reference to the initial circumstance which led to the systematic distortion itself.'[291] As Habermas perceives, his view leads to there being, within psychoanalytic practice, 'simultaneous hermeneutic understanding and causal explanation. . . . Clarification of a systematically inaccessible mean-

Eagle, *Recent Developments in Psychoanalysis*, above n. 201, at 148 (what psychoanalysts 'mean by clinical formulations or clinical theory is an explanatory account in which a person's behaviour or symptoms are explained by reference to his conscious or unconscious aims, wishes, and goals'); Benjamin B. Rubinstein, 'On the Clinical Psychoanalytic Theory and Its Role in the Inference and Confirmation of Particular Clinical Hypotheses', *Psychoanalysis & Contemporary Science*, 4 (1975), 3–57.

290 See text accompanying nn. 159–66 above

291 Jurgen Habermas, 'On Systematically Distorted Communication', *Inquiry*, 13 (1970), 205–18, at 209.

ing succeeds only to the extent to which the origin of the faulty or misleading meaning is explained'.[292]

So in both of these ways psychoanalytic therapy cannot evade the kind of questions that demand a metaphysics and an epistemology. Questions of truth, reference, reality, and justification must be asked at some point, no matter how distinct are interpretive activities from explanatory activities. Psychoanalysts might take to heart Robert Holt's warning to those of his fellow analysts seeking to avoid these kinds of questions: '[M]etaphysics . . . takes its revenge on those who ignore it. It is of the very nature of the questions metaphysicians tackle that everyone must take some implicit stand on them, and it is dangerous to remain unaware of that fact.'[293]

IV. LAW PRACTICE AND JURISPRUDENCE AS MODESTLY INTERPRETIVE

We have explored three basic forms of interpretivism on which lawyers might be tempted to base their own rejection of metaphysics and epistemology in law practice and jurisprudence. One is the very ambitious interpretivism of Rorty and Fish; if they were correct in their claim that all thought is interpretive in character, then thought about law would of course share that character. Another is the ambitious interpretivisms of the Diltheian, Heideggerian, or Rylean sorts; if they were correct in their various claims that all thought in the human sciences is interpretive, then so long as law is one of the human sciences it too would be interpretive. The third possibility is the modest interpretivism we uncovered at the close of our exploration of psychoanalytic interpretivism.

I have given what I hope are persuasive reasons why lawyers and legal academics should avoid the ambitious or very ambitious varieties of interpretivism. I have not given similar reasons to reject a modest interpretivism at least about psychoanalytic therapy; but we did explore why the legitimacy of such a modestly interpretive activity did not justify an antimetaphysical stance by psychoanalysts. What we should now explore is the possibility that law practice and jurisprudence are modestly interpretive activities and, if they are, whether that fact has any antimetaphysical, anti-epistemological implications. Since Ronald Dworkin has recently answered both questions affirmatively,[294] I will focus the discussion on his brand of interpretivism.

292 Ibid. at 216–17.

293 Robert R. Holt, 'The Death and Transfiguration of Metapsychology', *International Review of Psychoanalysis*, 8 (1981), 129–43, at 132 .

294 Dworkin, *Law's Empire*, above n. 66. Although few have argued that jurisprudence is an interpretive activity, many other than Dworkin have argued that the practice of law is interpretive in character. See nn. 59–65 above.

Keeping in mind how fruitful was our distinction between the claim that psychoanalytic practice (therapy) was interpretive, and the claim that psychoanalytic theory was interpretive, we should separate two interpretive claims that Dworkin wishes to keep together. One is that the practice of law by judges, lawyers, and citizens in our legal system is an interpretive activity. A second interpretive claim is that jurisprudence as practised by Hart, Raz, and other legal theorists is best viewed as an interpretive activity. Despite Dworkin's admonitions that jurisprudence is continuous with law practice in a culture,[295] I here provisionally separate the two interpretive claims because not to do so would be to beg some very important questions that we shall wish to examine. I find Dworkin's interpretive claim about law practice to be plausible as a description both of how we do practise law and how we ought to practise law. But, I shall argue, Dworkin's interpretive claim about jurisprudence is intimately connected to his ultimately antimetaphysical stance; and both fail for the same reason.

A. Dworkin's General Account of Interpretation

To see whether the practice of law and jurisprudence is interpretive, Dworkin first develops a general account of interpretation. He seeks to elucidate when we have an 'interpretive concept', when we have a community that shares an 'interpretive attitude', when we have an 'interpretive enterprise' or activity, and when we have an 'interpretive discipline'. Although he uses these terms without clearly defining or distinguishing them,[296] the most basic notion seems to be 'interpretive attitude' towards a practice. When there is such an attitude towards a practice, then the key concepts used in that practice will be 'interpretive concepts' and the arguments about what such concepts mean will be an 'interpretive activity'. Further, to the extent such interpretive activity is a central one for some discipline, that discipline will be an 'interpretive discipline'.

Seeking a general theory of interpretation poses something of a problem for anyone who thinks that all knowledge is interpretive, for how can he give a description of interpretive concepts, attitudes, or enterprises that is not itself an interpretation? Given (as we shall see) Dworkin's strong affinities to Rorty, he too faces this problem: 'Unfortunately, even a preliminary account [of interpretation] will be controversial, for if a community uses interpretive concepts at all, the concept of interpretation will be one of them.'[297] Like Rorty, Dworkin's solution is to see himself as inter-

[295] Dworkin, *Law's Empire*, above n. 66, at 90.

[296] Ken Kress's able review of Dworkin notes this also. Kress, 'The Interpretive Turn', *Ethics*, 97 (1987), 834–60, at 838 n. 10.

[297] Dworkin, *Law's Empire*, above n. 66, at 49.

preting our shared concept of interpretation when he gives us his general theory of what interpretation is: '[A] theory of interpretation is an interpretation of the higher-order practice of using interpretive concepts.'[298] Dworkin thus sees his work as internal to our practice of interpretation, not external to those practices. Thus, he does not claim to describe either the cross-cultural essence of interpretation or the most desirable concept of interpretation for us to employ, only to interpret the one we do in fact employ. Dworkin, like Rorty, thus carefully seeks to avoid committing himself to any external metaphysics as he lays out his hypothesis that legal knowledge is interpretive in character.

With this careful caveat, Dworkin's theory of interpretation distinguishes three species to the genus. First, he claims, 'scientific interpretation' is the activity of scientists giving meaning to the phenomena they observe.[299] Dworkin is unsure whether this is really interpretation or only metaphorically like interpretation,[300] presumably because he is not sure how ambitious an interpretivist he wishes to be.

Second, 'conversational interpretation' is the process by which readers and listeners understand their communicative utterances. A standard view of this kind of interpretation holds that a listener or reader reaches such understanding by duplicating within herself the propositional attitudes that the author intended to communicate.[301] Dworkin hesitates to adopt this standard view, since it would give interpretations truth values by virtue of their correspondence (or lack of it) to a historical person's state of mind. Dworkin plainly is tempted by some form of ambitious interpretivism, believing as he does that our understanding of authorial intentions is as much the product of our interpretive activity as the other way around.[302] These hesitations are important, for they colour how we are to understand both the breadth of Dworkin's interpretivism and the nature of his professed opposition to metaphysics.[303]

The species of interpretation Dworkin thinks most relevant to law is what he calls 'creative' or 'constructive' interpretation. Dworkin has made this method familiar in legal theory. It has two dimensions: the dimension of fit with the practice being interpreted, and the dimension of value, which requires the interpreter to impose a 'purpose on an object or practice in order to make of it the best possible example of the form or genre to which it is taken to belong'.[304]

When do we interpret this way? Early in his career, Dworkin seems to have thought that the justification for engaging in creative interpretation was linguistic in the sense that such interpretation was called for by the

[298] Ibid. [299] Ibid. at 50. [300] Compare ibid. at 51 with ibid. at 53.

[301] See e.g. Platts, *Ways of Meaning*, above n. 6.

[302] See Dworkin, *Law's Empire*, above n. 66, at 419 n. 2. [303] See n. 308 below.

[304] Dworkin, *Law's Empire*, above n. 66, at 52.

existence of 'essentially contested concepts'—concepts such as equality[305]—that can be distinguished from other concepts simply by the way they are used within the linguistic community. If usage reveals an agreement about the meaning of a concept—either in the way it is defined or in what constitutes a paradigmatic exemplar of it—and if usage also reveals a pattern of systematic disagreement over the competing understandings of that concept, it is 'essentially contested'.

Dworkin's more recent criteria for when creative interpretation is appropriate look sociological. Creative interpretation arises, Dworkin tells us, 'when a community develops a complex "interpretive" attitude towards the rules' of some social practice like courtesy.[306] Such an attitude has two components:

> The first is the assumption that the practice of courtesy does not simply exist but has value, that it serves some interest or purpose or enforces some principle—in short, that it has some point—that can be stated independently of just describing the rules that make up the practice. The second is the further assumption that the requirements of courtesy—the behavior it calls for or judgments it warrants—are not necessarily or exclusively what they have always been taken to be but are instead sensitive to its point, so that the strict rules must be understood or applied or extended or modified or qualified or limited by that point.[307]

This sounds like a sociological criterion because it makes creative interpretation's appropriateness depend upon the existence of certain shared attitudes within some society.

What Dworkin has to be up to here, however, cannot be this kind of external, descriptive sociology. In light of his own interpretivism about what is an interpretive concept, discussed above, Dworkin no doubt intends the interpretive attitude (the prerequisite for interpretive concepts) to be our own. If we regard some practice as having some value, and if we regard that value as penetrating the practice to particular cases, then we should regard that practice as an interpretive one.

This, of course, is very close to the notion of modest interpretivism we uncovered in psychoanalysis. The modest interpretivist generally thinks that interpretation makes sense only when some set of values justifies why we or others ought to engage in that nonexplanatory activity, which as we have seen translates into a demand for some value that justifies why we or

[305] W. B. Gallie, 'Essentially Contested Concepts', *Proceedings of the Aristotelian Society*, 56 (1956), 167–98. Dworkin early in his writings adopted this idea as his vehicle for justifying the theorizing a language user must do in order to use such concepts properly: see *Law's Empire*, above n. 66, at 70–3 (containing echoes of this conceptual justification of theorizing); Ronald Dworkin, 'The Jurisprudence of Nixon' (Book Review), *New York Review of Books*, 4 May 1972, at 27, reprinted in Dworkin, *Taking Rights Seriously* (Cambridge, Mass.: Harvard University Press, 1977), 131.

[306] Dworkin, *Law's Empire*, above n. 66, at 47.

[307] Ibid.

others ought to regard a text or practice as authoritative for our decisions in particular cases. This is one reading (and I think the best reading) of Dworkin's first criterion for an interpretive attitude.[308]

Admittedly, there are some difficulties in construing Dworkin's interpretivism as a 'modest interpretivism' in my sense of that phrase. One stems from Dworkin's imprecision in specifying what aspect of a practice must have a 'purpose' or 'point' before it can be considered interpretive. Dworkin seems to think that a practice (his example is the practice of courtesy) is interpretive because it 'does not simply exist but has value . . . that it has some point . . . that can be stated independently' of the practice itself.[309]

This is too crude a gloss to show us why the practice of courtesy is interpretive. Many social practices have value but are not interpretive. For

[308] Because Dworkin flirts with the idea of there being scientific and conversational interpretivism, it is possible to construe him as a less modest interpretivist. To understand him as a pragmatist interpretivist like Rorty or Fish, however, would require his commitment to the view that there is nothing distinctive about interpretive concepts, for all concepts are interpretive for the pragmatist interpretivist. Dworkin, however, like many others, thinks there is something specially interpretive about the concepts used in law and literary criticism. Alternatively, to construe Dworkin as an ambitious interpretivist in the Diltheian tradition would generate some views he plainly would reject. About morality, for example, he would have to commit to something like G. E. Moore's non-naturalist ethics with its separate-realm hypothesis about moral qualities. This separateness would then justify insulating the practice of interpreting moral concepts from external criticism. Dworkin has explicitly rejected any such view of morality. See *Taking Rights Seriously*, above n. 305, at 60 (Dworkin finding non-naturalism, which he misleadingly calls the 'natural model', very odd). Alternatively, to take seriously Dworkin's approving references to the Heidegger/Gadamer model of interpretivism, *Law's Empire*, above n. 66, at 419 n. 21, 422 n. 14, given Heidegger's and Gadamer's explicit refusal to countenance 'correctness' for interpretations, would be to give up one of Dworkin's central claims—that there is a right answer to every interpretive question in law. See Ronald Dworkin, 'No Right Answer?', in P. Hacker and J. Raz (eds.), *Law, Morality, and Society* (Oxford: Oxford University Press, 1978), 58; see also Ch. 8 above for a detailed reconstruction of Dworkin's right-answer thesis. Finally, one might construe Dworkin as an ordinary-language-style interpretivist who goes Ryle one better by discovering many categorical divides (not just one) in our discourse and uses that supposed linguistic fact to seal off the interpretive discourse in one category from the 'external' criticism originating in any other. Admittedly, Dworkin does sound like an ordinary language philosopher with his assumptions: (1) that meaning is use within a discourse and (2) that questions of real-world reference can be ignored once one discovers a category of discourse with its own sense of 'exist'. Dworkin makes the first claim when he tells us that 'moral or aesthetic or interpretive judgements have the sense and force they do just because they figure in a collective human enterprise'; he makes the second when he infers from this that 'such judgements cannot have a "real" sense and a "real" truth value which transcend that enterprise and somehow take hold of the "real" world'. Ronald Dworkin, 'My Reply to Stanley Fish (and Walter Benn Michaels)', in *The Politics of Interpretation*, above n. 155, at 300. Ryle couldn't have said it better.

I put aside all such alternative interpretations of Dworkin's interpretivism partly to avoid duplicating our earlier discussion but mostly because Dworkin does recognize the essential point of modest interpretivism: interpretation is not an activity we *must* perform but one we *can* perform when there is some point justifying our doing so.

[309] Dworkin, *Law's Empire*, above n. 66, at 47.

example, there are social practices of kindness that certainly have value but which are not interpretive in character. The practices of kindness could become interpretive only if there were some value or point that justifies why practitioners of kindness should treat the pre-existing forms of kindness as a type of authoritative text, interpretations of which are to guide how one is kind. The point or value that would make the practice of kindness interpretive, in other words, must not simply show why some practice is (or produces) good; rather, the value must justify something much more particular, namely, that using some text to give authoritative reasons for action is a good thing to do. There is no such text to kindness, for those who would seek to be kind only through interpreting the forms of kindness accepted in some society are some of the least kind people there are.[310]

By way of contrast, much of our practice of courtesy is interpretive by my 'authoritative text' criterion because there is a point justifying why practitioners of courtesy should grant authority to the existing social text (our existing rules of courteous behaviour). To be courteous, one must be understood as trying to be courteous, so that one needs to utilize the existing forms of courtesy to succeed at being seen as being (and thus as being) courteous. This justifies treating the existing rules of courtesy as a kind of text, interpretation of which is to guide courteous behaviour. If courtesy, however, were more like kindness—where no point justifies us in granting authority to the existing forms of kindness, even though there is a good deal of value to kindness—then courtesy would not be an interpretive practice.[311]

The second problem with forcing Dworkin's concept of creative interpretation into my 'modest interpretivist' category stems from Dworkin's second criterion for when we have an interpretive attitude towards some practice. A modest interpretivist should have no such criterion, for it would exclude as non-interpretive, for example, plain-meaning approaches to statutory interpretation (on the ground that such approaches purport to exclude the value behind a rule in its application to

[310] Thus, the lawyer in Albert Camus, *The Fall*, trans. Justice O'Brien (New York: Vintage, 1956), comes to realize that by aping the outward forms of kindness he was not being kind but simply preserving a falsely good opinion of himself.

[311] This particularity about what it is that must have value before a practice is interpretive is not a minor quibble, for Dworkin's sloppiness here misleads him about matters as important as justice. Thus, Dworkin concludes that 'justice is an institution we interpret' because '[l]ike courtesy, it has a history; we each join that history when we learn to take the interpretive attitude toward the demands, justifications and excuses we find other people making in the name of justice' (*Law's Empire*, above n. 66, at 73). Justice certainly has value, and our practices of it certainly have a history, yet that hardly means that our judgements of justice are or should be interpretations of prior historical practice. The value that justice possesses does not justify us in treating prior practices of justice as authoritative for our decisions.

particular cases).[312] Admittedly, if one distinguished 'interpretation' from 'application'—as many of the plain-meaning judges themselves do[313]—then such approaches are not interpretive. I think it preferable, however, to use a broader notion of interpretation that keeps such theorists on the playing field of competing interpretive theories. Doing so allows us to get rid of them on normative rather than conceptual grounds.[314]

B. Dworkin's Interpretive Claims About Law Practice and Jurisprudence

If we apply this modified Dworkinian account of interpretation to Anglo-American legal practice, then much of that practice is interpretive by Dworkin's first criterion. There is a persuasive argument that statutory texts should be authoritative for judges, lawyers, and citizens. Dworkin queries, 'Is there any point to requiring public force to be used only in ways conforming to rights and responsibilities that "flow from" past political decisions?'[315] That point may be either the maximal satisfaction of the rule-of-law virtues, as I would describe it, or Dworkin's value of integrity, or something else. But whatever the point, legal practice with regard to statutes in our legal system is interpretive precisely because of the moral fact that there is some set of values served by granting authority to those 'past political decisions' (texts) that statutes represent.

Whether legal reasoning in our culture is interpretive when it is not a matter of statutory construction is an interesting question that I shall not pursue. I have argued elsewhere, for example, that common law reasoning is not interpretive because there is no text to the common law as we practise it.[316] Constitutional reasoning, however, is interpretive in America because of the existence of an authoritative text.[317] However one decides these more problematic cases, Dworkin is on solid ground in claiming that much of our legal reasoning is interpretive in character.

Jurisprudence, by contrast, is not interpretive because there is no point making the practices of judges authoritative for legal theorists. Dworkin,

[312] Two famous 'plain meaning' cases are *Tennessee Valley Authority v. Hill*, 437 U.S. 153 (1978), and *Caminetti v. United States*, 242 U.S. 470 (1917).

[313] See e.g. *Caminetti*, 242 U.S. at 485 ('Where the language is plain and admits of no more than one meaning the duty of interpretation does not arise.'). More explicit was Justice Brandeis in *Dahnke-Walker Milling Co. v. Bondurant*,. 257 U.S. 282 (1921): '[I]n every case involving a statute, the state court must perform . . . two functions essentially different. First the court must construe the statute; that is, determine its meaning and scope. Then it must apply the statute, as so construed, to the facts of the case.' Ibid. at 294–5 (Brandeis, J., dissenting).

[314] The normative arguments against the plain meaning approach to legal interpretation are explored in Moore, 'Semantics of Judging', above n. 13, at 181–202.

[315] Dworkin, *Law's Empire*, above n. 66, at 94.

[316] See Moore, 'Precedent', above n. 52, at 183–8.

[317] Moore, 'Do We Have an Unwritten Constitution?', above n. 51.

to be sure, asserts the contrary. The general theories of law propounded by legal philosophers are, he tells us, also 'constructive interpretations: They try to show legal practice as a whole in its best light, to achieve equilibrium between legal practice as they find it and the best justification of that practice. So no firm line divides jurisprudence from adjudication or any other aspect of legal practice.'[318] This seems to mean that the point of the practice of jurisprudence is the same as the point of the practice of law, that is, that (in Dworkin's version) integrity demands that the practice of each be carried on in ways respectful of past political or jurisprudential decisions. Yet why should I as a legal theorist feel bound to respect any text as I seek to construct my own theory of the best way to practise law? There would seem to be three possible texts for jurisprudes: (1) the text that judges and others within a particular legal culture are obligated to interpret and obey ('the law' in this internal sense of 'law'); (2) the second order text created by judges within some particular legal culture, which consists of their judicial practices in construing statutes and constitutions (judges' implicit jurisprudential theories); and (3) the text of prior legal theorists, some of whom seek to describe the judges' jurisprudence within some particular legal system, and others of whom seek to do non-culture-specific, or 'general', jurisprudence. Are we to believe that there is a point to jurisprudence as an activity that could justify any of these texts as authoritative for me in the way statutes and constitutions are for judges?

The only way that Dworkin can have been led to a position this implausible is by a necessity claim: necessarily, legal theorists cannot 'get out' of their own legal culture, so they too must be interpretivists of that culture.[319] This necessity claim, it turns out, is part and parcel of Dworkin's antimetaphysical stance. To that stance we now turn.

[318] Dworkin, *Law's Empire*, above n. 66, at 90. Dworkin specifically treats jurisprudence as interpretive in 'Legal Theory and the Problem of Sense', in R. Gavison (ed.), *Issues in Contemporary Legal Philosophy* (Oxford: Oxford University Press, 1987), 9.

[319] As I explore in Ch. 3, such a necessity claim is imperialistic against any form of general jurisprudence, be it descriptive or normative. It implies that jurisprudes cannot get exernal to the practices of all legal cultures either to describe general features of law as such or to prescribe how we ought to conceive of law. The only thing jurisprudence can be, in this view, is a general interpretation of some culture's legal practices. One can imagine less imperialistic defences of interpretivist jurisprudence. One might argue, for example, that normative jurisprudential arguments are always directed at particular audiences. To be persuasive, it is usually a good rhetorical strategy not to bend too much the practices of your targeted audiences as you seek to persuade them to mend their ways. Perhaps the authoritativeness of Anglo-American legal practice for jurisprudes—when speaking to Anglo-American audiences—comes to no more than that. Alternatively, perhaps that authoritativeness can be justified in light of the need to apply any ideal jurisprudence to the less-than-ideal world. To be practical, jurisprudence must take into account certain features of existing legal cultures because those features themselves are morally relevant. It matters, for example, to what degree a legislature or a constitutional convention is truly democratic because its representativeness affects the degree of respect to which legislative or constitutional enactments are entitled.

Yet neither of these defences of interpretivist jurisprudence can work because neither

C. Dworkin's Antimetaphysical Stance About Literature, Morality, and Law

We should describe Dworkin's antimetaphysical stance as he himself presents it, as it applies to three parallel but distinct kinds of practice: literature, morality, and law. Dworkin thinks that metaphysics is bad for literary theorists, bad for moralists, and, for the same sorts of reasons, bad for lawyers.

Consider literature first. In his reply to Stanley Fish, Dworkin attacks what he takes to be a 'set of dogmas about truth and reference' within contemporary literary theory.[320] These are the metaphysical dogmas that truth is correspondence, and reference a relation between words and convention-independent things. A realist about literary interpretation would assert that 'meanings are "already in place" or "just there" '[321] to be corresponded to by a true literary interpretation; a conventionalist would assert that meanings are the inventions of the interpreter and his linguistic community, so that they are 'true' only in the conventionalist's sense that assertions of them are warranted in light of such-and-such conventions. Dworkin announces that these were 'both the positions I was trying to escape'.[322]

Dworkin's escape route uses the time-honoured expedient of denying sense to the question that the realist/antirealist debate in literature was trying to answer. Dworkin claims that he does 'not know what it means to say that meanings are "already in place" or "just there" or "self-executing" '.[323] Either asserting or denying the existence of such things as literary meanings puts us 'back in the land of the incomprehensible metaphors'.[324] Dworkin's doubt here is not ontological, that there is no realm of being for these objects, for that would just be antirealist scepticism. Rather, he thinks

justifies the authoritativeness of some culture's legal practices for a legal theorist. The only point the first argument establishes is that a normative jurisprude who wishes to be maximally persuasive to some audience should take their accepted practices into account as he frames his argument. This pragmatic consideration about how to be persuasive hardly makes their practices authoritative for him. Ethical arguments directed towards religious audiences are usually most persuasive when framed in terms of their beliefs about God; that hardly makes such audiences' beliefs about God authoritative for the ethical theorist. The only point the second argument establishes is that when normative jurisprudence is applied to some culture it must take into account the features of that culture that are morally relevant. The point is the same as would be made by a (non-interpretivist) moral realist: when judging the morality of slavery in Athens, take into account whatever features of Athenian culture (limited alternative economic opportunities?) as are morally relevant. This is only context-sensitive application of general moral truths to a less-than-ideal society; such context-sensitivity hardly grants authority to less-than-ideal practices. Nor does it make the moral theorist into an interpreter applying those practices in his judgements.

[320] Dworkin, 'Reply to Stanley Fish', above n. 308, at 287.
[321] Ibid. at 291.
[322] Ibid.
[323] Ibid. at 292.
[324] Ibid. at 299.

that 'the whole issue of objectivity . . . is a kind of fake'.[325] His advice to literary theorists is that '[w]e should stick to our knitting',[326] by which Dworkin means, stick to substantive arguments of literary criticism, not metaphysical arguments about literary criticism. Aside from these substantive arguments, 'we can give no sense to the idea that there is anything else we could do in deciding whether our judgments are "really" true'.[327]

Dworkin at one time held similar views about the lack of sense possessed by any metaphysical position about morality, realist or antirealist. Dworkin concluded about moral judgements, as about literary judgements, that he could 'see no point in trying to find some general argument that moral . . . judgments are objective'.[328] Again, this was because Dworkin could not understand the 'claims that the injustice of slavery is part of the furniture of the universe, that it is really "out there" in some way'.[329] Again, such claims take us 'back in the land of the incomprehensible metaphors'.[330] There is no metaphysical debate to have, Dworkin thought, on whether the injustice of slavery was or was not part of the furniture of the universe; only a non-metaphysical debate to have on whether slavery is or is not unjust. Dworkin thought that there is no debate to have on whether moral judgements describe an independent objective reality, for 'the question of what "independence" and "reality" are, for any practice, is a question within that practice, so that whether moral judgments can be objective is itself a moral question'.[331]

More recently, Dworkin has indicated some doubt about his earlier view that any metaphysical debate on the status of morality was meaningless.[332] He therefore draws a second arrow from his antimetaphysical quiver: even if there is a sensible inquiry called 'the metaphysics of morality', the outcome of that inquiry would be irrelevant to the practice of morality because no metaphysical answer could enter into our substantive moral argumentation that could either underwrite (if it is realist) or defeat (if it is sceptical) our moral convictions.

> What is the relation between my original opinion that slavery is wrong and these various 'objective' judgments I added to it? Here is one suggestion. The objective statements I added are meant to supply some special kind of evidence for my original opinion or some justification for my acting on it. They are meant to suggest that I can prove slavery is wrong the way I might prove some claim of physics, by arguments of fact or logic every rational person must accept: by showing that atmospheric moral quaverings confirm my opinion, for example, or that it matches a noumenal metaphysical fact. If this were the right way to understand my objective claims, then my claims would assert what external scepticsm denies: that

[325] Dworkin, 'Reply to Stanley Fish', above n. 308, at 298.
[326] Ibid.
[327] Ibid.
[328] Ibid. at 297.
[329] Ibid. at 299.
[330] Ibid.
[331] Ibid. at 300–1.
[332] See Dworkin, *Law's Empire*, above n. 66, at 80, and esp. at 426 n. 27.

moral judgements are descriptions of some special metaphysical realm. But it is not the right way to understand them. No one who says slavery is 'really' wrong thinks he has thereby given, or even suggested, an argument why it is. (How could quaverings or noumenal entities provide any argument for moral convictions?) The only kind of evidence I could have for my view that slavery is wrong, the only kind of justification I could have for acting on that view, is some substantive moral argument of a kind the 'objective' claims do not even purport to supply.[333]

In short, moral metaphysics neither adds to nor subtracts from our moral life, no matter how the debate between realists and antirealists might turn out.

In law, too, Dworkin thinks that it is a mistake to seek 'a thundering knock-down metaphysical demonstration no one can resist who has the wit to understand'.[334] Here too Dworkin thinks that the 'preliminary dance' of the metaphysician 'is silly and wasteful; it neither adds to nor subtracts from the business at hand'.[335] This opposition to metaphysics in legal theory echoes Dworkin's objections to metaphysics in moral theory: he claims that either (1) metaphysical support or criticism of legal theories is literally without sense and so must be ignored[336] or (2) such support or criticism is irrelevant to legal theory and practice because it cannot influence how we carry on these activities—even conceding that the metaphysical debate makes sense.[337]

D. The Inference from the Interpretive Claim About Law Practice to Dworkin's Antimetaphysical Conclusion

We now need to ask how Dworkin arrives at his antimetaphysical conclusions about literature, morality, and law, starting as he does with his interpretivist approach to all three areas of knowledge. Dworkin, like Rorty, was heavily influenced by Quine's work in epistemology.[338] For Dworkin no less than for Quine and Rorty, justification is never a matter of discovering foundational beliefs that stand in some primitive relation to brute reality. Only our other beliefs are available to support a belief we wish to justify.

333 Ibid. at 80–1.

334 Ibid. at 85. Notice that in both this and the previous quotation about morality, Dworkin, like Fish, confuses metaphysics with foundationalism in epistemology. He assumes that both antirealist and realist metaphysicians must claim that they have seen reality up close, unmediated by distorting theory, and have come back to give us new evidence of what it is like. Non-foundationalist metaphysicians make no such claims. Their metaphysics is not new evidence; it is, they think, a better way to think about what it is the evidence we all possess evidences.

335 Ibid. at 86.

336 See Dworkin, 'Reply to Stanley Fish', above n. 308, at 300–1.

337 See Dworkin, *Law's Empire*, above n. 66, at 266–7.

338 Although this has been evident from the first in Dworkin's coherence theories about law, for an explicit paraphrase of Quinean coherentism, see Ronald Dworkin, *A Matter of Principle* (Cambridge, Mass.: Harvard University Press, 1985), 169.

Also like Rorty, Dworkin employs two distinctions to draw his antimetaphysical and anti-epistemological conclusions from his non-foundationalism about justification. The first is the familiar external/internal distinction, which in Dworkin's hands is the distinction between arguments made within an interpretive practice and arguments made from the outside by non-participants. These latter arguments either affirm or deny the existence of the entities apparently referred to by the participants' internal discourse.[339] Dworkin claims there can be no such external arguments about an interpretive practice. They are either meaningless (Dworkin's first conclusion) or at least irrelevant to the interpretations offered within the practice (Dworkin's second conclusion). Second, Dworkin trades on the other distinction Rorty uses to bolster his antimetaphysical, anti-epistemological conclusions, the distinction between wholesale and retail points of view.[340] Even within an interpretive practice, Dworkin argues, we should distinguish wholesale from retail justifications or criticisms. The distinction, for Dworkin as for Rorty, is one of generality not internality. Dworkin uses the distinction to deny the possibility of wholesale (i.e. epistemological) justification or scepticism, either because it makes no sense or because it is irrelevant to the practice of giving retail interpretations.

Dworkin's arguments against (external) metaphysics and (wholesale) epistemology have some plausibility in Rorty's hands. After all, how does one stand outside all of our beliefs and theories to stare at a brute reality? How does one have an external judgement standard about such a reality when the standards to which it is external are all the standards we currently believe to be true? How does one meaningfully question all of our beliefs at once (wholesale), since that leaves none of our beliefs as the standard from which such questions may be asked?

[339] For Dworkin's use of the external/internal distinction to argue for the irrelevance of metaphysics to an interpretive activity, see *Law's Empire*, above n. 66, at 82–3; *Matter of Principle*, above n. 338, at 176; *Taking Rights Seriously*, above n. 305, at 282, 283–4; and Ronald Dworkin, '"Natural" Law Revisited', *University of Florida Law Review*, 34 (1982), 165–88, at 175–7. For Dworkin's use of the external/internal distinction to claim the senselessness of external (metaphysical) criticism, see 'Reply to Stanley Fish', above n. 308, at 297–303. In light of Dworkin's extensive use of this distinction, it may seem puzzling for Dworkin also to assert that the question of external objectivity is 'a fake because the distinction that might give it meaning, the distinction between substantive arguments within and skeptical arguments about social practices, is itself a fake' (*Matter of Principle*, above, n. 338, at 174). Yet this is just another way of using the external/internal distinction: to deny sense to the external and thus to the distinction itself. For a similar use, see Donald Davidson, 'On the Very Idea of a Conceptual Scheme', in J. Meiland and M. Krausz (eds.), *Relativism: Cognitive And Moral* (Notre Dame: University of Notre Dame Press, 1982), 66.

[340] We may trace Dworkin's gradually weakening use of this distinction in '"Natural Law" Revisited', above n. 339, at 177; *Matter of Principle*, above n. 338, at 175; and *Law's Empire*, above n. 66, at 78–9, 84, 266–75.

Those whom Rorty calls 'technical realists', such as myself, have argued that these intuitions of Rorty's, plausible as they are, cut no ice against naturalized epistemology or naturalized metaphysics. But Dworkin's use of these arguments, in connection with his modest interpretivism about discrete interpretive practices, is not even plausible. Notice that Dworkin makes Rorty's argument about each discrete interpretive practice that some society may have happened to have set up. According to Dworkin, we cannot criticize the practices of law, morality, and literary criticism, except by employing the standards of validity prevailing in that discipline, nor can we raise wholesale questions within such discrete practices.

Dworkin claims autonomy for each interpretive practice by consistently denying that there are any cross-disciplinary, cross-practice notions through which we could raise external (metaphysical) questions. Thus Dworkin tells us that each interpretive practice must be judged internally by its own standards of validity,[341] objectivity,[342] independence from convention,[343] and even truth,[344] meaning and reality.[345] For Dworkin, it is impossible to judge the propositions central to any interpretive practice by the (external) standards of science.[346] Rather, we should 'proceed more empirically'[347] by ascertaining what counts as a good reason within each such enterprise and judge the objectivity of its practice accordingly.

There are three things wrong with using Rorty's distinctions in this way: it is false, it is dangerous, and it is irretrievably paradoxical. It is false because the viewpoint external to moral practices, for example, is not some Archimedean place outside all of our beliefs and theories. For morality, the external viewpoint is our normal scientific viewpoint, with its normal notions of truth, reality, reference, and justification. If we put aside the 'special realm' picture that non-naturalism would bequeath to us about morality, then the existence of moral entities and qualities, the truth and the meaningfulness of moral utterances, the referents of moral terms, and the justifications of moral beliefs can all be judged by our normal (if external to morality) standards of ontology, meaning, reference, truth, and justification. The plausibility of Rorty's use of the 'impossibility of the external' argument depends wholly on Rorty's application of it to our knowledge as a whole. Once Dworkin applies the argument to discrete interpretive practices, it loses that plausibility.

Granting autonomy to each interpretive practice, so that it can be judged only by its own standards of judgement, is also dangerous. It requires us

341 Dworkin, *Matter of Principle*, above n. 338, at 153.

342 Ibid. at 162.

343 Ibid. at 174.

344 Ronald Dworkin, 'A Reply by Ronald Dworkin', in M. Cohen (ed.), *Ronald Dworkin and Contemporary Jurisprudence* (Oxford: Oxford University Press, 1984), 247, 277.

345 Dworkin, *Taking Rights Seriously*, above n. 305, at 174.

346 Ibid. at 153.

347 Ibid.

to license each complex, coherent, and publicly practised fairy tale that comes along. Presumably a Pegasus society could develop which became large enough to be called a linguistic community. If the society's numbers developed a complex set of standards towards which they also developed Dworkin's 'interpretive attitude', presumably the rest of us would have to admit that, in any meaningful (i.e. internal) sense of the words, that ancient winged horse really does soar through the skies.

Asserting the autonomy thesis is paradoxical for Dworkin because we are entitled to ask, from what vantage point does he assert the truth of this thesis? If 'true' is relativized to the practices of literary criticism, morality, and law, then with what truth concept does Dworkin assert the truth of that relativity thesis? Rorty, we should recall, had an answer to this ancient objection: Construed as an internal critic, Rorty asserted his truth from inside our practices, considered as a whole. Since Dworkin doesn't consider our practices as a whole, but instead relativizes truth to each sort of interpretive practice, Rorty's answer is unavailable to him. If Dworkin were to adopt Rorty's position, he would assert a cross-disciplinary truth (about the nature of truth in law, literature, and morality) from the perspective of either law or literature or morality. Dworkin wants to assert his relativized truth thesis from a point of view 'above' these three interpretive practices, but to do so falsifies his assertion while (and because) he makes it.

Dworkin must thus abandon his more ambitious conclusion that external criticism of claims made within interpretive practices is senseless. Can Dworkin's modest interpretivism sustain his more modest conclusion about external criticism? Dworkin, as we have seen, sometimes believes that a point of view external to an interpretive practice is not senseless but merely irrelevant to how practitioners do and should frame interpretations within the practice.[348] In this version of his antimetaphysical stance, Dworkin admits that from some point of view external to our practice of law, literature, or morality, one might well question whether the entities seemingly referred to by the discourse within these enterprises actually exist. Even so, Dworkin urges, such external criticism (or support) would be irrelevant once one began refereeing chess matches, writing literary criticism, making moral judgements, or deciding law cases. For in doing these things, the external critic must throw off her metaphysics, whatever it is, and get to work within the practice. Her metaphysical arguments are simply irrelevant to her interpretive claims within the practice because such external considerations do not affect such internal interpretive claims in the least.

This is a fair statement of the modest interpretivist claim that we saw before in psychoanalysis. If true, the claim seems to render academic (in

[348] See text accompanying nn. 339–40 above.

the pejorative sense of the word) any metaphysical inquiries. Such a claim is thus as much a challenge to the realist/antirealist debate as the less modest interpretivisms we have considered.

The problem for the modest interpretivist is whether he can maintain his line between interpretation, which is internal, and metaphysics/epistemology, which is external. I noted two problems for Dworkin's modest interpretivist cousin in psychoanalysis (who justified his interpretive activities by the non-explanatory aims of cure). (1) Successful therapy, while it is a process of interpretation, can itself become the subject of scientific evaluation, with all of its metaphysical trappings of truth, reference, and reality; thus the interpreter cannot stay only within his own interpretive practices but must at some point step out to explain them. (2) According to some psychoanalytic theories, an interpretation will be good only if it is also true both as description and as explanation. But in that case, the metaphysical and epistemological notions of truth, reference, reality, and justification have a central place within the interpretive practice itself.

Both points hold true on Dworkin's view of legal reasoning. In order to evaluate legal interpretations—whether particular acts or general types of interpretation—we must step outside of interpretive activity. We must seek both true descriptions of causal connections (e.g. does reliance on plain meanings enhance predictability and thus liberty?) and true evaluations of legal practices. This kind of description, explanation, and evaluation will indeed invoke our general notions of truth, reference, reality, and justification; but the mere fact that these notions are not purely legal is no reason to refuse to use them. As legal theorists, we need not be committed to some internal point of view such as that of a judge: texts like statutes that are authoritative for judges, lawyers, and citizens need not be authoritative for us qua legal theorists. An important part of legal theory, after all, is to argue for legal change. This is why I argued earlier that 'interpretive jurisprudence' is a mistake: legal theorists must examine the practices of their own legal culture and evaluate both the 'point' or values of that culture's interpretive practices and their success in realizing those values.

Moreover, this same argument also shows why Anglo-American legal practice, which is largely interpretive, cannot be insulated from external questions. For on Dworkin's own showing, the lawyers and judges who are internal to our interpretive practices must also ask these same evaluative, descriptive, and explanatory questions.[349] They too must ask how

[349] This has been one of Dworkin's consistent themes, see *Taking Rights Seriously*, above n. 305, at 14–130. Judges cannot rest content with following conventional practice but must ask the legal philosopher's questions: What is the authority of a statute? Why is legislative supremacy good? And so forth. Moreover, as Dworkin also consistently argues, these are not 'Sunday questions' for judges, to be put aside during Monday's judging; rather, the point the judge discovers on Sunday will guide the interpretation the judge does on Monday. The point of an interpretive practice should penetrate that practice to guide its application.

well their interpretive practices serve the point that justifies their engaging in such practices and thus join the legal philosopher in asking the metaphysical and epistemological questions earlier outlined.

The second reason why modest interpretivism cannot write off metaphysical inquiries as irrelevant is that our legal texts are implicitly metaphysical. Judges must interpret texts like those that award custody of a minor child to the parent who will maximize the 'best interest' of that child, that grant tort damages only against those who have 'caused' the harm complained of, that punish persons only if they 'intended' to do what they did, that allow organ transplants only from persons who are 'dead', and that grant each person 'equal protection of the laws'. As I have argued in other contexts,[350] the best interpretations of texts such as these are those that discover the most meaningful life for a person, the nature of the causal relation, the nature of an intention, the line between life and death, the nature of equality. These issues are inherently metaphysical, and the best interpretation is the one that comes closest to getting the metaphysics right.

An internal interpretation of prior legal practice hardly guarantees metaphysical success. In the case of causation, for example, judges must be free to discover the true nature of cause, not just parse prior legal discussions of 'cause'. Judges must examine not only 'legal paradigms' of the causal relation[351] but should also reach outward and determine whether, in the true sense of 'cause', one person caused another's harm. Only then can we maximally serve the corrective justice notion that people should pay for the harms they (really) cause.

Our legal system thus adopts something equal in effect to the Socratic therapy thesis in psychoanalysis, even if not strictly parallel. Although both disciplines may legitimately distinguish interpretive activities from explanatory activities initially, the way Freud and we carry on (and ought to carry on) our respective interpretive activities brings the external explanatory and evaluative viewpoints back inside. For us, accordingly, to interpret dreams or statutes is to seek true explanations and evaluations, where 'true' is not a term internal to our practice but brought to it from general metaphysical and epistemological positions.

[350] See Moore, above n. 5. The argument I there defend is that my 'natural law theory of interpretation' comes closer to maximizing the point that justifies interpreting statutory and constitutional texts—the rule of law values—than do competing interpretation theories that are less metaphysical in their demands. My argument parallels Freud's argument for his Socratic therapy thesis, for it is this thesis that commits the Freudian therapist also to seek the truth while he engages in the ultimately non-explanatory, non-truth-seeking task of interpretation.

[351] For an apparent example of a lawyer attempting this kind of internal, interpretivist analysis of 'cause' as used exclusively in the law, see Richard A. Epstein, 'A Theory of Strict Liability', *Journal of Legal Studies*, 2 (1973), 151–204, at 160–89. For a more realistic analysis, see Moore, 'Thomson's Preliminaries', above n. 43, and Moore, 'Causation and Responsibility', above n. 43.

I conclude that no interpretation of interpretivism can render either senseless or irrelevant the metaphysical debate about realism in science, morality, and law. Interpretivism in its less modest forms is just a thinly disguised metaphysical position, and an antirealist one at that. In the modest form it arguably assumes in Dworkin and clinical psychoanalysis, it is not metaphysical as an activity; but in that form it also cannot maintain the needed barrier between interpretive activities and those metaphysical inquiries that explain and justify good interpretations. It is thus time we end this debate with the interpretivist about the meaningfulness or worth of the metaphysical debate about realism. The real issues lie in the metaphysical debates among realists, sceptics, and idealists, not in the 'preliminary and wasteful dance'[352] of the antimetaphysical interpretivist.

[352] Dworkin, *Law's Empire*, above n. 66, at 86.

11
Interpreting Interpretation

I. INTRODUCTION

There is a simple life cycle for metaphors: they are born of fresh insight about an unnoticed similarity, wither with overuse, and die by becoming so familiar that they are treated as established senses of words. Intellectual fashions are like metaphors in this respect. Although they may begin life fresh and full of promise, they eventually become the tired counters in a patter that prevents insight rather than conveys it.

This has happened to the current intellectual fashion built around interpretation. Like the 'form of life' patter of the 1950s, and the 'paradigm' patter of the 1960s, some mention of 'interpretation' has become de rigueur in articles on just about any subject. Like the 'form of life' and 'paradigm' patters that Wittgenstein and Kuhn visited upon earlier decades, our 'interpretive' patter does very little work in either discovering or justifying any conclusion; such patter is most often merely the ornamental dressing put onto generally sceptical conclusions about law, literary criticism, psychology, physics, or just about anything. 'It is only your interpretation' has descended to the level of cocktail party conversation as our preferred way of expressing metaphysical or epistemological scepticism about anything, but it rarely does any work in justifying such scepticism.

All this is distressing to those of us who were interested in interpretation before it became so fashionable. This is not just the unhappiness one feels by having the symbols of one's personality appropriated by the masses—as when hippies made blue jeans a uniform, or when yuppies made BMWs a high status automobile. Rather, it is the dislike of seeing a useful concept turned into a piece of empty rhetoric. It is rather like the distress a surgeon might feel when, having honed his skills and his instruments to prepare for a delicate operation, he finds that others have thrown mud all over his scalpels.[1]

The mud in this case is what I have elsewhere called 'very ambitious interpretivism'.[2] What is so ambitious is the claim that all knowledge is interpretive, physics as much as psychology, astronomy as much as literary criticism. This is sometimes put into slogans, such as that 'all the world is a text', or that 'nothing exists outside the text', or that 'all understanding

[1] I owe the metaphor to David A. J. Richards, who at a conference many years ago when some very woolly comments were being directed to me leaned over to whisper, 'they're throwing mud on your scalpels'.

[2] Ch. 10, above.

requires the prejudices of interpretation'.[3] These Derridan, Barthian, and Gadamerian slogans create a great deal of sympathy in me for reactions like that of Michael Devitt: 'when someone starts talking about "interpretation", reach for your gun.'[4] Still, even with bathwater this dirty, there may be a baby worth saving. What I wish to examine is the concept of interpretation that should be saved when the bloated interpretivism of current post-modernist fashion has run its course and died.

II. GENUINE INTERPRETATION

A good first stab at defining a useful notion of interpretation is that it is the activity we engage in when we are trying to find the meaning of something.[5] To elucidate this definition, we should pursue three questions: first, what sorts of things have meaning? Second, does the validity of an interpretation consist in the discovery of such meanings, or can such validity exist even if we *create* such meanings by our interpretations? Third, why should anyone ever engage in this activity, i.e. what value is served by finding/creating a meaning for something? The first I shall call the basic question about interpretation, the second, the question of validity, and the third, the question of justification. Although these are analytically separable questions, the interrelations of any plausible answers to them prevent me from organizing this discussion around them. Rather, I shall ask all three of them simultaneously for each model of interpretation that I explore.

A place to start is by pursuing the basic question: what sorts of things have meanings? Let us sharpen this question before we try to answer it. The late Paul Grice once distinguished non-natural meanings from natural

[3] Some of these slogans are explored in Joseph Margolis, 'Reinterpreting Interpretation', *Journal of Aesthetics*, 48 (1990), 1–15, at 7. Recognizing that very ambitious interpretivism is 'notably, even peculiarly, fashionable in our own time' (ibid. at 1), Joe Margolis seeks to salvage what he can out of it.

[4] The realist metaphysician, Michael Devitt, is so quoted in W. Lycan, *Judgement and Justification* (Cambridge: Cambridge University Press, 1988), at 195 n. 7.

[5] Cf. Sigmund Freud, *The Complete Introductory Lectures on Psychoanalysis*, trans. James Strachey (New York: W. W. Norton, 1966), at 87: 'Interpreting means finding a hidden sense in something . . .' Note that Freud, like many others (e.g. Annette Barnes, *On Interpretation* (Oxford: Basil Blackwell, 1988), chs. 2–3, and Andrei Marmor, *Interpretation and Legal Theory* (Oxford: Oxford University Press, 1992), 21), adds something to this most general notion of interpretation that I leave out, namely, that interpretation is the finding of something that is hidden or not obvious. In this sense, statutes with a plain meaning can be said to need no interpretation. This unhelpfully narrows interpretation, as I argue in M. Moore, 'A Natural Law Theory of Interpretation', *Southern California law Review*, 58 (1985), 277–398, at 284–5. In Marmor's case, this restriction seems part of his general affirmance of the communicative model of interpretation, so that what is governed by semantics (and is thus obvious) is not part of interpretation.

meanings.[6] 'Clouds mean rain' was an example of the latter usage of 'meaning', while 'he means to hurt you' was an example of the former usage. With Grice, I take the natural meaning usage not to be of interest in this context, for 'natural meanings' are just animistic metaphors for causal connections between literally meaningless events. Causes and effects are natural signs for one another, but that just means that each is evidence for the other given the connection between the two. Clouds are a sign of rain, and if it rains, the raining is a sign that there were clouds from which the rain fell. In this uselessly broad sense of 'meaning', everything that is not causally inert (which is everything we know about) 'has meaning'.

Better for our purposes is non-natural meaning, what Grice called 'meaning'$_{nn}$. If we leave clouds for *talk* about clouds, for example, such talk seems to have a meaning that is not simply the causal connections between the clouds and other phenomena. Such talk may be an explicit utterance in ordinary, everyday conversation; it may be a legal utterance, such as a statute; it may appear in a novel or play; it may be part of an utterance of God; or it may form part of the manifest content of a dream. In all such cases, we are presented with phenomena that seem to possess meaning and seem to call for interpretation in order to be understood.

If we isolate what it is about ordinary conversational utterances, laws, novels, divine commands, and dreams that seems to give them meaning$_{nn}$, we come upon something that should be called a *text*. To say of each of these productions, that they have meaning, is to say that each of them consists of a text. This of course is not to say much until we say what a text is (in some way that is freer of question-begging than, 'possessor of meaning').

A first impulse might be to think that there are texts in nature. Geologists often say, for example, that the various layers of rock form a textual history of the earth and that to learn geology is to learn how to read this text. Such a reading of 'text', however, returns us to natural meaning. Layers of rocks are signs of past events—and thus, are texts 'about' those past events—only in the anaemic sense that such rocks are the effects of (and thus constitute evidence of) those earlier events.

The alternative that perhaps most readily suggests itself is to think that something can be a text only if a person or persons intentionally create it as a text. More specifically, one might think that *the* creative act of relevance here is that whereby persons create symbols that allow them to communicate what they mean to one another. On this view, texts are the medium (of representation devices) that author and audience share when one human agent is attempting to communicate to another. This, as I shall call it, is the communicative model of interpretation. The model has a

[6] H. P. Grice, 'Meaning', *Philosophical Review*, 66 (1957), 377–88.

powerful grip on our image of interpretation. Before showing how the model misleads, we need to understand the grip that it has on us.

The power of the communicative model of interpretation lies in its tidiness in answering my three earlier distinguished questions. To the basic question of what has meaning, the model answers, only those representational systems (texts) that are created by human agents in order to communicate with one another. A system of signs becomes a representational system, on this view, when agents use them to form the object of intentions which they wish to communicate, and when the signs so used by authors are also used by audiences as the objects of the beliefs formed in response. Ultimately, thus, what is a text on this model is a function of the symbol system used in those propositional attitudes that are the intentions of communicators and the beliefs of their audiences. Since the propositional attitudes are what they are by virtue of their Intentionality, that makes texts too a function of the Intentionality of those agents who use them in this way.[7]

The second question—about validity—also has a very tidy answer on the communicative model of interpretation. An interpretation of an utterance—be it in a novel, dream, statute, or holy text—is valid on this model if and only if the interpretation corresponds to the intention with which the utterance was produced. There is no question here about *creating* something by interpretation, the validity of which then becomes mysterious. Rather, an interpretation is valid only if one discovers the true explanation of why the text was produced. Such an explanation does not create anything; it reproduces the object of the intention that caused the utterance to exist.

Similarly, the third question of justification has a ready answer on the communicative model of interpretation. For interpretation becomes a species of explanation (namely, explanations of communicative utterances). We thus need have no special sort of activity, distinct from the normal descriptive/explanatory activities of science, that requires justification. Scientific curiosity about why some dream was produced, some novel written, some holy pronouncement made, or some statute passed, may suffice to justify interpreting these texts on this model of interpretation.[8]

[7] By Intentionality, I mean the directedness upon-an-object that Franz Brentano reintroduced to modern discussions. This rather technical notion is to be distinguished from the more ordinary, more idiomatic 'intentional'. For an introduction, see Daniel Dennett, *Content and Consciousness* (London: Routledge, 1969), ch. 2.

[8] On this view, interpretation is an activity in which one is justified in engaging on the normal scientific grounds: 'The basic reason for studying the cognitive processes has become as clear as the reason for studying anything else: because they are there' (U. Neisser, *Cognitive Psychology* (New York: Appleton–Century–Crofts, 1967), 12). On my view of interpretation developed below, interpretation is more like mountain-climbing than scientific explanation in that both mountain-climbing and interpretation require more than George Mallory's famous 'because it is there' answer to justify the doing of them.

The communicative model thus causes no ripples in the smooth waters of science. Moreover, the model no doubt accurately captures perhaps the most ordinary, most familiar usage of 'interpretation'. When we seek to 'find the meaning of something'—that is, when we engage in an activity properly called 'interpretation'—perhaps most often we are the audience of a communicative utterance by another. In which case our reasons and our methods are the standard reasons and methods of scientific description/explanation, with the only difference that what we describe (a text) and explain it with (authorial intention) are both Intentional phenomena.

This is all so happily unproblematic that some may wish to stop here. Yet to do so ignores the insight that I take to have motivated late nineteenth-century theology to coin the English word, 'hermeneutics' from the Greek. That insight is that there is something especially interpretive about disciplines like theology, literary criticism, law, and psychoanalysis. More precisely, the insight is that certain dominant *activities* within such disciplines cannot be forced to conform to the methods of ordinary scientific description/explanation, nor are such activities justified by the normal scientific goals of prediction/explanation/understanding.

If we examine how such activities within such disciplines are in fact carried on, this sense that interpretation is richer than the communicative model can allow is reinforced. A problem with the communicative model lies in the straitjacket it would force onto us about what we may properly conceive to be activities of literary, statutory, theological, or dream interpretation. For the model requires us to say that only when literary critics are seeking to recapture the intended meaning of the author of some novel are they *interpreting* that novel, only when lawyers are seeking to recapture the intended meaning of the legislature that created some statute are they *interpreting* that statute, only when theologians are seeking to recapture what God meant in causing the Bible to be written are they *interpreting* the Bible, and only when psychoanalysts are seeking to recapture the wish that caused the dream to have the content that it did are they seeking to *interpret* that dream. There are of course well-known versions of literary criticism, legal theory, theology, and psychoanalysis that promote just these intentionalist interpretive strategies. But there are other, competing interpretive strategies in each of these disciplines that do not seek to recapture authorial intention. Not only are these equally well-regarded strategies; not only, indeed, are these *better* interpretive strategies, as I have argued in detail about some of these disciplines;[9] but it seems a woefully parochial and narrow-minded view of interpretation to rule out these non-intentionalist strategies out of hand because they cannot—logically can-

[9] Moore, 'A Natural Law Theory of Interpretation', above n. 5.

not—be *interpretive* in character.[10] Even if one ends up being an E. D. Hirsch about literary criticism, a Robert Bork about statutory and constitutional interpretation, an intentionalist about theological interpretation, or a Freud about dream interpretation, it should not be for lack of any truly *interpretive* alternatives. Even those literacy critics, lawyers, psychoanalysts, and theologians who end up being intentionalists need a broader notion of interpretation than that allowed by the communicative model in order to have substantive (as opposed to conceptual) arguments against their opponents.

I thus propose that we regard 'interpretation' as ambiguous. One sense is that involved in communication, where 'interpretation' names the description and explanation of communicative utterances. Such social-scientific task is one sense of 'finding the meaning of something'. The distinct, non-communicative sense of 'interpretation' we have not yet described. Perhaps the most common analysis of this second sense of interpretation is that bequeathed to us by Dilthey and the other original 'hermeneuts'. I refer to the dualistic tradition that divides the world between natural, meaningless phenomena, and social, meaningful phenomena, that divides the sciences between the *naturwissenschaften* and the *geisteswissenschaften*, that divides cognition between knowledge and *verstehen*, or understanding, and that divides the manner of doing science between explanation and interpretation.[11] These dualistic divisions are then used by such theorists to create a ghostly realm in which they may mimic the communicative model of interpretation. To the basic question of what is a text, they say that meaningful texts simply exist as a distinct kind of thing in the world even though such texts need not be created by an author communicating to an audience. To the question of what makes an interpretation valid, they answer that an interpretation is valid if it corresponds to that meaning which is an essential feature of meaningful phenomena—even though that meaning is not to be equated with the datable state of authorial intention. To the question of why we should engage in interpretation, they answer that there need be no value justifying interpretation other than the value that motivates all science, namely to understand (in a special sense) the truth (in a special sense). What is mimicked is the communication model's subsumption of interpretation into ordinary scientific understanding, with the enormous caveat being added to the effect that this is a special sort of scientific understanding and a special sort of truth, to go along with this special sort of phenomena.

[10] As argued, for example, by Walter Benn Michaels, 'Response to Perry and Simon', *Southern California Law Review*, 58 (1985), 673–81.

[11] For description of this tradition and citations, see Ch. 10, above. Compare the differing views on dualistic interpretation in D. Hiley, J. Bohman, and R. Shusterman (eds.), *The Interpretive Turn* (Ithaca, NY: Cornell University Press, 1991).

This dualistic model provides an unnecessarily mysterious and extravagant answer to our question of whether there is some non-communicative sense of 'interpretation'. Special notions of truth and understanding are notoriously the first refuge of those intellectual scoundrels who seek to escape their obligation to relate whatever it is that puzzles them (such as interpretation) with the rest of the world as they understand it.[12] Surely we can do better than this.

The dualist hermeneuts were right to seek to free up another model of interpretation from the grip on the concept by the communication model, but the dualist tradition's 'special science' is no way to do this. Perhaps we can creep up on a better model, alternative to the communicative model, if we return to the basic question. What else might be a text besides a system of representations used by someone with the intention of communicating some intended meaning to others? To keep the communicative intentions of authors out of it, let us focus for the moment on examples where there are no authors. Imagine a formation of clouds in rare but suggestive shapes (we might call them 'Rorshach Clouds'). Suppose further a set of individuals who purport to see their deepest secrets revealed in such clouds. Should we say that the clouds are a text, that they have meaning, so that those who see themselves revealed by the clouds can properly be said to *interpret* them?

The tug of the communicative model may be strong here. As we have seen, the general insight behind the communicative model is right: meaning_{nn} is a function of the Intentionality of some human agents.[13] And if no human agent invested the clouds with meaning, how can they *have* meaning? Besides an author, there is of course the audience whose propositional attitudes of belief are eligible investors of meanings. A move tempting to some, such as the early Stanley Fish,[14] is to take the brute social fact that certain audiences ('interpretive communities') do regard certain phenomena as meaningful—do purport to form objects of beliefs by paying some kind of attention to such phenomena—as enough

[12] See Ch. 10, above, for an example in psychoanalysis, where psychoanalytic theorists attempt to insulate their theory from scientific criticism by taking refuge in the tradition of dualist hermeneutics.

[13] Which is not to buy into John Searle's notion that persons possess an original, primitive, or irreducible Intentionality that a Turing machine (such as the human brain) cannot possess. I assume that human brains are ultimately syntactic engines whose complexity nonetheless produces states with semantic (i.e. Intentional) properties. M. Moore, 'Mind, Brain, and the Unconscious', in P. Clark and C. Wright (eds.), *Mind, Psychoanalysis, and Science* (Oxford: Basil Blackwell, 1988). One can accept this reductionist view about minds while accepting, as do I in the text, that persons are truly possessed of Intentional states and that it is the Intentionality of persons' propositional attitudes that invests other objects in the world with meaning.

[14] Stanley Fish, *Is There a Text in This Class?* (Cambridge, Mass.: Harvard University Press, 1980).

to constitute such phenomena as a text. Yet this sociological kind of answer brings with it all the dissatisfactions aroused whenever social facts are substituted for analysis. We all recognize that others sometimes regard a phenomenon as meaningful, but if what we want to know is in what sense such a phenomenon *is* meaningful, it is no help to be told that 'many so regard it'.

My own answer is in a sense 'audience-centred', but it focuses, not on the actual propositional attitudes or actions people may have in response to a phenomenon, but rather, on the attitudes and actions they have *reason* to have or to do. A person or group of persons staring at Rorshach clouds can give the clouds meaning by finding some value (such as self-knowledge) in treating the clouds as a text. To treat the clouds as a text is to treat the clouds as potentially giving us either reasons for belief or reasons for action, if we can just figure out what they mean. If there are such reasons to treat the clouds as a text, the clouds *are* a text.

This sounds circular, but it is not. There is a text, and thus interpretation in the desired sense, whenever: (1) people have some good reason, (2) to treat some phenomenon they do not yet know the meaning of, as being meaningful, (3) in the sense that such meanings give them either reasons for belief or reasons for action. Let us unpack this one step at a time.

Let us start with the second element, treating some phenomenon as meaningful. People do this whenever they impose a syntax/semantics distinction onto the phenomenon, that is, whenever they find the phenomenon to be meaningful even without knowing what it means. I call this the imposition of a syntax/semantics distinction because in order to do this they must have some criteria for isolating meaningful phenomena that do not depend on knowing the meaning of the phenomena. If we call the meaning of the phenomena its semantics, we should call the criteria for text individuation its syntax, for 'syntax' is the name we give in linguistics to those rules that determine which strings of symbols are well-formed formulas and thus eligible to be the bearers of meaning.

Two examples: in theology there is an old debate about whether the consuming goodness of God consists in the fact that whatever God commands is good (because she commands it), or whether that goodness consists in the fact that God, being omniscient, makes no mistakes about what is good in her commandings.[15] Suppose a believer seeks to do what God commands. Under the first variation the believer is plainly interpreting God's commands, because he has a criterion of text individuation (God said it) independent of yet knowing what the text means. Under the second variation the situation is less clear. Eventually the believer may come to

[15] Notice how Aquinas splits the difference here: 'the divine law commands certain things because they are good . . . while others are good because they are prescribed . . .' (*The Political Ideas of St. Thomas Aquinas*, ed. Dino Bigongiani (New York: Hafner, 1953), 100).

interpret God's commands because eventually he will grant God the (theoretical) authority he also grants to a good weatherman: both God and the weatherman get it right often enough that they should be listened to when it comes to morality or picnics. When the believer under the second variation grants such authority to God, he then has a criterion of text-individuation (God said it) independent of yet knowing what the text means. But initially, when the correspondence between the good and what God commands is in doubt, the believer will have to understand what the commands mean, check them against his own understanding of the good, and follow them only if they check out. This is not interpretation because there is no criterion of text-individuation that is independent of knowing what the text means.

The second example is from law. While there is a debate in legal theory (about whether statutes possess practical or merely theoretical authority) that parallels exactly the above debate in theology,[16] another debate in legal theory reveals different aspects of this second criterion for the existence of a text. I refer to the debate about whether there is, can be, or should be a 'rule of recognition' that tests the validity of laws within any legal system. The late Herbert Hart's famous answer was that there is such a legal syntax, a set of rules that give the criteria for text-individuation independent of knowing the meaning of the text.[17] Critics of Hart have disagreed, arguing that one cannot know the text of the law without knowing (and judging to be good) what the law means. Somewhat ironically (given the rather different self-labellings of some of the critics), only the first of these positions about law reveals legal practice clearly to be interpretive. It takes some delicate footwork on the second of these views to make legal practice interpretive—one must talk about 'pre-interpretive data', 'obvious law (to be interpreted by non-obvious law)', 'rules (to be interpreted by non-rule-like principles)', 'concepts (to be interpreted by conceptions)', and the like to reintroduce the crucial notion of legal syntax in order for there to be something like a text to law.[18]

Why cannot one merge syntax and semantics so that whether there is a text, and what is the text, is a function of what such a text might mean?[19] The answer lies in the fact that with such merger one loses what is essential about interpretation, which is the guidance texts (and their correct interpretations) are to give us in what we believe and what we do. Interpretive reasoning is distinctive from ordinary moral or scientific reasoning in that it essentially involves a two-step dance: ask first whether

[16] See e.g. Heidi Hurd, 'Challenging Authority', *Yale Law Journal*, 100 (1991), 1611–77.

[17] H. L. A. Hart, *The Concept of Law* (Oxford: Clarendon Press, 1961).

[18] See e.g. Ronald Dworkin, *Law's Empire* (Cambridge, Mass.: Harvard University Press, 1986).

[19] Ronald Dworkin's kind of query. See ibid.

there is a text and what it is; ask second what that text means in the sense of how it applies to the situation at hand. One can allow for a kind of reflective equilibrium to be reached between text-individuation ('syntax') and text-interpretation ('semantics'), so that whether a text produces good interpretations bears on the questions of whether it is a text at all, and if so, what the text is; but even so, when the epistemic equilibrium is reached, the reasoning must be a two-step dance to be an interpretive dance at all.

This brings us to the third aspect of my three-part answer to the basic question about texts. This third aspect is the distinctive reason-giving nature of texts and their interpretations. What makes interpretive reasoning so distinct a method of reasoning about what to think or what to do is the unique sort of reasons (for belief or action) such reasoning seeks to discover. Because these text-based reasons are themselves different depending on whether they are reasons for belief or reasons for action, let us consider each separately.

There is some debate about how texts can give reasons for action to those subject to the authority of such texts. Joseph Raz has developed in elegant detail the idea that texts can give those subject to them what he calls 'protected reasons' for action.[20] Such protected reasons are dual in nature: they are first-order reasons to do the act described in the text, a reason that did not exist prior to the creation of the text; and they are second-order reasons excluding all other reasons that might bear on the action from having any influence on the actor's decision. Texts on this view give conclusive reasons to act in the way described by the texts, for the text itself is a new reason for acting in conformity with it and that new reason is protected from any competition.

If there were a God, and if we had the text of her commands, this is undoubtedly how we should conceive of her text's influence on our practical reasoning. For less divine texts, however, such as those we find in the law, this is surely too strong. Democratically enacted statutes in reasonably just regimes, for example, give at least some legal actors new first-order reasons for action in conformity with them, but these reasons are unprotected from competition with the other reasons that may argue against doing the action. Or so I have argued in some detail.[21]

Whether one adopts Raz's view or my own does not here matter. On either view, what is distinctive about texts is that they give actors reasons for action that did not exist before the text was created. When a friend requests an action, we promise to do an action, God commands an action, or a statute requires an action, we often have a reason to do the action

[20] Joseph Raz, *Practical Reason and Norms* (Oxford: Oxford University Press, 1975), *The Authority of Law* (Oxford: Oxford University Press, 1979), and *The Morality of Freedom* (Oxford: Oxford University Press, 1986), chs. 2–4.

[21] Ch. 5, above.

requested, promised, commanded or required just because such a text was created.

Reasons for belief are different. When a text creates a new reason for belief, it is because we grant the text a kind of expertise over its subject matter to which we are willing to defer. Weather reports are a good example. Because the weatherman has a better ability than do I to predict the weather, the texts he issues create for me new reasons for belief about the weather. The weatherman has no practical authority over me, so that his texts give me no reasons to act one way over another. Still, since my actions depend on what I believe, the weather-report texts can indirectly influence my actions by directly influencing my beliefs.[22]

Again, we can distinguish protected reasons for belief from unprotected but new first-order reasons for belief. And again, if there were a God, and if she were omniscient, God's texts would undoubtedly give us protected reasons for belief. For less divine texts, however, unprotected reasons for belief are more likely all we can expect. The important point again, however, is that such texts do give us reasons to believe that did not exist prior to the existence of such texts.

This notion of texts giving new reasons for action or belief must be sharpened if we are to use it in explicating text-hood and interpretation. For lots of things give us reasons for action or belief that are not texts. My decision in the past to allow my eldest child to attend a rock concert at age 14 created a reason, based in equality, to act now so as to allow my youngest daughter on her fourteenth birthday to attend her first rock concert; yet my past action is not a text. Similarly, the fact that a blade of grass is bent gives me reason to believe that some animal has passed recently; but the bent blade of grass is not a text. To be sure, the existence of such events and states give me reasons for action or belief only because there are true generalizations of morality and science that include both them and the future act or event I have reason to do or believe. Yet these moral and scientific generalizations are also not texts, at least on any non-relativistic view of ethics and science.

Needed is the Intentionality of some intervening human agency if we are to have the kinds of reasons for action or belief that are created by text. If my youngest daughter requests that she go to the rock concert, or if I promise her that she may go, the acts of requesting and promising are texts; they not only give me a reason to do the act requested or promised, but they do so as Intentional states. That is, to have a reason to do the act

[22] Reasons for belief can have a more immediate implication for action than that mentioned in the text. One very important kind of theoretical authority is practical wisdom, that is, moral expertise about reasons for action. The utterances of such a theoretical authority do give us reasons for belief, not of action, yet *what* we have reason to believe because of such utterances is what reasons for action we have.

requested or promised because the act was requested or promised means I have to figure out what my daughter requested, or what I promised to do. This is to enquire into the propositional attitudes expressed in the actions of requesting and promising.

Likewise for reasons for belief. The bent blade of grass has no Intentionality, and thus the reason for belief that it creates is not of the relevant sort. Contrast such ordinary evidence with the distinctive sort of evidence of relevance here: someone is holding the blade of grass and tells me that it will be bent because he intends to bend it; alternatively, an expert on the watering habits of animals at the waterhole around which the grass sits tells me that the blade of grass is bent because, at this time of the day, all of the grass is bent by animals watering. In both of these last cases, the expression of intention or of belief is a text because it gives me a reason for belief as the Intentional state of a person. That is, to know what it is this kind of evidence evidences, I will have to enquire into the propositional attitudes expressed by the relevant actors.[23]

It might seem that this reason-giving capacity of texts returns us to an intentionalist mode of interpretation.[24] For many examples of texts that give us new reasons for belief or for action do so only because the *authors* of those texts are either theoretical or practical authorities. And if the authority of the text wholly depends on the authority of the author of that text, one would usually interpret the text in a manner that seeks to elicit what the author *meant*.[25] One would, in other words, return to an intentionalist method of interpretation even while proceeding from a non-communicative model.

Are there then (syntactically individuated) texts that give us new reasons for belief or for action that do *not* depend on the authority of their author? This moves us to the first aspect of my three-part explication of what is a text—that is, to the question of value. We easily understand why we have reason to interpret requests, promises, and expert advice. Each of these give us reasons for action or belief, if we can only figure out what was meant by the requester, promisor, or expert; we thus in these instances have reason enough to engage in intentionalist interpretation. But our present enquiry is what reason there might be to treat some text as creating new reasons for us when we do not care what the author meant.

23 I am indebted in this discussion to the notion of 'content-independent' reasons developed by Joseph Raz and Herbert Hart. See e.g. Raz, *The Morality of Freedom*, above n. 20, at 35–7. I have avoided their vocabulary because the label is a quite misleading one when used to refer to essentially Intentionality-dependent reasons.

24 See e.g. Marmor, *Interpretation and Legal Theory*, above n. 5, at ch. 8.

25 But not always. Jeremy Waldron, in 'Legislators' Intentions and Unintentional Legislation', in A. Marmor (ed.), *Law and Interpretation* (Oxford: Oxford University Press, 1995) nicely explores a variety of reasons for thinking that statutes may possess theoretical authority without any individual legislator possessing such authority.

What values might be served by ceding authority to such texts when either they have no author, or the author they have lacks any theoretical or practical authority?

Suppose it were the case that clouds, like dreams, were in fact excellent devices for generating self-knowledge. Since self-knowledge is a good for persons, clouds and dreams should be treated as texts in the sense explicated, that is, they are treated as meaningful phenomena even before we know their meaning, and when we know their meaning we know the reasons for belief that they impart to us. The value of self-knowledge in such a case makes clouds and dreams a text even though there need be no author of them.

As another example, consider that used by Ronald Dworkin, the social practice of courtesy.[26] Social practices of courteous behaviour have no single author, and no intentional creation by anyone. They grow up gradually and unwittingly. Nonetheless, we have reason to treat such practices as a text in the sense explicated: we have a syntactic mode of their individuation (past practice), and we treat the interpreted practice as giving us a reason to act in conformity with it. The value served by doing this is the value of respect. It is a good to treat others respectfully, and since others are so treated only when they realize that respect is being manifested, we each have reason to follow the practices of respect-giving (courtesy) by treating those practices as a text.

There is an important subtlety here that requires emphasis since it is so easily missed.[27] It is not that a social practice like courtesy becomes a text just because the practice is a valuable one. Our practices of kindness and justice are valuable practices, but those practices are not themselves texts that we must interpret in order to be either kind or just. Rather, there must be a value justifying why we should treat a practice as a text in the sense I have explicated. The value must show us why it is good to regard the practice as meaningful before we know its meaning, and why it is good to treat the interpreted practice as giving us reasons to behave in one way rather than another. Because courtesy must be understood by its recipients as courtesy in order for the good of respect to be achieved, we have reason to treat our practices of courtesy as a text. Because kindness and justice do not require their beneficiaries to understand that they are being treated kindly or justly for the goods of kindness and justice to be realized, we have no reason to treat our practices of kindness or justice as texts.

For a legal example, consider the American Constitution. This is a text with an author, or at least a set of them. It has thus tempted American constitutional lawyers for decades to think that the authority of the text is due to the authority of its authors. This then leads to an intentionalist method

[26] See Dworkin, *Law's Empire*, above n. 18, at 46–9.

[27] For criticism of Dworkin on this ground, see Ch. 10, above.

of interpretation being applied to the document. Yet there is no good argument for why the framers of the Constitution had either theoretical or practical authority.[28] They were neither divinely inspired, nor notably more astute politically than are the educational elites of our own generation. They were not selected by us to lay down our fundamental law, nor have we in any meaningful sense consented, explicitly or tacitly, to their authority. I think it obvious that the framers had no authority over those of us who live two hundred years later, so that we have no reason to care what they may have meant by what they said.

Nonetheless, there is some value served by the present generation of Americans treating the written Constitution as a text. Like authorless clouds, dreams, and courtesy, that value has nothing to do with some supposed need to find out what the author of the document believed, wanted, or intended. Rather, that value has to do with the legitimation potential that the document has within American society. It is trite but true that the Constitution is America's civil religion. The result is that peaceful resolutions of fundamental disputes become easier if those disputes are framed as disputes about the meaning of Constitutional phrases like 'free expression', 'cruel and unusual punishment', and the like. Peaceful resolution of such disputes is a real good, giving each of us reason to grant the document the status of text even while we refuse to grant any authority to its authors.

These last examples, while freeing us from the inevitability of always seeking to discover an author's intention when we interpret, may seem to have flouted my earlier stated requirement that the reasons given by a text be Intentionality-dependent. With social practices like courtesy, the American constitution, and perhaps even with dreams (on a Freudian account), this flouting may not be so obvious, for at least these items were in some sense produced intentionally by someone or some group. But clouds, even Rorshach clouds, are intentionally produced by no one. In what sense can clouds give us 'Intentionality-dependent' reasons?

This worry leads many theorists about interpretation, such as Joseph Raz[29] and Andrei Marmor,[30] to disclaim such cases as instances of interpretation at all. Only items that are at least intentionally produced by their creators, and perhaps even intended to be a text by those creators, are eligible candidates for text-hood. This would include the American Constitution, perhaps dreams and courtesy, but certainly exclude clouds.

[28] See M. Moore, 'Do We Have an Unwritten Constitution?', *Southern California Law Review*, 63 (1989), 107–39, at 120–1.

[29] Joseph Raz, 'Interpretation Without Intention', in Marmor, *Law and Interpretation*, above n. 25.

[30] Marmor, *Interpretation and Legal Theory*, above n. 5, at ch. 6.

Yet notice how arbitrary is the line this view would draw. Once it is admitted that the meaning of texts such as dreams, courtesy, and the American Constitution is not to be sought in the propositional attitudes of their authors,[31] of what relevance is it whether a given phenomenon was intentionally produced, or intentionally produced as a text? Such a requirement seems an idle stipulation. If we have reason to treat dreams, for example, as a text, and if that reason justifies us in seeking a meaning to dreams *not* to be equated to any intention or wish that produced them, then surely it is irrelevant to their text-hood whether dreams are intentional productions or not.

One can of course seek to bolster this 'intentionally produced' criterion of text-hood by saying that we always do seek authorial intention when we interpret. Then the criterion is not idle. Yet one can only plausibly say this about dreams, courtesy, and the American Constitution if one fictionalizes the authorial intention a good interpretation recaptures.

Ronald Dworkin, for example, urges that when we interpret the American Constitution we seek the framer's intention—with the enormous *caveat* that such intention is not a psychological state.[32] Andrei Marmor likewise pays lip service to intentionalist interpretation when he proclaims that 'interpretation is essentially a matter of attributing intentions' but then allows the attribution of purely fictional intentions of fictional authors to fit the bill so that he can account for what he (rightly) regards as undeniably interpretive practices of artistic criticism.[33] Similarly unhelpful are the evasions common to American legal practice with statutes, whereby one pretends that the value a statute serves (and that is therefore maximized by correct interpretations) is the 'intention in the statute'.[34] Equally unhelpful is the wilful trading on the ambiguity of 'purpose', so that one actually interprets so as to serve the purpose (in the sense of function, or value) of the statute all the while pretending to be interpreting so as to serve the purpose (in the sense of further intended

[31] See e.g. ibid. Marmor distinguishes the use of intention to individuate the text from the use of authorial intention to find the text's meaning. According to Marmor, the latter use is occasional even while the former use is universal to all activities of interpretation.

[32] Ronald Dworkin, *A Matter of Principle* (Cambridge, Mass.: Harvard University Press, 1985), 34–57. See also *Law's Empire*, above n. 18, at 53–65.

[33] Marmor, *Interpretation and Legal Theory*, above n. 5, at 30–1. For yet another example, see Stanley Fish, 'Play of Surfaces: Theory and Law', in Gregory Leyh (ed.), *Legal Hermeneutics: History, Theory, and Practice* (Berkeley: University of California Press, 1992), at 300–1.

[34] The 'intention in the words alone' obfuscation may be found in *United States v. Goldenberg*, 168 U.S. 95, 102–03 (1911) ('The primary and general rule of statutory construction is that the intent of the lawmaker is to be found in the language that he has used'); Donald Gustafson, 'On Unconscious Intentions', *Philosophy*, 48 (1973), 178–82 ('Exegetical and critical work makes use of the notion of *intention in* when it tries to bring out the intention in a piece of art without reference to the intention with which the artist produced it'). See generally M. Moore, 'The Semantics at Judging', *Southern California Law Review*, 54 (1981), 151–294, at 258–62, and 'A Natural Law Theory', above n. 5, at 347.

consequence) of the authors of the statute.[35] Similarly misleading is Plowden's old ploy of pretending that one's value-laden interpretations are really the recapturing of the hypothetical intention the author would have had had he directed his attention to the problem.[36]

If one is willing to fictionalize the authorial intention a good interpretation seeks in these ways, why would one not also fictionalize the intentional production of a text? Why not say of clouds, for example, that we regard them as a text because God intended them to be so treated, qualifying the latter by disavowing any belief in God or his intent? Alternatively, and preferably, we should dispense with both fictions. It neither matters to the existence of a text, nor to its proper interpretation, that someone intentionally created the phenomenon as a text or that someone meant something by it. Justice Holmes' forthright disavowal of intention is preferable to the fictionalized evasions we have noted; with regard to legislative intent, Holmes noted, 'in fact intention is a residuary clause intended to gather up whatever other aids there may be to interpretation besides the particular words and the dictionary'.[37]

One might legitimately wonder at this point whether my own account doesn't fictionalize Intentionality in its requirement that texts give Intentionality-dependent reasons. In a sense this is true, for when I disavow the need for both authorial intention and audience belief I disavow the two obvious sources of Intentionality for texts. My notion of Intentionality-dependent reasons thus involves some fiction, but the fictionalization is not mine; rather, it is built into the relevant reasons themselves. Since this last sentence is hardly self-interpreting, let me explain.

Take the American Constitution. If I am right about it having authority while its authors have none, then one way to state the Intentionality-dependent reason the document gives us is to say that we have reason to treat the document as having more meaning than in fact it has. The reason itself is no fiction, because a real good is served by our treating the document as a text, interpretations of which legitimately resolve our political disputes. Yet the content of the reason contains a fiction, for what we have reason to do is to treat the document as if there existed a meaning

[35] For this ambiguity, and its use, see M. Moore, 'The Semantics of Judging', above n. 34, at 263–5.

[36] Plowdon's famous recommendation to look to the legislator's hypothetical intent is to be found in his reporter's remarks after *Eyston v. Studd*, 2 Plowdon 459, 75 Eng. Rep. 688 (1574). See also *Heydon's Case*, 76 Eng. Rep. 637 (Exch. 1584). For modern expressions, see Warren Lehmann, 'How to Interpret a Difficult Statute', *Wisconsin Law Review*, [1979], 489–507; Richard Posner, 'Statutory Interpretation—in the Classroom and in the Courtroom', *University of Chicago Law Review*, 50 (1983), 800–22.

[37] Letter by Holmes, quoted in Felix Frankfurter, 'Some Reflections on the Reading of Statutes', *Columbia Law Review*, 47 (1947), 527–46, at 538.

sufficiently authoritative and sufficiently determinate to resolve our controversies.

Consider clouds again. On my earlier suppositions, we have reason to treat clouds as texts and that reason is no fiction, mental health being a real good. Yet the content of the reason contains a kind of fiction, for what we have reason to do is to treat the phenomenon as if it were a description of our character, moods, and emotions, when of course the clouds are not a description by anyone.

This completes my general account of the basic question about interpretation, namely, what sorts of things have meaning. My answer, in terms of syntactically individuated texts whose interpretations give us new Intentionality-dependent reasons for belief or for action, also begins the answer to my third question, the question of justification. To that question (of what value is served by finding the meaning of something) the answer can be quite diverse: values of social peace, of treating people with respect, of knowing oneself, can justify treating different phenomena as texts requiring interpretation. Indeed, almost *any* value might give rise to treating *some* phenomenon as a text whose interpretations give us new reasons. The important point is that there must be some value justifying treating such phenomena as a text, else it is not a text nor is reasoning under it interpretation.

We have not yet answered the second of my three questions, that about validity. On the notion of interpretation here described, in what sense are interpreters discovering meaning (as opposed to creating it) and in what sense can their interpretations be true or valid? As we have seen, the communicative model of interpretation has an easy answer to these questions: interpreters discover meanings, not create them, and their interpretations are valid when but only when they discover what the author meant. But once we move to author-less texts, what are the analogous answers?

My own view about validity is this: an interpretation of some phenomenon is valid when but only when it maximally serves the value(s) that justifies the treating of the phenomenon as a text to begin with. In the case of clouds, the correct or valid interpretation—'what the clouds mean'—is that interpretation which maximally enhances our self-knowledge. In the case of a social practice like courtesy, the correct interpretation of our courteous practices is the one that maximally conveys respect to those to whom one is being courteous. In the case of the American Constitution, the matter is a bit more complicated. Prima facie, the correct interpretation of the Constitution is the one that maximally furthers the peaceful resolution of fundamental political disputes. I say 'prima facie', because the authority of the written Constitution only partly depends on the value of social peace. If the document made too many moral mistakes in what it required of us, we would not owe that text any allegiance; quite the contrary, amendment, civil war, or revolution would be our obligation. A more complete account of that document's authority thus includes some element of theoretical authority. This means that a correct interpretation of the Constitution is one that maximizes social peace while also seeking to eliminate moral mistakes.

In other cases the values that justify us in treating certain phenomena as texts justify us in interpreting those phenomena by reference either to what their author meant or to what their actual audience took them to mean. Two examples. In interpreting the request of a friend, we maximize the good of acceding to a friend's request—which is the reason that justifies us in treating it as a text at all—by seeking to discover what our friend meant by his request. In interpreting the defamatory utterance of another, courts maximize the good of corrective justice—which is (arguably) the reason that justifies courts in treating the utterance as a text at all—by seeking to discover, not what the speaker meant, but what any sizeable and respectable audience understood it to mean. In neither of these examples should one see a return to the communicative model of interpretation or to Fish's 'interpretive communities'. Rather, these author- or audience-centred interpretive strategies are instances of the more general, value-laden schema for interpretation that we have been examining. The same criteria for a valid interpretation hold even if those criteria sometimes yield intentionalist or belief-centred interpretive strategies.

The openly instrumental nature of this criterion of validity may give one pause. For how constraining can a text be if interpretations of it are valid simply because such interpretations maximally promote the value(s) justifying the treating of a text as a text? We should separate two strands to this worry. The first is nicely stated by Joseph Raz in his criticism of Ronald Dworkin's equally value-laden criterion of validity:

> If you regard the Constitution as an uninterpreted jumble of ink scratchings and regard legal theory [interpretation] as designed to give it meaning in accordance with the best moral theory there is, then there is no gap between ideal law and interpretation of existing law. Under these conditions one can interpret the Constitution to mean anything at all. It can be read to mean the same as Shakespeare's Hamlet.[38]

Raz worries that such instrumental interpretive reasoning ceases to be interpretive reasoning at all because the text in no way constrains doing what we would do if there were no text.

The answer to this worry lies again in the content of the Intentionality-dependent reasons essential to there being a text. When we have reason to

[38] Joseph Raz, 'Dworkin: A New Link in the Chain', *California Law Review*, 74 (1986), 1103–19, at 1103. I am indebted to both Joe Raz and to my commentator at the Tel Aviv Conference, Gilead Bar Elli, for stressing this point in the discussion on my paper at the Conference at Tel Aviv University.

treat some phenomenon as a text, it is not just that we have reason to treat it as *any* kind of text. The legitimization potential of the American Constitution, for example, not only gives us reason to consider that document as *some* kind of text; in addition, the kind of text it gives American citizens reason to interpret is one that respects the legitimizing potential of the document, which means that the ordinary English meanings of the words the document employs must be respected. Similarly, with the example of social practices like courtesy, the value of expressing respect gives us reason to take seriously the accepted parameters of courteous behaviours prevalent in a society, else the good of courteous behaviour expressing respect could not be realized.

At the level of generality of our concept of interpretation there is little to be said about these more particular constraints on interpretation. For these are local constraints, differing in their nature by the kind of text (and the kind of value justifying treating that text as a text). About the kinds of texts that appear in law, some generalization about these local constraints is certainly possible: because laws are framed in natural languages, and because one of the essential functions of all law is to realize the good of liberty (notice and opportunity to avoid legal sanctions) and substantive fairness (no retroactive surprises), the ordinary meaning of the words used in legal texts must always be given respect.[39] Yet even this generalization is better conceived as being part of a theory of interpretation, not part of the syntactic criteria of text individuation.[40] The local constraints (such as that of 'plain meaning' in law), in other words, are better thought of as markers of good versus bad interpretations, not of what is interpretation at all.

The second strand to this indeterminacy worry stems from the lack of there being any bright line blocking the slide down the slippery slope to fully instrumental reasoning, ignoring the text entirely. That is, granting the point just made—that local constraints such as plain meaning do constrain good interpretations—the distinct, second worry is that such constraints evaporate in the face of the pressure exerted by the values also guiding a good interpretation. This is the familiar worry about any form of what lawyers call 'purposive interpretation':[41] that the end or purpose

[39] Which is not to say that such meanings may not be disregarded entirely in favour of a technical legal meaning; only, that such ordinary meanings carry great weight. See Moore, 'A Natural Law Theory', above n. 5; see also Brian Bix, *Law, Language, and Legal Determinacy* (Oxford: Clarendon Press, 1993), for another account of the local constraints put on legal interpretation by the semantics of natural languages.

[40] Argued for in Moore, 'Do We Have an Unwritten Constitution?', above n. 28.

[41] See Moore, 'The Semantics of Judging', above n. 34, at 277–81. Some theorists seem to have imbibed so deeply of this fear that they refuse to conceptualize purposive interpretation of a rule to be following (or applying) the rule at all; according to Andrei Marmor, for example, when judges amend the ordinary meaning of the words appearing in a rule so as to make the rule better serve its purpose, they are 'disregarding', not 'following', the rule. Marmor, *Interpretation and Legal Theory*, above n. 5, at 136–7. There are good reasons not to adopt this

(in the sense of value, not in the sense of authorial intention) will so dominate the reasoning that the means chosen (the text) will be ignored entirely. 'And' can be interpreted to mean 'or',[42] for example, or 'black' can be interpreted to mean 'white',[43] 'death penalty' can be interpreted to mean 'life sentence',[44] once the validity of interpretation is made to turn exclusively on the ends served by the texts in which such words or phrases appear.

Yet this is a non-worry. Remember *what* it is that the value that guides interpretation first must justify: that the text be treated as a text by those who would interpret it. Even though, for example, a seeker of self-knowledge justifies his treatment of clouds or dreams as texts by the good of self-knowledge, and even though his interpretation of those phenomena is thus to be guided so as to maximize the self-knowledge attained, he must nonetheless pursue such self-knowledge indirectly. He must, in other words, focus on what the clouds mean, not on his own mental health, in order to serve the good of his own mental health. Similarly, the person who would be courteous must pursue respect for others indirectly. It does not maximize respect for others to ignore the forms of courtesy—say, by gushing constantly, 'I respect you'. Rather, one maximizes respect by behaviours that are recognizable interpretations of the forms of courtesy prevalent in that society. Similarly, the judge who would further the good of peaceful resolution of fundamental political disputes must pursue that good indirectly in his constitutional interpretations. It will not maximally serve that good to say that the constitution means whatever a majority of Americans want it to mean; rather, he maximizes political peace by seeking an objective meaning to the document.

There is, to be sure, no bright line to be drawn as to when some value is sufficiently disserved (by giving the words of some legal text their ordinary meaning) that ordinary meaning should be overruled. Yet this is no more of a worry here than are slippery slopes generally. The inability to

structural criterion of rules and rule-following and to adopt my functional criterion, namely, that doing the latter allows us to identify judicial obligation with following the (rules of the) law.

42 *People v. Skinner*, 39 Cal. 3d. 765, 217 Cal. Rptr. 685, 704 P 2d 752 (1985). (In the insanity defence, 'and' held to mean 'or' for purposes of conforming California initiative to the M'Naughten test.)

43 This was one of Jonathan Swift's worries about the casuistry (purposive interpretation gone awry) of lawyers: 'There was a society of men among us, bred up from their youth in the art of proving by words multiplied for the purpose, that white is black, and black is white, according as they are paid' (Swift, *Travels by Lemuel Gulliver*, 4, ch. 5, reprinted in C. V. Doren (ed.), *The Portable Swift* (Harmondsworth: Penguin, 1984), 472).

44 As I took the Chief Justice of the California Supreme Court to be doing in her vote to reverse 59 consecutive death sentences on allegedly procedural grounds. See Moore, 'Politics Is Not the Basis for Judging Judges', 'Justices' Personal Values Must at Times Give Way', 'Rose Bird Should Go', *Los Angeles Times*, 29, 30, 31 July 1985, reprinted, *USC Law* (Fall–Winter, 1986), 24–7.

describe in general terms the right place to draw any line hardly betokens that in individual cases correct judgements of whether the line is crossed are not possible. It is not the case that everything (or nothing) is a heap, even if no clear general rule can be stated about how many stones make a heap.

III. APPLYING MODEST INTERPRETIVISM

Where are we? Having put aside the uselessly general very ambitious interpretivist model so popular today, I then distinguished four other models of interpretation: the communicative model where necessarily one seeks authorial intention if one is interpreting anything; the metaphysical dualist model according to which objectively true interpretations are just there to be discovered in the special class of phenomena we call meaningful; the conventionalist or sociological model, according to which interpretation occurs whenever interpretive communities arise, developing concepts and practices of interpretation; and my own model, what I call the modest interpretivist model.[45] On this last model interpretation is an activity people do when they have some good reason to treat some phenomena as a syntactically individuated text, valid interpretations of which will give them new, Intentionality-dependent reasons for belief or for action. We now should apply this model of interpretation to a variety of interpretive, or allegedly interpretive, activities.

Consider first the ordinary, communicative use of language in everyday conversations. When we as listeners seek to divine what the speaker meant by some utterance, are we engaged in an interpretive activity (on my 'modest interpretation' model)? The answer, perhaps surprisingly, is that it depends on what reason we have for listening. In ordinary, everyday conversations often there is no value that justifies us as listeners treating interpretations of the utterance as giving us either reasons to believe the proposition uttered, or reasons to act in accordance with the utterance. Conversational use of language looks interpretive in my sense (and is interpretive in the communicative sense I put aside at the beginning) because we often do have reason to seek to find out what the speaker meant by some utterance, and the conventional meaning of the sentence uttered is good evidence of that speaker's intent. It is part of the art of conversation to discover what the other meant so that one can respond appropriately, and we may plausibly suppose such pleasure of conversation to be something intrinsically good. Yet to serve this good does not require us to regard our interpretations as reasons for belief or action for us. Only

[45] See Ch. 10, above.

when speakers are either theoretical authorities on the subject in question, or practical authorities (such as are friends with their requests), do we have reason to treat their utterances as giving us new reasons for belief or for action.

Ordinary, conversational use of language involves listeners in a standard, social-scientific task of description/explanation, not interpretation in the sense I have been attempting to isolate. Our curiosity in what such a conversational speaker meant is no different than our curiosity about what that speaker may have intended to achieve by saying what he did, or, indeed, from what he may have intended with any action, speech-act or not. In all such cases, we wish to know the mental states of intention that moved him to action. This is a standard descriptive/explanatory question of social science even though it involves Intentional states, not the kind of non-descriptive, non-explanatory interpretive question that interests me.

It might be objected that the discovery of what someone intended on a given occasion is itself a matter of interpretation,[46] and thus that the social-scientific, communicative model of interpretation should be subsumed under my or some other more general model of interpretation. Yet this too would be a mistake. Describing what someone intended does of course involve one in describing the object or content of their intention. This is true for all Intentional states, not just for intentions. Yet describing a propositional attitude by describing its Intentional object is still to describe something, even if the thing described is itself a linguistic phenomenon. If you intend to go downtown, my description of what you intend is accurate if it corresponds to that object of your intention. That is, my description, 'he intends to go downtown' is true if and only if the description in his head—the object of his intention—is also that he go downtown.[47]

[46] I discuss this possibility at somewhat greater length in M. Moore, *Law and Psychiatry: Rethinking the Relationship* (Cambridge: Cambridge University Press, 1984), ch. 1, and in *Act and Crime: The Implications of the Philosophy of Action for the Criminal Law* (Oxford: Clarendon Press, 1993), 63–5. The best working out of this possibility in the contemporary philosophy of mind is Dan Dennett's pragmatism about Intentional states. See Dennett, 'The Intentional Stance', in his *Brainstorms* (Cambridge, Mass.: MIT Press, 1978), and *The Intentional Stance* (Cambridge, Mass.: MIT Press, 1987). This pragmatic/interpretive construal of intentions is assumed without argument by Ronald Dworkin (*Law's Empire*, above n. 18) and by Dworkin's former student, Nicos Stavropoulos, *Objectivity in Legal Interpretation* (Oxford: Clarendon Press, 1996). For a similar scepticism about the intentions of individuals, see Bix, *Law, Language, and Legal Determinacy*, above n. 39, at 188.

[47] This view of Intentional objects is of course not that of current eliminative materialists like Dan Dennett, Steven Stich, or Paul and Patricia Churchland. Rather, my own bets here are with those defenders of the folk psychology who believe that there is a language of thought in the brain that will allow realism about the propositional attitudes and their objects. See e.g. Jerry Fodor, *The Language of Thought* (Cambridge, Mass.: MIT Press, 1975). Compare the divergent views collected in John Greenwood (ed.), *The Future of Folk Psychology* (Cambridge: Cambridge University Press, 1991).

It is true that we often refer to both utterances and propositional attitudes in the language of indirect discourse. Instead of direct quotation, as in 'Mary said, "John is a louse" ', we may paraphrase to, 'Mary said that John is a louse'. Likewise, instead of direct attribution, as in 'Mary intended, "Mary go downtown" ', we may paraphrase to, 'Mary intended that she go downtown'. This indirect manner of referring to both utterances and propositional attitudes misleads many into thinking that therefore there is no fact of the matter about what Mary said or intended, and that we listeners therefore must fill in with our own interpretive efforts. Yet this is to take far too seriously our use of indirect discourse. One of Paul Grice's pragmatic injunctions was to convey no more information than your listener needs. We use indirect discourse because usually a listener does not need the precise wording of an utterance or an Intentional object—usually 'the gist' is sufficient.[48] That we have this intentionally vague way of referring to utterances and propositional attitudes should not deflect us for a moment from the truth about both: there is a fact of the matter about both to which a description must correspond to be accurate.

If neither conversational use of language nor propositional attitude ascription are interpretive activities, what is? Quite a lot. Literary criticism, for example. There is (at least arguably—some literary critics make me doubt this) a point or value to treating novels, plays, poems, etc., as texts to be interpreted. If one has a moralistic view of literary criticism, such as that held by Mathew Arnold or John Gardner, then literature serves an educative function.[49] To the extent that the author is morally wiser than we the audience, we have reason to treat her productions as a text, interpretations of which give us new reasons to believe certain moral propositions to be true. This quickly leads to intentionalist literary interpretation. Alternatively, one might take certain literary productions to give us new reasons for moral belief (when those productions are correctly interpreted) even if the author of those productions is morally no wiser than are we. She may simply have hit upon a tale of compelling emotional power, allowing us to experience vicariously what life's lottery has not allowed us to experience directly in our own lives. For such novels, literary critics have reason to treat the novel as a text, interpreting it so as to further its experiential potential (and thus its capacity to give its audience new reasons for moral belief).

One might think literary criticism to have some quite different value justifying its interpretive attempts. One might think that literature can serve a therapeutic good, like clouds and dreams in my earlier examples. In

[48] Alternatively, we often do not know exactly what was either said or intended, so we use indirect discourse so as not to mislead as to the precision of our own knowledge.

[49] This view of literature is explored by Ron Garet, 'Comparative Normative Hermeneutics', *Southern California Law Review*, 58 (1985), 35–134.

which case it is the good of self-knowledge that justifies treating certain productions as texts, interpretations of which give us new reasons for believing truths about ourselves. Or the point of literary criticism might be beauty for its own sake (although this is more plausible for art than for literature), in which case it is the good of beauty (or appreciation of beauty, as G. E. Moore thought) that justifies literary critics interpreting the text so as to make it more beautiful (and thus to give its readers more reason to appreciate beauty).

Theology and psychoanalysis also contain activities properly thought of an interpretive by my modest conception of interpretation.[50] Rather than pursuing these, however, I shall consider another purportedly interpretive activity, the practice of law. Consider first statutory legal reasoning. This is plainly interpretive on the modest model of interpretation. There is a value served by judges regarding statutes as syntactically individuated texts, interpretations of which give judges reasons for belief or for action. On one view of the matter, legislatures are theoretical authorities whose utterances therefore are the fit subjects for interpretation.[51] Such utterances, when properly interpreted,[52] give judges reasons for believing certain decisions to be more desirable than others. On my own view of the matter, legislatures are practical authorities because of their democratic composition; in addition, certain rule of law values justify judges in treating statutes as texts.[53] Such texts when properly interpreted give judges reasons for deciding one way rather than another. (Neither democracy nor the rule of law justifies judges in using intentionalist interpretive methods, but that is a detailed argument I have undertaken elsewhere.)[54]

With common law (or precedential) reasoning, the situation is different. It is not difficult to imagine what an interpretive common law would look like. Indeed, with what is commonly called 'vertical precedent'—the deference lower courts give to prior opinions by courts higher in the appellate hierarchy—American courts regularly regard the prior opinions of higher courts as texts that they (the lower courts) have reason to interpret. Yet ordinary (or 'horizontal') precedent is not like this. Our courts do not treat prior opinions as texts. They broaden, narrow, reformulate, or throw out entirely the rule or the reasons stated by a prior court in its opinion,

[50] See Ch. 10, above.

[51] The view of Heidi Hurd and Donald Regan, among others. See Hurd, 'Challenging Authority', above n. 16; Regan, 'Law's Halo', in Jules Coleman and Ellen Frankel-Paul (eds.), *Philosophy and Law* (Oxford: Basil Blackwell, 1987).

[52] Either by finding what the legislature meant, or by some non-intentionalist interpretive strategy. Compare Marmor, *Interpretation and Legal Theory*, above n. 5, ch. 8, with Waldron, 'Legislators' Intentions', above n. 25.

[53] See Ch. 5, above; Moore, 'A Natural Law Theory', above n. 5 at 313–18.

[54] Moore, 'A Natural Law Theory', above n. 5.

even while they 'follow' the decision of the prior court in deciding the later case.[55]

Our practice of horizontal precedent is correct in not regarding prior court opinions as texts. Those who have urged the contrary have often done so for the kind of reason given by Lord Mansfield, that prior judges have 'worked the common law pure', so that their opinions possess a kind of theoretical authority for subsequent judges; alternatively, such proponents of an interpretive common law might think that being a judge in a legal system with a sitting legislature requires as little judicial law-making as possible and that therefore one's predecessors' opinions have some practical authority over one until changed by the legislature.[56] But neither of these views is very plausible. The value served by today's judges following precedent decisions is mainly the value of equality, but equality does not demand that cases that are alike *in the respects described in prior opinions* be treated alike; rather, equality demands that cases that are alike *in all morally relevant respects* be treated alike. Equality, thus, does not give a judge any reason to treat the opinions of his predecessors as texts he must interpret.[57]

Why are not the particular decisions of prior judges themselves a kind of text? For equality does give present judges reason to treat present litigants no differently than similarly situated, prior litigants were treated by prior judges. Why cannot we consider what was done to prior litigants to be a kind of text? The reason we cannot do so lies in the Intentionality-dependent reasons that must exist for there to be a text. Although we might be able to formulate a syntactical rule (a rule of recognition) for what sort of judicial actions are to form the text for today's judges,[58] what the rule recognizes as authoritative—past judicial actions—will not give new, Intentionality-dependent reasons for belief or for action to subsequent judges. When judges generalize their decisions into common law *rules* in their opinions, such rules subsequently could be regarded as a text, if there were some value justifying subsequent judges in so treating them (as I have argued there is not). But the decisions themselves are simply meaningless events in the world, not Intentionality-dependent, reason-giving texts.

[55] Explored in Moore, 'Precedent, Induction, and Ethical Generalization', in Laurence Goldstein (ed.), *Precedent in Law* (Oxford: Oxford University Press, 1987).

[56] The apparent view, for example, of Justice Heher in *Reimann v. Monmouth Consolidated Water Co.*, 9 N.J. 134 (1952).

[57] Argued in Moore, 'Precedent', above n. 55.

[58] Brian Simpson questions whether precedent as it is practised in Anglo-American legal systems in fact operates with such a rule of recognition. A. W. B. Simpson, 'The Common Law and Legal Theory', in Simpson (ed.), *Oxford Essays in Jurisprudence, Second Series* (Oxford: Oxford University Press, 1973).

Common law reasoning is simply flat-out moral reasoning when the latter is done in the non-ideal case that past history must be respected so as not to violate the demands of equality. Moral reasoning in the ideal case (that is, ignoring the history of past treatments) is not interpretive reasoning for anyone whose metaethics is not relativist. Moral reasoning in the actual world, where equality demands that we respect our history, is similarly non-interpretive. Like common law reasoning, non-ideal moral reasoning itself generalizes past treatments, but those treatments, as we have seen, do not give Intentionality dependent reasons for belief or for action.

American constitutional reasoning has long been thought to hover—or oscillate—between being like statutory reasoning and being like common law reasoning. We are in a position to understand this uncertainty, for recall that the authority of the document lies both in its ability to resolve peacefully fundamental disputes and in the fact that the content of the document makes sufficiently few moral mistakes that the costs of revolution/radical amendment outweigh the gains. Only the first of these values justifies why judges should treat the document as a text even before they know what it means. The second requires judges to figure out what it means and only then decide whether it is good enough for government work. American Constitutional reasoning is thus an uncomfortable blend between genuinely interpretive reasoning and the kind of non-interpretive reasoning we find in common law adjudication.

Now let us consider, not legal practice, but legal theory. Since the work of Herbert Hart,[59] it has become common to distinguish two perspectives on law: one is the internal perspective on the law of a given legal system, taken by those who (actually or vicariously) participate as legal actors in the system; the other is the external perspective on law in general, taken by those who do not participate as a legal actor under that law. Theoreticians about law can work from either perspective. One can write, for example, judge-centred jurisprudence, advising judges in the American legal system what they should accept as American law and how they should go about interpreting (or otherwise applying) it. Or one can disengage from such vicarious judicial role-playing, writing one's legal theory about the (conceptual or real) essence of law as such.

Is the practice of either form of legal theory (usually labelled, respectively, particular or general jurisprudence) interpretive in character? It is easy to blurt out an unthinking 'yes' here, on the ground that because some of law practice is interpretive, so too must a study of that law practice be interpretive. This is a crude mistake, however. It is like the mistake of thinking that to study metaphors, one must do so metaphorically, or that to describe vagueness, one must do so vaguely. One can describe,

[59] Hart, *Concept*, n. 17 above.

explain, and fully understand an interpretive practice without necessarily being engaged in an interpretive practice.[60] So there is no necessity that legal theory of either kind be interpretive just because some of the legal reasoning studied by legal theory is itself interpretive.

Indeed, legal theory done from a perspective external to any particular legal system is quite plainly not interpretive in character. For there is no text of which theoreticians must seek the meaning in order to theorize about law in general. Such theorists are not judges, nor are they advising judges in some particular legal system, so that statutory or constitutional law does not bind them as it binds judges in those legal systems. Other legal theorist's writings are sometimes good heuristics, although more often good foils, but in any case, not *texts* for legal theorists.

It is true that a descriptive, general jurisprudence aims to describe law by giving a theory as to the nature of law, and that like any description, such a description of law must correspond to that which it describes, namely, law. Yet that does not make the kind, law, into a text legal theorists must interpret—any more than similar truths about chemistry and descriptions of gold make chemists interpretivists about the periodic table. Describing something that has a nature hardly becomes interpretation just because the description must describe that nature in order to be accurate.[61]

All of this remains true for those general jurisprudes who seek to describe, not the thing, law, but a shared concept of law. When Herbert Hart and Joseph Raz wrote their justly celebrated books on this topic,[62] they were not interpreting anything. Rather, they like essentialists about law such as Aquinas, were seeking to describe something with a nature. In their case, that something was that set of shared propositional attitudes we call a concept, i.e. common beliefs about law's nature. As we have seen, such propositional attitude ascriptions are not interpretations, irrespective of whether the propositional attitudes being described are about law or about anything else.

Does the case for legal theory being interpretive become stronger when that legal theory is done from the internal perspective? Since the legal theorist is giving advice to legal actors such as judges, presumably if the advice is to be taken seriously it will be because real judges ought to heed

[60] Compare the often criticized view of Peter Winch, whose Wittgensteinian fascinations led him to assert that to understand a social practice one must join the natives in practising that practice, *The Idea of a Social Science* (London, Routledge, 1958). See also Dworkin, *Law's Empire*, above n. 18, at 55 ('a social scientist must participate in a social practice if he hopes to understand it').

[61] Such descriptions of law's nature remain just that, descriptions and not interpretations, even if the essential nature of law is given by the unique values ('functions') law serves and not by any structural features (like coercive sanctions). Functionalist description of law is not interpretive jurisprudence. For the difference, see Ch. 9 above, n. 79.

[62] Hart, *Concept*, above n. 17; Joseph Raz, *The Concept of a Legal System* (Oxford: Oxford University Press, 1970).

it. Since real judges are often engaged in interpretive reasoning, must the theorist who would advise them on how to reason also be engaging in interpretation? Since real judges have reason to treat statutes as texts, do not theorists who would advise judges how to judge not also have to treat statutes as texts?

Despite the appearances, these are not rhetorical questions. Indeed, the answer to them is 'no'. We must distinguish between advocates before judges—lawyers—from theorists advising judges how to judge. Lawyers arguing to judges must surely engage in the interpretive reasoning that they would have the judge himself go through in order to reach a result favourable to their client. But advising judges how to judge is not this sort of advocacy. For notice when I or other legal theorists advise judges how to interpret statutes—as I do regularly in my 'jurisprudence for judges' seminars in America—we are not interpreting statutes. Rather, we are trying to describe the best way to interpret statutes. Ours is a 'meta-' question. If there is any text for our meta-question, it would be the interpretive practices of judges, not the statutes being interpreted. And why should I, or the judges I advise, be bound (in how they do their interpretations) by how other judges have done their interpretations? Why should I or the judges I advise care a fig that American judicial practice is to interpret statutes by paying at least lip service to legislative intent? Surely I as a theorist, like the judges I advise, are free of any obligation to treat other judges' interpretive practice as having any authority to constrain my recommendations about how to interpret statutes.[63]

I conclude that no legal theorist should wish to think of his theoretical activity as an interpretive activity. Only when legal theorists become advocates for particular interpretations—only when we act like lawyers who themselves act like judges, in other words—do we engage in interpretive reasoning.[64]

IV. CONCLUSION

From what was just said, it should be clear that my title is misleading. I have not been interpreting interpretation—for such an activity would

[63] I can imagine that in a judicial world different from the one with which I am familiar—namely, a world in which there was some convergence of judicial interpretive practices—there could be a good of co-ordination giving each judge a reason to co-ordinate his interpretive practices with those of other judges. Presumably equality, enhanced predictability, and efficiency would be the goods served by such co-ordination. See Gerald Postema, 'Co-ordination and Convention at the Foundation of Law', *Journal of Legal Studies*, 11 (1982), 165–203, for suggestions in this direction.

[64] The conclusion that jurisprudence is not interpretive has been defended before, both by me and by Andrei Marmor, specifically against Dworkin's claims to the contrary, in Ch. 10, above; Marmor, *Interpretation and Legal Theory*, above n. 5, at ch. 3.

presuppose that I had some reason to treat our practices of interpretation as a kind of text, interpretations of which would give us reasons to believe certain facts about interpretation. And I can't think of any such reason that is at all plausible. Not being a very modest fellow, I am unwilling to grant any theoretical authority to the theories or practices of interpretation of others. Nor do I see any practical authority to such practices or to their practitioners. What I have been up to in this Chapter, thus, is *describing* a kind of activity. Even though that kind of activity is an interpretive one, that does not mean I have been doing anything other than describing the nature of this kind of activity. Such description becomes interpretation only on the very ambitious view that holds *all* descriptions/explanations to be interpretations or on the communicative sense of 'interpretation' that identifies all descriptions of Intentional states as interpretation. But that is to abandon the useful, distinct notion of interpretation that I have sought to analyse in this Chapter.

In closing, let me taxonomize the various models of interpretation around their views on the relation between description/explanation, on the one hand, and interpretation on the other. The very ambitious interpretivist sees no difference between the two, because everything is interpretation. With a nice symmetry, the communicative model also sees no difference, but in this case, because interpretation just is a description of a natural phenomenon (an intention) and the explanation of another natural phenomenon (production of a text) as the causal product of it. Both of these reductionist views are wrong. Interpretation is an activity that is distinct from the descriptive/explanatory activities characteristic of science. But one must be modest about this difference. It will not do to elevate this difference into a metaphysical divide between two kinds of being, each with their own brand of science. That is the mistake of the metaphysically dualist model of interpretation. Interpretation is just another activity—like sleeping, eating, teaching, or writing—that people sometimes have reason to do. None of such activities needs the justification of science to make them worthwhile, and none of them can have that justification—the generation of understanding—since they are not descriptions/explanations. Interpretation as an activity makes perfectly good sense in the restricted domains that I have mentioned without any more ambitious trappings.

Index